Praise for *The New Net Zero*

"*The New Net Zero* is a thorough philosophical and technical rendering of the subject. What makes it exciting and meaningful is that it is not just about the details and technology, it also demonstrates how it is essential to build on human and other natural-system relationships to succeed. There is hope in these pages; this book goes a long way to prove that a sustainable future is possible and practical."

—Bill Reed, COAUTHOR OF *THE INTEGRATIVE DESIGN GUIDE TO GREEN BUILDING* AND PRESIDENT OF THE INTEGRATIVE DESIGN COLLABORATIVE

"Design is the first signal of human intention. Thoreau once wrote, 'What's the use of a fine house if you haven't got a tolerable planet to put it on?' Bill Maclay thoroughly describes an intentional architect's Platonic search for truth in beauty and Aristotelian search for truth in science with a Hippocratic oath to seek to 'do no harm.' With this fine book he provides a robust foundation for buildings that can rise up to become beneficial to people, place, and planet."

—William McDonough, COAUTHOR OF *CRADLE TO CRADLE* AND *THE UPCYCLE* AND FOUNDER OF THE CRADLE TO CRADLE PRODUCTS INNOVATION INSTITUTE

"*The New Net Zero* is a treasure trove of design and construction knowledge gleaned over a forty-year career in creating leading-edge, net-zero-energy and near-net-zero-energy buildings of all types and sizes. Detailed, practical information on design is interspersed with beautifully illustrated case studies of Maclay's projects. If I could recommend only one book on low-energy, green building today, this would be it."

—Alex Wilson, FOUNDER OF BUILDINGGREEN, INC., AND PRESIDENT OF THE RESILIENT DESIGN INSTITUTE

"*The New Net Zero* is comprehensive, authoritative, beautifully written, well illustrated, and incredibly timely. With the effects of climate change escalating rapidly, moving away from fossil-fuel energy has become desperately necessary. The good news is that it has now become possible to cost effectively power our buildings entirely with renewable energy sources, and this is the best book yet about why and how to build net zero buildings. Maclay and his team have long been leaders in proving the net zero proposition, and he has gracefully delivered a detailed manual for the big design and building breakthrough that can happen now."

—Tedd Benson, FOUNDER OF BENSONWOOD AND UNITY HOMES AND AUTHOR OF *BUILDING THE TIMBER FRAME HOUSE*, *THE TIMBER-FRAME HOME*, AND *TIMBERFRAME*

"This book will become a game changer at a pivotal point in history. *The New Net Zero* is a technical manifesto that brings together engineering, ecology, architecture, energy, the construction industry, transportation, and design into a coherent whole. Its goal is to transform the built environment into landscapes that heal, while reversing climate change. Immensely practical, thorough, and technologically comprehensive: it is a masterful job."

—John Todd, FOUNDER OF JOHN TODD ECOLOGICAL DESIGNS

THE
New Net
Zero

THE New Net Zero

Leading-Edge Design
and Construction of
Homes and Buildings for a
Renewable Energy Future

WILLIAM MACLAY AND MACLAY ARCHITECTS

Chelsea Green Publishing
White River Junction, Vermont

Editor: Joni Praded
Project Manager: Patricia Stone
Proofreader: Eileen M. Clawson
Indexer: Shana Milkie
Designer: Melissa Jacobson

Printed in the United States of America.
First printing June, 2014
10 9 8 7 6 5 4 3 2 1   14 15 16 17 18

Our Commitment to Green Publishing

Chelsea Green sees publishing as a tool for cultural change and ecological stewardship. We strive to align our book manufacturing practices with our editorial mission and to reduce the impact of our business enterprise in the environment. We print our books and catalogs on chlorine-free recycled paper, using vegetable-based inks whenever possible. This book may cost slightly more because it was printed on paper that contains recycled fiber, and we hope you'll agree that it's worth it. Chelsea Green is a member of the Green Press Initiative (www.greenpressinitiative.org), a nonprofit coalition of publishers, manufacturers, and authors working to protect the world's endangered forests and conserve natural resources. *The New Net Zero* was printed on paper supplied by RR Donnelley that contains at least 10% postconsumer recycled fiber.

Library of Congress Cataloging-in-Publication Data
Maclay, William, 1948–
  The new net zero: leading-edge design and construction of homes and buildings for a renewable energy future/William Maclay and Maclay Architects.
    pages cm

Includes bibliographical references and index.
  ISBN 978-1-60358-448-7 (hardback)
1. Sustainable buildings. 2. Sustainable construction. I. Title.

TH880.M32 2014
690.028'6--dc23

                          2014002411

Chelsea Green Publishing
85 North Main Street, Suite 120
White River Junction, VT 05001
(802) 295-6300
www.chelseagreen.com

CONTENTS

PREFACE

We shape our buildings; thereafter they shape us.

—WINSTON CHURCHILL

We live in a time of cataclysmic transformation, a turning point in human existence. We hear constantly of climate change, ecosystem degradation, overpopulation, living beyond the earth's carrying capacity, and the peaking of fossil fuels and other natural resources.

Perhaps we stand at the beginning of a change that rivals the onset of the Dark Ages, the Renaissance, or the industrial and information revolutions. Perhaps the challenge before us is something even larger—a major evolutionary shift that could rival the disappearance of dinosaurs from the planet. Whatever the magnitude of change ahead, people are increasingly realizing that we as humans are now in a place of massive evolution—for both better and worse.

Is the threat exaggerated? Can the choices we make alter the future for good or ill? What actions can we take now that can lead us toward a more sustainable, nurturing, and inspiring future? If we, like Churchill in the quote above, acknowledge that our lives and our habitation in the environment are inextricably intertwined, can we alter our physical infrastructure and environment in a way that lessens the negative impacts of our living—and creates a positive way of life that supports and nurtures life and living systems?

In the broadest sense, the goal of this book is to help people explore and create a future without fossil fuels that supports and enhances all living systems and is renewably based. It is a vision beyond attainment by any individual, but we hope it provides a path for a meaningful journey each day and throughout a career.

I am an architect, and I think most architects share an underlying way of seeing the physical world—the places we live in—as intimately connected to who we are as human beings. Some might even claim we cannot separate from our surroundings who we are and what we do. When we walk in a redwood forest or in a medieval cathedral, our mood, our movements, and our thinking are all drastically altered. Compare those moods and feelings to walking into a crowded subway stop in New York or Singapore.

Surroundings matter. You may define your world based on your family life, work life, spiritual life, or any number of other possibilities, but the physical nature of your world molds the core of your existence, as it does for any living organism. But unlike other organisms, we have the ability to design our future worlds.

The pages ahead offer a vision of how net zero design can make our immediate surroundings—the homes and buildings we spend our days in, as well as our wider communities—fossil-fuel free. They also relay state-of-the-art information on how to achieve the highest net zero building standards possible; how to create buildings that are beautiful, comfortable, and healthy; and how to expand our current thinking about net zero buildings into thinking (and practice) about net zero community design.

My own journey on this path began in 1970, when I attended a lecture on renewable energy by Steve Baer. The founder of Zomeworks, Baer had built Drop City, a community of dome-like polyhedra in the southern Colorado desert. The small

FIGURE P.1. Simple, dome-shaped poly-hedra that opened in the daytime to catch sunlight and store its heat in water barrels, provided cost-effective, passively heated living space for residents—and inspiration for solar advocates—in the 1970s.

polyhedra had reflective panels that folded down on the south side of each structure during the day. These glazed surfaces allowed sunshine to enter the polyhedra, and the reflective surfaces increased solar gain inside the structures. Just inside the glazing, 55-gallon drums were filled with water to soak up and store the heat from the sun. At night the insulated reflective panels were pulled up to cover the south-facing glazing surfaces, minimizing heat loss, and the 55-gallon drums radiated heat back into the interiors of the polyhedra, main-taining comfortable temperatures in the cold desert nights. The incredibly simple design offered low-cost, renewably powered housing in a community connected to nature. Baer's lecture was so inspiring that right then and there, I committed to work for the creation of a renewably powered civilization and planet.

Less than nine months later, I was at work with two other first-year graduate students from the University of Pennsylvania designing and building a small, renewably powered community in Vermont, the first of its kind in the Northeast. When we began this project, Dimetrodon, my partners and I were twenty-one years old, with almost no knowledge of design and

construction but filled with visions of what a solar-powered world might look like. We believed that solar power was not just an energy source to replace fossil fuel but an opportunity to evolve a different and better quality of life.

We did not think that building solar-powered houses alone would be enough to create a renewable world. To make a viable impact, solar energy needed to be incorporated in construc-tion on a larger scale—at the community level at the minimum. Our vision was to create a small, vibrant neighborhood. We thought individuals should be able to design and build their own spaces, as they had over the millennia, so we designed a community structure within which people could easily build homes without architects and builders.

Dimetrodon was designed around a central courtyard, to bring the families together around a shared space. At the center of the courtyard was a community building and sleep-ing tower for shared meals, gatherings, and guest sleeping space. Surrounding the courtyard, were multiple trusses over 40 feet tall and 100 feet long. The trusses were 16 feet apart—the dimension wood framing spans easily without much engineering or cost. This allowed individuals and families to

FIGURE P.2. Dimetrodon's construction began in 1971 as a small-scale, renewably powered model community with compact homes, common spaces, and open land, similar in concept to more recent cohousing communities. The name of the project was inspired by the dimetrodon, a prehistoric animal with a sail on its back that was believed to be involved in its thermo-regulation.

easily design and build their own spaces between the trusses, even if they had minimal design and construction experience. At the time many people thought of Dimetrodon as a hippie commune, but the social principles involved were much the same as cohousing, a concept that did not arrive in North America until decades later. I lived at Dimetrodon for twenty-five years as I married and grew a family. Now occupied with a vibrant younger generation and evolving with new changes, it is an example of innovative, affordable, self-designed and -built housing and community.

While creating Dimetrodon, I took a six-month hiatus to take a motorcycle trip to Machu Picchu in Peru. This was the second experience that has inspired my work. I was able to glimpse the richness, diversity, and pure awesomeness in how people can live as a community. I also gained a deep appreciation of the role of beauty and wonder in building design.

When I returned to graduate school after three years designing and building Dimetrodon and other projects, I researched the interconnection of the primary sources of energy that power human settlement and the rhythms and quality of life. I observed how renewable energy connected to

farming and water mills in villages and towns; coal to railroads and cities; and oil to cars and suburbs. This research and the inspiration from Zomeworks and Machu Picchu has been the foundation for my work and the work of Maclay Architects over the past forty years.

Over those years, our firm has grown from handling small-scale design, construction, and land planning projects to becoming recognized throughout New England for innovation and leadership in ecological design. We focus on designing buildings and communities that are models for healthy, inspired living and demonstrate progress toward a carbon-neutral and ecologically sustainable future.

Over this time, we have worked on commercial, institutional, planning, historic preservation, multifamily, and single-family residential projects. Our projects are designed to the highest levels of environmental performance, minimizing consumption of energy and natural resources. We see buildings as organisms that must function not just individually but also within their larger ecosystem of office buildings, homes, institutions, communities, and natural systems. Our goal is to design and build with systems in mind, both within each building and without, so that we can make beautiful spaces that enhance people's lives and environment and create the kind of world we want to inhabit.

Our commitment has guided our journey. And our focus on renewable energy has led us to in-depth exploration of energy conservation, indoor air quality, materials research and assessment, healthy building design, and a myriad of green design strategies, including sustainable design, regenerative design, living systems design, and net zero design. It has also convinced us that creating renewably powered homes, buildings, and communities is our only viable choice, and the time for this shift is now, not some time in the future.

Human civilization has been powered by different primary energy sources over time. Transitioning from one energy source to another is and has been a part of human evolution, and when our energy sources change, so do our settlement patterns. Today we are transitioning from fossil energy to something else—and in our opinion the only current viable energy option is renewable energy.

In *The New Net Zero* we explore how a future without fossil fuel impacts the design of buildings, communities, and society. We show how to use net zero building strategies to avoid some of our current problems with buildings. And we demonstrate that creating renewable buildings, communities, and infrastructure is entirely feasible, both technologically and financially, today. There is no excuse to wait.

We also present a way to construct net zero buildings that not only perform well but are beautiful and can substantially improve our quality of life. The buildings and communities of the future, powered by renewables, will be more vibrant, human focused, and satisfying than what we inhabit in our fossil-fuel society today.

Informed by our own work in New England, *The New Net Zero* specifically focuses on cold-climate design, and while the general strategy and process for net zero design is similar for other climates, the specific metrics and details we present are suited for climates that experience 4,500 heating degree days (HDD) or greater on an annual basis. This is generally zones 4 through 7 on the climate map shown in figure P.3, or about half of the United States.

Although this map highlights these colder areas only within the United States, the specific building strategies and technologies in this book are equally suited to places with a similar climate and number of heating degree days anywhere on the planet, and broadly these strategies will make sense for any building where heating loads are predominant.

The more technical information in Part III details the nuts and bolts of cold-climate net zero strategies. But the overall tenets of net zero building and community design outlined throughout the book are applicable to all climates. Our twelve steps to net zero offer a simple, straightforward process for anyone undertaking a net zero project anywhere—from designers and builders to homeowners and building owners, environmentalists, and community planners. Currently, there are few books covering larger net zero projects; most of what has been written applies to homes and smaller-scale buildings. Yet it is larger and existing buildings that require our most urgent attention. To fill that void, we have covered buildings large and small, residential and commercial, as well as institutional buildings. We also explain how to apply net zero strategies to both new construction and renovations.

Designing buildings and communities around viable future energy sources is even more relevant today than it was over forty years ago when I began my journey on this path. Unfortunately, our society did not build on the strong beginnings of the renewable energy movement of the early 1970s. If we had, the crisis we face today could have been much less threatening.

Today we have a clear challenge and a clear choice. Our way of life is threatening all living systems. The solution is simple: lower CO_2 and end our addiction to fossil fuels.

To do that is also simple. We can make significant headway by ensuring that every new building lives within the planet's flow of renewable energy. We can decide to build and rebuild only buildings that are net producers of energy, either with renewables on-site or powered with nearby renewable community systems. From there, we can make our communities net producers.

We have the technology, tools, and knowledge we need to do this right now. We can do it one home, one building, and one community at a time.

So please join us in making net zero happen. Now.

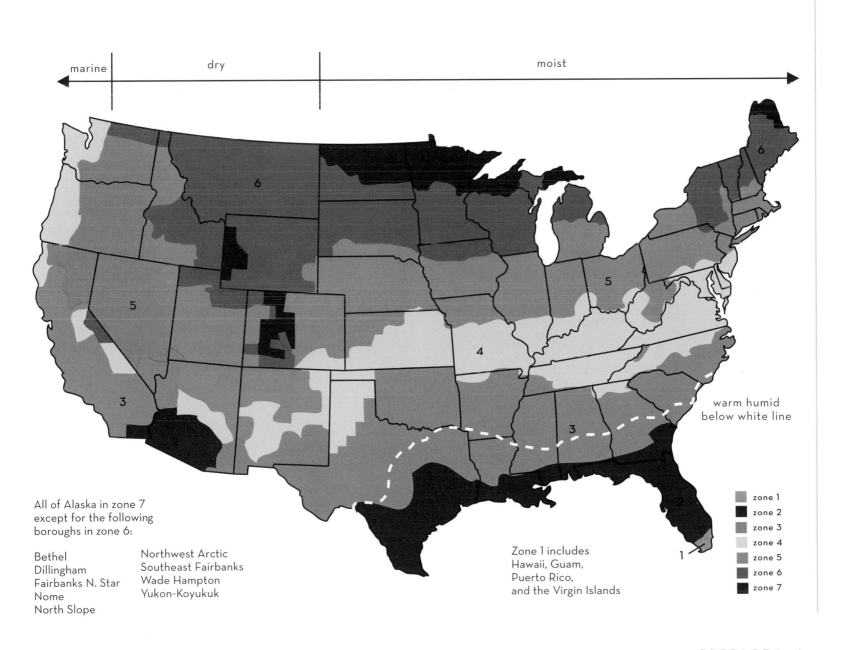

FIGURE P.3. The climate zones in the United States. The details and metrics in this book address the cold climates in zones 4 through 7.

marine

dry

moist

warm humid below white line

All of Alaska in zone 7 except for the following boroughs in zone 6:

Bethel
Dillingham
Fairbanks N. Star
Nome
North Slope

Northwest Arctic
Southeast Fairbanks
Wade Hampton
Yukon-Koyukuk

Zone 1 includes Hawaii, Guam, Puerto Rico, and the Virgin Islands

zone 1
zone 2
zone 3
zone 4
zone 5
zone 6
zone 7

FIGURE P.4. Maclay Architects' projects have an ecological foundation incorporating strategies. A green roof (*top left*) with stone elements placed on a ledge outcrop overlooking a fast-moving river. NRG (*top right*) demonstrates the feasibility of renewables to power workplaces and industrial uses. Similarly, at the Coastal Maine Botanical Gardens (*bottom left*) the design of an education building connects the interior to the surrounding botanical gardens in a daylit space using natural materials from the region. The Rubenstein School of Environment and Natural Resources at the University of Vermont (*bottom right*) engages students, faculty, and staff to embody their mission in a living building design that includes a solarium and an Eco-Machine™ for treating waste.

ACKNOWLEDGMENTS

The *New Net Zero* represents a long journey of exploration and the participation and inspiration of more people than I can appropriately acknowledge. However, I am deeply grateful for the support of all of those who have contributed in so many large and small ways. It truly has been a team effort that could not have happened without the engagement and support of my architecture firm, our larger design team, clients, builders and subcontractors, teachers and mentors, and friends and family throughout my education, practice, and career. Architecture is a unique and curious profession grounded in an integration of art, science, technology, social organization, culture, history, and much more. People, collaboration, and relationships are at the heart of the process.

My first thanks is to the people in my architecture practice who have contributed and supported the efforts that have generated our work—both the buildings that we have designed and the thinking and writing that have enabled our work and this book. This partnership has been with scores of people who have worked in our firm over the more than 40 years of its existence. For assistance writing this book, I want to thank Eileen Hee, who provided ongoing invaluable oversight, coordination, editing, and writing, and managed the book as well as our practice while writing a book, which turned out to be a much greater undertaking than any of us anticipated. I also want to extend my extreme appreciation and thanks for the work of Laura Cavin Bailey and Danielle Vitoff, who worked tirelessly on researching, documenting, editing, coordinating, and writing parts of the book over a two-year period—and to Tom Bodell, who quietly and persistently contributed his knowledge of building science and construction details to the technical parts of the book as well as with the execution of details and writing. Kevin Dennis provided graphic support that was invaluable. Chris Cook and Schuyler and Thayer Maclay provided graphic and general research, editing, and support. Pattie Lorraine, Marc Young, Bill Gallup, Megan Nedzinski, Cam Featherstonough, Will Grimm, and others in our office during this time assisted in making the project happen, either through support of the book directly, working on projects that are the foundation of the book, or completing projects in the office at the time. I would also like to specifically thank Steve Frey and Lisa Sawin Roy, who contributed to many of the projects in this book during their years in our office, and to express my appreciation to an innumerable number of other former employees for their work on projects and aspects of our thinking reflected in this book.

Consultants outside our office also were essential to the work that we have done and the knowledge we have gained with net zero buildings. We have been involved in leading-edge design, and that kind of design only happens in concert with others who are willing to take prudent and educated risks while spending significant volunteer time doing the research necessary to insure that innovative design is prudent and successful for clients and projects. Andy Shapiro of Energy Balance has worked on every innovative project our office has completed in the last 25 years, since our second double-wall project. He also has been a significant collaborator on this book—working on many of the projects featured, as well as providing valuable and generous information about content in the book. That said, the work in the book is our work, and Andy and others deserve credit for all positive aspects, but no responsibility for errors, omissions, or confusion that is generated. For that, I take all responsibility. Within our office, we think of Andy as a permanent team member. Our dialogues with him about ideas, strategies, and technologies have been essential to our growth and the work that we have done.

We have also worked with numerous other design professionals who have made significant contributions to our work. For more than 25 years, Dan Lewis, originally, and later others at Kohler and Lewis have provided innovative mechanical system design on many of our net zero projects and introduced our firm to air-source heat pumps at a time when few air-source heat pumps were in use in cold climates. LN Consulting has also contributed to innovative mechanical and electrical engineering solutions. For structural engineering, on almost all of our innovative projects we have worked with Engineering Ventures who have been invaluable in working with us to find creative, cost-effective solutions to the design of envelopes that minimize thermal bridging and thus conserve energy and avoid moisture-related problems. On our smaller projects, Ina Hladky has worked creatively with us to develop similar solutions. Lighting designers Naomi Miller and Jim Stockman have provided their expertise in high-efficiency lighting. For landscape architecture, Cynthia Knauf Landscape Design, T. J. Boyle Associates, Andropogon Associates, and SE Group have worked with us to expand from building design to the surrounding ecosystems. Artist Sarah-Lee Tarrat has collaborated with us on several projects integrating art into our design. Cx Associates and Zero by Design have provided important commissioning services on multiple projects. I apologize for not mentioning all of the other consultants we have worked with, as we have learned on every project and from everyone who has consulted with us.

It is not enough to come up with great ideas to create a net zero future. Collaboration with construction professionals is also essential to incorporate net zero strategies and technologies into the construction industry so that net zero practices become the industry standard on an ongoing basis. To accomplish this, design must be balanced with cost and constructability. We thank DEW, Engelberth, H. P. Cummings,

PC Construction Company, Bensonwood, and Naylor & Breen on larger projects and Brothers Construction, Reiss Building and Renovation, Estes & Gallup, Wright Construction, Cedar Tree Builders, Jonathan Klein, Mike Ellis, and Bill Parquet on smaller projects. In addition, Erickson Consulting and Steve Pitkin have provided valuable costing and constructability consulting on our projects to insure that the financial assessments of net zero are accurate and achievable.

The photographers we work with have made it possible to represent our projects on the pages of this book. Their patience and attention to detail allow us to share with you the beauty and details of these places. In particular, I would like to thank Jim Westphalen, Carolyn Bates, Robert Benson, and Carol Stenberg. In addition, sincere thanks to Pat Heffernan and Marketing Partners who have helped us spread our mission in Vermont and beyond.

Perhaps most important are clients. Without clients there is no building—net zero or otherwise. While net zero projects bring rewards, they are unfamiliar and new. They cost more and require more effort. They potentially add some additional risk (in addition to also offsetting and avoiding other risks). Successful net zero projects happen in partnership with clients, designers, and builders—all generating and contributing to a shared vision for a renewable future. While we have learned and grown with all of our clients, I will mention a few that have contributed significantly to our growth and learning. Jan Blomstrann at Renewable NRG Systems, Randy Smith at The Putney School, Yestermorrow School, Mark Biedron and the Willow School, the Coastal Maine Botanical Gardens, the University of Vermont, and the State of Vermont stand out as several of the clients who have placed the most trust and commitment in pursuing a net zero future. Others who have been influential in our pursuit of net zero on larger buildings are Dartmouth College, Phantom Labs, and Jeffry Glassberg. In the design of homes, Artemis Joukowsky, David and Karen Miller, Jon Larsen and Mary Peacock, Burt and Harriet Tepfer, and Ralph Earle and Jane Mendillo all stand out in working with us to go beyond typical design and construction practices. We are very grateful to all of our clients who have explored and collaborated with us to create places and projects beyond what any of us envisioned at the beginning.

In addition to those directly on our team, we have learned from others in our field of net zero and renewable energy design. This includes those we have worked with occasionally, spoken with at conferences, shared our experiences with, and consulted with informally or who have been mentors, teachers, and inspiration to us. This includes Marc Rosenbaum of Energysmiths; Gunnar Hubbard of Thornton Tomasetti; John Straube and Joe Lstiburek of Building Science Corporation; Bill Reed and Marcus Sheffer of 7group; Willy Osborn of Massachusetts Green Energy Fund, Murray Bookchin, Dan Chodorkoff, Joseph Kiefer, and others at The Institute for Social Ecology; Blair Hamilton and Beth Sachs of Vermont Energy Investment Corporation; John Connell, Mac Rood, Kate Stephenson, Robin Morris, Sylvia Smith, Bill Bialosky, John Ringel, Steve Badanes, Jim Adamson, Jim Edgcomb, Jeff Schoellkopf, Kyle Bergman, Rick Ames, Pat Pinkston, Jim Newman, and others at the Yestermorrow School; David Blittersdorf of AllEarth Renewables; and John Todd of John Todd Ecological Design. The following organizations have provided inspiration and leadership in the environmental movement: Rocky Mountain Institute, the Northeast Sustainable Energy Association, and Vermont Businesses for Social Responsibility, including Will Raap, Melinda Moulton, Terry Ehrich, Bruce Seifer, Julie Davis, Matt Rubin, Allison Hooper, and Jeffrey Hollender. Fellow architects and others in the design field have been sources of inspiration and knowledge including Dave Sellers, Jim Sanford and Richard Travers, Scott Simons, Mithun, Architerra, Bruce Coldham, Tom Horton, Bill McDonough, Tedd Benson, Steve Baer, Paul Eldrenkamp, Rick Renner, Amory Lovins, Ed Mazria, Victor Olgyay, Janine Benyus, Stephen Kellert, Katrin Klingenberg, Pliny Fisk III, Lisa Heschong, and William Lamm.

Beyond the environmental design community, I have learned and been inspired by many other thought leaders, educators, authors, innovators, and practitioners. These include Yves Lepere, Christopher Alexander, Louis Kahn. Leaders in the community of language, collaboration, and somatics have also contributed to our work and include Fernando Flores, Bob Dunham, Richard Heckler, Jen Cohen, and Gina LaRoche, as well as fellow partners in lifelong learning Suzanne Zeman and Dan Waldman. All of these people have contributed in different ways at different times.

We also have learned from all of the contributors to this book who generously gave their time, graphics, photographs, text, and advice. We have gained much support also from manufacturers, distributors, and material suppliers who have worked with us to make sure new and innovative products and new use of existing products offer durable and resilient solutions for construction.

Thanks to Chelsea Green and their support of this book. Joni Praded provided ongoing, thoughtful, and highly valuable support and assistance during writing and editing, making this book possible—particularly considering that writing this book was an entire new undertaking for me and my office. And special thanks to Pati Stone, who tirelessly assisted throughout the process in organization, design, graphics, editing, and all of the nitty gritty.

Perhaps most important are friends and family that have supported me in innumerable ways throughout my life. My mother taught me about vision and compassion, and my father was rigorous in his insight, clarity, and follow-through. Both showed me deeply the power, opportunities, and also challenges in these areas. My stepmother demonstrated that writing might even be possible for a person like me. My brother, David, and sister, Sherry, showed me other ways of seeing and experiencing that I have valued and benefited from. Without the support, love, and companionship of my wife, Alex, and two sons, Schuyler and Thayer, I never would have been able to complete this book or much of the other work that I have completed, as well as experience the richness and complexity of everyday life that is deeply meaningful and fulfilling. Lastly, I have been blessed to have lived in a community in a beautiful and caring valley in Vermont for the last 42 years, which has served as a daily reminder that living and working toward caring and nurturing communities connected to nature and all living systems within the flows of renewable energy and resources is meaningful, fulfilling, inspiring, and fun—and fully possible and necessary NOW.

PART I

What Is Net Zero?

1 | Energy and Transition

Everything in the universe may be described in terms of energy. Galaxies, stars, molecules, and atoms may be regarded as organizations of energy. Living organisms may be looked upon as engines which operate by means of energy derived directly or indirectly from the sun. The civilizations, or cultures of mankind, also, may be regarded as a form of organization of energy.[1]

—LESLIE WHITE

Energy is our fuel and foundation, the source of power for our civilization. It is ubiquitous in our patterns of daily living. It allows food to be produced and goods to be transported. It powers our cars, buildings, and industries and is essential in the creation of the materials we consume, from food and consumer goods to building products and technology. Everything, in fact, can be seen as energy in one form or another.

Look back in time, and the story was the same. Energy sculpted our settlement patterns. It was the force behind the birth of modern society. Short periods of human history may have been dominated by politics, war, individual demigods, or major climate upheavals, but the major factors shaping the evolution of civilizations stayed the same: energy, its form, its availability, and its cost.

Today the energy sources we rely on to fuel our society can be divided into two simple categories: nonrenewable and renewable. Nonrenewable energy refers to finite energy sources, those that, once exhausted, cannot be replenished. Nonrenewable energy sources include two major categories: fossil fuels such as coal, natural gas, and petroleum and radioactive fuels used in nuclear technology, such as uranium. Nonrenewable resources are currently being consumed at a rate much faster than they can be replenished by nature, and as resources decrease they will become too costly to harvest. Renewable energy refers to energy sources that renew through natural forces and processes, such as sun, wind, tidal waves, hydro, biomass, and geothermal energies. There is enough potential energy from renewable energy sources to cover all global energy needs thousands of times over.

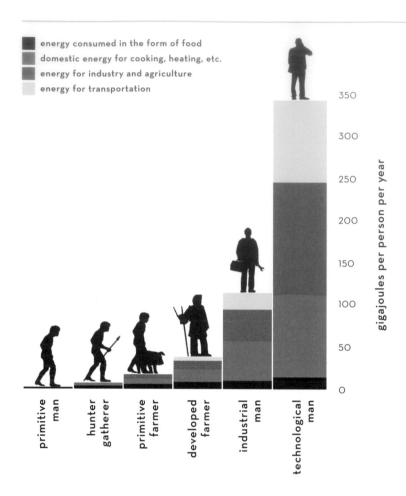

Where does the concept of net zero fit into this larger context of energy? We'll dive into the precise definition in chapter 2, but for now it's important to dispel a common misunderstanding. "Net zero" does not mean using no energy. That's impossible in our modern, high-tech world, just as it was impossible in ancient times and throughout the evolution of all life and the universe. Rather, "net zero" refers to producing, through renewable sources, more energy than is consumed—or becoming a net renewable energy producer. This new term broadly indicates a future without fossil fuels.

To most of us, net zero seems like an intriguing, new idea—a new paradigm for our energy future, one that functions on renewable resources only. But the reality is that with the exception of the historically brief fossil-fuel era in which we live today, humans have always lived in a net zero world. It is interesting how short our memories are.

Anyone reading this book will likely already know, though, that the fossil-fuel era had a profound impact on both civilization and the planet. To understand why, we need to understand that energy is to civilization what food is to biological organisms. If there is food readily available to biological organisms, the organisms grow and their population grows. We can all remember this fact from middle-school biology: if rabbits proliferate, so, too, do the foxes that eat them.

The same holds true for energy sources and the humans that depend on them. Only the story can get a bit more complex. The more energy we have, the more our populations grow, and the more energy each one of us uses. It now takes ten times more fossil-fuel energy than solar energy (as in photosynthesis) to feed us when you include the fertilizers, tractors, irrigation, transportation, processing, packaging, refrigeration, cooking, and all of the other energy-consuming

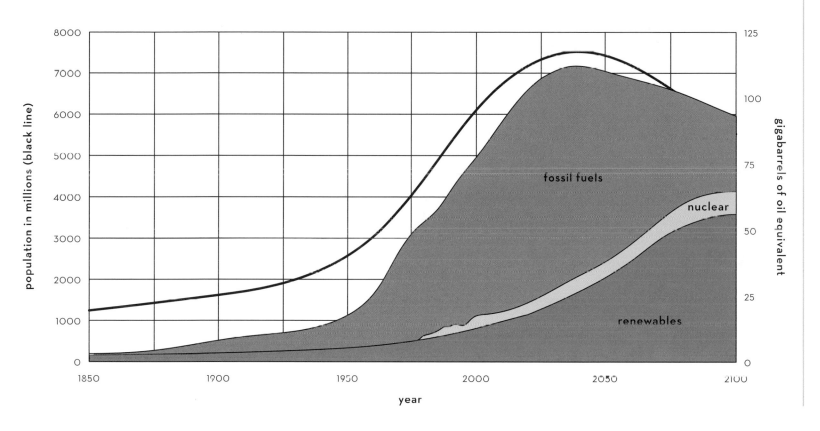

FIGURE 1.2. World energy consumption has increased rapidly with the rise in human population in the fossil-fuel era.

aspects of human food production. Over time, we've used more and more energy to produce and transport goods, services, and information. As figure 1.1 shows, our energy use per person has grown as we have evolved.

As energy became relatively easier to find and use, more people were fed with less effort, driving population growth and providing other human conveniences. Figure 1.2 shows the correlation in the historical growth of global energy consumption and population over the past few millennia, including the rapid increase in growth of energy and population in the fossil-fuel era.

The future population, quality of life, and wealth of our society will also likely relate to where our energy comes from, how it is transported to us, and ultimately how much it costs. Inexpensive energy not only fuels population growth but boosts the accumulation of wealth by society, businesses, and individuals. If energy costs rise, it will impact every aspect of

society, from the production and transportation of goods to population and settlement patterns.

Even when a society has the opportunity to transfer from a more expensive energy option to a less expensive one, the development of new infrastructure and the repatterning of human activities cause significant societal pressures and temporary additional costs.

The cost of an energy resource is related to its density and ease of collection, extraction, and transportation to where it is used. Fossil fuels are solar energy converted into plant materials and then compressed under pressure. Thus oil, coal, and natural gas contain significant energy in a relatively small volume of material that can be easily transported. Collecting solar, wind, and water power require large areas of land to collect the less concentrated forces of the sun, moving air, and water. We are arriving at a point where even fossil fuels are

FIGURE 1.3. Humans have always used diverse forms of renewable energy, including windmills, sail power, and water mills, for cooking, comfort, and production of goods and transportation.

becoming more difficult and therefore costly to access. But the predominant view remains that nonrenewable resources are much less expensive than renewable energy because they are relatively easy to capture in comparison.

Through constant innovation, we have always found better ways of using energy to serve our daily purposes. Consider the advent of the wheel, sail power, and water power; the domestication of animals; and the creation of steam engines, internal combustion engines, telephones, and computers. All these developments allowed humans to harness power in new ways. While many people believe that future innovation alone can solve our problems, including energy and climate change, the answer may not be evident until it is too late. Innovation will continue to be a critical factor in shaping human civilization, but selecting the appropriate energy source is equally or likely more important.

Social traditions can also affect the preference of one energy source over another. In general, social norms resist change, slowing down the transition from one fuel source to another. Today we see this in the resistance of big business, politicians, and most of the population to changing our primary energy source to renewables. Renewables are new and different, and people are understandably cautious. However, there are some cases where social pressures can hasten energy transitions. As an example, the Chinese government has been very aggressive in increasing the amount of their energy supply that comes from renewables, as they see the enormity of the global energy challenge and the advantageous position this transition might allow.

Our relationship with renewable energy is long indeed. As hunters and gatherers, humans used the solar energy stored in biological organisms for food, shelter, clothing, and all other material goods. Our most primary application of energy was the transference of power in the human body: we were fueled by food. Over time we began to develop additional ways of deriving energy from the environment, first with fire, which allowed the stored solar energy in wood to be used for cooking, warmth, and the production of goods. Technological innovations paralleled this growth in energy use. The development of tools in the Stone Age improved the efficiency of hunting.

The next major energy innovation came in the Neolithic revolution, which saw a major transition from hunting and gathering cultures to agriculture and settlement through the

FIGURE 1.4. Sprawl and highway-side development in the fossil-fuel era.

domestication of plants and animals. This innovation caused an enormous transition in lifestyle. Society could for the first time produce a surplus of food to store and trade, allowing for increased social complexity and the first population explosion on the planet. While the Neolithic revolution reached parts of the world at different times, archeological data of plant and animal domestication tell us that it started around 10,000 BC and continued to around 3000 BC. During that period the world's human population grew astronomically: before the Neolithic revolution it had fluctuated between 5 and 8 million, but by around 4000 BC it had grown to 60 to 70 million.[2]

The need for transportation spurred further innovations in renewable energy. Humans used newly domesticated animals to carry goods, allowing for trade over longer distances. The development of the wheel spurred greater use of domesticated animals, and primitive boats soon made transport by water more efficient than transport over land. Later sail-powered boats allowed for even larger volumes of goods to be transferred over greater distances with less energy.

The way we harnessed renewable energy to meet our needs and desires grew more and more diverse. Industry arose with the fabrication of stone and metal tools and weapons and expanded to the development of water mills and windmills to grind grain and produce textiles. Each of these innovations offered increased efficiency and levels of production that stimulated wealth and human population growth. In fact, renewable energy fueled our world until about the mid-nineteenth century, when nonrenewables took over. First came coal, surpassed by oil in the 1950s. Today our world runs for the most part on oil, natural gas, and coal, with smaller percentages of nuclear power and renewables.

The Current Energy Transition

It is easy to understand how rising costs for one fuel source drive the market for other fuel sources, but it's more difficult to predict the timing and understand how the transition relates to our everyday decisions. For that, it is useful to look at longer-term trends and past changes in energy sources. Figure 1.5 shows our past and current major energy transitions. Note that fossil fuels prevail for just a few centuries of human existence.

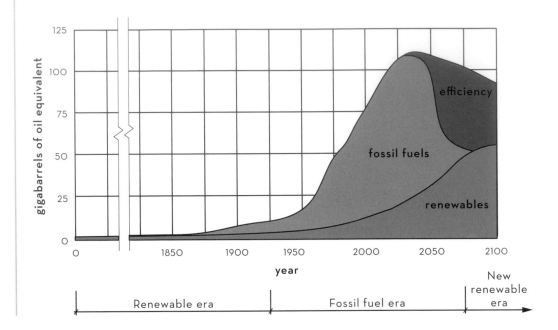

FIGURE 1.5. The gradually increasing use of renewables over millennia has been interrupted for several hundred years by the fossil-fuel era, which will wane as we return to renewables.

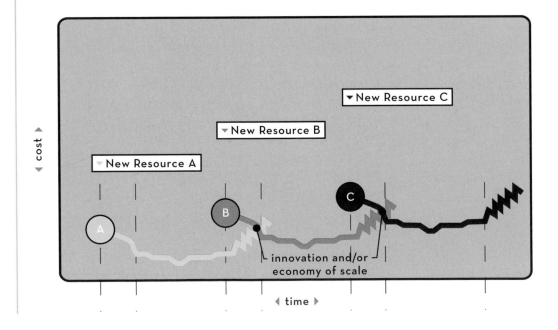

FIGURE 1.6. During energy transitions, the cost of the old energy rises while the cost of the new energy resource declines because of innovation and increased production.

Amory Lovins and others project that we can and should substantially transition off fossil fuels by 2050 by using efficiency measures to reduce consumption by 50 percent.[3]

When we shift from this overall look at the history of human energy use to the period of transition, we can see a pattern. Energy cost starts out expensive, then drops dramatically with ongoing innovation and improvement and remains relatively flat for a long time as the source is fairly easy to find. As the source becomes scarcer, the price typically increases inconsistently, with spikes and plateaus. When a new energy source emerges, the decreasing cost of the new energy and the increasing cost of the old energy source converge. As figure 1.6 shows, once this happens, consumers switch to the new source as it becomes less expensive than the old source.

For example, solar energy came into the market in the 1970s, was expensive relative to oil, and remains more expensive even today. However, the relative difference is less. The cost of all renewable energy sources including solar are decreasing as cheaper, more efficient technologies are being developed. Already today solar photovoltaic costs and large wind costs are less than nuclear, nearly competitive with oil, and slightly more expensive than natural gas.

Because fossil-fuel prices continue to rise, at some point (likely in the near future) the renewable sources will become less expensive than the fossil-fuel sources, and we will be at about a break-even point when comparing the costs of using fossil fuels to the costs of using renewables. We can argue about exactly where we are in this pattern of transition, but we do know that all of our fossil-fuel sources have finite reserves, and they will all peak—as oil already has. They could all be depleted at some point and will all increase in expense as demand grows and supply declines. We also know that in our near future there will be no energy resource as easy to access as fossil fuels have been. Drilling a hole and having black oil come spurting out of it is an incredibly inexpensive way to find energy.

Unless we happen upon some magical, cheap energy source, we can assume that our transition from one energy source to another will take many decades and consume many resources—as energy transitions have historically. Our current transition is particularly complex because it involves multiple fossil-fuel sources that are in use concurrently. We will need to switch to new supply and distribution systems and create a broad range of other energy infrastructure.

But with climate change upon us, we have no choice except to wean ourselves from fossil fuels as fast as we possibly can. We need solutions that are viable and practical and can start being implemented today. The only energy sources that seem capable of fulfilling this need are renewables.

Experts fluctuate on just how long we have before we encounter runaway climate change and its catastrophic results, but most agree that we have just four or so decades to make serious change. As we shift course, we'll need to rely on natural gas, oil, and coal as transitional fuels, though as these resources become less plentiful it will become even more difficult, risky, and costly to reach them, as we now see when extracting oil from tar sands or deep-sea wells or fracking gas from deep, ultrathin veins in the earth. During this transitional phase, biomass is likely to be a prominent renewable energy source for some time, but power from solar, wind, water, and other sources will eventually outpace it as demand for biomass for the production of material goods grows—which will happen when fossil fuels become less available for plastic production and agricultural operations.

However, we will need to conserve energy in every sector of our economy, including transportation, manufacturing, electric generation, and transmission. Energy efficiency and occupant behavior have big roles to play as well when it comes to buildings, which are responsible for about 40 percent of energy consumption in the United States.[4] Our work in net zero building design indicates that energy consumption in buildings can be cut by 70 to 80 percent with improved occupant comfort and satisfaction and increased building durability. These efficiencies, combined with renewables, currently raise building costs between 5 and 15 percent.

As we change our energy profile, how do we decide which energy sources to favor and in what circumstances? Earlier we said that the change happened when the cost of the old energy source exceeded that of the new energy source. Sounds simple, right? But maybe it isn't. Another question might be: What is the true cost of energy? Or how about the full cost of fossil-fuel use, including subsidies and health and environmental impacts? Or the full cost of climate change, including river and coastal flooding; ocean rise; hurricanes; tornadoes; melting glaciers; water loss to agriculture, ecosystems, and habitat; and other problems that we do not even know of yet? What is the full cost for nuclear energy, including subsidies, insurance by governments, waste storage, and pollution from meltdowns? There are real costs associated with these issues that are external to the direct use of fossil fuels and nuclear energy. These externalities, as they are called, do not appear in our modern economic accounting. Amory Lovins, in his book *Reinventing Fire*, estimates that the external costs—above the cost the consumer pays to purchase oil—of the US addiction to and dependence on oil was over $500 billion in 2008.[5]

We also need to consider the value of ecosystems in our global economy. The services ecosystems provide us are generally categorized into four areas: provisioning, supporting, regulating, and culture. Renewable energy is one example of an ecosystem service; others include seed dispersal, pollination, water, minerals, pharmaceuticals, fish, agriculture, air and water purification, carbon sequestration, flood mitigation, pest and disease control, recreation, and spiritual renewal.[6] A frequently referenced peer-reviewed paper assessed the value of ecosystems services in 1997 to be between $16 and $54 trillion.[7] However, one might assess the value as infinite, since life on Earth could not exist without ecosystems. The authors Paul Hawken, Amory Lovins, and L. Hunter Lovins have suggested a new economic model, natural capitalism, which restructures our economic system to value rather than exploit nature.[8]

Returning to energy, if we add the true costs of fossil-fuel and nuclear-power use and subtract for the value lost through

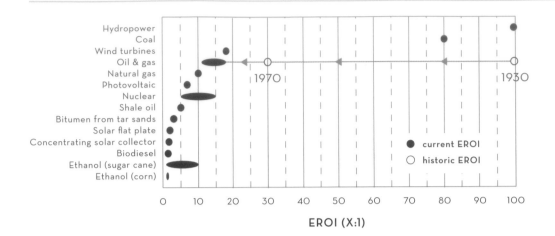

FIGURE 1.7. The energy return on investment (EROI) is a ratio that compares the amount of energy available from an energy source to the amount of energy it takes to find, extract, process, and deliver energy from that source. This graph shows the EROIs of resources in use today as well as the changes over time for some resources. It is evident that renewable energy sources are becoming competitive with nonrenewable sources.

destruction of ecosystems, our societal balance sheet and profit and loss statements would look very different. And the bottom line would very clearly point to renewables as significantly less expensive than nonrenewables and nuclear today.

But for the moment let's forget about these externalities and ecosystem services and just evaluate our potential future energy sources using the traditional method of analyzing the energy return on investment (EROI). In an EROI analysis, if an energy source generates a lot more energy than it requires to extract and process the energy, then the energy source is more valuable than another source requiring more energy output. When oil was first discovered, for instance, the EROI was approximately 100, meaning that it took an average of one barrel of oil worth of energy to extract 100 barrels of oil.

As figure 1.7 shows, current EROI analyses indicate that most of the conventional fossil-fuel sources provide the highest EROI. However, renewable sources are nearly competitive, especially when compared to fossil fuels extracted with some of the extreme processes now becoming more common. As the reserves that are the easiest to exploit are depleted and new reserves become harder to find or more difficult to exploit, the EROI has decreased to below 20, resulting in other sources' becoming comparatively more viable. Over time, fossil fuel EROI numbers have been declining and are likely to continue declining; at the same time, renewable EROI numbers are improving.

So even with a traditional and far less comprehensive way of analyzing the economics of an energy source, it is still clear that there is a time when the rising costs of one fuel drive the shift to another fuel. And right now the numbers point to a transition from nonrenewables to renewables. But even when we know the inevitable result, the timing is hard to predict.

Tomorrow's Energy Sources

Many people claim that renewables cannot power the planet. But a look at actual capacity seems to suggest otherwise. Figure 1.8 shows that in 2011 the world consumption of energy was 522 quads, and our nonrenewable reserves were more than seventy times greater than world energy consumption. So theoretically, if demand does not go up, we have seventy years of nonrenewable energy. Obviously, some new reserves will be found, but many of these will likely be in places such as the deep ocean or tar sands or the Arctic, making them too difficult, costly, and risky to extract and transport. If we powered the planet with just nuclear, the nuclear reserves, using today's technology, would be depleted in four years; with just natural gas, in fourteen years; with just oil, in twenty years; with just coal, thirty-five years. Is there a similar issue with renewable supply? No. In fact, renewables could produce more than 7,000 times as much power as is needed at today's world consumption levels—every year, forever.

So you might say this is feasible, but is it economically realistic? In the deserts of the Southwest there is adequate solar power to power the United States. There is hydroelectric power potential in the Northwest, wind on both coasts and

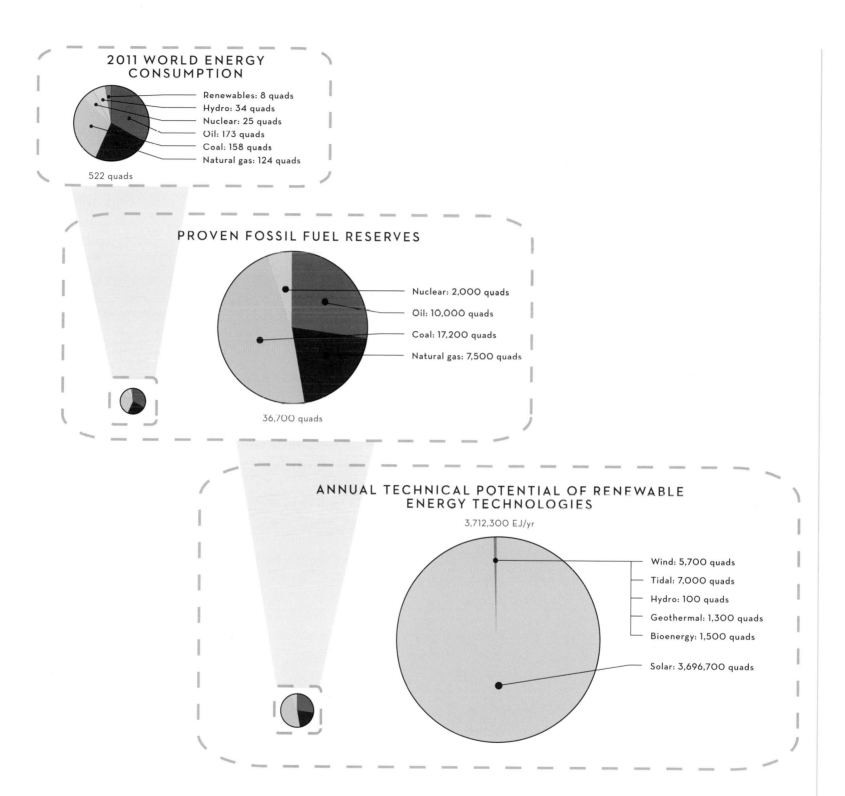

2011 WORLD ENERGY CONSUMPTION

- Renewables: 8 quads
- Hydro: 34 quads
- Nuclear: 25 quads
- Oil: 173 quads
- Coal: 158 quads
- Natural gas: 124 quads

522 quads

PROVEN FOSSIL FUEL RESERVES

- Nuclear: 2,000 quads
- Oil: 10,000 quads
- Coal: 17,200 quads
- Natural gas: 7,500 quads

36,700 quads

ANNUAL TECHNICAL POTENTIAL OF RENEWABLE ENERGY TECHNOLOGIES

3,712,300 EJ/yr

- Wind: 5,700 quads
- Tidal: 7,000 quads
- Hydro: 100 quads
- Geothermal: 1,300 quads
- Bioenergy: 1,500 quads
- Solar: 3,696,700 quads

FIGURE 1.8. Current world energy consumption is small in comparison to total proven fossil fuel reserves. Renewable energy sources offer millions of times more energy annually than what we need at our current consumption rate.

in the Midwest, and solar everywhere for local generation. Some researchers estimate that there is enough energy in the deserts of North Africa alone to provide forty times the global electric energy demand in 2006.[9] Availability is not the issue. What's lacking is the will to make change. Let's take a look at what the key renewables can offer.

SOLAR. The most abundant renewable resource, solar is available to some degree almost everywhere on the planet, and solar domestic hot water and photovoltaic (PV) systems are feasible options for local energy needs in most locations. While individual sites may have limitations, solar energy can be supplied at community, urban, and regional scales and fed into the global energy grid to be used almost anywhere. Large-scale installations that feed industrial, urban, and national needs are becoming more common around the world. Technological advances in PV, with associated rapid cost decreases, continue at an accelerating pace. By 2020 the US Department of Energy's SunShot Initiative hopes to reduce PV costs to around $1 per watt, the equivalent of six cents per kilowatt-hour, which is lower than coal.[10]

Other large-scale solar-powered technologies include solar furnaces and parabolic collectors. In the future we can expect to see photovoltaic installations along highways, in median strips, on parking meters, in traffic devices, and more. With installations of over 300 megawatts (MW), these systems can rival coal and nuclear power plants. In 2012 Germany had the largest installed photovoltaic capacity, at over 32 gigawatts (GW); China, the United States, and other nations are also increasing capacity rapidly.[11]

WIND. Global wind power demand and installed capacity, too, have escalated in the last decade. Wind costs were approaching grid parity in 2011, with onshore wind power down to $68 per MW in the United States, Sweden, Brazil, and Mexico at a time when coal in those same areas was about $67 per MW.[12] In 2012 the cumulative global wind power installed was 282 MW.[13]

TIDAL. While less widely recognized and less abundant than solar and wind, tidal power has significant potential and is a reliable and constant source of energy. Tidal mills use barrages, similar to dams, along rivers and bays with tide changes. Gates in the dams are regulated to allow the rising tide to enter a storage area and the falling tide to exit. Energy is generated as the water flows through turbines located at the gates. Tidal mills were common on the East Coast of the United States and Europe in the nineteenth century. The city of Boston had multiple mills where the Back Bay now is. The Bay of Fundy was proposed as a site in the 1930s but never developed. Tidal power has been used in France, South Korea, and other countries and is likely to be used increasingly in the future.

GEOTHERMAL. Geothermal power is produced from thermal energy generated below the earth's surface. The potential energy available from the earth's core is vast. However, this energy can be used most easily in places where the earth's heat bubbles to the surface, such as near natural hot springs or at tectonic plate boundaries where water heated with geothermal energy can be piped from a hot spring to a building for heating or to an electric-generating plant—a process that is common in Iceland, where geothermal energy is abundant. Recent technological advances could make geothermal energy available in other locations by drilling wells thousands of feet deep. While this geothermal energy from drilling is accessible and abundant, deep-well production is not yet a cost-effective approach.

The public often confuses geothermal energy with ground-source heat pumps. While geothermal power uses heat stored deep underground, ground-source heat pumps use annually supplied solar heat that is stored at the earth's surface. Thus, a ground-source heat pump is an efficient use of electricity for heating and cooling. (See chapter 7 for more information on heat pumps.)

HYDRO. Hydropower, available from falling or flowing water, has been used for millennia to power flour, textile, saw, and other types of industrial mills. Today hydro dams are most commonly used to generate electricity. Because hydro is an established renewable resource, most of the best sites have been developed; thus hydro does not have as much potential for new energy generation as other renewable options.

BIOMASS. Biomass is material grown by living organisms, typically plants. Some forms—such as wood, switchgrass, and agricultural waste—can be used as a direct energy source to produce heat and/or electricity through combustion.

FIGURE 1.9. The Solar Energy Generating System is a 354-megawatt solar thermal electricity generation facility located in California's Mojave Desert.

FIGURE 1.10. The eighty-eight-turbine Sheringham Shoal Offshore Wind Farm in the United Kingdom has a rated capacity of 317 MW.

FIGURE 1.11. The Rance Tidal Power Station, located in Brittany, France, has a peak rating of 240 MW. Built in 1966, it is the world's first tidal power station.

FIGURE 1.12. Geothermal energy is derived directly from hot springs, geysers, or volcanic hot spots or by drilling deeply into the earth's core, as at the Nesjavellir Geothermal Power Station in Iceland, which generates 120 MW of electrical power.

FIGURE 1.13. The Three Gorges Dam in China generates 22,500 MW. It was the largest such dam in the world when it was completed in 2012.

FIGURE 1.14. The Tracy Biomass Plant near San Francisco, California, generates 21 MW and uses agricultural and industrial biomass by-products as fuel.

Corn, sorghum, sugarcane, palms, algae, and many more plants also can be transformed into biofuels to substitute for liquid fossil fuels.

Tens of thousands of years ago humans burned biomass to cook, and it is still a significant part of the current global energy economy. Biomass use will likely continue to increase and will be more competitive in supplying energy for heating and electric generation. New technology has significantly improved efficiency and significantly reduced emissions, pollution, and maintenance in modern chunk, chip, and pellet applications. However, it is as a liquid fuel that biomass has the greatest promise. Since the transportation sector accounted for approximately 28 percent of US energy consumption in 2012 and renewables currently do not easily power vehicles and airplanes, the use of biofuels as an energy source for transportation is a critical element for any transition beyond fossil fuels.[14]

Even with technological improvements, though, biomass has potential downsides. It can still pollute when used for combustion if more expensive pollution and efficiency measures are not used. But when combustion is clean, the only significant carbon impacts come from harvesting and transportation, since decaying trees and vegetation release carbon anyway.

Perhaps the most important consideration revolves around land use. Biomass cultivation competes with agriculture, forestry, and ecosystems. Its conflict with food production became clear when the cultivation of corn for ethanol reduced land for food production and caused higher food prices.[15] A 2011 study found that the EROI of corn ethanol is close to 1, meaning that almost as much energy is consumed in making this fuel as is provided in the final product sold at the gas pump. And without government subsidies, corn ethanol would not be profitable.[16] Its conflict with ecosystems protection has similarly come to the public's attention: the increasing demand for palm oil in biodiesel fuel production is causing more tropical forest to be cleared for palm plantations. Also, the more wood we use for fuel, the less there is available to replace plastics, which will become increasingly expensive and difficult to produce as fossil fuels decline, adding to the many pressures already placed on forestland.

Solar, wind, and hydro are better suited than biomass for producing electricity, heating, and other direct energy uses. Even so, biomass is likely to continue to be used as a direct energy source during this transition period, then phased out over time. During that transition phase, there will likely be a major increase in biomass use both as a liquid fuel for vehicles and a substitute for fossil-fuel plastics.

However, algae—the newest frontier in biofuel production—may come with far fewer problems: it can be grown in artificial ponds; it does not need agricultural land for cultivation; and in terms of EROI, the US Department of Energy claims that algae production is thirty times greater per land area than that of other biofuels.[17] It has been estimated that all 250 million automobiles in the country could be powered by 18,750 square miles of algae production (approximately 0.49 percent of US land, or 17 percent of Nevada) if we drove our cars as many miles as we do today, fuel mileage remained the same, and algae energy production improves as projected.[18]

In another search for liquid fuels for the transportation sector, the Joint Center for Artificial Photosynthesis led by Caltech; the University of California, Berkeley; and Lawrence Livermore National Laboratory are working on an artificial photosynthesis project to convert water, CO_2, and sunlight into a fuel that can be transported and stored—a more direct solar fuel than biofuels.[19] While these solar-based fuels are still in the research and development phase, innovators, entrepreneurs, corporations, and governments are making significant investment in them.

EMERGING ENERGY SOURCES. In addition to deep-well geothermal, algae biofuel, and solar fuels, we are likely to see other trends emerge. Extremely large wind turbines will be more common off our shorelines. To avoid the cost and environmental impact of dams for tidal power, some have proposed tethering turbines to the bottom of rapidly moving water in rivers and along coasts with strong currents. The movement of waves is being used to generate electricity. And in other areas thermal gradients in water are being used to generate power. While these sources have less potential for power generation everywhere, they are effective in specific locations.

Smart Grid and Storage

Energy produced by fossil fuels can generally be stored for use when needed. But for renewables to power the planet, energy must be distributed to where it is needed at the time that it is needed, requiring storage as well as distribution. Hydro can be turned on and off very quickly—in fact more quickly than most fossil-fuel systems can be started and stopped for electrical generation. However, other renewable sources provide power when the renewable energy source is available—when the sun shines or the wind blows.

These differences demand new storage and distribution infrastructure. Fossil fuels have used a centralized distribution system: the power is produced centrally and transported to a large power plant located close to where it will eventually be used. Renewable power generation will create a decentralized grid with power coming from decentralized renewable sources. This decentralized grid will be combined with integrated distributed storage.

New strategies and technologies are on the horizon. In the meantime, the traditional grid can balance renewable energy sources to some degree, allowing renewables to be produced where available and consumed far away where needed. For instance, the excess solar electric generation in a sunny or windy area can be used in a cloudy or calm area without storage. Most grid experts agree that renewables can provide up to 20 percent of the energy in the grid with no complications. Experience in Europe indicates that it is likely that renewables can provide up to 50 or 60 percent of the grid's power, probably higher with a smart grid, before there is a problem. In the United States, where the outdated national electrical grid causes frequent major brownouts and blackouts, we need serious innovations that allow electricity to be efficiently moved over larger distances and stored.

The emerging smart grid allows user loads to be adjusted to grid needs, significantly increasing the grid efficiency. Just as communications devices deliver digital communications to Internet protocol (IP) addresses, the smart grid delivers power to individual addresses as well, allowing power to be turned on and off at every user location to control grid power loads. So if the grid needed power, and my building had an agreement with the utility that allowed them to juggle my power supply in exchange for lower rates, the grid could turn off power at my building and use it for other specific needs. These smart-grid agreements specify what can be turned on or off so that a building's critical functions aren't cut off.

This smart grid also allows for other innovative distributed energy storage strategies. For instance, in the winter water could be heated at night, at low, off-peak rates, in homes or other buildings with a domestic hot water load and then used during the day when the building calls for hot water and when rates are higher. Or electric cars could have oversized batteries that allow for storing energy from the grid. Batteries could be charged at home at night, on cheaper, off-peak rates, and then the car could be plugged in during the day, and the power company could get the stored power back. These batteries could also supply other electrical needs in the home to modulate grid loads. These innovations require larger household and/or car batteries but are likely, given continuing improvements in battery storage over the last decade. The increased storage prospects of a smart grid would also help encourage the use of PVs for both net zero and non-net-zero buildings.

The growth of this kind of distributed energy production technology has been encouraged by relatively recent federal regulations that opened the door to net metering across the nation. Net metering allows individual customers who generate their own power at their site, or on other sites within the same utility service area, to access power from the grid when they need it and sell their own power back to the grid, at the same price, when they produce it—essentially running the meter backward and earning a credit on their utility bill for the energy they produce. In some states customers can only earn credits for as much as they consume each month. In other states customers can earn credit for more than they consume each month.

That's why, with renewables, we will end up with a highly flexible and smart integrated, distributed, energy production, storage, and distribution system, which will likely be as transformative in the energy sector as the Internet has been in communications. In addition to being highly efficient, this distributed energy production system will be less expensive and much safer from terrorist threats.

FIGURE 1.15. Mesa Verde: The beauty of human creativity is amazing and inspiring.

The Big View: Energy, Beauty, and Human Settlement

In our ongoing journey from hunter-gatherers to computer users, energy and settlement patterns have been intertwined. When humans were totally dependent on the wild ecosystem, they continually moved in small groups in search of food. There was little or no settlement, and humans traveled in small family or extended family groups.

With the advent of agriculture and animal husbandry, which were innovations that used the sun's energy to cultivate crops and animal power to work the fields, humans began to stay in one place, first in small tribal settlements and then in large villages with stored food. Later, water mills and windmills allowed for the expansion of industry beyond earlier farm and animal-based industrial activity. This also fueled the movement of goods, spawned villages catering to increasingly specialized trades, and eventually gave rise to larger urban centers. While the renewable energy was still dispersed, various forms of storage, including crops, water power, firewood, and wind, all allowed for the more concentrated use of energy along with the denser human settlement that accompanied it.

Eventually, in the nineteenth century, coal came on the scene, creating the industrial city and associated urban lifestyle. With coal came trains, large-scale manufacturing, more movement of goods, dense concentrations of housing, and retail trade. This new, inexpensive energy source fueled dramatic wealth and population growth.

The discovery of significant amounts of oil in the late nineteenth century set the stage for the next major transition in daily life and settlement. Since this time oil has become civilization's primary energy source. Oil, similarly to coal, was an intensely concentrated form of energy, which meant it could be transported and used almost anywhere. But because oil in its liquid form was far more easily distributed than coal, energy and settlement no longer needed to be as intimately connected.

Today most of us live in a world shaped by oil, in cities and suburbs strewn with parking lots, shopping malls, and uniform architecture. With people enslaved to their cars, the interaction and cohesiveness of earlier community life has been significantly reduced and lost, and our community structure has been drastically altered.

As anthropologist Joseph Tainter points out, "Energy flow and sociopolitical organization are opposite sides of an equation. Neither can exist, in a human group, without the other, nor can either undergo substantial change without altering both the opposite member and the balance of the equation. Energy flow and sociopolitical organization must evolve in harmony."[20]

There are, however, a few other drivers of human lifestyle that have remained fundamental for as long as we have existed. Everyone from yesterday's hunter-gatherers to today's nine-to-fivers has been concerned with survival (whether physical or

FIGURE 1.16. Hammarby Sjöstad, Sweden: This urban redevelopment is part of the Stockholm municipality and is an example of the integration of human and natural communities. Here, the restoration of ecosystems connected to a pedestrian-oriented community offers a healthy, nurturing, and inspiring quality of life.

emotional), community (whether family, tribe, or Facebook), materiality and economy (whether arrows and food or computers, SUVs, and 401(k)s), and spirit (whether organized religion or simple wonder). The prominence of each of these concerns may have ebbed and flowed over the course of our history, but they have never vanished.

Another constant in our evolving history is the role of beauty. Whether found in nature, art, or the built environment, beauty reminds us that we are just an infinitesimal part of an awesome and inspiring world. We can see it in artifacts dating back to ancient civilizations in Mesopotamia, India, and China. We can find it in the diverse evolving empires of China, Greece, Rome, Egypt, Babylonia, and Mesoamerica. Walking through ancient remains, we can visualize the richness of daily life—of growing and finding food; of prayer with others; of living closely connected within the larger community of families, tribes, city-states, and empires. Additionally, we can see the interconnections with surrounding regions and ecosystems in providing food, resources, energy, and trade.

What was it like living in these beautiful places? What went on in daily life? What did the inhabitants really care about, dream about, or fear? What did they value, and what gave their lives meaning? And how does all this connect to the physical world they created?

There exists a continuous interplay between physical space and human activity that generates and evolves the future. Whether now or thousands of years ago, our quality and way of life gives us purpose and meaning, and our human-built, physical world supports and expresses this way of life.

So how might our needs for survival, community, spirit, beauty, and more come together in a world shaped by renewables? Paul Hawken, Fritjof Capra, David Korten, Ken Wilber, and many other modern thinkers believe we are at a turning point as powerful as the one that occurred between the Middle Ages and Renaissance. There is a growing consensus that our current scientific and technological framework will not get us out of the massive challenges we face on a global scale. As Albert Einstein once said, "The problems that exist in the world today cannot be solved by the level of thinking that created them."[21]

There is great hope that the emerging paradigm—the force that determines how we live and how we design and inhabit our world in the future—will be grounded in an understanding and appreciation of life and living systems and a desire to restore and regenerate them.

Building individual dwellings and communities that can evolve in harmony with ecosystems and restore connections between people and nature is step one in this process. But whether you are a designer, builder, homeowner, or building owner, remembering your connection to this larger shift is key. We should be thinking about net zero communities and infrastructures if we're going to build the world we want to live in.

2 | Defining the New Net Zero

A Net Zero Energy Building is proof that it is possible to live within our means.
—INTERNATIONAL LIVING FUTURE INSTITUTE

To us, the definition of a net zero project at any scale—a building, a community, a country, or a planet—is simple: it produces more energy than it consumes on an annual basis using only renewable energy in the process.

Yet there has been much discussion about how to define "net zero" and what standards a net zero project should meet. The debate has become quite detailed and in some cases even nitpicky—not atypical for an emerging discipline. But the question of how we build a net zero world can be answered only when we all agree on the standards that support that goal. So to advance the definition debate, in this chapter we will lay out a new net zero paradigm, including metrics and definitions that promote development of net zero not only for buildings but also for larger projects, such as communities and beyond.

A building's energy performance is traditionally evaluated by relative metrics; it is ranked based on a percentage reduction in energy consumption in relation to a level of existing building or code-compliant performance. Thus, someone might claim a certain building is 10 percent or 40 percent better than code or than the building before renovation. While relevant, this does not tell us much about how far along the path to a fossil-fuel-free, net zero, and carbon-neutral goal this performance is getting us. As global climate change and peak oil assume a larger role in the development of our policies and our future, absolute metrics must replace the relative metrics of the past—and the absolute standard of net zero can move the building profession toward a renewable future.

The Definition Debate

Any definition of "net zero" requires that the energy produced to power a building or project must come from renewable sources. The differences lie in each definition's

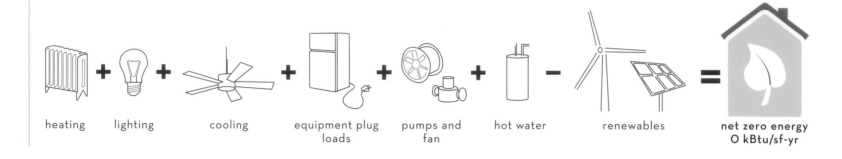

FIGURE 2.1. The concept of net zero is simple: a building meets the requirements of net zero if all energy loads in the building are matched by renewable energy production on an annual basis.

heating + lighting + cooling + equipment plug loads + pumps and fan + hot water − renewables = net zero energy O kBtu/sf-yr

requirements for where the energy consumed by a building must be generated and whether or not a building can consume any fossil fuels and still be considered net zero.

Various sustainable-building authorities have developed their own "net zero" definitions and metrics. Most of these, though, relate only to the design and performance of a single building. Some standards require that all energy consumed or generated come directly from the building footprint or from the building property. Other definitions allow for a building to be powered by fossil fuels (as when burning natural gas in the building boiler to provide heating) as long as the building produces an equivalent amount of energy from renewable sources to offset its fossil-fuel consumption. There are ongoing questions about how this offset is calculated: does one kBtu of electricity supplied by the grid really equal one kBtu of renewable energy produced on the property? Is all electricity created equal? Should differences between the generation of energy from fossil fuel and renewable sources be considered?

Additionally, some definitions allow biomass to be considered as a renewable energy source. However, while there are opportunities to create carbon-neutral projects using wood sourced from the property, that kind of long-term, on-property wood supply is rare. For that reason, our own net zero standards do not allow the use of biomass.

Let's review some of the definitions. The American Society of Heating, Refrigerating and Air-Conditioning Engineers (ASHRAE), an international leader in energy and engineering,

defines a net zero energy building as "a building which, on an annual basis, uses no more energy than is provided by the building's on-site renewable energy sources."[1] Similarly, the European Council for an Energy Efficient Economy states that "a net zero energy building is where, as a result of the very high level of energy efficiency of the building, the overall annual primary energy consumption is equal to or less than the energy production from renewable energy sources on site."[2]

Under these current definitions, a building's property is a major factor in determining whether the building will be able to achieve net zero or not. It is quite easy to achieve net zero on a wide-open rural property but quite challenging in a dense urban environment. To acknowledge these limitations, other definitions recognize off-property energy production as feasible for creating a net zero project.

The National Renewable Energy Laboratory (NREL) outlines a more detailed and tiered definition, with four separate distinctions for classifying a net zero energy building (NZEB) based on energy supply options. They start with a building that reduces energy use for all projects through energy efficiency. The goal is for that building to meet its energy demands with renewable energy generated on the building footprint (NZEB:A). If demand cannot be met through renewables on the building footprint, additional energy production can be installed on the property (NZEB:B). When options are limited on the property, the third distinction allows for renewable energy sources, such as wood chips, to be brought in to power systems connected to the building's electricity or hot/chilled water distribution (NZEB:C). This option would also apply to renewable energy projects built specifically for the project but located off-site and net metered. The last classification, if the first three criteria cannot be met, is that renewable energy certificates can be purchased through a certified source (NZEB:D).[3]

The International Living Future Institute (ILFI), the organization currently offering third-party certification of net zero energy projects, defines a net zero building as one where "one hundred percent of the building's energy needs on a net annual basis must be supplied by on-site renewable energy."[4] While the definition states renewables must be on the property, there is room to adjust these requirements and achieve net zero through "the implementation of solutions beyond the individual project scale that maximize ecological benefit while maintaining self-sufficiency at the city block, neighborhood, or community scale."[5] This solution strives for an elegant way to address property limitations, one we agree with for creating a net zero project that allows net metering and installing renewables in appropriate locations.

These definitions for net zero buildings do not put a limit on energy consumption as long as the consumption is matched by renewable production, but some do encourage energy efficiency as the first step. This means that new or existing buildings that consume high amounts of energy can qualify as net zero just by adding large numbers of renewables.

But again, do standards like this put us on the best path to a net zero world? It is this question that we believe should frame the discussion around how to define "net zero."

Framing a New Net Zero Strategy

To address this gap in current net zero thinking, we need to redefine the ideal net zero building as a net zero project that extends beyond one building or one property, anchoring its end goal not just in building performance but also in its contribution to a net zero community and a net zero future. In other words, we need to look differently at how to design and build homes, offices, institutional buildings, industrial centers, and other structures or complexes. So let's begin.

A net zero project is any project that generates more energy from renewable sources than it consumes, period. That said, a net zero project, in our thinking, needs to meet some additional criteria.

- It also must reduce energy loads of the building to a minimized level. Just installing massive renewables to power inefficient buildings does not make sense.
- The renewable energy systems it uses need to be created specifically for the project. In other words, if not for the project, the renewable energy system would not have been built. However, this renewable energy system does not need to be located on the specific building footprint or property—a particularly important distinction when we consider the immensity of existing building stock that may not have adequate resources on the property for renewable-energy generation. The 1970s idea of the energy-independent building will not generate an energy-independent world since we rely on the electric grid for reaching net zero on an annual basis. Rather, we must consider a larger scale and context for the location of renewable energy built for a specific project, which focuses on how we use renewable energy and connect it to the energy load of our buildings.
- We also define "net zero" as not using biomass or fossil fuels that get offset through renewable energy. However, using biomass can help achieve a carbon-neutral building (different from a net zero building), as discussed later in the chapter.

The first step to a net zero society is load reduction—the reduction of society-wide energy consumption. Instead of focusing singularly on the metric of net zero, we should focus on the energy performance of all new and existing buildings. This means we must first measure energy consumption for each building using an energy-use intensity (EUI) number (see the sidebar "Understanding Building Energy") and benchmark performance against similar building types—comparing schools with schools, single-family homes with single-family homes, offices with offices, and so on. We should establish EUI numbers that are cost effective for net zero buildings based

To understand net zero buildings, you need to understand building energy and energy use intensity (EUI). EUI is a critical metric that describes building energy use in total energy consumption relative to the building's size. An EUI number for a building is calculated by taking the total energy consumed in one year, measured in kBtu, and dividing it by the total conditioned square footage of the building.

To understand this concept in greater detail, you must understand the measure of kBtu, which we calculate in order to normalize energy sources into one unit. One kBtu refers to 1,000 Btu, or British thermal units. One Btu is the amount of energy in one matchstick and is further defined as the energy required to increase the temperature of 1 pound of water by 1°F. This is a relatively small unit of measure when considering building energy use, so to reduce the number of zeros we instead use the kBtu.

EUI numbers are reported in kBtu/sf-yr (or kWh/sm-yr in its metric equivalent). A lower EUI number refers to a building with a better energy performance. So the goal is to produce buildings with the lowest EUI numbers that are cost effective for a renewably powered civilization.

on renewable energy costs and build consistently to these standards. We call buildings with low EUI numbers that do not yet have the renewables installed net zero ready buildings.

Reducing energy on a building-by-building basis is essential. Only if we build and renovate our building stock to net zero ready standards will buildings be economical to power when fossil-fuel prices rise and our fossil-fuel energy sources disappear.

How do you know how much to reduce a building's energy load? We recommend assessing the renewable energy production needs and cost for each building to determine the proper load. There is a balance point between the amount of renewables needed and the building load that must be found for a net zero project to make financial sense.

No matter how much the energy load is reduced, buildings will still need some energy. Under almost all definitions of "net zero" (including ours), this energy must be produced from renewable sources. Yet the best renewable energy sources are often not located where buildings are. To build a net zero city we cannot meet net zero goals individually on each building property, nor should we, as this individualistic approach does not provide for the best use of resources. Approaching the goal of a net zero world by making each separate building meet net zero standards guarantees failure.

Instead, we should look at the installation of renewable energy systems to meet net zero building goals as a two-step process. Step one should be the incorporation of whatever renewable energy options are available on the building property—the typical net zero strategy, which is also the easiest to implement. Where it is possible to provide the needed energy from sources on the property, that option should take precedence. If it is not possible to generate the needed renewable energy on the property, don't abandon your net zero goal. Rather, move on to step two and investigate options to locate renewable energy generation for your project on a different property.

Perhaps you could find renewable energy generation on another property and get credit for the electricity generated through net metering. Or you could investigate building a larger-scale, community renewable project. You could form a partnership of local residents to develop this community energy project, and with the net zero building as a catalyst, you could instigate a larger renewable energy project that could benefit many other people in your community. Although renewable energy production on another property encourages the growth of larger-scale renewable energy generation within your community and therefore takes an even larger step toward a net zero world than does a single net zero building, the challenges and time frame involved in a successful project increase. Therefore, you should pursue this second step after you have maximized use of renewable energy sources on the property.

What is key in this discussion is taking responsibility for the energy impacts of all projects. If we meet net zero ready building standards with every project, whether new or renovated, and we install renewable energy systems to power the project, whether on or off the property, then we are being responsible by not increasing society's energy demand. From our point of view, this is the most important consideration.

It is not a major leap to realize that the renewable-energy-generation side of the net zero equation is really about assessing energy resources as a town or region or on a more global scale rather than just at a specific property. It is still best if the renewable energy can be generated as close to the building as possible, thus reducing line losses and increasing the efficiency of the systems as a whole. If this is not possible, then it is appropriate to consider net metering from renewable installations on another property or power purchase agreements (PPAs) to meet the net zero goal.[6] However, in our opinion the purchase of renewable energy certificates (RECs),[7] otherwise known as green tags, should not count toward this net zero goal, as this approach does not create a new renewable energy source specifically connected to a building.

The definition of "net zero," then, is not black and white but varying shades of gray. It is challenging to outline all of the specific requirements for meeting the goal. But using the following set of guidelines to approach any building project can bring the goal of a net zero world much closer:

- Build every building, whether new or renovated, to the net zero ready metrics identified throughout this book.
- Build renewable energy systems to power as many buildings as possible by maximizing power generation on the building's footprint, on the property, or as close by as feasible.
- Consider partnering with others in the community to encourage renewable energy development beyond the needs of your building.

- If a renewable system is not feasible at the time of construction, at a minimum reduce building loads to net zero ready standards and begin to look for opportunities to provide renewables later.

Energy Conservation Standards

There are many terms that describe the varying levels of energy performance and energy conservation in building standards. The following are the energy conservation standards we use to distinguish different energy performance and intensity levels in our work and in this book.

TYPICAL EXISTING STANDARD

This classification includes the average performance of all existing buildings. Historically, energy codes were nonexistent or significantly less stringent than they are today, and energy prices were much lower, resulting in an existing building stock with lower energy performance than new buildings. Energy performance data indicate that many existing buildings are consuming five to ten times more than what we recommend for a net zero building. To find energy consumption data for typical building types, refer to the Commercial Buildings Energy Consumption Survey (CBECS) or the Building Energy Data Book, which draws on data from the CBECS.[8]

CODE-COMPLIANT STANDARD

This classification encompasses buildings and projects built to meet current energy code standards. While there currently is not a consistent code standard across the United States, code-compliant building projects almost always perform better than typical existing buildings because current building codes are more stringent than past standards. Buildings designed to these current standards usually consume three to four times what we would want to see for a net zero building.

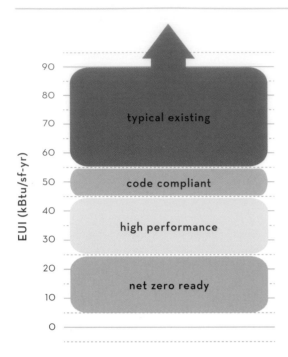

FIGURE 2.2. To assess energy performance of buildings, we quantify the energy consumed per square foot to supply all energy consumed in a building. Comparing the different energy use intensities, we can classify different standards of energy conservation. This chart describes the different standards we use, from typical existing buildings to net zero ready buildings.

HIGH-PERFORMANCE STANDARD

The high-performance standard covers a broad spectrum, ranging from projects that are just better than code-compliant to those approaching net zero ready or microload, as defined below. These buildings often include additional insulation or higher-performance windows but still follow standard building practices. Though their energy performance is slightly better than code-compliant buildings, they still consume two to three times what we recommend for net zero buildings. When we refer to high-performance building projects in this book, we mean an average building in this category, with energy performance about 20 percent better than code.

NET ZERO READY/ MICROLOAD STANDARD

Buildings in this category meet the level of energy conservation appropriate for a financially feasible net zero building but lack renewable energy production. The building is therefore ready for the addition of renewables in the future, after which it could become classified as a net zero project. When the

cost of reducing energy loads within a building is less expensive than powering those loads with renewables, you have reached an energy performance level where it is cost effective to add renewables. At lower energy performance levels, it is much less expensive to reduce energy consumption through increased insulation and more efficient mechanical systems than it is to cover the loads by renewables. Also, once further energy conservation measures require the use of more uncommon technologies, the cost per unit of energy saved to further reduce loads is no longer cost effective. This concept is illustrated in figure 2.3.

Distinctions of Net Zero

A net zero project is one that meets the net zero ready/ microload energy conservation standard and then adds enough renewable energy production specifically for the project to cover annual building energy consumption. Seems simple, right? Here we distinguish three levels of net zero differentiated by the location of the renewables: net zero project, net zero property, and net zero footprint.

FIGURE 2.3. Net zero buildings optimize energy conservation levels. For typical buildings, the optimum and most cost-effective level is 10–20 kBtu/sf-yr—for all building loads, including heating, air-conditioning, lighting, ventilation, and plug loads. Lower EUI numbers than this level mean a disproportionate expense for renewable energy. Higher EUI numbers mean a disproportionate expense for energy conservation. (Note that buildings requiring atypical amounts of energy—such as laboratories, manufacturing sites, and hospitals—will require higher EUI levels and more detailed assessment and conservation measures.)

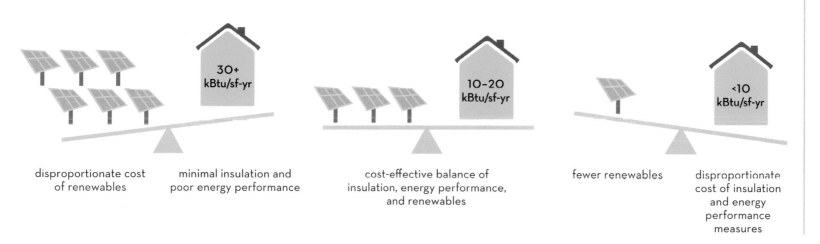

NET ZERO PROJECT. This accounts for projects where some or all of the renewables providing energy to the building are located beyond the confines of the building property. While many net zero definitions do not allow for the inclusion of renewables off the property boundary, our definition does, if and only if the renewables are installed specifically for the project.

NET ZERO PROPERTY. A building qualifies as net zero property if all the renewables used to cover the building's consumption are located within the confines of the project property. While this classification is easier to meet on a rural location not restricted by tight site boundaries, it is still possible on a tighter urban location.

NET ZERO FOOTPRINT. The net zero footprint classification is the most stringent of the net zero classifications. To meet this classification, all of the renewables used to cover the building loads must reside within the footprint of the building itself, most often on the roof of the building.

So the concept of net zero is really quite simple, but with multiple energy sources to consider, both for consumption and production, and the variety of locations where renewable sources can be located, the verification of net zero can be complex. Researchers at the National Renewable Energy Laboratory assembled a clear comparison of net zero energy buildings in a 2006 paper titled "Zero Energy Buildings: A Critical Look at the Definition."[9] They outline four criteria for determining if a project meets the net zero requirements:

SITE ENERGY. Site energy is easily understandable: it is the amount of energy consumed by a building as reflected in utility bills. A site net zero energy building meets verification of the net zero metric by producing enough energy on an annual basis to cover the site consumption of the building. In this case 10 kBtu in equals 10 kBtu out.

SOURCE ENERGY. Source energy takes into account the reduced efficiency of producing the energy and delivering it to the site. All energy delivered to a building is depleted as it moves from where it is generated to the building where it is eventually used. While the actual conversion from site to source energy can vary at different locations because of extracting and transporting fuel sources in that region, average national conversion factors for fuel delivered to a building are as follows: electricity, 3.365; natural gas, 1.092;

In 2010 the largest commercial net zero energy building in the United States opened in Golden, Colorado. Owned and operated by the National Renewable Energy Laboratory (NREL), this 222,000-sf building uses cutting-edge, energy-efficient technology and design strategies to meet stringent energy requirements.

The EUI goal for the Research Support Facility (RSF) building was 35.1 kBtu/sf-yr. This goal is 50 percent lower than the commercial energy code required at the time of design.[10] This building energy will be produced by the 1.6 MW of installed solar PV on the property, including 450 kW of rooftop PV. Actual performance data since the building has been occupied show the energy consumption of the building is 35.4 kBtu/sf-yr and is meeting the net zero building EUI design performance goal before adding renewables.[11] Because this energy consumption is 100 percent offset by the PV production on the property, this building meets our definition of a net zero project.

Multiple passive strategies reduce energy consumption compared to a typical office building. These strategies include daylighting, natural ventilation, preheating of ventilation air through a transpired collector, and exposed thermal mass to store thermal energy. The building massing and shape take advantage of the climatic conditions and optimize passive energy strategies. The main office wings are only 60 feet wide,

FIGURE 2.4. NREL's Research Support Facility, as seen from the front entrance.

FIGURE 2.5. This rendering of the NREL Research Support Facility shows the solar PV installed to cover all available roof surface. Additional PV will be located on the property to offset the remaining building use.

FIGURE 2.7. High windows and open floor plans allow for optimized daylighting throughout the open workspace.

FIGURE 2.6. Exterior courtyards provide pleasant spaces for employees and highlight the air intake that brings cool night air into the data center.

which means that they can take full advantage of daylighting and passive ventilation, and minimize unwanted solar gain from the east and west. This narrow footprint results in two office wings elongated on the east-west axis and linked by a central corridor that houses the lobby and conference facilities.

Although this building has normal office functions, it also houses a data center, which provides a significant challenge to energy conservation because of the high internal process loads. However, because of the ideal bioclimatic influences in Colorado, outside air cools the data center equipment, and evaporative cooling meets nearly all cooling requirements. In addition a heat recovery unit extracts hot air from the data center, which can be reused throughout the building when necessary.

Beyond showcasing a revolutionary net zero energy design, the facility is adaptable to future changes. The 1,300 full-time occupants work in open offices that contain low partitions that do not block daylight and views, are within 30 feet of an operable window, and have modular workstations for flexibility and collaboration. Wind-tunnel testing helped generate the geometry of the building with the best options for the operable windows, cross-ventilation, and pedestrian comfort in the exterior courtyards. Additionally, the RSF provides an ongoing resource for learning about office building energy use.

fuel oil, 1.158; propane, 1.151.[12] For example, 10 kBtu of fuel oil used on-site is really 10 kBtu multiplied by the conversion factor 1.158, which equals 11.58 kBtu of actual energy delivered from the source. The source-net-zero energy building verification accounts for total energy use of a fuel from the extraction, delivery, and use on-site. The challenge of verification under this definition rests in the varying site-to-source conversion factors for different locations.

ENERGY COSTS. To achieve the cost net zero metric, a building must produce enough energy to generate $0 on the balance sheet at the end of the year. In this case, 10 kBtu in does not necessarily equal 10 kBtu out, because the costs of energy from different sources vary greatly, but $1 spent on energy equals $1 paid by the utility for energy produced. While this approach appeals to the bottom line, this method of verification can lead to situations where a building is producing more energy than it consumes but does not meet the net zero cost goal. Conversely, the building may reach the net zero cost goal but does not produce enough energy to cover the building consumption. How the utility company charges for electricity impacts the calculations for this metric. When utility companies add a premium for peak loads, this metric can require producing more energy than necessary for meeting other definitions of net zero. And in cases where the utility pays a premium for all energy produced on the property, this can result in an under-production in comparison to other net zero definitions.

EMISSIONS. This fourth criterion is based on the non-energy differences among fuel types. A building is net zero under this verification strategy if it produces at least as much emissions-free renewable energy as it uses from emissions-producing energy sources. The most common emissions to offset are carbon, nitrogen, and sulfur oxides. However, similar to source net zero energy buildings, 10 kBtu in does not necessarily mean 10 kBtu out: conversion factors are used to relate the carbon impact of different energy sources, such as the following: natural gas, 116.39 lb CO_2/MMBtu; distillate fuel oil #1, 2, and 4, 159.66 lb CO_2/MMBtu; liquefied petroleum gas, 138.75 lb CO_2/MMBtu; US average of electricity, 1.34 lb CO_2/kWh.[13]

Although the conversion factors for fossil-fuel emissions are pretty well agreed upon, those for electricity can vary dramatically from place to place. For example, the emissions factor for electricity in Idaho is 0.03 CO_2/kWh and in North Dakota 2.24 CO_2/kWh.[14] These differences occur because of the mix of energy sources used to produce electricity in different areas: coal has much higher emissions than hydro from a CO_2 standpoint, for instance. However, we could argue that since we are all connected to the same electric grid, we are really using a mix of electricity from across the United States. In all cases the national average should be used.

All four of the above criteria of net zero have become acceptable in the marketplace, but we will use the site energy definition throughout this book because it is measurable and verifiable without using any conversion factors. The information and metrics that we present in this book are therefore related to on-site energy consumption and can be easily adjusted to source energy requirements based on the conversion factors for your specific location.

What's a Carbon-Neutral Building?

Another distinction frequently used in the high-performance building community is that of carbon neutrality. As with net zero, the definition of a carbon-neutral building is complex and carries different meanings in different groups. In some cases carbon-neutral metrics are more stringent than net zero metrics, and in some cases they are less stringent.

By most definitions, though, a carbon-neutral building is one that achieves a net zero carbon footprint by sequestering or offsetting as much carbon as it is responsible for releasing. In other words, the building has no net carbon production when considered over an annual period.

Our definition of a carbon-neutral building matches these same criteria. In fact, it is not that much different from the definition of a net zero building—just slightly more inclusive. By definition, a net zero building cannot count the burning of biomass on the renewable side of the equation because, except in very rare cases, biomass is not a renewable resource harvested from the property. A carbon-neutral building can, however, count biomass use on the renewable side of the equation. While there has been much discussion about whether biomass is really carbon neutral because there is some carbon impact from harvesting, processing, and transportation, we consider it close enough.

Carbon-neutral buildings often have higher energy consumption levels than their net zero counterparts because the cost per unit of energy for biomass is usually less than that for other renewables, changing the balance point illustrated in figure 2.3. However, we recommend designing carbon-neutral buildings to the microload/net zero ready standard because biomass costs will likely increase. The cost of wood, for example, will likely rise as it is increasingly used for fuel and also as it begins to be used as a replacement for the construction of material goods when rising fossil-fuel prices cause a decline in the use of plastic.

Embodied energy in the building is not typically considered in calculating carbon neutrality. Carbon impacts from embodied energy include the carbon generated to build a building, including material extraction, processing, and transportation. Therefore, a full accounting of carbon impacts must include both embodied energy of materials and operational impacts.

Beyond Net Zero

We have been looking at net zero from a narrow energy input-output model because we believe that energy concerns will be the single greatest challenge to civilizations and living systems in the twenty-first century. However, a more inclusive definition of net zero buildings takes into account that these buildings protect the environment, pay for themselves through improved efficiency, provide stable energy costs, and avoid the need for fossil-fuel-based energy sources. Implied but often not specifically noted in the definition is that along with the reduced energy load, net zero energy buildings minimize adverse impacts on the environment. A net zero energy building is environmentally friendly: no matter its specific function, its construction and operation are examples of good environmental stewardship.

Furthermore, while the term "net zero" may refer to one building, nothing restricts the definition to this small scale. The term can extend to an office complex, a residential neighborhood, a college campus, an entire town, a state, a country, or the whole world. Once net zero is viewed on the scale of a larger project, we can share efficiencies between buildings and place renewable sources to allow for more efficient energy production. Ultimately, our buildings, villages, regions, and planet need to live within a homeostasis where all flows and cycles are in balance.

In other words, we need to think beyond net zero buildings and also consider net zero waste, net zero water, net zero food, and other aspects of a net zero society so that we can achieve the ability to truly live within our means.

FIGURE 2.8. Net zero buildings can be classified in each of three categories, providing options to meet net zero requirements for almost any location.

NET ZERO PROJECT

Renewables are located at a remote location and energy produced is attributed to the project site.

NET ZERO PROPERTY

Renewables are contained within the building site.

NET ZERO FOOTPRINT

Renewables are an integral component of the structure and do not impact the site outside the building footprint.

The Leopold Legacy Center in Baraboo, Wisconsin, is a net zero, carbon-neutral Leadership in Energy and Environmental Design (LEED) Platinum project located on the Leopold Memorial Reserve. Completed in 2007, this 12,000 sf project includes three one-story buildings that make up the new headquarters for the Aldo Leopold Foundation. The goal of this project was to remain true to the land use, ecological ethic, resource conservation and management, and scientific spirit of Leopold's land ethic: one that reduces humans' impact on our natural resources.

The process of designing the Leopold Legacy Center started with the development of an energy budget. This energy budget accounted for the total amount of renewable energy that could be produced on the property. The design team then took this information and worked backward to ensure that the building would operate within these constraints. The resulting building uses 70 percent less energy than an office building of its size that is built to code.

The project was designed to produce over 110 percent of the building's annual energy needs from solar PV on the buildings. The 39 kW of solar PV produces over 61,000 kWh annually, yet the building uses only around 54,000 kWh annually. The reduced energy consumption of the building was achieved through passive strategies for heating and cooling and efficient technical systems solutions. Ground-source heat pumps provide heating and cooling through radiant slabs, while woodstoves provide spot heating and passive survivability in the event of a power outage. The separate ventilation system results in energy savings of two to five times that of a combined system, part of which is attributed to an earth-tube system that provides 100 percent fresh, tempered air in all seasons.

The Leopold Legacy Center used resources available on the property for much of its construction. Trees on the 1,500-acre Leopold Memorial Reserve were suffering from overcrowding. In order to boost the health of the forest and enable the trees to increase their capacity to sequester carbon, the forest was

FIGURE 2.9. The net zero and carbon-neutral Leopold Legacy Center is composed of three one-story buildings clustered around a central courtyard.

FIGURE 2.10. With daylight streaming through clerestory windows and a small floor plate, electric lights are used minimally in the main administration wing. The interior is finished with wood harvested from the property, including the innovative round wood structural system of the rafters.

thinned. The harvested wood influenced the building design, structure, and interior finishes: because most of the timber from the property was relatively small, the center, with the help of the US Forest Service Products Laboratory, developed a round wood truss system for structural members.

Designers developed a carbon-neutral calculation for the building based on the World Resources Institute's Greenhouse Gas Protocol. This inventory indicates that the project emits 13.63 tons of carbon from building operations, waste, travel, and commuting; the roof PV system offsets 6.24 tons of carbon; and the managed forest sequesters 8.75 tons of carbon each year. When all is accounted for, the building is responsible for the net offset and sequestration of 1.36 tons of carbon per year.[15]

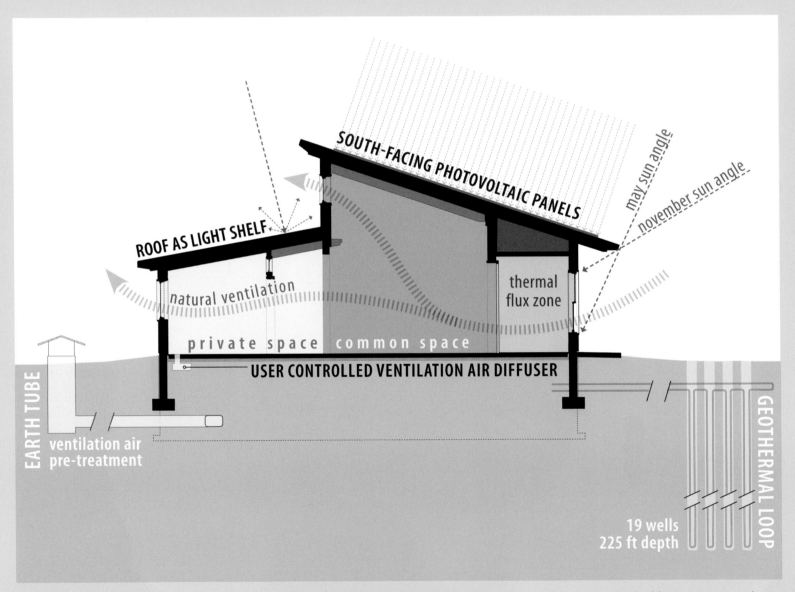

FIGURE 2.11. Passive strategies allow for daylighting and natural ventilation, low-tech solutions that reduce the building's energy needs.

3 | The Roots of Net Zero Design

Net zero building design has its roots in the principles, strategies, technology, and experience of the environmental and ecological design traditions of the last forty years, as well as in renewable design practices dating back through millennia. These design traditions are varied and carry many labels: integrated, regenerative, restorative, green, healthy, renewable energy, living building, sustainable, and biophilic. In this chapter we focus on aspects of these traditions critical to the design of net zero buildings, beginning with an exploration of living building design.

The New Building Paradigm

We tend to think of buildings as objects of bricks and mortar created to serve societal and personal functions and needs. Le Corbusier, an icon of the modernist movement, even described the home as "a machine for living."[1] In contrast to this mechanistic paradigm, a new worldview is emerging. There has been a revolution in scientific, social, and philosophical thought. Leaders across many disciplines have integrated chaos and complexity theory, the Gaia hypothesis, and a slew of other principles that take their inspiration from the complex, integrated processes we see in nature. We are turning toward a more holistic, whole-systems approach to investigating organisms, ecosystems, and social systems—and to generating a sustainable future for the planet and all living systems. This paradigm shift is central and critical to creating a powerful and inspiring way of thinking about our buildings, communities, and ecosystems—and our way of being in the world.

From this larger paradigm shift, we can reinterpret our human-generated physical world of buildings and communities as living systems and ecosystems. Structures and the people occupying them interact and evolve together to form one unified system that produces an active, vibrant, and healthy environment. If the structure changes, the activities inside it are affected, and vice versa. When we are in a room with glare on our computer screen or poor acoustics, we are less productive. If we want an engaged

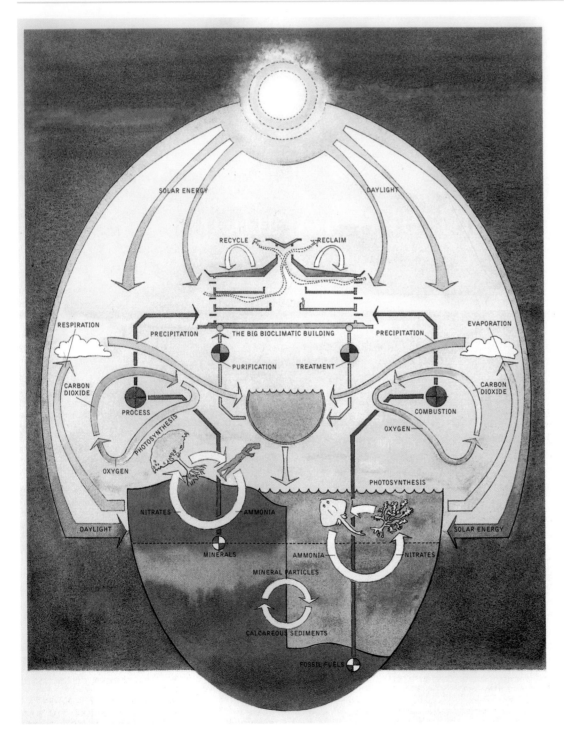

FIGURE 3.1. The intent of the living-building paradigm is to generate buildings that operate within the cycles and flow of nature and natural processes, including energy, materials, waste, water, and air.

discussion and are in an auditorium, our conversations are less effective than in a small meeting room. Just orienting chairs in a room encourages different kinds of interaction. While we do not typically observe and analyze our spaces, we are often drawn to different places for different activities. When consciously designed and planned, this connection between space and activity enhances not only our productivity but also our satisfaction and inspiration in our daily life. This design of building and communities can even change the outcomes produced by society, individuals, and organizations.

Theorists like Dutch architect N. J. Habraken have long explored the relationship between humans and their dwellings, pointing out that the people-place connection is an active not a static phenomenon. In his book *The Structure of the Ordinary*, Habraken explains this dynamism:

> The intimate and unceasing interaction between people and the forms they inhabit is a fundamental and fascinating aspect of built environment. We are all players: agents who inhabit the environment, transforming it to our liking and making sure things stay as we choose, within the territory we claim. Few are passive. Office workers arrange flowers, adjust picture frames and books, set down a cup of coffee; students hang posters on the wall. Such humble impulses of inhabitation lead to maintaining and adapting building forms, and ultimately to erecting, demolishing, or replacing buildings and settlements.[2]

The philosopher Martin Heidegger connected our urge to build to a similar deep notion that changing and molding our environment is fundamental to our feeling settled, safe, and even fully human, fulfilled, and vital.

As people interact with their built environment, they shape it, and it in turn shapes them. In one way or another, we bring all the experiences we have in our work, social, recreational, and spiritual lives to our dwellings—molding them to reflect our aesthetics and values and meet our needs. In turn, the physical spaces we spend our time in can transform our moods, our productivity, our comfort, and much more. They can also connect us to the natural world more fully when designed to link to the natural systems around us.

But just how do we reinforce our connection to nature via our built environment? We make sure we're preserving ecosystems. We connect our buildings to the nature around them. We bring nature inside through view, material selection, and design integration. Evolutionary biologist E. O. Wilson and social ecologist Stephen Kellert have written much about biophilia over the past two decades, asserting that our need to connect to nature is both fundamental and instinctual, and without that connection it is difficult, if not impossible, to live a fulfilling and satisfying life.[3] They point out that humans have lived in nature—in forests and savannahs, primarily—for hundreds of thousands or even millions of years, while we have lived inside buildings in substantial towns and cities created by humans for only a few thousand years or less. Throughout our evolution, we have mostly been outdoors during our waking hours. It is no surprise, then, that spaces that feel natural make us happy. In fact, until the last century or two, most people still lived in rural environments directly connected to nature and its rhythms and cycles. Research has even shown that hospital stays are reduced in time when patients have window views and can see nature or even when they have plants in the room.[4]

Just as nature-centric buildings can improve our well-being, nature-inspired concepts can improve our buildings. Janine Benyus, another leading thinker in the emerging field of design based on living systems, coined the term "biomimicry" and laid the foundation for the emerging discipline of the same name.[5] Biomimicry looks at how nature solves design problems and attempts to imitate nature's solutions when designing everything from buildings to products to systems.

Scientists have researched the aerodynamics of flippered ocean creatures to get clues on how to enhance lift and reduce drag in new airplane wing designs.[6] They have studied lotus plants with water-repellent leaves to see how microprotrusions on their petals create a layer of air that causes water to

Opened in 1996 in Harare, Zimbabwe's city center, the Eastgate Centre, is a leading example of biomimicry in building design. This 592,000 sf mixed-use building, designed by architect Mick Pearce, uses passive building strategies to keep occupants comfortable year-round with minimal mechanical air conditioning or heating (10 percent of what is normally used).

The inspiration for Eastgate's cooling strategies came from termite mounds, or termitaria. These mounds control their environment and maintain temperatures of 30 to 31°C using the earth's moisture and thermal mass, internal ventilation shafts, and diurnal shifts in external temperature. The Eastgate design team studied the termites' complex living systems and applied key principles throughout their design.

The center's passive ventilation system relies heavily on the exposed thermal mass of the precast concrete elements throughout the building to maintain constant temperatures throughout the day. This strategy mimics the termite mound's network of mud composite chambers that capture the heat generated during the day for release at night. At Eastgate, heat

FIGURE 3.2. Eastgate as viewed from the southeast, with the center of Harare beyond.

FIGURE 3.3. The atrium extends the full height of the building, creating a public spine through the center of the building and facilitating natural ventilation from each level.

from people, equipment in the interior space, and the sun hitting the structure is absorbed by the thermal mass. At night cool air passes over the thermal mass, which cools through heat transfer.

The Eastgate Center and termite mounds also have ventilation shafts that draw in cool air from low intake holes and expel it out of the top through stack ventilation throughout the day. Additionally, the building's double precast concrete floor functions as a heat exchanger, cooling incoming ventilation air before it moves through occupant spaces. At night heated air from the day is vented out of the building assisted by fans, and the process restarts with cold night air flowing through the cavities in the floor slabs, cooling the thermal mass of the building. As a result, Eastgate uses 35 percent less energy than a similar air-conditioned building in Harare.[9]

Lessons from the natural world show us that smooth exposed bodies absorb heat quickly and have less surface area to emit heat to space at night. In contrast, jagged bodies, which shade themselves, absorb less heat by day and have greater surface area to emit more heat at night. As a result, the external façade of the building has many jagged edges and features green walls on the north and south to enhance shading.

Offices are cooled with integrated design. A vaulted concrete ceiling works with uplighting fixtures so that heat generated by the light fixtures is reflected upward and absorbed by the slab above instead of dispersing into the room. Additionally, lighting fixtures are placed near air exhaust ports to minimize loading the room with their heat. The concrete structure absorbs heat in the inside and shades and disperses heat on the outside. Displacement ventilation provides cooling and fresh air.

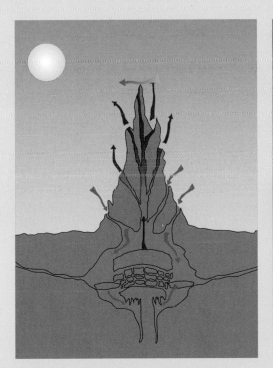

FIGURE 3.4. The chimneys exhaust warm air through the roof of the building, mimicking the passive cooling systems of a termite mound (*left*) by drawing in cool outside air down low and expelling hot internal air through stack ventilation in the roof. Additional roof features (*right*) include a glass roof daylighting the interior atrium space and solar hot water panels used for water heating.

FIGURE 3.5. A jagged façade with green plantings helps the Eastgate Center eliminate direct solar gain to the building. The concrete structure is used for cooling with integrated ventilation.

bead and wash away surface dirt. This process has been used on paint, glass, and fabric to create easier-to-clean surfaces in buildings.[7] Entrepreneurs are now developing products using mushrooms and agricultural waste to form an insulated panel resistant to mold.[8] Ideas like these are just the tip of the iceberg when it comes to changing our current world from one where (nearly) everything we touch is made of fossil fuels to one where materials are biologically based: the paradigm shift from fossil fuels to living systems is tangible.

Because animals in their dwellings have to tackle some of the same problems we do—staying warm or cooling off, for instance—looking to the natural world can solve a host of building and community design dilemmas as well. Perhaps the most famous example of biomimicry in building design can be found in Harare, Zimbabwe, where the Eastgate Centre (see sidebar) regulates its temperatures naturally with minimal mechanical heating or cooling, thanks to lessons learned from termite mounds.

In fact, new frameworks and ideas about our built environment and how we relate to our world are transforming the design profession. Architect Bill McDonough introduced a cradle-to-cradle design concept for architecture, stressing that "waste equals food."[10] McDonough reminds us that waste does not exist in nature. In all ecosystems organisms evolve to grow on the decay and by-products of other organisms. McDonough and other pioneers helped architects see that human processes and buildings could leave air and water as clean or cleaner than they were when they entered the building, serve as net generators of energy, and create nutrients and otherwise support living beings and systems. Even before

McDonough articulated this hypothesis, ecological designer John Todd and others designed sewage treatment plants to produce clean water, recover valuable nutrients for agriculture, and fertilize crops.[11] We've come to realize, at least on some levels, that traditional large-scale modern sewage and waste treatment has created pollution rather than encouraging a reuse of nutrients.

Others are looking for areas where environmental problems can become opportunities. Sustainability strategist Bill Reed, among others, is exploring ways to engage in regenerative design—design that helps restore ecosystems as it creates a human environment that supports rather than depletes the natural world and enhances human quality of life.[12]

As these design innovations emerged, the US Green Building Council created a building rating system, Leadership in Energy and Environmental Design (LEED), to improve the environmental performance of buildings.[13] While based in the old mechanical worldview, the LEED system improved the environmental performance of many buildings constructed since 1998, and its influence has improved the environmental performance of the entire construction community.

The International Living Future Institute has recently introduced a new building assessment system more rooted in the living-systems paradigm. Their green building certification program, the Living Building Challenge, recognizes that today we tend to think of buildings not simply as bricks and mortar but as living organisms in a connected web of life, and it requires buildings to perform as positive forces in the future. They must produce more energy than they consume, improve water, eliminate waste, eliminate toxic materials, be beautiful,

FIGURE 3.6. At the University of Guelph-Humber in Canada, an interior living wall biofilter is integrated into the building's air-handling system. The biofilter, designed and built by Nedlaw Living Walls in conjunction with Diamond & Schmitt Architects, biologically removes air contaminants and cleans indoor air, acting like the lungs of the building.

FIGURE 3.7. *Left,* in the city of Fuzhou in China, canals were used to transport sewage and waste, causing health and odor issues. *Right,* John Todd designed and built floating aquatic restorers in the Baima Canal, converting raw sewage into clean water by using living organisms and plants in an ecological processing system for wastewater rather than dredging or modern chemically based solutions.

and more. This system does not rate individual characteristics or different levels of performance but rather requires that new buildings be net contributors to society and make the world a better place. The program asks challenging questions, such as: "What if every intervention resulted in greater biodiversity; increased soil health; additional outlets for beauty and personal expression; a deeper understanding of climate, culture and place; a realignment of our food and transportation systems; and a more profound sense of what it means to be a citizen of a planet where resources and opportunities are provided fairly and equitably?"[14]

This program challenges us to rebuild our framework of what constitutes a green building and provides opportunities for thinking on a community scale, making communities that are net ecological producers and utilize integrated, community-wide energy systems.

The Adam Joseph Lewis Center at Oberlin College in Ohio is one of the first buildings of any large scale to be designed following living-building ideals. Intended to house the environmental studies program, the center was conceived during a long-term design process between 1993 and 1998 by a group of students led by professor David Orr with a design team led by William McDonough + Partners. The 13,600 sf building, completed in January 2000, serves as a model of sustainability for the Oberlin community and beyond.

Before the center was built, few people had imagined a building that produced more energy than it consumed, increased biological diversity, and treated waste like food. This groundbreaking building shifted the thinking on sustainable design.

The design evolved from three questions Orr framed: "Is it possible—even in Ohio—to power buildings by current sunlight? Is it possible to create buildings that purify their own wastewater? Is it possible to build without compromising human and environmental health somewhere else or at some later time?"[15]

The original goal for the building was to be a net energy exporter through careful design, load reduction within the building, and renewable energy. Reaching the net zero goal involved

FIGURE 3.8. Oberlin. The intent of the living-building paradigm is to generate buildings that operate within the cycles and flow of nature and natural processes—including energy, materials, waste, water, and air. *Left*, the exterior; *right*, the interior atrium and gathering space.

FIGURE 3.9. Ken Yeang's EDITT Tower in Singapore shows ecological system integration through vertical landscaping that connects building occupants to beautiful and vegetated spaces typically experienced only at street level.

FIGURE 3.10. The Milwaukee Art Museum by Santiago Calatrava, with the brise-soleil open (*top*) and closed (*bottom*).

FIGURE 3.11. The Bullitt Center located in Seattle is projected to meet the Living Building Challenge.

FIGURE 3.12. A view of the Phipps Center for Sustainable Landscapes, with the lagoon, part of the water management system, in the foreground.

ongoing learning, monitoring, and adjustments of the systems. The rooftop and carport PV have made the building a net energy exporter since 2006—a remarkable achievement that demonstrated to others that larger-scale net zero energy and zero-waste water goals were possible and should be pursued.

In the wake of Oberlin's success, many others began to see that even loftier goals were both viable and necessary. Ken Yeang, an internationally recognized Malaysian architect, ecologist, and author, has been creating high-rise buildings that incorporate ecological systems. Yeang's integration of green pathways and sky terraces gives rise to many energy and social benefits in the urban environment.

In a different way the architect and engineer Santiago Calatrava is transforming static buildings into structures that move and adapt to their surroundings. At the Milwaukee Art Museum, the sun shade (or brise-soleil) opens and closes, bringing and filtering daylight in the building. With its organic shapes and the winglike brise-soleil (with a 217-foot span), the museum looks and acts like a living organism, one that opens and closes daily or in response to wind.

The Bullitt Center is a six-story, 50,000 sf office building widely regarded as the greenest office building in the world. Currently in the monitoring phase, it plans to generate its own energy on-site, collect its own water, and process its own waste

NET-ZERO WATER DIAGRAM

A. Rooftop Capture
B. Storage Tank
C. Lagoon
D. Rain Garden
E. Pervious Asphalt
F. Pump Station
G. Non-Potable Well

Storm Systems
Green Roof

FIGURE 3.13. Net zero water diagram showing multiple water systems that manage storm water for irrigation and reuse at the Phipps Center.

in order to meet the stringent criteria of the Living Building Challenge. It is projected to have an EUI of 16 kBtu/sf-yr, and has a 242 kW PV system as a dominant feature on its roof. The building designers drew inspiration from living organisms and sought simple, beautiful, and integrated solutions to the challenging urban environment. The building systems and structure are separate entities, which enable easy changes and updates as necessary in the future.[16]

The Center for Sustainable Landscapes at Phipps Conservatory and Botanical Gardens in Pittsburgh is a 24,000 sf mixed-use building integrated into an ecological and beautiful landscape. It is designed to meet the Living Building Challenge

as well as LEED Platinum and the landscape-equivalent Sustainable Sites Initiative (SITES). The center houses education, research, and administrative components and is a leading example of innovative, integrated design that reveals the beauty of living buildings and sites. Particular care was taken in the design of water systems for storm water treatment, irrigation, and water reuse. Ecological site strategies include pervious paving, roof water collection, green roofs, bioswales, lagoons, and rain gardens that manage water and contribute to the beauty of the site. All of the building users' water is captured on-site or reused without chemicals, and 100 percent of the storm water and water discharged from the buildings is managed on-site.

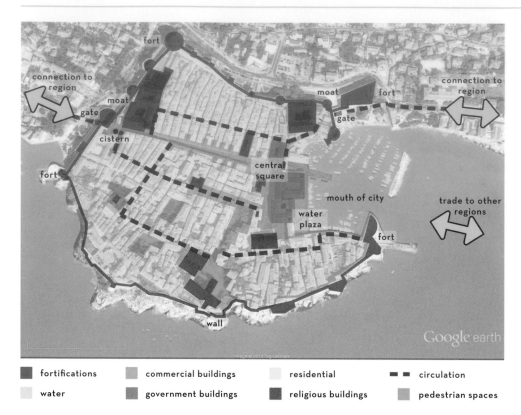

FIGURE 3.14. Dubrovnik: A functional medieval city that looks much like a living organism.

Legend:
- fortifications
- commercial buildings
- residential
- circulation
- water
- government buildings
- religious buildings
- pedestrian spaces

Ecology and Infrastructure

The city of Dubrovnik in Croatia grew to prominence as a port in the Middle Ages. Protected by a moat, an enclosing wall, and numerous forts and heavy fortifications, the city was originally surrounded by fields and agriculture. Although the land around the city has slowly evolved from open lands to buildings, the inner city of Dubrovnik escaped modernization and remains one of the best-preserved medieval cities in Europe. The structure of the city can be seen in the patterns of buildings, circulation, and gathering spaces used for spiritual, governance, and commerce purposes. With these functions expressed by colors in figure 3.14, the city of Dubrovnik looks similar to a simple living organism. The fortifications are like the skin or shell, clearly defining the organism from its surrounding environment. The major concentration of public, commercial, and spiritual spaces is at the harbor. The harbor looks and acts like a mouth of an organism, exchanging goods and products from the Dubrovnik region to other ports around the Mediterranean Sea. Two major gates control movement of goods and people from Dubrovnik to the surrounding region. Throughout the city are the living spaces for inhabitants, supporting and filling out the city much like the muscles of an animal. Within the residential areas, there are small neighborhood open spaces for gathering. Providing citywide cohesion and energy are the civic, spiritual, and commercial buildings, which expand out into public spaces and plazas. Running throughout the city is an intricate network of larger and smaller alleys. Along the major thoroughfares are shops and stores energizing the city with human exchange and interaction. Between the west gate and the harbor is a street where the prime commerce of the town is centered. From all of this we can observe Dubrovnik behaving like a living organism, its physical layout and structure manifesting the operations and life of the people, culture, and city.

Franklin Becker and Fritz Steele, in their book *Workplace by Design: Mapping the High-Performance Workscape,* coined the term "organizational ecology," proposing that organizations act like organisms in an ecosystem and that the physical environment and its systems can support and enhance the mission and actions of organizations.[17] While their book focuses on businesses, the organizational ecology concept is equally suited to families, neighborhoods, villages, cities, and other social organizations.

Buildings, towns, and cities share many characteristics with living organisms. We can compare a building's structural system with an animal's skeleton. The enclosure or skin of the building is similar to the skin of a living organism. In both cases the skin insulates, protects, senses, and mediates between the internal and external environments. And people in buildings act like cells in an organism. People have different roles, moods, and metabolisms in a workplace just as cells are differentiated and specialized in our bodies. We can think of certain places in buildings, like common rooms and public spaces, as similar to organs in living beings. What, then, is the heart or soul of a building? What keeps an organization acting as one unified entity? We can compare hallways and movement systems in buildings to arteries and veins in living beings and the flow and production of goods and services to the flow of food and nutrients through a digestive system. In the midst of these places and systems are people engaged in conversation and the coordination of movement and activity almost like the cells in blood, structures, and organs. From this we can understand the analogy of living buildings and living beings. And we can see how they relate to the world around it: every building, town, or city, like an organism, extends outside itself to get resources, energy, and food and dispose of waste and is coordinated by people in the midst of natural processes.

These components together act as a whole—a single organism that exists as a force in society and civilization well beyond the individual people that inhabit its parts. In her book *The Death and Life of Great American Cities,* Jane Jacobs explains the seamless integration of parts with human activity energizing and enlivening urban streets as the essential veins and arteries of a city bringing life and vitality to every corner:

Under the seeming disorder of the old city, wherever the old city is working successfully, is a marvelous order for maintaining the safety of the streets and freedom of the city. It is a complex order. Its essence is in intricacy of sidewalk use, bringing with it a constant succession of eyes. This order is all composed of movement and change, and although it is life, not art, we may fancifully call it the art form of the city and liken it to the dance—not to a simple-minded precision dance with everyone kicking up at the same time, twirling in unison and bowing off en masse, but to an intricate ballet in which the individual dancers and ensembles all have distinctive parts which miraculously reinforce each other and compose an orderly whole.[18]

When we view the city as an organism, we see that the city's health depends on the dance of city life in the streets with its movement of goods and exchange of services. This dance is what connects the urban organs of government, spiritual, and commercial centers and extends them to a larger region. Food, goods, and services flow in and out from around the region and around the globe. The conversations to coordinate, stimulate, and energize these flows occur in the buildings, streets, and public spaces throughout the city. Human waste flows out through sewage treatment plants into nearby water bodies; other waste goes into landfills and recycling centers. This is the ecosystem and environment that supports the city as an organism with diversity of human culture, commerce, spirituality and governance.

Thus, we can consciously change our future by making our buildings, towns, and cities symbiotically enhance our productivity and happiness as individuals and as a society.

The Essence of a Living Building

We might think that a biological perspective toward design is an interesting idea but question its value in influencing the design of buildings. However, as more design professionals realize that the life of a building is not in its structure but rather in the activities that go on inside, the role of the designer may be changing. As designers and builders, we create the support systems for the life of the building—such as the structure, circulation, systems, and envelope—that surround and enclose these activities. What is "real" is not the structure we design but the operations, energy, and life that happen in the space of the building. This is a new way of thinking about our trade, and there are certain basics to keep in mind as we begin our journey toward designing and building better buildings.

PURPOSE

First, all buildings have a purpose. They would not have been built without one. The purpose might be creating a home, a workplace, a recreation space, or a spiritual place. That purpose can go beyond direct function. Renaissance buildings, for instance, were intended to support social and community life and cultivate art, literature, and architecture. In other cases a building's purpose might be to connect its users to each other or to nature, be it the path of the sun, fields outside, a river that goes by, a pond, or a mountain. All these elements can become a part of the purpose of a home or any other building. In the case of a living building, purpose is expanded: the goal of the building also includes positive contributions to the environment, not just in terms of energy but in terms of all of a building's flows, such as waste, water, resources, beauty, spirit, and community. We work to make the building give back more than it takes—just as any healthy organism or ecosystem does. Why shouldn't the physical world made by humans contribute to the planet and play by the rules that have allowed life to flourish and evolve for living systems for billions of years?

SYSTEMS AND OPERATION

Systems theory and thinking is helpful in understanding buildings. From a systems perspective, a building has an overall purpose composed of components and parts that are connected as an integrated and fully networked system. Any change to a part of the system impacts all other components of the system. This system is engaged in a symbiotic interrelationship with a larger ecosystem: the system and ecosystem are continuously changing, adapting, and evolving. The skin of a building or organism interacts with its surroundings to maintain its health. Windows allow view, light, and air; walls and roofs keep out rain and maintain temperature and comfort. The structure holds up the building so that activities can occur inside. Key spaces and rooms allow the building to fulfill its purpose. A living organism's operating systems include systems for treating waste, digesting food, and circulating nutrients. In a building the systems include recycling, heating and cooling, ventilation, and circulation of people and resources.

INTERCONNECTION

The success of biological systems, organisms, and living buildings depends on both internal connections and connections to the surrounding environment. Without symbiotic relationships to the environment, natural systems and buildings alike will decay. In the human brain, for instance, the nervous system connects all organs, blood flow, food and waste processing, muscles, and ultimately every cell in the body. At the same time, the brain, through the nervous system, is connected to our surrounding environment through the five senses of touch, smell, sight, sound, and taste.

Similarly, in buildings humans are interconnected through rooms, hallways, and doors as well as through telephones, computers, mechanical control systems, and so on. Occupants in buildings are also connected to the outside world by the same communications technology but also physically through windows to gardens, public spaces around buildings, automobiles and mass transit, waste systems, energy, and resources delivered to buildings. These connections extend regionally and even globally to supply goods, services, and food. And as Jane Jacobs points out, this interconnected universe of buildings and ecosystems is even more clearly seen when we look at our cities that are teeming with life and vibrant interactions on all scales.

REGENERATION, GENERATION, AND AUTOPOIESIS

What distinguishes a living system from a nonliving system, and how might that relate to buildings? In the book *Autopoiesis and Cognition: The Realization of the Living*, Humberto Maturana and Francisco Varela coin the term "autopoiesis" to describe self-creation or self-generation.[19] They claim that a living organism's ability to maintain itself and recreate cells and components of itself is the central distinguishing feature of a living system. Others have used the term "regeneration" to distinguish between biological and mechanical systems. Mechanical systems are distinguished by production processes, like making cars, computers, and other products of our consumer society. Biological systems involve living organisms that grow and reproduce. Think about a termite mound, where termites build their own home or even city that grows, evolves, and survives beyond individual generations of termites.

Similarly, think of humans who renovate, add onto, and keep up their homes by assembling and replacing building materials, equipment, and furnishings to maintain comfort and support activity inside. Or think of our cities that grow and decline, with some areas that deteriorate and others that expand. Thus, in one sense, over time, all buildings act like living buildings or an organism larger than one individual. In our building structure we can see an organism such as a family, business, or community reflected in the plan and section as we did with the termite mound. So what makes a net zero living building or city different from a non-net zero building or city? The net zero building or city lives within the flow of the renewing and renewable resources of the planet and is not fueled by nonrenewable resources. Using this perspective, we think of building systems and components and how they will operate, change, and be maintained over time.

As we explore later in this chapter, we think of the human intervention needed to maintain the building's structure, envelope, systems and services, human activity, and human comfort. As in a living organism, which develops from a single cell into an adult, building design begins with the seed of an idea around which designers orient the components and elements and develop the details. And with a living building, the final structure spurs new ideas to evolve the next generation of buildings.

LEARNING, ADAPTION, AND EVOLUTION

We can put systems theory to work in buildings and use feedback loops to leverage change. A feedback loop is a cycle that returns to its source in a way that alters the future actions of the system, either maintaining or changing the system to optimize performance.

A simple example of a feedback loop is waste treatment. Current strategies concentrate wastes at sewage treatment plants, landfills, and animal feedlots, where they either still pollute or have polluted water, and those responsible try to contain wastes in order to limit this pollution. In a positive feedback loop, waste is used as a nutrient through reuse or recycling. With human and animal waste, this means using waste for fertilizer or energy generation such as methane gas production that fuels a biodigester. Instead of a negative loop of pollution, there is a positive loop of potential energy, food, and/or resource production. In the design of living buildings and communities, we look to enable these positive loops that nourish and enrich life rather than cause pollution and degrade life.

From these examples, it is evident that feedback loops can both enhance and detract from building and ecosystem performance. Ultimately, it is positive feedback in living systems and living-system thinking that generate successful biological adaptations and evolution. Living buildings and communities investigate and use similar strategies and systems to adapt and evolve into organisms and ecosystems that thrive in their environments.

HEALTH AND BEAUTY IN LIVING

A successful biological organism is one that thrives. Health is the indication of success or failure both in natural systems and in buildings, towns, cities, regions, and the planet. So once we start looking at buildings as living buildings, we need to consider the issue of health. How well does the building sustain its own health and the health of the occupants? Is there optimal indoor air quality? Is the water in the building pure? Is the daylight in the building plentiful and balanced? Do all these factors combine to create a healthy place for people to be? Do we feel comfort, ease, and positive emotions?

What is beauty? Should we consider beauty in our buildings and communities? Sometimes beauty is seen as some abstract physical pattern and buildings as pure sculpture. However, beauty can also be seen as a manifestation of health and vibrancy that emerges from the inside of an organism—just as we see beauty from the inside when we look at people.

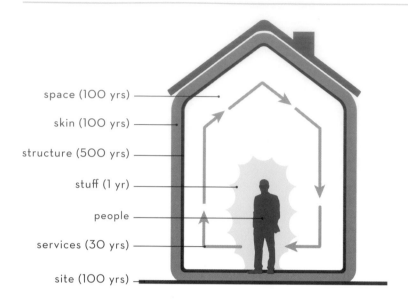

space (100 yrs)

skin (100 yrs)

structure (500 yrs)

stuff (1 yr)

people

services (30 yrs)

site (100 yrs)

FIGURE 3.15. Buildings can be looked at in separate layers serving different purposes, each with an expected lifetime. Although these layers may be combined, it is useful in net zero building design and construction to distinguish them and their specific roles.

Our buildings and communities should be aesthetically pleasing, but the beauty on the surfaces should be an outward manifestation of the building's inner health, the activities that take place there, the building's connections to nature, and the quality of its public spaces, views, light, and air.

Building Organization

We can observe buildings in different ways. While we think of buildings as permanent, the reality is that buildings change, adapt, and deteriorate over time, a fact that has led architects such as N. J. Habraken and Frank Duffy to look at buildings as a series of layers in different time frames.[20] Author Stewart Brand builds upon their classification of layers of buildings and distinguishes six s layers—site, structure, skin, services, space, and stuff—that typically change and evolve at different rates and frequencies.[21] Recognizing these layers and their time limitations is helpful in the planning and design process for all buildings and for net zero living buildings in particular. If it is likely that interior space requirements will change frequently, for example, then we should allow for that in the design of the interior walls. When we build the structure and skin, we should design for durability and longevity. When we think about the services required in the building, such as the mechanical

equipment, we should consider their life cycle and create a design that allows them to be changed without compromising the components that have not reached their end of life, such as the structure. Let's take a look, then, at Brand's six layers and see how they relate to net zero and living-building design.

SITE

A living building's site extends beyond its geographical setting and lot lines. It includes both physical and biological characteristics such as geology, soils, climate, topography, and ecosystems, as well as surrounding buildings, roads, utilities, regulations, and community. On the physical and geological level, the site is permanent or nearly permanent; at the biological and human community level, it is evolving more rapidly. Understanding the visions, master plans, and regulatory requirements that affect it will give a designer an idea of how its surrounding environment might evolve in the future. It will also help point to opportunities to influence and affect the future of the site and its surroundings.

STRUCTURE

The structure is what holds up the building. It comprises the foundation, walls, columns, and roof components that carry occupants, wind, snow, earthquakes, and other loads to the ground, making the building safe to inhabit. The walls that carry loads are called load-bearing walls in structural terminology. Structure does not include walls and other elements if they are not carrying loads. This can be confusing when we look at a building and think about changes to the building design and layout, a good reason for building design to differentiate what is structural and what is not.

Ultimately, the structure must generate a long life for the building, and if it must be changed, it must still hold the building up. Particularly in living and net zero buildings, the life of the structure should be hundreds of years, as the intent and purpose of living and net zero building design is to make high-quality and durable buildings that are prudent long-term investments. This stands in contrast to many twentieth-century fossil-fuel-based buildings that are designed for the life of a mortgage or loan, which may be only twenty or thirty years. In net zero and living buildings, the structure should be located within the heated envelope to be protected from deterioration from moisture and pests and preferably visible from the inside so that problems can be seen and addressed. Again, this is in contrast to most twentieth-century buildings, where the building structure may be hidden, allowing moisture and pests to go undetected.

SKIN

The skin is the enclosure that wraps the structure and separates the inside of a building from the outside. In net zero building design, the skin is a critical component, providing a controlled environment for human activity. The skin protects occupants; keeps water out of the building; maintains human comfort through temperature, fresh air, and humidity control; provides security and protection; controls views to the outside; and controls sound and fire.

In net zero construction, our focus is primarily on control of the envelope in terms of temperature, moisture, humidity, and air movement. Of lesser importance but still significant is sound and sight. Sound varies in a building. In the wintertime, with the windows closed, the sounds from the outside are almost entirely eliminated. In the summertime, with open windows, it is quite different. Sight is connected to our experience of nature. Through windows we see beyond our building, most commonly to nature or vegetation. Even in an urban environment we connect to places beyond our building, including the sky and street trees. Daylight rather than artificial light connects us to the rhythms and changing light levels that benefit health. And windows impact solar gain, which affects the interior temperature and energy loads. All of these temper the interior environment for human comfort.

Brand suggests that the skin of a building changes relatively frequently, roughly every twenty years, for cosmetic or maintenance reasons.[22] While this is true for many buildings today, it is not true for most buildings built before fossil fuels, where the time frame and building materials enabled a much longer lifespan. For net zero buildings, we propose that the building envelope be designed to be resilient and durable, to last for 100 years or longer (even if it may require maintenance on some components in a shorter time frame).

SERVICES

Brand distinguishes services as "the working guts of a building: communications wiring, electrical wiring, plumbing, sprinkler system, HVAC (heating, ventilating and air conditioning), and moving parts like elevators and escalators."[23] As he explains, the lives of these services are relatively short, perhaps five to thirty years. Having access to services is important to minimize ongoing expenses as the services need to be replaced or maintained.

SPACE

Brand defines the spatial plan as "the interior layout—where walls, ceilings and floors and doors go."[24] It is this layout of internal components that creates and defines the boundaries and spaces that support human activity in a building.

It is worthwhile to think about which spaces in a building should have walls that are potentially movable and which should have walls that are fixed and not easily movable without an extensive renovation. Brand suggests that a commercial building's spatial plan can change every three years based on tenant needs. Office buildings are often reconfigured frequently, while the layout of homes and institutional buildings

Tedd Benson and Bensonwood Homes are innovators in quality housing and leaders in applying Brand and Habraken's thinking about building layers to homes and buildings. Bensonwood creates panelized buildings supported with wood post-and-beam frames provided with all interior and exterior finishes, with access panels installed, and designed to last and look beautiful.

The exterior roof and wall panels are designed with insulation, air, moisture, and vapor control up to net zero standards. Interior panels have what Bensonwood calls an "open-build system" to allow for building services, including electrical and mechanical services, to be changed over time. Walls and ceilings include a chase space with access panels so wiring can be altered. Ceilings also are separated from floors so plumbing and mechanical systems can be adapted to suit future occupant needs.

Thus, these buildings have durable and lasting envelopes and frames. All of the structures and prefinished panels are built with computer-aided design (CAD) and computer-aided manufacturing (CAM) in a controlled environment. This drastically reduces construction time and ensures better control of construction conditions. These buildings demonstrate the practicality and effectiveness of the kind of layered design that Brand and Habraken suggest. Bensonwood Homes, the MIT House_n research consortium, and other industry partners have collaborated to develop the OPEN Prototype Initiative to improve how homes are built in the United States as well as to make them more affordable and adaptable while reducing environmental impacts.[25]

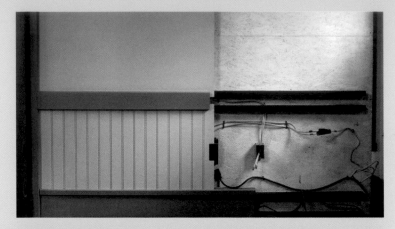

FIGURE 3.16. *Top*, a wall access panel easily accommodates future changes in wiring. *Center*, by separating the floor and ceiling assemblies, leaving a deep open area, designers create another, larger chase space for mechanical, plumbing, and electrical services. *Bottom*, easily removable ceiling panels make access simple and inexpensive.

with significant spaces for meetings, circulation, gathering, and performances last longer. When we renovate historic spaces or design spaces that could become important landmarks, long-term function and beauty are important to plan for, maintain, and preserve. Thus, some walls are best designed as fixed to create important public spaces that last and other walls should be expected to have a shorter life for functions that change.

When flexible design informs the structure, enclosure, and occupant activities of the building, the building has a greater chance of functioning like an organism or ecosystem.

STUFF

Finally, Brand designates as "stuff" everything that is not fixed in place in a building—furniture and equipment that move around and change yearly, monthly, or even daily. Stuff reflects the everyday activities of the occupants and allows for flexibility. The central purpose of a building is to provide a place for human activity. And this activity is supported by the ephemeral stuff that is in the building. In looking at stuff and its arrangement, then, we get a picture of why a building exists in the first place.

The People Factor

We have been exploring building components of all kinds, but at the center of this are the people who occupy the buildings. Our ultimate goal is to make buildings that are comfortable for people. Comfort covers a very broad range of well-being, including physical, emotional, psychological, spiritual, and social. Our buildings should provide comfort in all of these ways, but our main focus with net zero buildings is to provide a climate-controlled interior space that enables people to perform tasks and be protected from the elements in a healthy environment. Every building layer that we have explored should account for and address how it affects the comfort zone inside the building.

This comfort zone is determined by the combination of temperature, humidity, and air movement. It, too, must be adaptable and flexible, as there is not one comfortable temperature, humidity level, or amount of ventilation that is optimal for everyone. All individuals have different tolerances and accept different conditions in summer and winter. We can affect the comfort zone by balancing air temperatures and the radiant temperatures of surfaces as well as designing to encourage air movement, which makes us feel cooler in hot temperatures.

The psychometric chart is an engineering graph that documents how temperature and humidity levels determine the range where most people feel comfortable and to establish set points for building systems. Adding air movement increases the upper thresholds of the comfort zone, while solar access and radiant heat can expand the lower range of comfort. An individual's ability to control surroundings by opening a window or turning on a fan enables a more adaptable and potentially efficient building design, but this requires building services coordination that accounts for individual adaptation, especially in larger buildings with central heating or cooling services.

Life Cycle, Durability, and Resilience

Once we view the site and building as interconnected, we can see how the structures of buildings can be interwoven into human and ecological communities—connecting the human life inside them to the web of surrounding ecosystems. Pueblo Bonito, Machu Picchu, Angkor Wat, and other preserved archeological ruins showcase the way human intervention over time created symbiotic sites and structures, successful living patterns, and adaptable environments. These ruins also illustrate Brand's six s's and the longevity of each. Walls that are not structural are shorter-lived than the overall structure and fabric. The building layout and space plan are somewhat less durable. The building services have a still shorter life and are less evident, and the stuff in the building has the shortest life and is rarely found or has been removed from these ancient sites.

It is interesting to observe how these life cycles change depending on whether buildings and civilizations are powered by renewable or nonrenewable energy. In the millennia of human existence before the predominant use of fossil fuels, significant buildings were typically made out of stone and built to last hundreds and even thousands of years; all elements of the building were built to last as well. Less important buildings were made from less durable materials. With the advent of fossil fuels, the life cycle of buildings has shortened significantly. This has sometimes been due to our financing cycles, other times to fashion or less permanent materials, and often to rapid growth fed by oil. We can think of 100-year-old homes torn down to make room for McMansions and perfectly adequate buildings removed for shopping malls or high rises, even if the structures and skin of the older buildings were fully serviceable. With more sustainably focused community planning and allocation of resources, this would be less common.

Design parameters for space planning changed radically with the use of fossil fuels, and this impacted a building's life cycle. Fossil-fuel-powered buildings, particularly offices, have very large, wide floor plates (often 100 feet wide) that feel more like warehouses, where workers have no visual connection to a window and spaces are lit from artificial light sources. Pre-fossil-fuel buildings relied primarily on daylighting spaces with narrower floor plates (typically 30–50 feet) to allow for light penetration to all of the workstations. Buildings using renewable energy are designed with careful attention to daylight, views, passive solar, and indoor air quality, so the prevalence of frequently moved walls is less likely. As we explore in greater detail later, renewably powered buildings are narrower, use skylights and light wells, or have an atrium space to allow daylight to illuminate the building and connect people to daily light rhythms.

The reduction of energy consumption in buildings is changing the norm for building skins, or building enclosures, in ways that provide human comfort with much less energy consumption. Also, investment in envelope construction with more durable materials extends the life cycle of building enclosures. A skin life cycle of fifty or 100 years is a more prudent investment when using renewable energy.

As energy becomes more expensive, the cost of building operation and maintenance also becomes a more important concern. Stone buildings from the pre-fossil-fuel era are among the least expensive buildings from a structural life-cycle perspective. They require far less maintenance than the typical short-lived and less durable buildings of the fossil fuel era. However, their energy costs are significant. What we need is the structural and envelope durability of past buildings combined with energy efficiency.

Moving toward a renewable future is a move toward resilience. Buildings are a great place to start, but even if we make all buildings net zero, we will be less than 50 percent of the way toward creating a net zero society. As we design, build, and renovate, then, we need to consider the interconnection of our buildings to the larger fabric of human settlement and natural systems so that we can spur change there as well.

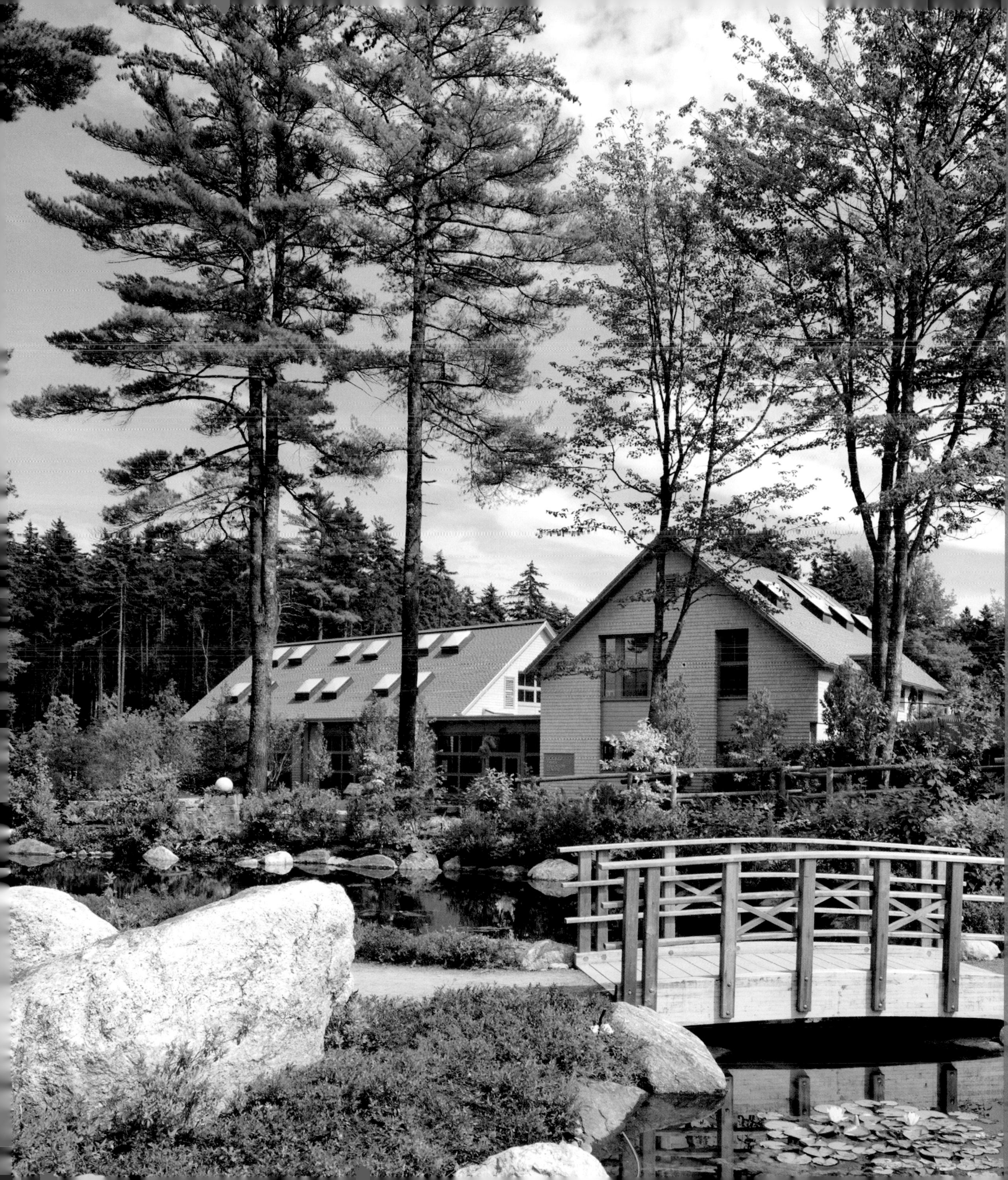

BOSARGE FAMILY EDUCATION CENTER

DESIGN PROFILE

Building Profile	Building Name:	**Bosarge Family Education Center at the Coastal Maine Botanical Gardens**	
	Location:	Boothbay, Maine	
	Occupancy Date:	July, 2011	
	Square Footage:	8,200	
	Certification:	LEED-NC 3.0 Platinum	
Energy Profile	Energy Reference Year:	November, 2012–October, 2013	
	Total Energy Consumption:	46,040 kWh (actual)	
	Total Energy Production:	56,395 kWh (actual)	
	Energy Intensity:	Actual:	19.2 kBtu/sf-yr
		Modeled:	20 kBtu/sf-yr
		Actual with Renewables:	-4.3 kBtu/sf-yr
Building Envelope	Construction Type:	Wood panel	
	Insulation Values:	Walls:	R-40, dense-pack cellulose in 11⅞" I-stud cavity
		Roof:	R-60, dense-pack cellulose in 16" I-stud cavity
		Foundation (slab perimeter):	R-20, 4" XPS rigid insulation
		Foundation (slab-edge joint):	R-20, 4" XPS rigid insulation
		Foundation (sub-slab):	R-20, 4" XPS rigid insulation
	Air Infiltration:	Final Blower Door:	0.115 cfm50/sf exterior surface area
	Windows/Skylights:	Windows:	Low-e, tri-pane, argon-filled
			U-value 0.16, SHGC 0.24 or 0.14, VLT 0.57 or 0.629
		Skylights (Type 1):	16 mm nanogel-filled polycarbonate inner layer
			U-value (max) 0.154
		Skylights (Type 2):	Triple-glazed, low-e, argon-filled
			U-value 0.27
Mechanical/ Electrical Systems	Heating System:	Daikin, single-phase air-source heat pump	
	Cooling System:	Provided by the ASHP if needed	
	Ventilation System:	Manual and automatically operated clerestory windows and skylights; ERV with automatic CO_2 and airflow sensors to recover about 70 percent of heat from exhausted air	
	Lighting System/Controls:	LED, high-efficiency, and super T-8 throughout; daylight dimming and cutoff in classrooms in all public spaces, bilevel (manual on and auto off) in offices and other small spaces	
	Hot Water:	Solar domestic hot water with electric backup	
	Renewable System:	45 kW installed on-site peak, 25 kW roof mounted and 20 kW ground mounted	

BOSARGE FAMILY EDUCATION CENTER
at the Coastal Maine Botanical Gardens

n the mid-2000s, a group of Maine residents, sharing a belief that Maine needed a botanical garden, acquired a 248-acre parcel of tidal shoreland with nearly a mile of tidal saltwater frontage. The Coastal Maine Botanical Gardens (CMBG) are the largest botanical gardens in New England and one of only a handful of waterfront botanical gardens in the United States. By 2009 the rapid growth and popularity of the gardens led to the need for additional indoor space for educational programs, events, and administration. A dedicated group of garden members joined together to explore the possibility of creating a model environmental building on the campus of the gardens. A major donor challenged the gardens to build a net zero building.

Project Overview

The result of this effort is the Bosarge Family Educational Center, which serves as a model of sustainable, energy-efficient design and is the first net zero public building in Maine. The building exemplifies CMBG's commitment to environmental sustainability and helps to fulfill its mission to protect, preserve, and enhance the botanical heritage and natural landscape of coastal Maine through horticulture, education, and research.

The building is intimately connected to nature and its site through natural materials and its views and access to its surroundings. The building has two wings joined by a central transparent gallery that serves as a gateway to the gardens along a central circulation route for visitors. The two wings meet distinct program needs. The classroom wing functions

as three acoustically separate classrooms, each opening to an outdoor teaching space, or as one larger event space. It connects to the outdoors on both the north and south through floor-to ceiling windows. Passive solar is maximized through extensive glazing, and the south-facing roof supports a photovoltaic array. The two-story office wing is oriented at an angle to allow views to the gardens from both floors as well as solar gain into the offices. The staff is visually engaged in the activity in the adjacent gardens through the large windows.

Vision and Goals

From the outset, the client set a high environmental bar, asking that the building meet LEED Platinum and net zero standards, while also being beautiful. The building was to be an active teaching tool, outwardly demonstrating energy and resource conservation to visitors and influencing the future of energy and sustainability in Maine and beyond. The client also wanted the building to fit into Maine's heritage and to complement the surrounding gardens and the existing visitor's center. With thousands of yearly visitors, the facility is expected to have a significant impact on the public.

The solar panels that cover the south-facing roof are clearly visible from the parking lot, a prominent display of the building's sustainability. Other high-performance characteristics are highlighted throughout the education center by signage and an interactive building dashboard. A window cut into a wall to create a "truth wall" allows visitors to look inside to understand its highly insulated assembly. These educational tools provide

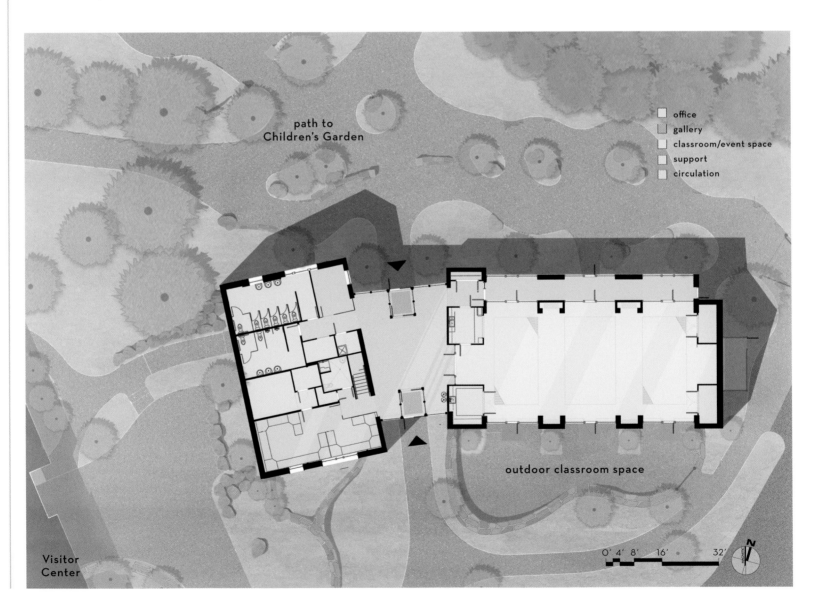

FIGURE CS1.1. The floor plan shows the two wings of the building with the transparent connector.

path to
Children's Garden

office
gallery
classroom/event space
support
circulation

outdoor classroom space

Visitor
Center

0' 4' 8'   16'   32'

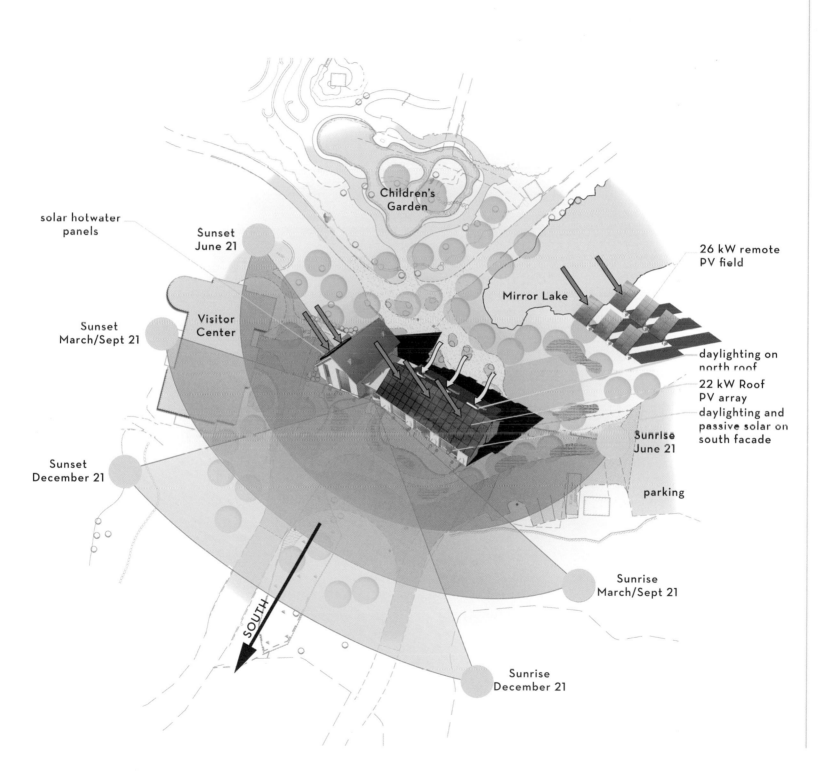

FIGURE CS1.2. This three-dimensional representation shows the building's orientation to the sun's path.

solar hotwater panels

Sunset June 21

Sunset March/Sept 21

Sunset December 21

Children's Garden

Visitor Center

Mirror Lake

SOUTH

26 kW remote PV field

daylighting on north roof

22 kW Roof PV array

daylighting and passive solar on south facade

Sunrise June 21

parking

Sunrise March/Sept 21

Sunrise December 21

FIGURE CS1.3. View from the main entrance.

opportunities for visitors to learn about the design process, green features installed in the building, the building's energy production and consumption, water consumption, and daily use patterns.

Energy

Because of the garden's master plan and garden layout, the education center's site was predetermined, adjacent to the existing visitor's center. With the site located in a valley, maximizing the solar access critical to net zero performance presented a challenge. In addition, the client wanted to preserve as many of the large coniferous trees as possible. Extensive study of the site was undertaken to maximize solar access, views, and pedestrian and vehicular access. This effort resulted in a design that maximizes passive solar heat gain on the south wall as well as south-facing photovoltaic production on the roof, while establishing a connection to the existing visitor's center so staff can easily connect between the two buildings. The entry, located along the visitor's central circulation path, also allows the staff to be connected to the arrivals and departures of guests. It was a complex site planning effort.

The building enclosure is superinsulated, featuring R-20 below-grade insulation, R-40 above-ground walls, and an R-60 roof. Triple-glazed R-6.25 windows, manufactured in Germany, provide passive solar gain in the winter. Detailed energy modeling assessed numerous envelope and building system configurations that led to an optimized design for the best long-term benefit and investment.

To meet the tight budget and schedule, reduce waste, and minimize site impact, the client and design team elected to use a panelized construction system. This allowed for the majority of the building envelope to be fabricated off-site and assembled rapidly on-site. With the shell in place, construction inside continued through the winter months, allowing the center to be completed before the botanical garden's busy summer season.

Daylighting strategies contribute to the overall beauty and performance of the building. South-facing windows with light-guiding blinds and north-facing windows and skylights provide even light to the educational space. Glazing in the connector creates a light-filled space, while skylights highlight wall-mounted displays. The office wing is organized to take advantage of solar access. High windows allow for deep daylight penetration. High-efficiency lighting and daylighting strategies provide an estimated 60 percent reduction in energy use for lighting. Window treatments include roller shades that allow for views even when blocking glare and light-guiding blinds on higher windows to reduce the need for artificial lighting.

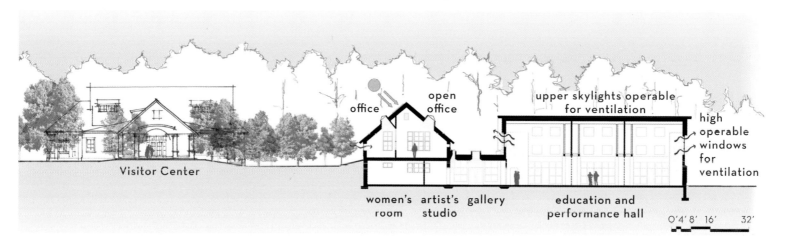

office
open office
upper skylights operable for ventilation
high operable windows for ventilation

Visitor Center

women's room   artist's studio   gallery   education and performance hall   0' 4' 8' 16'   32'

FIGURE CS1.5. Daylit entry gallery with building dashboard.

Mechanical systems include a variable-volume refrigerant heat-pump system that provides for both heating and cooling. This air-to-air heat pump extracts heat from the outside air and pumps that heat into the building in the winter; it rejects heat to the outdoors in the summer. Ventilation is provided in summer by operable windows and in winter by energy-recovery ventilators, which recapture about 70 percent of the heat from exhaust air and deliver it back into the fresh incoming air stream.

To meet the net zero goals, a 45kW PV array was specified based on load analysis and reduction. Although the design team discussed the possibility of locating all the required PVs on the building roof, programmatic needs for the office space as well as concerns about the aesthetic aspect of a single large roof for the entire building daylighting and view led to the decision to break up the roof massing. The team decided to supplement PV on the education center roof with ground-mounted PV on nearby garden property.

Energy monitoring tracks real-time and cumulative energy consumption and renewable energy production. The design team monitored building performance to ensure that it was meeting its projections for the first two years. Meters inside the building and online track real-time data for lighting, mechanical systems, water use, and electricity production to educate staff and visitors.

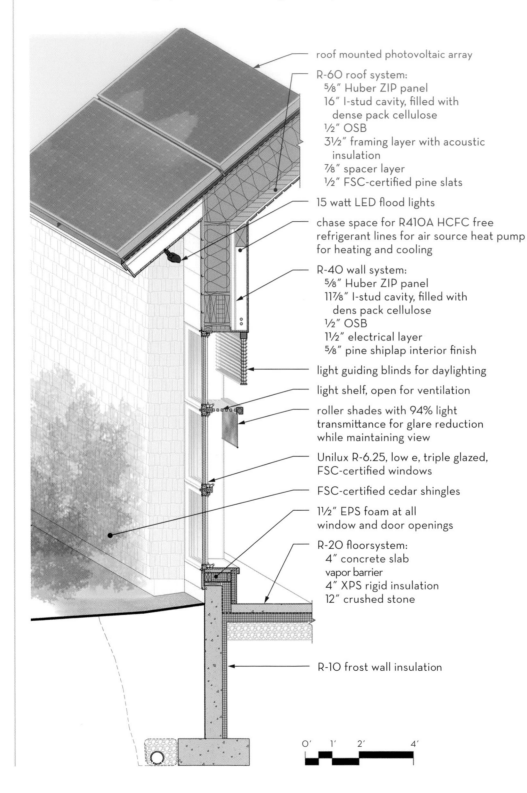

FIGURE CS1.6. High-performance building assembly.

roof mounted photovoltaic array

R-60 roof system:
⅝" Huber ZIP panel
16" I-stud cavity, filled with
  dense pack cellulose
½" OSB
3½" framing layer with acoustic
  insulation
⅞" spacer layer
½" FSC-certified pine slats

15 watt LED flood lights

chase space for R410A HCFC free
refrigerant lines for air source heat pump
for heating and cooling

R-40 wall system:
⅝" Huber ZIP panel
11⅞" I-stud cavity, filled with
  dens pack cellulose
½" OSB
1½" electrical layer
⅝" pine shiplap interior finish

light guiding blinds for daylighting

light shelf, open for ventilation

roller shades with 94% light
transmittance for glare reduction
while maintaining view

Unilux R-6.25, low e, triple glazed,
FSC-certified windows

FSC-certified cedar shingles

1½" EPS foam at all
window and door openings

R-20 floorsystem:
  4" concrete slab
  vapor barrier
  4" XPS rigid insulation
  12" crushed stone

R-10 frost wall insulation

0'   1'   2'   4'

Healthy and Sustainable Strategies

The team carefully selected materials and finishes for the building to meet the owner's goals of beauty, character, high-recycled content, low or no toxicity, durability, and low environmental impact. A total of 85 percent of the wood in the building is FSC-certified, and wood for flooring, ceilings, and trim is locally harvested. Natural finishes were used wherever possible, including clear wood finishes, mill finish aluminum, and polished concrete. A total of 90 percent of on-site construction waste was recycled. The interior is finished with non-VOC and nontoxic paints and stains.

Water-saving technologies and water reuse contribute to a 75 percent reduction in building water usage when compared to a typical building. Runoff from over half of the roof area is collected in a rainwater collection tank for reuse in the building. The adjacent bioswales channel stormwater runoff into the ground and gardens, minimize garden irrigation needs, and filter polluting runoff before it reaches the ocean.

Collaborative Process

The Bosarge Family Educational Center was designed collaboratively and equally by two architecture firms who together

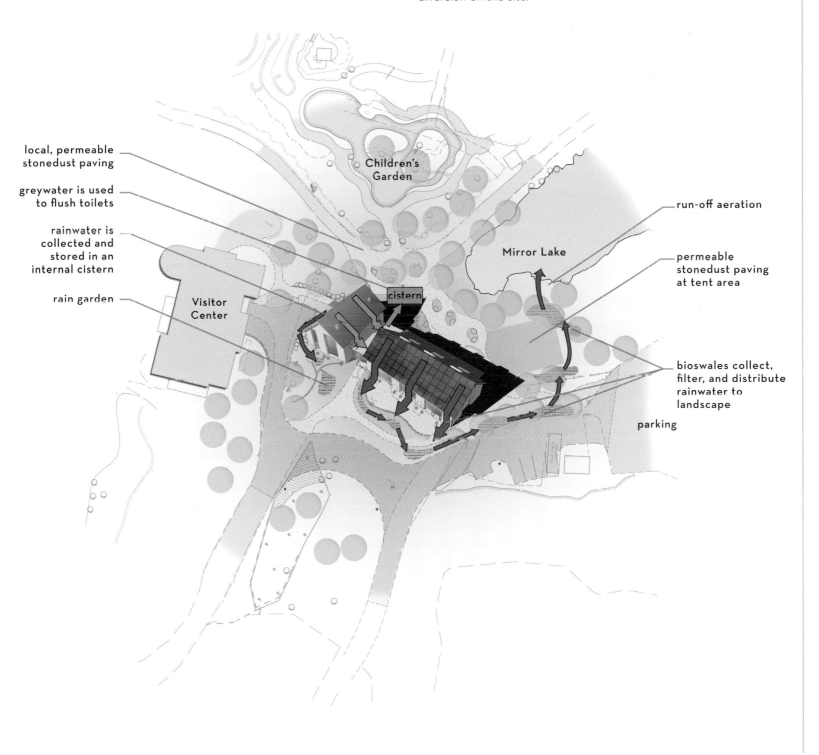

local, permeable stonedust paving

greywater is used to flush toilets

rainwater is collected and stored in an internal cistern

rain garden

Children's Garden

cistern

Visitor Center

run-off aeration

Mirror Lake

permeable stonedust paving at tent area

bioswales collect, filter, and distribute rainwater to landscape

parking

FIGURE CS1.8. Building entrance.

FIGURE CS1.9. Scupper directs roof runoff to rain gardens.

led an integrated design and construction team, beginning at the permitting stage and continuing through construction administration. At the onset a division of responsibilities was outlined: the local firm, Scott Simons Architects, was responsible primarily for construction documents and construction administration, while our firm, Maclay Architects, led the net zero portion of the project and developed the building envelope. While this division remained relatively intact, both firms participated heavily in all aspects of design and were able to learn from each other's expertise.

An integrated design process, spearheaded by the owner's sustainability consultant, included highly interactive and collaborative design work sessions. The sustainability consultant helped the owner set and retain the project goals, select the architects, and successfully fulfill the LEED Platinum documentation requirements. Additional team members were an energy consultant, a structural engineer, a mechanical and electrical engineer, a civil engineer, a landscape architect, a lighting designer, an electrical engineer, a construction manager, a building systems fabricator, and numerous CMBG staff, board members, donors, and community members. On-site design

charrettes enabled the team to make informed choices about the site, building systems and materials, renewable strategies, and budget alignment.

The client, a nonprofit institution, was restricted by a tight budget and a short schedule, as it was intent on preserving garden visitors' experience during the summer season. The design team brought a construction manager on board early during the design process to explore different ways of meeting the client's performance and design goals while performing the majority of construction out of the busy summer season. Using a panelized construction system proved to be the most effective way to construct the building on time and within budget. What would typically have been a twelve- to fourteen-month construction project was completed in less than ten months.

Through this integrated design process, the client's strong environmental goals were realized, complete with a teachable mantra, "If a plant designed a building. . . ." Visitors to the gardens can now complete that sentence with firsthand observations: "It would be powered by the sun, it would use natural materials as its building blocks, and it would harness the daylight."

PART II

Net Zero Design

4 | Integrated Design Fundamentals

Living buildings. Biomimicry. The kind of new building paradigm we've been exploring rests on a key strategy: integrated design, which views the building as an interconnected system whose parts and whole are designed to work together synergistically within the larger environment. Integrated design is central to the design of net zero buildings and relies on principles that have long been part of the architectural design process, though only recently named as such. Core principles include letting nature do the work, conserving energy and resources, and encouraging passive systems before active systems. The foundation of integrated design rests on systems thinking, in which changes in one part of a system are studied to determine how they may change other parts of that system or the entire system. Designing within this framework allows for innovation and the ability to achieve net zero goals more easily and cost-effectively.

Integrated design and the systems thinking that supports it are important to the design of net zero buildings and communities because they allow the design team to look at a building as part of larger environmental, ecological, economic, spiritual, and social systems. This way of thinking encourages the design team to ask critical questions: Is this building even necessary? Is there a way that the uses can be shared and create synergies that will enhance operation? How can we maximize solar energy utilization on the site? If we insulate to a very high level, can we eliminate mechanical systems or at least radically reduce their costs?

The end result is that each net zero project is unique. A net zero building design cannot be replicated on multiple sites without attention to the specific characteristics of each site. Before any design even occurs, the designer must research and understand the environmental factors interacting on the individual site. Consequently, a net zero design reflects an understanding of site influences so deeply that a preliminary understanding of the site—from the path of the sun and the direction of prevailing winds to the availability of water and renewable resources—can be understood from the design features of the completed building.

In implementing integrated building design, there is no list of strategies that can be checked off one by one. An integrated approach requires much more complexity

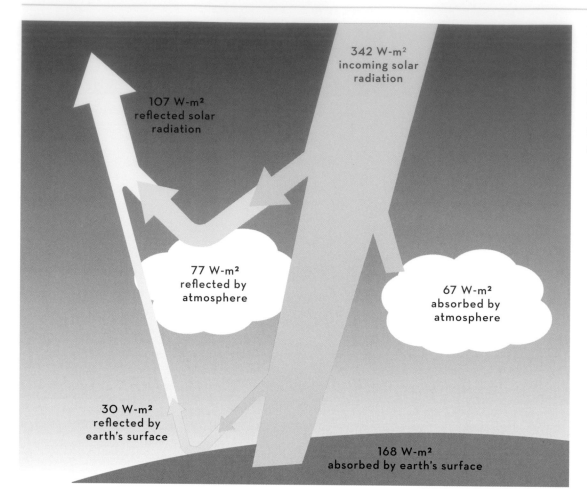

342 W-m² incoming solar radiation

107 W-m² reflected solar radiation

77 W-m² reflected by atmosphere

67 W-m² absorbed by atmosphere

30 W-m² reflected by earth's surface

168 W-m² absorbed by earth's surface

FIGURE 4.1. Only about half of the solar energy from the sun makes it to and is available at the earth's surface. The rest of the solar energy is reflected back into space by the atmosphere, absorbed in the atmosphere, or reflected by the earth's surface itself.

to accommodate the interplay of site influences and building requirements. In this chapter we cover the various influences of the site and the potential strategies to work them into an integrated design. In the following chapter, we walk through the integrated design process.

It is worth repeating here that the assumption throughout this book is that we are designing for the Northern Hemisphere; specifically, cold northern latitudes. The concepts described in this chapter are applicable to other locations but must be modified. For those with knowledge of passive solar building design, this chapter will be familiar. For those with limited solar knowledge, it will provide only an overview. But for both readers, the discussion in this chapter will highlight the specific aspects of integrated design important to the design of net zero buildings.

Understanding the Sun

Understanding the sun's movement and position during the day is fundamental to site planning, daylighting, passive solar design, and controlling unwanted heat gains. Through its design, a net zero building maximizes the use of free, renewable energy from the sun and in turn reduces its dependence on fossil fuels.

The sun is located 93 million miles from the earth and sends off a steady supply of heat energy toward the earth's surface; this is called the solar constant, equal to 433 Btu/sf-hr.[1] If 100 percent of the sun's energy could be harnessed in the outer atmosphere, there would be enough energy to keep

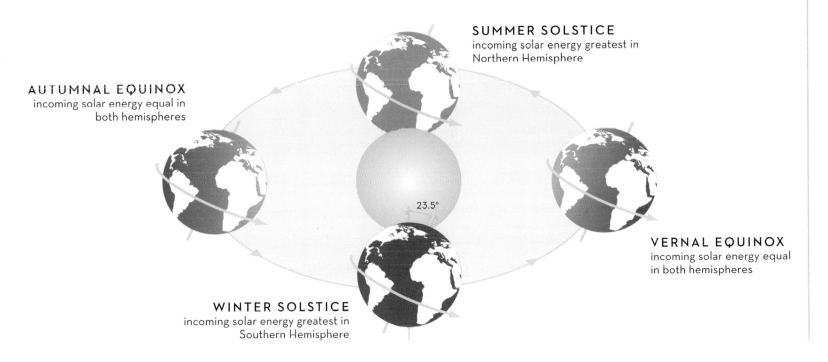

FIGURE 4.2. The earth annually travels around the sun in an elliptic path. Its axial tilt on this path is responsible for seasonal variations. When the Northern Hemisphere tilts away from the sun, the sun angle is low, and less solar radiation reaches the earth's surface, resulting in winter. In contrast, when the Northern Hemisphere tilts toward the sun, the sun moves to a higher altitude in the sky and more solar radiation hits the earth's surface, resulting in summer.

SUMMER SOLSTICE
incoming solar energy greatest in
Northern Hemisphere

AUTUMNAL EQUINOX
incoming solar energy equal in
both hemispheres

23.5°

VERNAL EQUINOX
incoming solar energy equal
in both hemispheres

WINTER SOLSTICE
incoming solar energy greatest in
Southern Hemisphere

a 120-watt bulb burning constantly on every square foot of the earth's surface—approximately 55 trillion 120-watt bulbs. The solar constant varies annually because the earth travels in an elliptical orbit around the sun, but this variation is imperceptible at the building level. What is measurable at the building level is the difference between the solar constant and the portion of this energy that actually makes it through the atmosphere to the earth's surface. The measure of solar radiation received on any one point of the earth's surface over a given time is called solar insolation, or irradiation. The difference between the solar constant and solar insolation relates to how much of the sun's energy is reflected or absorbed by the atmosphere.

AXIAL TILT AND THE SEASONS

The earth's axial tilt, at 23.5°, creates seasons. This tilt, along with the fact that the earth travels around the sun in an elliptical orbit, causes the hemisphere tilting toward the sun to experience summer, while the hemisphere tilting away from the sun experiences winter as shown in figure 4.2. The rotation of the earth impacts the amount or depth of atmosphere the heat energy from the sun must pass through to reach the surface. The rules of trigonometry mean that at a more oblique angle a given square meter of sun is spread out over more surface area. The combination of these effects determines how much solar energy any given point on the earth's surface receives at one time.

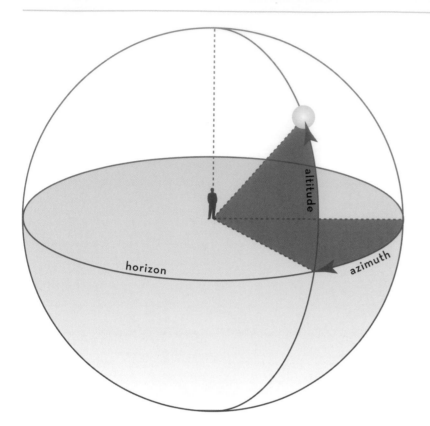

FIGURE 4.3. The altitude angle is a measure of the height of the sun vertically above the horizon, while the azimuth angle is a measure of the position of the sun along the horizon from true, or solar, south.

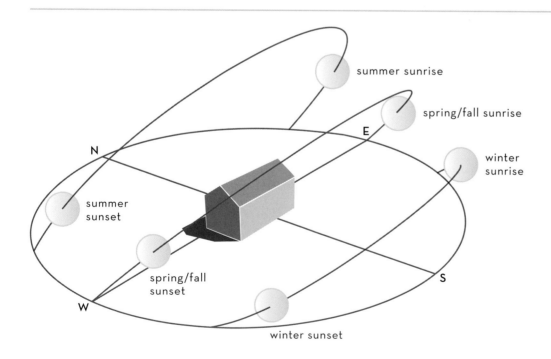

FIGURE 4.4. In the Northern Hemisphere the sun rises north of east during the summer, due east on the equinoxes, and south of east during the winter. This changing location of the sun requires design solutions that address both summer and winter sun paths, depending on heating, cooling, daylighting, and other needs during these periods.

FIGURE 4.5. While the location of true north is dictated by the geometry of the earth itself, magnetic north is defined by flows and deposits of metal ores deep below the earth's surface. Compass readings point to magnetic north and can therefore vary significantly from solar, or true, north. To determine true north, you must adjust your compass reading by the angle of difference between magnetic and true north (*red lines*), which is specific to your location on earth.

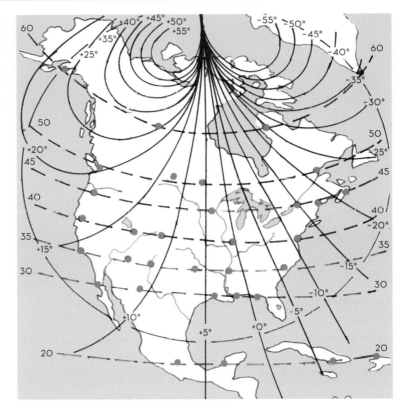

ALTITUDE AND AZIMUTH

At any given time the position of the sun can be defined by its altitude and azimuth angles, depicted in figure 4.3. The altitude angle, the angle between the horizon and the sun's position above the horizon, begins and ends at 0° at sunrise and sunset and peaks at solar noon. The daily maximum altitude varies throughout the year and in northern climates reaches its yearly maximum on June 21, the summer solstice, and its yearly minimum on December 21, the winter solstice. Additionally, the altitude angle depends on the observer's position on the earth; the daily maximum altitude of the sun increases as the observer travels closer to the equator.

The azimuth angle of the sun is dictated by the time of day and the season, it is the angle along the horizon of the sun's position relative to due south. In the Northern Hemisphere the sun rises north of east during the summer, due east on the equinoxes, and south of east during the winter. This large azimuth range, combined with the altitude, results in the longer summer days, as shown in figure 4.4. It is important to understand the measures of altitude and azimuth for your site, as the location and angles of the sun factor into building orientation, shading devices, daylighting, passive solar heating, and the location of activities within the building.

TRUE NORTH AND SOUTH

When we refer to north and south in building design, we are referring to the true, or solar, directions. Depending on the geographic location, the solar direction can vary significantly from a compass reading at the site. As a reference, a traveler moving across the United States from one coast to another would experience a 30° variation, attributable to the fact that a compass is oriented to magnetic north (see figure 4.5) and is affected by irregularities in flows or deposits of iron and ore deep under the earth's surface. When we work with daylighting and passive solar design in net zero building design, it is solar, or true, north that is relevant, not magnetic north. To determine the location of solar north based on a compass reading, we must adjust the magnetic reading by the angle of declination for the specific site. It is therefore critical to understand the difference between true and magnetic north and to make the needed adjustments in reference to the sun's location. In many cases land surveys indicate only magnetic north. In our work we indicate both magnetic and true north on all documents so that all team members are sure they are using the correct true north for design and construction.

Collecting and Analyzing Site-Specific Data

In addition to the overall ecological site opportunities and constraints in any design process—including views, access, and natural features—there are site considerations specifically related to net zero design. Because weather patterns at different sites can vary dramatically and have a major affect on the design, the first step in any design process is to collect site-specific data. For instance, consider the cold and relatively cloudy weather of New England compared with the sunnier and equally cold weather of Colorado. Although the temperatures at these two diverse locations are relatively similar, overall the environmental forces vary dramatically, especially in terms of humidity and solar access. The differences in the environmental factors have a significant impact on building design and performance and will result in different design solutions for each location.

The National Oceanic and Atmospheric Administration (NOAA) provides the most accurate weather data for sites in the United States. City-specific data can also be found at city-data.com. Accurate weather/climate data have not been collected for every town, so if you cannot find data for your specific site, then substitute data that is most similar. In most cases this would be data for the closest town, but differences in elevation or lake and ocean effects should be considered in picking the most appropriate substitutions. While all weather data help to provide a comprehensive picture of a specific site, the elements critical to net zero building design are the temperature, sun, wind, rainfall, snowfall, and humidity. Other data points you need to collect to understand the net-zero-specific climatic influences are heating degree days, cooling degree days, solar access, direct solar radiation and percentage of sunshine, humidity, and wind direction and speed.

HEATING DEGREE DAYS (HDD)

Heating degree days (HDD) indicate the heating requirement, or the relative coldness, for a specific location. In calculating heating degree days with a base temperature of 65°F, it is assumed that a building does not need to be heated when temperatures are 65°F or higher.[2] One heating degree day means that the average outside temperature for one day was one degree lower than the base temperature of 65°F. For example, if the average daily temperature is 35°F, then the HDD65 is 30, and if the average daily temperature is 85°F, then the HDD65 is 0, because the average temperature is higher than the base temperature and no supplemental heating is required. The

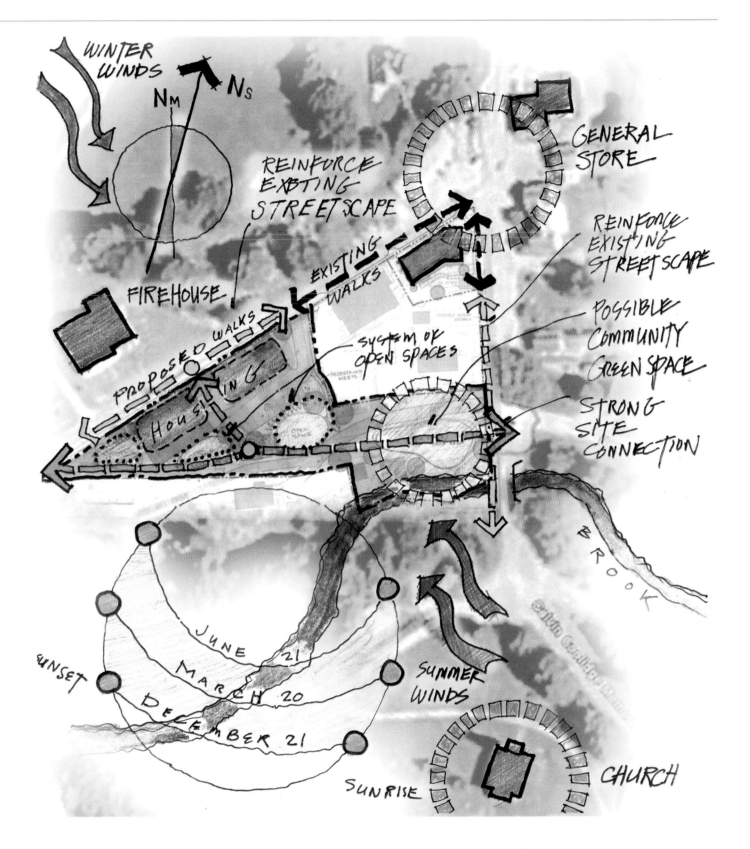

WINTER WINDS

N$_M$ N$_S$

REINFORCE EXISTING STREETSCAPE

GENERAL STORE

EXISTING WALKS

REINFORCE EXISTING STREETSCAPE

FIREHOUSE

POSSIBLE COMMUNITY GREEN SPACE

PROPOSED WALKS

HOUSING

SYSTEM OF OPEN SPACES

STRONG SITE CONNECTION

BROOK

JUNE 21

MARCH 20

DECEMBER 21

SUNSET

SUMMER WINDS

SUNRISE

CHURCH

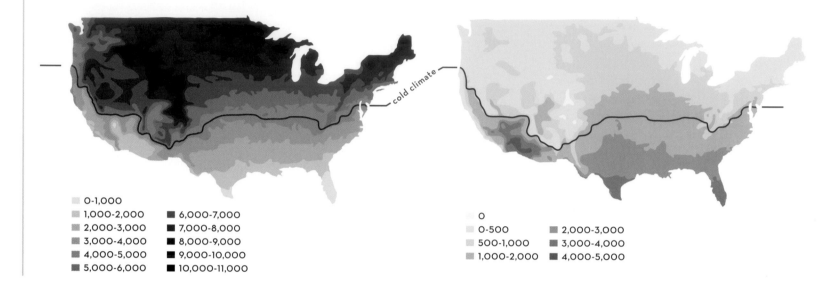

FIGURE 4.7. HDD (*red map*) in the continental United States range from less than 500 to greater than 10,500. CDD (*blue map*) range from less than 500 to greater than 4,000. Areas above the black line are considered cold-climate regions, the focus of this book.

cold climate

☐ 0–1,000	
☐ 1,000–2,000	■ 6,000–7,000
☐ 2,000–3,000	■ 7,000–8,000
☐ 3,000–4,000	■ 8,000–9,000
☐ 4,000–5,000	■ 9,000–10,000
☐ 5,000–6,000	■ 10,000–11,000

☐ 0	
☐ 0–500	■ 2,000–3,000
☐ 500–1,000	■ 3,000–4,000
☐ 1,000–2,000	■ 4,000–5,000

sum of the HDD for a month (or even an entire year) is used to compare the need for heating or the relative coldness of a site. The total annual HDD is used to calculate the annual energy load requirements for a specific building.

COOLING DEGREE DAYS (CDD)

Cooling degree days (CDD) are analogous to HDD but measure how many degrees the average temperature is higher rather than lower than a given base temperature, calling for additional cooling. The measure of CDD gives a relative understanding of when cooling is needed for a specific site. CDD in NOAA charts are calculated from the same base temperature of 65°F as used for HDD, but the thermostat should be set at 75–80°F to conserve energy. This will depend on air movement, humidity levels, and personal comfort preferences of occupants. In figure 4.7 you can see that even in the regions we consider as having cold climates, with 3,000 or more HDD, there are upward of 1,500 CDD. In these areas where our focus is on heating, we do need to address cooling in some cases.

SOLAR ACCESS

To accurately determine total solar access and consequently shading on a site, a solar measuring device such as the Solar Pathfinder or smartphone-based application can be used.[3] The data collected help determine the opportunities and accurate potential for passive solar, daylighting, and active solar production technologies.

We use a Solar Pathfinder to determine the the existing and potential solar on a site. To use the Pathfinder, center it along the true north–south axis of the site location where a building or solar array would be positioned. You will see a reflected sky dome in the Pathfinder lens; the image depicts the annual shading for all of the months and times of day throughout the year based on your latitude. From this reading, you can figure the percentage of solar access on the site.

Figure 4.8 (*top*) shows the Pathfinder reading of the existing trees that shade the specific location. Trees blocking the prime solar access are identified in red and indicated in the photograph in figure 4.8. By calculating the percent of solar access

FIGURE 4.8. The Solar Pathfinder (*top*) shows the reflection of the sky dome over the sun path for your latitude. This reveals obstructions to the solar access, such as trees, outlined in black. Trees to be kept on-site are shaded in green; those to be removed are shaded in red. A photograph of the site (*bottom*) shows which trees are to be removed.

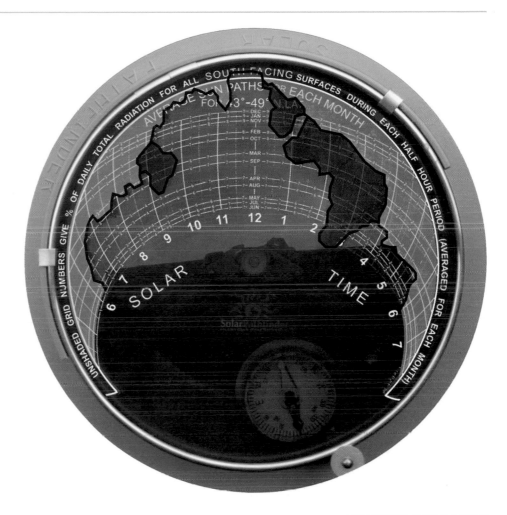

TABLE 4.1. SOLAR ACCESS ON A GIVEN SITE

	EXISTING SOLAR	PROPOSED SOLAR
January	47%	63%
February	43%	80%
March	41%	83%
April	86%	95%
May	99%	99%
June	92%	97%
July	94%	99%
August	98%	96%
September	76%	92%
October	50%	80%
November	47%	70%
December	47%	64%
Total Potential Solar	68%	85%

per month, you can determine the existing annual solar access, in this case 68 percent (table 4.1). To achieve the proposed solar access of 85 percent, the indicated trees would need to be removed. Depending on your project goals, you would propose a plan that identifies trees to be removed and retained to balance solar access, aesthetics, and other concerns. With the final tree removal plan in place, you can calculate the anticipated solar energy to be harvested by multiplying the

FIGURE 4.9. This map indicates the predicted annual average solar production from a solar collector oriented south with a tilt angle equal to the local latitude, measured in kWh/m^2-yr. A solar collector located almost anywhere in the mainland United States is capable of producing more energy than a solar collector located in Germany.

percent of open solar access from the Pathfinder analysis by the PV efficiency and by solar radiation data for the site.

DIRECT SOLAR RADIATION AND PERCENTAGE OF SUNSHINE

The measure of direct solar radiation and percentage of sunshine are important in determining potential solar thermal and PV production. Research these for the geographic location of a specific site. While solar thermal and PV production is financially feasible in locations with lower levels of direct solar radiation, the higher the direct solar radiation is, the higher the thermal and/or electricity production per installed area of collecting surface.

The sunniest part of the United States, the Southwest, experiences on average 6.8 kWh/m^2-day of direct solar radiation and is ideal for thermal and PV installation. In comparison, Alaska receives only half that amount. Germany, which boasts 36 percent of the global installed PV capacity and the highest PV generation per capita in the world at 302.8 W of installed capacity per inhabitant in 2011, receives less direct solar radiation than any state in the United States other than Alaska, as shown in figure 4.9.[4] Germany's high PV generation supports the conclusion that PV is feasible across the United States.

With appropriate building design responses, both passive solar and daylighting can be viable in cloudy locations. In fact, with proper design a cloudy day can be better for daylighting than full sun, which causes glare and is challenging to regulate.

HUMIDITY

It is important to understand humidity at a site in order to determine how to provide a comfortable environment for building occupants and select appropriate building materials. Most people are more comfortable in hot and dry conditions than hot and humid conditions, and it is much the same for building

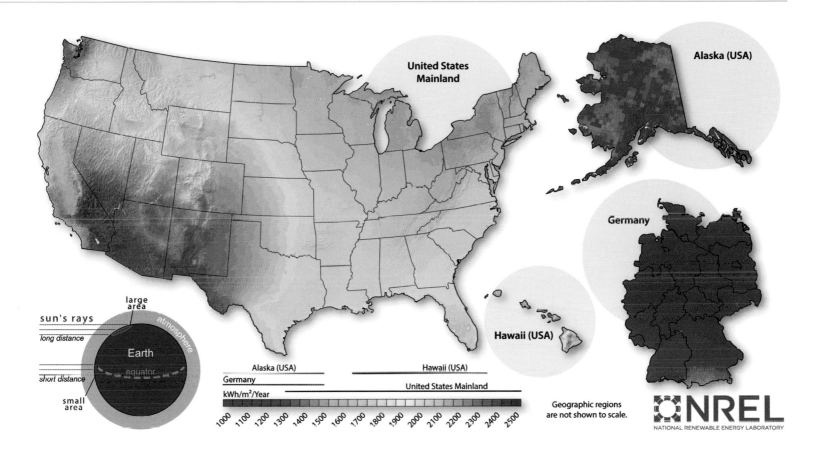

materials. Hot and humid conditions can lead to mold and mildew, degrading building materials, and unhealthy conditions for the building's occupants. Rot is more often a result of rain getting into the building enclosure through inadequate water detailing rather than humid conditions, as discussed in chapter 6. However, once building materials are wetted by any source, mold germinates and then can grow in high-humidity conditions.

WIND DIRECTION AND SPEED

Understanding wind speed and direction is important in the development of ventilation and passive cooling strategies in hot weather, as well as for heat loss due to air movement through the envelope in winter. It is also critical in assessing the viability of wind power on specific sites. Wind roses depict wind speed and direction (see figure 4.10). Wind data from standard resources such as NOAA or a local airport often do not give a full picture for the specific site, as topography

can have a significant impact on wind direction and speed. If wind data is critical to the building design strategy, additional observations or measurement might be necessary.

Energy Conservation through Integrated Design Strategies

Once the design team has collected and understood site-specific data, they can begin to look for the simplest solutions to construct the most efficient building at the lowest cost.

The design of a net zero building is driven by two key components: energy conservation within the building itself and renewable energy production. Energy conservation and the reduction of loads is the most essential step to developing a financially feasible net zero building. For effective and reproducible net zero building solutions, building loads must be

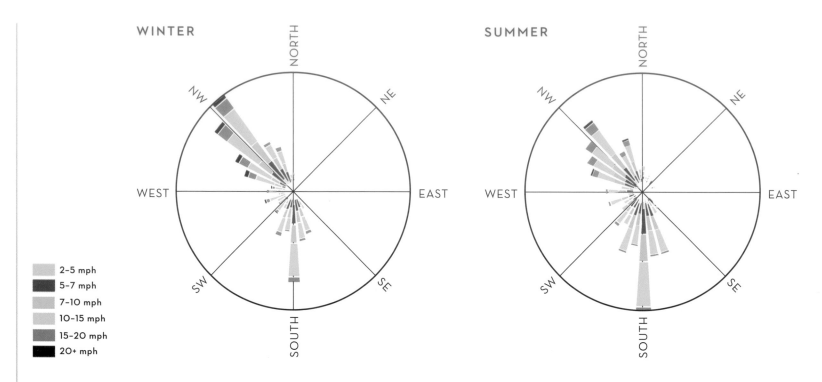

FIGURE 4.10. A wind rose indicates the typical distribution of wind speed and direction for a particular location and season. The length of the spoke indicates the wind frequency, and the direction of the spoke shows the direction of the wind. The color indicates intensity. These two wind roses show that prevalent wind patterns are from the northwest in the winter and the south in the summer for this location. It is important to look at separate summer and winter wind roses when designing buildings that respond to wind, have outdoor spaces, and/or use natural ventilation to cool. Wind roses can also initially evaluate possible wind potential for energy generation. Wind intensity and frequency data are plotted on a polar coordinate system.

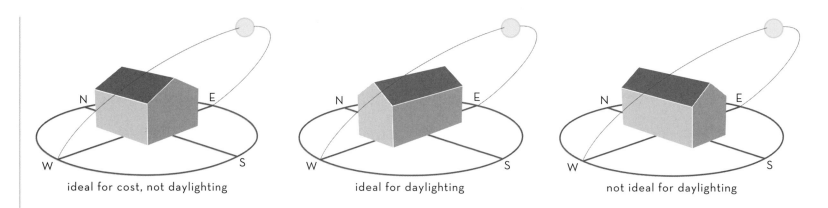

FIGURE 4.11. A perfect cube is often cheaper to build but is not ideal for daylighting because daylighting at the exterior may not penetrate to the building's interior. A building elongated over the east–west axis is ideal for both daylighting and passive solar heat gain and is therefore generally the best orientation and massing for a net zero building. A building elongated over the north–south axis is not ideal because it provides larger areas for glazing to the east and west, which are harder to control for consistent daylighting and can cause overheating.

reduced by around 80 percent of those in existing buildings of the same type. This load reduction is generally accomplished through integrated passive strategies and smart design, including orientation, elongation, massing, daylighting, passive heating and cooling, increased insulation, and decreased air infiltration through the building enclosure.

Load reduction by the measures indicated above also provides an opportunity for a major decrease in both the size and complexity of the mechanical systems that heat, cool, and ventilate the building. This further reduces the overall energy loads of the building and the size of the renewable system needed to power the building. Because the reduction in size and complexity of the mechanical systems is so integrally related to any load reduction accomplished through the building enclosure design, the designers of each must work together to develop a solution that will maximize the benefit to each.

ORIENTATION, ELONGATION, AND MASSING

Determining the size and shape of the perfect building enclosure while balancing heat loss, heat gain, building use, and construction cost can be complicated, but some general rules can help shape most net zero buildings.

When the goal is to optimize solar heat gain, the best strategy is to spread the building out over the east–west axis, orienting one of the longer elevations to face due south (see figure 4.11). A building thus elongated also minimizes overheating because more wall area is available for glazing on the ideal glazing façades of the north and south and less area is located on the east and west façades, where low sun angles can cause challenges related to shading and overheating. When the goal is to minimize heat loss through the building enclosure, the total surface area of the building should be minimized. The optimal form to do so is a half-sphere, but this is not the most practical and cost-effective option, as rectangular geometry creates spaces that can be occupied more efficiently and reduces construction costs. So a cube is the next most logical shape to consider. However, when we balance the effects of maximizing solar heat gain with reducing heat loss, we return to a rectangular shape. In most cases this rectangle will not be as elongated along the east–west axis as it would be if it were

created considering solar heat gain alone, but it will still be more elongated than a cube. As a general rule for the northern latitudes, the ratio of north and south walls to east and west walls should be approximately 1.7:1, but with today's advanced energy modeling and daylight calculations, building and site-specific calculations are preferable.

Another consideration when siting the building is to locate the long axis perpendicular to the prevailing summer wind direction to maximize natural ventilation during the summer, fall, and spring. While the building orientation should first be guided by solar gain and daylighting, the ideal solar orientation can be adjusted by 10–20° to the east or west with very little impact on solar gain or daylighting.

Cost should also be considered when determining a building's massing. Complex and spread-out forms increase building surface area, increasing the quantity and complexity of materials and assembly needed to construct the building. A more compact building mass can be more cost effective since net zero building enclosures include higher than normal insulation values and therefore more materials per square foot of building enclosure than a traditional building design. Compact, smaller buildings can also perform better and use minimized mechanical systems. A point-source heating system is a viable option for a compact building, while a more spread-out building will require a more complex distributed heating system.

DAYLIGHTING SCIENCE AND PRACTICES

Daylighting is a cornerstone of integrated building design. The overall purpose and goal is to use controlled natural light to enhance indoor living and working environments and reduce the need for electric lighting. Because we can so easily use artificial lights in our buildings today, we often pay little attention to designing for daylighting. But diverse research has linked daylit spaces to increased learning rates, reduced error rates, and increased retail sales (see chapter 17 for additional information on the benefits of daylighting). Minimal changes in light levels have been connected to eyestrain, headaches, and fatigue. Our transition from living outside in constant connection to nature to living inside in artificial environments has had multiple impacts for better and worse, many of which we do not understand.

In the United States we tend to assume that the idea of orienting a building to take advantage of the sun for daylighting and passive solar heating was a product of the 1970s energy crisis and the resulting passive solar craze. But in fact the idea has been understood since humans first began designing homes and communities. Pueblo Bonito in Chaco Canyon, New Mexico, and Mesa Verde in Colorado are two excellent examples.

Chaco Canyon was a major center of the ancestral Puebloan culture from around 800 AD to 1100.[5] Pueblo Bonito, the most thoroughly investigated and celebrated site in the canyon, is designed with ideal massing for a solar community. The building site, which covers 2 acres and includes 650–800 rooms, is a huge, D-shaped building divided into two sections by a precisely aligned north-to-south wall through the central plaza. The large, curved masonry wall to the north reduced heat loss from within the enclosure, while the orthogonal walls and roofs stepping down to the south captured the sun's heat and created a protected plaza oriented to the south to take advantage of the available winter heat from the sun.

At Mesa Verde the Puebloan people took a different but equally successful solar strategy. They sited their buildings in a carved-out section of a south-facing

FIGURE 4.12. An artist's representation of Pueblo Bonito during its height of occupancy.

FIGURE 4.13. Mesa Verde as it exists today. The photograph shows the shade created from the overhanging cliff above the buildings in the summer.

cliff, which created a warmer microclimate in the winter and partly shaded the buildings in the summer, helping to passively condition the buildings in the extreme temperature changes of the desert Southwest. The buildings were elongated on the east–west axis and stepped down to the south, again maximizing solar gain in the individual structures.

The Puebloan people understood the relationship between their buildings and the sun; both solar and lunar cycles are marked in petroglyphs on the surrounding cliff and architectural walls.

As fossil fuel began to power mechanical, heating, cooling, and lighting systems, this relationship between the building and the sun was mainly forgotten, though there are a few examples of modern buildings that refine the passive-solar design principles of the Puebloans. One of the most famous is the Jacobs II House, the second home Frank Lloyd Wright designed for Herbert and Katherine Jacobs in Wisconsin. In this house, which he called the Solar Hemicycle, Wright reused many of the space principles from his Usonian I home but adapted the orientation to a semicircular design to take advantage of passive solar strategies.

The semicircular plan of the Solar Hemicycle faces south, creating a warm and sunny microclimate in the courtyard. Large expanses of glass to the south maximize solar heat gain in the winter and have a wide roof overhang to shade them in the summer. An interior concrete floor slab and masonry walls bermed to the west, north, and east provide protection from the cold winter winds and thermal mass for solar storage. The curved plan and glazing connect the daily living of the owners to the flow and path of the sun, the environment, and natural systems.

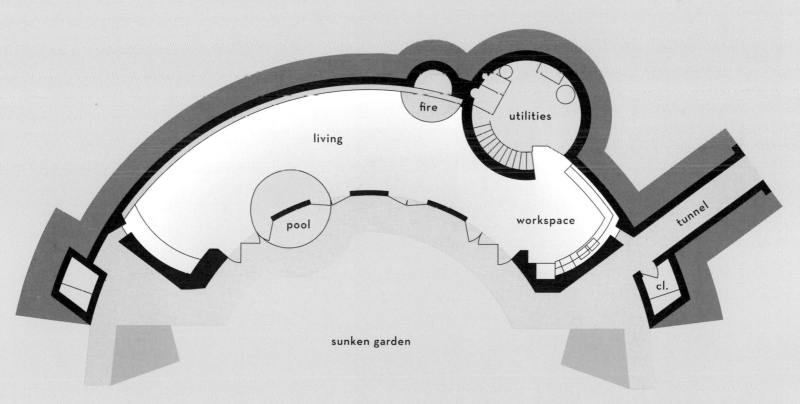

FIGURE 4.14. The plan of the Solar Hemicycle was designed to maximize passive heating.

FIGURE 4.15. The Hovilanhaara paper mill in Finland (*top*) and the Cologne cathedral in Germany (*bottom*) demonstrate the art and science of daylighting before the twentieth century.

FIGURE 4.16. A typical twentieth-century workspace, with small-perimeter windows, a low ceiling, and a wide floor plate.

Throughout most of our history, we humans lived outside, in starlight to brilliant sunlight. In the morning and evening, our eyes adapted to lower light levels and then to fire as an "artificial" means of lighting. In most of today's buildings, we experience far dimmer lighting levels during the workday and barely change them until we go to bed. During our day we typically see much less variation in lighting levels than we did when humans lived mainly outdoors, where lighting levels constantly change. It is documented that human daily patterns and internal clocks are connected to the twenty-four-hour rhythm of the sun's rising and setting. With the advent of computers, LEDs, and fluorescent lights, our night lighting is often bluish or white rather than the more orange hues of the setting sun and fire.[6]

Research is showing that these changes are affecting our health and circadian rhythms.[7] White or blue light at night triggers abnormal levels of melatonin, which interrupts daily sleep patterns.[8] This research reveals a need for greater understanding of the effects that a diversity of lighting levels in our buildings can have on occupant health. The variation from bright to dim connected to human daily rhythms appears to be a particularly crucial design requirement for buildings—just as views of nature, sun, and sky are critical to maintaining other human health needs. It is this complex synergy of varying lighting level needs, connections to nature, and energy consumption that have fed the active dialogue in the design community about how to determine the optimal levels of glazing and light in buildings.

Before the advent of electricity in the nineteenth century, artificial lighting was limited to candles, whale oil lamps, and coal gas lamps, all of which were expensive and provided minimal, low-quality light. These low-quality artificial lighting sources resulted in building design that maximized daylight in all buildings, from religious spaces to homes to manufacturing sites (see figure 4.15).

With the advent of relatively cheap and available electricity in the twentieth century, buildings no longer needed to rely on the sun for lighting. This change radically altered building design and the interior built environment. Many buildings, particularly office and manufacturing facilities, were created with large floor plates that received little or no natural light, which has become standard for lighting design (see figure 4.16). This change, which on its own seemed relatively logical at the time, consumes substantial energy and, more importantly, increases eyestrain, decreases occupants' connection to the rhythms of nature, lowers productivity, and results in a less satisfying human experience.

Returning daylight to buildings is easy. It can be accomplished by returning to the design practices in use before artificial lighting was so widespread: designing narrower floor plates and increasing floor-to-floor distances and areas of glazing so that daylight can penetrate through buildings. Daylight can also be brought in from all sides with interior courtyards, atriums, light wells, and skylights.

Daylight comes from the sun, and our eyes can adapt to widely varying light levels, but different light levels facilitate different uses of our eyes and thus human activity. We prefer bright light for detailed tasks and manipulation, another level for reading, meeting with people, having dinner, and so on. Outdoor light intensity levels are very different depending on the time of day, the time of year, and the cloud cover. In building design we are concerned with lighting levels for specific user tasks. Adjustments to the building enclosure can match use and lighting levels.

Light creates a mood that affects us. We are drawn to it. Dimmer and varied lighting in religious spaces or a forest, for example, can create a quality of mystery and spirituality. For working at tasks, we want even light, but for other activities we want a diversity of lighting levels making for a richer and more inspiring place to live, work, and play.

Daylighting design is both art and science. The art is in modulating light connected to the use of space and desired mood, quality, and feeling—essential to creating buildings that are satisfying and inspiring. The science relates to achieving specific lighting levels and characteristics appropriate to the intended use so that artificial light is eliminated and/or minimized during the day while providing the healthiest and most effective lighting to occupants. Although this book doesn't fully cover the art of daylighting, we offer some initial guidelines.

Lighting intensity on a flat surface is measured in foot-candles (fc). Light levels outside on a sunny day in northern climates are typically 8,000–10,000 fc at midday and 500–5,000 fc on an overcast day. Optimal light levels for human functioning vary: simple tasks with only occasional reading require 10 fc; normal visual tasks in most buildings need 30–100 fc.[9] So daylight would be more than enough for optimized human functioning in buildings. The challenge lies in guiding, controlling, and directing daylight so that there are appropriate and consistent light levels and quality for the varied human activity in buildings. For example, detailed manufacturing work requires higher light levels than hallways. Recommended lighting levels vary by the age of users as well: older people need higher lighting levels than younger people. Since spaces serve people with different ages, lighting levels for specific uses are selected based on the age of the majority of users. The Illuminating Engineering Society provides extensive tables on light levels for different functions and age groups in their lighting handbook.[10]

To understand lighting levels outdoors and lighting levels striking the wall and roof surfaces of buildings, we can imagine our building as a sky-dome, or hemisphere. We can visualize that light of different intensities strikes the dome's surface, depending on the sun's altitude and azimuth. On a clear day, light is more directional from the sun. This is typically called direct-beam sunlight. Direct-beam sunlight casts clear and distinct shadows inside buildings. On a cloudy or overcast day, the sun's rays are scattered and diffused so that the light on a sky-dome (or building) is more uniform on all surfaces. This is called diffuse sunlight. Shadows cast in diffuse light are not clear or distinct. This obviously has significant impact on building design. Buildings in primarily cloudy climates offer different daylighting opportunities and challenges than buildings in sunny climates. However, even in cloudy climates daylighting must be designed for sunny and for cloudy weather. Figure 4.17 illustrate these two conditions.

WHOLE BUILDING DAYLIGHTING STRATEGIES

When we make glazed openings in buildings, we can bring in sunlight and illuminate interior spaces. We can select clear glazing that allows direct-beam sunlight to enter while maintaining the directionality of the light and casting clear shadows. We can also select other types of glazing that scatter sunlight so it is diffused, as on a cloudy day. Because direct light can cause glare, light-diffusing glazing is often used in skylights where there is exposure to direct light from the entire sky-dome. Other treatments inside and outside of a glazed opening can be used to control the quantity and quality of illumination. Through careful design of the size and location of openings in the building envelope, as well as the glazing materials and filters, daylight can be used to provide efficient, productive, and pleasing lighting for human use.

In net zero buildings the goal is to use daylight for lighting all occupied spaces as much as possible. When daylight is used for lighting spaces all day, these spaces are said to be 100 percent daylight autonomous. If all occupied spaces in a building are 100 percent daylit, then the building is classified as a 100 percent daylit building. Typically, only a portion of the spaces are daylit, and that portion is measured and identified as a percentage of the overall occupied spaces.

All buildings have roofs and walls. Thus, there are separate strategies for daylighting through the roof (top lighting) and the walls (sidelighting). Single-story buildings allow for 100 percent top lighting no matter what size the building is. Since daylighting from building walls typically penetrates only 15′ from the periphery of a building, after 15′, supplemental artificial lighting is required. Generally higher ceilings and windows

FIGURE 4.17. These diagrams show lighting intensities, with direct light from one direction on a clear day (*top*) and diffuse light from multiple directions on an overcast day (*bottom*).

direct beam radiation from
one direction

diffuse radiation from
multiple directions

allow deeper light penetration (as far as 30′). These numbers are good for general planning purposes.

PLANNING AND MASSING OPPORTUNITIES

The plan and section of a one-story building in figure 4.18a shows how it can be daylit using a combination of top and sidelighting, no matter what the building's size.

Because multistory buildings cannot use skylights except on the top floor, daylighting in multistory buildings is limited to sidelighting. A typical modern high-rise is 100′ or more wide, which means that much contemporary interior space cannot be daylit.

DAYLIGHTING OPPORTUNITIES IN MULTISTORY BUILDINGS

Figure 4.18b shows a multistory building indicating typical areas where full, partial, and no daylight is available with proper daylighting strategies and techniques. This diagram shows how daylight is available everywhere on the top floor

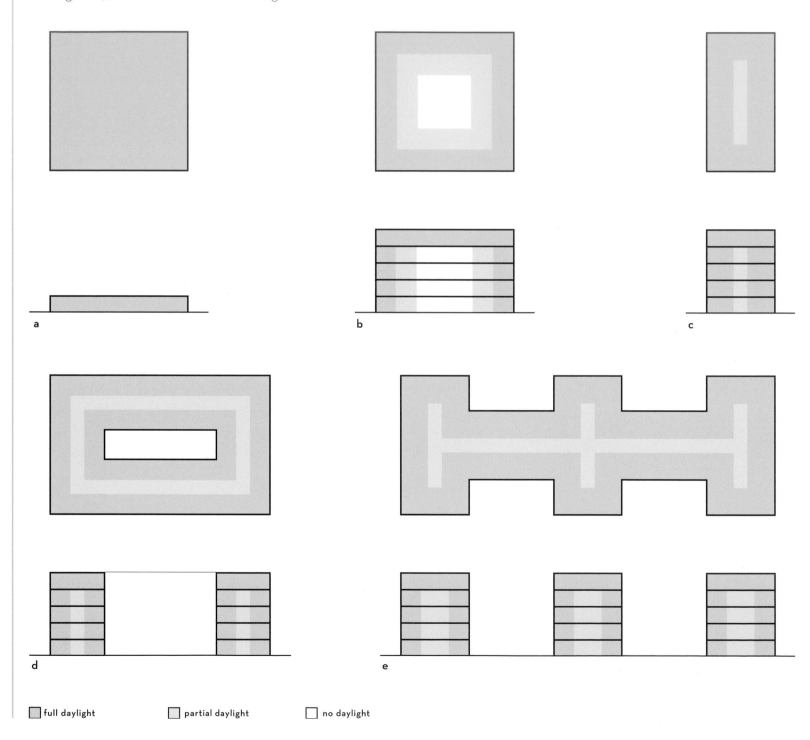

FIGURE 4.18. The diagrams show how building shape and configuration affects the ability to daylight (a) a single-story building, (b) a wide multistory building, (c) a narrow multistory building (d) an atrium building, and (e) an articulated narrow building.

full daylight   partial daylight   no daylight

TABLE 4.2. ADVANTAGES OF TOP-LIGHTING STRATEGIES

SKYLIGHTS AND LIGHT TUBES
Greatest daylight efficiency (light per glazed sf)
Lowest cost
Good for daylighting in overcast conditions
Even, well distributed light

CLERESTORIES, DORMERS, AND MONITORS
Greater control over glare
Better for including ventilation and rain protection
Easier to create more interesting quality of life
Potential for directional light

by using skylights. Where only sidelighting is available, on the lower floors, full daylight can reach just 15' into the building perimeter. Partial daylight suitable for corridors and partially occupied spaces is available from approximately 15–30' from the perimeter. Beyond this depth there is no useful daylight available through sidelighting. Thus, figure 4.18c shows that multistory buildings using daylighting should be a maximum of 40–50' wide, with corridor, storage, or less-frequent functions taking up the middle of the buildings. These were typical dimensions of buildings before artificial lighting. If buildings are wider, then they can have interior light courts, as depicted in figure 4.18d.

These planning, massing, and daylighting principles can be used for articulated, curved, and combined layouts and massing. To achieve daylight autonomy, buildings can be kept narrower, with central light wells, atria, and articulated massing.

TOP LIGHTING

There are two basic approaches to top lighting: either you can use skylights and light tubes or you can use vertical glazing in clerestories, monitors, and dormers. The primary difference between these two categories is the distinction between flat or sloped glazing for skylights and light tubes and vertical glazing on clerestories, dormers, and monitors, as shown in figure 4.19. We also can distinguish between top-lighting strategies for single-story buildings and multistory buildings.

Skylights in general are glazed surfaces that are set into a flat or sloped roof with minimal alteration to the building massing and structure other than a simple curb that supports the glazing and allows for waterproofing. Light tubes are a variation of skylights that include a reflection surface inside the light shaft that brings light through a deep roof structure or even down multiple stories. Clerestories, dormers, and monitors are different types of structures added onto the roof that change the building massing to bring daylight and/or ventilation into a building. Table 4.2 indicates the advantages of skylights and vertical roof-glazing options. Depending on the application, one option or another might be more appropriate.

Open to the entire sky-dome and able to provide light throughout the spaces below the roof, skylights generally provide uniform lighting and daylight autonomy and so are appropriate for warehouse and office space. However, if uniformly spaced, they don't allow for the varying light levels that make the daily experience of living and being in buildings enjoyable, enlivening, surprising, and maybe even poetic.

Depending on the size of the skylight, the rule-of-thumb spacing changes: small skylights should be placed one times the height of the room from center to center, and larger skylights should be placed two times the height of the space, as shown in figure 4.20.[11] This allows even distribution of natural light in the space at the work surface. Individual skylights may

FIGURE 4.19. Various top-lighting strategies include (a) clerestory windows, (b) dormers, (c) monitors, (d) flat skylights, (e) light tubes, and (f) angled skylights.

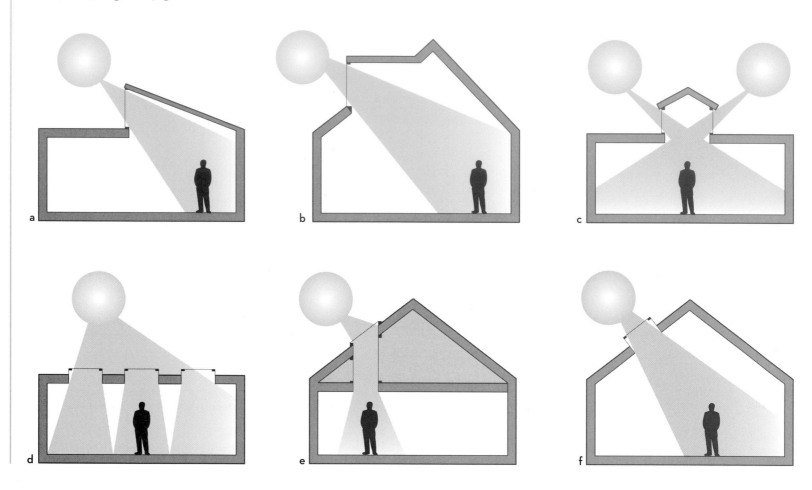

have differing photometrics, so the spacing may be altered due to the reduction in daylight available, but in general, for areas with a need for higher light levels (offices, classrooms, gymnasiums), skylights should be closer together or larger in size. In areas with less need for light (warehouses, field houses, and corridors), skylights can be farther apart. Sizing the number and area of glazing for skylights depends on light-level goals balanced with the resulting heat gain. Overall, skylights should be between 3 and 4 percent of the floor area for typical uses with typical-height rooms and work surfaces.

Whether you bring light in via skylights or with more complex clerestory, dormer, and monitor designs, it is critical to use either computer-modeling programs or physical models combined with light meters to determine appropriate size, location, and spacing.[12]

SIDELIGHTING

In multistory buildings or buildings where roof penetrations are not desired, sidelighting is always available. Sidelighting simply involves putting windows in walls. It is the easiest and most commonly used means of bringing daylight into buildings. Sidelighting also provides abundant access to views, fresh air, and ventilation. However, in daylighting terms, windows are limited by the depth that light penetrates horizontally into a

FIGURE 4.20. Skylights should be spaced on center at one to two times the height of the space, depending on the size of the skylight. Diffusing material in the skylight itself or below the opening will even out daylight throughout the space and reduce internal glare.

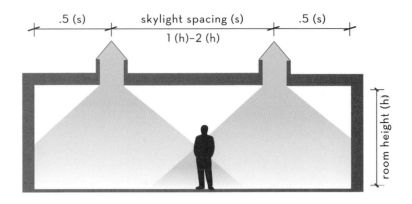

FIGURE 4.21. Effective daylighting penetration is equal to about 1½ times the window height, which means more daylighting as the window height increases.

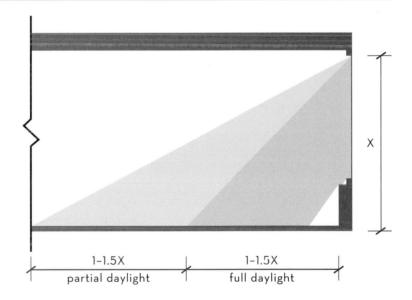

space, as depicted in figure 4.21. Generally, this means that daylight from sidelighting provides 100 percent of lighting needs along the perimeter of a room where the windows are located and into the room for a distance on the floor about 1 to 1½ times the height of the top of the window opening, assuming a room with light-colored and more reflective surfaces. Some light penetrates into the building an additional 1 to 1½ times the height of the window opening, but not enough for full daylighting and turning off all electric lights.

Dark surfaces, furnishings, carpet, or objects lower the effectiveness of windows (or skylights) for daylighting. To get light to penetrate the space more deeply, you can raise the top of window heights, add light-guiding blinds (see figure 4.22), install light shelves, raise the roof, add skylights, and/or use lighter interior surface colors (other strategies are shown in figure 4.23).

However, all of these options for daylight autonomy and even interior light conditions may not be adequate on cloudy days unless lower light levels are tolerated or walls are overglazed. Such overglazing would cause excessive light on sunny days and require diffusing material to reduce the daylight.

Windows and skylights can also be a source of glare. Occupants may like the view and light that come from windows but may want to avoid the glare, particularly in spaces where

FIGURE 4.22. Light-guiding blinds are effective at reducing the window contrast and bouncing light onto the ceiling from the perimeter windows. Light green areas show brighter areas from bounced daylight and light fixtures.

TABLE 4.3. OPTIMAL GLAZING AREAS FOR DAYLIGHTING

	HOUSE (%)	OFFICE (%)
Overall Building Glazing Area	10–15	20–30
North	5–10	15–20
South	25–30	25–30
East	5–10	10–15
West	5–10	10–15

computers or other screens are in use. In these cases glare can be minimized if the glazing in skylights is designed to provide diffuse top light and window shades are made of diffusing material. Effective sidelighting also requires an appropriate amount of glazing on differing building elevations. The goal is to maximize daylight and minimize glare and cooling loads. Table 4.3 shows rough glazing-to-wall percentages, which can be considered for preliminary design; however, detailed energy modeling should be performed to determine the ideal glazing percentages for your specific building. Generally, south-facing glass is best, north-facing glass is second best, and east and west glazing is the worst due to the potential for overheating and difficulty of control of light beams at low angles.

While the human benefits are often the primary driver for daylighting in integrated building design, there also are connections between daylighting and energy consumption. Proper daylighting provided by controlled south and north windows, with few east- and west-facing windows and skylights, can reduce building energy loads related to lighting and smaller mechanical systems, resulting in energy and cost savings. In small buildings (less than 5,000 sf) daylighting is easily accomplished, but the impacts on energy loads are often not that large. In larger buildings implementing proper daylighting strategies can save more energy, but the design considerations are much more complex.

For these larger buildings, modeling should be used to accurately determine the energy impacts of daylighting. Daylighting effectiveness and quality can be determined by using either a computer simulation system or a light meter to test a scale model with a simulation of wall lighting levels. When daylighting strategies are properly integrated into the building design, the result can provide appropriate levels and quality of lighting without any artificial sources and with minimal energy impacts. If, however, daylighting strategies are not properly designed, dramatic differences in lighting levels and glare can create an unwelcome living and working environment and energy costs can increase.

A rule of thumb for the even distribution of light for daylighting is to have the brightest surface in the room no more than four times brighter than the darkest area. In addition, no direct-beam sunlight should fall on work surfaces, or in some cases on any surface, unless specifically intended to diffuse

FIGURE 4.23. Progressive sidelighting strategies for daylighting spaces. A typical 8-foot window height (a) with full daylight projecting 12 feet into the room. A raised window head height of 10 feet (b), which results in additional areas of the room that can be daylit. A light shelf or light-guiding blinds on the outside or inside of the buildings (c) give deeper penetration and reduce the high concentration of direct light on the perimeter of the room. A skylight next to the wall opposite the windows with a deflecting wall (d) enables daylight to reach both sides of the room for indirect daylighting. The deflecting wall also reduces glare.

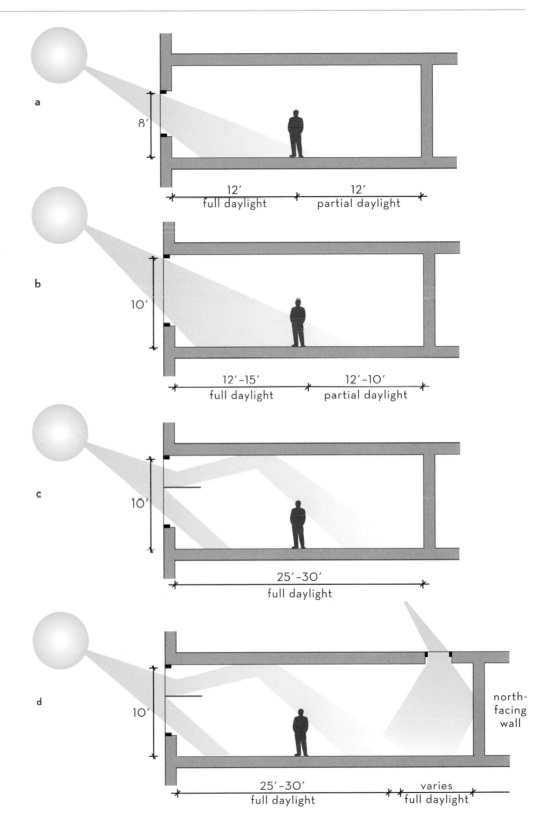

and/or bounce light deeper into workspaces. Providing light evenly through equally balanced glazing on walls and ceilings enhances optimal energy and daylighting performance, and larger areas of glass enhance building users' views and their connection with the outdoors. When designing glass openings on building façades, you must balance these sometimes conflicting integrated design goals. In circulation and some public spaces, light levels can be lesser or greater to create differing moods and aesthetic qualities. Beyond these daylighting design goals, net zero building design should include the added goal of achieving 90–100 percent daylight autonomy in all occupied spaces with no artificial lighting used during typical workday hours, excluding support spaces such as bathrooms and storage.

Even with 100 percent daylight autonomy, artificial lighting is needed at night, of course, and it, too, should support occupant needs for appropriate lighting levels, mood, and quality. Artificial lighting should be integrated with the daylighting strategy, planning, and design. Some of the most common control solutions for daylit spaces include artificial lighting using zones, dimmers and photocell controls, and multiple-level switching and occupancy sensors. In larger and deeper buildings, lighting zones are defined by distance from daylighting windows. Photocell sensors turn on or modulate artificial lighting when adequate lighting levels are not reached naturally. Lights at the interior of the building illuminate, while spaces toward the outside can remain fully lighted by natural sources. Artificial lights can also be set up with dimmers or multiple lighting levels so they provide just the needed levels of lighting, reducing their energy use as compared to a standard on/off setup. Occupancy sensors, a simple form of lighting control, are used to provide light only when spaces are occupied, further reducing energy consumption. An optimum design strategy is to require occupants to turn on lights with sensors in place to turn off lights when spaces are not occupied.

PASSIVE SOLAR HEATING

Passive solar heating harnesses the sun's energy without the use of mechanical systems and equipment. At the simplest level, passive solar heating is achieved by placing windows on the south façade of a building; more complex variations include heat storage systems. South-facing glazing is the most cost-effective renewable energy available for any project—unless your site is completely shaded by trees, hills, or other buildings. Almost all sites have some solar potential, and passive solar should always be used first to the maximum extent appropriate.

As we pointed out earlier, although humans have practiced passive solar design for thousands of years, the idea didn't garner much interest in the United States until the 1973 oil crisis, which triggered a boom in the construction of solar houses and the publication of books advocating the benefits of passive solar design, including Ed Mazria's classic, *The Passive Solar Energy Book*. The principles are simple:

- Orient the building along the east–west axis.
- Place the majority of glass on the south-facing façade.
- Provide mass related to the amount of glass to prevent overheating.

This last point is critical. If you are locating your project in a sunny, cold climate, then you may want to maximize solar heat gain and south-facing glass. If so, you will need to carefully calculate the mass required to store the sun's energy. If your project is in cloudier, colder locations such as the Northeast and Midwest, then you do not want too much glass on the south, because the lack of consistent winter sunshine does not justify the expense of adding more. In general, in cloudy locations you want 30 percent or less of glass area on the south façade compared to your floor area. Minimal or no mass is necessary with this lower percentage of glazing. However, mass is always beneficial in moderating thermal change. And if this percentage of glazing is exceeded, you'll need to calculate the mass required to store energy to avoid overheating of the building.

Within these simple passive solar principles there are numerous simple and more complex passive solar strategies. These strategies generally fit into one of five categories or combination of categories. The most basic (figure 4.24a) we call sun-tempered space. It is simply south-facing glass sized so that no additional mass is needed. If more glass is added, then additional mass is needed, which can be integrated

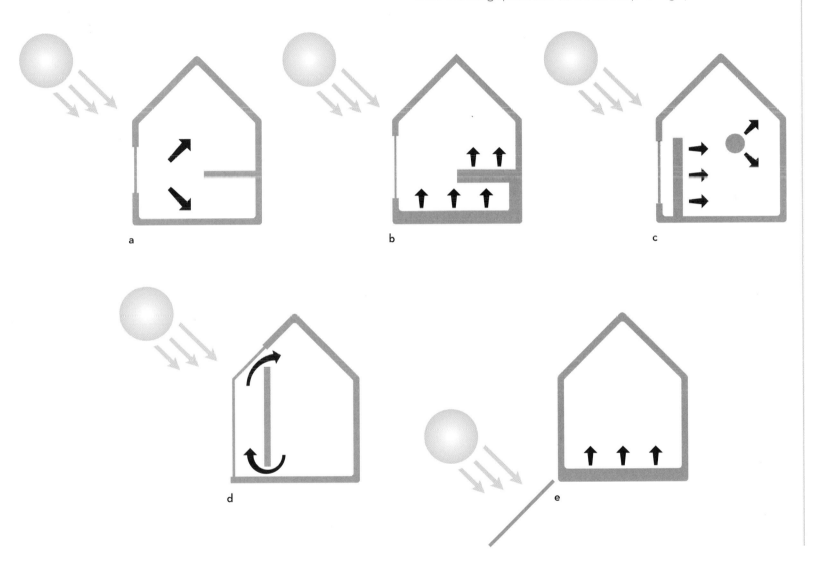

FIGURE 4.24. Passive solar heating through a variety of design strategies. Sun-tempered space (a) with reduced glass and minimal mass, (b) integrated mass in the structure in sun-tempered spaces and additional glazing, (c) mass separated from the structure in a sun-tempered space with additional glazing, (d) sun space separated from the living space, and (e) a thermosiphoning system.

a

b

c

d

e

into the building structure in one or more floors or walls so that the building structure holds more heat from the sun and releases the heat at night (figure 4.24b). Mass can also be added as a separate element in the building rather than integrated into the structure (figure 4.24c). Typically, this is water in freestanding tubes, concrete walls, or elements placed in the living space so that when sunlight strikes them, they store heat, and then release the stored heat at night. One variation of this is an internal mass wall behind south-facing glass, with an airspace between known as a Trombe wall. The wall stores the concentrated heat during the day, and at night the heat is transferred into the interior space.

A passive sun space (figure 4.24d) is a solar room on the south side of the building that collects solar energy during the day. When needed, the heat from the sun space can be circulated into the building through openings that connect the two spaces. The sun space and/or building may or may not have thermal mass to store heat. This space may be a greenhouse for food production, a place to sit in the sun, or other space not occupied at all times, as the temperature variation within it can be great. To maximize solar collection, the most windows possible are installed, which means little to no insulation. It is not heated at night. Depending on use, this can be a complicated space to model energy performance and can have complex humidity conditions if plants are growing there.

Finally, a passive thermosiphoning system involves a solar collector below the living level of the building where hot air or liquid rises in the collector and transfers the solar energy to thermal mass either directly into the living space such as a concrete floor (figure 4.24e) or to a water storage tank connected to a radiant heating system. This system may be successful in climates with daily sunshine. In other locations larger storage tanks and likely pumps or fans (making this an active system) are needed to provide reliable comfort. (Active solar systems are also important in net zero buildings and are covered later in this chapter.)

While the principles of passive solar design remain the same today, current recommendations for energy conservation levels for net zero buildings exceed earlier recommendations and standards for passive solar design. Because net zero buildings are insulated to higher standards, the glazing recommendations from many of the older passive solar books will cause overheating and glare on sunny days. The general trend in net zero building design is to better insulate, significantly reducing south-facing glass compared to 1970s recommendations, and to use glazing on other orientations for daylighting and view.

This current trend to reduce glass and mass is called sun-tempering as opposed to passive solar. Sun-tempering combined with a microload enclosure significantly lowers backup energy needs. For residential sun-tempered projects, the backup heating is approximately one-third passive solar, one-third internal gain, and one-third from either a nonrenewable or renewable energy source. Internal gains come from things like lights, cooking, body heat, and equipment. Regardless of the amount of glazing, it is beneficial to have mass in buildings, as it helps to modulate temperature fluctuations connected to sun, internal gains, and/or exterior temperature changes. But run the numbers: mass is cost-effective only if you can add it inexpensively—with a slab-on-grade with south-facing glass or by using ⅝″ gypsum board instead of ½″ gypsum board.

In larger commercial and institutional projects such as schools and office buildings, both passive solar and sun-tempering are likely to be counterproductive. In these buildings internal loads from equipment, computers, servers, people, and lighting add enough heat so that even buildings in cold climates need very little heat year-round and likely have cooling loads much of the year. Even in cold climates these buildings may have larger cooling loads than heating loads. Careful analysis of load and envelope is required in the design of internal-load-dominated buildings to minimize energy consumption.

WINDOW ORIENTATION

Window orientation is key for passive solar heating in net zero building design. As with daylighting, the seasonal variations of the sun's path and angle create opportunities for design.

South glazing is the most critical in terms of passive solar heating. The low angle of the sun on the south side of buildings in the winter allows deep penetration of sunlight, helpful for both heating and daylighting. At the same time, summer solar gain through south glazing can be easily controlled by overhangs, louvers, or awnings, addressing the concern of overheating. When overhangs and other shading devices are used, the impacts on daylighting should be balanced with undesired solar heat gain to achieve the best combined performance. In order to develop an optimum level of southern glass, you must evaluate not only the size of south-facing windows but also the size of the room or space to which they will be connected. Generally, the larger the space, the larger the amount of south-facing glass that can be accommodated without overheating. It is not effective to place large expanses of glass in small rooms, such as closed offices or conference rooms; bigger expanses of south-facing glass work only in sizable rooms, open offices, and/or circulation or gathering spaces.

You want the least amount of glazing on east and west orientations. East- and west-facing windows gain heat year-round in the early morning and late afternoon, when the sun is low on the horizon. This means horizontal shading devices do not work well for stopping solar heat gain in the warm months when heat is not wanted, making it difficult to control overheating. East windows are generally better than west windows as they add heat in the morning, when it is cooler. Even in a cold, northern climate, using the superinsulated strategies suggested in this book, overglazing can lead to considerable overheating in the summer and sometimes in the spring and fall. However, there often is no other alternative. Some building sites and/or existing buildings can only be oriented on a north–south axis with east–west windows.

Northern glass plays a smaller role in the equation. Only during long summer days do the sun's rays penetrate through north-facing windows, making them effective for daylighting without the associated overheating concerns. This is particularly useful for daylighting large commercial and institutional buildings that are internal-load-dominated.

Skylights add the most daylight and least cost for any given amount of glazing area. However, skylights also add more heat gain in the summer, when the sun is high in the sky. In terms of energy savings, although heat gain and the subsequent need for cooling could offset the energy savings of daylighting, the daylight still has qualitative benefits. In roofs vertical glass can be used as clerestory windows instead of skylights. Although the light gained to the interior space per square foot of glazing area is substantially reduced than with skylights, control of overheating, weather protection, easier ventilation, and lighting quality are potentially offsetting factors.

In all events, the windows should be oriented and sized to accommodate activities inside the building. For instance, in a home it is often beneficial to have a breakfast area facing east to get the first light and heat of the day. And bedroom location also can satisfy individual preferences to let in or avoid morning light.

INTEGRATED COOLING

Even in cold climates the ability to cool buildings is important. We recommend beginning with the simplest and least energy-intensive strategies (such as simply opening windows in smaller buildings) and using more intensive and complex strategies as loads increase in larger buildings. As climate change intensifies, so, too, will cooling demands, and designers should be careful to plan systems that can be added to with time.

Passive cooling provides cooling without the use of energy-consuming mechanical components such as pumps, air conditioners, and fans. It is first accomplished by slowing heat transfer into a building, or avoiding unwanted solar gain, and then by removing unwanted heat from the building. If passive strategies such as natural air movement through the building are not adequate for comfort, then passive cooling can be supplemented with ceiling fans, mechanical ventilation, dehumidification, or air-conditioning. In a net zero building, such supplemental cooling will of course add to the load requirements for PV or other renewable energy sources. Figure 4.25 illustrates ventilation strategies.

NATURAL VENTILATION

Natural ventilation is the process of moving air through an indoor space without the use of any mechanical systems. There are two forms of natural ventilation, both the result of pressure or thermal differences: cross-ventilation, which is driven by wind, and stack ventilation, which is buoyancy driven.[13] In cross-ventilated spaces (figure 4.25a), wind flows through open windows located on opposite sides of the spaces. Cross-ventilation suits buildings with small floor plates and large ventilation openings on either side—typically residential or small commercial buildings. Its effectiveness depends on wind direction during the cooling season, so summer breezes should be taken into account when considering siting and window operation.

In stack-ventilated spaces, low windows bring in cool air from outside and high windows exhaust hot air from the building (figure 4.25b). Stack ventilation works because of the stack effect, the rising of hot air. It is not dependent on site-specific wind conditions. However, cross-ventilation and stack-ventilation effects can be combined for maximum benefit. While stack ventilation is effective, it is not as powerful as steady breezes. Stack ventilation can be magnified with solar chimneys to increase ventilation, but this tends to be relatively costly compared to the benefit.[14]

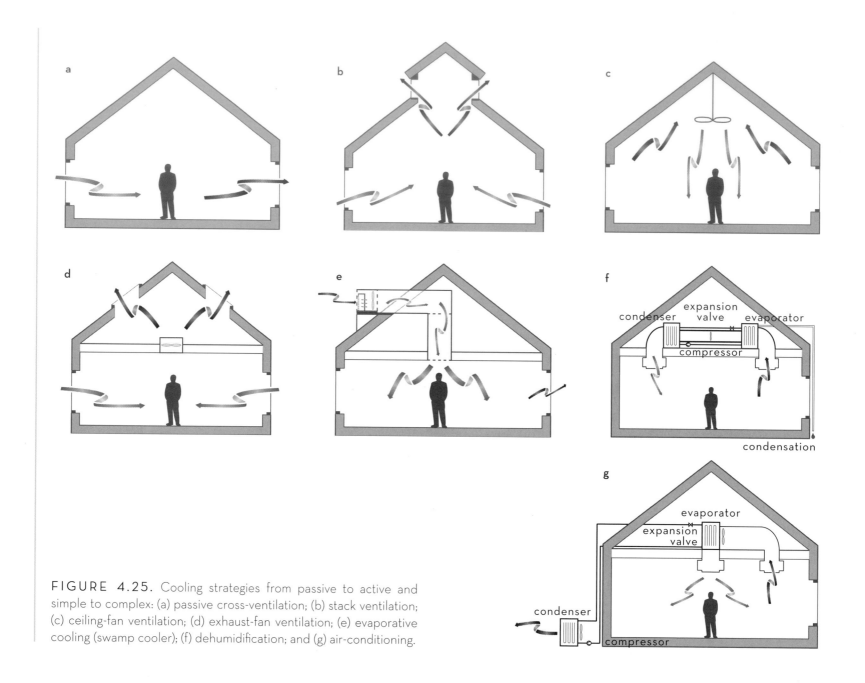

FIGURE 4.25. Cooling strategies from passive to active and simple to complex: (a) passive cross-ventilation; (b) stack ventilation; (c) ceiling-fan ventilation; (d) exhaust-fan ventilation; (e) evaporative cooling (swamp cooler); (f) dehumidification; and (g) air-conditioning.

SIMPLE MECHANICAL VENTILATION

In addition to natural ventilation strategies, there are simple mechanical ventilation, or hybrid, systems that require some energy but much less than typical cooling systems. These systems should be investigated and employed to the greatest extent possible before incorporating traditional air-conditioning and after maximizing passive strategies. The simplest version of hybrid cooling, shown in figure 4.25c, uses fans to enhance the natural ventilation strategies of cross-ventilation and stack ventilation. Ceiling fans circulating inside air are the simplest and most cost-effective strategy. Or an exhaust fan, as shown in

The Zion Canyon Visitor Center, located in Springdale, Utah, is a creative example of a high-performance, sustainable building. This 7,600 sf building includes integrated passive strategies that reduce energy by 70 percent and provide an enhanced building for the over 2 million visitors per year to Zion National Park.[15] Some of the passive features include daylighting, Trombe walls for solar heat gain, and natural ventilation through clerestory windows.

To supplement natural ventilation during the heat of summer, the building's prominent cooling towers offer additional cooling. A low-horsepower pump brings water to the top of the tower and through cooling pads. When hot, dry air is drawn into the evaporative cooling pads, it picks up moisture, becoming denser and causing it to sink and spill out into the building. These towers provide over five air changes per hour.

The Zion Visitor Center cost less to build than a comparable National Park visitor center, and the sustainability measures save around $14,000 in energy costs per year.[16] A roof-mounted PV system provides 30 percent of the total building load of 39 kBtu/sf-yr.

FIGURE 4.26. The cooling towers at Zion National Park passively cool the visitor center.

figure 4.25d, can be placed in a wall or roof and ducted to the outside to draw away air when inside air is hotter than outside.

Additional hybrid cooling strategies include night ventilation and evaporative cooling. Night ventilation uses cold night air to cool the structure or mass of a building supported by stack or cross-ventilation. Sometimes it requires simply opening windows at night, but in many cases it makes sense to add fans, as shown in figure 4.25d, to boost the airflow and to cool the structure as much as possible. In order for night ventilation to work effectively, four conditions must be met: the building must be thermally closed during daytime hours and thermally open during nighttime hours; nighttime temperatures must be lower than the desired daytime temperature; there must be enough thermal mass in the building that it can function as an effective heat sink for internal heat gain during the daytime hours; and humidity levels must be low enough that cooling does not cause condensation and moisture problems.

Night ventilation is most effective in areas with dry summer conditions, since bringing humid outside air into the building can cause condensation and mold. In small buildings humidity can be controlled by human observation and alleviated by insulating massive elements from the earth so that all interior building surface temperatures are consistently above the dew point in summer and therefore don't cause humidity to condense. In buildings with air-conditioning during the day, night flushing with humid air means the moisture introduced into the building must then be reevaporated by the air conditioner during the day, wasting at least some of the energy gained by cooling the structure at night. Building control systems in larger buildings can be programmed to monitor humidity and discontinue night flushing when it is too humid outside, allowing this strategy to be effective even in more humid environments.

Evaporative-cooling strategies—most commonly associated with swamp coolers in larger buildings—require careful analysis (figure 4.25e). Evaporative cooling functions by adding moisture to the air, which increases humidity and consequently decreases the dry-bulb temperature, creating perceived cooler temperatures. In general this is not the most effective strategy in moist climates. In very dry climates, in contrast, the added moisture is not an issue because it evaporates and adds to the cooling effect. These systems are limited to areas where conditions are uncomfortably hot and dry, rather than uncomfortably humid. Added drawbacks are that these systems require significant amounts of water and most often use fans, which can create noise and high air velocities.

Dehumidification systems (figure 4.25f) remove humidity but do not cool the air. If the air is less humid, we feel comfortable at higher temperatures, even without cooling. In some cases dehumidification alone can work, which is less energy-consuming than air-conditioning, the last option (figure 4.25g). Besides conventional air-conditioning systems, there are mini-split systems, window units, and heat-pump-based systems.

The most efficient cooling will combine passive and active cooling systems to minimize energy consumption. For instance, internal-load-dominated buildings often require cooling when outside temperatures are lower than temperatures desired inside. Simply using outside air to cool is not only economical but also the first level of mechanical cooling in larger buildings.

In large buildings with operable windows, where temperature-control systems are more complex and regulated, a green light can tell building occupants when windows can be opened and a red light when the cooling system is on and therefore windows should remain shut.

More complex control systems can also lock windows when air conditioners are in use. While these systems can be quite effective and use minimal electricity if properly designed, there can be issues with the windows closing tightly. Specifically, electrically operated windows have no latches to pull them in tightly. Thus, when they are used, they should be carefully researched and priced to ensure effective performance and minimize energy losses. It is also critical to test all windows at the end of construction to ensure that they shut properly.

Energy Harvesting: On-Site Renewable Production

The three fundamental components of a net zero building are the reduction of energy loads, the incorporation of mechanical and electrical systems for human needs and comfort, and the production of renewable energy to cover any remaining loads. You should evaluate renewable energy options early in the design process to determine which systems will make the

FIGURE 4.27. Solar PV comes in many forms. *Left,* PV integrated into a curved roof at the Kaohsiung National Stadium. *Right,* PV integrated into the front glass wall at the Lillis Business Complex at the University of Oregon, allowing views to the outside and filtering light into the atrium.

most sense for the project—selecting from solar, wind, hydro, geothermal, biomass, and biofuels. While PV has been the renewable of choice for most of the net zero buildings to date, other options may be more suitable for a particular project because of the availability of on-site resources, site constraints, the goals of the owner, and/or economic factors.

HARNESSING THE POWER OF THE SUN

After passive resources have been exhausted, active solar processes can provide energy to cover remaining loads in a net zero building. There are two types of active solar technologies: those that convert the sun's energy into electricity (PV) and those that trap and distribute solar radiation in the form of heat.

PHOTOVOLTAICS (PVS)

PV systems are increasingly the most common renewable energy production strategy for net zero buildings. They are simple to install, reliable, and inexpensive to maintain. Commercially available since the 1970s, PV materials and technologies have grown in number and improved considerably over the last forty years, with some examples shown in figure 4.27.

PV systems produce direct current (DC), while the appliances and electronics in your home require alternating current (AC), so an inverter must convert the electricity from DC to AC, with some energy loss.

Building-mounted PV systems can often offset all of the energy needs of smaller, lower-energy-consuming buildings such as homes, offices, and classrooms. Our definition allows all buildings to be net zero even if limited by the site, by using net-metered off-site renewables installed for a specific

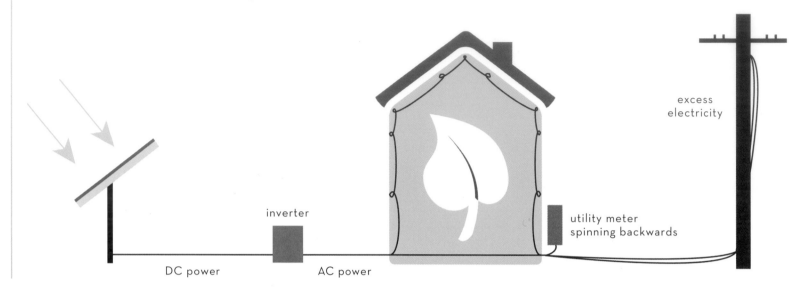

FIGURE 4.28. Net metering allows excess energy to return to the grid when it is not needed to power the building. The building can then draw on the grid during times when the photovoltaics are less productive, resulting in net zero energy use.

excess electricity

inverter

utility meter spinning backwards

DC power

AC power

building and possibly as a part of a community energy system. Net metering is described in figure 4.28.

Net metering provides the basis for financially feasible, grid-connected, net zero buildings and allows for the generation of off-site renewable energy for net zero projects. With the passing of the Energy Policy Act of 2005, net metering must be available upon request to customers by all public utilities. In cold climates where large winter heating bills are the norm, this allows the consumer to generate electricity in the summer when the sun is plentiful and develop credit toward larger winter energy bills. In some states energy that is generated on one site can be credited to another electric account, assuming both sites are within the territory of the same power company.

While the construction of PV panels and the inverters is technical and complex, the function of generating electricity is quite simple and reliable. With no moving parts, PV systems need virtually no ongoing maintenance other than the readjustment of orientation angles by season in tracker systems. Most PV panels come with a warranty of twenty years, but the life of a PV panel is closer to fifty years and may be longer. Over time the efficiency of PV systems will slowly decrease and

may need additional panels to maintain a net zero building. The only component of the PV system that will likely require shorter-term replacement, the inverter, which needs to be replaced every ten to twenty years, is a fraction of the total PV system cost. New PV technologies keep evolving, including PV modules that have mini-inverters at each panel. This adaptation will simplify installation and in some cases, particularly where part of the array is shaded, provide greater electricity output.

ACTIVE SOLAR HEATING

In contrast to passive solar heating and PV systems, active solar heating uses pumps, fans, controls, and other energy-consuming mechanical equipment to capture and distribute the sun's energy. Active solar heating systems use solar radiation to heat a fluid, either liquid or air, which transfers this heat directly to the interior space or to a storage system for later use, typically for space heating or domestic hot water (DHW). Air systems have been successful in industrial, commercial, and residential projects, particularly in Canada, but water systems are much more common today and will be the focus in this book. For more information, see chapter 7.

HARNESSING THE POWER OF THE WIND

The viability of wind power for net zero building applications is based on wind speed, cost, turbine size, location, environmental impact, and public opinion or policy. Power produced from a wind turbine is related to the cube of the wind speed, so incremental increases in wind speed result in exponential increases in power. The location of turbine installation is thus critical. An average wind speed of 10 mph is the minimum requirement for cost-effective wind generation, but investment in wind really makes sense where speeds are closer to 20 mph. Keep in mind that these are averages, so an average of 10 mph requires a windy site, typically at a high elevation or on a coastline. In addition to wind speed, which is essential for financial viability, the distance from major power lines is a significant capital cost. When any new power source is installed, the power lines must have adequate capacity to carry the new power, requiring upgrades and/or new lines. Wind turbines require maintenance, which is relatively minimal for large turbines compared to the power generated. However, for small turbines it is a relatively significant cost. Environmental impacts and public opinion are also considerations in any new installation.

There are two types of wind-generated renewable energy production: stand-alone turbines and building-integrated systems. Examples of each are shown in figure 4.29. Stand-alone turbines can supply the energy needed for a net zero building if there is adequate wind on the site, which is unlikely. With net metering, turbines can be located off-site. Building-integrated systems involve wind turbines mounted directly on buildings. Although there are a lot of creative designs for building-integrated wind systems, they are currently not cost-effective and unlikely to become so.[17]

The cost of erecting a wind turbine, per kBtu produced, decreases as the size of the turbine increases. Wind speed increases significantly the higher you get above ground level. Also, because optimal wind sites are usually located farther away from human settlement and larger wind turbines are most cost-effective, wind power often makes the most sense in larger-scale installations—wind farms. While wind is one of the cheapest renewable energy resources, it is usually most appropriately used to supply energy for communities and fill the larger societal need for renewable energy rather than to cover the smaller loads of an individual net zero building. Connecting to community wind systems is an excellent way to power net zero ready buildings and a key strategy for powering larger buildings, particularly in more urban areas. However, we do not recommend or count buying green power credits as a way to claim that a building is net zero. And while generally not justifiable, small wind turbines of 10 kW or smaller in plains, shorelines, island, and other unique locations may be a sound investment and appropriate choice.

HARNESSING THE POWER OF WATER

There are numerous innovative, renewable ways that water power is being developed and used. However, for the scale of net zero buildings and community projects we cover in this book, typical hydropower is most appropriate.

Typical hydropower, from the flow of water in streams and rivers, is limited to building sites with on-site or nearby water-powered energy production. Because of the relatively small number of undeveloped hydro sites, it is not a typical option for powering net zero buildings. If you happen to have a site where hydropower is a possibility, it is worth evaluating two options: small-scale dams that have a low drop in elevation but a large quantity of water (as we more commonly see at existing small hydropower operations) and small microturbines suited for residential applications. Microturbines require minimal or no dams, a consistent but small amount of water, and a large drop in elevation. Specifically, micro turbines are an option for off-grid development and can complement PV for smaller projects. Repurposing old mill sites is perfect for small-scale hydro applications, as seen in figure 4.30.

Hydropower is complex, and expensive and requires ongoing maintenance. With larger hydro systems, permitting, engineering, and cost are significant hurdles. Smaller flows that have higher drop or head can be appropriate for smaller net zero projects but do require an involved construction and operation process. In most cases hydropower, like wind, is more viable as an option for community-scale net zero operations and may be worth investigating for larger projects if there are regional opportunities. If you believe that your site might be a

FIGURE 4.29. At a good wind site, a stand-alone wind turbine can provide electricity for small buildings. For larger buildings, building-integrated turbines can help supply power, though the economics and percentage of building electric load met by wind is usually small. Vibration, insurance, and liability if blades malfunction are other significant issues that can be difficult to solve. *Left*, a 1.8kW Southwest Windpower turbine at a suburban home site. *Top right*, the Bahrain Trade Center with three 225 kW wind turbines located between two buildings. *Middle right*, a series of wind turbines mounted on the roof parapet on the Museum of Science, Boston. *Bottom right*, the Strata SE1 building in London displaying building-integrated wind systems.

FIGURE 4.30. The energy generated by this water turbine in Warren, Vermont, was sold to the local utility and fed directly into the grid. The turbine had an installed capacity of 70kW.

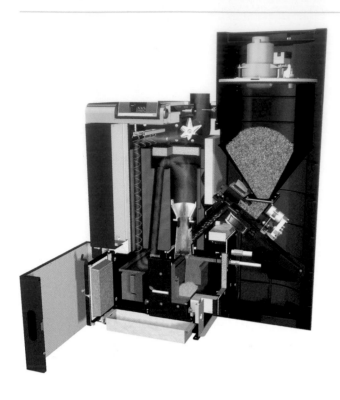

FIGURE 4.31. A wood pellet boiler.

good candidate for hydro, first contact an experienced hydro consultant or company that can perform a detailed evaluation of the resource.

HARNESSING THE POWER IN BIOLOGICAL GROWTH

Chunk wood, wood chips, wood pellets, and agricultural-based pellets are all biomass products.[18] Biomass is a renewable resource when sustainably harvested or generated from waste products. Although biomass is not "renewed" on a daily or annual basis such as the other renewable resources we have discussed (aside from switchgrass), it is a natural product, and its renewal process is vastly shorter than that of fossil fuels. Through a combustion process, biomass can generate electricity or thermal energy that can be distributed by water or air through a building. For our purposes, we will not consider biomass as a source for powering net zero buildings. (For a detailed explanation, see chapter 2.) However, if a project seems well suited to the use of biomass, it is an option worth discussing with engineers who are experienced with biomass.

Biomass technology has evolved significantly in the last few decades. European wood pellet boilers have drastically reduced labor for feeding fuel, cleaning, and maintenance in general from older wood combustion devices. Wood chips and chunk wood offer excellent options for large projects and small projects, respectively. And all of these devices have reduced emissions to safe and reasonable levels. While biomass is renewable and carbon neutral and is considered by some to be a net zero energy resource, we believe biomass is more important in the long term, both environmentally and as a resource for making wood products when fossil-fuel-based plastics become more expensive. In the short term biomass is likely to play a role in the full transition to renewables. Not everyone, of course, shares our opinion about the future of biomass.

Once you understand the integrated-design options for net zero buildings, you can begin the process of evaluating and implementing them. The next step, then, is to understand the overall net zero design process—from assembling the design team, to communicating with owners, to establishing construction protocols.

GEORGE D. AIKEN CENTER

DESIGN PROFILE

Building Profile	Building Name:	**George D. Aiken Center**	
	Location:	University of Vermont, Burlington	
	Occupancy Date:	January, 2012	
	Square Footage:	40,003	
	Certification:	LEED-NC 2.2 Platinum	
Energy Profile	Energy Reference Year:	2009	
	Total Energy Consumption:	388,000 kWh	
	Total Energy Production:	110,000 kWh	
	Energy Intensity:	Modeled: 31 kBtu/sf-yr (not counting renewables)	
Building Envelope	Construction Type:	Cast-in-place concrete structure, light-gauge metal wall studs	
	Insulation Values:	Walls:	R-32, 5″ of XPS board and 3½″ existing fiberglass batt cavity insulation
		Roof:	R-54, 9″ minimum polyisocyanurate board
		Foundation:	R-10, 2⅜″ rigid fiberglass board
	Air Infiltration:	Final Blower Door:	3,700 cfm50
			0.11 cfm50/sf above-grade surface area
			0.08 cfm50/sf total surface area
	Windows/Skylights:	Windows, Operable:	U-value 0.20, SHGC 0.24, VT 0.41
		Windows, Fixed:	U-value 0.15, SHGC 0.28, VT 0.49
		Skylights:	U-value 0.22, SHGC 0.57, VT 0.48
Mechanical/ Electrical Systems	Heating System:	Two-pipe fan coil and campus steam	
	Cooling System:	Two-pipe fan coil and campus-chilled water; economizer through increased volume of ventilation of air; automatic natural ventilation for cooling of solarium, Eco-Machine™ space, green conference room, and north atrium	
	Ventilation System:	Demand-controlled, dedicated-outside-air ventilation system for all spaces; displacement ventilation serving the first floor; enthalpy recovery on ventilation air to recover heat and moisture	
	Energy Recovery System:	Cambridgeport, with Thermotech 3A molecular sieve wheel	
		Minimum Effectiveness: 82 percent	
	Lighting System/Controls:	High-efficiency, super T-8, automatic daylighting cutoff; occupancy sensors in all occupied spaces	
	Hot Water:	Indirect-fired 80-gallon Hubbell water heater, 170 gph recovery at 6 gpm, 200° F hydronic supply	
	Renewable System:	68kW PV system installed off-site (17 dual-axis trackers at 4kW each)	

GEORGE D. AIKEN CENTER
A National Model for Green Renovations

You wouldn't know if you just passed by, but the Aiken Center at the University of Vermont (UVM) in Burlington is among the most energy-efficient renovations in American higher education. Faculty, staff, and students are amazed by the transformation of the formerly outdated and uninviting building. Now, large windows allow daylight into the once dark building, offering naturally lit classrooms, offices, and gathering areas. Just inside the entrance doors at the southern façade, visitors experience the gentle trickling of water from the irrigation system for the plants filling the sunlit space, as the Eco-Machine™ cleans 100 percent of the building's wastewater. Local boulders, including ones discovered on the project construction site, are placed throughout the ground floor, offering casual locations for students and faculty to pause, while wood paneling certified by the Forest Stewardship Council (FSC) and sourced from UVM's sustainably managed research forest in Jericho, Vermont, ribs nearly every interior wall. And beyond the visual cues, the Aiken Center boasts a highly insulated building envelope and new HVAC equipment, which together allow the building to achieve a 63 percent reduction in energy usage over the existing building, while adding approximately 2000 square feet and air-conditioning, which was sorely lacking in the existing facility.

Project Overview

This building provides a home for UVM's Rubenstein School of Environment and Natural Resources (RSENR), which includes 600 undergraduates, 130 full- and part-time masters, and Ph.D. students, 40 full-time faculty members, and 30 research and administrative staff. Located prominently on the main pedestrian circulation spine through the UVM campus, the center is designed as a model for a sustainable future and acts as a green beacon for the university, the Burlington community, and visitors. This deep energy retrofit, net zero ready project received LEED Platinum certification in August 2013.

The 41,000 gross sf space is organized around two public spaces: the solarium and the north atrium, with its monumental stairway. The solarium is the primary addition to the existing building envelope, along with the adjacent Eco-Machine™ room. This 2,000 sf sliver of added space focuses south toward the existing Davis Center Oval as a welcoming invitation to the building. With operable windows for natural ventilation, greenery-filled planters with integrated seating, extensive daylighting, and a view of the Eco-Machine™, the solarium was envisioned as a multifunctional space and a virtual beach on sunny days in the winter when snow covers the campus. The previously dark, tight, and uncomfortable circulation spaces have been transformed, creating an engaging and enlivening area for social interaction. The existing stairway was widened; skylights were added; and the awkward, three-level, north-facing curtain wall, angled at 45°, which facilitated dangerous ice avalanches over the entry, was moved to a vertical position, generating a more spacious feeling and beautiful views of the historic campus buildings.

Moving through the building from these core circulation spaces, the first floor houses three general-purpose classrooms, a renovated computer laboratory, a conference

room with new windows, and an undergraduate lounge. The main entrance is located on the second floor, along with the solarium, the Eco-Machine™, the dean's suite, administration and faculty offices, and three teaching/research laboratories. The third floor consists of more faculty offices; informal meeting spaces, including a faculty lounge; graduate workstations; and the Green Conference Room, which extends over the second-floor entry, with internal windows into the solarium and Eco-Machine™ room.

The central theme—celebrating natural systems, ecology, and biophilia—is continued throughout all details in the building. A recycled-content terrazzo floor in the hallways introduces a story of earth, water, and air. The first-floor colors are deep reds and earth tones to mimic the earth's core. Greens on the second floor are reminiscent of grasses and trees on the earth's surface. Blue on the third floor brings to mind the earth's atmosphere. And finally, a deep, flowing blue connecting all floors and cascading down the stairs simulates water. Building users speak of a pleasant warmth and joy when experiencing the plants, rocks, trees, and nature-based themes throughout the building and extending into the surrounding site.

Vision and Goals

From the outset, the Aiken Center renovation was envisioned as a national model for higher education: an example for low-energy-consuming buildings, the responsible use of natural resources, the development of a healthy learning and work environment, and an inspiration for future generations. It was also intended to expand the University of Vermont's demonstrated commitment as a leading environmentally focused university. From these starting points, the main goals for the project were born.

A LIVING BUILDING. The idea to design the Aiken Center as a "living building" was inspired by the Eco-Machine™, which employs a technology developed by recently retired UVM

FIGURE CS2.2. The building section highlights the natural light in the two-story solarium space and the Green Conference Room.

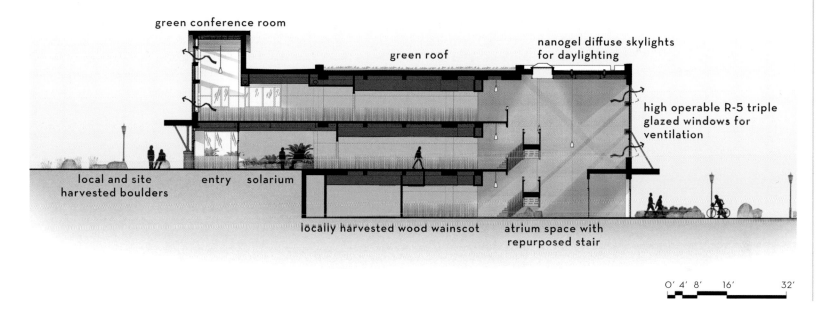

green conference room

green roof

nanogel diffuse skylights for daylighting

high operable R-5 triple glazed windows for ventilation

local and site harvested boulders

entry   solarium

locally harvested wood wainscot

atrium space with repurposed stair

0' 4' 8'   16'   32'

professor John Todd to transform wastewater into clean water. With the Eco-Machine™ as the seed, the design team based the building design on a model of a living organism within an ecosystem, with active water collection and monitoring, a green roof, and the integration of natural materials.

DEEP ENERGY/NEAR-NET-ZERO RENOVATION. The design team wanted to prove that it is possible to complete aesthetically pleasing yet economically viable renovations in cold climates. From the project's inception, the main goal was to demonstrate that a dark, uninviting, high-energy-consuming building could be transformed into a vibrant, engaging, interactive, and inspiring hub of research, learning, and education. A related goal was to reuse as much of the existing building as possible—preserving its embodied energy and demonstrating that existing buildings can cost-effectively attain as high an energy performance as a new building. To date, we know of no other cold-climate university building, either new or old, with as low an EUI number for energy conservation.

ENGAGING OCCUPANTS. It was important to RSENR to design a building that would bring people together as an active community for research and learning. The school building was visualized as a living system with informal hangouts and gathering, learning, and office spaces. Circulation and public spaces were designed to bring the community together, while allowing classroom learning, research, and office functions to serve the occupants as well.

AESTHETICS. The aesthetics of the building embody the mission and vision of RSENR. The ambition was to reflect the natural world of Vermont and to bring this connection into the daily life and activities of the students, faculty, and staff. The goal was to create a daily experience within the building that was beautiful and inspiring for occupants and visitors.

TEACHING LABORATORY. The building was meant to be a teaching laboratory in itself, engaging students even outside the RSENR program and immersing them in opportunities to learn from the built environment as well as the natural environment.

Energy

The Aiken project is expected to achieve a 63 percent reduction in energy consumption over the existing building, reducing the total building load from 89 kBtu/sf-yr to 33 kBtu/sf-yr while slightly expanding the building footprint and also including air-conditioning from the university's central chilled water plant, which the original building lacked.

BUILDING ENCLOSURE

The energy performance and building science of the exterior envelope were critical areas of analysis and investigation. The existing brick-and-concrete structure had structural components running from inside to outside that were a significant source of heat loss through the envelope. These thermal bridges made typical insulation retrofit strategies on the interior ineffective. A holistic wall-assembly assessment was conducted, including thermal, materials, and durability analyses. When the final analysis was completed, including cost estimates of the proposed new envelope, it was evident that removing the existing exterior brick and insulation system and installing a new, combined moisture, water, and air barrier, as well as new insulation to the walls and roof, was the prudent choice and investment for UVM. The new system allowed for significantly higher efficiency levels and lower energy costs in the future. The following include the main upgrades to the building enclosure to increase energy performance.

- All windows were upgraded to triple-glazed, R-5 windows.
- 5″ of rigid insulation was added to the building's exterior, which along with the 3.5″ of fiberglass insulation already existing in the building walls brought the walls up to an R-32 assembly.
- 9″ (minimum) of polyisocyanurate insulation was added to the roof, bringing the roof to an R-54 assembly.

In addition to the high-performing insulation and building enclosure components, a spray-applied barrier combined with membrane layers in corners and nonadhesive surfaces was specifically detailed to make the center one of the tightest commercial buildings in Vermont. A commissioning consultant hired by the university carefully inspected the installation to ensure that the construction precisely followed ambitious specifications, drawings, and installation requirements. A blower door test gave a result of 0.11 cfm50/sf exterior surface area, one of the best such test results for this size building in the Northeast.

RENEWABLES

Seeking all sources of innovation for the project, the research staff worked with faculty and students to submit a proposal for solar PV trackers to the University Clean Energy Fund. The fund is a self-imposed fee of $10 per student per semester, established to advance renewable energy research, education, and infrastructure on campus. The proposal was approved, seventeen 4kW PV AllSun Trackers were installed at the school's adjacent US Forest Service site, and the university entered into a power purchase agreement with a local renewable energy provider.

The trackers have generated over 100,000 kWh annually to date, which accounts for over 25 percent of the Aiken Center's energy needs by cost. When the contribution of the trackers is taken into account, the EUI is further reduced from 34 kBtu/sf-yr to 24 kBtu/sf-yr. The school also installed a small PV tracker near the building entrance to represent the off-site trackers.

LIGHTING AND DAYLIGHTING

One of the major challenges (and opportunities) of the existing building was the low levels of daylighting and views through windows. By dramatically increasing the size and particularly the height of existing windows, increasing the total number of windows in the building, and removing existing dropped ceilings, the use of daylighting in the building has been substantially enhanced. Careful consideration was taken during the design process to ensure that all offices and classrooms have access to direct natural light or have interior window access to rooms that do. This was accomplished both by strategic programming

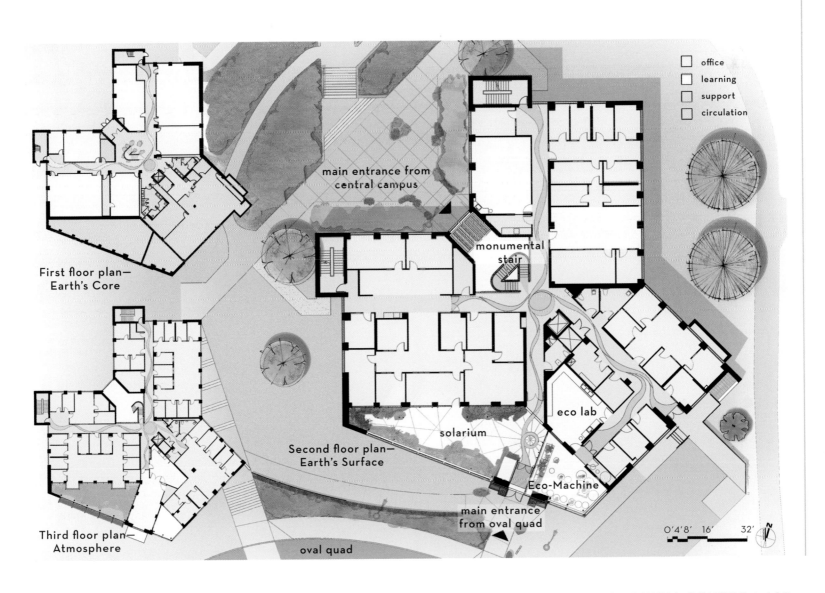

FIGURE CS2.3. The floor plan shows the connections to the campus from the north atrium and the solarium space.

office
learning
support
circulation

main entrance from central campus

monumental stair

First floor plan— Earth's Core

Second floor plan— Earth's Surface

solarium

eco lab

Eco-Machine

main entrance from oval quad

Third floor plan— Atmosphere

oval quad

0' 4' 8' 16' 32'

FIGURE CS2.4. The solarium addition.

FIGURE CS2.5. The patterns and colors in the terrazzo floor mimic elements of the earth—air, water, land, and core—with a river of blue connecting all three floors.

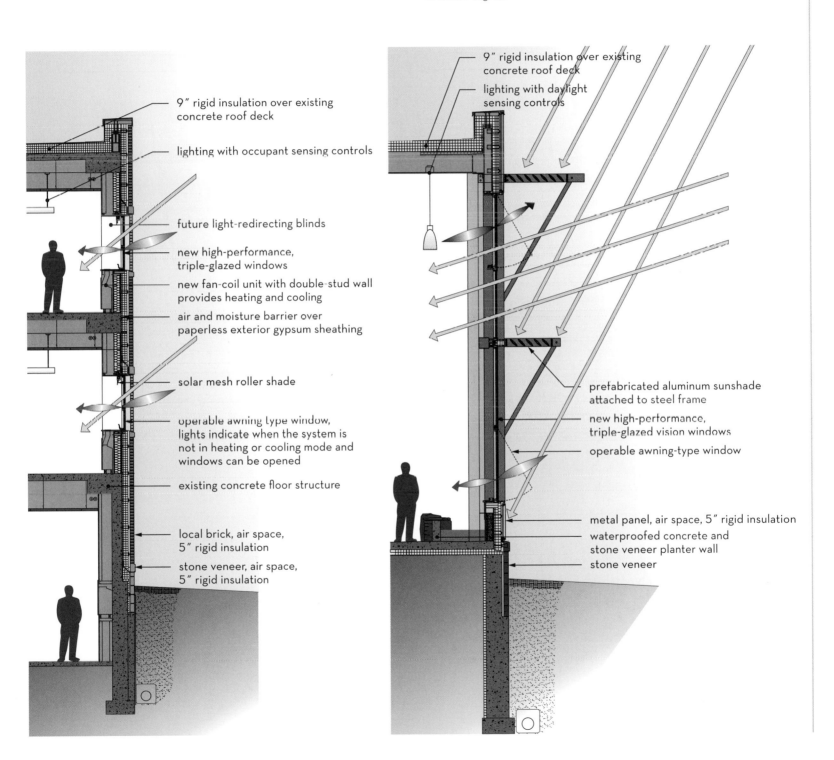

9" rigid insulation over existing concrete roof deck

lighting with occupant sensing controls

future light-redirecting blinds

new high-performance, triple-glazed windows

new fan-coil unit with double-stud wall provides heating and cooling

air and moisture barrier over paperless exterior gypsum sheathing

solar mesh roller shade

operable awning type window, lights indicate when the system is not in heating or cooling mode and windows can be opened

existing concrete floor structure

local brick, air space, 5" rigid insulation

stone veneer, air space, 5" rigid insulation

9" rigid insulation over existing concrete roof deck

lighting with daylight sensing controls

prefabricated aluminum sunshade attached to steel frame

new high-performance, triple-glazed vision windows

operable awning-type window

metal panel, air space, 5" rigid insulation

waterproofed concrete and stone veneer planter wall

stone veneer

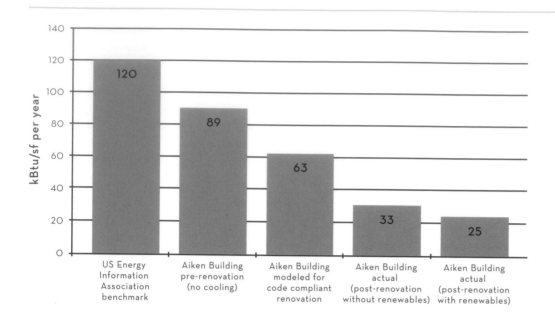

FIGURE CS2.7. Energy performance of typical university buildings compared to the existing Aiken Center and the modeled energy intensity of the renovated building.

FIGURE CS2.8. Monumental stair flanked by local boulders.

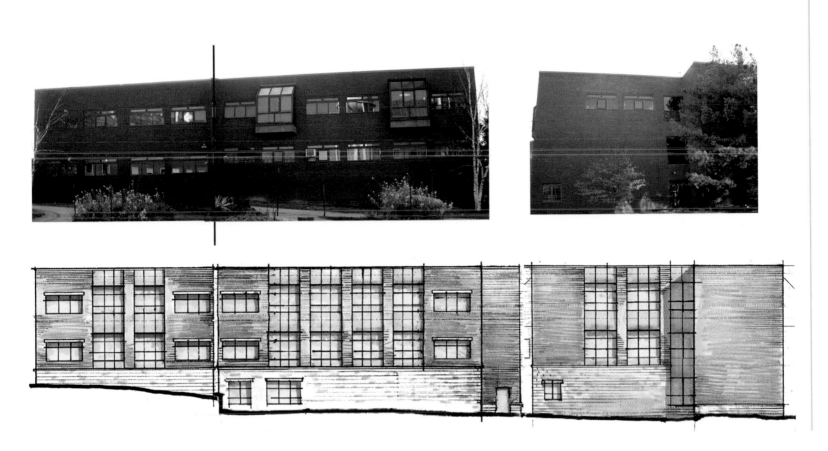

as well as increasing window heights and removing acoustic ceiling tile to allow daylight to penetrate deeper into the building. The focus on daylighting extended to paint-color selection: light colors were used throughout the building, and all wall surface above 7 feet is painted white to better reflect the light to the interior spaces.

HEATING AND COOLING

A building assessment at the start of the project identified major deficiencies with the existing heating and ventilation systems.

The existing building did not provide cooling, which resulted in major comfort issues for building users, especially during the summer months. The new HVAC system separates the heating and cooling functions from the ventilation function, lowering fan costs and resulting in a more energy-efficient system. Demand-controlled CO_2 sensors provide variable amounts of air to meeting spaces to provide adequate fresh air for varying room occupancies. Other spaces use occupancy sensors to control ventilation rates. To the extent possible, existing ductwork was used for ventilation to maximize resource reuse and minimize cost. In the larger classrooms, displacement ventilation is introduced at the floor and rises to the ceiling, where it is captured by return ducts. This saves energy by taking advantage of the stack effect, enhances air quality by improving the flow of air through spaces, and reduces noise from air distribution by using slower-moving air. The mechanical system is designed to use outdoor air when temperature-appropriate to supplement heating and cooling and further reduce energy loads. The outdoor air passes through an energy recovery ventilator, which tempers the incoming outside air by exchanging energy with outgoing, conditioned exhaust air, thereby conserving energy.

When outdoor air conditions are appropriate according to temperature and humidity set points in the control systems, windows in four locations automatically open and close. Users are also encouraged to participate in the daily fluctuations of heating and cooling: amber and green lights located throughout the building tell occupants when conditions are optimal to open manually operated windows. The connection between the building users and the building systems helps to encourage strong stewardship for the building and understanding of how the building operates.

Healthy and Sustainable Strategies

The project prioritized locally sourced materials. Bricks for the exterior envelope, for instance, were made by Vermont Brick Manufacturing in Highgate Center; boulders for seating came from the project site and a gravel pit in Jonesville, Vermont; and wood wainscoting, featuring nine species, came from UVM's own research forest and are FSC certified (the certification process was undertaken for this project but certain to be of benefit to future UVM projects as well).

The project focused intently on using water wisely. In the paradigm of a living building, reduced water usage is as important as reduced energy use. The Eco-Machine™ mimics the natural wastewater treatment of a wetland ecosystem and is installed adjacent to the entrance and solarium. The system includes three research-based "trains," or parallel pathways for treatment, to allow for comparison of different methodologies and techniques, further serving the educational mission. The treated water (cleaned to potable water standards) is reused in the building's toilets and urinals, reducing the amount of water needed from the city water system by up to 80 percent.

A green roof filters rainwater on-site, reducing runoff to the municipal stormwater system and reducing the chemicals needed to clean the water in the water treatment process.

Collaborative Process

UVM held a national design competition to select an architect for the renovation of the Aiken Center. Our submission included a collaborative design process to maximize stakeholder engagement. Rooted in the educational mission, goals, and desires of RSENR, the process included facilitating charettes, teaching classes, giving lectures, and ensuring ongoing student, staff, and faculty involvement. More than 500 UVM students over nearly a ten-year period played a role in the design of the greened Aiken Center.

Active learning takes place in the hallways, on the roof, in the Eco-Machine™ laboratory, and in the classrooms. More than 200 sensors and meters in the building measure everything from heated and chilled water consumption for heating and cooling to water and electricity use. The information is displayed on a Building Dashboard, where students and visitors alike can view, compare, share, interact, and learn. Additionally, the extensive experimental green roof, partially funded by a grant from the Environmental Protection Agency, includes eight microwatersheds for research and stormwater management.

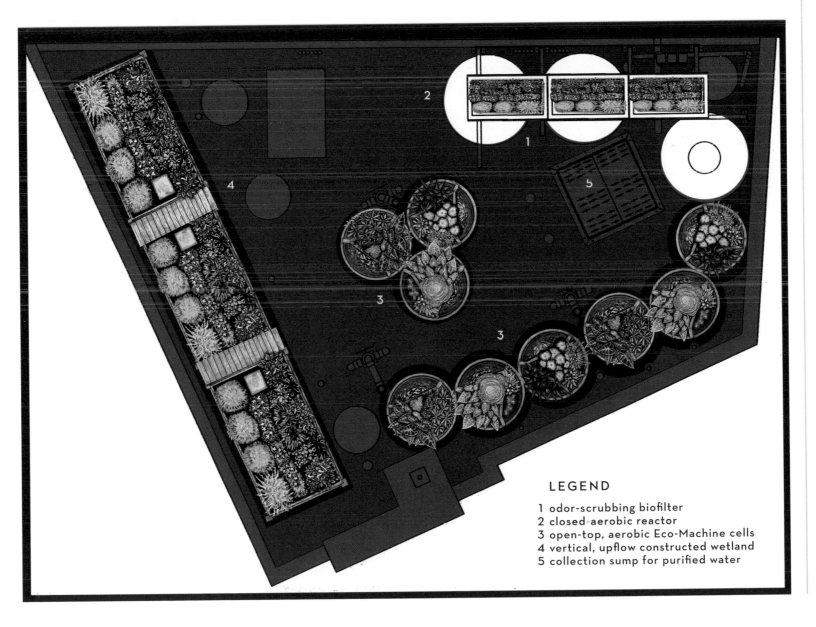

FIGURE CS2.10. The Eco-Machine™ purifies all the wastewater generated in the building. It is a web of life with plants and animals grown on the waste, leaving clean water to reuse for toilet flushing.

LEGEND

1 odor-scrubbing biofilter
2 closed-aerobic reactor
3 open-top, aerobic Eco-Machine cells
4 vertical, upflow constructed wetland
5 collection sump for purified water

5 | Integrated Design Process

This chapter focuses on the critical components of an integrated design process for creating net zero projects that are beautiful, efficient, and prudent long-term investments.[1] The conventional design process follows a linear flow, from programming through schematic design, design development, construction document development, bidding, negotiation, and construction. The integrated design process frontloads the design process more, giving a strong focus to generating clear project goals, objectives, and metrics at the beginning of the process. The integrated design process also involves developing a deeper understanding of the context, purpose, site, client, and project needs prior to initiating schematic design. It includes in-depth programming focused on energy consumption in addition to function and occupant needs.

Building a Team for Success

The success of a net zero project is critically affected by team selection. An effective team must have the appropriate expertise in the field of ultra-high-performing building design, experience with one another, openness to collaboration, and a shared alignment, commitment, and purpose. While not all team members have to meet all criteria, the majority should to ensure a successful outcome. It is more challenging for teams that have not worked together before to be productive, timely, and successful in meeting net zero goals cost-effectively. To succeed on innovative projects takes trust and collaboration, which can be developed only over time.

The entire design team must have a foundation in whole-systems thinking. For instance, in designing a net zero building the mechanical system design must work with the envelope design and vice versa. All team members need to be responsible for the specific interests and concerns of their field, but they also need to be aware of how their individual concerns connect to the whole building. Team members must actively search for ways in which they can adapt their designs to benefit the project

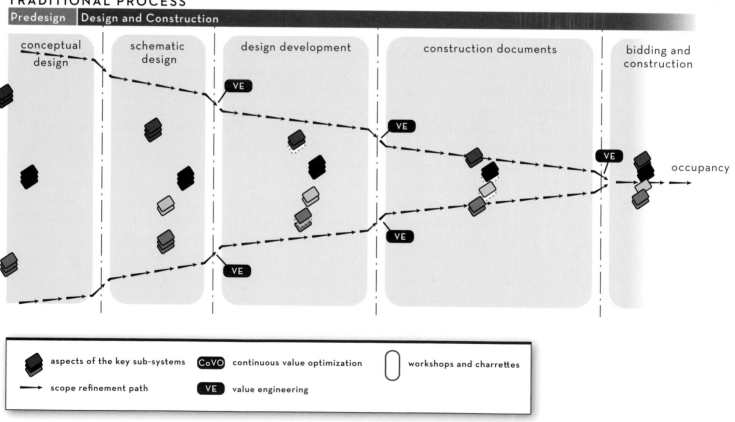

INTEGRATIVE PROCESS

| Discovery | Design and Construction |

CoVO

CoVO

CoVO

occupancy,
operations, and
performance
feedback

prep | evaluation | conceptual design | schematic design | design development | construction documents | bidding and construction

TRADITIONAL PROCESS

| Predesign | Design and Construction |

conceptual design | schematic design | design development | construction documents | bidding and construction

VE

VE

VE

VE

VE

occupancy

---

aspects of the key sub-systems **CoVO** continuous value optimization **workshops and charrettes**

scope refinement path **VE** value engineering

FIGURE 5.1. The integrative design process includes diverse project parameters, including environmental goals and concerns. During a discovery and project understanding phase, the team establishes project goals, metrics, and outcomes as a foundation, prior to the start of any design work. This contrasts with the traditional design process, which does not include the broad parameters and flows in a more direct path, often leading to challenges at the end.

as a whole. At the end of the day, the project needs to meet the goal of net zero energy. The path to get there requires a design process that reflects the visions and concerns of each of the building users and owners as well as all team members.

The integrated design process requires a broad group of participants, especially early in the process. In addition to the traditional design team of the architect, contractor, engineers, and specialty consultants, the integrated design team includes members that will address the project goals and stakeholder concerns. Stakeholders include customers, adjacent landowners, the public, and/or funders of the project. For a net zero building, the pool of stakeholders extends to the silent stakeholders: the environment and its ecosystems.

A successful process engages stakeholders in a conscious manner in the discussions and decisions where each stakeholder or team member can most benefit the project. It begins with engaging all stakeholders at the initiation of the process to generate the overarching goals and principles for the building and continues by including specific individuals at appropriate parts of design and construction. As the integrated design process moves from larger goals and principles to metrics and the development of concrete design ideas, there are also times when the process is opened back up to the entire group. Bringing the stakeholders back into the process at multiple later dates ensures that individual concerns are addressed and the design process is on track. It also provides an opportunity to establish consensus on design decisions. If carried out effectively, this ongoing process of stakeholder engagement allows the evolution of an integrated design, one that complements the interests of occupants, building systems, and operations.

A project that follows an integrated process reflects the collective knowledge, experience, needs, and desires of each individual stakeholder participating in the process with a broad base of ownership and support.

The composition of the team and the need for specific, individual members depends on the size, complexity, and goals of the project. Very different teams are needed to design a small house and a 200,000 sf office building or a large hospital. Regardless of its size, the team must have a designated leader, in most cases the architect. The role of the team leader is to develop and orchestrate the overall process so that outcomes are consistent with goals and metrics. The leader ensures that the process is inclusive and recognizes all concerns. With the input and agreement of the team, the leader coalesces these concerns into a unified vision that guides the process through completion.

In the ideal scenario, each team member should have well-documented experience with net zero projects or ultra-high-performing-projects. Although it is important for such individuals to further the development of this knowledge in the building community, it can also be very challenging to bring aboard a team member with little or no experience on similar projects. Teaching on the job can be frustrating to other team members, especially owners, and can result in schedule and budget challenges. Yet there are situations in which the best project teams are not the most experienced but those with the openness and flexibility to experiment and support the project purpose and goals. Effective team members are critical; they challenge, question, investigate, and vet new ideas. They possess knowledge and diligence to ensure

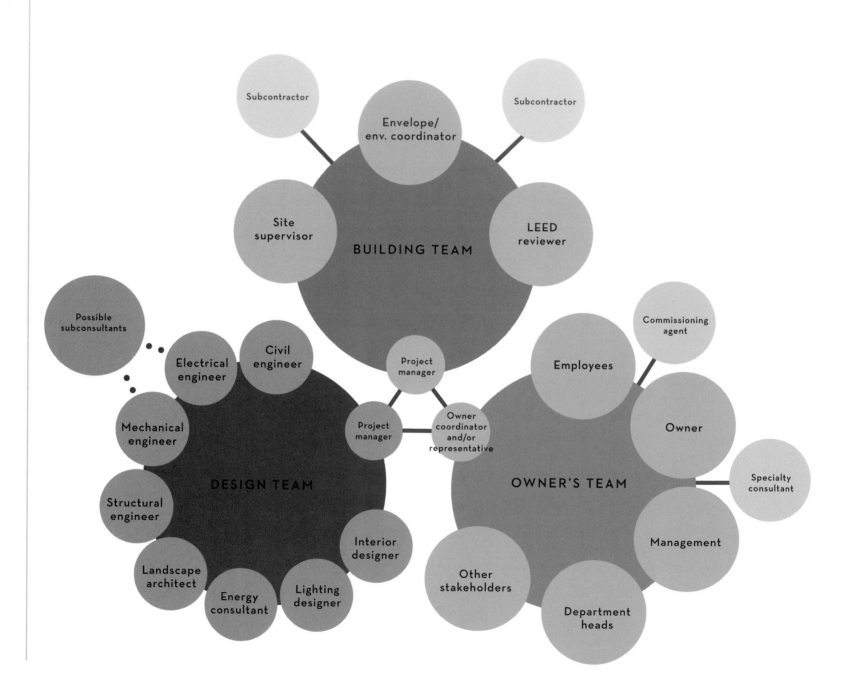

FIGURE 5.2. The integrated team is composed of three main teams: the design team, the building team, and the owner's team. Each individual member of the team participates within one of these three smaller teams, and all three teams work as a whole to deliver the project.

that decisions are based on thorough, in-depth analysis and solid assessment. A net zero project is by nature innovative. As a result, it requires a team with a collaborative attitude and the unique skills developed through experience working on high-performance projects.

THE OWNER'S TEAM

The most critical player for any project is the owner. The owner is footing the bill for the project, and it is the owner's needs and desires that must be held in the highest regard throughout the process. Sometimes the owner is an individual, but in most cases the owner consists of a multiperson team. On smaller projects, such as a home, the owner is often a couple or a family, while on larger projects the owner may be the board of directors at a company or school. It is important to clarify at the beginning who the owner is, who makes the decisions, and who is the point person for the duration of the project.

While there is often a single person who has the final say in financial decisions and to whom the designer is ultimately responsible, the designer must understand the dynamics of the owner's team in order to gain teamwide commitment to the net zero goal. This team may include facility personnel, administrative personnel, a very active local leader, a distant president, or what seem to be random, varying personalities. Each additional individual, and especially his or her interactions with the others, can make the process more complicated. In order for the process to function effectively, the design team must balance the needs of these individuals by providing clear documentation of costs, benefits, and constraints that will lead to stronger buy-in and direction from the owner's team.

For a net zero project to be successful, the owner must be completely on board with the net zero goal. In many cases the owner's understanding of the goal and ability to communicate a commitment to the entire team can be the difference between the success and failure of the project. Achieving net zero is a challenge. In the design process many hurdles will arise, including conflicting pressures for resources and budget, which can cause energy goals to be forgotten along the way. A project in which the owner's commitment to net zero is solid will experience these challenges as surmountable hurdles rather than roadblocks to achieving the net zero goal.

The owner may completely support the net zero goal from the beginning of the project, or this commitment may grow incrementally. The owner may be open to considering a net zero goal but not ready to commit until they understand the cost and design implications. In some cases the owner asks for net zero as one of multiple options, while in others the owner has the vision of an environmentally responsible building but is not yet familiar with the idea of net zero. Whatever the owner's stance, the design team must create a thorough and transparent process to allow the owner to make informed and prudent decisions in determining the goals and approach best suited to the project.

The process of evaluating options is often worthwhile even if the owner is committed to the net zero goal from the beginning. Completing the analysis to compare different levels of building performance helps the owner evaluate whether or not the net zero goal is realistic or fiscally prudent. This analysis also provides background documentation and reasoning that can help to convince stakeholders, including users and donors, that a net zero project is the right choice. Without the grounded and explicit decisions of this comparative process, concerns may later arise as to whether the right assumptions were made in the beginning. These concerns can delay the project or realization of the net zero goals.

The owner's team typically includes an owner coordinator, or owner's team leader, a commissioning agent, and sometimes an owner's representative. There may also be additional specialty consultants.

OWNER COORDINATOR

For most small projects, owners usually represent themselves; on larger, more complex institutional and commercial projects, however, there is typically one contact person—the owner coordinator—through whom all work and decisions are communicated. This person is a direct employee of the owner, coordinates with the owner's team, knows the owner's organization well, and ensures the owner's interests are addressed. Frequently, there also is a committee representing the diversity of interests and organizational knowledge. This committee provides useful knowledge of project needs, input in decision-making, and communication within the larger organizational and community context. When there is a committee, the coordinator is the primary point of contact between the owner and the design team.

OWNER'S REPRESENTATIVE

More and more often, the owners are not involved in every aspect of the design process and instead hire a consultant with extensive construction and project management experience to represent their interests. This occurs either because the owner does not have the time to participate fully in the process, the owner does not have the experience to lead the design process, or the project is large and complex. The owner's representative tends to be someone with documented experience leading the design or construction of similar-size projects. The owner's representative may be involved in the project throughout its entirety or only in specific phases. For example, a clerk of the works is an owner's representative responsible for the inspection of construction work who is usually not involved in the project as a whole. In many cases, because of the owner representative's close interaction with the design team, it is more important to have the representative fully on board with net zero goals than to have the owner on board.

COMMISSIONING AGENT

The commissioning agent ensures that the project is designed and constructed to meet project goals and that it functions as it was designed. While this sounds simple and obvious, most completed buildings do not perform as designed. Typical project completion practices such as punch lists and start-up procedures often do not pick up all problems. It is not uncommon for mechanical systems in large buildings to have deficiencies that go unnoticed for years after project completion.

As a result of these obstacles, it is increasingly common to use the services of a commissioning agent. Ideally, the commissioning agent is an owner's consultant, directly accountable to the owner rather than the design team or contractor to ensure objectivity. When selecting a commissioning agent, the owner should consider experience with net zero design, expertise in the proposed building type, and an attitude that allows for collaborative work as a team member while raising challenging and critical questions in support of project goals. The design process functions most effectively when the commissioning agent is on board from the beginning (or at least from the end

of schematic design). Joining the team early in the process allows the commissioning agent to review concepts and raise questions before construction begins. When brought on to the team later in the process, an agent often raises relevant and legitimate concerns at a time when it is very expensive to address them.

Under different project scenarios a commissioning agent can assume different roles. Most commonly, a commissioning agent reviews mechanical and electrical systems for intended function. Because these are complicated systems requiring precision, this is the likeliest place, even on conventional projects, for the commissioning agent to make improvements. While net zero practices often reduce the complexity of the mechanical system, making effective installation easier, it requires a higher degree of precision for proper performance, reinforcing the benefit of including a mechanical commissioning agent on the team.

Commissioning of the building envelope, too, is becoming more commonplace. The envelope design for a net zero project can be as complex and essential as the mechanical-system design, so its proper execution is essential for net zero performance. An envelope commissioning agent can make a critical difference in whether a project achieves its net zero goals.

ADDITIONAL SPECIALTY CONSULTANTS

For a larger project or a specialty building type, an owner may well add further consultants to the team. For example, an owner might hire a manufacturing consultant for an industrial project, a programming consultant for an educational project, or a food consultant for a restaurant or dining facility. These additional team members need to understand and embrace net zero goals. As they may be less familiar with integrated and net zero design, the designer should encourage them to ask questions and bring to light concerns that relate to their specific discipline so as to discover and address any issues as early as possible.

THE DESIGN TEAM

Design teams may differ slightly depending on the scale and purpose of the building, but certain members are critical in any net zero project.

ARCHITECT

The architect is the leader of the design team and is responsible for coordinating the work of team members. The architect is also responsible for the schedule throughout design and must coordinate with subconsultants to ensure the project is completed with high quality, on time, and on budget. As the leader of the design team, the architect is ultimately responsible for meeting the net zero goal and needs to keep that goal at the forefront of the subconsultants' and owner's minds to ensure that the decisions and resultant work align with this goal. It is important to the success of the project that the architect orchestrate effective communication and interaction among team members for the duration of the project.

ENERGY CONSULTANT

The energy consultant is engaged in all aspects of the design process and is accountable for energy modeling, determining the energy consumption of the design, and tracking performance-related decisions to ensure that the design will achieve the net zero goal. From the beginning of the project, the energy consultant provides input on orientation, massing, and daylighting. The energy consultant will also help to set energy goals and metrics and provide modeling of multiple energy performance levels. As design progresses, the energy consultant makes recommendations for envelope design and coordinates the right sizing of mechanical systems with the mechanical engineer. On some projects the mechanical engineer may assume the role of energy consultant, but it is preferable to separate these responsibilities to allow for oversight as well as dialogue and exploration that are likely to lead to more creative solutions.

The energy consultant develops overall building metrics and submetrics for HVAC, lighting, and plug loads. When you design a net zero building, confirm that the selected energy consultant will provide this detailed level of energy-metric investigation and analysis and ask for a comparison of energy modeling data to actual monitored energy data for completed projects, using at least twelve months of data. Within the high-performance building field, it is not uncommon to find discrepancies between modeled and actual performance; careful selection of an energy consultant based on performance on past projects is important to the success of a net zero project.

MECHANICAL, ELECTRICAL, AND PLUMBING (MEP) ENGINEER

Net zero buildings boast dramatic energy-load reduction compared to typical buildings. In terms of mechanical systems, the net zero building is therefore quite different, allowing for significantly simpler and smaller systems than are usually designed and specified. In order to provide the mechanical systems for a net zero building, a mechanical, electrical, and plumbing (MEP) engineer needs to be creative and flexible. Old methods and solutions for mechanical design often result in systems that are substantially oversized because innovative building envelopes frequently perform better than a conservative mechanical engineer would expect. An overly cautious approach to the engineering, while understandable, may hinder the achievement of project goals and metrics.

To create an environment in which the engineer can trust that the envelope will perform as designed requires a team with competence in integrating envelope and mechanical-system design, preferably a team that has a history of working together. It also is important to ensure that the owner and/or contractor will not downgrade the envelope in a value-engineering process during construction. If the envelope's insulating value is reduced, the engineer will need to resize the system. In addition to being open and flexible, the MEP engineer must carefully document the design so the systems perform as intended and the owner has a comfortable building.

LIGHTING CONSULTANT

For larger and more complex building projects, the design team should include a lighting consultant accountable for developing a design strategy that connects daylighting and artificial lighting so the two work together seamlessly and efficiently. The lighting consultant also sets specific lighting levels for the building type and individual room uses. After the lighting layout is developed, the lighting consultant coordinates the daylighting strategy with a control strategy to minimize artificial light use. To select a consultant, you should find out the consultant's experience with net zero design and lighting energy metrics for completed projects of a similar building type.

STRUCTURAL ENGINEER

A structural engineer is a critical member of the net zero building team because of the need to minimize thermal bridging in the enclosure. Larger buildings, usually made of steel and concrete, must be designed and detailed carefully to minimize or eliminate thermal bridging. This requires creative structural design strategies for net zero buildings. When selecting a structural engineer, choose one who has experience with net zero buildings, the ability to collaborate with a team, and flexibility with design strategies.

CIVIL ENGINEER

While past net zero experience is less critical for the civil engineer, it can be helpful for certain site conditions. Not only does the civil engineer need to offer the best environmental design strategies and measures, such as erosion control and ecological stormwater strategies, but the civil engineer is also responsible for coordinating this work with net zero project requirements.

OTHER SPECIALTY CONSULTANTS

As with the owner's team, the design team may decide to include other specialty consultants, particularly for a project with a highly specific use. A retail consultant could be brought in for a store design, a food consultant for a restaurant, or a laboratory consultant for a lab project. Frequently, consultants specify the sort of energy-intensive equipment often required for food service, laboratory, or manufacturing work. Therefore these consultants must understand and support the net zero goal and be willing to work with others to find creative solutions.

THE CONSTRUCTION TEAM

For net zero projects, how the construction team is selected can impact the success of the project. There are two standard means of selection: the traditional bid process and a construction-management process.

In the traditional bid process, the design team completes the final design and the project is put out for bids. Each interested contractor returns a bid number, or price for completing the work, and the owner chooses which bid to accept. Under this process innovative technologies and construction strategies inherent to net zero buildings are sometimes overbid because they are misunderstood. At other times unique net zero design elements are missed altogether, which can cause major budget and schedule hurdles later in the project. The bid process can also lead to disagreements and additional expense with change orders. In today's competitive market, this process can be very challenging for all team members. If you use a bid process, you should prequalify contractors and develop a short list of those best suited to deliver a net zero project with the care and quality that is required. Also in the bid process, you can prequalify subcontractors and/or include rigorous experience and/or certification requirements for the trades that are particularly important for constructing a net zero building, such as air barrier, insulation, and mechanical subcontractors. You can also require that the contractor list the three lowest bids for critical subcontractors so the owner and design team can participate in the selection process, selecting from the most qualified low bidder.

A construction manager is selected preferably at the beginning of design to give feedback on design decisions regarding constructability and cost, to help the builder develop in-depth knowledge of the project and understand the critical or innovative project components. The construction manager can be hired through a competitive process using requests for proposals that clearly ask for information on high-performing expertise, experience, commitment, project approach, company values, markups, general conditions, rate structures, billing procedures, and general process. From this, as well as information about past work, the owner, in coordination with the design team, can choose the best construction manager to meet the project requirements.

Understandably, building owners are concerned about construction costs and what seems to be a lack of competitive pricing under the construction management process. The construction management firm is hired well before other members of the construction team. Subcontractors to do the majority of the project's work are selected later through competitive bidding. The construction manager provides only administrative cost and project management services for the project. But by being brought on board from the very beginning of the project, the construction manager can help optimize design and managing project costs effectively. The process also offers a smooth transition between the design and construction phases. The money spent on hiring a construction manager may be saved through improved constructability and time savings, which create a more efficient process and project and avoid costly change orders. If the decision is not to follow a construction management process but rather to go to bid, then it is particularly crucial to include someone, as a part of either the owner's team or the design team, responsible for developing accurate estimates throughout the design process. This role can be filled by a cost estimator who has experience with net zero or ultra-high-performing buildings, an owner's representative who is experienced with estimating, or a contractor hired specifically for preconstruction services. With any of these options, the project will benefit from early input on cost and constructability, ensuring that the project heads in a successful direction.

SCHEDULE AND COSTS

The design of a net zero building takes both more work and more time than the design of a conventional building. It takes time to educate the team on the innovative technologies and construction practices, and the more thorough drawings and specifications, a more detailed decision-making process, the selection of more alternatives, and the detailed financial analysis of energy choices all take more work. During the construction process the expanded time frame includes additional coordination between the contractor and the design team to ensure the project is completed as intended because the net zero details require additional effort and care. These measures add time and expense for the construction team as well.

In developing a budget for net zero projects, it is important to remember that the additional costs for the design and construction of the project will be offset in the long term by reduced operating costs. The owner will financially benefit from the additional up-front cost. Some professionals suggest calculating design and/or construction fees based on energy performance: the better the building's performance, the higher the reward is to the design and/or construction team. This rewards the team as they share in a small percentage of the building owner's savings that they helped create.

Predesign: Energizing the Team, Orienting Design, and Developing a Vision for Success

Once a team is selected, the next step is to get the members to work as one unified team, oriented to the project purpose, vision, goals, objectives, and metrics. There are many steps that can generate alignment in a team.

INSPIRE TEAM MEMBERS

The team is selected specifically for their knowledge, experience, and commitment to net zero design. It is important to explain and clarify the owner's aspirations, commitment, vision, and goals for the project and discuss the challenges and ambitions with team members. This helps team members see the project as an opportunity. It is critical that team members are aware of the effort required to meet the net zero goal and are willing to take the additional effort that a net zero project entails. Including a construction manager at the beginning of design is optimal for aligning the entire design and construction team. If the project is bid, similar measures at the beginning of construction are helpful in energizing and inspiring the team. On low-bid projects, the general contractor and subcontractors typically do not have the same commitment to the net zero vision and goals. It can be helpful to emphasize how the experience from the net zero project will benefit the construction team in getting and completing future work and identifying them as leaders in the industry.

ORGANIZE A KICKOFF CHARRETTE WORKSHOP

A full team charrette or workshop is a great way to energize and inspire the team from the start. By developing vision, purpose, goals, objectives, metrics, schedules, and outcomes, a charrette provides a chance to build an understanding of the

FIGURE 5.3. The design action report assists in ensuring that projects progress smoothly, effectively, and with mutual satisfaction. It is used to document the conversations, commitments, and promises with clear responsibility for completion. As such, it differs from traditional minutes, which simply record a conversation.

challenges and opportunities for the project and team and a boost in overall energy.

COMMUNICATE AND MEET REGULARLY

During predesign, the process of meetings, communication, and documentation should be established with a core internal team; there should be design team and client meetings on a regular basis and larger charrettes or workshops at design milestones. The frequency and lengths of meetings vary depending on the size and complexity of the net zero project. Establishing clarity of meeting purposes as the project evolves generates more productive meetings. Typical meeting purposes might be to develop site concept, establish overall building concept, define exterior and/or interior character, and refine building details. Key questions might include: How do we balance conflicting goals, like a desire for west windows toward view and our energy goals? What is the character and feeling of space that fits a specific organization or client's culture? How can desires for collaboration and productivity be addressed in the design and layout of an office project? The flow of meetings reflect issues critical for moving the design forward at that specific point in the design process. Clear outcomes of these meetings generate decisions that keep the design process on track.

Setting up a meeting framework and a team communication process is critical to achieving ambitious net zero goals. Clear documentation of communication and action contribute to the success of a project. Our firm uses a project action report, similar to meeting minutes but specifically focused on actions

and accountability. In this practice we identify a topic with a short title and then indicate the action needed and agreed to at the meeting, including who is accountable and the completion date. These items stay on the action report until the team agrees that they are complete.

CHECK ON TEAM SATISFACTION

Discussing how the team is working together can be beneficial in overcoming difficulties that arise due to the innovative and challenging nature of the project. To facilitate this, team satisfaction should be an agenda item at regular design and construction meetings or at separate meetings. With ongoing communication, problems and dissatisfaction within the team can be avoided, minimized, or resolved quickly.

ESTABLISH PERIODIC CHARRETTE WORKSHOPS

Throughout the design process there should be meetings with key stakeholders to get broad-based input and project support. Typically, these occur at the transition of phases—closing out one phase of design and opening up discussion about the next phase.

UNDERSTAND THE CONTEXT OF YOUR PROJECT

Any new project, even a revolutionary one, must be designed to function within an existing world. Although Frank Lloyd Wright and others have encouraged the myth that the great

MaclayArchitects
CHOICES IN SUSTAINABILITY

PROJECT PURPOSE: To create a long-lasting, beautiful net zero building with a heart

DESIGN ACTION REPORT #3

PROJECT	XXXX
MEETING DATES	April 2, 2013
ATTENDEES	Owner, Architect, Energy Consultant

Architect _X_ does ___ does not anticipate completion of (current phase) by 04.15.13
The Project Design schedule _X_ is ___ is not current.

A. Due Dates / Milestones

Date	Project milestone
By 4.05.13	Meet with selected CM to determine assemblies and systems for pricing
4.26.13	Initial Cost Estimate

B. Budget

Item #	Issue/Date/Action	Responsibility/Due Date
B1	Construction Budget: (10.26.12) Project budget is xx.xxx. Include alternates in schematic design and phasing options that will meet budget.	OWNER 04.15
B2	Initial Estimate: (10.26.12) Builder (once selected) to provide initial cost estimate based on schematic design.	CM May

C. Permit / Regulatory / Land Use Issues

Item #	Issue/Date/Action	Responsibility/Due Date
C1	Permitting: (03.17.13) Architect to develop permitting summary with civil engineer	ARCH April

D. Owner Issues & Approvals

Item #	Issue/Date/Action	Responsibility/Due Date
D2	Contract: (03.06.13) Architect to issue draft CM contract	ARCH May

E. Existing Conditions

Item #	Issue/Date/Action	Responsibility/Due Date
E2	Utility Wires/Pole: (03.06.13) Architect to include relocation of utility pole in outline specifications. CM to coordinate options with power company.	ARCH April

F. Project and Environmental Goals

Item #	Issue/Date/Action	Responsibility/Due Date
F2	Current Energy Consumption: (10.26.12) Owner will provide energy data. (03.06.13) Architect to use as appropriate in energy modeling calculations.	Architect May

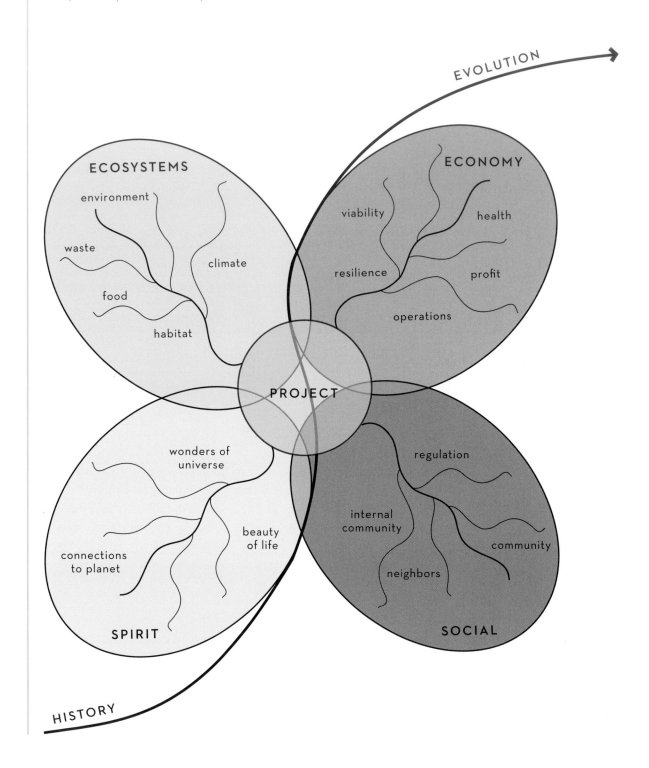

FIGURE 5.4. Project understanding: Projects evolve in an existing background and set of circumstances in the areas of economy, ecosystems, spirit, and society.

artist creates a new reality out of nowhere, that idea is not valid. Everything is already in existence; a great artist or innovator can generate a new reality with his or her creative work only by taking what already exists and organizing it in a new way, a new order. This is the basis of the design process. Therefore, the designer must undertake two critical processes: the first involves understanding the context and environment in which a project will exist, and the second involves synthesizing and structuring the elements in the environment to generate a new organism and pattern of living that can be in symbiosis with its environment. It is only through a deep understanding of a project's context that a designer can lead a project to emerge and coalesce into its final form.

Understanding the background for a project requires exploring its context and how it will extend out into its universe. This overall universe typically can be seen as a multiplicity of worlds, contexts, areas of concern, or ecosystems. Some common project context areas worth exploring include environment, society, economy, and spirit (connection to something larger). And then we think of the subcontexts of these areas as ecosystems, which would have energy, waste, resources, and so on as subareas. And each project has its own particular forms and manifestations. The design team needs to ask questions like: Where do materials come from? What are the environmental and carbon impacts? Are there stakeholder concerns? How will this project impact the existing surrounding community? Will it encourage new vitality and health? Will it improve or impact social equity? Will it encourage community intersection and collaboration? Who are the stakeholders who will be affected by this project, and how can their involvement and collaboration be encouraged? How is the project enhancing its surroundings?

These questions help define how a project fits into its environment and community to make a positive contribution to its surroundings. This broad understanding also creates a foundation for net zero design. The investigation of and connection to the project's context and universe enables the project team to accomplish the project's purpose, mission, objectives, and beyond to succeed and thrive. When the design team internalizes the project context, the project can respond appropriately to the world around it. If a project is contributing to its surroundings socially, environmentally, and economically, it is contributing to making the world a better place and providing positive impact. We use a process called mind mapping to synthesize visually how a project interacts with its environment.[2] A diagram similar to figure 5.4 can be used to summarize the project context graphically by showing major areas of interaction and connection, which are linked through branches and pathways of influence to other parts.

ECOLOGICAL UNDERSTANDING

The project team needs to develop an in-depth understanding of the ecosystem in which the project will be located: sun and weather patterns; water flow; pollution and contaminants; soils; geology; flora and fauna. Generative design ideas are often discovered through an exploration and developed understanding of the site ecology.

SOCIAL UNDERSTANDING

It is important that the project team understand the social context by learning about the community; existing and past land use; land use regulatory requirements; transportation: pedestrian, mass transit, and automobile connections to the site; and the connection to utilities and infrastructure. These pieces are critical to generating a project that fits into the human community.

ECONOMIC/OPERATIONS UNDERSTANDING

The project team should determine how the project operates as a model of positive change and how it will fit into or improve the organization and community's economy and function. This evaluation should include the cost of operation and life-cycle cost, not just the construction budget, to identify how the project can be a generative economic influence to its surroundings.

SPIRITUAL UNDERSTANDING

While much of society today seems to be caught up in science and consumerism, net zero and living buildings are concerned with the planet, living systems, and beauty—matters that are often overlooked in everyday life.

BUILDING AND ENERGY PROGRAM

There are two aspects to a program for a net zero building project: a building program and an energy program. While the building program is typical for all building projects, the energy program is unique to net zero constructions. This two-part program provides the backbone of the building design.

The building program includes the desired spaces with information related to size, capacity, character, adjacencies, lighting, mechanical, technical, and any other special needs. Make sure you thoroughly understand the use characteristics and requirements prior to beginning design. Careful program review will reveal overlap or inefficiencies that you can eliminate to reduce square footage. Add the room sizes to calculate the net usable space. To determine the overall building size, multiply the net square footage by an efficiency percentage, wall thicknesses, circulation, and other minor support spaces.

An energy program for each room and/or use in the building estimates average and peak occupancy; required equipment and specific user requirements for interior conditions such as temperature and humidity; and daily, weekly, and seasonal occupancy patterns. This energy program provides the basis for appropriate mechanical and electrical design. With occupancy patterns and equipment loads, you can accurately estimate and include energy consumption for every space in the energy load calculation.

VISION

The project vision should encompass more than just the building; it should evoke a future way of life and world of activity and energy. Design creates the future. Designing buildings, places, and communities is the act of proposing a new reality or world. The design process creates a new structure that affects how we live and experience our world. More concretely, design generates a new physical building with associated structures of skin, support, and finish, and the physical structure supports daily living and activities. The net zero building combines the elements of lifestyle, beauty, and energy and is a focused vision for a new reality and world. The net zero building offers a vision founded on renewable energy and the flow and rhythm of natural forces. This vision contributes to building a planet where people and nature cohabit and evolve together, intertwined in a growing web of codependence.

Beyond the building, it is important to connect the project vision to the larger context of infrastructure, lifestyle, and transportation and to explore a vision for a larger net zero community. While this process includes simple but important choices such as site selection, it can also look for opportunities to incorporate more mixed-use functions, to connect to public transportation, walking, and bicycling, or it can find local resources for building and consider the future needs of building occupants. Ideally, the vision involves a holistic and evolving way of life rather than one that would create a building suited to a singular use at one point in time.

This vision should include the development of a healthy future and a better quality of life. For instance, if you are designing a new office building, do you envision the overall character for the office as a functional "cube farm" or as a vibrant neighborhood that encourages collaboration, innovation, community spirit, and inspiration? This vision must encompass the full environmental impact of the project—the cycles for waste, water, neighbors, and materials—beyond that of just energy. Establishing a plan for how these cycles function in the context of the net zero building is a critical aspect of designing a sustainable path for all buildings. It is through encompassing these externalities beyond our building that we can enhance our planet, including all living systems.

The vision should also include an emphasis on beauty. People often think of beauty as the surface of the built form. But while making buildings and places that appear beautiful on the outside is important, it is even more important that our buildings help support users and stakeholders to have a more productive, healthy, enlivening, and satisfying day inside spaces. We recommend mapping out a vision for beauty in a broader way, asking how all of the stakeholders can be supported so that their daily living is rewarding and meaningful.

In other words, we ponder how to create a built environment that improves our quality of life and living. The goal is to generate a singular, vibrant vision that begins to synthesize all of the diverse project ideas and all the forces acting upon a project into a cohesive and inspiring vision that can carry the project through the inevitable peaks and valleys of its evolution. This vision needs to be broad enough to include the diversity of stakeholders' needs and desires and yet defined enough that the components and elements of the project are unique and contribute to an overall project that is cohesive and successful.

One possibility for generating this vision is to imagine the project as a living organism. Think about how this organism breathes, eats, and disposes of waste within the ecosystem around it.

Another way to develop the overall vision for the project is to reflect on how the occupants will go about their daily lives and interact with the building and the surrounding environment. In an office setting, do people see their roles as performing work and completing tasks in private offices with occasional meetings in larger meeting rooms? Or do the workers see the environment as an ecosystem with a diversity of spaces that encourage creativity and interaction? How can the environment encourage chance encounters with others that lead to new ideas and innovation? How can this lead to productivity, satisfaction, and overall value generation? All of these questions can generate a better understanding and overarching vision for this space and its daily use.

The best projects use the overall vision to fuse two or three overarching key elements, such as energy, the human use and purpose for the project, and possibly a strong stakeholder need or desire for the project. This vision is further articulated by specific project goals.

SET NET ZERO OBJECTIVES AND METRICS

As the overall design vision is generated, goals, objectives with metrics, and strategies specific to the net zero goal need to be developed. While project goals include program, environmental, energy, and budget, the energy goal for a net zero building is simple: net zero performance. Objectives for overall energy intensity and energy components such as heating, cooling,

ventilation, lighting, and plug loads are tied to concrete metrics that can be checked during design and later after construction. Strategies include design ideas like passive solar heating, radiant slabs, daylighting techniques, and similar ways to achieve goals and objectives. In this generation of goals, objectives, and strategies, questions arise: What are the most effective strategies for energy conservation: passive solar technologies or ground-source or air-source heat pumps? What are the most effective renewable energy production strategies to achieve net zero: PV, on-site biomass, wind, hydro, or solar hot water? How do we address transportation energy and energy not fully connected to the building use? How do we address embodied energy?

The nuts and bolts of the net zero design are derived from these questions and discussion around them. Within this, the overall vision remains the driving force for the building. For these goals and metrics to be realized in the design process, the entire project team needs to be involved in developing them. The goal setting process should be broad and include all project aspirations and visions, covering user, social, financial, and environmental needs of the project. For each goal, concrete objectives with metrics and strategies need to be established so that the team can measure performance through the project development.

As it evaluates the concrete goals and metrics of design, the team should evaluate and reflect upon the project vision. Is the vision reasonable? Is it possible to achieve?

DEVELOP THE OWNER'S PROJECT REQUIREMENTS (OPR)

The owner's project requirements (OPR) document the goals and metrics set by the project team and agreed to by the owner. This document develops owner buy-in agreement on the operational performance of the building and requirements for user satisfaction. The OPR should include criteria for temperature, humidity, lighting levels, and indoor air quality and establish permissible levels of fluctuation for internal environmental conditions. For example, net zero buildings minimize mechanical systems, which can mean fluctuations in interior conditions, particularly in extreme conditions. The OPR indicates to the owner that mechanical equipment for the building is not over-sized, so at extreme design conditions, which might occur for several days a year, internal temperatures might vary from set points by a degree or two. It is critical to establish clear criteria for the building operational parameters at the beginning of the project so the building owner is on board with the expected function of the building and there will be no major concerns about operation once the building is completed.

DOCUMENTATION

At the end of the predesign process, you will want to document all your key decisions. Create a comprehensive overall predesign document that includes detailed information on the following:

- Building and energy programs
- Vision summary
- Goals, objectives, and metrics
- OPR

Design

The design process generally moves from establishing overall vision, concepts, order, and structure to more specific details. Throughout design of a net zero building, we balance functional use and the net zero goals. The design process flows from an initial concept or schematic design into detailed design.

Throughout design we offer choices to explore the diversity of options and to establish clarity about what is and what is not desired. We generate scenarios from business as usual to visionary approaches so that stakeholders can imagine what living in the new design paradigm could be like at an experiential level. We do this connected to the daily living in the new building and specifically with regard to energy alternatives. This allows the design team and clients to explore choices and make prudent and thoughtful decisions based on a thorough evaluation of the best information. In the design of a net zero building, this is particularly relevant for making informed energy-related choices. We provide energy modeling at a minimum of four levels: code-compliant, high-performing, net zero ready, and net zero. To assist the client in making good choices, we begin this analysis early in the process.

The energy analysis includes varying levels of envelope and systems energy conservation measures, annual energy costs, and construction costs for these four levels of performance. We use these data to estimate capital and operating costs over twenty years based on alternative fuel escalation rates. We also provide internal rate of return and net present value analysis so that cash flow and value can be evaluated. Integral to this process is generating cost estimates so budget parameters are met prior to beginning construction documents. We explore this in greater detail in chapter 17.

Giving information at multiple levels is effective for the following reasons:

- The client and entire team are able to make the best choices for the project.
- When the client and/or team question whether the best decisions were made later on, they can refer back to the earlier analyses.
- The data can later be used with potential donors, investors, and/or the public to demonstrate prudent and cost-effective choices.
- When the project is complete, the data are available to the public and press to educate others on the prudence of net zero buildings.

During design, documentation includes project action reports for decisions and agreements made at every meeting as well as drawings, models, sketches, and specifications reflecting design progress. While these are requirements for success on any project, for success on a net zero project, which includes innovative and atypical design, the design process and communication need to be more inclusive, thorough, and clearly documented.

On joining the team, the construction manager can immediately develop a concept-level budget for the project, based on square footage estimates. At each subsequent phase of the project schematic design, design development, and construction document development, the construction manager or a cost estimator updates the estimates based on more detailed design decisions so that anticipated costs can be tracked accurately. Throughout initial design phases it is important to develop construction cost estimates for both a code-compliant and a net zero building design at a minimum so that financial analysis can be provided. In order to complete the analysis accurately, it is important that the construction manager or cost estimator have experience with high-performance projects. When those generating the cost estimates either miss cost related items or are overly conservative due to their lack of knowledge about the specific considerations in net zero construction, over- and underestimating is common, particularly at the beginning of the project. An inaccurate estimate of costs can throw off the client's budget and threaten the feasibility for the project to achieve net zero.

Construction Documentation

Clarity is incredibly important in the development of construction documents, especially when dealing with innovative and unusual requirements and specifications. This is true whether the construction is performed under a construction management process or a bid-delivery process, and even more so for the latter.

During the construction documents phase, it is critical to have coordination meetings with the owner, design team, and (if there is one) construction manager. Owners need to be engaged in the process so that the design fully suits their needs. The construction manager's input during the construction documents phase can be invaluable in providing clear, coherent, practical, and cost-effective drawings and specifications.

In the drawings and specifications, specific attention needs to be paid to envelope, mechanical, electrical, renewable energy, and all other specialized net zero requirements. In terms of the water, air, vapor, and thermal control layers, any information different from typical projects that will be used to determine compliance with the specification should be outlined in detail, including clarification of oversight and required metrics. Clarity regarding requirements from the beginning ensures that these control layers can be properly installed with the least effort, lowest cost, and fewest problems.

In addition to providing clear details, the design team should establish a comprehensive construction process in the drawings and specifications, including the following essential procedural elements and critical meetings:

- Subcontractor qualifications
- Pre-bid meeting
- Preconstruction meeting
- Pre-installation meetings
- Submittal review
- Mock-ups
- Inspections
- Blower door and smoke testing
- Infrared scans
- Commissioning
- Ongoing action reports and meetings

The purpose of these measures is to ensure that procedures occur during construction and that the owner and the construction and design teams understand the process prior to beginning construction.

As in other phases, regular meetings and communication are needed to ensure well-coordinated drawings and specifications. Typically, review meetings should happen at 50 percent and 90 percent of construction document completion.

Construction

Following the design phase, the next challenge is translating the design into the physical building. Adding innovative design strategies, technologies, products, and practices to this already demanding process can cause even greater challenges. Although the net zero design practices and details we are proposing will likely become common in the construction industry in the future, they are not common practice today. When beginning construction, then, keep in mind that the construction industry has learned and become used to standard procedures. You will need to take the time necessary to address concerns by all construction professionals working on the project.

Throughout construction, the design team should build strong ties with the construction team. If the design process has had the participation of a construction manager from the beginning, it is important to reaffirm the commitment to the net zero goals and the communication practices mentioned earlier in this chapter. These goals and project requirements also need to be communicated to all subcontractors and suppliers for the project. And if it is a bid project, it is even more important to build the team and communicate effectively. This includes clarity and firmness regarding net zero requirements and helpfulness in anticipating and resolving challenges. At the beginning of construction, it is important to confirm that the owner is still fully supportive of net zero goals and that this support is conveyed to the construction team. It is essential that the design team and owner work seamlessly together supporting net zero goals. For the success of net zero projects, commitment and teamwork are as important as good drawings and specifications.

Critical Meetings, Requirements, and Procedures

For successful net zero building construction, the following specific meetings and procedures are useful in making construction run as smoothly as possible. While these elements are important on all projects, we orient these measures for net zero projects. The critical meetings and requirements discussed here are the level appropriate for larger and more complex projects. For smaller projects, the same issues need to be addressed, but the manner can be less formal. Also the construction management delivery process makes this process less onerous during construction, as the construction manager is involved in design decisions and conversations.

PRE-BID MEETING

During the contractor and/or subcontractor selection and/or bidding process, the building team should be aware of all of the unusual and innovative procedures that are a part of the drawings and specifications, including the special meetings during construction. At the pre-bid meetings, these can be explained. This helps to generate accurate bids and minimizes cost increases in change orders.

PRECONSTRUCTION MEETING

The preconstruction meeting allows the design and construction teams to thoroughly review, evaluate, and discuss the requirements of producing the high-performance building envelope. It also allows the team to anticipate potential coordination, schedule, and other conflicts. This is a chance for the owner and design team to reinforce the net zero project requirement and purpose. This communication at the beginning of the project establishes the rules of the game to ensure that when issues arise later in the process, there are procedures and lines of communication for resolving them quickly.

PRE-INSTALLATION MEETINGS

Prior to the installation of any net zero components, pre-installation meetings should be required in the specifications to include detailed review and the discussion of net zero building design components. Some of the specific times when pre-installation meetings are important include the installation of insulation; mechanical systems; windows; doors; and water-, vapor-, and air-control layers.

All subcontractors involved with each specific material or system need to be part of these pre-installation meetings. For example, the pre-installation meeting for the air barrier should include the exterior cladding installer or mason, the window installer, the air-barrier installer, the insulation subcontractor, and the general contractor. Additionally, mechanical and electrical subcontractors may be appropriate to include because their work involves penetrations through the air barrier. These meetings ensure that all parties are aware of the requirements and are working together to achieve the air-barrier goal.

REGULAR CONSTRUCTION MEETINGS

During construction, weekly meetings should be held to discuss construction-related issues. Net zero requirements should be tracked regularly at these meetings. Specific emphasis should be placed on critical lead-time aspects of the work so material ordering and mock-ups do not hold up construction (specifically, windows and water, air, vapor, and thermal components). These meetings should be documented following a similar action report process outlined during the design phase, with actions, dates, and responsible parties.

FIGURE 5.5. An enclosure mock-up, with many of the components and finishes complete, confirms the assembly. This mock-up was made as a corner of the building, with wall, window, and roof conditions, so that it could be blower door tested. Mock-ups help ensure proper water drainage and air-barrier connection from typical wall conditions to windows.

TEAM ASSESSMENT MEETINGS

To ensure that the construction team continues to work together as well as possible, set aside a part of a regular construction meeting every couple of months to assess how the project is going overall and with the net zero components. These opportunities for open conversation help alleviate misunderstandings that can arise due to the innovative and challenging aspects of net zero projects.

Compatibility Matrix

To choose the best compatible materials for water, air, vapor, and thermal barrier layers, the contractor develops a compatibility matrix that includes all the products used for the control layers. This ensures that there are no warranty, responsibility, or other compatibility problems. It is critical that the builder fill out a compatibility matrix with the final products that will be installed so there are no misunderstandings. Table 5.1 shows the different components of the control layers and the compatibility between the layers to ensure the integrity of the building envelope layers over time.

Mock-ups

Often construction mock-ups focus mainly on aesthetics, particularly color and material choices. In addition to these concerns, mock-ups on a net zero project help to ensure that the materials and installations procedures will work as designed and that the construction team understands the drawings and specifications. This is the chance to establish clear installation procedures, solve problems before the overall installation, and test the components and assembly before installation.

Two types of mock-ups are useful on net zero projects. The first are freestanding mock-ups not connected to the building; the second are building-installed mock-ups (see figure 5.5). Freestanding mock-ups can be built earlier in the construction process than is possible when the mock-up is part of the building. In mock-ups involving the roof, having a mock-up on the ground is easier for the construction team to build and for the design team to review. On larger projects we often specify a freestanding mock-up in addition to the building-installed mock-up. On smaller projects a building-installed mock-up can be used with the installation of the first window or a corner of the building that includes the roof conditions. Building-installed mock-ups should

TABLE 5.1. COMPATIBILITY MATRIX

| ITEM | MATERIAL | RESPONSIBILITY | SPECIFICATIONS SECTION | ITEM | |
				Underslab Vapor Barrier	Underslab Rigid Insulation
Underslab Vapor Barrier	Stego Wrap	general contractor	07 2100		
Underslab Rigid Insulation	Shelter Enterprises Shelterfoam EPS	general contractor	07 2100		
Foundation Waterproofing	Tremco 260	barrier subcontractor	07 1200		
Drainage Board and Rigid Insulation	2⅜" DPI board	barrier subcontractor	07 1200		
Exterior Sheathing	Lafarge exterior sheathing	framing and sheathing subcontractors	08 5700		
Air Barrier	Tremco ExoAir 110/120	barrier subcontractor	07 2200		
Window Angle	Grainger UHMW polyethylene angle	window subcontractor	08 5700		
Membrane Flashing at Grade	Hyload flashing system	masonry subcontractor	04 8100		
Metal Flashing	masonry: Sandell's SS metal flashing; windows: LEED Himmel	masonry and window subcontractors	07 6200		

proposed material   approved material   material compatible with itself

compatibility confirmation required   compatibility confirmed by manufacturer   compatibility not required

also include wall penetrations, such as structural, mechanical, and electrical penetrations as appropriate to each project.

Submittal Review

During construction, the builder provides documentation (called submittals) that the products and systems installed in the building comply with requirements in the construction drawings and specifications.

Careful review of submittals for net zero products and shop drawings by all parties is particularly important to ensure that the contract drawings and specifications are followed. In general, substitutions on net zero components should be discouraged unless significant improvements or cost savings are anticipated and passed on to the owner without compromising net zero goals. Specified materials are carefully selected for certain properties and characteristics that may not be obvious to those unfamiliar with the requirements for net zero buildings.

ITEM							ITEM
Foundation Waterproofing	Drainage Board and Rigid Insulation	Exterior Sheathing	Air Barrier	Window Angle	Membrane Flashing at Grade	Metal Flashing	
			▓		▓		Underslab Vapor Barrier
			▓				Underslab Rigid Insulation
	▓		▓		▓		Foundation Waterproofing
	▓						Drainage Board and Rigid Insulation
			▓				Exterior Sheathing
					▓		Air Barrier
				▓			Window Angle
						▓	Membrane Flashing at Grade
						▓	Metal Flashing

Inspections

Frequent inspections should be scheduled throughout net zero building construction to avoid problems. Especially on larger projects, a clerk of the works or specialty envelope consultant should perform inspections. In particular, the installation of air, water, and vapor barriers and insulation require thorough inspections. With these layered components it is important to ensure that individual layers are not covered by the next step of the construction process without inspection. Other specialized net zero mechanical, electrical, and renewable-energy requirements also demand careful attention and inspection.

Commissioning

Commissioning on net zero projects is twofold, involving not just the mechanical and electrical systems but also the building envelope. Commissioning begins in design with review of systems and envelope design and continues through construction documents and construction, even though it is considered primarily a part of building start-up to ensure operation that is consistent with design.

The first step in commissioning is making sure that both the envelope and mechanical agents are selected during schematic design so they each can have input into the building design

FIGURE 5.6. Careful inspection of window flashing is a critical part of the enclosure performance because of the conjunction of many different materials.

FIGURE 5.7. The process of air-infiltration testing, which includes fog testing, helps to ensure proper assembly of materials.

For the George D. Aiken Center at the University of Vermont, the university hired an envelope specialist to do the envelope commissioning. His work included inspections and testing, beginning with the construction of the mock-up and continuing daily during the course of the construction of the envelope.

Because mock-ups are constructed sequentially and subsequent layers of materials can obscure previous work, it is important that the envelope commissioning agent be present during mock-up construction to observe and inspect installation of materials. The work of the mock-up often serves as a learning experience for the contractor(s), and since it serves as an example of how the remainder of the project is to be constructed, deficiencies are corrected on the spot.

The first few instances of window installation on the building were inspected and tested for airtightness and water-infiltration resistance in order to detect and correct any deficiencies before proceeding with further window installation. The portions of the building containing the windows were depressurized; then the windows, mullions, and sealed perimeter were checked with a fog generator to detect air currents caused by infiltration. Water-penetration testing was also performed under depressurization, by applying a broad, constant stream of water over the outside surface of the window assembly.

The envelope commissioning agent supervised the testing of the Aiken Center's airtightness, including inspection of the contractor's pretest preparations and blower door testing for verification of the building's performance. The building's airtightness exceeded the specified requirement by a significant margin, due in no small part to the envelope commissioning agent's diligent inspection and progress testing as well as the owner's commitment and the care and effort of the design and construction teams.

throughout the process. This input is regarding the intent, the details for execution, and the delivery process. For reference, use NIBS Guideline 3-2012 along with ASHRAE Guideline 0-2005, *The Commissioning Process*.[3] In the commissioning process the owner's project requirements should also be followed. For mechanical systems commissioning, it is particularly critical that the commissioning agent review the design intent, the OPR, the systems design concept, and detailed drawings, and then finally provide inspection and final testing during construction.

Testing

For successful commissioning and to ensure performance, testing is necessary. For mechanical systems, appropriate testing procedures relate to specific mechanical systems design. Mechanical-systems testing has been a standard construction industry practice for long enough that we will not address detailed procedures here. But we do recommend that commissioning and testing of lighting and lighting controls be included in the commissioning scope of work, as lighting controls may require some care to ensure proper operation.

Envelope commissioning and testing involves several critical areas: air leakage, water penetration, visual inspection, and moisture content of materials. Blower door tests, which we discuss in chapter 6, gauge air leakage. Typically, we use either a mock-up or a corner of the building to set up blower door tests and water-penetration tests. That way, multiple tests, inspections, and review can occur simultaneously so the owner, design team, and trades all can participate more easily.

In 2009 and 2010, South Mountain Company designed and built a cluster of eight net zero and near-net-zero single-family homes on Martha's Vineyard in Massachusetts for the Island Housing Trust. These houses exemplify a quote by energy consultant Andy Shapiro: "There is no such thing as a net zero house, only net zero families." Of the eight houses, half are 1,447 sf three-bedroom units, and half are 1,251 sf two-bedroom units. All have full basements. The homes were designed to be capable of net zero performance, and each includes a 5.04 kW PV array to power the all-electric systems of the houses.

FIGURE 5.8. The houses at Eliakim's Way on Martha's Vineyard, each with PV panels on the south-facing roof to produce electricity and south-façade glazing to provide solar heating.

After the first year, two households were net zero, two were within 20 percent of net zero, and four others consumed more energy. Measured in energy intensity, the houses varied in total energy use by nearly a factor of two, meaning one house consumed almost twice as much energy as another. These buildings were built to the following standards: R-50 roofs, R-31 walls, R-20 below grade, R-5 windows, and very low air-infiltration rates. Heating and cooling is provided by a single-zone, minisplit heat pump with a single wall cassette in the main living area. Supplemental bedroom heating is provided with radiant heating panels. The single-source wall cassette provides adequate heat except in the coldest weather as long as bedroom doors are left open. As the graphs in figure 5.10 indicate, use of radiant ceiling panel varied significantly, although all heating ranged from 15–30 percent of total energy consumption. Domestic hot water is provided by highly insulated, direct electric water heating. Domestic hot water is typically the largest load, indicating that either solar hot water or a heat-source water heater could improve overall energy performance. Cooling use varied by a factor of twenty-six to one, indicating that the perception of need for cooling varies significantly among different occupants. However, cooling was a relatively small part of the overall load. Figures 5.9 and 5.10 show the variation in total use as well as different types of use.[4]

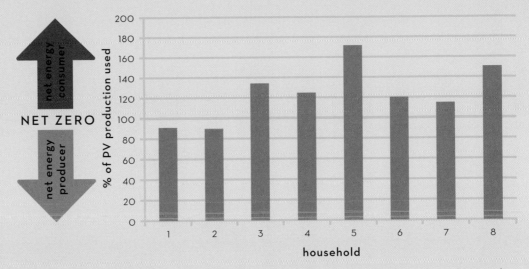

FIGURE 5.9. The annual energy use of each home compared with the average PV production varies by household: some are below net zero while some are above.

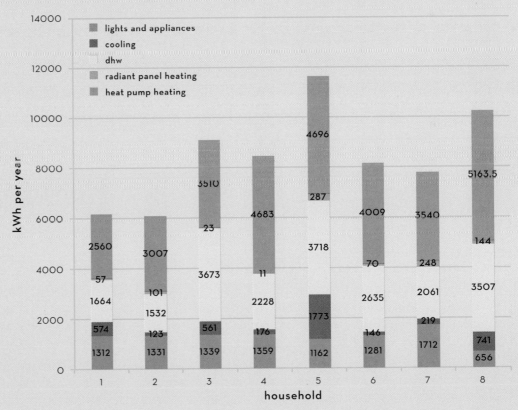

FIGURE 5.10. The breakdown of energy by use in each of the eight houses shows domestic hot water use is higher than heating use.

In addition to testing, it is critical that there is daily inspection of thermal, water, vapor, and air barrier work. On large projects a clerk of the works trained to understand building enclosure project requirements is invaluable. If not a clerk, a consultant or other specialist can be hired. The builders should also employ someone with the explicit responsibility for overseeing air, water, vapor, and thermal envelope details.

Occupancy and Operation

Net zero performance requires connecting people with their buildings. Up to 20–25 percent variation in energy consumption can occur when different people use the same building. Educating building owners is key to success, as net zero buildings employ new technologies and require user interaction. Owners need to learn about daylighting, the reduction of artificial lighting, natural ventilation for increased comfort, and the associated reduced energy consumption. Understanding how the daylighting systems work may give building users a greater appreciation of natural light and its benefits. Mechanical systems are often less complicated in net zero buildings than conventional buildings and therefore easier to operate and understand for the user.

Monitoring System Choices: Low and High Tech

Continued monitoring is a critical component of all net zero buildings to make sure they perform as designed—and they should be designed to monitor performance easily. In the first year of operation, performance should be reviewed every month to uncover any problems and allow for system adjustment. During the first heating and cooling season, data can reveal if there are any glitches requiring attention. For the life of the building, the total building energy consumption should be reviewed annually, at a minimum, to confirm ongoing performance. As part of the monitoring process, heating degree days and solar insolation data for the year should be compared with typical years to see if atypical annual weather conditions are impacting performance.

FIGURE 5.12. There are numerous ways to engage occupants and visitors in the environmental design, features, and performance of net zero buildings. *Left,* exposed piping and tipping buckets for rainwater collection at the University of Vermont's George D. Aiken Center. *Middle,* signage explaining unique, net-zero-related aspects of the building at the Bosarge Education Center at Coastal Maine Botanical Gardens. *Right,* a "truth wall" showing wall construction and an exposed insulation cavity, also at the Bosarge Education Center.

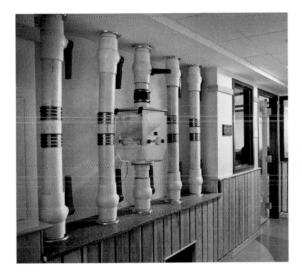

There are two basic approaches to monitoring: low tech and high tech. The lowest-tech option uses analog meters like those used by electric companies, shown in figure 5.11. You can buy them inexpensively, refurbished and in excellent condition. With all electric net zero buildings, this is an easy solution. When circuits and panels are laid out, there can be separate subpanels specified for lighting, ventilation, heating, cooling, plug loads, and hot water, making it easy to identify and monitor different building loads. This system does require that someone record the meter readings on a monthly basis.

The high-tech route includes expensive, complex digital systems. For larger projects, direct digital control (DDC) systems commonly monitor and control the building. Simpler digital systems can be connected to the Internet, enabling detailed data to be downloaded anywhere and, if desired, made available to the public. These Internet-based systems require additional wiring but can be operated from both on- and off-site and are very useful in tracking energy. In addition, there are monitoring systems that simply attach to individual circuits so each circuit can be monitored. There are simple programs that track the loads and generate graphs that function well as educational tools. For many situations, the simple monitoring systems with electric metering are suitable. These can be located in the public lobby area, so building users can see the impact of their use on an ongoing basis. All of these monitoring systems require electrical layout in order to collect useful data.

Celebrating and Educating for Inspiration

The accomplishment of the net zero goal through an integrated design and construction process presents the exciting opportunity to share the experience, educate others, and promote net zero projects. Of course the first part of this is the education of the building users and owners, but this process can extend into physical and Internet communities. The following are a few options for celebration and education.

FIGURE 5.13. At the Coastal Maine Botanical Gardens, Gunnar Hubbard of Thornton Tomasetti, the project's sustainability consultant, addresses those gathered to celebrate the opening of the net zero Bosarge Family Education Center.

NET ZERO CHEERLEADER/ADVOCATE

Designate a net zero advocate for the building, a building user who is knowledgeable and excited about the building, can act as a resource, and can point out to others its net zero mission and purpose.

SIGNAGE

Because net zero buildings do not necessarily look different from other buildings, users and visitors can be unaware of its unique features. Simple signage can educate visitors and remind occupants to use the building properly.

PUBLIC OUTREACH

When your net zero building is first occupied, host an open house. Inviting legislative members and other local policymakers can spur future legislation, funding, and interest in similar projects. Newspaper, Internet, and other media coverage can spread the word that net zero buildings are feasible now. Virtual tours, websites, and blogs exploring and explaining the project are all positive modes of outreach. Ongoing and/or intermittent tours can also be very successful in reaching the public. Thousands of people a year come to visit the NRG Systems building, for example, perhaps because the public is looking for examples of a net zero future for our buildings, communities, and planet. When visitors walk into a 70,000 sf renewably powered building that is healthy and beautiful, they are inspired. It gives them hope that a net zero future is not only possible but practical.

ONE-YEAR CELEBRATION

After a year of documented net zero performance, throw a party celebrating the achievements of all involved—the design and construction teams, the stakeholders and donors, and the owners and users of the building. Sharing and celebrating success inspires others to take concrete action now.

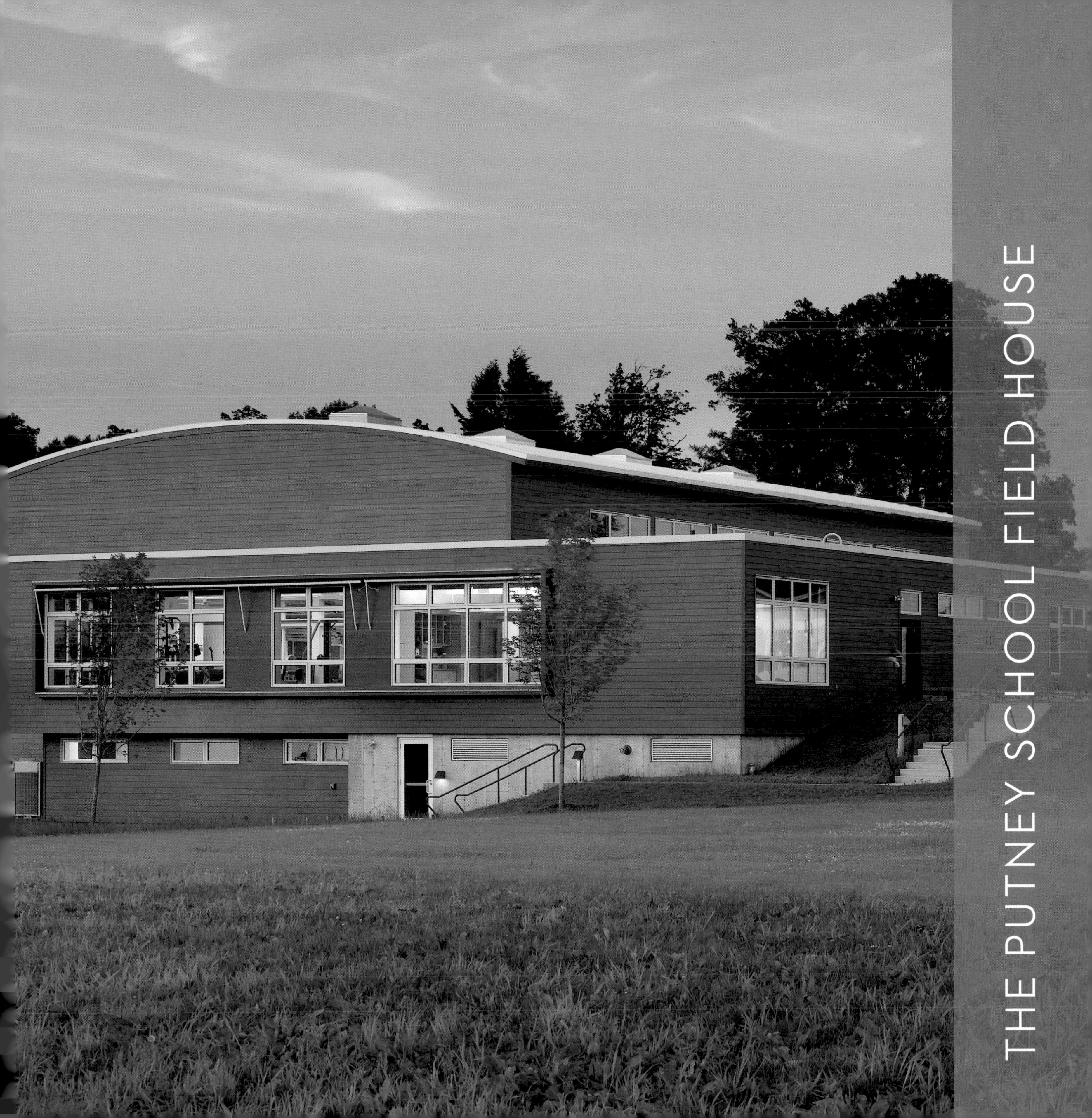

THE PUTNEY SCHOOL FIELD HOUSE

DESIGN PROFILE

Building Profile	Building Name:	**The Putney School Field House**	
	Location:	Putney, Vermont	
	Occupancy Date:	November, 2007	
	Square Footage:	16,814	
	Certification:	LEED-NB 3.0 Platinum	
Energy Profile	Energy Reference Year:	November, 2011–November, 2012	
	Total Energy Consumption:	42,805 kWh	
	Total Energy Production:	54,405 kWh	
	Energy Intensity:	Actual:	9 kBtu/sf-yr
		Modeled:	11 kBtu/sf-yr
		Actual with Renewables:	-2 kBtu/sf-yr
Building Envelope	Construction Type:	Composite—steel and wood	
	Insulation Values:	Walls (gym):	R-45, 17" of cellulose
		Walls (all other spaces):	R-45, 8" of cellulose, 2" of polyisocyanurate
		Roof:	R-60, 9" continuous polyisocyanurate
		Foundation (slab perimeter):	R-10, 2" EPS panel to 48" depth
		Foundation (slab-edge joint):	R-15, 3" EPS
		Foundation (sub-slab):	R-20, 5" EPS under whole slab
	Air Infiltration:	Final Blower Door:	1,625 cfm50
			0.065 cfm50/sf exterior surface area
	Windows/Skylights:	Windows:	U-value 0.12, SHGC 0.55 or 0.33, VT 0.57
		Skylights (offices):	U-value 0.39, SHGC 0.30, VT 0.47
		Skylights (gymnasium):	U-value 0.35, SHGC 0.74, VT 0.66
Mechanical/ Electrical Systems	Heating System:	Daikin VRVIII Heat Recovery air-source heat pump	
		Annual COP (estimated):	2.3
		Annual HSPF (estimated):	7.8
	Cooling System:	Heat pump disabled for cooling with the exception of the internal office	
	Ventilation System:	Dedicated ventilation, constant volume in small spaces, variable volume in gym with CO_2 and RH control; manual boost provided in exercise, locker, and bathrooms, which are ventilated only when occupied, via occupancy sensor	
	Energy Recovery System:	SEMCO enthalpy wheel	
		Average Effectiveness:	75 percent
	Lighting System/Controls:	High-efficiency super T-8, automatic step-dimming in gym, daylighting cutoff in other spaces; occupancy sensors in all occupied spaces	
	Hot Water:	Electric hot water	
	Renewable System:	16 Zomeworks tracking PV arrays	
		Installed System Size:	36.8 kW

THE PUTNEY SCHOOL FIELD HOUSE
The First Net Zero, LEED Platinum Secondary-School Building in the United States

This is not just a gym. . . . We want this to be a place where our students can learn about being environmentally responsible, so that later in life, when they are making choices, they can say it's possible.

—RANDY SMITH, CFO, THE PUTNEY SCHOOL

t began with a vision. The Putney School in Vermont wanted to design a field house that would support its independent and creative academic and environmental tradition, serve as a central social space for students as well as an indoor athletic facility, and meet the sustainability goals outlined in the school's forward-thinking strategic plan. But like all visions, this one had a challenge to overcome: it had only a $3 million budget.

Project Overview

The Putney School had long yearned to build its field house, and when the opportunity finally arose, they thought long and hard about how to create a long-term asset for students, staff, faculty, and community. Their top priority was to build a model environmental building that would become a center for health on the campus. But the school also wanted the new building to enhance social energy and draw students into it. The field house was to be a core building on the campus, not a distant destination but an inviting central meeting place to encourage the development of strong connections between students, faculty, and staff.

FIGURE CS3.1. View of field house from playing fields.

So the building was sited at the heart of the campus, next to their dining hall—easy access that would ensure more frequent use. The design included both an outside courtyard space and an inside social space for students to hang out and play games, all near the fitness facilities, allowing exercise to be integrated into daily community life.

Upon entering the field house from the dining hall, you first encounter the social space, which is connected to the gymnasium one story below by bleachers—creating a continuous flow from the dining hall, through the outside courtyard, social space, and bleachers to the gym. Close-by but separate, a flexible space for yoga, movement, and aerobics; a strength and conditioning room; locker and shower facilities; and offices fill out the upper floor. Glass between the gym and the strength and conditioning room further reinforces the connection of spaces and activities and provides views to the outdoors. The lower floor contains the gym space, which includes a rock-climbing wall; a waxing room for cross-country skiing; and a mechanical room that contains the composters for the composting toilets, electrical and PV utilities, water heaters, and an energy-recovery ventilator (ERV) unit.

Vision and Goals

Not only did the school envision an ultra-green building that encouraged social networks and enhanced community life, it also wanted to make sure that the design fit in aesthetically with the existing campus facilities—an eclectic mix of old Vermont farm buildings and more modern buildings.

In keeping with a tradition of including students in planning the school's built environment, the larger community of students, faculty, and staff were involved in the decision-making process and even designed and built some parts of the building.

Energy

From the beginning, the Putney School's budget and vision for the project were not aligned. As we told the school, "We know we can design a great field house for $3 million, and we know we can produce one of the best environmental buildings in the country, but we don't know if we can achieve the two together."

But we could promise the school that we would design the field house at three different performance levels and provide comparative capital and operating costs for the three design options over a twenty-year period, so that they would have the information they needed to make an informed and prudent decision about the direction of their new building. We designed a $3 million building following conventional practices but built to a slightly higher standard than most new secondary school construction at that time. We also designed what we called a high-performance building that would perform 20–30 percent better than code. And we designed a net zero building, or the best environmental building we could envision.

Randy Smith, CFO of the Putney School, recognized that future energy cost increases and price volatility could threaten the school's ability to provide high-quality education to their students. The board of trustees agreed and realized they could either raise another $1–2 million for an endowment to pay for continued energy and operation costs for their new building, or they could raise the same amount before construction to build a building with no energy costs that would be

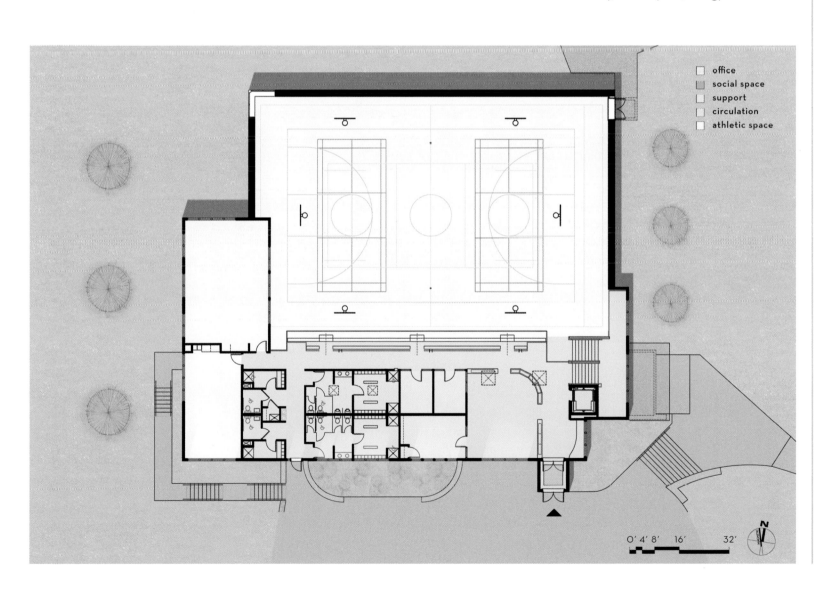

FIGURE CS3.2. The main floor plan of the field house highlights the connection between the entry, social space, and gym.

office
social space
support
circulation
athletic space

0' 4' 8' 16'   32'

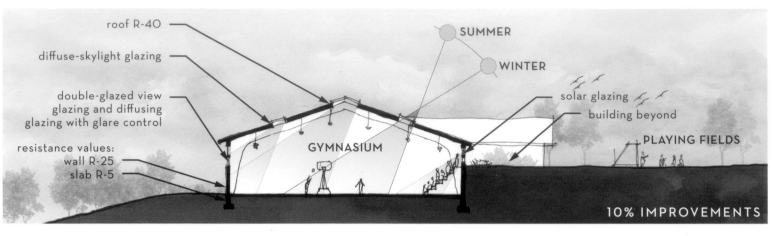

roof R-40

diffuse-skylight glazing

double-glazed view glazing and diffusing glazing with glare control

resistance values:
wall R-25
slab R-5

SUMMER

WINTER

solar glazing

building beyond

GYMNASIUM

PLAYING FIELDS

10% IMPROVEMENTS

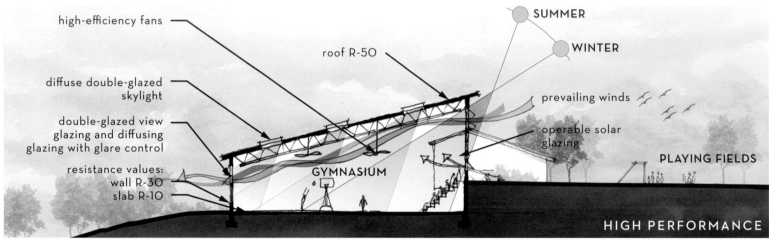

high-efficiency fans

roof R-50

diffuse double-glazed skylight

double-glazed view glazing and diffusing glazing with glare control

resistance values:
wall R-30
slab R-10

SUMMER

WINTER

prevailing winds

operable solar glazing

GYMNASIUM

PLAYING FIELDS

HIGH PERFORMANCE

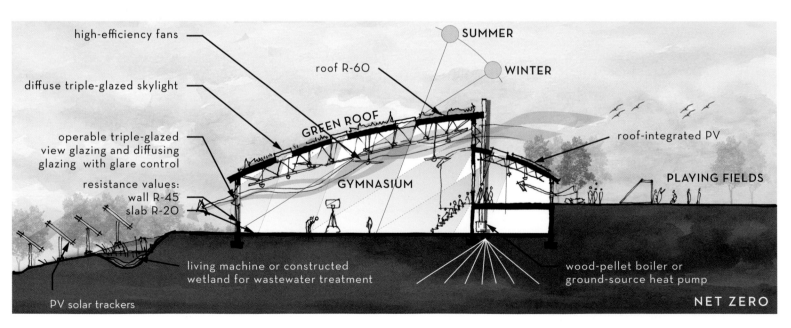

high-efficiency fans

roof R-60

diffuse triple-glazed skylight

operable triple-glazed view glazing and diffusing glazing with glare control

resistance values:
wall R-45
slab R-20

PV solar trackers

living machine or constructed wetland for wastewater treatment

GREEN ROOF

GYMNASIUM

SUMMER

WINTER

roof-integrated PV

PLAYING FIELDS

wood-pellet boiler or ground-source heat pump

NET ZERO

FIGURE CS3.3. During the design process, the team evaluated multiple building performance options, including 10 percent better than code complaint, high performance, and net zero (*left*). The team analyzed the construction and operating costs for each building option as they addressed the school's short-, medium-, and long-term goals for environmental and energy sustainability. *Below*, the estimated costs for the building options ranged from $3.5 million to $5 million; the projected first-year energy costs ranged from $22,500 to $0; and estimated total CO_2 emissions ranged from 130,000 lb to 0 lb per year.

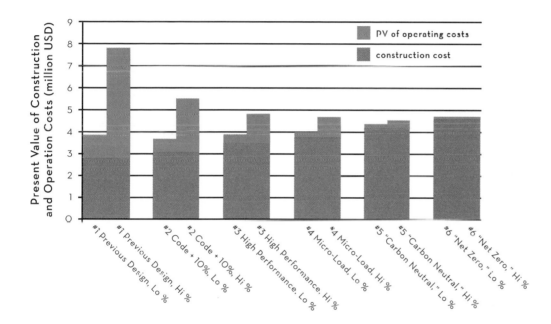

FIGURE CS3.4. Flex space/yoga room

an environmental model for students and other schools. Framed in this way, it became an easy choice for the board to support the net zero option, exciting and inspiring donors and the entire Putney School community.

BUILDING ENCLOSURE

To achieve the net zero goal, the field house was superinsulated, with extensive attention to air sealing and minimizing thermal bridging in the enclosure. High insulation levels, including an R-60 roof, R-45 above-grade walls, R-20 below grade slab and foundation walls, and R-5 windows, contributed to a 77 percent reduction in heating energy use as compared to ASHRAE Standard 90.1-2007 baseline building.[1] All insulation used in the field house was chosen with the additional goal of minimizing global warming and ozone depletion: the wall insulation is primarily cellulose, the roof insulation is isocyanurate foam boards, and below-grade insulation is zero-ozone depleting, low-global-warming-potential, high-density (2pcf) expanded polystyrene. To minimize thermal bridging, a unique composite structural system was used, combining wood-framed exterior walls with a steel structure and roof.

A prime factor in the high energy performance of the field house is its low air leakage, accomplished through careful envelope design and execution. It has a spray-on air barrier with compatible self-adhesive waterproof membrane where appropriate on the exterior of the sheathing; airtight connections of this spray-on barrier to the roof

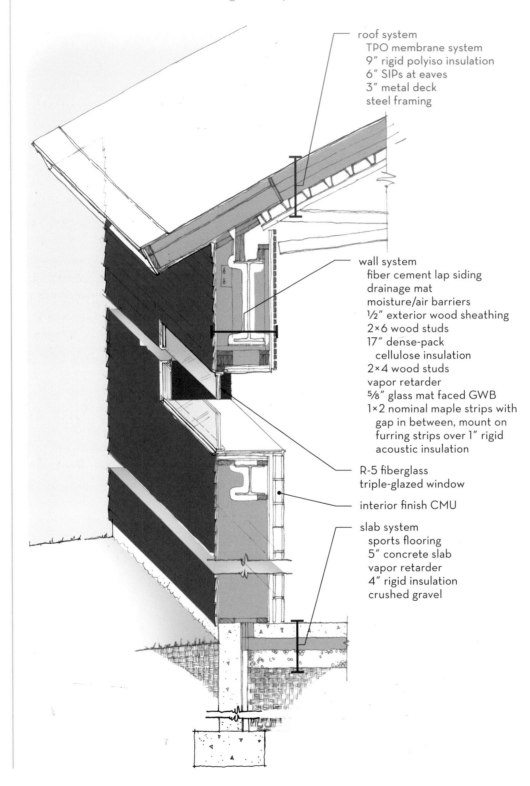

FIGURE CS3.5. Standard building assembly.

roof system
  TPO membrane system
  9" rigid polyiso insulation
  6" SIPs at eaves
  3" metal deck
  steel framing

wall system
  fiber cement lap siding
  drainage mat
  moisture/air barriers
  ½" exterior wood sheathing
  2×6 wood studs
  17" dense-pack
    cellulose insulation
  2×4 wood studs
  vapor retarder
  ⅝" glass mat faced GWB
  1×2 nominal maple strips with
    gap in between, mount on
    furring strips over 1" rigid
    acoustic insulation

R-5 fiberglass
triple-glazed window

interior finish CMU

slab system
  sports flooring
  5" concrete slab
  vapor retarder
  4" rigid insulation
  crushed gravel

sheathing and to the foundation; tightly sealed, operable windows; and ultra-low-leakage dampers on all ventilation penetrations. The field house achieved an impressively low air-leakage rate of 0.065 cfm/sf of building shell above-ground at 50 pascals test pressure.

PASSIVE SOLAR AND DAYLIGHTING

Located on a north-facing hillside with spectacular views to the north and west, the site is not optimal for passive solar design. South-facing clerestory windows in the gym use high-solar-heat-gain glass to maximize solar gain. Additionally, light-guiding blinds bounce direct sunlight up onto the ceiling, where it contributes to ambient lighting rather than direct-beam lighting (which would be disruptive to gym users). Triple-layer, semidiffusing skylights in the gym, totaling approximately 4 percent of the floor area, also contribute to daylighting.

When the gym space is occupied and daylighting is not sufficient, a minimum of 30 fc of illumination is maintained by three-step, T5 light fixtures with automatic, open-loop daylighting controls. A third pair of lamps in each of these T5 fixtures can be turned on for 50 fc of illumination. North-, east-, and west-facing windows provide additional daylight and views to the pastoral surroundings. These windows all use low-solar-heat-gain glass, and the west-facing glazing is controlled with awnings to reduce the potential for overheating during the summer.

HEATING AND COOLING

In order to achieve net zero performance with on-site renewable electricity generation, the field house uses heat pumps. The initial design included a ground-source heat-pump system, but the engineer suggested switching to an air-source system. This change saved $100,000 in the initial mechanical system cost, but to make up for the decreased efficiency of the air-source system, an additional $35,000 of PV was required, resulting in net savings of $65,000. (See *Heat-Pump Choices: The Putney School* in chapter 7.) An additional benefit of the air-source system is that it is much simpler to operate.

Although air-source heat pumps can provide air-conditioning, the field house relies on natural ventilation to provide passive cooling. The direct digital control system automatically opens windows if the building requires cooling when the outdoors is cooler than the indoors. If building users want to open windows, when it is warmer outside, they can do so only by engaging a manual override and the windows will automatically close after a certain period of time to maintain control of the indoor temperature. Even without the use of air-conditioning, because of the sun control and the high levels of insulation, this building is one of the coolest spaces on campus during the summer.

VENTILATION

An energy-recovery ventilator serves CO_2-controlled variable air-volume terminals in each space. Because the general occupancy is typically low but can swell quickly, incorporating a variable-volume ventilation system significantly reduces energy usage. On cold days outdoor air entering through the ventilation system can be electrically preheated to keep frost from developing, though this system rarely operates because of low relative humidity indoors.

Air to the large gym and social space is recirculated to the toilet rooms and locker rooms to provide makeup air for these spaces, reducing the total outdoor air required. CO_2 sensors regulate the amount of air supplied to the gym and social space, and occupancy sensors control the air for the locker rooms if they are occupied while the gym and social space is not. The three small offices in the building are ventilated with small, individual ERV units controlled by occupancy sensors. Because these offices may be in use when the rest of the building is not, the small ERVs avoid the need to run the larger ERV when only a few individuals are present.

ENERGY-PERFORMANCE MONITORING

Intended as a learning and teaching tool, a submetering system more complex than is typical of this kind of building was installed in the field house. Watt meters connected to a DDC system tally the energy use of all subsystems, including heat pumps, lighting, and ventilation. In addition, the total building import of electricity from the grid, export of electricity to the grid, and generation of electricity by the PV system is monitored. These monitored data have been used to make adjustments to the ventilation algorithm; identify and solve lighting-control issues; and spotlight the amount of energy being wasted by the electric hot-water tanks. Monitoring has indicated that the energy intensity of the building is extremely low, at 9 kBtu/sf-yr (30 kWh/sm-yr). This includes energy for all building uses, but it should be noted that the field house temperatures fluctuate more than those of a typical building. Heating energy consumption is less than 1.0 Btu/sf-HDD.

RENEWABLE ELECTRICITY

To achieve the net zero goal, a substantial investment in on-site, renewable energy was required. The design team studied, priced, and assessed various building-mounted and site-mounted PV options for performance, long-term value, construction cost, and aesthetics. From these options, the team chose 36.8 kW of tracking solar collectors and installed them on the north side of the field house in an open field with full southern exposure.

Healthy and Sustainable Strategies

To provide a healthy indoor environment, the building was designed to optimize indoor air quality, daylighting, and views. Automatic and manually operable windows allow for natural ventilation and nighttime flushing to recirculate interior air. CO_2

sensors control ventilation in the majority of interior spaces, providing the appropriate ventilation to building occupants.

The fixed, light-redirecting louvers installed in the gym clerestory windows deliver daylight deep into the field house. Adjustable light-redirecting blinds in the social space enhance and control daylighting according to the daily needs of the space. Solar glare control is provided by EcoVeil roller shades, located on all south-facing windows. An exterior-mounted, motorized fabric window awning on all west-facing windows reduces solar gain and undesirable glare.

All materials for the field house were specifically chosen for durability, environmental performance, LEED

point contributions, and cost. Site-harvested, locally milled, character-grade maple was used for wainscoting and paneling in the gymnasium space. All composite wood materials are formaldehyde-free, reducing the off-gassing of toxic chemicals.

Composting toilets and waterless urinals reduce water consumption by 64 percent over a typical building.

Collaborative Process

As Emily Jones, the director of the Putney School, put it, "The Putney Field House is not only a shining example of sustainable architecture and not only a beautiful space, but it is a wonderful testament to the power of collaboration."

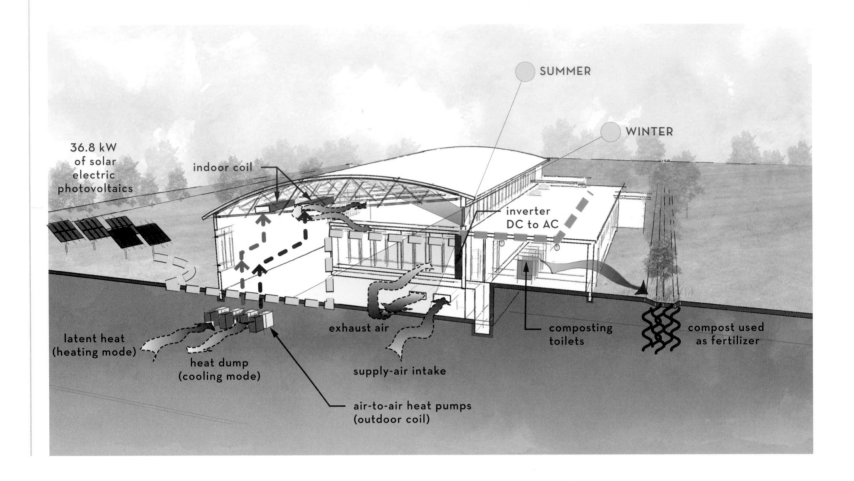

36.8 kW
of solar
electric
photovoltaics

indoor coil

SUMMER

WINTER

inverter
DC to AC

latent heat
(heating mode)

heat dump
(cooling mode)

exhaust air

composting
toilets

compost used
as fertilizer

supply-air intake

air-to-air heat pumps
(outdoor coil)

Lessons Learned

Including faculty, staff, board members, students, and local community members in the design process turned out to be key to the project's success. The integrated design process began with a kickoff meeting and continued throughout the project with design workshops, charrettes, and presentations. Daylong work sessions were integral to the collaborative design process. Each session began at the school's morning assembly with the design team presenting past work and inviting the community to an afternoon charrette. Other collaboration efforts included meetings with the school's facility committee, further generating and refining ideas and strategies.

Innovative projects happen when the ambitious vision and goals of a client are combined with a committed and caring design and construction team experienced in the challenges of trying out new ideas. Perhaps one of the most rewarding aspects of the project was that it inspired the school to initiate a master planning process for a net zero campus. As the school had hoped, the field house has become a favorite spot on campus and an inspiration to students, faculty, staff, and visitors. The field house supports the school's underlying goal: to inspire and engage the students in making a better world.

6 | Principles for Net Zero Building Enclosures

The purpose of the building enclosure is to provide a controlled, comfortable environment for human activity separate from the outdoor environment. From the time when we called caves home and constructed tepees from animal skins, humans have sought out or made places that temper the natural environment, providing protection from rain, snow, cold, heat, and sun. But the complexity of accomplishing this goal has expanded exponentially. In the past, one or two layers of stone, animal skin, or wood separated people from the outdoors. In the modern world, our diverse desires for function and comfort have generated exacting demands regarding temperature, humidity, light, sound, and on and on. The choice of materials, technologies, and construction assembly offer millions of choices where there were once only a few options.

To maintain a comfortable interior environment and separate humans from external environmental pressures, the building enclosure relies on four specialized layers: a thermal-control layer, an air-control layer, a water-control layer, and a vapor-control layer. These control layers are critical to achieving a building's net zero goal, though they are required in any building project, net zero or not. These layers are analyzed in this chapter in terms of their ultimate purposes: providing thermal comfort to the building's occupants, controlling air movement, keeping water out, and controlling vapor infiltration or diffusion.

These layers also provide the basis for what makes a building durable—its ability to survive and remain productive and enjoyable for centuries. In order to achieve the higher levels of performance that a net zero project requires, the control layers are precisely detailed and often use higher-performance products or different assemblies of products than traditional projects.

The study of enclosures, interior environmental conditions, and occupant/building health is referred to as building science. Building science has recently become

FIGURE 6.1. Primitive shelters have for centuries provided human comfort by creating a separation from the environment. *Top*, the beehive huts on the island of Skellig Michael off Ireland. *Bottom*, a tepee summer home on the Red Lake Indian Reservation, Minnesota, 1923.

popular and continues to evolve as buildings become more and more complex and our energy performance goals become more stringent. Because our understanding of the effects of new building systems has not kept pace with their growing complexity, there has been a rise in building-related problems such as degradation from moisture and occupant health concerns. It is becoming increasingly important to understand all facets of the buildings we are constructing in order to understand the effects of each decision on building durability, occupant health, and energy conservation. We need, in other words, to know our building science.

As illustrated in detail in chapters 8–14, the location of the four control layers within the building enclosure depends on the mechanisms of air and water movement and the effect of temperature gradients. The materials used for these control layers are located and specified because of their ability to meet their particular functions: to provide thermal control, limit air infiltration, control water, and prevent vapor migration. Because they are often not durable when exposed to conditions such as UV rays, wind, and other detrimental external environmental forces, many of these products require additional protection. If the control layers are located within the building enclosure system and underneath finish layers, they can be protected from environmental conditions, increasing their lifespan and improving their ability to function as designed. A tempering layer is sometimes used to provide further control of the transition between the interior and the exterior environments of buildings.

None of the ideas on thermal, air, water, and vapor control layers as well as the mechanisms of water, air, and energy movement laid out in this chapter are radical. Any competent design and construction team can accomplish the goals presented here. However, all of the control layers and optional tempering layer must be designed in a thoughtful way in order to meet the net zero energy goal.[1]

Thermal Control

The thermal control layer is generally the easiest to understand, as the mechanisms of heat flow are constant and uncomplicated. Thermal control is probably what first comes to mind when one thinks of occupant comfort. It is the thermal control layer that allows a building to use less energy for heating or cooling while still maintaining ideal internal temperatures. Insulation, which provides thermal control, is a low-thermal-conductivity material that reduces heat movement. In most cases, the more insulation the better the thermal control and the easier it is to maintain internal occupant comfort.

R-VALUE

Conduction is the primary mechanism of heat transfer through a building enclosure, and the reduction of this transfer is the primary function of insulation. A material's resistance to heat transfer is called its R-value, reported in $ft^2 \times °F \times hr/Btu$, a term proposed in 1945 by Everett Shuman, a researcher at Penn State.[2] Before this time, the U-factor, which is the inverse of the R-value ($Btu/ft^2 \times °F \times hr$), was the primary gauge of insulation's effectiveness. U-value measures the rate of heat flow through a material, which made understanding the U-factor challenging to laypeople: as the insulative value of a material improved, the U factor got smaller. Because of this confusion, R-value is now more commonly used in comparing insulative properties: the thicker the material, the higher the R-value. Materials are typically rated as an R-value per thickness (per inch in the United States).

Because still air is a relatively effective insulator, most insulation products tend to be low-density, porous materials with a large proportion of small, air-filled voids. For example, fiberglass batt insulation is made of a generally conductive material, glass, but it is produced in such a way as to be mostly air voids. In fact, fiberglass insulation is 99.4 percent air.[3] On the other hand, foam insulations made from plastics have lower conductivity and a lower percentage of air-filled voids. Most materials create their insulating value by making sealed-off airspaces. The highest level of insulating value for perfectly still air is about R-5 per inch, thus most insulations are R-5 or less, depending on how well they stop air movement. Insulations can also use gases instead of air to achieve higher R-values per thickness, as do polyisocyanurate and urethane foam. Since these foams lose some of the gas over time due to outgassing, you should take into account the aged insulation R-value rather than the R-value when the foam is first installed in your building design and energy calculations.

The building enclosure must be designed in such a way as to address three mechanisms of heat transfer: conduction, convection, and radiation.

CONDUCTION. Conduction is the transfer of energy from atoms or molecules to neighboring atoms or molecules. Because this is the most significant means of transferring heat in solids, it is a prime concern in a building enclosure where a combination of materials are in contact with one another, bridging from inside to outside. The conductivity of different solids, even different metals, varies greatly. For example, a bar of copper conducts very well. If you hold one end in the fire, the other end will get very hot. In contrast, a plastic bar conducts very little. If you hold one end of a plastic bar in the fire, it will melt before the other end gets hot. Conduction in a building enclosure is addressed mainly through insulation.

CONVECTION. Convection involves the flow of gases or liquids in moving heat from one location to another. A common example of convection is a hot shower, which warms your body because the moving fluid (water) transfers its heat to you. In a building enclosure convection is controlled primarily by making any air gaps very small—so small that air can't move. The tiny bubbles in foam insulation or the tiny airspaces between

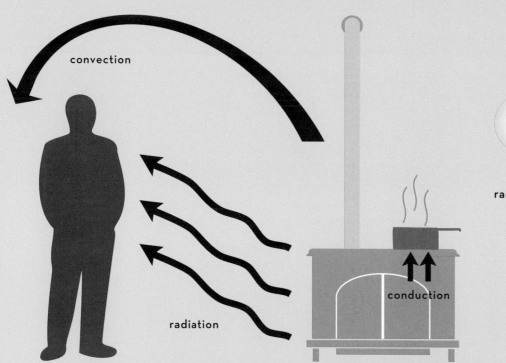

FIGURE 6.2. Heat is transferred from a woodstove to its surroundings by three mechanisms: conduction (direct contact), convection (air movement), and radiation (electromagnetic waves).

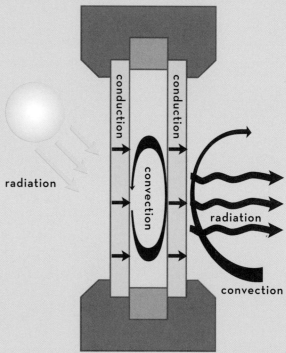

FIGURE 6.3. Convection between two panes of glass and radiation of the sun through the glass.

particles of cellulose insulation don't allow air movement and therefore stop convection through the building envelope.

RADIATION. Radiation is the transfer of energy by electromagnetic radiation, which is how we get heat from the sun. A woodstove gives off a lot of radiant heat in addition to creating heat by convection, which results in the warm air's rising. This mechanism of heat transfer can occur only in a direct line of sight through a gas or a vacuum, as electromagnetic waves cannot move through opaque solids. Since radiant heat can be transmitted through transparent glazing, heat-reflective or low emissivity (low-e) surfaces can be applied to windows to reflect or reduce emissions of radiant heat, respectively.

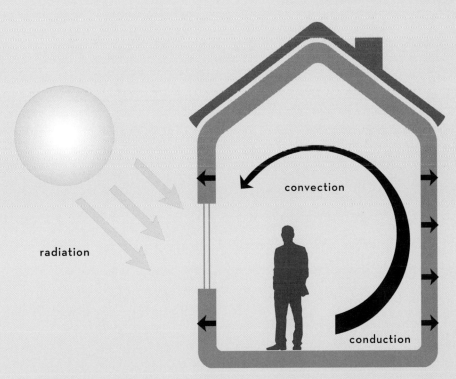

FIGURE 6.4. Heat flows through the building enclosure following the three mechanisms of heat transfer: conduction, convection, and radiation.

FIGURE 6.5. In some cases thermal bridging in the wall is very apparent. In the winter, when buildings are warm on the inside and cold on the outside, humidity can cause dew to settle at wood stud locations, creating thermal bridges through the insulated wall.

Of course the building enclosure is not made entirely of insulation but contains other materials less resistant to heat transfer, so we need two different R-values to adequately explain the thermal layer. The material R-value takes into account only the R-value contributed by the insulation itself and assumes that the insulation layer is unaffected by other materials in the assembly with different heat-transfer resistance. The assembly R-value accounts for the entire building assembly, including structural components and, as much as possible, inconsistencies related to installation. It is the assembly R-value that we use for accurate net zero energy design. The assembly R-value of each building system provides the raw data needed to perform accurate calculations to ensure the building energy performance of a net zero building. Cellulose and fiberglass are both commonly used as insulations that are blown into wall cavities and/or ceilings, whether under pressure (dense pack) or gravity (loose fill). Because cellulose is recycled paper, it is environmentally the best insulation and our first choice of insulation where it is appropriate. Blown-in insulation is appropriate for new and retrofit installations.

THERMAL BRIDGING: THE CHALLENGE

Structural materials are usually far more conductive than insulative materials. In order to design a building that will both stand up and limit heat transfer in the building enclosure, the design must use both conductive and insulative materials. Because of their higher conductivity, structural members—whether wood, metal, or concrete—can act as thermal bridges, creating short-circuits for heat flow through the building enclosure. The challenge for a well-designed net zero building is therefore to maximize insulative value and minimize thermal bridging.

Thermal bridging in an assembly causes cold spots that are sometimes even visible. It may also be possible to feel the location of structural members within a wall assembly by the cold spots. In cold climates thermal bridging is evident in the pattern of melting snow on the roofs of poorly insulated buildings. This can cause moisture issues in the building enclosure through condensation as the cold materials come into contact with warm, humid air. In the worst cases in steel or concrete structures, thermal bridging can cause increased heat loss of 50–80 percent.

No matter what type of insulation you intend to buy, in the United States it will have a product label similar to a nutrition label. In order to protect consumers, the Federal Trade Commission has enacted very clear rules about what information must be included on all residential insulation products. Insulation labels include an R-value for the material, as well as information about health, safety, and fire-hazard issues.

The market for insulation products, categorized by material and form (rigid, semirigid, batt, or loose), can seem overwhelming. When choosing which of the multitude of insulation materials to use, you should consider method of installation, durability, cost, toxicity, flammability, and environmental impact.

GLASS WOOL AND OTHER BATTS. Glass wool, more typically called fiberglass, is what comes to mind when most people think about insulation. But batts of fluffy insulation, often faced with paper or foil, can also be rock wool, sometimes cotton and recycled denim. The batt, or blanket of insulation, is installed between framing members and held in place either by friction or by stapling the facing to the framing members themselves. Because batts are almost impossible to install with a perfect fit at their perimeter, they create thermal short-circuiting: air currents next to framing or at joints allow air movement directly from the outside to the inside, which significantly lowers the real R-value below the advertised R-value. Glass and rock wool are not combustible products, but the paper facings are, so there can be a small fire hazard associated with these products as well. And because air can move through the batts, fire can also move through them, in contrast to cellulose, which has so little air that it stops fire migration as long as it is densely packed. Some batts, such as fiberglass, are relatively inexpensive but need to be properly protected against air movement and moisture.

CELLULOSE AND OTHER BLOWN-IN INSULATIONS. Although cellulose is the most common, fiberglass is also available for blown-in applications. Such insulations are a good choice for

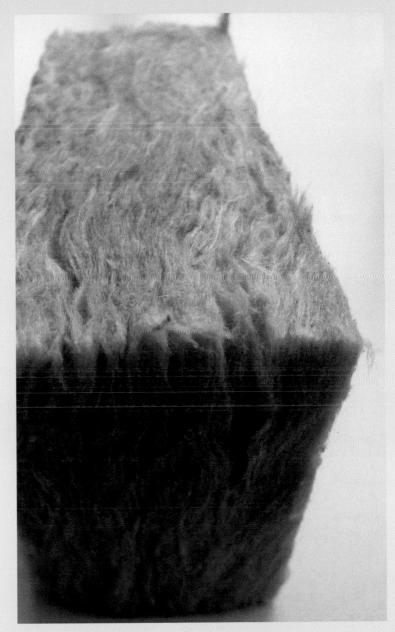

FIGURE 6.6. Rock-wool batt insulation, or stone wool, is made of naturally spun stone fiber.

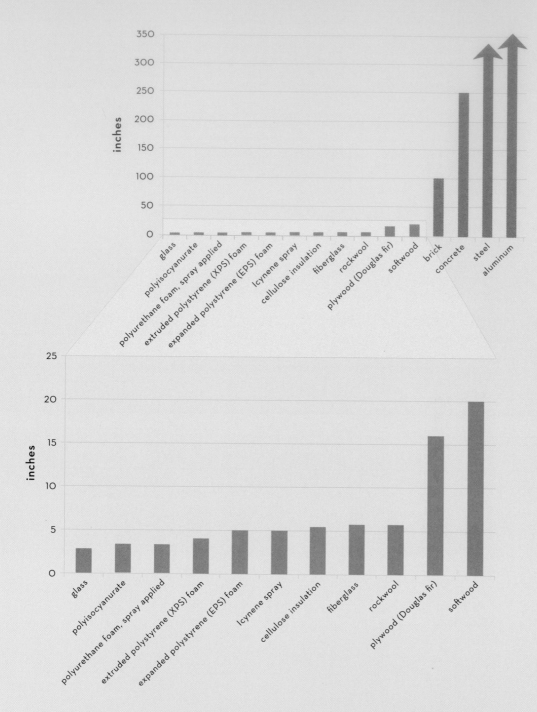

retrofit installation because they can be forced into existing cavities or through small holes drilled into either the exterior or interior of the building enclosure or added to attics as loose fill. They are also relatively low in cost and fairly high in R-value per thickness. Because air can move through loose fill, its use should be combined with careful air-control-layer installation. A challenge with blown-in cellulose insulation is that it can move or settle over time, which can cause the creation of cold spots in the building enclosure. This is solved by densely packing at 3.5 lb/sf pressure for cellulose. Cellulose can also be applied to open-wall cavities as a self-adhering, damp spray at a density that makes it self-supporting, so settlement is not a concern. Cellulose is chemically treated, typically with nontoxic borates, to be fire and pest retardant, and it does not generally pose a fire hazard, although it

FIGURE 6.7. Every building material has an R-value, a description of its heat-transfer ability. The higher the R-value, the higher the material's resistance to heat flow. This graph indicates the thickness of a material required to reach R-20. The higher the R-value of the material, the less material is required to achieve net zero.

FIGURE 6.9. Dense-pack cellulose is sprayed into open-stud cavities and tested for density to prevent gaps that can occur from settling over time.

FIGURE 6.10. Foam insulation is sprayed onto framing cavities and will expand to fill the entire cavity.

should not be used in contact with chimneys or flue pipes, or in any other locations not rated for direct contact with insulation.

SPRAY FOAM (POLYURETHANE/POLYICYNENE). Spray foams are mixed from two components and injected in place to adhere to the surrounding surfaces. Spray foams generally have high R-values but are also relatively expensive and require an experienced installer. There are two general categories of spray foam: closed-cell foam and open-cell foam. Closed-cell foam, usually available in medium or high densities, provides excellent R-values at higher densities and can serve as an air-control layer and stop moisture and vapor migration. Open-cell foam works as an air-control layer as well as an insulator but does not resist vapor migration. The embodied energy of spray foams is relatively high, and many use hydrofluorocarbons (HFCs), which are potent greenhouse gases. We recommend other products currently on the market, such as Icynene, that use only water as the blowing agent rather than harmful HFCs or chlorofluorocarbons (CFCs). More options will continue to evolve as the market demands less harmful solutions and superior performance. The chemical components used on-site to install spray urethane foams are hazardous, requiring protective gear for the applicators. If properly installed, however, the product is inert once the components have reacted to form the final material. Off-gassing

of volatile organic compounds (VOCs) from the cured material is negligible as well. Spray-foam insulation must be protected from fire by means of a thermal-barrier finish such as gypsum board or, in unfinished areas, with a spray-applied thermal barrier such as intumescent paint or cementitious coating.

RIGID FOAM BOARD. Most options for rigid insulation are easy to install, moderate in cost, and provide good insulating value. The three types used most often, in order from highest R-value per thickness to lowest, are polyisocyanurate (commonly referred to as polyiso), extruded polystyrene (XPS), and expanded polystyrene (EPS), though the R-value of polyiso is impacted by adjacent temperatures.[4] All are vapor permeable to differing extents (EPS being most permeable, at 3.5 perms/inch), though permeability declines, of course, with increasing thickness. They differ in their absorption of moisture, too, with XPS being the least absorptive. Water absorption of the other two types is greatly affected by their facing materials. All three types represent high-embodied energy. XPS insulations use ozone-depleting chemicals in their manufacture to some extent and represent high global-warming potential, while EPS and polyiso foams have low global-warming potentials. All are inert in their final form and do not off-gas VOCs. However, like spray foams, they are combustible plastic foam products and must be protected from fire by a thermal barrier.

FIGURE 6.11. To see the effects of thermal bridging, we use computer simulations. This graphic shows existing and proposed concrete slab and wall connections. In the existing wall (*left*) the cool colors penetrating into the building show where heat is lost with the potential for mold and moisture problems. In the proposed wall (*right*), with added continuous insulation, the joint is protected and heat loss is more uniform and reduced at the floor slab.

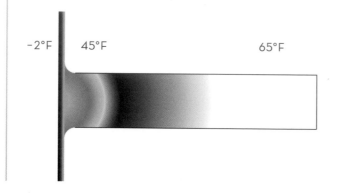

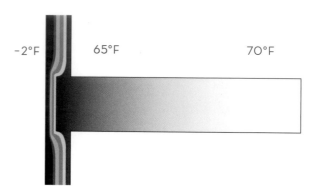

For high-performance buildings, wood is the preferred structural material because it is less conductive than metal or concrete, causing less concern for thermal bridging in the enclosure system. Even so, wood is still significantly more conductive than insulation, and any thermal bridging can decrease the assembly R-value.

The standard strategies for combating thermal bridging all rely on the same principle: developing a continuous layer of insulation somewhere within the building enclosure. Usually, this insulation layer is located to the exterior or interior of the structural assembly, functioning to eliminate thermal bridges that occur through the structural members. On a double-framed wall assembly, the continuous insulation layer is between the two stud walls, creating a thermal separation within the structure. While it is never possible to completely eliminate thermal bridging in a building enclosure, with careful planning it can be dramatically reduced.[5]

THERMAL PERFORMANCE FOR NET ZERO SUCCESS

We hope that by now we have established that insulation—and lots of it—is important to the success of a net zero building. Still,

the question almost always comes up, how much is enough? More specifically, what is the most cost-effective amount? It is true that each additional incremental amount of insulation is less cost-effective than the previous amount. However, if we are committed to constructing net zero buildings, then we need to determine the level of energy conservation that is cost-effective for the project based on the renewable energy source utilized to cover the loads of the specific building project. Renewables have a higher cost per kBtu of energy produced than fossil fuels, so a much higher level of conservation becomes cost-effective.

The R-values noted in table 6.1 depict the minimum assembly R-values we recommend for net zero buildings. While careful modeling analysis may change these levels for your climate and specific building, these rule-of-thumb measures will work for the preliminary analysis of most net zero building projects in cold climates. If the building is not insulated to this level, then the cost of adding PVs to achieve the net zero goal will be more than the insulation costs to further reduce the building loads. Insulating much beyond these levels will mean that you will spend more money on energy conservation than it will be possible to get back in reduced PV costs. These levels of insulation are also needed to create the indoor comfort required while reducing the size of heating systems.

Determining the assembly R-value for the building enclosure involves a rather detailed calculation. Since R-value is reported per inch of material, to find the material R-value for each component of the building enclosure, multiply the per-inch R-value by the thickness of the material. Once you know the total R-value for each individual material, you can combine these to determine the assembly R-value.

To get an accurate assembly R-value metric, the R-values should be combined in two different ways based on the order and combination of the materials. If materials are continuous across an entire building system, such as in a system of structural insulated panels (SIPs), then the R-values are additive. On the other hand, if materials are not continuous, such as insulation interspersed by framing members, then the R-values must be combined based on their relative percentages. The additive R-value found in the first case is relatively easy to understand, but the second case becomes more challenging. In order to better understand these principles, let's look at the example of a wood-framed wall.

A standard wood-framed wall includes insulation in the voids between 2×4 or 2×6 framing members. In typical wood-frame construction, 15–20 percent of the wall area is wood framing, but this number would need to be calculated specifically for any particular wall system. For the sake of this example, we will consider a 2×6 wood-framed wall (actual measurements 1.75" × 5.5") with fiberglass insulation filling all voids and framing making up 20 percent of the wall area. We know that wood's R-value is 1 per inch and fiberglass insulation's R-value is 3.5 per inch. To calculate the assembly R-value of the insulation and framing, the material R-values must be combined based on their relative percentages, according to the following formula:

Fiberglass Insulation: $R 3.5 \times 5.5" \times 80\% = R 15.4$
Wood Framing Members: $R 1 \times 5.5" \times 20\% = R 1.1$

Total: R-16.5

In comparison, if the insulation were 5.5" deep and there were no framing members, the assembly R-value would be R-3.5 × 5.5" = R-19.25. This number is what is considered material R-value, or the R-value for just the material. When accounting for the thermal bridging of the structural members through the calculation above, we see a 14 percent reduction in the effective insulation value.

Next we include the other materials in the building enclosure—to the inside and the outside of the insulation and wood-framing members. On the interior of the assembly is drywall; on the exterior is sheathing and exterior siding. Because none of these materials are specified for their insulating properties, the additional R-value from these materials is almost incidental, but we will go through the calculations here in line with the example.

Insulation Layer Including Framing (from above)   R-16.5
Drywall: $R 0.5 \times 0.5" = R 0.25$
Sheathing: $R 0.5 \times 0.5" = R 0.25$
Siding (wood): $R 1.0 \times 0.5" = R 0.5$

Total: R-17.5

The R-value of the wall is significantly affected by the framing members but not greatly affected by the drywall, sheathing, or siding. If this example used metal studs, the R-value of the wall assembly would be substantially lower.

TABLE 6.1. RECOMMENDED R-VALUES FOR NET ZERO PERFORMANCE

	TOTAL ASSEMBLY R-VALUE
Wall (to 2' below grade)	R-40
Roof	R-60
Window	R-5
Below Grade	R-20
Heated Slab at Grade	R-30
Radiant Slab	R-40
Air Leakage Rate	≤0.10 cfm50/sf above-grade exterior surface area

The R-values presented in table 6.1 can be used for typical homes, apartments, offices, retail, classroom buildings, and any other building with standard energy usage. These values are initial design suggestions only, and you should perform energy modeling for your own project to ensure that overall building-energy-intensity numbers are met. When designing buildings with large, unique loads, such as restaurants, hospitals, manufacturing, and labs, you would want to evaluate these numbers even more carefully with energy modeling. To achieve our net zero goals, the following practices are necessary in terms of the thermal-control layer.

- Insulate to net zero standards: use the R-60, -40, -20, -5, -0.1 guidelines and adjust them based on energy modeling for the specific project.
- Use assembly, not material insulation values, for all energy modeling and all reporting on the building.
- Minimize thermal bridging, which can cause heat movement through the building enclosure and other problems.

Air Movement

There are three primary reasons to stop air movement through the building enclosure: conserving energy, limiting vapor migration, and maintaining indoor air quality.

The basic mechanism of air movement is really quite simple. Air moves from a location of higher air pressure to a location of lower air pressure. However, extrapolating from this simple mechanism of airflow to how air moves within and around a building enclosure is much more complex. Airflow through a building is multidirectional and time-dependent, based on wind forces, thermal effects, and the operation of mechanical systems within the building. Each of these forces function to either pressurize or depressurize one side of the building enclosure, causing air to move from the pressurized side to the depressurized side—either into or out of the building enclosure. When air is moving into the enclosure in one spot, it is likely that it is moving out in another. Through this process, conditioned interior air is replaced by unconditioned exterior air, which can be warmer or colder than desired, laden with humidity, or carrying pollutants from the exterior. A well-designed air-control layer conserves energy by reducing this airflow across the building enclosure.[6]

In addition, air can carry much more water vapor into the building enclosure than is typically transported by vapor diffusion. Since water can be detrimental to the building structure, it is very important to keep moist air out of the building enclosure. This is particularly true in the winter, when damp interior air needs to be prevented from entering the exterior wall assembly, where the moisture can condense on colder surfaces and cause significant structural damage and problems in indoor air quality. A good air-control layer also improves indoor air quality by controlling the exchange of interior and

FIGURE 6.12. Fluid-applied air- and water-control product is put over the exterior wall sheathing, later to be covered and protected by rigid board insulation.

exterior air. In urban environments we may want to keep out automobile fumes and industrial pollutants, in rural locations pollen and other allergens.

AIR-CONTROL LAYERS

An air-control layer is a system of materials that controls airflow through a building enclosure between the outside (unconditioned) space and inside (conditioned) space. An air-control layer also defines the location of the pressure boundary of the building enclosure, the location where 50 percent or more of the air pressure drops across an assembly. The goal for an air-control layer in a net zero building is to keep the air within a building enclosure and ensure that the building's mechanical system is controlling air movement in the building. To accomplish this, the air-control layer must resist the air-pressure differences acting upon it. The Building Science Corporation identifies four characteristics for an effective air-control layer: it must be impermeable to airflow, continuous, able to withstand forces during construction, and durable over the life of the building.[7]

IMPERMEABLE TO AIRFLOW. The air-control layer must eliminate air movement. To do so, it can be made of fluid-applied (usually sprayed-on) membranes specifically designed to resist air (or water and air); peel-and-stick membranes designed as self-healing water- and air-control layers; and building sheathing like plywood or oriented strand board (OSB), with taped or fluid-applied systems used to cover all joints. Housewrap systems that are commercially sold as air-control layers, such as Tyvek and Typar, are not impermeable as typically installed. Although these products are impermeable to airflow on their own, their installation requires the stapling and taping of joints. Holes and gaps can substantially reduce performance, and in some assemblies wind pressures can cause seams to separate over time.

CONTINUOUS. The air-control layer must continuously surround all six surfaces of the building enclosure: the roof, walls, door and window openings, and below-grade walls and slabs. In the past the basement and slab were often not included in the air-control layer because it was believed that air would not move through the ground at any significant rate. However, drainage and radon systems can cause extensive airflow through the basement or slab. Because it is so important, it is worth stating again: the air-control layer must be completely continuous; it cannot have any gaps. Even very small holes can allow enough airflow through the enclosure to impact performance. It is crucial to limit all penetrations through the air control layer, including those for mechanical or electrical equipment or structural fasteners. If holes are required in the construction process, they must be patched or sealed with sealant or mastic that is compatible with the material for the air-control layer so that no holes exist in the final product.

DURABILITY DURING CONSTRUCTION. Construction is a disruptive process, and care must be taken to maintain the integrity of the air-control layer. Try to limit the ripping and tearing

FIGURE 6.13. Blower door testing is imperative to determine if an air-control layer is functioning as designed. Testing should be completed before finishes are installed to ensure that any problems the test reveals can be fixed without additional delay and cost. If permanent doors and windows are not yet installed, these openings must be temporarily sealed airtight for the testing. To complete testing, a fan with measuring equipment is inserted into a door opening.

of housewrap systems by environmental factors, such as wind. Because UV radiation can degrade some products as well, plan the construction sequence carefully so that air-control layers are not left exposed to sunlight longer than recommended by the manufacturer. When the air control layer is disturbed during construction, it must be repaired with patches, sealant, or tape or even replaced. Holes can and often do get covered up before they are found and fixed, greatly reducing the effectiveness of the air-control layer. To protect the air-control layer throughout the entire construction process, follow construction practices that go beyond today's standard practices.

DURABILITY OVER THE BUILDING'S LIFE. A building enclosure should be designed to withstand the deteriorating forces of sun, wind, water, freezing, and building changes for 100 years or longer. As an internal component, the air-control layer should be designed and installed to function as long as the building enclosure itself. This is most easily accomplished by sandwiching the air-control system between more durable building-enclosure components to protect it from these environmental and other factors.

BLOWER DOOR TESTING BASICS

A blower door test assesses the effectiveness of the air-control layer by measuring the amount of air movement through the building enclosure. For larger buildings, the blower door equipment can get more complicated, but the general strategies remain the same: a calibrated, variable-speed fan mounted in an airtight way in a door or window opening creates a pressure differential between the interior and exterior of the building. This causes air to be forced through holes or cracks in the building enclosure in an effort to reach the area of lower pressure. The amount of air the fan must move in order to maintain a specific pressure is related to the aggregate area of the gaps in the enclosure that the air is moving through—and is thus a measure of the effectiveness of the air-control layer.

Before the blower door test begins, it is important to establish a baseline pressure differential between the interior and exterior of the building. This value is then subtracted from all pressure-differential measurements during the test. Often only a depressurization test is performed. For the best results, however, both pressurization and depressurization tests should

MYTH BUSTING:
DO AIR-CONTROL LAYERS LEAD TO SICK BUILDINGS?

Traditional building construction has suggested that air-control layers are unhealthy for occupants because in an airtight building indoor air is recirculated. Following this logic, sealing the building with a high-performance air-control layer is like sealing the entire building within a plastic bag, creating an unhealthy environment. This kind of thinking led some people to believe it was better to design a leaky building enclosure that would let air filter through. This notion does not stand up to building science.

As an example, the New England farmhouse is a typical leaky building, but on days when there is no wind and very little exterior air movement, almost no air moves within the house, and the occupants do not receive adequate fresh air. Natural convection currents inside the house can further reduce indoor air quality. Hot air rises and escapes out of the leaky roof, drawing new air in through the lowest levels of the house. In many of these older houses, the foundation is stone; incoming air thus passes through the frequently wet and damp basement and picks up mold spores and other pollutants, which get dispersed throughout the house.

That said, most newer, conventionally constructed houses are tight enough that they do not provide occupants with adequate fresh air. Designing a house to be leaky to address this concern is not the answer. Not only would this waste energy, but in houses with attached garages, uncontrolled air movement between the garage and house risks bringing in carbon monoxide or other pollutants.

A building with a high-performance air-control layer and a properly sized mechanical ventilation system allows for controlled air movement through the building enclosure and maintains healthy indoor air quality. And with heat-recovery ventilators, fresh air need not mean heat loss. Problems with indoor air are more the fault of improper ventilation systems than tight wrapping. Net-zero-engineered homes and buildings provide properly designed envelope enclosures to minimize moisture problems with carefully calculated and sized mechanical ventilation and optimized indoor air quality.

---

be done, as the building enclosure may respond differently to airflow in different directions.

BLOWER DOOR TESTING STANDARDS AND METRICS

The blower door test is reported as the number of cubic feet of air per minute that must be blown into or out of a building or space to maintain a specific pressure differential, measured in pascals (Pa), an SI-derived unit of pressure. As testing depressurizes or pressurizes the building, readings are taken at every 5–10 Pa to create a pressurization curve in order to understand how airflow occurs across the building enclosure. A standard upper pressure for blower door testing is 50 Pa, and the test result is then given in cubic feet per minute at 50 Pa (cfm@50 Pa, or—the further abbreviation we prefer—cfm50). Some tests use 75 Pa, a pressure no building is likely to experience under normal conditions but one that may result in a more accurate test.

Another common metric is based on the number of times per hour that the volume of air in the building will be exchanged, or air changes per hour (ACH), at a pressure differential of 50 Pa (given as ACH50). This metric is therefore dependent on a building's volume, but the test results using this metric will not always be comparable between different buildings because of potential differences between volume and surface area. For example, if you have two buildings with the same volume—one a one-story building and the other a two-story building—the one-story building has a significantly higher surface-area-to-volume ratio. The one-story building would need to have a significantly tighter building enclosure (per unit of surface area) to achieve the same ACH measurement as the two-story building.

The cfm50/sf surface-area measurement therefore allows for a better comparison between different buildings. It also encourages the design of more compact and efficient building massing, while concentrating attention on improving the air-sealing measures of the building enclosure.

There are two accepted ways to calculate surface area for the assessment of air infiltration. One method assumes that the earth below the enclosure stops air movement and so calculates only the above-ground surface area. A second method includes all six sides of a building's surface area, taking into account that there may actually be air movement through the enclosure below grade (through underslab stone fill, for instance, which is often connected to foundation drainage), if care is not taken with the installation of underslab air-control layers. In the past, we have calculated surface area using above-ground measurements. For all future projects, however, we will use total building surface area to measure the effectiveness of the underslab as well as above-ground air control.

We commonly set a goal of 0.1 cfm50/sf for our net zero projects. Although we include this metric in preliminary design discussions, we always calculate the blower door reading, in cfm, that needs to be achieved to meet this metric based on our calculations of surface area. The cfm reading is calculated by multiplying the cfm50/sf number by the exterior surface area. This cfm number becomes the requirement that we list in our specifications and is readily verified in the field without the need for further calculations.

BLOWER DOOR TESTING PROCEDURE

For our net zero projects, we recommend a minimum of two blower door tests for air leakage: one to be performed as soon as the air-control layer is complete (and before insulation or finishes are installed over the control layer) and a final blower door test when the building is complete. For smaller projects,

this is often sufficient. For larger and more complicated projects, we also recommend an envelope mock-up air-leakage test and progress testing of components or junctions of the control layer as the first instance of each is installed.

The specifications must include the number of blower door tests, their timing, and the metrics that must be met for each test. The specifications need to make clear that achieving these test results is a requirement of construction and that air-sealing measures must continue until this criterion is met. In addition, the specifications should note that any retesting that may be required to ensure that the metrics are met will be the responsibility of the contractor.

EXTERIOR WALL ENVELOPE MOCK-UP TEST. The purpose of this blower door test is to check that the procedures developed for installing the air-control layer work and that any problems are found early in order to inform the rest of the construction process. This should be the first test for larger projects and should take place before beginning installation of the control layer on the building. The mock-up should be constructed to assess a portion of the roof, typical wall conditions (including corner and base of wall conditions), and at least one window. The mock-up must be sealed off to provide an enclosure that can be pressurized or depressurized.

This test will indicate whether the air-control layer installation is on track for meeting the air-leakage test criterion in the specifications. If the test shows that installation of the air-control layer is not up to par, procedures can be revised or clarified to improve the air-control layer before its installation on the building itself, when there may be greater challenges for meeting the air-infiltration test metric.

PROGRESS TESTING. We also highly recommend testing air-barrier components and air-control layer intersections as they are installed or completed on larger projects. By testing these early on, you can detect problems before they have been replicated at multiple locations throughout the building, thus potentially saving much trouble and expense later on. We typically specify testing the first instance of building corners, base of walls, roof-wall intersections, floor-wall intersections, and window, skylight, and door openings. Often one location in the building can be selected that will provide most or all of these conditions, reducing the amount of tests that need to be performed.

To perform progress testing, you will need to isolate the subject area of the building (with a temporary enclosure if permanent partitions do not exist) and pressurize the area with a blower door. When the area is pressurized, a theatrical fog generator creates a fog that will be forced by the pressure differential to follow any air-leakage pathways, making them readily visible so that problems with the control layer can be located and corrected. Occasionally, you may want to use depressurization, especially if air-leakage testing is taking place at the same time as moisture-leakage testing of windows, for instance.

AIR-CONTROL-LAYER TEST. Because insulation and finishes are typically installed after (in other words, over) the air-control layer, it is important to test the effectiveness of the air-control layer before it is covered with these other materials. This allows for easier inspection of the air-control layer and thus the detection and correction of installation problems or defects. This test should occur as soon as the air-control layer and windows, doors, and louvers have been installed and any miscellaneous penetrations of the air-control layer have been air-sealed.

The specific air-leakage metric requirements in this test must be met: by the time of the final test, it is much more challenging and expensive to improve the air infiltration. This test is therefore sometimes referred to as the compliance test.

FINAL BLOWER TEST. The final blower door test, when construction is complete, provides the air-infiltration metric that will be reported for the building. With proper design and installation of the air-control layer, this test should be only slightly improved from the previous, air-control-layer test, because the addition of insulation and finish materials should not significantly change the performance of the air-control layer. If the final blower test results were worse than the compliance test results, it would be reason for concern (though the likeliest cause is apt to be poor pretest preparation). At this point the only thing that can be done to improve the effectiveness of the air-control layer would be to block tiny holes by sealing and weather-stripping around windows, doors, baseboards, access panels, mechanical systems, ductwork penetrations, and dampers. Pretest prep work such as sealing open louvers, closing windows, and opening all interior doors is usually required and should be included in the specifications. To ensure that this prep work is completed prior to the final blower door test, remind the contractors that the testing specifications make it their responsibility for any additional costs if the building needs to be retested.

NET ZERO AIR-CONTROL-LAYER PERFORMANCE

We need clear procedures to achieve the design and construction of an air-control layer that supports net zero goals. The three following design measures are the most important for a high-performance air-control layer:

- Design the air-control layer to be impermeable to airflow, continuous, able to withstand forces during construction, and durable for the life of the building.
- Set a strict requirement for air infiltration in the specifications.
- Test as many times as necessary to ensure that the air-control layer meets the requirements of the specifications.

The minimum air-infiltration requirement recommended to achieve the net zero goal cost-effectively is 0.1 cfm50/sf, calculated using total surface area.

Water Control

The importance of water control in the building enclosure may seem obvious. Keeping dry is one of the primary reasons humans started constructing shelters in the first place. No one likes sleeping in a wet bed or listening to the plunk, plunk of water dripping through a hole in the ceiling. In addition to lowering comfort and creating annoyance, water can rot buildings and cause sickness in their occupants. Controlling water is a fundamental requirement for all buildings, including net zero buildings. If the buildings we design use no energy but do not control water, we have failed. While water control may seem separate from our net zero concerns, the design of a water-control layer needs to be integrated with the other building-enclosure layers.

The largest source of moisture that affects most building enclosures is driving rain on the walls and roof. Other sources of water and moisture are below ground. Water presents one of the greatest challenges to control because of its ability to change form, from water to vapor to ice and snow. This variability means that there are multiple ways water can attack a building enclosure. In this section we primarily address the solid and fluid forms of water; we cover vapor in the next section, even though vapor can condense in the building enclosure and must also be controlled as a fluid.

WATER MOVEMENT

As water is deposited on the surface of a building, it begins to form a film. Once water has accumulated in a film over the building enclosure, there are really five forces that govern its movement: gravity, surface tension, capillarity, air-pressure differences, and momentum.[8]

GRAVITY. The force of gravity pulls water downhill most of the time but can also cause it to flow horizontally when it encounters a small bead of water built up on a horizontal surface.

SURFACE TENSION. Surface tension occurs because water molecules are attracted to other water molecules, and this attraction is stronger on the water's surface. Surface tension can cause water to adhere to another material's surface or to be directed along a surface. It can also enable water to span gaps up to ⅜".

CAPILLARY ACTION. Capillary action can draw water into small voids in porous materials or between two adjoining hydrophilic materials due to the attractive force of surface tension, even counter to the force of gravity. The latter type of capillary action occurs only in small gaps, generally less than ⅛".

AIR-PRESSURE DIFFERENCES. If there is a great enough air-pressure differential across a material or an assembly, then water from a surface film is driven through to the side of lower pressure. By equalizing air pressure, this movement is stopped.

MOMENTUM. Individual droplets of rainwater can be carried through openings by wind-driven momentum—as long as there is a difference in air pressure and an opening that is larger than the droplets.

While all five of these forces can cause water to move into a building assembly, the greatest impact occurs when the forces act in combination.

WATER-CONTROL LAYERS

To stop water everywhere, a layer of water-resistant materials must be installed correctly and continuously around all six sides of the building enclosure.

Because in most cases gravity causes water to move downhill, water-control layers must have vertically lapped joints out of a flashing material, a sheet product, siding, or roofing, to direct the water from the top of the building to below the foundation. Lapping is a relatively easy process; you just need to ensure that the lapping is done in the right direction and that the materials shed water rather than collect it. Materials are typically lapped only one or two inches, but different materials and applications have different requirements and tolerances. At windows and doors the water-control layer will wrap into the opening, providing one continuous membrane to resist water movement into the building enclosure.

Water-control layers need a minimum drainage gap or drip edge when flashing is used at roof overhangs or other locations. To overcome surface tension, where water can go uphill a small amount, the minimum gap is ¼". If there is no airspace, the lap should be an inch or more, as indicated above.

The water-control layer must be constructed of a nonwicking material. Although rosin paper was once used as both an air- and water-control layer, it was not effective because it allowed water to seep into the building assembly. The traditional asphalt-impregnated or tar paper has generally been replaced by modern products such as Typar and Tyvek, peel-and-stick membranes, or sprayed-on coatings.

WATER-CONTROL-LAYER TESTING

To test the water-control layer, after window installation and prior to the installation of any interior or exterior finishes, depressurize the building and use a wide-spray hose at multiple

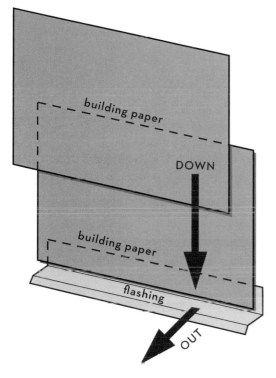

FIGURE 6.14. All joints in the water-control layer must be lapped, upper material over lower, so that all water sheds to the building's exterior.

FIGURE 6.15. Informal water testing of a window and flashing while the interior space is depressurized. Such testing and inspection for water intrusion is recommended on a random sampling of windows.

locations. In particular, carefully test windows and joints that are susceptible to moisture problems. Monitor testing for any water infiltration, address any issues, and retest.

BUILDING DESIGN

The design of a building's water-control layer must address all four types of water movement in order to control moisture across the building enclosure. Each component of the building enclosure—the roof, the walls, and the foundation—restricts water in a different way.

THE ROOF. Above ground, the roof plays the largest role in protecting the building enclosure from water intrusion from rain and snow. The main focus of the designer here is in developing and selecting durable strategies, materials, and installation practices to effectively shed water from the roof to the perimeter of the building. Particular care in design and construction is required at all roof penetrations, changes in roof plane, and wall intersections.

THE WALLS. Because walls are in most cases vertical, the drainage of water off the walls seems quite simple. But wind-driven rain can be horizontal or even cause water to go uphill. Drainage-plane wall design, as discussed in the next section, is used to overcome these challenges. In addition, walls typically have numerous penetrations, including windows, doors, and penetrations for mechanical systems. Any water-control layer must address these penetrations and effectively keep water from moving through the building enclosure at these weak points. In the past the exterior finish materials were used as the water-control layer. Generally, these were lapped to provide drainage, but because of wall openings and trim details, the water-control layer was not fully continuous. Caulking was used in many of these spots, including where siding meets trim, around windows and doors, and along flashing joints, to connect all parts of the water-control layer. But caulk deteriorates over time, and most caulking products fail in only five to ten years. Since the goal of a net zero is to last 100 years or longer, a material with such a short lifetime is inadequate. Thus, rather than rely on caulk, detail the water-control layer and drainage plane so that it is continuous everywhere, then use metal flashings to cover membrane flashings.

The ground surfaces around buildings can carry significant amounts of water, especially during rain, snow, or times of snowmelt. These can all lead to problems at the intersection between the ground and the wall. Specifically, with increased handicapped accessibility, there can be a significant potential for water intrusion at doors and other unique areas.

THE FOUNDATION. Below grade, seasonal groundwater movement must be addressed when designing and building foundation walls and slabs. A perforated pipe (called a footing, perimeter, or French drain) located at the base of the building footings and another pipe below the slab both direct all subsurface water away from the building. Backfilling around the entire building foundation with permeable fill such as sand, gravel, or crushed stone allows the water along the foundation wall to drain to the footing drain. The subsurface water level is thus effectively lowered around the building so that the building is not floating like a boat in the subsurface groundwater, creating inward water pressure on foundation walls. Grades around buildings should be sloped away from the building to direct surface water away from the foundation, and the foundation walls and adjacent soil need to be designed to eliminate potential problems from groundwater below surface grades. Foundation walls should be designed similar to above-ground walls, so that water moves downhill with gravity.

Because water in the foundation assembly can also be drawn up the entire height of the foundation walls by capillary action, a water-control layer should be installed between the footing and the foundation walls. The foundation also needs a water-control layer system around the outside: a continuous membrane, where any joints are lapped—in most cases simply a fluid-applied membrane. This water-control layer needs to shed water but not resist water pressure. Traditional dampproofing mostly stops water-vapor migration but does not necessarily shed water and thus is not adequate for the foundation. "Waterproofing" implies resistance to water pressure and is expensive, so in all but the most extreme cases it is more than is needed. For purposes of clarity, we will use the term "moistureproofing" for the appropriate level of water control for foundation walls.

DRAINAGE-PLANE WALL DESIGN

In a net zero building, the walls incorporate what is called drainage-plane design and detailing practices. The drainage-plane water-control system is composed of multiple elements that function together to combat the mechanisms of water movement and keep water out of the building enclosure.

FINISH/CLADDING MATERIAL. In drainage-plane design, the exterior siding materials need to be lasting and durable but do not need to act as the water-control layer. While the finish material sheds 90 percent or more of the water that hits the building enclosure, the exterior finish serves mainly to protect the interior assembly of the building enclosure and as an aesthetic feature. Because of their exposure to the elements, finish materials should shed water and resist deterioration from UV rays, insects, mold, freeze-thaw cycles, and any other environmental conditions that could adversely affect the interior wall assembly. You should also consider maintenance, replacement, resistance to fire, durability, cost, and environmental impacts when you evaluate exterior finishes.

DRAINAGE GAP. It is nearly impossible to detail the exterior finish to stop all water movement into the wall assembly, so an unobstructed airspace behind the finish material and in front of the drainage plane allows drainage of water that finds its way behind the exterior siding. This drainage gap also acts as a ventilation space, allowing any moisture absorbed by the finish material to evaporate. This gap

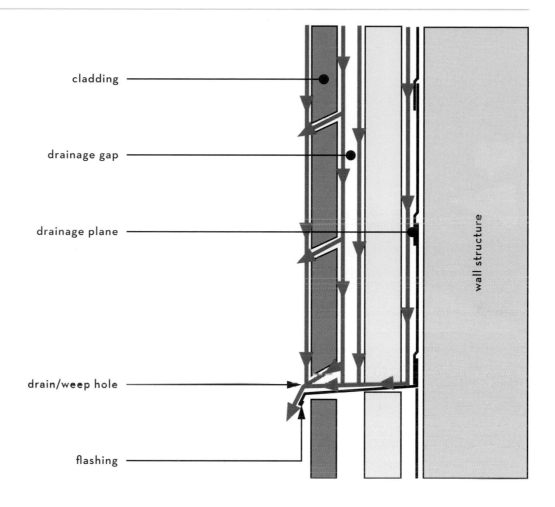

FIGURE 6.16. The drainage-plane water-control system is composed of multiple elements, including the finish/cladding material, drainage gap, drainage plane, flashing, and drain/weep holes to keep water out of the building enclosure.

cladding

drainage gap

drainage plane

wall structure

drain/weep hole

flashing

is generally a minimum of ⅜″ thick in metal-panel and wood-frame construction and 1″ or greater in masonry construction. If the drainage gap does not need to provide ventilation, it can be smaller, but this width should be sized to allow for dimensional variations encountered in construction and large enough to create a capillary break for preventing water movement.

DRAINAGE PLANE. The drainage plane, located to the interior of the drainage gap, must be constructed of a water-impermeable material. As this is the barrier against water migration into the wall assembly, all joints must be lapped and detailed following the principles described above. Since it is behind the exterior finish material, the drainage plane is protected from the elements and need not be chosen for aesthetics or durability.

FLASHING. Flashing is made of a waterproof material and used to direct water out and away from the building enclosure. It is used in various instances in the wall and roof assemblies, including at the base of the drainage plane; around any openings in the building enclosure, such as windows and doors; at the intersection of roof and wall planes; at most changes in plane of the building assembly; and at the base of the walls where they meet the foundation. Flashing is nearly horizontal and therefore must be installed with a continuously outward slope in order to shed the water. Because most flashing materials are made in limited lengths, all joints must be sealed, not just lapped, to stop any leaks in the joints between separate pieces of flashing, and water must be diverted from the wall interior where the flashing ends.

FIGURE 6.17. To stop water at the back of the sill, the flashing needs to be formed into a dam. A proper flashing "pan" also turns up at the jambs, like the sides of a pan, to prevent water from seeping into the corners.

In the past, flashings made of copper were soldered, allowing the building trades to connect multiple pieces of flashing with waterproof joints. Metal flashings must be joined properly to avoid failure. However, typical modern joints use caulk or lapped joints, which do not last. At doors, windows, and roof-to-wall intersections—all notorious locations for leaking—one-piece pan flashings or flexible-membrane flashings are preferable. It is easier to create an impenetrable, waterproof layer with membrane flashings than with their inflexible counterparts that are difficult to seal together, but these products tend to deteriorate in sunlight. Best practice is to use a metal or other flashing to cover and protect the membrane flashing from the environmental forces that cause degradation. This also provides a crisp detail on the exterior finish/cladding layer. At corners we recommend a material such as FlexWrap that stretches and is more effective for wrapping around corners than plastic systems that require glues, tapes, caulks, or liquid materials to hold multiple pieces together and may end up with holes. Regardless what system the design team finally chooses, a careful inspection of these flashing details is necessary to ensure that water is kept out of the building enclosure.

DRAIN/WEEP HOLES. Drain holes, or weep holes, allow water to escape out of the drainage gap as quickly as possible without traveling down the entire side of the building enclosure before exiting the assembly.

While these methods of controlling water flow are generally effective, especially in simpler building designs, most buildings have atypical conditions and joints where problems with water can still occur. At any interruptions or joints in the surfaces, such as seismic joints, the connection of a deck, and the connection of the wall to the foundation, the water-control layer can be interrupted and water can penetrate the building enclosure. Membrane flashing and/or drainage holes at these spots must be designed and constructed to direct water to the exterior of the enclosure.

Managing Vapor

Moisture vapor in a building enclosure can be absorbed into building materials and, at certain temperatures and indoor and outdoor humidity levels, condense into liquid and cause mold, mildew, and rot. Besides affecting building health, vapor can also compromise occupant health.

VAPOR MOVEMENT

Moisture vapor moves into and through the building enclosure by two different mechanisms: diffusion and air transport. Diffusion moves vapor through materials, from an area of high vapor pressure to one of low vapor pressure as a result of a vapor concentration gradient that usually shifts the vapor from the warm side of an assembly to the cold side. The movement of vapor by diffusion can be controlled in the building enclosure by a vapor-control layer.

The air transport of vapor follows the same mechanisms as any other movement of air. Air moves across the building enclosure from areas of higher pressure to areas of lower pressure, transporting the vapor with it. Air movement through the building enclosure, in either direction, can carry moisture vapor with it, altering the moisture levels inside the building enclosure. To prevent trapping moisture vapor within the exterior enclosure, you will need to consider the predominant direction of vapor movement and where the air-control layer is located in the building enclosure. If the air-control layer is on the "wrong" side of the assembly or climate conditions are such that there is no predominant direction of transport, you should use vapor-permeable air-control layers.

PERMEABILITY

In order to design a building enclosure that controls moisture vapor, we need to understand permeability, the capability of a material to allow liquids and/or gases to pass through the material via pores or openings. All materials absorb moisture at different rates. Table 6.2 indicates the relative permeability, or the perm ratings, for different materials. Materials that retard vapor flow are classified as impermeable, while materials that allow vapor to pass through are considered permeable. Most materials fall somewhere in the middle of these two extremes, and some materials' permeability characteristics vary depending on the conditions: they may retard vapor when vapor levels are low and allow diffusion when moisture levels rise (see sidebar for specifics). Some materials are also hygroscopic, meaning they absorb and retain water.

VAPOR CONTROL

Often the strategies used to keep vapor out also tend to trap vapor in. Our challenge is to reduce vapor intrusion into the enclosure while allowing vapor to escape. We can do this by using a variable-permeability vapor retarder such as MemBrain, which allows the building enclosure to breathe to either the interior or the exterior of the system, or with gypsum wallboard and low-permeability latex paint.

The goal is to design and construct enclosure systems whose drying potential is greater than their wetting potential. To do this, take the following steps:

- Reduce vapor intrusion by convection through the enclosure.
- Reduce vapor intrusion by diffusion through the enclosure.
- Control enclosure permeability to allow vapor to escape from the building enclosure.
- Ensure that the water-control layer keeps all water outside the building enclosure.

Separate building strategies, including air-control layers, vapor-control layers, and water-control layers, manage the movement of vapor. Below, we describe the design of each of these to control vapor. Additionally, this enclosure must be permeable to allow for drying when moisture does penetrate the assembly. While vapor movement can sometimes be controlled with one material, such as a membrane on the exterior of a masonry wall, it often needs to be managed by different layers and materials in the assembly. In order for the vapor-control system to perform properly, it must be continuous around the entire building enclosure.

AIR-CONTROL LAYER. As discussed earlier in this chapter, the air-control layer stops vapor intrusion by exfiltration or infiltration. Proper air-control layer design and installation is critical not only to energy conservation in the building but also as a first step in controlling potential vapor migration through the building envelope.

VAPOR-CONTROL LAYER. A vapor-control layer can restrict the entry of vapor into the building enclosure from the interior, the exterior, or both. In cold-climate construction, the vapor-control layer is typically employed to limit moisture diffusion

In the United States we measure water-vapor transmission by US perm, defined as one grain of water vapor per hour, per square foot, per inch of mercury pressure differential. Materials can be tested to determine their perm rating under two different sets of conditions. A dry-cup test is performed with 0 percent relative humidity on one side and 50 percent relative humidity on the other side of the material, similar to what the material might experience in a dwelling that does not experience high relative humidities. A wet-cup test is performed with 50 percent relative humidity on one side and 100 percent relative humidity on the other side of the material, to simulate the high relative humidities that may be encountered in some situations. Most building codes define a vapor barrier as a material that has the permeability of less than 1 perm using the dry-cup testing method.

Some materials' vapor permeability depends on relative humidity levels. For nonhygroscopic materials (those that do not tend to absorb water), there is little difference in the results between the two tests. For hygroscopic materials (those that hold water), the wet-cup test results are much higher than the dry-cup test results. As an example, plywood, a hygroscopic material, has a dry-cup test result around 0.75 perms and a wet-cup test typically closer to 3 perms, a sixfold increase in permeability.[9] There is also a "smart" vapor retarder (MemBrain, by Certainteed) designed to have a variable permeability, so that it can react to a buildup of moisture vapor within a wall assembly and adjust its permeability to allow diffusion of water vapor out of the assembly. The perm rating of this sheet product slides from less than 1 perm to greater than 10 perms as needed. All materials are classified by their vapor permeability from class I to class III and beyond. Only class I materials are considered true vapor barriers. Table 6.2 shows typical building materials and their permeability.

from the warm, moisture-laden interior air to the drier, cold exterior air. In heating-dominated buildings in cold climates, the vapor control layer is thus located on the inside of the building assembly, to stop moist air from moving from the interior of the building into the building enclosure.

When buildings are cooled by air-conditioning or dehumidification systems, however, the opposite situation occurs: the drier air is inside, and the damper air is outside, driving vapor from the outside of the building enclosure into the inside of the building. With summer temperatures rising in currently heating-dominated climates, future buildings will likely call for more cooling. Building enclosure design must accommodate that likelihood.

WATER-CONTROL LAYER. If the water-control layer fails, water may enter the building enclosure, which obviously can cause significant problems relatively quickly. Thus, a reliable water-control layer is necessary for proper vapor control in the building envelope.

ENCLOSURE PERMEABILITY. Building-enclosure design must select the appropriate materials for the vapor retarder

TABLE 6.2. VAPOR PERMEABILITY OF VARIOUS MATERIALS

VAPOR RETARDER CLASS	VAPOR PERMEABILITY	MATERIAL	PERM RATING	
			Dry cup	Wet Cup
I	Impermeable (≤0.1 perms)	Glass	N/A	N/A
		Sheet metal	N/A	N/A
		Rubber membrane	N/A	N/A
		Polyethylene sheet	0.06	0.06
II	Semi-Impermeable (>0.1–1.0 perms)	MemBrain	<1.0	N/A
		Bitumen coated kraft paper	1	N/A
		Unfaced extruded polystyrene (1″ thick)	1.0	1.0
		Unfaced expanded polystyrene (1″ thick)	3.5	N/A
II	Semi-Permeable (>1.0–10 perms)	OSB sheathing (³⁄₈″ thick)	0.75	2
		Plywood (CDX, ³⁄₈″ thick)	0.75	3.5
		Oil based paint	1.0–3.0	N/A
		Concrete block, 8″ thick	N/A	N/A
		Board lumber (per inch thickness)	0.4	5.4
		Traditional stucco	3.8	5.8
		Latex paint	3.5–6.1	~17
Not Classified as a Vapor Retarder	Permeable (>10 perms)	Brick	N/A	1.7–13.7
		MemBrain	N/A	12+
		15# asphalt coated paper	31	N/A
		Gypsum board (paper-faced, ½″ thick)	40	N/A
		House wrap	5	54
		Cellulose insulation	N/A	75
		Fiberglass insulation (unfaced)	120	168

N/A = not available

and locate them in the right order within the assembly to ensure that vapor can escape if it manages to get in. Vapor retarders are typically defined as materials with perm ratings of less than 1. However, in practice, semipermeable and variable-permeability membranes are most often used as vapor retarders to allow some breathing of the building enclosure and moisture to escape. On the exterior of our building enclosures, we use a material that stops water movement but allows vapor movement, such as Tyvek, Typar, and some fluid-applied membranes. An exterior enclosure with layers of semipermeable materials on the exterior side may limit the overall permeability, so the interior vapor retarder should have variable permeability or semipermeability to allow moisture to diffuse to the inside. This can be a chemically engineered product such as MemBrain or Sheetrock and typical latex paint, which is semi-vapor-permeable. In any case, it is essential that air movement and associated vapor transport has been stopped through the proper installation of an air-control layer, with testing to ensure performance.

Windows

Making the right choice in window technology is critical in a net zero building. In the parts of the building enclosure where windows are installed, they become the control layer for water, vapor, air, and thermal energy. Because of this, the sequence of window installation and method of window connection to all the various enclosure control layers becomes of paramount importance. Windows also must resist wind. As discussed earlier, they provide daylight to the interior of the building and views to the outdoors, enhancing the aesthetics of the building and experience of the users. They can provide ventilation for cooling or passive solar heating in the winter. Conversely, overglazing of a space can cause overheating.

In all of these functions, windows need to be durable and easy to install, use environmentally friendly materials, and withstand difficult environmental conditions and operator abuse. High-performance windows are often a significant portion of the building cost, so the project's budget plays a role in their selection. Windows likely will be replaced before the rest of

the building enclosure, but windows are still a major investment and should last thirty years or longer.[10]

WINDOW RATINGS AND PERFORMANCE

The National Fenestration Rating Council (NFRC) rates windows for structural, water, vapor, and energy performance. NFRC ratings include information on the solar heat gain coefficient (SHGC), thermal performance, visible-light transmittance, and sometimes condensation resistance. Another rating agency, the North American Fenestration Standard (NAFS), classifies windows by performance level, including structural and thermal performance, as well as air and water resistance.[11] Manufacturers' product specifications also provide performance data on specific window products, including air leakage. For more information on choosing the correct window for your project, see the "Window Selection" section in this chapter.

To allow for comparisons, the NFRC has developed testing procedures and whole-product performance ratings for windows. Some metrics must be included for certification and some characteristics are at the option of the window manufacturer. Almost all major North American window manufacturers have their windows rated by NFRC. Windows from Europe, including high-performing Passive House windows, are not certified by NFRC and have their own rating system.[12] The window-performance metrics that NFRC rates include:

- U-factor, a measure of thermal performance.
- Solar heat gain coefficient (SHGC), a value from 0 to 1 that represents the fraction of incident solar radiation that is admitted through a window. The lower the number, the less solar heat it transmits.
- Visible-light transmittance (VLT), which indicates the amount of visible light that is transmitted through the window, expressed as a value between 0 and 1. The higher the number, the more visible light it transmits.
- Air leakage (AL), an optional rating that gives a value from 0.3 cfm/sf to 0.01 cfm/sf, with the lower numbers indicating less air leakage and thus better performance.
- Condensation resistance (CR), another optional rating, expressed as a number between 0 and 100, with the higher values representing a better ability to resist condensation.

STRUCTURAL PERFORMANCE

The NAFS table identifies four performance grades for windows, ranging from residential to commercial applications in low-, mid-, and high-rise buildings. This rating includes structural, wind, and water assessments.

WATER CONTROL

Windows need to keep rain and water out of the building. Many windows also open, creating a hole in the water-control layer. There are two aspects of water control of windows: the

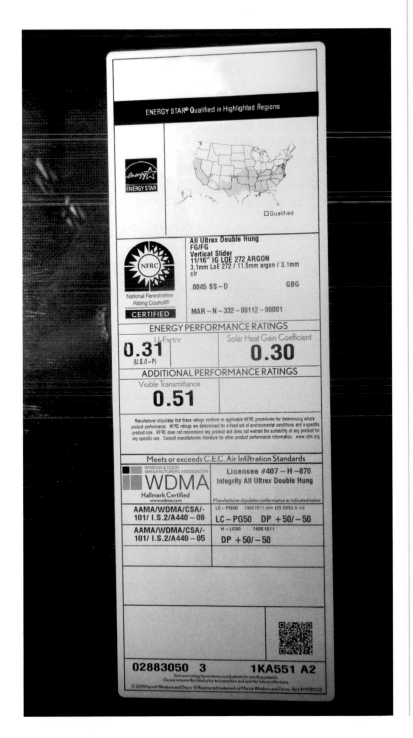

window unit itself and the window installation in the wall (or roof for skylights). Water potentially can get through the frame or through the joints and seals at the edge of the window. Water testing of windows is recommended on larger buildings.

Windows need pan or sill flashing under the window, as well as jamb and head flashings to maintain the building water-control layer where the windows meet the water-control layer. In chapters 8–14, detailed drawings depict window and door installation with continuous water-, air-, vapor-, and thermal-control layers at these openings.

VAPOR CONTROL

Windows in net zero buildings are the coldest surface on exterior walls because of course windows are less insulated than walls. Condensation occurs when the air film next to the window reaches the dew point. Therefore, high R-value windows are less likely to have condensation in cold climates. With triple glazing, condensation is unlikely unless the interior air is very humid, such as in bathrooms and other high-moisture areas, where condensation can be minimized with an exhaust fan. Occasional condensation is no cause for concern; frequent condensation can present a problem and should be investigated. Warm-edge spacers and installation of windows nearer the inside of the wall lower the likelihood of condensation, though the latter also reduces daylight and solar gain. Thus, we typically install windows closer to the exterior of the building enclosure. This is fine with triple-glazed or better windows. In the NFRC rating system, a CR rating of at least 50 is recommended in cold climates to avoid moisture concerns.

AIR CONTROL

Windows can be fixed or operable to allow for ventilation. Placing operable windows for good cross-ventilation and/or vertical (stack-effect) air circulation should be part of a cooling strategy. In certain building types, night flushing can also be an effective energy-saving measure. Obviously, operable windows need to seal properly when closed to minimize winter heat loss. Air-control design needs to take into account not only air movement at the window unit but also where the window unit connects with the enclosure air-control layer. Windows can be compared based on ASTM E283 testing, which provides results varying from a maximum of 0.3 cfm75/sf to as low as 0.01 cfm75/sf. For net zero

buildings, we generally recommend 0.03 cfm75/sf as a minimum, though you should consider the potential impact of windows as an aggregate on the overall air-leakage rate. In general, window casement and awnings have lower air-leakage rates than double-hung and sliding windows. If available, single-hung units, where half of the glass is fixed, perform better than double-hung windows and are often a good solution for historic renovations and retrofit projects, where the goal is for the aesthetic of a double-hung unit.

In addition to air leakage of the window unit, air can flow between the window unit and the rough opening. This gap is normally closed with minimal expanding foam, but air may still flow through the foam, and the window may move over time, allowing small cracks and gaps. For net zero buildings, sealant and a backer rod serve as the air control at these locations. The air-control layer needs to wrap into the rough opening so that the sealant joins the wall's air-control layer to the window frame.

THERMAL CONTROL

In selecting windows for net zero buildings, thermal control is the primary concern. Ideally, windows lose minimal energy in the winter, gain energy in the winter if needed, and minimize cooling in the summer by being operable and cutting heat gain through low-e glazing, shading, and other devices. These thermal controls do not always work together, though, and windows on different sides of a building call for different strategies. Glazing design requires balancing multiple considerations.

In any climate, a window's thermal conductivity is the first thing to consider. Heat transfer is controlled primarily through the number of layers of glazing, which create airspaces, as well as the type of gas fill that is used. The airspaces create the insulating value, as glass on its own has a very low R-value. The optimum airspace is ½" for most insulated glass. Both narrower and wider airspaces generally lower the performance. Some gases and vacuums in the glazing allow smaller airspaces. If the airspaces are filled with argon gas, the cheapest and most readily available gas fill, the R-value improves by ten times or more. Krypton further reduces heat loss, and xenon insulates the best.

Some window manufacturers are now offering up to five layers of glazing, and there is research on evacuated glazing, in which the airspace is actually a vacuum, that may offer R-values up to R-12 or higher. To minimize the weight of high-performance windows, windows with more than three layers typically use a thin, heat-energy-reflecting film in between two outside layers of glass. Heat Mirror by Southwall Technologies, for example, is a transparent film with a specialized nano-coating of metal. In the heating season, this film reflects the heat back into the building, and in the cooling season the heat is reflected outside. One drawback of using heat-reflecting films in glazing is that the films have a lower visible-light transmittance than standard 3 or 4 mm glass, so windows with multiple films can appear darker than traditionally glazed units.

In addition to multiple layers of glazing and gas, low-e coatings are used to reduce heat loss through windows by reflecting heat back into the building interior and decreasing the quantity of radiant heat emitted from the glass. There are different types of low-e coatings, depending on how they are applied: pyrolytic and sputtered. Pyrolytic (generally referred to as hard coat) is applied to glass in its molten state in a chemical vapor deposition process. Sputtered (referred to as soft coat) is applied to the glass in a physical deposition process in a vacuum chamber. Soft coat low-e coatings are most frequently applied where control of solar gain is desired, whereas the hard-coat forms have generally been used where a higher solar heat gain coefficient is desired, such as in passive solar buildings. There are soft coatings, though, such as Cardinal Glass, that allow for moderate or high solar heat gain.

In order to attach two layers of glass with airspace, the edges need to be sealed, and windows lose heat through these edges. The most common edge sealer is aluminum, which has high thermal conductivity. Stainless steel performs better thermally than aluminum, but butyl rubber and silicone outperform any metal, with silicone foam the best-performing edge seal. These improved nonaluminum edge spacers are part of the new warm-edge technology. Because multiple glazing layers, low-e coatings, and gas-filled spaces raised the performance at the center of the glass, heat losses at the edges of insulated glass have become disproportionately larger. As a result, the NFRC now rates windows as a whole window unit, not just the center of the glass. Whole-unit thermal performance is used to assess windows for net zero buildings.

Another innovation in window technology is installing PV in glazing so that windows generate electricity while they allow views and light. To accomplish this, PV cells are embedded in the insulating glass. This glazing looks somewhat like fritted glass; the transparency can range between 10 and 30 percent. In curtain-wall building-enclosure systems, the PV can be put in spandrel glass. Because it requires electric wiring to each panel of glass, units with larger glass are more cost-effective. Currently, though this strategy is expensive, it has been used on multiple projects.

COOLING

Where mechanical systems for cooling are part of net zero buildings, installing windows with a high insulating value may be effective in reducing cooling loads. Limiting the solar heat gain coefficient will further lower incoming energy. Balancing and tuning windows for optimum performance requires analysis of glazing by orientation for all net zero projects. Commercial and institutional applications with high internal loads call for additional care.

DAYLIGHTING

For optimum daylighting, we prefer insulating glazing with high visible-light transmittance. To minimize energy consumption, however, selecting the optimum VLT involves evaluating daylighting, heating and cooling needs, and glazing performance.

WINDOW SELECTION

Beyond ratings, factors from preferences in materials to historic standards may influence the choice of windows. Table 6.3 shows key areas for comparison between windows, including frame and glazing features, gasketing, performance factors, and environmental considerations. The same kind of matrix can be used to compare skylights, in which case there are other factors that should be included, such as fall impact resistance (important for commercial applications), daylight diffusion, and frame materials.

WINDOW SIZE

In addition to the glass specifications and the edge sealing, the size of the glass affects thermal performance. Because the edge seals perform significantly worse than the glazing, smaller units of glass lose more energy for the same area of glass than larger units. However, allowing some percentage of the glass to be in operable units is effective for cooling, and operable units are limited in how large they can be made. Thus, you should specify the appropriate amount of glazing for ventilation, then

TABLE 6.3. WINDOW COMPARISON MATRIX

CATEGORY	MANUFACTURER		
	Manufacturer 1	Manufacturer 2	Manufacturer 3
Components			
Frame Material	wood, aluminum	insulated fiberglass	insulated fiberglass
Glazing	double or triple; argon or krypton; low-e outer and inner pane	302 HM TC88, #3, #4; T=triple glazing, with two low-e coats and argon gas fills	AF TRI 1 COMARGON (2)
Glazing Thickness	⅞″	1⁵⁄₁₆″	1⅜″ (measured)
Weather Seal	polypropylene	thermoplastic	santoprene rubber seals
Edge Spacer	Cardinal XL Edge	Edgetech's Super Spacer	Tri-pane Super Spacer
Sash Material	wood, aluminum	fiberglass	fiberglass
Nailing Flange	flange on all four sides of frame	nailing fin	flange on all four sides of frame
Hardware and Gaskets	Truth	Truth	Truth (Maxim)
Screen	fiberglass or aluminum; retractable option	fiberglass mesh	fiberglass mesh
Environmental Considerations/ Materials	fiberglass, aluminum, vinyl	fiberglass, polyester resin, expanded polystyrene, nylon, aluminum	fiberglass, resin, nylon, aluminum
Performance			
Unit U-Value	0.19–0.20	0.2	0.24
SHGC	0.16–0.36	0.36	0.45
Visible Transmittance	0.37–0.45	0.65	0.48
Design			
Maximum Frame Width (awnings)	72″	47″	54″
Detail Compatibility	coordinate attachment for oversize units	modify existing brickmold die	brickmold needs mechanically fastened nailing flange from new die
Color Options	6 wood interior species; 9 finish options; 19 standard exterior colors; custom color matching	custom color matching	12 interior and exterior options
Cost and Warranty			
Lead Time	8–10 weeks	8–10 weeks	10 weeks
Product Warranty	10 years glazing: 20 years	frame: lifetime finish: 10 years hardware: lifetime all other: 5 years	fiberglass frames/window system: lifetime, nonprorated Hardware: lifetime
Shipping and Crating Warranty	warranty for product and shipping to point of sale	warranty for product and shipping to point of sale	warranty from warehouse to door, if shipped through manufacturer
Total Price	$XX,XXX (shipping included)	$XX,XXX (shipping included)	$XX,XXX (shipping included)

The solar heat gain through a window or windows is a complex calculation best done with computer software. The first step is determining solar intensity based on location. Then the direct, diffuse, and reflected solar gains are calculated based on window orientation and ground reflectance (the *2009 ASHRAE Handbook—Fundamentals* provides a methodology for this). The resulting value is multiplied by the SHGC of the window to determine the fraction of the total that is transmitted to the building interior; this result is then multiplied again by the percentage of possible sunshine for the locality. These figures must be calculated for every ten-minute interval during the day for six days of each month, then averaged to provide hourly, monthly, and annual output values, expressed in Btu/sf (or W/sm, in SI units). These calculations can be useful as one factor in determining the optimum size and number of windows for a home or building (along with daylighting, views, and code regulations).

leave the other glazing as fixed. Glass size is a major factor in heat gain, heat loss, glare, view, and daylighting. Overglazing is a common mistake in net zero buildings.

EXISTING AND HISTORIC WINDOWS

Sometimes, for reasons of aesthetics or historic preservation, windows with divided lights are part of the building design. If these have muntins and multiple small panes of glass rather than one large pane, their energy performance is greatly reduced. Muntins that are on either one or both sides of the insulated glass so that it still looks like a divided window, do not lower energy performance, but when viewed up close it is clear that they do not extend through the insulated glass layers, which looks odd. Another option is spacers inside the glass, which make it look like the muntins extend through the window. Unfortunately, these muntins are usually metal and therefore compromise the energy performance. All of these options also add significantly to the expense of the windows.

In new net zero buildings, it is most cost-effective to minimize the use of muntins and to use operable and fixed glass in an honest and aesthetically pleasing layout. In existing and particularly in historic buildings, it is appropriate to respect the existing glazing pattern. Energy performance can be enhanced with interior and/or exterior glazing panels that are added to the existing windows. Or if the windows have deteriorated significantly or have already been replaced, some of the true divided lights or possibly divided lights with muntin bars and/or additional panels are appropriate solutions. On historic buildings, you should research and model different options to evaluate historic impacts, costs, durability, and so on.

WINDOW FRAMES

The glass needs to be held in a frame, whether operable or fixed. Most window frames are made of wood, vinyl, or aluminum. Fiberglass is becoming more common but is still a small part of the market. These materials vary in energy performance, durability, and cost.

WOOD WINDOWS

With an R-value of 1 per inch, wood has a reasonable energy performance. Along with foam insulation, wood is used on many Passive House–approved windows to enhance the performance. Although wood is less desirable in exterior applications, many window manufacturers offer a wood frame with aluminum extrusions on the outside to improve durability. Wood and glass expand and contract similarly, which is a benefit.

VINYL WINDOWS

Vinyl windows are typically the least expensive option in the residential market, where their use is common. In North America, they are generally thinner and less durable than in Europe, but there are now some vinyl windows with excellent energy performance on the market. Vinyl windows have multiple airspaces in the frame that add some insulation value. But vinyl expands and contracts more than glass, so there is more differential movement than is optimal. And vinyl involves a toxic manufacturing process that is an environmental detriment.

ALUMINUM WINDOWS

Aluminum is a very common window-frame material, particularly for larger commercial and institutional projects and for curtain-wall applications. Because it is an excellent conductor, aluminum is one of the worst insulating materials available, but it is very durable. In older windows aluminum extends from the interior to the exterior, causing significant heat loss and even allowing ice to form on the inside of frames. In newer windows polyamide or polyurethane is used to create thermal breaks in the aluminum, significantly lessening heat loss. Still, even with this improvement aluminum alone is generally a poor choice for window frames from an energy perspective. When aluminum on the outside is combined with wood or fiberglass for most of the frame, performance can be excellent and appropriate for net zero buildings.

FIBERGLASS WINDOWS

Recently, pultruded fiberglass has become an excellent choice as a material for window frames. Pultrusion is a process whereby woven or braided glass strands are impregnated with resin and pulled through a heated stationary die, where the resin undergoes polymerization. Although the resin in the fiberglass composite is a petroleum product, the manufacture of fiberglass is not nearly as environmentally harmful as the manufacture of vinyl. Fiberglass frames are thick and durable and expand and contract similarly to glass. Fiberglass frames have airspaces that many manufacturers fill with foam, providing excellent insulation value.

CURTAIN WALLS

Curtain-wall systems are common in large commercial and institutional projects and can be made with thermally broken aluminum, but they perform poorly. They typically have an R-value of 3 or lower, and even the best systems are usually only R-4. Curtain-wall systems are about 90 percent glazed and significantly increase heat loss, glare, and overheating. We recommend against them. If you do use curtain walls, however, install spandrel panels for portions of the wall so you can at least add insulation on the inside to improve energy performance and reduce glare and overheating.

A better solution is to have your window manufacturer gang multiple window units together to configure a glazed area that looks like a curtain wall. Still, these multiple window units need to be held together and often reinforced to deal with wind loading, and the reinforcement details, which tend to be metal, create thermal bridges. If you can, substitute engineered wood or fiberglass pultrusions. You can also include spandrel panels to offer the look of a uniform curtain wall while maintaining net zero standards for wall insulation. In general, you will want to give extensive review to curtain walls to avoid significant potential energy and/or durability problems.

Tempering Layer

While using windows in the thermal-, water-, air-, and vapor-control layers is the primary means of designing a building enclosure that is comfortable and healthy for occupants and durable and resilient for the structure, you can take certain measures on the outside of the building, and to some degree on the inside, to improve the interior building performance and create a transitional environment between inside and outside for human benefit. So far we have implied a hard boundary between the inside and outside of the building enclosure. However, many of the most livable, beautiful, and loved buildings blur this transition between building and site.

When we return to our living-building paradigm, we can think of this layer as the fur on an animal, feathers and wings on birds, quills on porcupines, or clothes, an umbrella, or a parasol for a human. With buildings we can distinguish three tempering layers. On the inside and outside of the building enclosure (at windows, doors, or skylights), we may have devices to filter or control sun, heat loss, view, and ventilation, such as blinds, light shelves, shades, curtains, and brise-soleil awnings. Activity

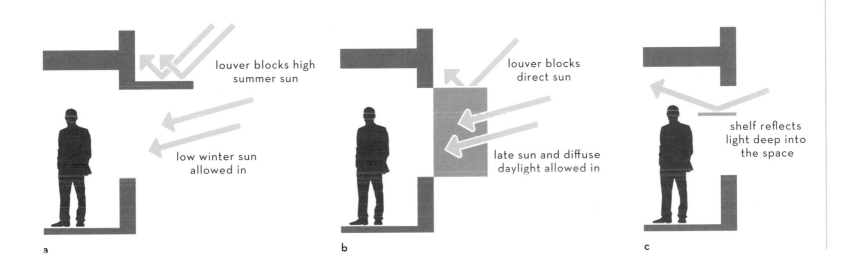

FIGURE 6.20. Sun tempering with devices to control heat gain, reduce glare, or enhance daylighting: (a) horizontal louvers, used on the south façade; (b) vertical louvers, used on the east and west façades; and (c) light shelves.

FIGURE 6.21. Sun tempering by creating a transition space, also called activity tempering.

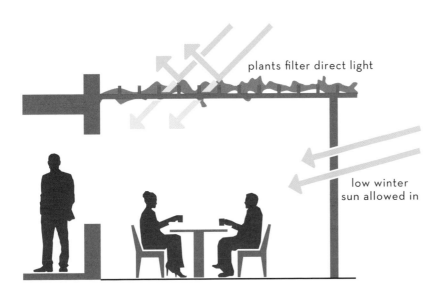

FIGURE 6.22. Sun tempering using vegetation for wall and roof tempering.

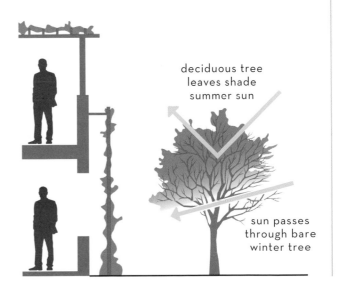

spaces on the outside of buildings, such as porches, balconies, arbors, terraces, roof gardens, and breezeways that create transition space and may modify light, view, glare, and temperatures. The third layer is vegetation—shade trees, shrubs, vines—at various distances from the building that can similarly create space and alter temperatures, views, and lighting. All of these combinations of structures and plantings can be used to temper activity, air, light, heat gain, and view, enhancing both quality of life and energy efficiency. Figures 6.20, 6.21, and 6.22 indicate some of the diversity and beauty in design within what we call the tempering layer.

Movable treatments and fixed devices can augment window performance in new and existing buildings. These enhancements can be used to address some of the conflicting energy-related functions, such as limiting solar heat gain, reducing heat loss, and controlling glare. These can also serve non-energy-related functions, such as insect control, security, aesthetics, UV light blocking, and noise reduction. Window enhancements include natural and horizontal brise-soleils, light shelves for daylighting, awnings, shades, and blinds.

Exterior devices are generally more effective than interior ones at stopping unwanted heat gain. Once sunlight goes through glass and is inside the building, at least some of the heat that has entered the building is trapped. To reduce summer heat gain on the exterior, horizontal shading devices are best on south-facing façades, while vertical devices work better on east and west façades because the sun is lower on the horizon during the cooling season.

Fixed devices such as brise-soleils do not call for any operation to work. Movable devices such as awnings and exterior blinds can be more efficient as they can be adjusted, but because they require operation and are exposed to harsher environmental forces, they demand more maintenance. Although awnings can be reset twice a year, users typically want to adjust exterior blinds more frequently because of their own preferences and daily changes in weather conditions; thus, exterior blinds have operational challenges that may limit their use.

To enhance daylighting, exterior light shelves can be used to reflect light in the upper part of windows while shading the lower portion of the window that allows views. In northern climates with snow conditions, exterior light shelves are exposed to harsher weather conditions than interior light shelves.

Interior devices have the advantages that they are not subject to harsh weather conditions and can be more easily adjusted by building occupants. But they are less efficient at controlling unwanted heat gain, as not all heat that enters the inside space is reflected back. Interior devices may include light shelves, light-directing blinds, and blinds to limit glare and heat gain. In cold climates interior light shelves or other light-guiding devices are less exposed to harsh weather, and there is no shading of lower glass, thus helping winter solar heat gain. Fixed and operable light-guiding blinds allow for light to be reflected onto the ceiling deep into the building. Light-guiding blinds look like typical blinds that are upside down so that they reflect light back onto the ceiling (see figure 6.23). For maximum benefit, the ceiling should be white, without any structure or mechanical system blocking it. The blinds must be spaced and curved to maximize light, meaning that view through the blinds is limited unless the blinds are installed on the upper portion of the windows.

Roller shades can limit glare on lower, view windows. They typically have a fabric screening that allows for view and some sunlight; the percentage of sunshine filtered through can be selected within a range of 3 to 30 percent (see figure 6.23). These shades can have different colors on the inside and outside so that the outside is reflective and the inside is dark, for better viewing. The shades can be manually or electrically operated and are typically mounted inside and rolled up into a valence. Blackout shades eliminate all light when room darkening is required.

Interior insulating blinds can be used to block sun in the summer and insulate windows at night in the winter. While this sounds effective, they have some limitations. Unless they are well sealed along the edges, the insulating value is significantly diminished by convection. In the winter they also often cause condensation on windows. To offer energy savings they must be manually operated, which often does not happen. And finally, shades that offer good performance are relatively expensive. If you are buying new windows, it is more cost-effective to go to R-5 to R-10 windows than to spend money on a combination of lesser windows and insulating blinds.

Other window devices for security, sound, and other uses are not covered here, as their energy contribution to net zero buildings is not great.

FIGURE 6.23. *Left,* light-guiding blinds are composed of highly reflective blades oriented upside down to redirect sunlight upward onto the ceiling of a room, reducing the need for electric lighting in the space without causing glare on work surfaces. *Right,* specially designed roller shades reduce glare while maintaining some daylight and view.

Assembling the High-Performance Building Enclosure

So far in this chapter we have considered water-, vapor-, air-, and thermal-control layers with optimal tempering layers as separate components of the building enclosure. While this can be useful in understanding the purposes, principles, functions, and design strategies related to each control layer, the building enclosure is an integrated assembly of materials that, when properly combined, is energy-efficient and durable and avoids potential moisture problems that could threaten building and occupant health.

CONDENSATION IN THE BUILDING ASSEMBLY

Avoiding condensation in the building assembly requires interrelated focused and integrated design of the vapor-, air-, water-, and thermal-control layers. The interaction of these control layers can cause challenges associated with humidity and dew point. These factors can cause vapor to condense within the building enclosure, which is like having rain enter into our walls and roofs. If the building assembly is composed of materials that can deteriorate, rot, or cause mold, this condensation can create a major problem for our building occupants.

HUMIDITY

Depending on its temperature, air has the ability to hold different amounts of vapor at different humidity levels. In general, cold air holds less moisture than warm air. Thus, in the winter the air inside our buildings can hold more moisture than the air outside. When we shower, wash dishes, and cook with gas, we increase the humidity on the inside of our buildings.

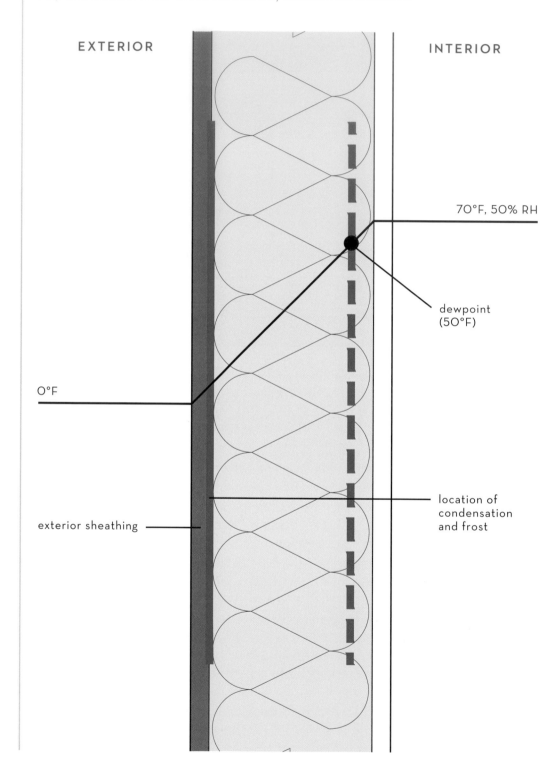

FIGURE 6.24. Temperature varies through a wall assembly. Dew point calculations can help to determine where within the assembly moisture will condense.

EXTERIOR

INTERIOR

70°F, 50% RH

dewpoint
(50°F)

0°F

location of
condensation
and frost

exterior sheathing

CONDENSATION

When the air cannot hold more moisture, the vapor in the air condenses into fluid. This is the phenomenon you see in the summer when water condenses on the exterior of a cold glass of water. The cold glass causes the air around it to get colder; once the air is colder, it cannot hold the same amount of moisture it could when it was warm, causing water to condense on the outside of the glass.

DEW POINT

The temperature at which vapor condenses and changes to a fluid is called the dew point. If our building enclosure is not properly designed, water condenses in the wall assembly and causes damage. The location of the dew point temperature in the enclosure needs to be calculated so that any area of potential condensation can be confined to a place in the enclosure that will do little harm.

As we design a building enclosure, we must consider the outside temperature, the inside temperature, and the humidity levels of both the interior and exterior of the assembly. Depending on the temperatures inside and outside of the enclosure, the temperatures within wall and roof assemblies vary throughout the seasons. This temperature variation determines exactly where within the wall assembly the dew point is likely to be reached.[13]

Rigid insulations on the outside of the structure make for the most forgiving assemblies and are really the only effective solutions for projects with thermally conductive steel and concrete structures. Dew points also need to be

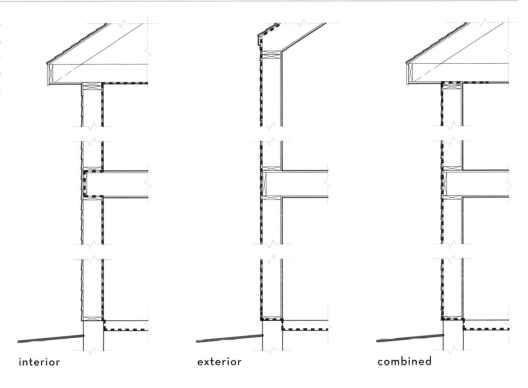

FIGURE 6.25. The air-control layer can be located anywhere within the wall assembly as long as it is continuous around the entire building enclosure. This diagram indicates some of the most common orientations of the air-control layer within a wood-framed wall cavity.

interior exterior combined

calculated on a seasonal basis, so that the assembly avoids condensation under all possible temperature and humidity variations. WUFI is a software program that can calculate seasonal heat and moisture changes in building components and generate graphs showing the temperature and water content through the thickness of the assembly over a range of conditions.

In the design of our building enclosure, we need to make sure that we have not created a situation where condensation can occur in a place that harms the envelope. Generally, we want to keep vapor out of any moisture-vulnerable parts of the building enclosure to the extent that is practical. We also need to allow a means of escape for vapor when it does get in. As mentioned previously, the best way to do this is to install a semi-permeable vapor retarder combined with an air-impermeable air-control layer. In a cold climate, this semipermeable vapor retarder goes on the interior of the assembly to keep moisture in the interior air from moving into the building enclosure. A vapor-permeable water-control layer should be installed on the exterior of the assembly.

LAYERING THE BUILDING ASSEMBLY

Now that we have considered the key design and performance aspects of building enclosure assembly, including the four control layers critical to the long-term performance of the net zero building, we need to take up the construction of this assembly. To be successful, the building enclosure needs to be designed, installed, and commissioned in an integrated and holistic manner.

The orientations of the control layers described here are specific to cold climates and need to be considered in this light. In most cases, the water-control layer is placed toward the outside of the building enclosure assembly, and the vapor retarder is located toward the inside. The air-control layer can be located anywhere within the building enclosure assembly.

In some cases it may seem wise to use one material to accomplish two or more control functions, but is this the best solution? Joseph Lstiburek, a principal of Building Science Corporation, notes that "it is possible and often practical to use one material as the air control layer and a different material as the vapor retarder. However, the air control layer must be continuous and free from holes, whereas the vapor retarder need not be."[14] While it might be possible to save expense by combining, for instance, the air- and water-control layers, keep in mind that each of these control layers is there for a different reason, such as air permeability, water permeability, vapor permeability, continuity, cost, or durability. In most cases, then, it is best to keep all four of the control layers separate, even if they are layered one against another, in order to best accomplish each of their functions. However, keeping all four layers separate can also have its own challenges, such as dealing with the thickness of the layered materials, which can affect the appearance of the finish.

MATERIAL SELECTION AND COMPATIBILITY

Typically, the water-, air-, vapor-, and thermal-control layers are composed of various materials, and it is critical to determine even at the concept design phase that they are compatible with one another and that warranties for the products in each individual layer can be upheld if they are paired together. Like most modern materials, the products that make up the control layers will be composites, multiple materials that when combined have specialized characteristics, thanks to the wonders of chemistry and fossil fuels. For instance, housewraps like Tyvek and Typar stop water and air movement but allow vapor migration. MemBrain and other variable-permeability vapor retarders allow vapor migration under high-humidity conditions but not under low-humidity conditions, allowing moisture-laden assemblies to dry. Our building products are like many of the food products on the market today: composed of multiple chemicals, with their composition generally unknown to the average consumer.

While these highly formulated products have unique and useful characteristics, they can also have compatibility issues. Two materials could deteriorate or destroy one another just by touching each other. To ensure that products are compatible, we typically have to have multiple conversations with manufacturers' representatives to minimize potential problems. This is a time-consuming and sometimes confusing process, and on complex projects it may take the preparation of matrices showing that the compatibility between all materials that come into contact with each other has been verified.

It is also common for a manufacturer to void the warranty of its product if used with another manufacturer's product. While sometimes these warranty issues are related to real compatibility issues, sometimes it seems that they are no more than market-protection strategies. However, as designers, we need to make sure that warranties are upheld for our clients, and therefore we need to follow all product requirements. Verifying product warranties is therefore an important part of the compatibility verification process as well.

MIDDLEBURY SOUTH VILLAGE

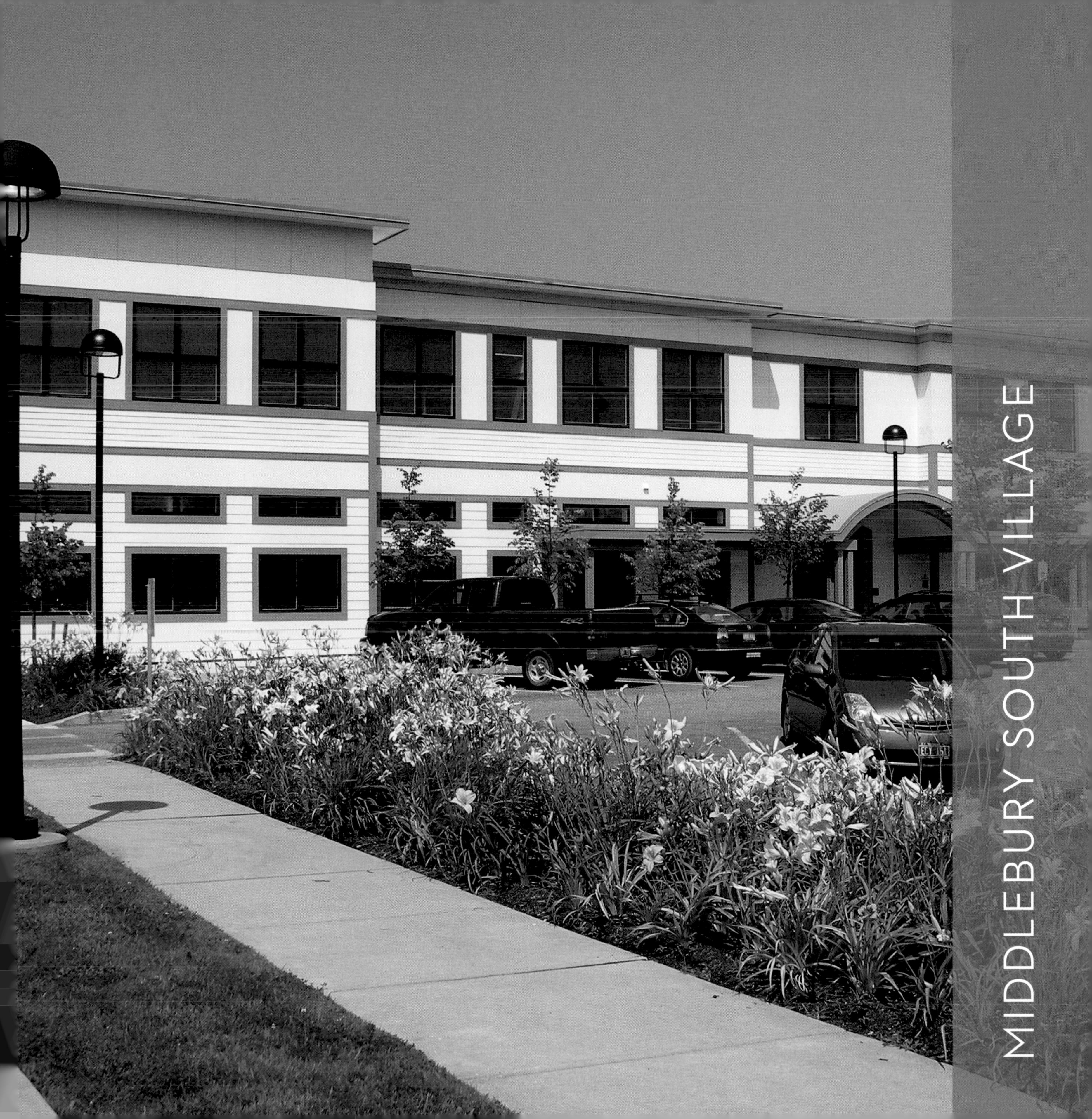

	DESIGN PROFILE		
Building Profile	Building Name:	**Middlebury South Village Professional Office Building**	
	Location:	Middlebury, Vermont	
	Occupancy Date:	May, 2011	
	Square Footage:	17,000	
Energy Profile	Energy Reference Year:	July, 2011–June, 2012	
	Total Energy Consumption:	479,078 kBtu	
	Energy Intensity:	28 kBtu/sf-yr	
Building Envelope	Construction Type:	Steel structure	
	Insulation Values:	Walls:	R-30, 1.5″ rigid, 4″ spray foam
		Roof:	R-70, 24″ cellulose
		Foundation (sub-slab):	R-10, 2″ rigid under whole slab
	Air Infiltration:	Final Blower Door:	1,250 cfm50
			0.06 cfm50/sf exterior surface area
	Windows/Skylights:	Windows:	U-value 0.28
		Skylights:	Nanogel diffuse skylights
Mechanical/ Electrical Systems	Heating System:	Ten high-efficiency propane furnaces with exposed spiral ducts for air distribution, located in mechanical closets adjacent to the spaces they serve	
	Cooling System:	Each furnace with matching condensing unit mounted on the roof to provide cooling; two minisplit cooling systems located in the conference rooms for additional capacity during meeting times	
	Ventilation System:	Ventilation through heating and cooling distribution system	
	Energy Recovery System:	Four HRV units delivering ventilation air to the furnaces	
	Lighting System/Controls:	Occupancy and daylight sensors in all rooms; in open office and lobby areas, daylight harvesting and time-control technologies to turn off lighting outside of business hours or if the spaces are receiving adequate daylighting from the exterior	
		Light level (1st floor):	0.81 watts/sf
		Light level (2nd floor):	0.72 watts/sf
	Hot Water:	Electric hot water	

MIDDLEBURY SOUTH VILLAGE PROFESSIONAL OFFICE BUILDING
High-Performance Energy for a Low Cost

From the outside, the Middlebury South Village (MSV) Professional Office Building looks like a typical office building in Vermont. But this 17,000 sf, two-story structure boasts one of the lowest-tested air infiltration numbers on any project of its size in the state, and the building's energy performance is better than any comparable commercial office building in the Vermont rental market, bringing savings to the owner and tenant alike. What is more, the construction cost in 2012, at $139/sf, was very competitive with costs for office spaces that are much less energy-efficient.

Project Overview

At the southern gateway to Middlebury, Middlebury South Village, winner of Vermont's 2008 Smart Growth Award, is a 31-acre, mixed-use development. For more than ten years prior to its acquisition in 2005 by a group of local investors, the site lay dormant and mired in controversy. Rather than constructing one or two large buildings fronted by a sea of parking, as is typical of highway-type development patterns, the investors took a different approach, implementing the town plan by creating a new village center and neighborhood for the southern end of Middlebury. This energy-efficient new construction is in a well-landscaped setting within walking distance of schools, recreation, major employers, and the county's largest shopping center. Sidewalks throughout MSV connect it to other neighborhoods and the larger Middlebury community.

The MSV Professional Office Building was envisioned as an integral part of this smart-growth community. The office supports the mixed-use goals of both the town planners and the developers, complementing the surrounding residential and retail uses. In addition to designing the office building, Maclay Architects worked with a landscape architecture firm to develop the project master plan.

Vision and Goals

The MSV Professional Office Building was not intended to be the highest-performing building possible; rather, it was designed as an energy-efficient building on a budget restricted by the fact that the developer needed to rent the office space in a competitive rental market. Although this building does not quite achieve the standards we recommend for net zero building projects, it is very close, at 28 kBtu/sf-yr. These levels point to a market-ready approach to very high-performing and very near net zero buildings. The following goals were identified for the project:

SMART GROWTH. The MSV Professional Office Building was meant to be part of the larger smart-growth community, part of a hundred-year solution for continued adaptable

FIGURE CS4.1. The site plan shows the mixed-use village planned for Middlebury South Village.

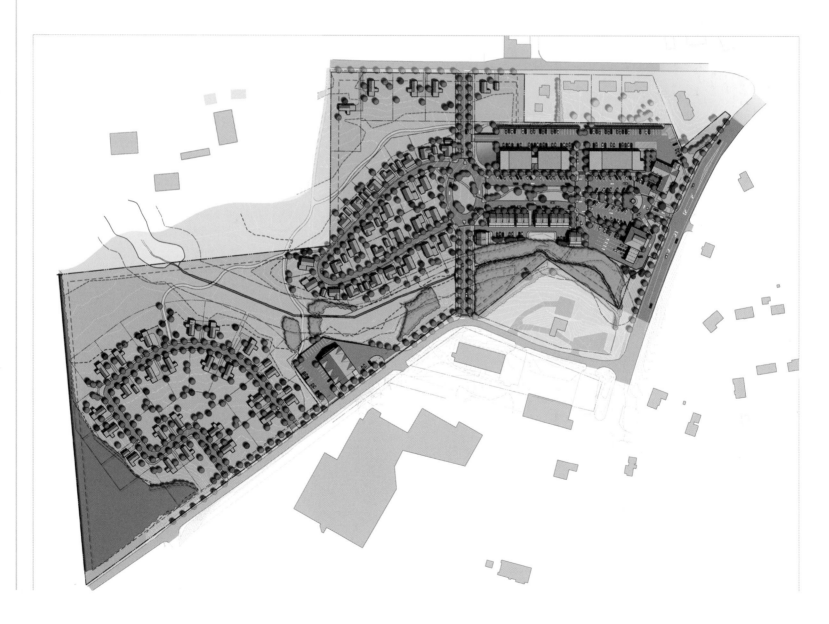

FIGURE CS4.2. The floor plan depicts the mix of shared and private office space in the building.

office
support
circulation
shared

open office

atrium

conference room

0' 4' 8'   16'   32'

use. Currently home to State of Vermont offices, the building was designed so the space can be adapted. Higher-than-normal ceilings on the first floor, for instance, allow the building to be redeveloped as premium-quality retail space should market conditions change.

COST-EFFECTIVE ENERGY PERFORMANCE. Because the project was designed as rentable commercial space, the cost needed to be competitive with other rental properties in the marketplace. Though the owner was committed to designing an energy-efficient and environmentally healthy building, value was the most important factor. Given the performance, which exceeded expectations, this project demonstrates the current viability of net zero commercial buildings today.

HEALTHY WORKPLACE. Part of the environmental focus of this building was creating a healthy workplace. This was accomplished by maximizing daylighting and views while developing open, flexible workspaces rather than small, closed offices. In addition, efficient mechanical systems optimized indoor air quality for users.

Energy

Energy conservation in this project encompassed smart-growth planning and site design; a near-net-zero building envelope; exceptional air-sealing performance; maximized daylighting; and efficient, right-sized mechanical systems.

The relationship of the MSV Professional Office Building to the larger neighborhood might be the most important energy consideration in the entire project. Although the decision to elongate the building along the north–south axis is contrary to ideal solar orientation, it does uphold holistic, smart-growth thinking. This orientation accommodated the construction site, reinforced the central town green, and allowed for increased site density for continued smart-growth development. The increased density on the site—reinforcing the pedestrian-focused community—will conserve more energy than an optimal east–west orientation. This strategy addresses the need for focusing on net zero communities rather than individual buildings and conserving energy by encouraging mass transit and pedestrian access while reducing sprawl and automobile use.

The building assembly developed for the MSV Professional Office Building bridged the gap between cost and energy efficiency. While at slightly lower than net zero levels, the insulation levels are well beyond that of a code-compliant building and almost all high-performing buildings. The high-performance building/near-net-zero assembly has the following components:

- An R-70 roof assembly with an average of 24″ of cellulose insulation
- An R-30 wall assembly with 1.5″ of rigid foam insulation outside of 4″ of polyurethane spray foam in the wall cavity
- R-3.3 fiberglass and wood windows with fiberglass frames and low-e, argon-filled, double glazing
- An R-10 foundation and underslab with 2″ of rigid foam insulation

Sandy LaFlamme, an energy consultant for Efficiency Vermont, noted that the MSV Professional Office Building is one of the tightest commercial buildings her organization has tested, and it also achieved Core Performance, a nationally recognized set of high-performing building standards.

The building had its highest efficiency metric for intensive air sealing, which is one of the most cost-effective ways to boost energy efficiency. The project set an air-sealing requirement in the specifications of 0.20 cfm50/sf of above-ground surface area, well beyond that required by the Vermont energy code. Although this was an ambitious goal, blower door tests at the completion of the project verified an air-infiltration rating of 0.06 cfm50/sf of exterior surface area, a rating 70 percent better than what was required in the specifications. The resulting propane savings, from reducing the air infiltration from 0.20 cfm50/SF to 0.06 cfm50/SF, is $1,600/yr at $3.40 per gallon per the Vermont Fuel Price Report average retail cost for propane for February 2011.

Multiple factors helped us exceed the air-sealing goal by such a significant margin, but most important was the integrated team process that included multiple meetings, mock-ups, and testing to ensure all team members were fully committed to and understood how to reach our goal. The air-sealing measures included careful attention to maintaining the continuity of the air and water barrier on all six sides of the building enclosure.

Lighting and daylighting strategies contributed to both energy conservation and a healthy workplace. The design team maximized views and connections to the outdoors, using daylighting for as much of the interior lighting as possible. To achieve this, windows were located around the entire perimeter of the building. EcoSmart shades block glare and provide user control. High-R-value, diffuse, nanogel skylights provide effective daylight harvesting while maintaining the high-performing envelope on the second floor.

All rooms in the building are controlled both by occupancy and daylight sensors. The open office and lobby areas apply both daylight-harvesting and time-control technologies to regulate lighting outside of normal business hours. While Vermont building energy codes allow for 1.1 watts/sf for lighting, through the use of T-8 fluorescent fixtures this project accomplished lighting efficiencies of 0.72 watts/sf on the second floor and 0.81 watts/sf on the first floor.

Ten propane-fired, high-efficiency furnaces with exposed spiral ducts for air distribution provide heating and cooling. The furnaces are located in mechanical closets adjacent to the areas that they serve and have matching condensing units mounted on the roof to provide cooling. Great care was taken in detailing the air barrier around these roof penetrations to ensure these junctures are as tight as possible. In addition to the full building mechanical system, two minisplit cooling systems are located in the conference rooms to provide additional cooling capacity during large meetings.

FIGURE CS4.3. High-performance wall section.

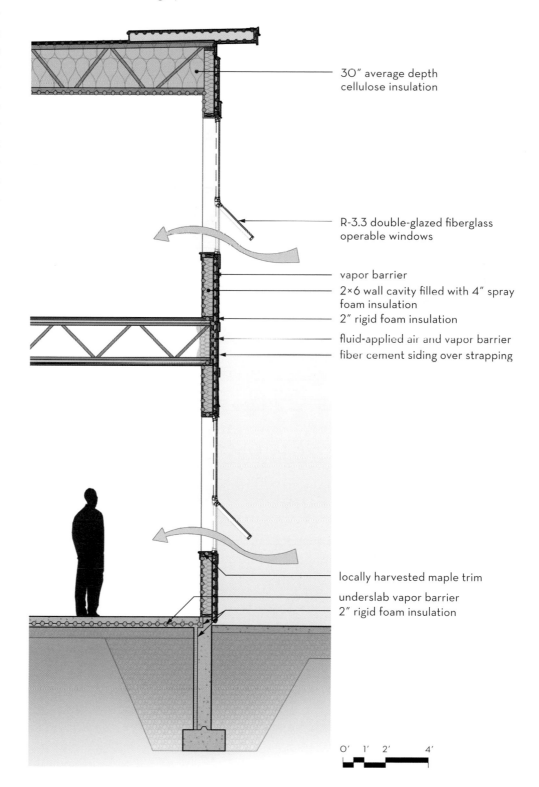

30" average depth cellulose insulation

R-3.3 double-glazed fiberglass operable windows

vapor barrier

2×6 wall cavity filled with 4" spray foam insulation

2" rigid foam insulation

fluid-applied air and vapor barrier

fiber cement siding over strapping

locally harvested maple trim

underslab vapor barrier

2" rigid foam insulation

0' 1' 2'   4'

FIGURE CS4.4. ExoAir, a liquid membrane, was applied at every seam of the exterior wall sheathing to create a continuous, impenetrable air barrier, which was instrumental in delivering the high performance in air-infiltration tests.

FIGURE CS4.5. Entrance of the Middlebury South Village Professional Office Building.

Healthy and Sustainable Strategies

Throughout the course of the design, we took special care to increase the durability of the building envelope, reduce water usage, and use local materials, including Vermont slate as a floor finish for the lobby and locally harvested maple lumber for cabinetry and interior trim.

Collaborative Process

The MSV Professional Office Building is an example of how a collaborative approach leads to the successful completion of an award-winning, high-performance project. While there are many instances where this process benefited the project, the most significant is the successful design, installation, and performance of the air-barrier system. On other projects our design team had set and achieved lower blower door–testing numbers, but the goal in this case was far below what is considered standard for the design and construction industry. Because they were responsible for meeting the goal, the construction team was understandably concerned. The owner, the design team, and the construction team held meetings, reviewed mock-ups, discussed strategies and alternatives, and weighed costs. Along with the owner, the construction manager, the air-barrier subcontractor, Efficiency Vermont (the state energy efficiency utility), and the architect all were part of critical discussions about the air barrier. And in the end the project exceeded everyone's expectations.

7 | The Essential Elements of Net Zero Buildings

n 2007 the construction and renovation of buildings in the United States cost $1.82 trillion, accounting for 12.4 percent of the GDP.[1]

As gas prices continue to soar and performance is brought to the forefront of every car commercial, there are very few consumers who will buy a car without taking its fuel efficiency into account. In comparison, very few owners and operators know how much energy their buildings use, even though they will invest much more money over their lifetime in their buildings than their cars. Of the small percentage of building owners or facility managers who do know how much total energy their buildings use, an even smaller percentage has any idea whether the usage is typical, high, or low for a similar building.

Equally important, very few building professionals know what level buildings need to be designed to in order to kick our addiction to oil. Many are aware of ways to reduce consumption by 5 or 10 percent but not the 50 to 80 percent necessary to transition to net zero buildings and ultimately a net zero planet.

We've found that generating a beautiful, resilient, healthy, and ecofriendly net zero building is a twelve-step process, and we outline that process in chapter 18. But at the heart of those twelve steps are three essential elements:

- Minimize energy loads to renewable-ready EUI metrics;
- Optimize systems for comfort and efficiency consistent with EUI metrics; and
- Provide power with renewable energy systems, sized to meet EUI-determined energy consumption.

All of these deal with energy, and rightly so. The successful path to a net zero building is defined by setting and meeting strict energy-consumption goals, which need to be around 80 percent less than a typical building's consumption in order to make renewable installation cost-effective. This load reduction needs to be supported by the installation of ultraefficient, low-complexity mechanical and electrical systems that ensure comfort and health for building occupants. Once building energy loads are understood and building performance is maximized, renewable energy systems need to be installed to cover the annual energy consumption of the building. To meet net zero cost-effectively, you must achieve the EUI principle and each of these three steps; if you leave out any of the elements, you will have major challenges in meeting the goal.

EUI Metrics: The Secret to Net Zero Building Success

During the design process, architects and engineers are more frequently beginning to estimate annual building energy consumption and the associated costs. Even so, there is a need for still greater understanding in the field to verify whether a building is being designed to the appropriate metrics. The design team rarely goes the next step and compares the predicted performance of the design to the actual performance of the finished building to understand how their projects are doing once they are built. After construction, often the only person who tracks a building's energy performance is the building owner, and often only as part of the budgeting process. This annual tracking of energy costs could provide valuable information to someone experienced in building metrics but often gives the building owner no more than an idea of energy price fluctuations.

Our hope is building owners will one day compare this annual energy data against a set of national or regional building energy metrics as a standard practice, providing them with a more complete understanding of how their buildings perform in relation to others and encouraging them to continually improve this performance. Just as an auto manufacturer would hardly brag about a car's performing in the lowest 50 percent of automobiles, owners will not want their buildings' performance to be in the bottom 50 percent.

In the future a building's energy performance will be a strong factor in determining a building's market value and lease rate; having predictable fuel bills can make a property more valuable, pushing up the selling price (see chapter 17 for more information).

Just as it is easy to calculate the fuel mileage of a car, it is relatively easy to calculate the energy performance of a building. The EUI number is found by taking the total energy consumption per year and dividing it by building size. We typically refer to the resulting metric as energy intensity, and what it is really telling us is the "fuel mileage" of the building. But because the EUI number takes into account only the energy consumed by the building and does not include the energy produced by the building, it tells only part of the net zero story. The focus on the demand side is critical in order to establish a cost-effective, energy-conservation metric. We address the energy-production side of the equation separately, later in this chapter.

CALCULATING THE EUI NUMBER

The EUI number is calculated from two numbers: the total annual energy consumed by a building from all sources and the base of standardization—typically the total conditioned, or heated and cooled, square footage of the building. In order to find the EUI number, we first need to determine these component numbers.

The annual energy consumed includes the total amount of energy used to run systems within the building as well as limited energy use outside of the building footprint, such as for site lighting. Most buildings use multiple energy sources to run their systems, such as electricity, oil, natural gas, propane, wood, or others in limited applications. To determine the total annual energy consumed, the energy use from all sources must be combined. The challenge in doing this is that each energy source is generally measured by a different set of metrics. For example, electricity use is reported in kWh, oil in therms, and wood in cords. In order to compare or combine the energy use from different sources, we need to convert to a consistent metric. The most common choice is British thermal units (Btu). One Btu is defined as the amount of energy required to raise the temperature of one pound of water by 1°F, at a constant pressure of one atmosphere. Because the energy unit of a Btu is so small, this conversion of annual energy loads results in very large numbers. To make the numbers more manageable, we use kBtu, or thousands of Btu, as our reporting unit, as you will see in the conversions factors listed in figure 7.2. All energy use can be converted to Btu through the process described in the sidebar "Calculating Annual Energy Consumption."

Conditioned area is defined as the space within the building that is heated and/or cooled. This is measured to the outside of the thermal enclosure. This calculation includes some spaces that may not be part of other square-footage calculations, such as storage areas and mechanical rooms when they are in the middle of other conditioned spaces. Any spaces that exist within the conditioned building enclosure should be included in this calculation. However, in smaller buildings and residential construction there are frequently basement spaces that are inside the thermal enclosure of the building but are not occupied by building users and are not heated or cooled. In these cases we do not include them in our calcuations. But if the basement is occupied—for instance, as a walkout—do count that square footage.

To determine the EUI number, reported in kBtu/sf-yr, we divide the annual energy consumed by the conditioned area (see sidebar "Calculating the EUI number"). Although the EUI number can be given in other units, the calculation is always based on a measure of the total energy consumed divided by a unit of standardization, which in most cases is the conditioned square footage of the building. The other most common unit for reporting EUI is kWh/m²-yr (to which, of course, we can convert our number). In order to accurately compare EUI numbers, you must verify that all units are the same.

THE LIMITATIONS OF EUI

The EUI number is the best way of evaluating and comparing energy consumption between buildings. It is relatively easy to calculate during preliminary design stages, based on projections, and so can inform design decisions. However, the EUI number has some important limitations that are critical to understand when using it as a metric for net zero design.

BUILDING USE

The EUI number can vary significantly between buildings with different uses. For instance, restaurants, laboratories, manufacturing facilities, and hospitals have much higher energy intensities than buildings such as offices, homes, and classrooms. Comparing the EUI numbers of buildings of unlike use is similar to comparing the miles per gallon of cars to that of trucks or buses. Most groups that collect building-energy-use data categorize their data by building function. This point is especially important to remember if you are designing a building that is not typical of its use category.

To address the issue of comparing the EUI numbers between buildings with different uses, we disaggregate the building loads to isolate specialty uses. When designing a building with high-energy function, such as one of those mentioned above, we separate the process load and consider only what we call the enclosure load, which includes the heating and cooling load, ventilation load, lighting load, domestic hot water load, and plug loads. However, the enclosure load may be all that the design team has control over, since manufacturing, laboratory, or commercial kitchen equipment specific to the building use is often brought in from existing facilities or not specified by the design team.

Many question whether investing in energy conservation is cost-effective in a building with large process loads. In fact, the benefit of investing in energy conservation is often the same across the board: saving 100 kBtu in one building is the same as saving 100 kBtu in another building regardless of the process loads. But the equation can change dramatically if excess process energy can be used to supplement heating and cooling production. When designing buildings with larger process loads, it makes sense first to invest money in energy conservation related to the process loads, where it can be cheaper and easier to make a greater dent in the total energy consumption of the building. Both the process and enclosure loads should be evaluated for their energy conservation options, however, and a cost-benefit analysis should be performed to determine the best options for energy conservation in both areas. EUI numbers are greatly affected by the building use. Table 7.3 indicates typical existing EUI numbers for multiple common building types as well as expected EUI numbers for code, high-performance, and net zero buildings of each type.[2]

INTERNAL VS. EXTERNAL LOADS

To determine the best energy conservation strategy for a building, you need to understand whether the building is

To determine the total energy consumption of a building in kBtu, you need to convert the total consumption by each energy source to its kBtu equivalent and then add these amounts together.

Tables 7.1 and 7.2 provide information that will allow you to easily calculate the annual energy consumption for your building. Table 7.1 indicates the average energy content of various fuels. Table 7.2 is a chart that can be used for most buildings as a guide to determining the total annual energy consumption in kBtu. For each energy source that is used in your building, enter the annual use in the correct units, multiply by the conversion factor, and sum the results to determine your annual energy consumption.

For example, if a building uses 16,000 ccf of natural gas and 25,000 kWh of electricity in a year, you can use the conversion factors in table 7.1 to find the total building consumption of 101,805 kBtu/year.

$$16,000 \text{ ccf of natural gas} \times \frac{1.03 \text{ kBtu}}{1 \text{ ccf natural gas}} = 16,480 \text{ kBtu}$$

$$25,000 \text{ kWh} \times \frac{3.413 \text{ kBtu}}{1 \text{ kWh}} = 85,325 \text{ kBtu}$$

$$\text{total} = 101,805 \text{ kBtu}$$

Each energy source has specific considerations:

- Electric: Electric bills for businesses will often include kWh usage as well as kW demand. For this exercise, we are interested only in annual kWh usage. Add together kWh readings for a twelve-month period to get annual kWh use.

TABLE 7.1: CONVERSION FACTORS FOR ENERGY SOURCES

BASE UNIT	kBtu
1 kWh of electricity	3.413
1 cubic foot of natural gas	1.008–1.034
1 therm of natural gas	100
1 gallon of liquefied petroleum	91.676–95.475
1 gallon of crude oil	138.095
1 gallon of gasoline	125
1 ton of coal	16,200–26,000
1 ton of wood	9,000–17,000
1 standard cord of wood	18,000–24,000
1 pound of low-pressure steam (recoverable heat)	1

internal- or external-load dominated. In external-load-dominated buildings, the majority of the need for heating or cooling is derived from the external environment; internal-load-dominated buildings are ones with large internal process loads. Even buildings with small or no process loads can have significant internal loads, including the heat generated from computers, lights, motors, pumps, and even the body heat of occupants. These all become more significant as buildings

are built to conform to net zero standards, in which added insulation and tighter building enclosures prevent any heat generated inside from escaping.

As uses within the building become denser or the buildings get larger, internal loads can become quite substantial. Even in cold northern climates, internal-load-dominated buildings—like computer server buildings and manufacturing facilities—that require three-season cooling are common. Whether the load is

- Natural gas: Natural-gas usage is measured in ccf (100 cubic feet). Sum your natural gas usage for twelve months to get annual use.
- Fuel oil: Fuel-oil usage is reported in gallons. Fuel-oil fill-ups often do not follow a monthly schedule, so make your best estimate as to how to sum reported fill-ups to get to annual usage.
- Propane: As with fuel oil, propane usage is reported in gallons. Fuel fill-ups often do not follow a monthly schedule, so make your best estimate as to how to add together reported fill-ups to get to annual use.
- Cordwood: It is important to count how much wood you used, not how much you purchased. At the beginning of the heating season, determine how much wood you have stored, add any purchases during the season, and then subtract how much wood is left at the end of the season.
- Wood pellets: Wood pellets, like cordwood, are often delivered intermittently and so call for the same method as indicated for cordwood to determine annual use.

Summing all of the results in the annual consumption (kBtu) column will give you the total annual energy consumption for the building to be used in the calculation of the EUI number. With all of these sources except electricity and natural gas, it is helpful to look at multiple-year consumption, since annual consumption varies based on delivery methods, especially for wood.

TABLE 7.2: CALCULATION OF ANNUAL ENERGY CONSUMPTION

SOURCE (UNITS)	ANNUAL USE			ANNUAL CONSUMPTION
Electricity (kWh)	_____ kWh	×	3.413 kBtu/kWh	_____ kBtu
Natural Gas (ccf)	_____ ccf	×	1.03 kBtu/ccf	_____ kBtu
Fuel Oil (gal)	_____ gal	×	130 kBtu/gal	_____ kBtu
Propane (gal)	_____ gal	×	92 kBtu/gal	_____ kBtu
Cordwood (cord)	_____ cords	×	19,600 kBtu/cord	_____ kBtu
Wood Pellets (ton)	_____ tons	×	13,600 kBtu/ton	_____ kBtu
				_____ Total kBtu

primarily externally or internally generated is not visible in the EUI number, though, which in its simplicity does not differentiate between heating and cooling loads.

SURFACE AREA VS. FLOOR AREA

The EUI number uses floor area as its unit of standardization and does not take into account the layout of the building, whether it is compact and has a small surface-area-to-floor-area ratio or is a complex, highly articulated building with a high surface-area-to-floor-area ratio. Because the energy use of a building is greatly affected by the amount of heat that is allowed to escape through the exterior surface area, the extent of surface area can have a large affect on overall energy consumption. It is better to design a high-performance building with a compact shape, as it allows for the most efficient heating and cooling with the least amount of materials. However, there are some

CALCULATING THE EUI NUMBER

To calculate the EUI number for a building, you divide the annual energy consumed by the conditioned square footage. To understand this, let us take the example in the previous sidebar, "Calculating Annual Energy Consumption," which found a total energy consumption of 101,805 kBtu for a building that uses 16,000 ccf of natural gas and 25,000 kWh of electricity annually. Let's now assume that this building is an office building with 10,000 sf of conditioned area (space that is heated and cooled for occupant use). The EUI number is calculated as follows:

The annual energy use of this building can now be compared against the annual energy use of other office buildings even if they are not the same size. Although it makes no sense to compare the annual energy consumption of 101,805 kBtu for a 10,000 sf building to that of 190,000 kBtu for a 20,000 sf office building, the EUI number lets us show that the larger building actually has a smaller energy intensity per square foot of conditioned area, at 9.5 kBtu/sf-yr compared to the 10.2 kBtu/sf-yr for the smaller building.

$$\frac{\text{annual energy consumed}}{\text{conditioned square footage}} = \frac{101,805 \text{ kBtu}}{10,000 \text{ sf}} = 10.2 \text{ kBtu/sf-yr}$$

TABLE 7.3. EUI NUMBERS BY BUILDING TYPE

BUILDING TYPE	TYPICAL EXISTING[a] (kBtu/sf-yr)	CODE[b] (kBtu/sf-yr)	HIGH-PERFORMANCE (kBtu/sf-yr)	NET ZERO (kBtu/sf-yr)
Office	92.9	45–55	25–45	10–25
Education	83.1	45–55	25–45	10–25
Single Family Home	55.4	35–45	20–35	5–20
Multifamily Home	78.3	35–45	20–35	5–20

[a] Typical existing building EUI numbers are sourced from the 2009 *Buildings Energy Data Book* published by the US Department of Energy tables 2.1.11 and 3.1.13, http://buildingsdatabook.eren.doe.gov/ChapterIntro2.aspx

[b] Code numbers are estimates.

In designing for cold climates, we are typically considering buildings with larger heating energy demands than cooling energy demands. However, in larger, more massive buildings, particularly in the southern range of cold climates, cooling demands are frequently larger than heating demands, particularly in net zero ready buildings, because internal building loads begin to grow larger than external building loads. Inside loads (which include lights, servers, computers, equipment, people's body heat, and cooking) all produce heat within the building that can require cooling year-round. With global climate change making temperatures rise, internal-load-dominated buildings that require constant cooling will become more common.

There are some ways to combat this constant need for cooling. In larger buildings, for instance, you can design narrower floor plates to increase the building's surface area and reduce the likelihood of the building's being internal-load dominated.

Internal-load-dominated buildings involve energy-saving strategies different from those for external-load-dominated buildings. For instance, for an internal-load-dominated building, it might not make sense to include as much insulation as you would otherwise. Because energy conservation for internal-load-dominated buildings is becoming increasingly complex, you will want to investigate multiple measures with computer modeling.

restrictions to this rule, based on daylight penetration and the effects of process loads, as mentioned above. To achieve the same EUI number with a higher surface-area-to-floor area ratio means employing greater energy conservation measures, which means in turn more resources and higher cost to achieve the same result.

PROGRAM EFFICIENCY

The EUI number does not take into account the efficiency of space use in the building. Both the number of users per room area and quantity of circulation spaces affect building efficiency, so it is possible for two buildings to accommodate the same program designed for the same number of people but for one to be twice as large as the other. While the smaller building serves the same number of people and provides its programmed use much more efficiently, this efficiency is not reflected in the EUI number. Though the larger building likely has a higher heating and cooling load associated with a greater surface area, plug and equipment loads may be close to the same between the buildings, as those are more closely related

to the number of users than the size of the building. It is therefore possible that the building with the less-efficient space usage may have a better EUI, even though it requires more materials to construct and likely has a higher construction cost.

Even if the larger building does have a lower EUI, when you compare the total energy consumed by the building, it will use more energy overall to perform the same function as the smaller building. While some of the additional spaces in this larger building might increase the beauty of the space and the occupant comfort, in general more efficient space utilization is a positive goal in the design of high-performance buildings.

DENSITY OF USE

The density of use—the number of building users per square foot of building area—is also not figured into the EUI number. A 5,000 sf home that houses only a couple could have a better EUI number than a 2,000 sf home for a family of six. Though the numbers alone suggest that the larger home is more energy-efficient, the smaller home is a better use of resources per person. Some energy experts advocate the evaluation of building performance based on the number of people accommodated per square foot, in particular for homes. The goal would be to curtail the green McMansion phenomenon, where big, expensive homes are designed to be energy-efficient but are far from ideal with a larger view to energy and resource consumption.

This concept has been discussed in the commercial and institutional market as well, and it is especially relevant for educational buildings, where it makes sense to evaluate energy use on a per student basis. For instance, it would be useful for colleges to evaluate energy consumption according to student capacity on a campus. While there is a valid argument to move toward evaluating energy consumption on a per occupant basis, our use of an EUI number based on building size comes back to the fact that building size remains constant: it is an easily measurable number that does not change. The occupant number goes up and down over time. Even for programs that use the occupant number in their evaluation of metrics, such as LEED, the calculations to get to the occupant number are not simple. For a home or a school, the occupant number might be relatively constant and possible to use, but for most commercial buildings occupant numbers reflect expected use patterns and can therefore be dramatically different from what actually happens as uses evolve. As energy costs increase, so may the occupant density.

WHY BOTHER WITH EUI?

Hoping to improve energy performance without metrics and measurements is like trying to drive a car blindfolded. While the draftiness of the building or how much we pay in monthly fuel bills might give us some general idea of how our buildings are performing, our assessments are often anecdotal and inaccurate, leading to a reduced likelihood of our improving their performance. We must understand how our buildings perform and compare to similar buildings in order to set meaningful and effective design goals to get to net zero buildings and communities.

The EUI number, as it is discussed in this chapter, is developed in two different ways and serves two different purposes. The performance EUI, as we have seen, is based on the actual energy consumption of the building. The design EUI is the goal set during design; it is developed in reference to known building uses and based on energy modeling.

SETTING A DESIGN EUI

The EUI number helps develop a clear metric that will act as a foundational goal throughout the entire design process. This number should be reevaluated at every subsequent design phase with modeling updates to determine if it is still the right goal and can be successfully achieved. The design EUI number helps evaluate potential performance options, such as changes in the mechanical systems design, higher-cost insulation options, and choices for renewable systems. The final design metric should also be compared against the performance EUI number—calculated after a year of data is collected—to determine how the building actually performs as opposed to the modeled performance expectations.

The design EUI should be developed by a qualified individual or team experienced with energy metrics for high-performance buildings—specifically, someone with a track record of actual, documented energy performance consistent with energy modeling. Since this number is so critical to achieving net zero goals, it is essential to have a member of the design team responsible for monitoring the achievement of this number throughout design and the first year of operation. Generally, the first iteration of this number is based on the energy use of the specific building type in relation to performance metrics for net zero buildings. The EUI numbers in table 7.3 can be useful in setting metrics for building performance because they document an initial benchmark for assessing net zero performance EUI metrics. When establishing an EUI number for a net zero building, we aim for 10 kBtu/sf-yr, with 20 kBtu/sf-yr as the upper end. This goal generally is related to enclosure loads only, and any large process loads are added to this EUI number to establish a total energy load for the building.

Minimizing Energy Loads

Once we've established a design EUI goal, we can begin designing the building to meet that goal. To accomplish this, we disaggregate our total building energy load into component

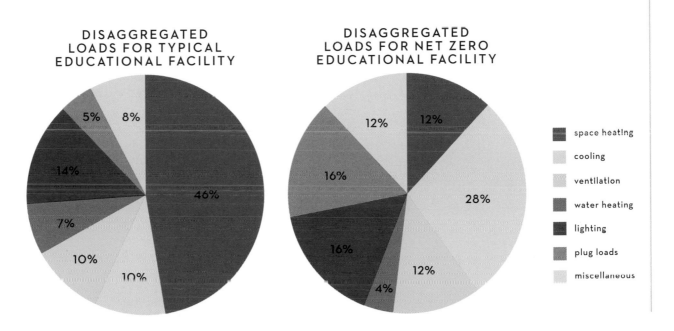

FIGURE 7.1. A typical educational facility uses almost 50 percent of its energy consumption for space heating. On the other hand, a net zero facility will use approximately 12 percent of its energy consumption on space heating.

DISAGGREGATED
LOADS FOR TYPICAL
EDUCATIONAL FACILITY

DISAGGREGATED
LOADS FOR NET ZERO
EDUCATIONAL FACILITY

■ space heating
□ cooling
▨ ventilation
■ water heating
■ lighting
■ plug loads
▨ miscellaneous

loads, including heating, cooling, ventilation, lighting, hot water, plug, and miscellaneous loads. A sample for a typical educational building is shown in figure 7.1. We disaggregate the loads to better understand energy use in the building and to optimize energy-conservation measures. We then set goals for each component of the disaggregated load to ensure the building will meet the total EUI goal. During preliminary design we initially develop energy goals for each component load; throughout design we use energy modeling to ensure that design decisions align with these preliminary targets. If energy modeling indicates a significant discrepancy between model and design goals, we revise the expectations for each component load and the overall design strategies until modeling numbers meet the EUI goal.

We also conduct room-by-room programming analysis to determine building and occupancy requirements in more detail (table 7.4). This analysis documents total energy use in the building by people, room, and equipment as well as solar heat gain and any unusual loads. With this detailed understanding of the individual building loads, we confirm that we have a reasonable estimate for the total energy load of the building.

When we disaggregate building loads, we typically consider heating, cooling, lighting, domestic hot water, ventilation, plug loads, and process loads. Heating and cooling loads as well as domestic hot water are discussed in greater detail later in this chapter. Other component loads, including particular challenges and basic load reduction strategies, are discussed below.

LIGHTING LOADS

Lighting loads are all electrical uses that provide lighting within the building. This includes electricity to power lighting and lighting-control systems, such as dimmers, occupancy sensors, and mechanical daylight-harvesting technologies. To reduce this load, daylighting should supply all or nearly all of the lighting

TABLE 7.4. ROOM-BY-ROOM ENERGY PROGRAMMING

		AREA/LOADS				
Room	Area (sf)	Function	Number of Occupants	Hours Occupied	Equipment	Window(sf)/ Orientation	Notes
		Primary/Secondary	Min/Max	Min/Max	Computer/Copier/Printer/Other	N/S/E/W	
Total	_____ sf		____/____	____/____			

for occupied spaces in the building during daytime hours. Net zero buildings, depending on their programming and security requirements, should be close to achieving 100 percent daylight autonomy—a term that means all occupied spaces are entirely lit by daylight when available. As discussed in chapter 4, building massing should optimize daylighting. Once the building massing is so designed, then the lighting designer decides how the lighting can meet specific watt/sf requirements based on functional requirements for each space.

DOMESTIC HOT WATER

The domestic hot water load is the energy consumed to heat water for the bathroom, kitchen, laundry room, and needs other than the heating system. In most buildings this use is relatively small, but in food-service buildings, laboratories, and manufacturing facilities the domestic hot water load can be sizable.

VENTILATION

Because net zero buildings are designed to have very little air infiltration, it is particularly important to provide adequate ventilation for the building occupants. The fans and motors used to do so can cause significant ventilation loads. ASHRAE establishes general ventilation rates based on building types, which are incorporated into building codes. These standards, however, frequently lead to the calculation of excessively large ventilation loads. For all buildings, you should consider the following reduction strategies:

- Accurately estimate room-by-room occupancy and diversity of use.
- Use occupancy-, manual-, and demand-controlled ventilation controls.
- Separate heating and cooling distribution from ventilation.
- Use 100 percent outside air with a heat or energy recovery system.

Ventilation loads need to match up with occupancy. A room without occupants needs no significant ventilation. A room such as a conference room can sit vacant for most of the day but swell to a large occupancy for short periods. If the room is ventilated at that maximum rate at all times, the ventilation load will be much higher than needed.

Even workstations or offices may have varying ventilation needs. *Science Daily* reports, "In a typical working week, people spend on average 5 hours and 41 minutes per day sitting at their desk,"[3] highlighting the lack of need for maximum ventilation at all times. Ventilation strategies that match the diversity of use within spaces can be much smaller than those that require maximum ventilation at all times.

The ASHRAE calculation method allows for an assumption of a diversity of space uses to ensure that the sizing of ventilation loads are realistic and not grossly overestimated. This takes into account the fact that a conference room is often filled by occupants of other spaces in the building. This sort of appropriate sizing saves on both initial capital cost by not calling for a larger, more complex ventilation system and operating costs in comparison to running the larger system. While the overall building ventilation load may be reduced on the assumption that not all rooms will be filled to maximum occupancy at the same time, individual rooms need to be designed for variable occupancy, such that each space is able to meet its ventilation requirements at maximum occupancy. By using occupancy sensors, CO_2 sensors, and manual controls, you can design a ventilation-control strategy that ensures occupant health without excessive energy consumption.

To further reduce energy loads, ventilation distribution is typically separated from the heating/cooling distribution system so they both operate specifically when needed. To provide the best indoor-air quality and reduce energy consumption, we typically do not use recirculating air systems. Instead, we use 100 percent outside air but only the required amount. By not oversupplying fresh air to the building, we can reduce energy consumption related to ventilation and still maintain the best indoor air quality for the occupants.

EQUIPMENT AND PLUG LOADS

Plug loads are created by computers, appliances, and other equipment plugged into outlets. These loads are not affected by high-performance enclosure design and are usually not included in the design process. In typical buildings, however, plug loads are significant, and in net zero buildings they represent an even larger proportion of energy consumption. While this is a user issue and usually out of the building designer's control, you do need to address the matter in net zero buildings. Plug loads have expanded significantly with the digital revolution, so for

homes you will want to research and specify the lowest-energy-consuming Energy Star appliances. In a densely populated office, if two monitors are used with a desktop computer the load factor could be as high as 2 W/sf; laptop computers can bring this down as low as 0.25 W/sf.[4] You should also evaluate and eliminate phantom power loads—the electricity appliances and electronics consume when they are turned off or in a standby mode—by using separate power strips with controls. Plug-load recommendations must incorporate design specifications and the OPR. You should also include an estimate of the plug loads in the energy model, because these systems produce heat and therefore affect the assumptions for the heating and cooling system.

PROCESS LOADS

When developing design metrics for net zero buildings, we are mostly concerned with the typical loads we have identified above, those that are standard in every building. In fact, the envelope loads and other loads for office spaces, educational buildings, and/or homes tend to be reasonably close. As we have said, our EUI goal of 10 kBtus/sf-yr includes all typical loads but not process loads, the unique loads required for specific buildings. These process loads could include manufacturing equipment, commercial kitchen equipment in a dining facility, or fume hoods in a laboratory. For any of these processes, we specify high-performance equipment to reduce loads and/or use the waste heat to reduce heating and/or cooling loads. During the net zero building design process, we keep these base and process loads separate so we can disaggregate loads and evaluate performance later.

Once we have designed the building to meet the overall EUI number, we can investigate how to provide occupant comfort with high-efficiency technology and how to power the building with renewables.

Optimizing Environmental Systems

By following the load reduction strategies discussed above, we have reduced loads by 80 percent or more over typical existing

When the Willow School in Gladstone, New Jersey, needed additional classroom, multipurpose, dining, and food-service space, they decided to build their project to LEED Platinum and Living Building Challenge standards, which required documented net-zero energy.

Because the kitchen had significant process loads, the Willow School put together a team to find a unique approach to achieve their energy and other Living Building Challenge goals. The team included the lead firm, Farewell Architects, in conjunction with the Maclay Architects (envelope consultant), 7group (green-building consultant), and other engineering firms. The team broke the kitchen loads out separately as a process load generating an additional process EUI of 6.02 kBtu/sf-yr; the projected building total was 21.9 kBtu/sf-yr.

Original designs called for all domestic hot water to be provided by solar thermal with direct electric backup. The design and engineering team then looked at reducing loads and replacing the solar thermal and direct resistance heat with a more targeted, PV-based delivery system. By reviewing energy use and time of use, reducing piping runs and storage, eliminating pumps, and carefully selecting equipment, including lower-temperature dishwashers with alternative disinfecting technologies the team cut anticipated loads by 50 percent.

The team cut an additional estimated 10 percent by changing use patterns and instructing building users. They elected not to use their teaching kitchen during dining hours when the main kitchen runs at capacity, thereby reducing peak loads.

The revised distribution and storage design included a more networked approach to domestic hot water as opposed to a single, central system. Specifications included direct, electric point-of-use water heating for small, remote loads, such as classroom sinks and janitor closets, and an interior air-to-water-source heat pump for kitchens and bathrooms. This will add slightly to the building's heating load in the winter, but the system was evaluated to be the most efficient for the needs of the project. Another option would have been a water-to-air-source heat pump with the compressor outside, increasing initial costs but possibly lowering the operating costs and PV required.

Overall, changing from a solar domestic hot water system with centralized storage to a more decentralized system powered with PV lowers annual energy consumption; reduces distribution, piping costs, and line losses; and provides hot water more efficiently. The approach of separating loads and evaluating different solutions applies to other projects with a variety of hot-water heating needs.

buildings, which can have some significant positive implications for the design of our mechanical and building-support systems. This is one place where we can save expenses.

RIGHTSIZING YOUR MECHANICAL SYSTEMS

The design of mechanical systems for net zero buildings offers two opportunities for increased efficiency and performance while saving operational costs: the first is rightsizing the systems, and the second is minimizing the mechanical distribution systems. Mechanical engineers often oversize mechanical systems, partly for good reasons: they do not want a client complaining that heat or air-conditioning is inadequate. If temperatures fluctuate beyond typical design parameters, it could cause litigation, so designers add a margin of safety to ensure occupant comfort. Then they add a factor of safety to cover potentially overly optimistic envelope insulation numbers from the architect, as well as possible changes to the design in the "value engineering" process to meet budgets. These factors can cause systems to swell to twice the size they need to be. Oversized systems are less efficient and more expensive and may malfunction or not perform as designed.

One exception to this rule is variable-volume air-source heat pumps, where some oversizing is fine, as these systems are efficient at partial loads. In fact, to maintain adequate heat and ensure reasonable recovery times when temperatures are below 0°F and efficiencies decline, some oversizing is important. You should add capacity of 15 percent or so beyond the calculated peak load. Heating equipment comes in specific sizes, so typically the next size up from the calculated peak heating load will work well.

This balancing of envelope design and mechanical design is why it is critical for a team to have experience together and trust one another. Design engineers must be confident that the building will be built to what they have assumed for their mechanical systems. To alleviate the concerns of the mechanical engineer and the design team, we inform the owner in writing that we are not oversizing the system and that the building temperatures may vary from design by two or three degrees in extreme weather. We then confirm that the owner accepts that small amount of risk. These assumptions should be included in the OPR.

The risk of over- and underheating or -cooling is significantly reduced because the net zero building envelope conserves energy so well. In typical buildings the loss of cooling or heating causes rapid temperature variation. In net zero buildings, by contrast, the temperatures fluctuate very slowly without heating or cooling even in extreme weather; the peaks and valleys of daily outside temperature fluctuations have little impact on interior comfort. When there are power outages or other issues, net zero buildings are not immediately threatened with freezing pipes or related problems. Temperatures may drop a few degrees a day for larger buildings with large internal loads; smaller buildings, particularly with more glass, will fluctuate more in colder temperatures.

In summary, first reduce the loads and then rightsize the building's mechanical system. This strategy is particularly effective for buildings where air-conditioning is required because we can potentially reduce the size of the cooling system for additional savings.

MINIMIZING YOUR MECHANICAL DISTRIBUTION SYSTEM

In typical buildings with significant heating and cooling needs, it is important to get heating and cooling distributed quickly to all corners of buildings for user comfort. This is partly because of large loads, partly because of perceived drafts, and partly because exterior walls and windows feel cold or hot due to radiant-heat exchange between our bodies and interior surfaces of the building enclosure. The standard strategy for mechanical-system design is to supply heating and cooling at the exterior envelope, usually below or near the windows, where the greatest amount of heat gain or loss is occurring, in order to provide continuous comfort. This strategy also means more energy is lost to the outdoors.

Due to reduced envelope-conditioning loads in a net zero building, there are lower heating and cooling demands along with less temperature stratification and fluctuation. The heating and cooling systems in net zero energy buildings don't need to go all the way around the exterior perimeter of the building to provide comfort. The systems can be smaller and provide heating and cooling near the center of the building with enhanced occupant comfort.

Heating/Cooling System Design

When we combine the downsized equipment with the reduced distribution systems, the savings can be significant, particularly if there is cooling and heating in a building. In some cases the savings can be enough to offset the cost of the extra insulation required to downsize the equipment. Although this is not true in heating-only climates, it is still critical to the cost-effectiveness of the net zero building that the heating and ductwork are minimized.

The size of the cooling system is not only reduced by a superinsulation strategy but by limiting solar gain into the building in summer. This calls for a combination of exterior shading and tuning glass to have enough solar transmittance on the south for passive gain (in northern climates) while reducing gain on other orientations.

SELECTING YOUR HEATING AND COOLING SYSTEM

After reducing loads and minimizing distribution, select systems to deliver heat and possibly cooling, depending on program, occupant, and building needs. The technology of mechanical systems is in a state of innovation and flux likely to continue for some time, but mechanical system technologies and equipment already offer reliable, cost-effective, and durable solutions for net zero buildings. As previously mentioned, net zero building envelopes should last for 100 years or longer and are very expensive and difficult to upgrade once built, whereas the expected lifetime of mechanical equipment is generally twenty years. This means that longevity and innovation in mechanical systems is slightly less of a concern than building envelopes. With mechanical improvements over time, this means future replaced equipment will only lower the energy consumed in the long term, which is of course a plus.

There are five potential systems to consider for net zero building heating and/or cooling: passive solar, solar water or air heating, direct electric space heating, variable air-source heat pumps, and ground-source heat pumps—with the last two being the most common. You may wonder why biomass and geothermal are not on this list. True geothermal has limited net zero building applicability, except in Iceland or similar locations where it can be profitably exploited, and we see biomass as a transitional fuel, applicable only in limited regions.

Passive solar should be used wherever possible but is not appropriate to meet 100 percent of heating needs. And solar water and air heating systems are typically no longer used in net zero buildings and net zero ready buildings for three reasons:

- To meet net zero goals and provide a significant percentage of annual loads, solar thermal requires massive and expensive storage systems.
- Solar thermal systems are mechanically more complex, with higher maintenance costs.
- PV costs are now low enough that PV for heating and cooling is cost-effective.

Although electric heat is 100 percent efficient at converting energy to heat once it is delivered to the location where it is used, and it is the easiest and initially the least expensive way to condition buildings with electricity, its losses in production and distribution are substantial. Even so, direct resistance heat is sometimes used—often with a radiant floor or ceiling system, baseboards, or convection heater—for supplemental heating or to heat small areas such as a bedroom or bathroom for short periods of time.

Heat pumps, on the other hand, are between two and three times more efficient than direct resistance heat. They are also more cost-effective over time. Net zero buildings generally use heat pumps not only because they are efficient but also because they use electricity, which can be linked to renewable energy resources such as solar, wind, or hydro. There are two types of heat pumps: ground source and air source. In cold climates ground-source pumps have been in use longer than air-source pumps in the United States.

AIR-SOURCE HEAT PUMPS

Air-source heat pumps extract energy from ambient air to provide conditioned air or water for heating and cooling buildings.

When in heating mode, the refrigerant in the outside heat exchange coil (evaporator) extracts heat from the ambient air, which is then compressed. The refrigerant circulates to the interior heat exchange coil (condenser) and condensed, releases heat into the interior. In cooling mode, the direction of the refrigerant flow is reversed. An air-source heat pump has four components:

- An outside compressor and heat exchanger that extracts or exhausts heat from the air
- An indoor heat exchanger that transfers energy to heat or cool occupied spaces
- An indoor distribution and/or delivery system, which could be the same as the heat exchanger or other air- and water-distribution systems
- Refrigerant lines, which transfer the energy between the outside and the inside heat exchangers

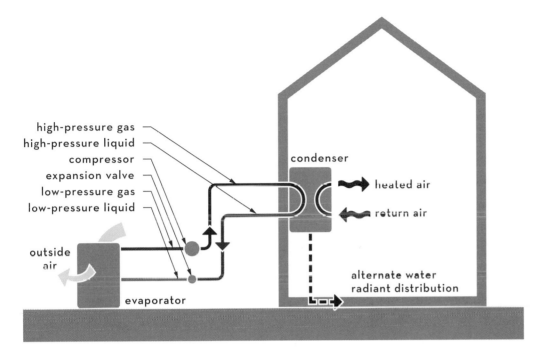

FIGURE 7.2. In the heating mode of an air source heat pump, the refrigerant flows outdoors, extracts heat from ambient air at the heat exchanger and is compressed. It then circulates through the coil indoors, releasing heat. In cooling mode the process works backwards: the refrigerant in its liquid phase circulates back into the house, where it evaporates into gas, absorbing heat in the process.

FIGURE 7.3. An air-source heat pump compressor unit.

Outdoor air contains some heat at any temperature higher than absolute zero. However, in the past air-source heat pumps did not function efficiently at temperatures around or below freezing and stopped functioning altogether at particular temperatures below freezing. Air-source heat pumps thus always needed backup heating, making them a poor choice in cold climates. Several manufacturers now offer heat pumps that operate at −15°F or lower because of variable refrigerant flow (which some manufacturers call variable refrigerant volume). When we use air-source heat pumps, we are always referring to models with variable refrigerant flow, as they are the only ones appropriate for cold-climate net zero buildings.

If you use an air-source heat pump in cold climates, make sure the unit is designed for subzero operation and oversize the system to ensure adequate heating at colder temperatures, when system efficiencies drop. This can require some estimation, as some manufacturers do not publish performance curves at low temperatures.

However, with extrapolation and estimation, air source heat pumps can be appropriately sized for low temperatures. Other air source heat pumps may turn off at low temperatures such as −18°F and not turn on until −13°F. However, with highly insulated net zero and net zero ready buildings, even if the heat shuts off, temperature drops are only a degree or two until the air source heat pump turns on again. This small risk is usually acceptable to owners. If not, backup heat, even small amounts of direct resistance heat, can accommodate this issue. And with all of these caveats, we have had 100 percent success in net zero and net zero ready buildings with air source heat pumps as the primary heating source with no noticeable drops in temperature and comfort.

GROUND-SOURCE HEAT PUMPS

Ground-source heat pumps extract energy from the ground; namely, the soil, rock, or water below the earth's surface.

FIGURE 7.4. An open-loop ground-source heat pump extracts water from a pond or well and injects this water back into a pond, stream, or well.

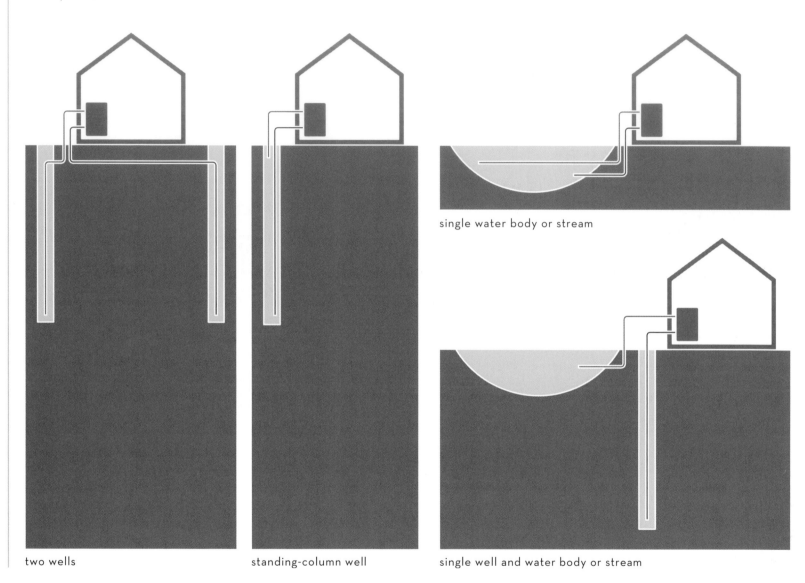

single water body or stream

two wells

standing-column well

single well and water body or stream

Depending on depth, the earth's temperature below ground remains relatively constant year-round, and closer to desired indoor temperatures. As a result, ground-source heat pumps are more efficient than air-source pumps, which are impacted by highly variable outside air temperatures. Ground-source systems have a heat exchange coil inside the building for energy transfer; pumps to move water or fluids from the ground, wells, or water to the coil; and pipes to move the fluid. This energy distribution system is much like that of an air-source heat pump. While there are numerous ground source heat pump systems, the two most common heat pumps are closed loop and open loop. Each of these

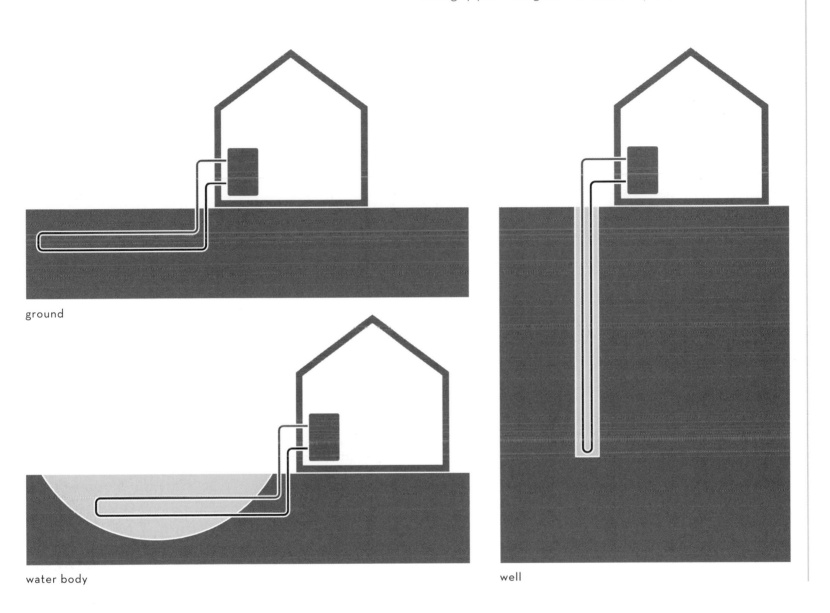

ground

water body

well

systems can extend either horizontally under water or near the ground surface or can extend vertically to greater depths in wells. There are two basic types of ground-source heat pumps: horizontal and vertical, and the heat pumps can be open-loop (figure 7.4), closed-loop (figure 7.5), or pump-and-dump systems.

An open-loop system pumps water from a well or water body into a heat pump and transfers energy to be used in the building. The outside pumped water is then returned to a water body or well in a different location to allow thermal recharge of the source. This requires one heat transfer inside the building as water from a well or water body is used directly.

FIGURE 7.6. This mechanical room contains the ground-source heat pump and controls.

In an open-loop horizontal system, water is pumped from one location in a water body and returned to a different location. In open-loop vertical ground-source systems, water may be recirculated in and out of the same or different wells.

A standing-column well is an open loop that returns the water back to the well it came from: taking water from the bottom of the well and returning it at the top. Open loops can also take water from a pond or water body and return the water in a different place. Or water can be drawn from a well and be returned to a pond or stream. All ground source systems using wells and water bodies require water quality, temperature, and yield testing to ensure adequate water supply, temperature, and quality.

A closed-loop system has a loop of tubing immersed in the earth, a well, or water. Closed-loop systems pump antifreeze through tubing in a loop from a heat pump located inside a building. Thus, there are two heat transfers: one from the ground or water that is in contact with the subsurface tubing and another in the heat pump to provide heat and or cooling distribution inside the building.

A horizontal closed-loop system is spread out in a layer of piping that is typically buried within 5' underground or in a body of water. A vertical closed-loop system consists of a long U

of piping inserted into a vertically drilled well up to several hundred feet deep and grouted in place with conductive material.

So how do you pick a system? The more direct the energy transfer, the more efficient the system in general. Open loop systems, where applicable, thus tend to be more efficient, but they have other drawbacks. If silt, corrosive materials, or other damaging ingredients occur in the water, they can contaminate the water or deteriorate equipment and piping, offsetting any benefits. Open systems in wells require a higher well yield. Some of these systems require a more complicated permitting process and may not be permitted at all. As a result, the often less-efficient closed-loop systems, with fewer unknowns and potential problems, are the most commonly used.

CHOOSING BETWEEN AIR- OR GROUND-SOURCE HEAT PUMPS

Even when you include pumping costs, ground-source heat pumps have efficiency benefits over those of air-source pumps. These can be eliminated, though, by additional PV at a reduced, combined capital cost of heat pumps and PV on net zero buildings. In addition, air-source systems are simpler, less expensive initially, and easier to maintain, and they have

There are many different efficiency ratings used in the marketplace for heating and cooling equipment, making it difficult to compare different units. Usually, equipment of the same type uses the same efficiency ratings, but to compare across system types, you need to have at least a general understanding of the efficiency metrics.

The coefficient of performance (COP), used for heat pumps, provides a ratio that determines the amount of heating or cooling from an initial energy input. When referring to cooling, the COP is the ratio of the rate of heat removal to the rate of energy input in consistent units for a complete cooling season. When referring to heating, the COP is the ratio of the rate of heat delivered to the rate of energy input in consistent units.

The seasonal energy-efficiency ratio (SEER) is used to show the efficiency of air conditioners but does so based on the cooling season load requirement. It is determined by the total cooling output in Btu during its normal usage period divided by the total electric energy input during the same period in W/hr.

Annual fuel utilization efficiency (AFUE) is found on fossil-fuel furnaces and shows the seasonal average efficiency of the unit. The AFUE is less than 100 percent because of the energy losses from converting fossil fuels into heat, but the higher the AFUE, the more efficient the furnace.

The SEER and AFUE ratings account for variable energy use of equipment by taking a full season's energy use and dividing it by the energy input to run the unit. Many equipment manufacturers rate a unit during set conditions, which does not represent how the unit will perform on an annual basis.

sole-source responsibility if problems do occur. Table 7.5 summarizes the differences between the two kinds of pumps.

While not a major concern on larger projects, ground-source heat pumps are less appealing to single-family homeowners and systems installers who may not want to deal with a more complex system. On the other hand, air-source heat pumps require oversizing and careful design when used at the lowest temperatures. Overall, at this time we generally recommend air-source heat pumps. In order to determine the system that best fits your project, use a spreadsheet similar to table 7.6.

HEAT-PUMP DISTRIBUTION SYSTEMS

Both ground-source and air-source heat pumps use similar distribution systems. Heat-pump systems are not able to produce comparably high temperatures: their distribution temperatures range from only around 100°F to as high as 120°F. So all heat-pump systems need to be designed with these lower temperatures in mind.

Heat pumps have the same choices for distribution as do the conventional systems: air and hydronic, but air-source heat pumps with hydronic distribution are less common than air-source heat pumps with air or ground-source heat pumps with water or air.

Air- and ground-source heat pumps that rely on air distribution typically use either a wall- or ceiling-mounted fan-coil vent to deliver heating and cooling without ducts, or they use concealed fan-coil units with minimal ducting. In both cases these units have a refrigerant line to deliver hot or cold fluid from the compressor to the individual indoor unit(s). Then air is blown around the refrigerant coils to transfer heat to air, which is then circulated

TABLE 7.5. HEAT PUMP PROS AND CONS

AIR-SOURCE HEAT PUMP (VARIABLE REFRIGERANT FLOW)		GROUND-SOURCE HEAT PUMP	
Benefits	Liabilities	Benefits	Liabilities
Simpler system	Lower efficiency	Higher efficiency	More complex
Minimum pumping efficiency	Tax credits likely not available	Better tax credits	Multiple system responsibilities: engineer, driller, installer
Sole source provider	Increased capacity required if used at lower temperatures		More engineering, analysis, and maintenance needed
Needs less engineering			Higher initial cost
Less and simpler maintenance			Pumping energy can be excessive if not carefully engineered
Lower initial cost			

TABLE 7.6. HEAT PUMP CHOICES

	AIR-SOURCE			GROUND-SOURCE	
	air-to-air	air-to-water, without cooling	air-to-water, with cooling, (radiant heating/ducted cooling)	without cooling	with cooling
Heating System Design					
Cooling System Design					
Comments					
Capital Cost					
Operating Costs					
Tax Credits[a]					
Other					

[a] See the Database of State Incentives for Renewables and Efficiencies (DSIRE) for additional, state-specific tax credits and updated federal tax credits: www.dsireusa.org.

to the conditioned space. This system thus eliminates most of the ductwork of the typical air-distribution system as well as the large energy loads for fans circulating air. When the units are wall mounted, they can be left exposed, though they are not aesthetically pleasing. You can locate the unit in an attic, a basement, or other space with conventional ductwork, conceal it, or integrate it into cabinetry and wood. If you want to hide the unit, be sure the manufacturer approves the proposed grill design so that operation complies with product warranties, and keep in mind that certain placements create hot or cold drafts, which can cause discomfort. Examples of installation are shown in figure 7.7.

Both air- and ground-source heat-pump systems can also be used with hydronic distribution, such as baseboard and radiant systems. These need to be sized for the use of lower-temperature hydronic fluids and based on lower building heat losses. Radiators need to be about four times the size when using 110°F–120°F water rather than the 160–180°F water a fossil-fuel boiler delivers. However, since net zero buildings conserve so much energy, moderately sized distribution can be used cost effectively. A drawback of hydronic delivery systems is that unless they are carefully designed and controlled, they are not appropriate for cooling (except perhaps with radiant slabs and/or ceilings specifically designed to control condensation) because radiant cooling can cause water to condense, creating mold or other moisture-related problems. To use a hydronic delivery

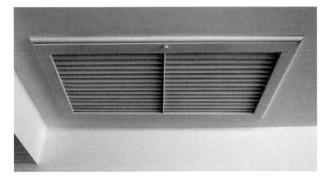

FIGURE 7.7. The air-distribution units for heat pumps are relatively small and can be left exposed in a wall-mounted cabinet (top *left*), integrated into cabinetry with a built-in grill (*right*), or become part of a concealed ducted system with a metal grate for delivery to occupied spaces (*bottom left*).

system, then, you would need to add a separate air system for cooling—another expense.

Radiant cooling, then, is appropriate only for large projects with extensive control and monitoring systems designed by experienced professionals. The same might be said for projects using hydronic distribution systems for heating—a plan that most likely will require two distribution systems, one for heating (hydronic) and one for cooling (air). Typically, for cooling, refrigerant is delivered to a fan-coil type of unit, adding another layer of complexity and expense.

To keep systems simple and reduce costs when both heating and cooling are needed, we usually prefer air-source heat pumps with an air-distribution system. In designing mechanical systems for net zero buildings, the first step is determining how cooling can be reduced and how much is needed. As discussed in chapter 4, if your project is located in a colder, breezier, or more northerly location, you may need minimal cooling that can be provided passively or with simple fans. If you are farther south, more active cooling may be warranted. If your building is a residence or small office, passive ventilation and fans may be adequate. However, if your building is larger and/or has more intensive uses, as with an internal-load-dominated building, you may need cooling even in a more northern climate. Initial energy programming, modeling, and analysis determine what type and intensity of cooling are appropriate.

The Putney School Field House was originally designed to use a ground-source heat-pump system, but during the design process we evaluated switching systems and calculated a capital savings.

For the ground-source system, the cost of the boreholes and the water-source heat-pump system inside the building were estimated at a total system cost of $376,000. The cost of the air-source system was estimated at $200,000. The cost of the extra PV array required to offset the added electrical load of the air-source system compared to the ground-source system was $38,000, based on the additional electric consumption of 6,400 kWh/yr due to the slightly lower efficiency of the air-source heat pump.

In the end, the net savings by going with air-source instead of ground-source heat pumps was $68,000, including the PV area required, so we decided to proceed with design of the air-source system. Since then, we have typically used air-source heat pumps on projects.

We decided to use heat-pump electric heating because our goal was to achieve net zero performance with on-site electricity generation. We created a spreadsheet analysis to compare the annual performance of an air-source heat-pump system with variable refrigerant flow to a ground-source heat-pump system. This model predicted an annual coefficient of performance (ACOP) of 2.3 for the air-source heat pump (inclusive of indoor fan power), based on weather in Concord, New Hampshire. This compares to an assumed ACOP (based on experience) of 3.5 for the ground-source heat pump (including groundwater and distribution energy). The size of the system was calculated to be approximately 28 heating tons.

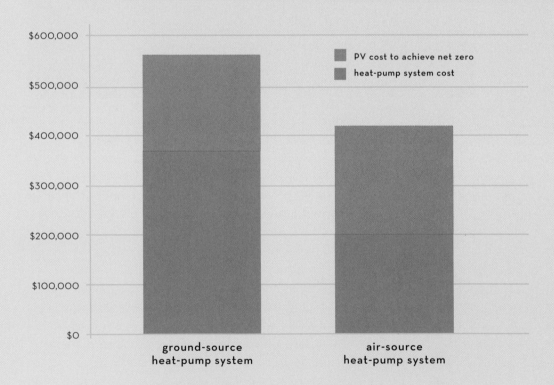

FIGURE 7.8. It was determined that the Putney School Field House could save $68,000 by installing an air-source heat-pump system rather than a ground-source heat-pump system, even including the additional PV needed for the system.

If you want active cooling, this will influence the selection of the heat-pump distribution system and perhaps also the choice between an air-source and a ground-source heat pump. While either a ground-source or an air-source heat pump will work fine for heating and cooling with air distribution, the choices are more complex if you choose a hydronic delivery system. You may want to avoid ductwork because of indoor-air-quality concerns (in which case you can use wall-mounted or short-ducted distribution systems). The owners may prefer radiant heat, as is often the case with smaller buildings and particularly homes. Or in an existing building, you may want to reuse existing radiant baseboard or a radiant-floor heating distribution system to save on costs.

RESIDENTIAL HEAT-PUMP CONSIDERATIONS

Smaller residential heating and cooling systems have some significant differences from larger commercial and institutional heating and cooling systems. In general, smaller systems should be substantially less complex and easier to understand. Cooling passively or with simple fans is likely to be adequate. If a home is less than 2,000 sf and insulated to net zero standards, it can be designed with one interior air-source wall-mounted distribution unit for the entire home. With one interior unit, temperatures in bedrooms are likely to be a few degrees cooler than in the living area, where the heating unit is typically located. While homeowners often prefer radiant heat to an air-source heat pump, it adds costs with little additional comfort. An air-source heat pump also provides cooling, if the homeowner ever wants it, which would be an additional cost if radiant heat were used. In summary, an air-source heat-pump system is simple and saves capital.

Ventilation

All buildings, including net zero buildings, should provide healthy indoor air. Many buildings recirculate air inside the building and replace a portion of the recirculated air with fresh air. It is difficult both to assess exactly how much fresh air is delivered with these systems and to get the air where it is needed. We therefore do not recommend mixing ventilation air with space-conditioning air and specify separate, 100 percent outside-fresh-air systems with ventilators to recover energy so as to supply the correct amount of ventilation air and conditioned air without wasting energy.

Heat-recovery ventilators (HRVs) and energy-recovery ventilators (ERVs) provide adequate fresh air to occupants and conserve energy in net zero buildings. In larger buildings these systems may be paired with space-temperature-conditioning systems, but it is better when these two systems are separated. The energy savings occur as the result of heating or cooling being transferred from exhausted indoor air to incoming air supplied to the inside of the building. In a flat-plate type HRV or ERV, this transfer occurs through the thin walls between layers of flat surfaces that are similar to layers in corrugated cardboard. Thus, alternating layers have ingoing and outgoing air traveling through them that then transfer energy. An enthalpy wheel transfers energy through a rotary that moves between exhaust and incoming air, scavenging heat and moisture from outgoing air in winter and transferring those to the incoming outside air. In summer this works in reverse, to cool and dehumidify incoming air.

HRVs transfer only energy between supply and exhaust streams, whereas ERVs transfer both energy and moisture. In small, tight houses in the winter, relative humidity can be too high, so an HRV may be best. In a large home or commercial space, where winter humidity levels may be low in heating mode, an ERV is best. In the summer, where air-conditioning or dehumidification help lower humidity levels, an ERV is also beneficial in maintaining lower humidity levels inside. The engineer and the design team should select an HRV or ERV on a case-by-case basis depending on climate and building use.

Domestic Hot Water

In net zero buildings, as space-conditioning loads are significantly reduced, domestic hot water loads are proportionately greater, although varied based on building use. In commercial kitchens and homes, domestic hot water use can be a larger load than heating, while in offices domestic water heating is very small.

FIGURE 7.9. A heat-recovery ventilation (HRV) system uses a heat exchanger to transfer heat between the inbound and outbound airflow.

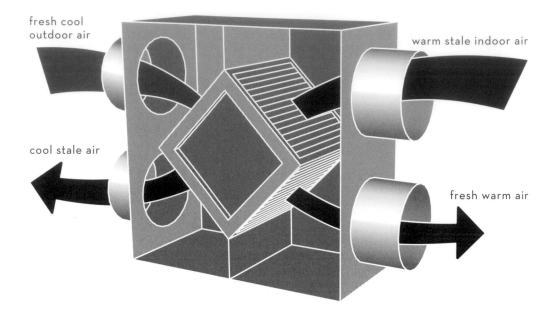

fresh cool
outdoor air

warm stale indoor air

cool stale air

fresh warm air

FIGURE 7.10. An energy-recovery ventilation (ERV) system typically uses an enthalpy wheel to transfer heat and moisture between inbound and outbound airstreams.

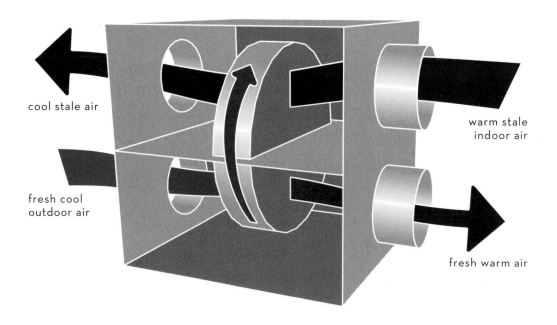

cool stale air

warm stale
indoor air

fresh cool
outdoor air

fresh warm air

The first task should be to reduce hot-water consumption. Use greywater-heat-recovery systems, low-flow aerators and shower heads, horizontal-axis clothes washers, and the highest-energy-performance dishwashers (figure 7.11). Then heavily insulate storage and distribution piping. Rightsize storage tanks to needs or consider point-of-use water heating, which eliminates storage losses. Generally, group loads as much as possible and provide storage rightsized for grouped loads.

Concentrate fixtures and minimize the length of hot-water lines. Sometimes running separate smaller lines to individual fixtures can help. Larger homes and buildings typically use recirculating loops so hot water is always available. In these instances consider a distributed system with point-of-use water heaters. Use controls and/or thermostats so that hot water is not constantly recirculated. More specifically, generate a DHW load reduction strategy based on a clear understanding of system requirements, including quantities and timing of use.

Once hot water loads are reduced, there are two different options to provide hot water with energy derived from the sun: solar DHW systems with hot-water collectors or PV collection with an electric water heater.

Solar hot water collectors use the same basic system for DHW and space heating (figure 7.12). However, since DHW loads are smaller than space-heating loads, the collection, storage, and distribution requirements are smaller, too. Solar hot-water systems still require a solar hot-water storage tank as well as a backup electric hot-water tank to meet user temperature requirements.

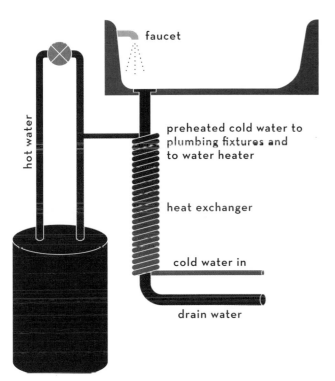

FIGURE 7.11. This system has tubing wrapped around greywater drainpipes to recover waste heat, reducing domestic hot water loads.

faucet

hot water

preheated cold water to plumbing fixtures and to water heater

heat exchanger

cold water in

drain water

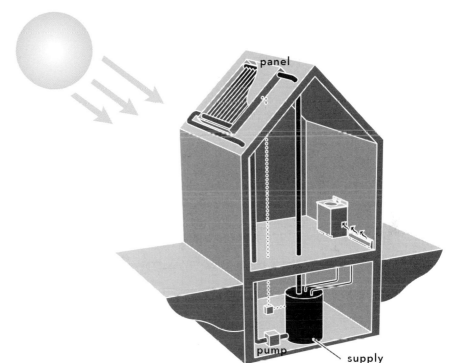

FIGURE 7.12. Active solar water-heating systems have a solar collection surface, a storage system, and a distribution system. These systems are most common for solar domestic hot water and are similar for solar space heating.

panel

pump

supply

Solar DHW systems are most cost effective in buildings where there are constant large annual loads, as in multifamily housing projects, buildings with commercial kitchens, and some manufacturing facilities. In contrast, solar DHW systems are less cost effective when used for smaller office and classroom buildings where there is minimal demand for hot water. For single-family residences, offices, and other loads of a similar size, we typically specify electrically heated hot water powered by PV.

Options for supplying DHW from renewable electricity include a traditional, direct electric heating system, an air-to-water-source heat-pump system located inside the building, or an air-to-water-source heat pump with an outdoor compressor that either supplies heat and DHW or is dedicated to DHW needs.

Indoor heat pumps called heat-pump water heaters are a good option when cooling requirements are larger than heating requirements. They usually are not an effective alternative in cold climates, though, as they cool the buildings in the winter and offset their efficiency advantages.

Our usual recommendation for single-family homes is PV with direct electric heating in the best available, well-insulated storage tank. Where loads are larger, such as with multifamily or kitchen loads, we recommend air-to-water-source heat pumps with the compressor located outdoors. Or if a home or other building is using an air-to-water-source heat pump for building heating, it can also be used for domestic hot water.

Electrical Systems

Electrical systems provide power to buildings for loads such as equipment, lighting, appliances, plug loads, and building automation or control systems. Equipment typically includes pumps and motors for heating, ventilation, cooling, and/or process loads. The highest-efficiency pumps and motors should be used to reduce loads.

When specifying lighting and appliances, use the lowest energy systems you can afford. For lighting, use LED if you can afford it and fluorescent if you cannot. Appliances should be as energy-efficient as possible.

Building automation can be incredibly complex. Our recommendation is to select automation and control systems that are as simple as appropriate. For homes, use simple and robust systems that match the owners' ability to manage complexity. Direct digital control systems are typically used for large and complex commercial, industrial, and institutional buildings.

Powering with Renewables

Once we have developed an EUI goal and calculated the total building energy load through energy modeling, we need to determine how the remaining energy will be supplied to the building. Since the net zero building is defined by producing as much energy as the building consumes on an annual basis, we must install renewable energy systems to cover the expected energy consumption of the building.

RIGHTSIZING RENEWABLES

Evaluate what renewable resources are available on-site and the potential generation of each option. Although you may need to bring in specialty consultants for larger or more complex systems, your own evaluation may be adequate for smaller systems. First, determine whether you can meet the net zero goal with on-site renewable-energy generation. If adequate renewable resources are not available on-site, then assess if further load reductions are feasible. If not, you will need to turn to off-site and net-metering alternatives.

The amount of energy your net zero building needs to generate from the renewable-energy system(s) is the total calculated energy load for the building based on your energy modeling. This figure is an average load and will vary year to year, based on annual weather fluctuation. Production by the renewable systems will also vary. The numbers used to size renewable systems are estimates of use and will vary from the actual consumption of the building, user consumption, and production of the renewable systems. You can assume these variations in consumption and production will average out over time, so the net zero goal will be met in an average year. If the goal is to meet the net zero goal every year, the renewable systems must be oversized. Generally, we oversize systems by 10 percent to address these variations. Once the goal is established for annual renewable-energy production, then potential renewable resources can be evaluated for meeting the goal.

EVALUATING RENEWABLE OPTIONS

Incorporating renewable energy into a project requires an analysis of the energy available and a review of the options for incorporating that energy into the project to determine the best strategy. Performing this evaluation early in design maximizes the potential for renewable energy for each project.

To compare the different domestic hot water and renewable electric generation alternatives, use a simple spreadsheet similar to table 7.7. This will help to assess how to provide renewable energy systems for your project.

SOLAR ENERGY

Solar is typically the most viable renewable option because sun is available at every site—at least to some degree. While some places might seem too cloudy for effective solar use, this is not the case.

Investigate all of the solar PV options on your site. Determine all of the possible locations that PV could be located, starting with your building. Begin with the south-facing

TABLE 7.7. RENEWABLE ENERGY GENERATION CHOICES

RENEWABLE OPTIONS	INSTALLED COST	ANNUAL ELECTRIC (OR Btu) GENERATION	MAINTENANCE/ OPERATING RELIABILITY/ COST	SERVICE-PROVIDER RELIABILITY/ COST	AESTHETICS	PERMITTING	FINANCING OPTIONS	OTHER
On-Site								
Rooftop PV								
Ground-mounted PV								
Carport PV								
Wall-mounted PV								
Wind turbine								
Small hydro								
Off-Site								
Project-specific renewables								
Shared renewables								
Community renewables								
Power purchase (on- or off-site)								
Renewable Energy Certificates (not recommended)								
Domestic Hot Water								
Roof-mounted solar DHW								
Ground-mounted solar DHW								
Direct-electric DHW								
Dedicated ASHP DHW								
Combined solar heating and DHW								
Combined A/W HP and DHW								

roof and façade as the simplest locations. Also investigate other south-facing wall areas and roof orientations—a carport over parking, an outbuilding, or ground mounting. Try different orientations and pitches. Determine areas and orientations for all options. In general, roof or ground mounting are the easiest and most cost-effective. For one- and two-story buildings, the roof area can be significant. Supplying all energy from building-integrated PV systems is challenging for buildings of four to six stories and nearly impossible for taller buildings.

Work with solar installers to determine the relative cost. You may discover that you have more flexibility than what you first imagined. Consider the aesthetics of different alternatives: in general, larger, simpler areas can be less expensive and more appealing than many small, broken-up areas. If it is well designed, solar can add to the value of your building; if it is poorly designed, it may detract from your building.

COLLECTION SURFACES

All solar systems, including active and passive, require a collection surface to gather the solar radiation from the sun. Solar collectors provide the highest levels of production if oriented within 20° of due south, but if there are no other viable choices, it is still feasible, if less cost effective, to orient collection surfaces up to 90° from due south. Since the goal for active solar-collection surfaces is to maximize the return on investment by optimizing the solar energy collected, choosing the best installation orientation and location is important.

The optimal angle of collector surfaces depends on the purpose of the collector, such as active or passive space heating, domestic hot water heating, PV, or combined uses. When the installation angle is combined with the percent of sunshine at a specific location and shading unique to a site, shading and monthly and yearly estimates for energy collection can be determined. Solar books and computer programs provide detailed information on the amount of solar radiation that falls on different collector orientations and angles.[5] For buildings in historic neighborhoods, optimal collector angles may need to be adjusted so that the building fits in better with surrounding buildings. In cold climates snow is slow to slide off collectors even with a 45° sloped collection surface, so some of the winter radiation is not collected unless the snow is removed. In locations where sunlight can be reflected upward from snow

on the ground, vertically mounted collectors may make sense. On sites with shading, maximizing energy production may also require altering the orientation of the collector surface. For all projects, you should obtain a solar assessment and estimate based on your specific site and needs. Calculate potential shading by buildings, trees, and other present or future landscaping and/or buildings by using a Solar Pathfinder or similar device, as described in chapter 4.

Depending on collection uses, such as thermal heating and PV, solar collection may be prioritized for different seasons, which affects the optimum tilt of the collecting array. Surfaces tilted up from the horizontal at an angle of latitude minus 15° maximize summer solar gains but reduce winter gains. Surfaces tilted at latitude plus 15° maximize winter solar gains and result in a solar delivery that is more uniform throughout the year. A tilt angle equal to the local latitude provides close to the maximum year-round solar gains and is usually appropriate for solar water heating and PV.[6] In general, this angle is steeper for active space heating than for domestic hot water and PV because space-heating systems are used only in the winter while domestic hot water and PV are used year-round.

While the best PV orientation and tilt is generally the same as for solar domestic hot water, staying closer to south and to the optimum tilt angles has a greater financial benefit than with solar domestic hot water because of the usually increased capital costs. And while not typically reflected in utility rate structure, PV production benefits utilities because the maximum PV production is in the summer, when utilities experience their peak loads due to seasonal building cooling loads—even in northern climates. In many northern areas, the percentage of sunshine is much higher in the summer than in the winter. And utility peak loads are also higher in the summer, so maximizing PV production in the summer may match utility needs. Systems can be installed outside of these parameters, but efficiency and cost effectiveness will be lessened.

Passive solar heating typically uses vertical windows as the solar collection surface. This is because angled glazing causes substantial overheating during the summer, fall, and spring and is not easily controlled. Thus, while vertical glass collects slightly less energy than angled glazing in the winter months, when heat is desirable, vertical glass collects much less energy in the summer, when the sun is higher off the horizon and heat gain is a liability.

Solar for space heating and hot-water systems generally follows similar orientation guidelines as solar PV but needs to be located on or very close to the building, generally within 100 feet. Solar thermal systems that produce hot air or water experience much higher rates of line loss than solar PV systems. This means these systems should be installed close to where the hot water will be used.

ACTIVE SOLAR HEATING SYSTEMS

While not a renewable source, active solar heating systems are covered in this section because the principles discussed for collection surfaces apply to these systems. In general, active solar heating systems include collection and distribution loops connected through a storage system. Once the heat from the sun has been collected, it is almost always transferred to a storage system so that the heat can be used later rather than transferred directly into the building and used for space or domestic hot water heating. DHW and space-heating systems may use collectors on roofs of buildings or sometimes south-facing walls.

With water systems there are three types of solar collection:

THERMOSIPHONING. Thermosiphoning solar collectors are passive, as they avoid the use of pumps and controls to circulate water between collection and storage. Instead, they depend on the force of solar heating of water to move water. Typically, thermosiphoning systems are very simple and do not use antifreeze and heat-transfer systems. Because of this, they typically are not used in cold climates.

ANTIFREEZE. A liquid with antifreeze is used to move the captured energy. Although antifreeze is less efficient in transferring heat than water and requires a heat transfer to the internal building distribution system, the antifreeze prevents freezing of the water in the collector. Antifreeze systems are reliable and the most frequently used systems in cold climates.

DRAINBACK SYSTEM. With a drainback system, water (not antifreeze) drains out of the collector when the collector is cold so that water does not freeze. This system should have staged pumps to minimize pumping energy but can be reliable and efficient if designed and installed properly. Drainback collectors have significant advantages in system simplicity, reliability, and overheating prevention. They are an excellent choice in cold regions.

In a space-heating system, a distribution system delivers heat to the occupied spaces as well as the storage system. This distribution system is radiant, with low-temperature hydronic (oversized baseboard), and/or low-temp fan coils. Pipes, pumps, and controls are used for distributing heat. The solar-heating distribution system is insulated so that energy is not lost.

A storage system is needed in order to provide heat at night and during cloudy weather. Water storage with fluid systems is relatively easily accommodated in tanks, but needing excessively large amounts of water for storage for cloudy weather is expensive. While most sunshine typically occurs in the summer, heat is needed only in the winter, making the seasonal balance of energy supply and demand poorly matched. Solar collection use is thus less efficient, more difficult, and more expensive for space heating, as much of the heat collected in the summer is lost. Because of this, there are two options for solar hot-water space heating: solar space heating with seasonal storage and space heating with reduced storage and backup electric heating powered by PV. Using a backup wood heating system can make a project carbon neutral but not net zero according to our definition. If you store heat seasonally, the investment in storage and insulation usually does not justify the expense and requires careful calculation for a net zero building.

Due to the expense of storage for solar space-heating systems and the advent of less expensive PV systems and more efficient ground- and air-source heat-pump systems, active solar heat systems are uncommon in net zero buildings. Assuming that PV costs stay relatively low and that storing heat via solar water systems remains more costly, it is likely that PV will be used for space heating and that active solar hot-water space heating will likely remain uncommon in net zero buildings. PV makes energy that is transferred through power lines and can be net-metered.

BIOMASS

In rural areas biomass is often a good alternative for heating. On large community projects it may be a possibility for cogeneration of electricity, although the economics are usually hindered because there tend to be unevenly distributed loads in the summer and winter, so that the capital investment cannot be spread over a full year. In terms of heating only, biomass is typically chunk wood (least expensive, labor intensive to use, and likely very locally sourced), wood chips (most expensive; needs a large load and space for wood handling), or pellets (moderate expense and requires very little effort to use). Other than this very brief overview, we will not go into biomass in depth, as we see this as a likely localized transition fuel. We classify biomass as carbon neutral.

OTHER RENEWABLES

Wind and hydropower are not typically cost-effective renewable resources on the site of net zero projects. As discussed elsewhere, they may be appropriate at a community scale. If you think that wind or hydro is potentially cost effective at your site, talk to the appropriate installers to estimate annual electrical production, cost, maintenance, and operational parameters. This will allow for a prudent evaluation of renewable alternatives.

CONNECTING YOUR RENEWABLES TO YOUR LOAD

Our definition of "net zero" does not distinguish how you connect your renewable resource to supply power for your project. A building can meet the net zero requirement either connected to the electric utility grid or off the grid. A grid-tied net zero energy building uses the grid instead of including a storage system to store energy for when the sun, wind, or water cannot meet the building-load requirements. With a grid-tied system, your renewable power provides energy to the grid when you are overproducing, and your building draws energy from the grid when you are underproducing. On the other hand, an off-grid building requires an energy storage system. The only other option for off-grid buildings is to use energy only when it is being produced, but this is not very practical for occupants. The options for storing renewably generated power on-site are currently inefficient and add significant additional expense to projects.

Because of these factors, unless the project location makes grid connection unachievable or cost-prohibitive due to distance, or if the building owner or user has a particular need to provide its own energy at all times, the decision to build an off-grid net zero building is uncommon. One option for grid-intertied net zero buildings is to have battery backup sized for only a few days for critical functions such as heat, refrigeration, and minimal lighting. This is a simpler and less expensive approach than full battery backup. It also is more costly than just a grid-tied approach. However, it does offer power during shorter periods of power outages and thus resiliency.

SHARED AND COMMUNITY RENEWABLE SYSTEMS

Renewable energy resources are not necessarily optimal at all sites. Larger-scale renewable development is more cost effective than smaller development. Larger buildings and existing buildings are less suited to on-site power generation. If our goal is a net zero world and future, we need to create a renewable infrastructure. Once our building is net zero ready, then we can look for nearby sites with either renewable resources for our project or the capacity to share the renewable resources with several other partners or as a part of a larger community system. Either the shared or community options produce more renewable power than just for your project and help reduce fossil-fuel dependence on a larger scale.

Group net metering allows multiple electric users to jointly own a common renewable system. Community systems are financially complex methods of renewable investment. They require agreements with a landowner, shareholders, and possibly a financial institution. However, there is little reason not to use renewable power, if you can find an appropriate site for the renewables.

In summary, throughout design, all building energy loads are reduced to match EUI metrics. Then building systems are rightsized and simplified with an appropriate reduced distribution network. With these steps completed, net zero buildings can be efficiently and cost-effectively powered with the appropriate renewable energy resource, either on- or off-site.

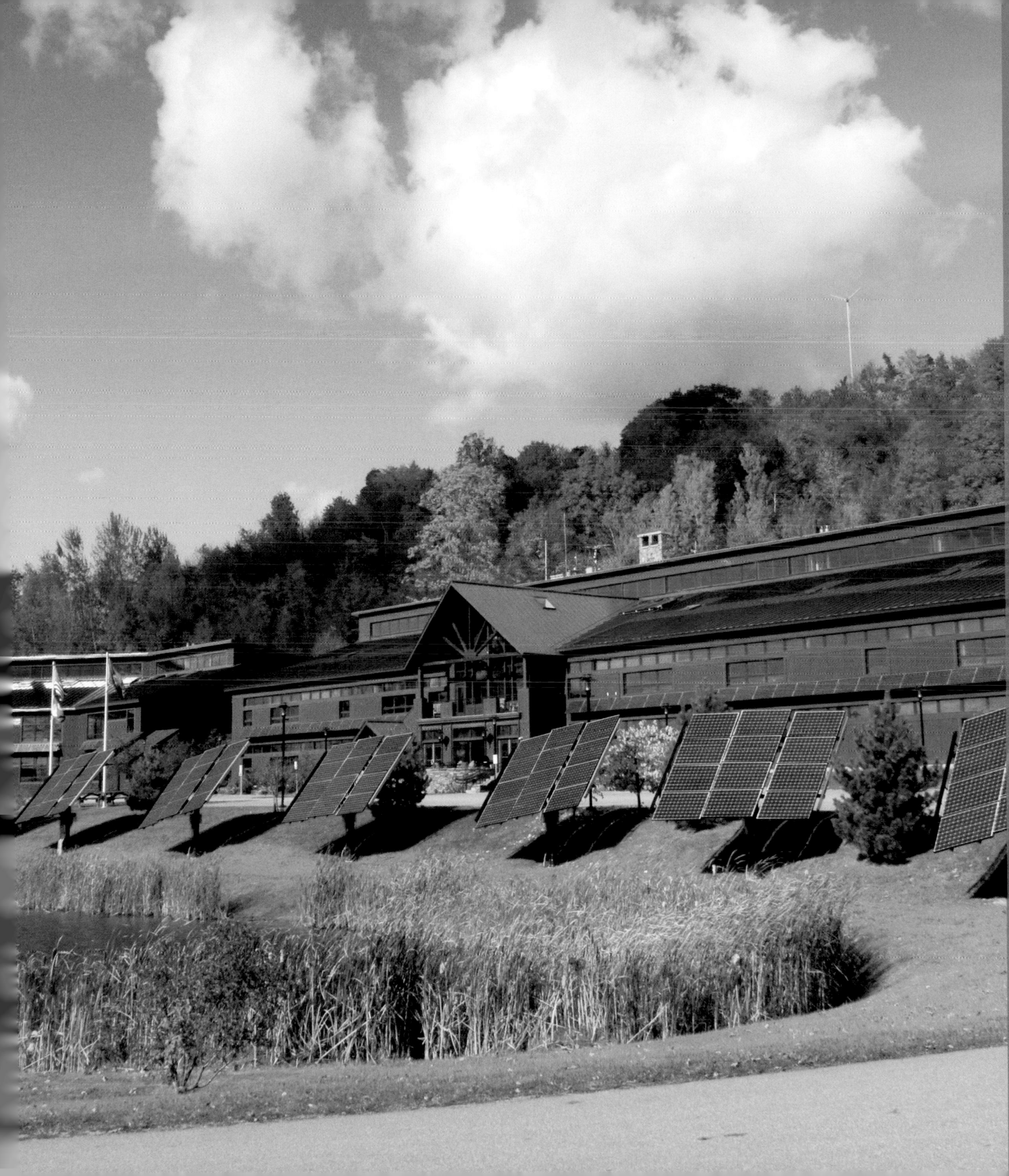

RENEWABLE NRG SYSTEMS

RENEWABLE NRG SYSTEMS

A renewably powered office and manufacturing facility

n 1999 NRG Systems' owners decided to build a new headquarters that would embody their core mission. The company, a world leader in wind measurement equipment, designs, sells, and manufactures the equipment in their Vermont location. The goal was for a building near to carbon neutral and powered by renewables, and a productive and beautiful workplace for the employees. After the completion of the first building, NRG Systems grew rapidly, soon outgrowing the building. A second building was designed, creating a campuslike setting on the outskirts of Hinesburg, Vermont. The second building capitalized on the lessons learned during the design and construction of the first and is a smarter and even more energy-efficient building.

Project Overview and Vision

NRG Systems brought to us a vision for their project with two equally important components: to follow NRG's renewable mission, the primary goal was 100 percent or near 100 percent renewable power for all energy use. The second but equal goal was providing a model healthy and productive workplace. And while not a specific goal at the beginning of the project, education of the larger community about renewable energy and exploring options for a larger renewable mixed-use project later evolved as further goals.

This clear and simple vision for the project provided the organizing purpose that defined and inspired the entire building design and process. From this purpose and vision, the building organization emerged from a living-organism paradigm. The life of the building revolves around a central "heart": a café commons with a wood post-and-beam structure and a fireplace—a place for eating, informal conversations, accidental meetings, and whole-company gatherings. From that heart, "arteries" extend through the workplace to quiet, small meeting rooms at the extremities, connecting all parts of their company to the warm heart at the core.

- CAFÉ/COMMONS AREA: The café commons, the heart and soul, is located at the center of each building. It provides a place for interaction, with different qualities and features in each building, including a stone fireplace, library, plants, trickling water, art and art floors, and a wood structure and wainscoting for warmth.
- INTERIOR "STREET": Transparent walls, "green" planters, and interior openings connect common areas to all workspaces.
- DAYLIGHTING: Skylights and windows with light-guiding blinds provide abundant daylight, ventilation, and views for connection to nature.
- RECREATION: Outdoor trails, an interior pool, and exercise areas foster employee health and wellness.
- ART: Art on walls and stained and polished art floors with embedded objects, hand-painted concrete, and tiles depicting the history of wind energy bring beauty throughout the space.
- CONNECTION TO ECOSYSTEM: Siting, stormwater management, earth berms, preservation of existing agriculture land use, and native vegetation integrate the building into the surrounding rural landscape.

DESIGN PROFILE

Building Profile	Building Name:	**Renewable NRG Systems Building One**	
	Location:	Hinesburg, Vermont	
	Occupancy Date:	June, 2004	
	Square Footage:	46,000	
	Certification:	LEED-NC Gold	
Energy Profile	Energy Reference Year:	2011	
	Total Energy Consumption:	394,055 kBtu electric use 153,143 kBtu propane use 292,220 kBtu wood pellet use	839,418 kBtu total annual energy consumption
	Total Energy Production:	73,678 kWh	251,389 kBtu
	Energy Intensity:	Actual:	18.2 kBtu/sf-yr
		Actual with Renewables:	12.8 kBtu/sf-yr
Building Envelope	Construction Type:	Composite—steel and wood	
	Insulation Values:	Walls (office):	R-26, 3″ spray foam, 2″ insulated panel
		Walls (manufacturing):	4″ thick foam, steel skin panels
		Roof:	R-38, two layers of foam insulation (6″ total)
		Foundation (sub-slab):	R-20, 4″ rigid foam underslab
	Air Infiltration:	Final Blower Door:	0.18 cfm50/sf exterior surface area
	Windows/Skylights:	Windows:	R-5 tri-pane fiberglass windows
Mechanical/ Electrical Systems	Heating System:	Radiant heating from pellet-fired boilers with a 90 percent efficient backup propane boiler; the heat-pump system utilizes an artificial cooling pond at the front of the building	
	Cooling System:	Radiant-floor cooling system and networked DDC system to control automated windows that open and close and provide nighttime cooling; two large "barn fans" in the warehouse area to supplement	
	Ventilation System:	Demand-controlled energy-recovery ventilation, variable volume with CO_2 and RH control for open spaces; closed offices and other small spaces ventilated on a schedule	
	Energy Recovery System:	Enthalpy wheel (75 percent efficient)	
	Lighting System/Controls:	South-facing glazing, skylights, and open floor plan to maximize natural light	
		High-efficiency fluorescent general lighting with automatic dimming ballasts and occupancy sensors; south-facing windows with light-guiding blinds	
	Hot Water:	6 solar hot-water collectors with 240-gallon storage (80 percent hot water needs)	
	Renewable System:	Installed System Size:	PV system 149.1 kW total—twenty-seven 2.2 kw trackers, 89.7 kW of building-mounted PV (silicon PVs are adhered on the standing seam metal roofing, awnings made of high-efficiency crystalline silicon PV panels, and roof-mounted SHW collectors)
			10 kW wind turbine
			Wood pellets made from lumber-milling waste

DESIGN PROFILE

Building Profile	Building Name:	**Renewable NRG Systems Building Two**	
	Location:	Hinesburg, Vermont	
	Occupancy Date:	June, 2008	
	Square Footage:	31,000	
	Certification:	LEED-NC Gold	
Energy Profile	Energy Reference Year:	2011	
	Total Energy Consumption:	381,805 kBtu electricity use	548,436 kBtu total annual energy consumption
		12,831 kBtu propane use	
		153,800 kBtu wood pellets	
	Total Energy Production:	74,949 kWh	255,725 kBtu
	Energy Intensity:	Actual:	17.7 kBtu/sf-yr
		Actual with Renewables:	9.4 kBtu/sf-yr
Building Envelope	Construction Type:	Composite—steel and wood	
	Insulation Values:	Walls (office):	R-40, 1″ EPS, 7″ cellulose, 2″ metal panel
		Walls (manufacturing):	6″ thick foam, steel skin panels
		Roof:	R-54, three layers of foam insulation (9″ total)
		Foundation (sub-slab):	R-20, 4″ rigid foam underslab
	Air Infiltration:	Final Blower Door:	0.092 cfm50
	Windows/Skylights:	Windows:	R-5 tri-pane fiberglass windows
Mechanical/ Electrical Systems	See NRG One for systems description		

FIGURE CS5.1. Aerial view of Renewable NRG Systems headquarters.

FIGURE CS5.2. The site plan shows the building nestled into the hillside to the north and connected to the pond to the south.

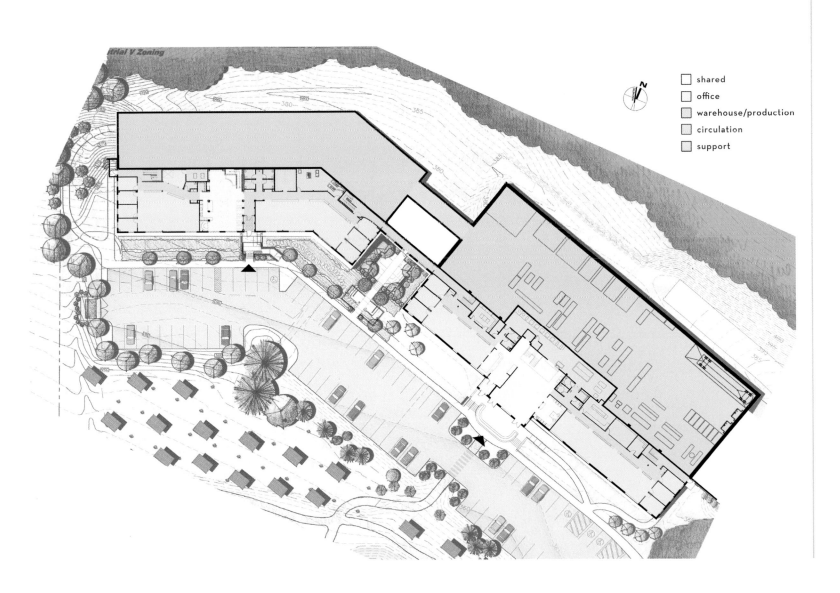

FIGURE CS5.3. The main floor plan depicts shared spaces and open offices to the south, with warehouse space to the north.

shared
office
warehouse/production
circulation
support

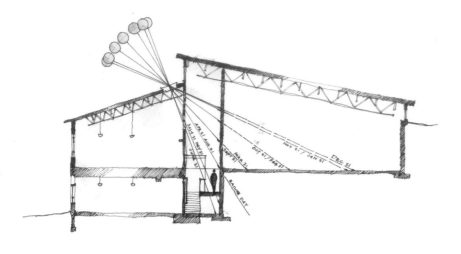

FIGURE CS5.4. These sketches are representative of the ideas explored during the design process. *Top*, proposed seasonal sundial at stairwell connects to living systems (not included in final design). *Middle*, living wall at building heart. *Bottom*, floor design connecting central heart and street circulation.

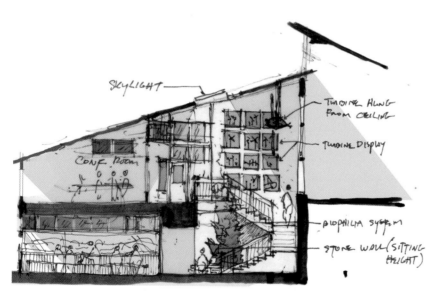

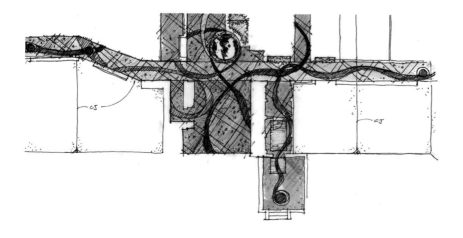

Energy

For the structure for both phases, we selected steel because of its fire rating, structural capabilities, high recycled content, recyclability, and durability. In the design of the exterior envelope, energy conservation, moisture control, and durability were primary considerations, however, these were addressed very differently in the two buildings.

BUILDING ONE. The steel structure was changed to a heavy timber frame in the common areas to provide a feeling of warmth. All insulation is outside the layer of steel structure, so there is no thermal bridging of the structural system. Outside the structural system, minimal connectors were used to fasten the exterior finishes through the insulation to the structure inside. An air barrier is located between two 3" layers of foam insulation on the roof to reduce air leakage. The roof overhang is made of OSB-skinned insulated panels to avoid thermal bridges caused when steel passing from the inside to the outside insulation carries heat out during cold weather. The warehouse walls consist of 4" of thick foam, steel-skinned panels. The office walls have 3" of spray-on foam, plus a 1½" metal panel, forming a tightly insulated wall system. Six air-leakage tests over the course of construction, combined with infrared scanning, confirmed the building's very low air-infiltration numbers. The warehouse's white thermoplastic polyolefin (TPO) roof helps reduce summer heat gain without the use of vinyl compounds. The fiberglass windows have an R-value of R-5, with low-solar-gain triple-glass, low-e layers, and argon gas. Ground-floor slabs are insulated with 4" of high-density expanded polystyrene.

BUILDING TWO. The second building incorporates the same basic design but also includes improvements. All insulation levels were increased and air-infiltration levels decreased. R-values in the roof assembly were increased from R-38 to R-54; 6" foam panels with steel skin were used in lieu of 4" in the manufacturing facility; and the R-value in the walls in the office portion of the building was increased from R-26 to R-40 from Building 1 to Building 2.

PASSIVE DESIGN STRATEGIES

The siting and design of the buildings maximize the effectiveness of passive and integrated strategies, including passive solar, natural ventilation, and earth berming. The buildings are elongated along the east–west axis to maximize solar gain in the winter and to capture daylight all year. The majority of the glazing is located on the south façade, capturing desirable winter sun while limiting direct solar gain in the summer. Glazing types specific to orientation were used to minimize active systems. Trees to the east and west of the building provide summer shading to reduce cooling loads. The north side of the building is bermed into the hillside to minimize heat loss and locate the building off agricultural soils, and the north-facing roof is white to reflect solar heat gain. Operable windows combined with vertical air circulation through the clerestory windows promotes natural ventilation, minimizing cooling loads.

DAYLIGHTING AND LIGHTING

The building's southern orientation and numerous windows and skylights provide office and warehouse areas with natural light. A high strip of south-facing windows in the offices is equipped with German light-guiding blinds to redirect sunlight up into the ceiling and diffuse the light for general illumination. Open floor plans and glass in interior partitions further distribute light. Skylights in the second-floor offices supplement and balance light coming from the windows. Direct sun from the skylights is diffused by white north walls most of the year.

In the offices, zoning of lights and automatic dimming ballasts on T-8 lights dim or brighten the lights as sunlight increases or decreases.

In the warehouse, skylights and large windows mostly eliminate the need for artificial lighting on sunny days. The south-facing clerestory windows bring direct sunlight into the warehouse space. Acrylic prismatic skylights diffuse light in the warehouse. Three lamp-dimming fixtures direct most of the light downward for higher efficiency. Occupancy sensors in every room of the building except closets and mechanical rooms turn lights off when they are not needed. Fluorescent lighting in the parking lot is also controlled with occupancy sensors.

FIGURE CS5.5. Shared interior spaces: *left*, fireplace in central heart of Building One; *top right*, two-story central library with art floor in Building Two; and *bottom right*, street walls with planters lining corridors.

FIGURE CS5.6. High-performance wall sections for Buildings One and Two.

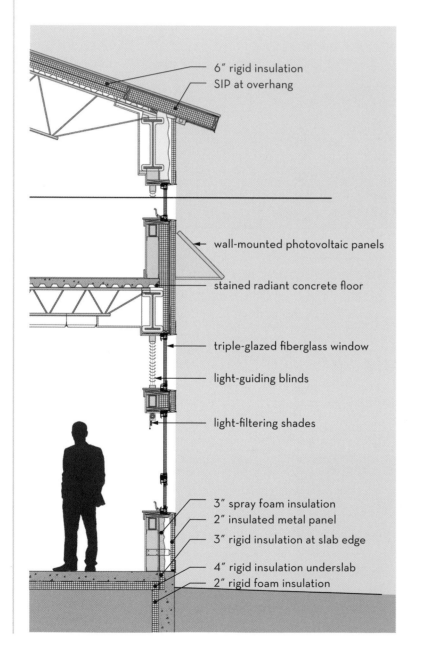

6" rigid insulation
SIP at overhang

wall-mounted photovoltaic panels

stained radiant concrete floor

triple-glazed fiberglass window

light-guiding blinds

light-filtering shades

3" spray foam insulation
2" insulated metal panel
3" rigid insulation at slab edge
4" rigid insulation underslab
2" rigid foam insulation

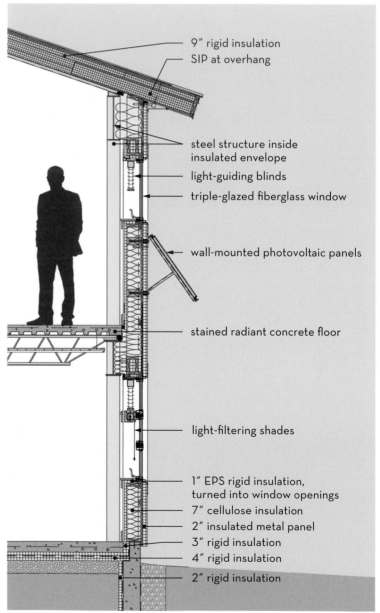

9" rigid insulation
SIP at overhang

steel structure inside insulated envelope
light-guiding blinds
triple-glazed fiberglass window

wall-mounted photovoltaic panels

stained radiant concrete floor

light-filtering shades

1" EPS rigid insulation, turned into window openings
7" cellulose insulation
2" insulated metal panel
3" rigid insulation
4" rigid insulation
2" rigid insulation

MECHANICAL SYSTEMS

A high-efficiency radiant heating and cooling system provides optimal comfort and climate control in the building. In the winter radiant slabs provide heat; in the summer the same radiant slab is used for cooling but is supplemented with ducted cooling in meeting rooms. High-efficiency heat pumps provide chilled water to the radiant floors and the ventilation system for cooling.

In Building One heat pumps reject heat from the building through 2 miles of tubing in the bottom of the heat-sink pond located in front of the building. In Building Two cool water is pumped from wells to be used directly in the slabs for cooling, then moves to the pond for Building One to cool it.

To improve the cooling system, the electricity-consuming heat pumps used for cooling the first building were replaced with a well-water system that draws cold water out of the ground, filters it, and uses it directly to cool the slab in the summer. The cool water is then released to the pond, where it helps cool the water temperature, effectively improving the efficiency of the heat-pump system in the first building.

Two wood-pellet-fired boilers provide primary heating for the building's radiant heating system with 90 percent efficient propane backup. In the fall and spring, when the pellet boilers take more effort to start and stop, solar hot water provides most of the domestic hot water. A wood-pellet silo located in the warehouse holds enough for a year's worth of heating. The pellets are gravity fed into the boilers located on the floor below by an automated auger system. Other than initial firing of the boilers and weekly maintenance checks, the system maintains building temperatures automatically.

The ventilation system provides fresh air to all the office working spaces and at the same time removes stale air to provide superior indoor air quality. An ERV recovers 75 percent of the heat and moisture energy required for fresh air in winter and in summer. The boilers add more heat in winter when it

is needed, and the heat pumps further cool and dehumidify the air in the summer. With its large open space and ample windows, the warehouse uses natural ventilation for fresh air.

Office spaces include operable windows so employees can have fresh air and natural cooling. Green and red indicator lights let employees know when windows may be opened and when the air-conditioning is operating. During the summer, Vermont weather is often cool enough to cool the building during the day or to precool the building at night for the next day, avoiding the use of air-conditioning and saving a significant amount of energy. Several automatically operated windows open when conditions are right. Two large barn fans in the warehouse area supplement this natural airflow when needed.

ENERGY PERFORMANCE MONITORING

A networked, computer-based DDC system orchestrates the building's heating, cooling, and fresh-air ventilation systems. The system is programmed to provide the most comfort at the lowest energy consumption. It also tracks overall building and subsystem energy use to maximize energy efficiency over time. In cooling mode the DDC system tracks temperature and humidity levels in slabs and the air to ensure that the system operates without condensation on the radiant slab.

RENEWABLE ELECTRICITY

When it was put in, the 67 kW solar installation for Building One was the largest in Vermont. Twelve 2.2 kW trackers use unique nonelectric "thermal motors" (by Zomeworks) to track the sun and improve the collection of solar energy by about 30 percent compared to fixed solar panels. On the south-facing roof, 35 kW of Uni-Solar amorphous silicon PVs are adhered directly to

FIGURE CS5.7. Living building and systems diagram

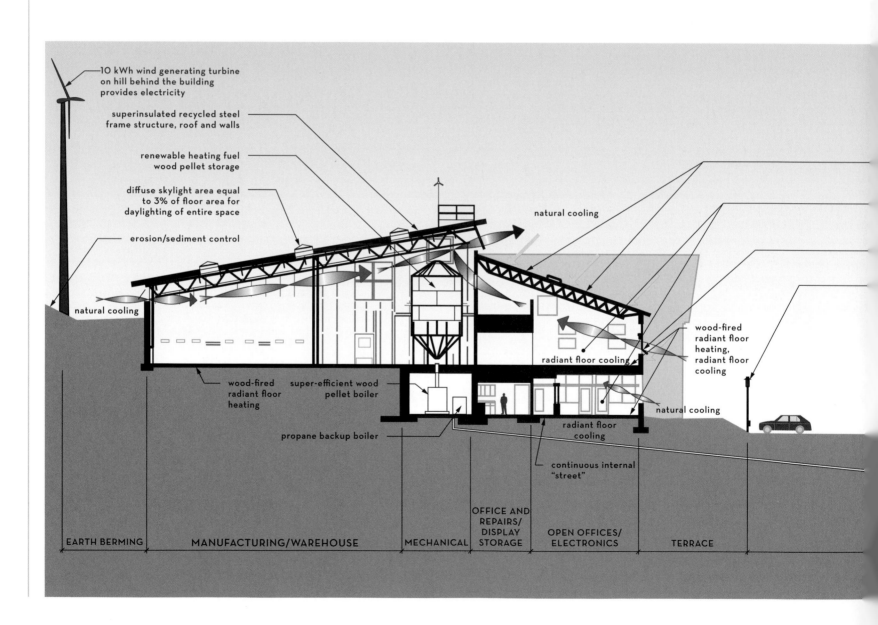

10 kWh wind generating turbine on hill behind the building provides electricity

superinsulated recycled steel frame structure, roof and walls

renewable heating fuel wood pellet storage

diffuse skylight area equal to 3% of floor area for daylighting of entire space

erosion/sediment control

natural cooling

natural cooling

natural cooling

radiant floor cooling

wood-fired radiant floor heating, radiant floor cooling

wood-fired radiant floor heating

super-efficient wood pellet boiler

propane backup boiler

natural cooling

radiant floor cooling

continuous internal "street"

EARTH BERMING

MANUFACTURING/WAREHOUSE

MECHANICAL

OFFICE AND REPAIRS/ DISPLAY STORAGE

OPEN OFFICES/ ELECTRONICS

TERRACE

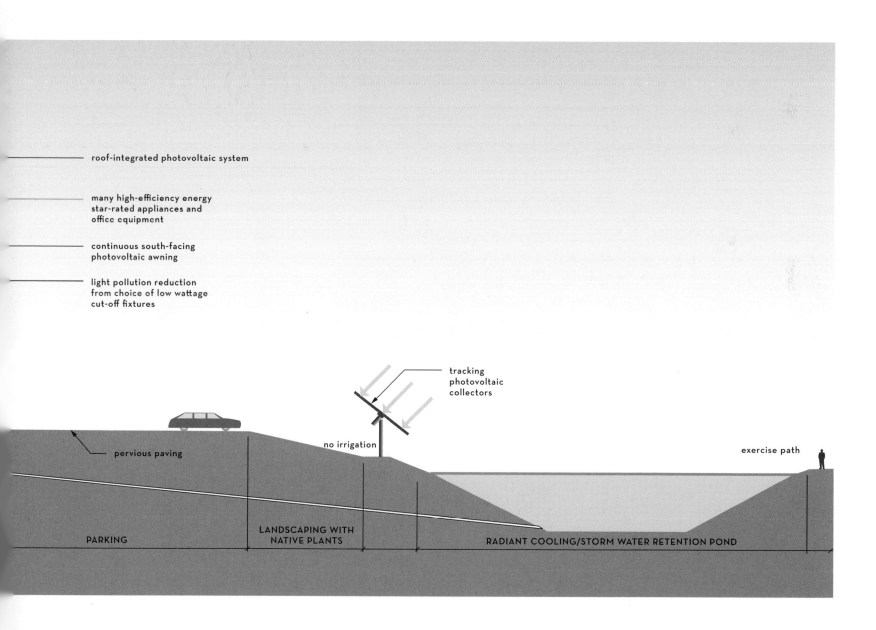

roof-integrated photovoltaic system

many high-efficiency energy star-rated appliances and office equipment

continuous south-facing photovoltaic awning

light pollution reduction from choice of low wattage cut-off fixtures

tracking photovoltaic collectors

pervious paving

no irrigation

exercise path

PARKING

LANDSCAPING WITH NATIVE PLANTS

RADIANT COOLING/STORM WATER RETENTION POND

FIGURE CS5.8. Daylighting in south-oriented office spaces.

FIGURE CS5.9. Daylighting in warehouse.

FIGURE CS5.10. PV trackers along the south of the building with cooling pond in the foreground.

the standing-seam metal roof. On the building's south wall is an awning made of 7 kW of high-efficiency crystalline silicon PV panels. Roof-mounted solar thermal collectors use the sun's energy to meet the building's domestic hot water needs. A 10 kW wind turbine on the hill behind the building was added to further increase the renewable power for Building One. Building Two uses the same strategy, with trackers and building integrated PV on the roof and as awnings on walls. In addition, through group net metering NRG purchases approximately 70 percent of the power generated from a 150kW solar-tracker farm located on a neighboring property.

Healthy and Sustainable Strategies

We selected building materials and finishes based on assessments of durability, indoor air quality, environmental impacts, capital and operating costs, and embodied energy considering a cradle-to-cradle life cycle. FSC-certified wood was used for

a glulam structure in the center of the facility. Interior trim and furnishings were fashioned from both certified and local wood. Recycled-content materials such as tile, ceiling tiles, fly ash, and insulation board were used in addition to the steel structure. To enhance indoor air quality, low-VOC paints, adhesive sealants, and carpet were used along with formaldehyde-free cabinets, furnishings, and interior doors. Over 330 tons (88 percent) of construction waste was reused or recycled. Strategies for minimizing waste generation included requesting minimal product packaging, worker education, and reuse/giveaway programs. Dedicated recycling stations and in-house programs promote employee recycling.

Landscaping and water systems design focused on water conservation strategies. Existing trees that do not require watering were preserved, and new landscaping is composed of native plants that require no irrigation once established. Plumbing fixtures were selected for water conservation, including 0.5 gpm faucet aerators, 2.0 gpm showerheads and dual-flush toilets. These conservation measures result in a 43 percent reduction in water use over a building with EPA-approved fixtures.

FIGURE CS5.11. Master plan for possible future mixed-use development on property.

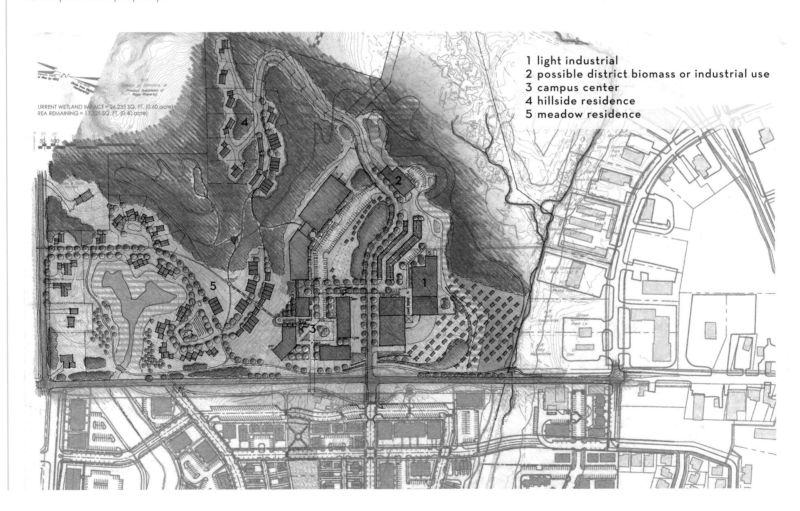

1 light industrial
2 possible district biomass or industrial use
3 campus center
4 hillside residence
5 meadow residence

Core Construction Practices

8 | Building Enclosure Fundamentals

n part 3 we apply net zero principles to the most common construction assemblies. By drawing upon the principles discussed in chapter 6 and using the drawings that appear in chapters 8 to 13, you can also generate details for other types of assemblies.

A Review of Basics

In the chapters that follow, we'll explore five types of construction. Let's quickly review the basics of each. Below-grade net zero construction practices can be applied to any above-grade construction type. The fundamentals include insulating below grade to net zero levels; maintaining continuity of the water-, air-, vapor-, and thermal-control layers; and connecting these layers as the construction transitions above grade. Poured-in-place concrete is the most common approach to below-grade work and is the basis of the net zero construction approaches in chapter 9.

Steel and concrete construction is the most common construction type for larger commercial and institutional buildings due to its durability and ability to meet the code requirements for noncombustible materials. Aside from achieving the thermal values necessary for net zero buildings, controlling thermal bridges in steel and concrete construction is most critical when working with this construction type.

Wood-frame construction is the predominant construction method for smaller buildings, including single- and multifamily residences, as well as many small-scale commercial, industrial, and institutional projects. Wood is a renewable resource that is relatively inexpensive, is easy to work with, and has an insulative value that exceeds other structural materials. Unfortunately, its use comes with a few drawbacks. Wood is a very attractive food for termites, carpenter ants, and other insects particularly when combined with some insulation and materials. It makes a great nesting environment and home for rodents and small animals. And when exposed to moisture, wood can rot and/or become an excellent food for mold. Furthermore, it is not dimensionally stable,

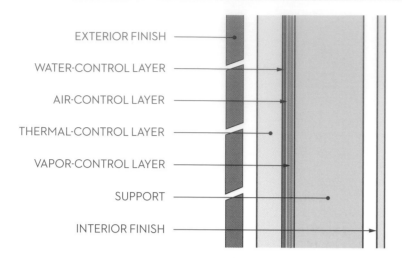

EXTERIOR FINISH

WATER-CONTROL LAYER

AIR-CONTROL LAYER

THERMAL-CONTROL LAYER

VAPOR-CONTROL LAYER

SUPPORT

INTERIOR FINISH

FIGURE 8.1. The perfect wall assembly, with continuous control layers on the exterior of the building structure.

moving over time and shrinking and swelling with changes in ambient humidity. Structurally, it is not consistent and frequently has defects such as large knots. These drawbacks aside, wood construction is prevalent, and the sound construction techniques covered in this book make it an appropriate and desirable choice for net zero building construction.

Steel and wood composite construction takes advantage of simple and economical wood construction with the strength of steel to create larger spans for floors and roofs. This may be desirable for certain types of buildings, typically 20,000 to 25,000 sf in size. This is a niche construction type, as buildings constructed as such are still classified under code definitions as wood-frame buildings. But these buildings can contain larger spaces that would not be feasible in all-wood-frame construction. This construction type allows all of the insulation to be on the outside of the structure and reduces the thermal bridges that are a challenge with all-steel construction, making it a good choice for net zero construction. This hybrid structure is not common but provides an opportunity for use with net zero construction.

The final construction type covered in the pages ahead is not really a construction type but rather the renovation of existing buildings to net zero standards. Progress toward a net zero society includes revamping our existing building stock, which consists of buildings that are by and large poorly insulated and inefficiently heated. The first step in successful renovations is an existing-building assessment. This needs to be followed by

a study of options in terms of building science, cost, durability, and feasibility to develop an appropriate net zero renovation strategy. In many cases the strategies depicted in the other four construction types are applicable in renovations. While the principal strategies and techniques are mostly the same, unique existing conditions offer significant challenges and opportunities that are different from new construction.

The drawings in the following chapters depict a wide range of conditions for each of these construction types. Common to each construction type are the below-grade conditions, covered in chapter 9. Chapters 10, 11, 12, and 13 demonstrate assemblies for constructing the ideal wall and roof for each of the different construction types. These four chapters also include drawings for common intersections, openings and penetrations, and atypical details such as seismic joints, exterior decks, porch roofs, and expansion joints. Chapter 14, "Net Zero for Existing Buildings," explores conditions unique to renovations. The drawings in these chapters all clearly describe and illustrate the components and connections necessary to assure the continuity of the water-, air-, vapor-, and thermal-control layers around the building envelope.

We have designed the illustration details in this part of the book in our office with assistance from Andy Shapiro of Energy Balance. We have also drawn on the work of Building Science Corporation. Their publications, in particular the book *High Performance Enclosures* by John Straube, are excellent resources for pursuing this topic in greater depth.

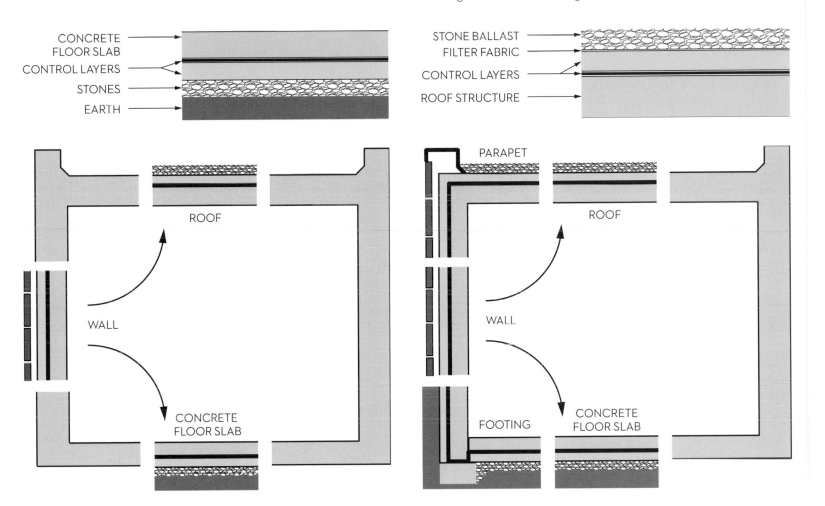

CONCRETE FLOOR SLAB
CONTROL LAYERS
STONES
EARTH

STONE BALLAST
FILTER FABRIC
CONTROL LAYERS
ROOF STRUCTURE

ROOF

WALL

CONCRETE FLOOR SLAB

PARAPET

ROOF

WALL

FOOTING

CONCRETE FLOOR SLAB

The "Perfect Wall" and the Ideal Building Assembly

Building Science Corporation's "perfect wall" is based on clear principles created to be used as a foundation for specific conditions or more detailed development. Figure 8.1 depicts their "perfect wall" with finishes on the interior, covering a layer of structure, over which are located the water-, air-, vapor-, and thermal-control layers, with a finish layer on the exterior. In this and other "perfect" assemblies, the thermal layer is on the outside of the structure, which minimizes thermal bridging. Figure

FIGURE 8.3. This diagram, included in the construction document set, illustrates how the air-barrier system is composed of multiple products, systems, and connections between products and systems that provide continuity around the entire building envelope.

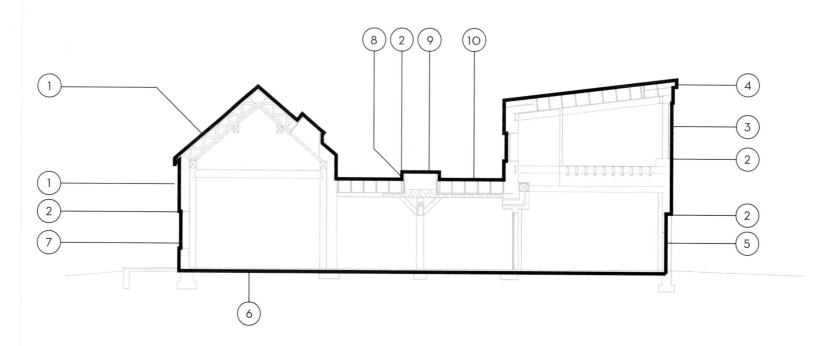

1. fluid-applied air barrier over joints in plywood
2. air-barrier sealant at perimeter of openings
3. translucent fiberglass glazing panel
4. 2-lb closed-cell spray-foam insulation between framing members
5. door unit with certified-infiltration rate
6. underslab-vapor retarder, lapped and sealed at wall
7. window unit with certified-infiltration rate
8. self-adhering waterproof membrane
9. skylight unit with certified-infiltration rate
10. fluid-applied air barrier, continuous and monolithic over roof sheathing

FIGURE 8.4. These graphic representations indicate the continuous water-, air-, vapor-, and thermal-control layers in diagrams for chapters 9 through 14, as well as the abbreviations used in these details.

LEGEND

▬ ▬ ▬ ▬ ▬ ▪ Air-control layer

▬ ▬ ▬ ▬ ▬ ▪ Water-control layer

▬ ▬ ▬ ▬ ▬ ▪ Vapor-control layer

▬ ▬ ▬ ▬ ▬ ▪ Combined air/water /vapor-control layer

Thermal Control Layer:

Cellulose insulation

Rigid foam Insulation

Spray-foam insulation

Mineral wool insulation

ABBREVIATIONS

EPS = Expanded polystyrene

GWB = Gypsum wallboard

LVL = Laminated veneer lumber

MIL = Thousandth of an Inch

POLYISO = Polyisocyanurate

P-T = Pressure-treated wood product

SAWM = Self-adhering waterproof membrane

XPS = Extruded polystyrene

8.2 shows how the perfect wall can evolve into the perfect slab and roof and eventually the perfect net zero assembly by reorientation, use of appropriate materials, and appropriate connections at intersections.

Building on the perfect assembly and other work by Building Science Corporation, the assemblies in the following chapters of the book are what we call "ideal" assemblies. We decided to use the term "ideal" rather than "perfect" because "perfect" implies a static world. As Building Science Corporation points out, perfection can be difficult to achieve in real-world applications. There are also likely to be changes or alterations due to budget, material availability, owner preferences, or existing conditions in the case of renovations. Although research and product development will certainly mean further innovation and evolution, the detailed and layered drawings we offer here will create resilient, durable, and lasting buildings for our generation and beyond.

While the individual junctures of components and materials are critical details for the integrity of the building enclosure, the continuity of the control layers must be maintained around the entire perimeter. During design and construction documentation, it is important to examine the enclosure at the macro- and micro-levels and document the continuity at both. Figure 8.3 depicts this continuity of the air-control layer at the

perimeter and identifies the specific junctures. This drawing should be included in the construction documents and supported by specific details in the construction document set. This drawing is particularly helpful in communicating the intent of the continuous air-control layer to the contractor and subcontractors, as they are often focused on individual aspects of the building construction. Air sealing for continuity of the air-control layer is critical. Infiltration/exfiltration affects the energy use of the building and creates a pathway for moisture-vapor transmission, which can lead to condensation within the wall assembly.

If the thermal layer is not addressed properly, it can of course have a significantly adverse affect on the energy performance of the building. If the water-control layer is not addressed properly, moisture intrusion can cause corrosion and rot that affect the durability of the building and may encourage mold growth that can affect occupant health. If you explain and describe the significance of each aspect of the work, the contractor and subcontractors will be more likely to take greater care to achieve the desired continuity to create a unified net zero building enclosure.

The details in the following chapters identify the major components of the assemblies, and they highlight the location and continuity of the water-, air-, vapor-, and thermal-control layers. The key in figure 8.4 applies to all of the details.

9 | Net Zero Below-Grade Construction

Below-grade construction is subject to significantly different environmental conditions than above-grade construction. Below grade walls and slabs do not encounter rain and/or sun or the extreme temperature variations that above-grade construction does. However, they do encounter moisture vapor and condensation, as well as groundwater. They are subject to water pressure, just like the hull of a boat would be. They also encounter lateral forces from the earth and from the soil's freezing and thawing cycles, as well as pests that can include termites, carpenter ants, and other insects and organisms. For obvious reasons, it is best to build below-grade construction so that it requires no maintenance and minimal oversight.

Water from the roof, ground, and buildings and from below grade must be addressed so it does not cause problems. Roof and surface water must drain away from the building, and water must be shed from below-grade walls. Since it is difficult and expensive to make basements fully watertight, like a boat, walls should be protected with permeable fill to promote drainage, a protective moisture coating, and a perimeter drain. The control layer on the basement wall should withstand water pressure and be continuous—usually achieved by spray coating. For this function, we will use the term "moistureproofing" instead of "waterproofing," which can be expensive and not always necessary, or "dampproofing," which does not provide the ability to withstand water pressure. Once there is adequate moisture protection, the air, vapor, and thermal layers can be provided; all are detailed in the drawings and descriptions that follow. The below-grade assemblies in this chapter are applicable to all of the building construction types in the following chapters.

With simple foundation walls, the foundation wall lines up with the building envelope. In larger and/or more complex structures, there may be extensions of or connections to the foundation on the interior or exterior of the building, such as piers for columns, shear walls, exterior entrances, exterior retaining walls, or unheated spaces such as garages or truck loading docks. Generally, structural engineers want to connect concrete foundation walls structurally so the building is as strong as possible. This then leads to problems with maintaining a continuous insulation layer. The first step to address this is to assess whether the insulation should go on the inside or outside of the foundation, which is often determined by the number of places where these thermal conditions occur and the difficulty of solving them. The most common foundation connections on the interior are piers for columns, which can be solved relatively easily with a concrete pier separated from the wall with insulation but tied together at the footing level (see figure 10.9). If there are lots of difficult intersections on the outside of the foundation, it is preferable to insulate on the inside, minimizing thermal bridges. Therefore, in this book the majority of the details of these intersections show the insulation on the inside of concrete wall.

The thermal-control layer as the foundation wall transitions from below grade to above grade is another critical area because the foundation walls extend below frost (usually 2–5′ in cold climates) to at least 8″ or more above grade, exposing a portion of the wall to the cold. The details in this and the following chapters illustrate multiple ways to address this transition.

We recommend continuing the above-grade R-40 insulation levels down 2 feet below grade. Beyond that depth, the thermal layer for a net zero assembly may be reduced in R-value from R-40 to a minimum of R-20, because of the insulating effect of the soil. There are two approaches to the thermal layer in below-grade wall construction: the insulation can be on either the inside or the outside of the wall. While extruded polystyrene (XPS) is the most common insulation material used in this situation, there are some concerns with using XPS on the exterior of the foundation. Most significantly, insects and animals can burrow into the insulation, destroying the insulation value. XPS is also susceptible to degradation from contact with petrochemicals, which can exist undetected as contaminants in the soil. For these reasons, we recommend using foam insulation products only on the interior side of the foundation wall. If rigid insulation is used on the outside of the building, we prefer rigid mineral wool or rigid fiberglass designed for below-grade applications, as they are more resistant to chemical and pest degradation. However, under slabs where we do not suspect oil contamination in the fill, we do use foam insulation.

When the insulation on the exterior of the foundation wall extends above grade, it needs to be covered. This is typically a plastered covering that resembles stucco, but there are panel products that can be used as well. If there is foam insulation below grade, make sure it is separated from above-grade foam with metal flashing, with sealed lap joints, to eliminate a path for insects migrating from the ground up.

While basement wall conditions are described below, simple frost walls can be insulated using similar strategies, with the insulation on the exterior or interior of the frost wall. When insulating on the inside of frost walls, you can use rigid foam insulations, since they are then protected from pests and contaminants.

Below-Grade Wall and Slab Assemblies

The following discussion examines the construction of various typical below-grade assemblies, including their control layers and other special requirements.

BELOW-GRADE BASEMENT WALL WITH EXTERIOR INSULATION. The ideal below-grade basement wall with exterior insulation is shown in figure 9.1a. The soils next to the wall should be sand, gravel, or stone, which are all permeable materials, allowing groundwater to flow downward. A drainage mat, or a water-permeable thermal layer, also facilitates the free flow of water down along the wall and protects the moistureproofing applied to the face of the foundation. The thermal layer should be of pest- and chemical-resistant insulation, as discussed above. On the interior side, the stud wall is held away from the concrete to prevent any moisture in the concrete wall from wicking into the wood.

In this assembly moistureproofing provides the water- and vapor-control layers, while the concrete itself is the air-control layer.

BASEMENT WALL WITH INTERIOR INSULATION. Given that mineral wool and rigid fiberglass exterior insulation are not typically used in the construction industry, an interior approach to basement insulation is often used to protect the insulation layer. Interior insulation allows the concrete, which is durable and economical, to be the exterior finish. While the interior of the basement should be dry and protected from water vapor by the continuous water- and vapor-control layers, there is always

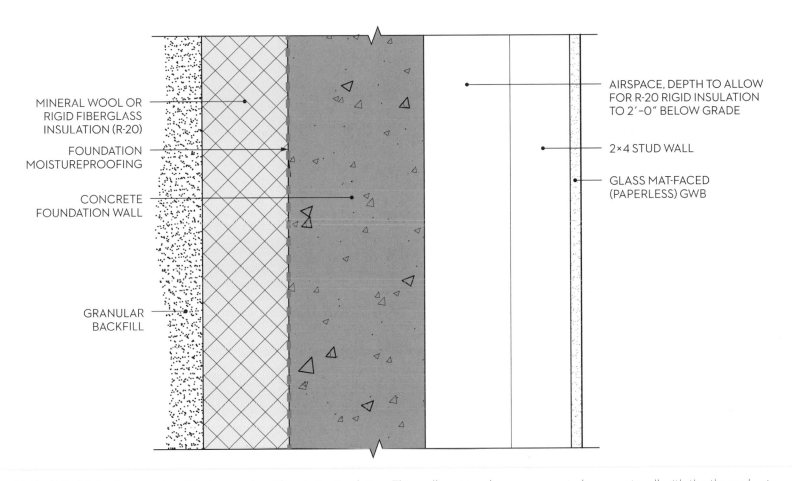

MINERAL WOOL OR
RIGID FIBERGLASS
INSULATION (R-20)

FOUNDATION
MOISTUREPROOFING

CONCRETE
FOUNDATION WALL

GRANULAR
BACKFILL

AIRSPACE, DEPTH TO ALLOW
FOR R-20 RIGID INSULATION
TO 2'–0" BELOW GRADE

2×4 STUD WALL

GLASS MAT-FACED
(PAPERLESS) GWB

FIGURE 9.1A. Basement wall below grade with exterior insulation: This wall section shows a concrete basement wall with the thermal-, air-, water-, and vapor-control layers on the outside and finishes on the inside. In this case an insulation that allows water to drain through it eliminates the need for a separate drainage/protection layer.

FIGURE 9.1B. A basement foundation with exterior, pest-resistant board insulation. Not visible is the layer of foundation waterproofing applied to the basement walls before the insulation.

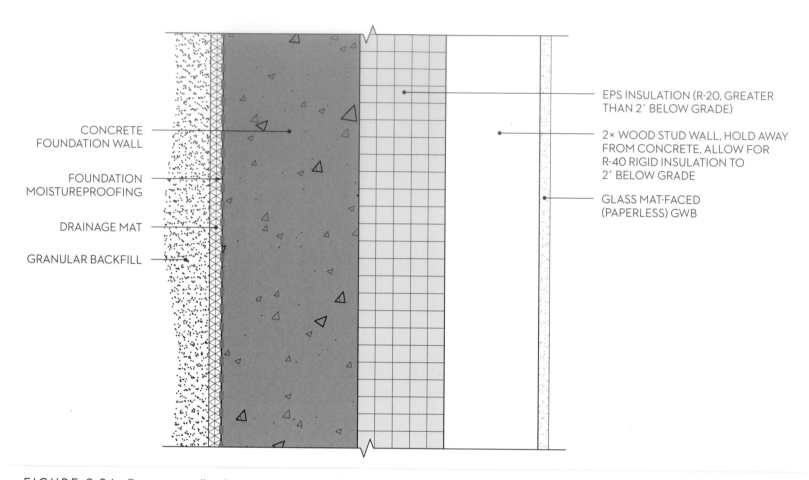

CONCRETE
FOUNDATION WALL

FOUNDATION
MOISTUREPROOFING

DRAINAGE MAT

GRANULAR BACKFILL

EPS INSULATION (R-20, GREATER
THAN 2' BELOW GRADE)

2× WOOD STUD WALL, HOLD AWAY
FROM CONCRETE, ALLOW FOR
R-40 RIGID INSULATION TO
2' BELOW GRADE

GLASS MAT-FACED
(PAPERLESS) GWB

FIGURE 9.2A. Basement wall with interior insulation: The thermal-, air-, water-, and vapor-control layers are installed on the outside of the concrete basement wall, and a thermal-control layer and finishes are installed on the inside. A drainage/protection layer is added for the exterior control layers as well.

FIGURE 9.2B. Basement walls under construction (before gypsum board finish is installed), with insulation installed on the interior side.

the possibility that plumbing equipment or basement drainage could fail at some time, causing substantial basement damage. Therefore, it is strongly recommended to use basement insulation that will not be damaged by water, which limits the choices to plastic foam board, mineral wool, or spray-foam insulation. EPS is the preferred insulation due to its reduced environmental impact, as discussed in chapter 6. All plastic foam insulations, except for those that are manufactured with foil or other special facings, require protection in order to meet code requirements. This can be either gypsum board for a finished space or intumescent paint for an unfinished space. The gypsum board can be fastened directly to wood strapping, which is fastened to the concrete through the insulation. On below-grade, basement, and exterior walls, glass mat-faced gypsum board is recommended because it is paperless and therefore not susceptible to holding moisture, which could lead to mold. As with the exterior insulation, suitable backfill, perimeter drainage, and grading away from the building are critical to keep water away from the walls. Figure 9.2a shows such an assembly.

BASEMENT WALL, AT AND BELOW GRADE, EXTERIOR AND INTERIOR INSULATION.

Since net zero buildings require an R-value of 40 above grade and only R-20 below, a transition must occur at the upper part of the basement wall, which is partially above grade. As mentioned previously, exterior insulation generates the ideal assembly below grade as well as above grade. Given the lower R-values of mineral wool and rigid fiberglass (approximately R-4/inch), it is not always practical to install the thickness required for R-40 on the exterior. Figure 9.3 shows a recommended approach, using 5″ of insulation on the exterior of the foundation wall and 5″ of EPS foam insulation on the interior above grade and continuing 2′–0″ below the grade line. For walls 2′–0″ or more below grade, the R-20 exterior insulation alone is sufficient.

SLAB ASSEMBLY.

The ideal concrete slab assembly is shown in figure 9.4a, and it is essentially the ideal below-grade wall turned 90°. The concrete slab can be used as the interior finish floor, or other floor material can be added on top of the slab assembly. A single-membrane product below the slab can serve as a combined water-, air-, and vapor-control layer, with the thermal-control layer below them. All joints in this membrane, any penetrations for piping, and all edges where the slab meets walls or footings must be sealed very carefully in order for it to perform as the air-, vapor-, and water-control layer. This means there should be no holes. Because this membrane is above the insulation, it must be a tough and durable product. Sheet polyethylene, 6 mils thick, is commonly used, but it can easily tear or be punctured and can degrade when in contact with alkali-containing materials. Stego Wrap, a polyolefin product available in 15-mil thickness, or equivalent product must be used to ensure durability during construction and for the life of the building. EPS below the water-, air-, and vapor-control layer provide a minimum R-30 thermal-control layer at conditioned spaces. This thermal layer must be continuous, including underneath locations where the slab is thickened to provide a strip footing for interior bearing walls. This means foaming all joints.

CRAWL SPACES.

Crawl spaces present some unique challenges and therefore would not be a first choice for a first-floor system. There is a strong likelihood of moisture migration from the soil below, which can cause problems with mold and rot. Because of this, building codes typically require the crawl space to be passively ventilated to the outside or mechanically conditioned. If the foundation is insulated, whether interior or exterior, ventilation to the outside will short-circuit the insulation, resulting in very significant heat loss. The floor can be insulated to avoid this, and in such a case we would recommend insulating the floor to the same level as the roof, R-60 (see figure 9.5). However, this still leaves concerns about moisture buildup and the potential for long-term damage to the building. Insulating on the exterior foundation walls and mechanically conditioning the crawl space (see figure 9.6) is not efficient in the sense that it is an added cost and uses energy to condition an uninhabited space, but it is preferable to insulating the floor and venting to the outside in terms of long-term durability and occupant health.

With either option, measures must be taken to limit the migration of moisture from the soil below. The soil should be leveled, and a heavy-duty vapor-control layer should be laid over it and sealed to the concrete or masonry around the perimeter. A ballast layer of round stone, sand, or concrete slab should then be installed over the vapor-control layer to weigh it down and protect it. This assembly will do much to reduce, but not necessarily eliminate, the potential for moisture issues.

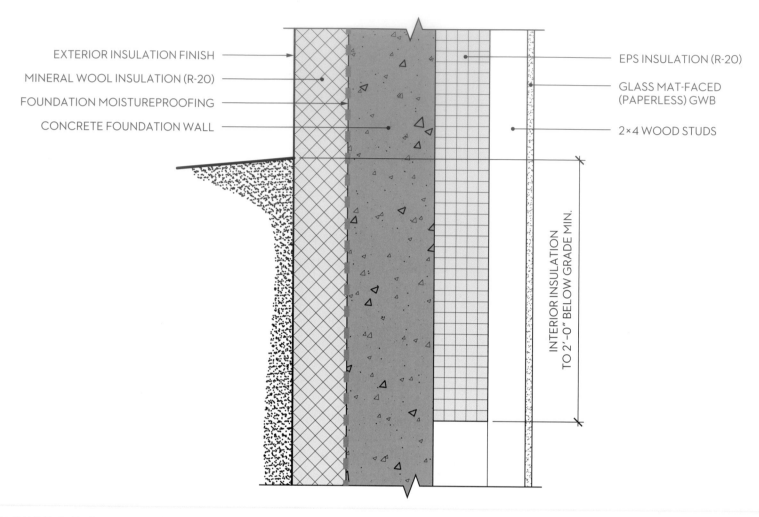

EXTERIOR INSULATION FINISH

MINERAL WOOL INSULATION (R-20)

FOUNDATION MOISTUREPROOFING

CONCRETE FOUNDATION WALL

EPS INSULATION (R-20)

GLASS MAT-FACED (PAPERLESS) GWB

2×4 WOOD STUDS

INTERIOR INSULATION TO 2'-0" BELOW GRADE MIN.

FIGURE 9.3. Basement wall, at and below grade, exterior and interior insulation, with a combination of exterior and interior insulation used to provide a combined R-40 to 2 feet below grade. Below that, the exterior insulation provides the required R-20.

Common Below-Grade
Intersections

The intersection between the basement wall and slab differs based on whether the below-grade wall construction contains insulation on the exterior or the interior.

SLAB-WALL INTERSECTION BELOW GRADE WITH EXTERIOR INSULATION. It is possible to wrap the entire footing on the exterior of the

below-grade wall with insulation so there is no interruption of the insulation layer, but since this could expose the insulation to soil contamination or other factors that could degrade insulation, we generally do not do this. When the insulation below and around the footing is omitted, it does create a thermal bridge at the intersection of wall and footing. While

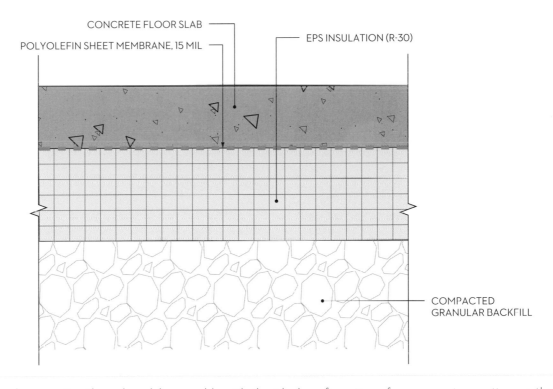

CONCRETE FLOOR SLAB

POLYOLEFIN SHEET MEMBRANE, 15 MIL

EPS INSULATION (R-30)

COMPACTED GRANULAR BACKFILL

FIGURE 9.4A. Slab on grade: a section through a slab assembly with the ideal configuration of components—continuous thermal-, air-, water-, and vapor-control layers below the slab.

FIGURE 9.4B. The carefully taped and sealed Stego Wrap is the vapor-, air-, and water-control layer. The wire reinforcing that will be embedded when the concrete is cast is installed as well. Care must be taken not to puncture the sheet membrane prior to and during concrete placement.

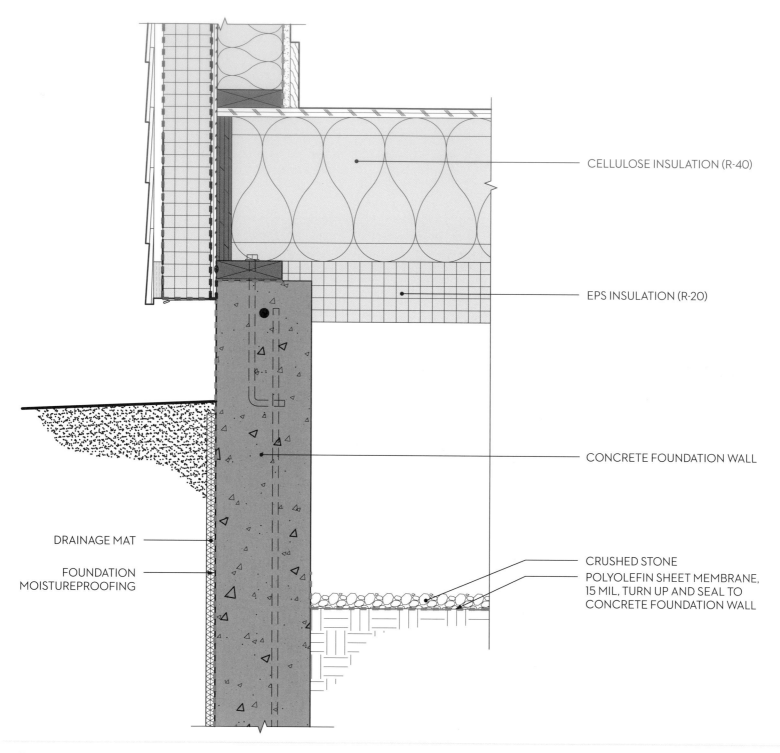

CELLULOSE INSULATION (R-40)

EPS INSULATION (R-20)

CONCRETE FOUNDATION WALL

DRAINAGE MAT

FOUNDATION
MOISTUREPROOFING

CRUSHED STONE

POLYOLEFIN SHEET MEMBRANE,
15 MIL, TURN UP AND SEAL TO
CONCRETE FOUNDATION WALL

FIGURE 9.5. Crawl space assembly with insulated floor: In this approach, the crawl space is treated as exterior, unconditioned space, requiring insulation of the floor to R-60. Passive ventilation to the exterior would be used in this case to try to control moisture.

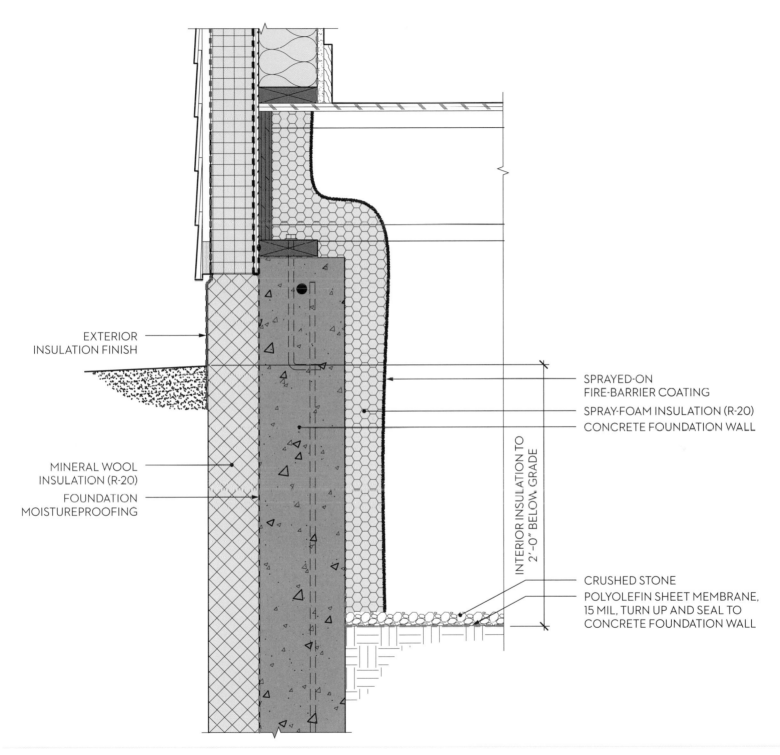

EXTERIOR
INSULATION FINISH

MINERAL WOOL
INSULATION (R-20)

FOUNDATION
MOISTUREPROOFING

INTERIOR INSULATION TO
2'-0" BELOW GRADE

SPRAYED-ON
FIRE-BARRIER COATING

SPRAY-FOAM INSULATION (R-20)

CONCRETE FOUNDATION WALL

CRUSHED STONE

POLYOLEFIN SHEET MEMBRANE,
15 MIL, TURN UP AND SEAL TO
CONCRETE FOUNDATION WALL

FIGURE 9.6. Crawl space with insulated exterior walls: This section shows the top portion of a foundation wall with crawl space, using insulation on the exterior and interior of the wall. This approach allows for a tempered crawl space and can also use mechanical conditioning to provide a moisture-controlled space.

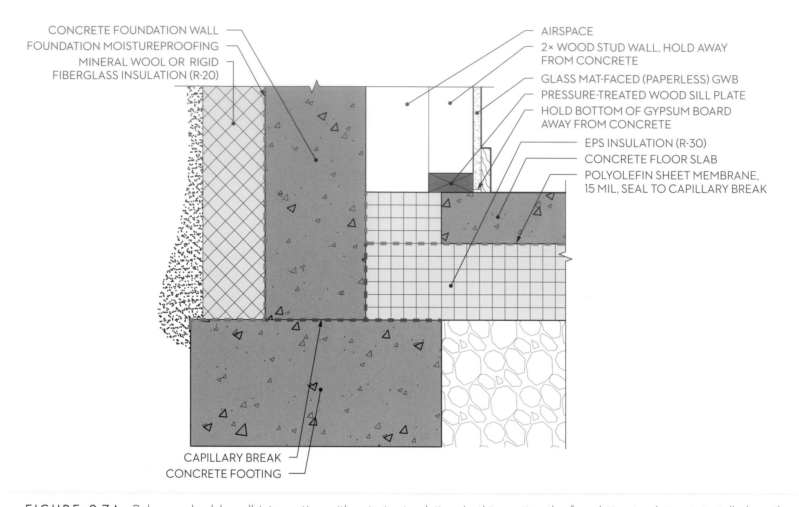

CONCRETE FOUNDATION WALL
FOUNDATION MOISTUREPROOFING
MINERAL WOOL OR RIGID FIBERGLASS INSULATION (R-20)

AIRSPACE
2× WOOD STUD WALL, HOLD AWAY FROM CONCRETE
GLASS MAT-FACED (PAPERLESS) GWB
PRESSURE-TREATED WOOD SILL PLATE
HOLD BOTTOM OF GYPSUM BOARD AWAY FROM CONCRETE
EPS INSULATION (R-30)
CONCRETE FLOOR SLAB
POLYOLEFIN SHEET MEMBRANE, 15 MIL, SEAL TO CAPILLARY BREAK

CAPILLARY BREAK
CONCRETE FOOTING

FIGURE 9.7A. Below-grade slab–wall intersection with exterior insulation: In this section the foundation insulation is installed on the exterior. We still recommend a thermal break between the foundation wall and floor slab. The polyolefin sheet membrane under the slab must be overlapped and sealed to the wall's capillary break to provide continuity of the water-, vapor-, and air-control layers.

FIGURE 9.7B. An underslab air/water/vapor-control membrane is installed, overlapping and sealed to the capillary break at the bottom of the wall. A strip of rigid foam insulation provides a thermal break between the slab and the wall.

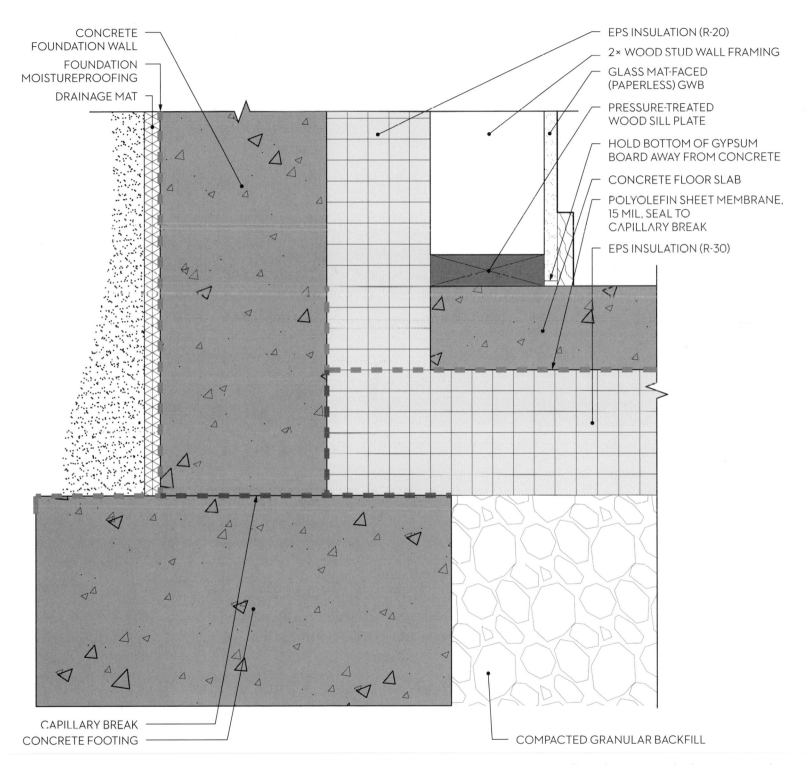

FIGURE 9.8. Slab-wall intersection below grade, interior insulation: In this detail the interior-wall insulation extends down to provide a thermal break between slab and wall and create a continuous thermal layer with the underslab insulation. Note that a capillary break is still required, providing continuity with the underslab control layer.

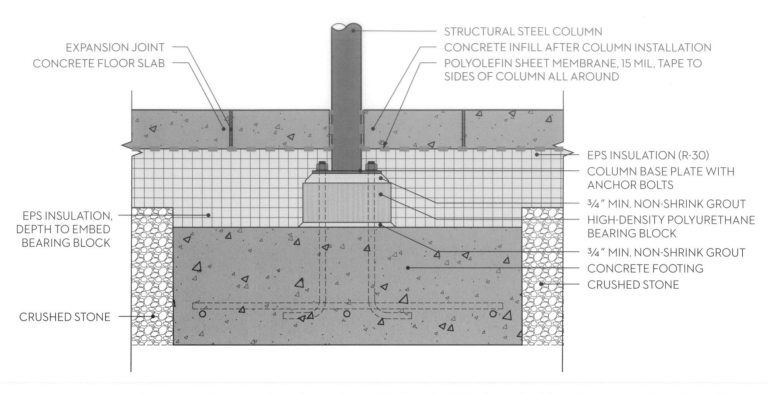

EXPANSION JOINT
CONCRETE FLOOR SLAB

STRUCTURAL STEEL COLUMN
CONCRETE INFILL AFTER COLUMN INSTALLATION
POLYOLEFIN SHEET MEMBRANE, 15 MIL, TAPE TO
SIDES OF COLUMN ALL AROUND

EPS INSULATION (R-30)
COLUMN BASE PLATE WITH
ANCHOR BOLTS
3/4" MIN. NON-SHRINK GROUT
HIGH-DENSITY POLYURETHANE
BEARING BLOCK
3/4" MIN. NON-SHRINK GROUT
CONCRETE FOOTING
CRUSHED STONE

EPS INSULATION,
DEPTH TO EMBED
BEARING BLOCK

CRUSHED STONE

FIGURE 9.9A. Interior basement column: a column footing located below the slab. The underslab insulation provides a thermal break between footing and slab and a high-density polyurethane bearing block under the column bearing plate isolates the footing from the conductive steel column.

FIGURE 9.9B. A column and footing with polyurethane block installed between to provide a thermal break. Rigid insulation will be installed over the footing and gravel fill (not yet placed) to provide the underslab thermal-control layer.

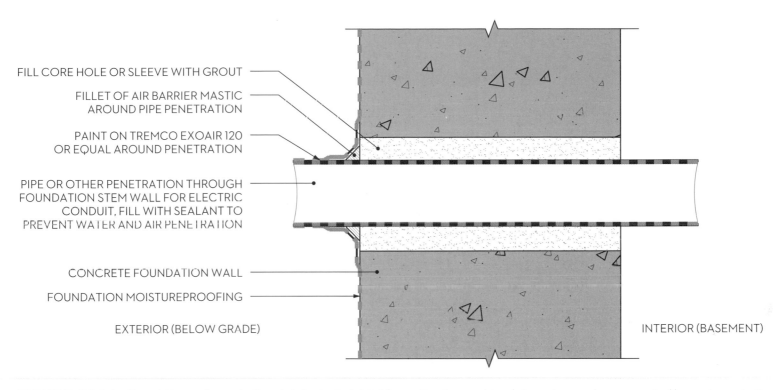

FILL CORE HOLE OR SLEEVE WITH GROUT

FILLET OF AIR BARRIER MASTIC
AROUND PIPE PENETRATION

PAINT ON TREMCO EXOAIR 120
OR EQUAL AROUND PENETRATION

PIPE OR OTHER PENETRATION THROUGH
FOUNDATION STEM WALL FOR ELECTRIC
CONDUIT, FILL WITH SEALANT TO
PREVENT WATER AND AIR PENETRATION

CONCRETE FOUNDATION WALL

FOUNDATION MOISTUREPROOFING

EXTERIOR (BELOW GRADE)

INTERIOR (BASEMENT)

FIGURE 9.10A. Foundation wall penetration detail: a typical detail for sealing the combined air-, water-, and vapor-control layer at penetrations.

FIGURE 9.10B. A typical through-wall penetration, prior to being grouted and sealed.

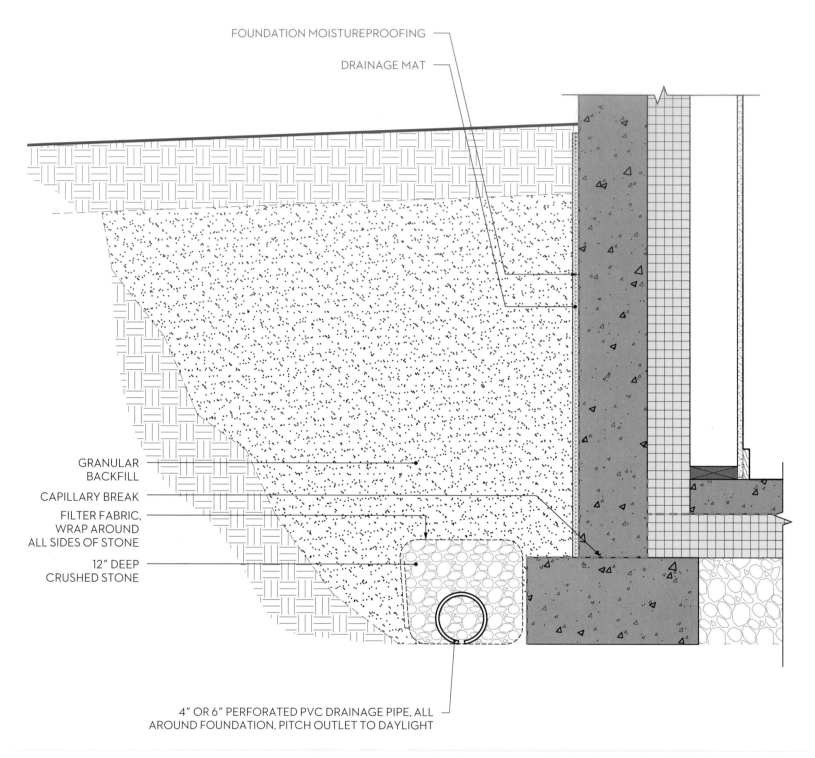

FOUNDATION MOISTUREPROOFING

DRAINAGE MAT

GRANULAR
BACKFILL

CAPILLARY BREAK

FILTER FABRIC,
WRAP AROUND
ALL SIDES OF STONE

12" DEEP
CRUSHED STONE

4" OR 6" PERFORATED PVC DRAINAGE PIPE, ALL
AROUND FOUNDATION, PITCH OUTLET TO DAYLIGHT

FIGURE 9.11. Foundation drainage: a section showing a typical foundation drainage system, which allows surface water and roof eave runoff to drain down through granular fill next to the foundation, to the perforated pipe that will drain the water away.

not desirable, this is an acceptable compromise only because of the lack of good alternatives. Figure 9.7a, a detail of this condition, therefore does not show insulation under footings. Additional insulation is installed around the perimeter of the foundation, creating a thermal break between the slab edge and the foundation wall. There is also a capillary break on top of the footing to stop water from wicking from the footing to the wall. Dampproofing can be used; however, foundation subcontractors do not like to place reusable forms on damp-proofing, as it sticks to them. Another capillary-break material commonly used is latex waterproofing paint. This capillary break also acts as the water and vapor retarder. The underslab water-, air-, and vapor-control layers must connect to this capillary break between the footing and wall to provide continuity from below the slab to the outside of the wall.

If the decision is made to wrap the footings with insulation, it will require the use of high compressive strength extruded polystyrene (XPS) insulation under the footings. XPS is available with compressive strength up to 100 psi, so loading can be calculated to ensure that XPS with the proper compressive strength is specified and installed. The higher the compressive strength, however, the more expensive the product.

SLAB-WALL INTERSECTION BELOW GRADE, INTERIOR INSULATION

Where the insulation is on the inside of the exterior below-grade wall, as in drawing figure 9.8, the thermal-control layer is continuous. The water-, air-, and vapor-control layers can be carried from the outside of the wall through the top of the footing as the capillary break and connect with the air/water/vapor-control membrane under the slab.

INTERIOR BASEMENT COLUMN.

In net zero buildings it is important to address all thermal bridges. This means creating a thermal break below any structural steel columns by pouring the footing separate from the slab so insulation can be continuous, except directly below the steel column, where high-density polyurethane blocks can be used. Figure 9.9a depicts this kind of slab assembly. Occasionally, separate strip footings may be required, such as for interior masonry bearing walls. Where used, strip footings should be depressed below the slab just as for isolated column footings, so insulation can be continuous above. Where

masonry walls bear on such strip footings, the bottom course of masonry (aligned with the insulation layer) should be a masonry product with low thermal conductivity, such as autoclaved aerated concrete (AAC) block or a cellular glass block.

FOUNDATION WALL PENETRATION DETAIL.

When piping or conduit penetrates a waterproofed concrete wall, the piping or conduit should be cast into the foundation or fed through a sleeve that is then grouted solidly into the concrete. This provides a structural surface for the application of the water- and vapor-control layer. Where the pipe exits the wall, the treatment should be as recommended by the manufacturer. To ensure air, water, and vapor sealing, it commonly involves installing a fillet of mastic or compatible sealant around the pipe, then sealing with the waterproofing material. The fillet creates a transitional surface from the wall to the pipe, eliminating sharp angles that are hard to seal properly.

FOUNDATION DRAINAGE.

Perimeter, or foundation, drainage is one of the best ways to passively drain water from the soil at the bottom of the foundation or frost wall and divert it away from the building. Figure 9.11 shows the ideal foundation drainage condition. A perforated drainpipe is laid in a bed of clean stone at the bottom of the excavation around the building perimeter, at the level of the base of the footing. The perforations in the drainpipe allow water to seep in; the drainpipe carries the water around the building to a solid drainpipe that pitches below ground to a surface drainage point or collection structure. The perforated pipe and stone are wrapped in filter fabric, which allows water to pass through but restricts the passage of fine soil particles that could clog the spaces between the stones or the holes in the drainpipe. Above the filter fabric and along the outside of the foundation wall, clean granular fill is installed, which allows water to drain from above to the footing drain. Filter fabric is also installed between the clean granular back and the remainder of the backfill to prevent the migration of fine soil particles into the granular fill that could prevent it from draining. Against the face of the basement wall, we recommend the use of protection and drainage board to protect the waterproofing membrane on the face of the basement wall from damage during backfilling and to help ensure that the water flows to the drainage pipe at the base of the footing.

10 | Net Zero Steel and Concrete Construction

Steel and concrete construction types are prevalent in new construction of commercial and institutional buildings. We are combining the two because in both types of construction the ideal enclosure assembly is the same. The structure is easily and most appropriately kept inside of all four control layers: water, air, vapor, and thermal. With the thermal layer on the exterior, there is a straightforward approach to achieving the ideal net zero assembly, though the details and intersections do require careful attention to reduce and eliminate thermal bridges and optimize air sealing.

Figure 10.1 is a section through a typical wall assembly with a steel above-grade structure. The exterior wall finish in this example section is brick veneer, though many options exist for exterior wall finishes, including metal panels, metal panels with a honeycomb core, metal panels with an insulated core, cementitious boards, stone panels, resin panels, and so on. This exterior wall structure is composed of a structural steel frame, with wall infill provided by light-gauge steel studs. The upper floor is a concrete slab poured on a galvanized steel deck, supported by the structural steel frame. The roof is supported by a steel deck and structural steel framing. For steel construction, the structural framing that supports the metal roof or floor deck can be either steel joists or steel beams, as indicated here. A cast-in-place concrete structure would be similar, with the structural steel elements replaced by concrete columns, beams, joists, and slabs. These are typically poured in place into removable forms with steel-rod reinforcement or precast.

The highly thermally conductive steel structure is located on the inside of the thermal-control layer. However, attached structures such as balconies, canopies, and sunscreens may create thermal bridges across the insulation layer. In addition to heat loss, these thermal bridges often cause condensation and associated mold problems, as well as creating cold spots in occupied spaces. Details at these conditions should

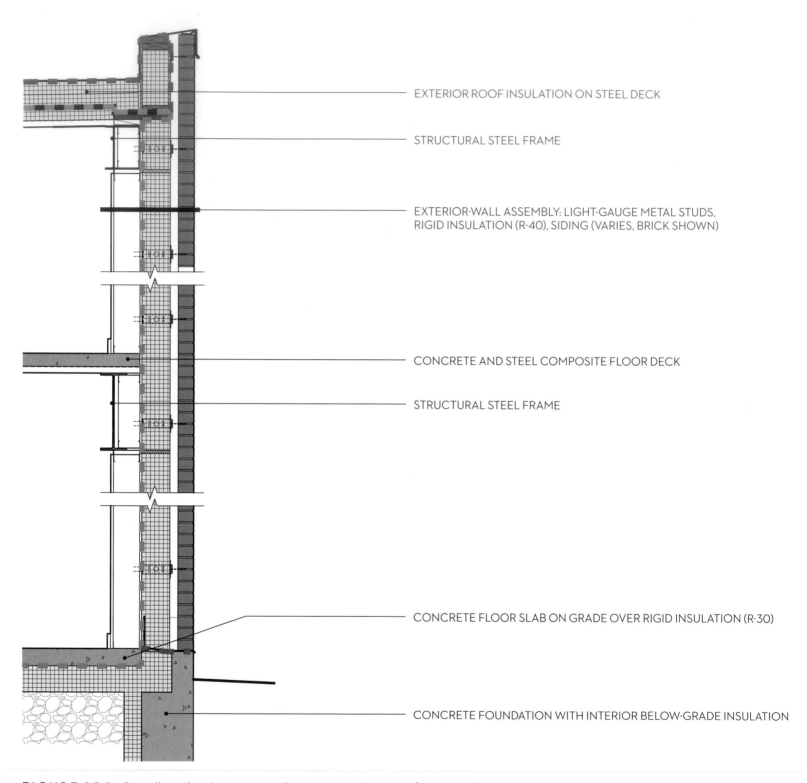

EXTERIOR ROOF INSULATION ON STEEL DECK

STRUCTURAL STEEL FRAME

EXTERIOR-WALL ASSEMBLY: LIGHT-GAUGE METAL STUDS, RIGID INSULATION (R-40), SIDING (VARIES, BRICK SHOWN)

CONCRETE AND STEEL COMPOSITE FLOOR DECK

STRUCTURAL STEEL FRAME

CONCRETE FLOOR SLAB ON GRADE OVER RIGID INSULATION (R-30)

CONCRETE FOUNDATION WITH INTERIOR BELOW-GRADE INSULATION

FIGURE 10.1. Overall steel and concrete wall section: a wall section for a typical steel and concrete building, with a structural steel frame, concrete floor slabs, steel roof deck, and light-gauge steel stud walls.

be carefully investigated to minimize heat loss through the envelope and are depicted in later detail drawings (see figures 10.16 and 10.29–10.32).

Steel and Concrete Roof and Wall Assemblies

In commercial/institutional construction it is relatively easy to create an ideal wall assembly. In this construction type, our ideal wall from the inside to the outside has interior finish, steel structure without insulation, and an exterior sheathing layer that functions as a surface to support the layers for controlling water, air, vapor, and energy movement. Outside the water, air, and vapor layers is the thermal layer. Beyond this is an airspace for water drainage behind the insulation layer. Outside the drainage space is the exterior finish layer that protects the inner layers from damage and serves as a rain screen, which deflects the bulk of the moisture striking the wall. Because the vapor-, water-, and air-control layers all are located inside the insulation and the insulation can withstand water, this wall system will provide optimum performance in warm and cold climates with or without heating and air conditioning.

The insulation can be mineral wool, extruded polystyrene foam, or polyisocyanurate foam board insulation. Spray urethane foam insulation is often used instead of board insulation, but spray urethane foams vary greatly in their global warming potential and must be chosen carefully (see chapter 6). A single membrane, either fluid-applied or as a peel-and-stick sheet, creates the water-, vapor-, and air-control layers.

Fluid-applied membranes can conform to irregular surfaces and bridge over small gaps. However, you may need to do multiple applications to cover window and door details. Typical problems with these membranes include application thickness, quality control, and sequencing, as the multiple applications require a series of visits from the installer. The gaps between sheathing may also need preparation, and other conditions can cause complications. Peel-and-stick applications have greater difficulty accommodating multiple bends at window and door openings, so installers sometimes have to rely on caulks. Peel-and-stick sheets may also fail to adhere at joints and may require priming before installation over many materials. They must also be lapped in the proper sequence on walls and sloped roofs to shed water. Small holes, in either application, are difficult to find and can cause water- and/or air-leakage problems. In addition, neither system can be exposed to weather for long periods of time, because they are subject to degradation from exposure to UV rays. Also, there may be compatibility issues between materials, particularly if they come from different manufacturers. Thus, careful installation, inspection, and protection are necessary with both systems. Neither is foolproof.

In designing the wall assembly, you must address several challenges to avoid thermal bridging.

INSULATION SELECTION AND INSTALLATION. To achieve a net zero-ready level of R-40 entirely on the exterior of the water- and air-control layers requires a minimum of 6.5" of polyisocyanurate or sprayed urethane insulation (R-6+), 8" of extruded polystyrene insulation (R-5), or 10" of mineral wool insulation (R-4.) If the building is internal-load-dominated, it is possible to reduce insulation thickness to provide R-30 or R-35 and still have an optimal assembly for a net zero building. Early modeling and costing can determine the optimum level. If using board insulation, you will need multiple layers of insulation to achieve the overall thicknesses.

It is critical to ensure that air can't travel through the insulation layer. With board insulation, potential air pathways exist between layers and through joints between boards within the same layer. The specifications must require that joints be staggered between boards from one layer to the next and that the joints between boards be filled with spray foam and/or caulk (for joints ⅛" wide or less). Penetrations such as exterior finish anchors and flashing need to be sealed as well. If using sprayed urethane, you will need multiple spray layers. Two to three inches of urethane is generally the maximum thickness that can be sprayed in a single application without shrinkage or other application problems (depending on the formulation). Careful daily inspection during construction is crucial to ensure proper performance.

EXTERIOR FINISH ANCHORS. Many exterior finishes require anchors to support the finish out from the wall and provide an airspace and plane of drainage behind the finish. In masonry veneer walls, support is provided by bearing the masonry veneer on the foundation or other structure below, but anchors are still necessary to brace the veneer from lateral forces such as wind and earthquakes. The thicknesses of insulation required means that for the exterior finish you must use anchors long enough to extend through the foam and leave an appropriate airspace behind the exterior finish material. For metal panel and other materials, this space can be ¼" or more. However, for masonry 2" is preferred, and 1" is the minimum to prevent blocking of the airspace by excess mortar that can ooze and drip from the backside of the brick or stone during construction. If spray foam is used, more space is required because the minimum distances must be maintained from the uneven exterior surface of the insulation. Another consideration for anchors is the penetration of the air- and water-control layers. After anchor installation, these penetrations need to be sealed, or the whole base of the anchor sealed, with a fluid-applied membrane or sealant.

TYPICAL WALL ABOVE GRADE, MASONRY EXTERIOR FINISH. Masonry veneer is a common exterior finish for commercial and institutional building construction. Masonry materials are durable and provide lasting protection for the insulation and water- and air-control layers. The masonry anchors that provide an airspace and laterally brace the veneer must also allow for differential vertical movement between the structure and the masonry (figures 10.2a and 10.2b). The steel structure supporting the anchors deflects under changing load conditions, and masonry, particularly brick, expands and contracts depending on temperature and moisture. One of the most common anchors of this type uses two pieces: a wire tie that is embedded in a brick mortar joint and an anchor that is fastened to the wall studs. The wire tie is hooked through a vertically slotted hole in the face of the anchor before being bedded in the mortar joint, which allows the tie to move up and down with the masonry (or the anchor to move up and down with the wall), but not in and out of the plane of the wall assembly.

Anchors must be screw-fastened to a wall stud, which means they create small thermal bridges through the insulation layer. For this reason, use the maximum anchor spacing possible. Engineering is usually required to determine the maximum spacing for anticipated lateral loads. When determining exterior stud spacing, remember that anchors are fastened directly to wall studs. If available, use anchors that have been drilled or punched to reduce their cross-sectional area to reduce thermal bridging, as shown in figure 10.3. Some anchors can also be used to retain board insulation in place, by using plastic plates or wedges that are attached to the anchors.

A relieving angle is typically used to support most tall brick veneer walls, often at every floor level. However, the relieving angle is a continuous steel angle that is connected to the structure, causing a continuous thermal bridge through the insulation layers. In addition to heat loss, these thermal bridges often cause condensation and associated mold and can create cold spots in occupied spaces. Therefore, we strongly recommend eliminating relieving angles in walls less than 30' high and minimizing them in taller walls. When used, a relieving angle is detailed with a sealant joint that flexes with the expansion and contraction of the brick. The expansion and contraction of the brick veneer relative to the steel and/or concrete structure must be calculated in order to size this expansion joint properly.

Details at windows, doors, parapets, and other features also need to be resolved to allow for differential movement. This movement needs to be calculated and taken into account early in a building's design, and it does require additional care in detailing. However, the thermal improvement that results is worth the added effort.

TYPICAL WALL ABOVE GRADE, NON-MASONRY EXTERIOR FINISH. Non-masonry veneer options such as metal, stone, or resin panels must be evaluated for performance. The type of joints between panels is an important consideration. Joints that overlap or interlock to prevent water intrusion with little or no reliance on sealants are preferable. All joints should allow for expansion and contraction between panels.

Care must be taken in the design of panel attachment to minimize thermal bridging, comply with manufacturer requirements, and adequately support the panels through the thickness of the insulation. Some panels have clips that fasten to wall anchors or metal furring channels; some are fastened over a double layer of metal furring channels running in opposite directions. As shown in figure 10.4a, the furring channels are best attached to the wall studs with intermittent

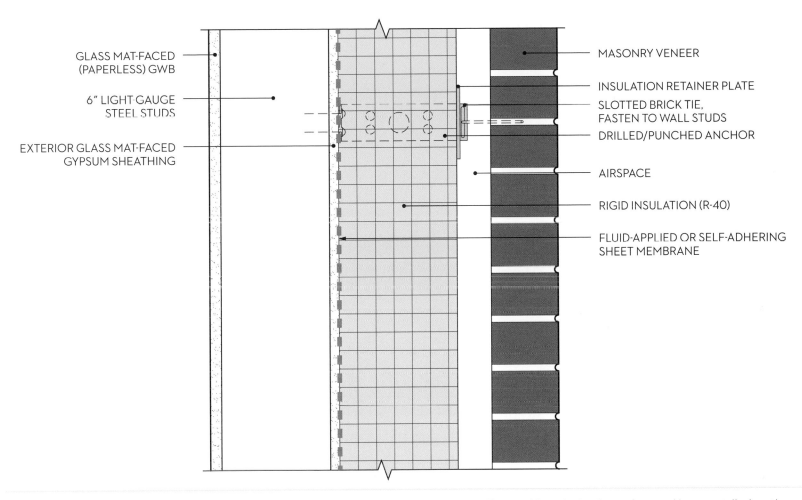

GLASS MAT-FACED (PAPERLESS) GWB

6" LIGHT-GAUGE STEEL STUDS

EXTERIOR GLASS MAT-FACED GYPSUM SHEATHING

MASONRY VENEER

INSULATION RETAINER PLATE

SLOTTED BRICK TIE, FASTEN TO WALL STUDS

DRILLED/PUNCHED ANCHOR

AIRSPACE

RIGID INSULATION (R-40)

FLUID-APPLIED OR SELF-ADHERING SHEET MEMBRANE

FIGURE 10.2A. Above-grade wall with masonry veneer finish: a typical steel-stud wall assembly with the thermal-control layer installed on the outside of the sheathing, over the air-, water-, and vapor-control layer. Masonry anchors tie the brick veneer to the wall studs for lateral support.

FIGURE 10.2B. A masonry veneer wall assembly with the masonry anchors installed as well as a fluid-applied air-, water-, and vapor-control layer to seal all penetrations.

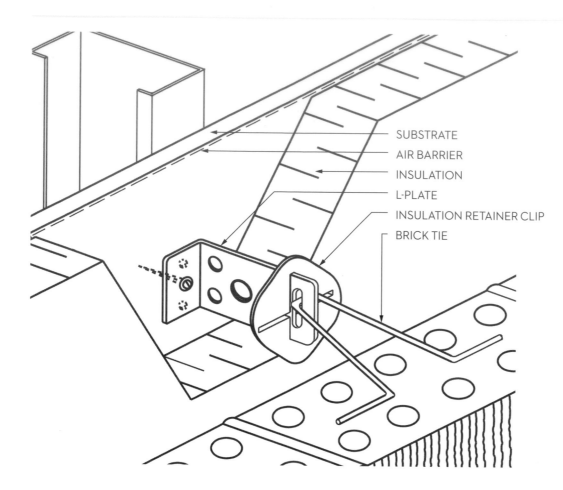

SUBSTRATE
AIR BARRIER
INSULATION
L-PLATE
INSULATION RETAINER CLIP
BRICK TIE

FIGURE 10.3. A masonry anchor is installed to tie the brick veneer to the wall studs and to hold the insulation boards in place at the same time. The holes in the anchor where it passes through the insulation reduce its cross-sectional area and therefore minimize thermal bridging.

Z-shaped anchors on the inside of the insulation layer. You can also fasten hat channels directly to the studs with long screws through the insulation thickness. Some panel manufacturers advocate using continuous metal Z-shaped purlins to anchor the system to the wall, but this creates continuous thermal bridges through the insulation. The anchorage concept and design require engineering analysis to determine gauge or thickness of supports, their spacing, and fasteners. When you fasten anchors directly through the insulation, the compressive resistance of the insulation becomes a factor in the equation.

ROOF ASSEMBLY WITH WATER-CONTROL LAYER ON TOP OF INSULATION.

Figure 10.5a shows a roof assembly with the water-control layer on top of insulation in a conventional application. This assembly allows for conventional fastening of the insulation layer into metal decking or the fastening of the lower layer and

the adhering of the upper layers and roof membrane to that. Polyisocyanurate is typically used for the board insulation on roofs because of its high R-value. A minimum thickness of 9″ will provide the desired R-60 insulation value. Joints between boards should be offset between successive layers of insulation to minimize air movement through the insulation. All joints should be inspected and caulked or foamed. This assembly also has a cementitious board installed on top of the insulation to protect the insulation from damage due to foot traffic. The roof membrane, which serves as the water-control layer, can be adhered to the protection board.

The air/vapor-control layer is sandwiched between insulation layers, so that it is protected. Placing the air/vapor-control layer in the lower portion of the insulation, below where the dewpoint is likely to occur, reduces the risk of condensation. It is important that the air-control layer be fully supported as well.

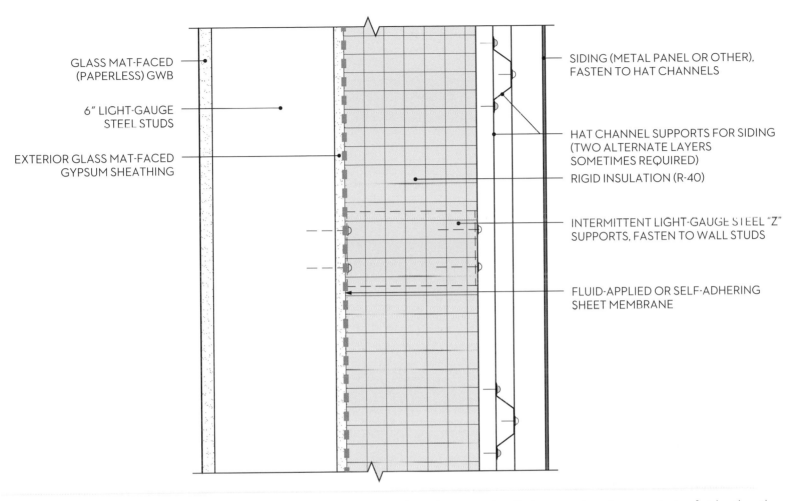

GLASS MAT-FACED (PAPERLESS) GWB

6" LIGHT-GAUGE STEEL STUDS

EXTERIOR GLASS MAT-FACED GYPSUM SHEATHING

SIDING (METAL PANEL OR OTHER), FASTEN TO HAT CHANNELS

HAT CHANNEL SUPPORTS FOR SIDING (TWO ALTERNATE LAYERS SOMETIMES REQUIRED)

RIGID INSULATION (R-40)

INTERMITTENT LIGHT-GAUGE STEEL "Z" SUPPORTS, FASTEN TO WALL STUDS

FLUID-APPLIED OR SELF-ADHERING SHEET MEMBRANE

FIGURE 10.4A. Above-grade wall, non-masonry siding: a section through a typical wall above grade using an exterior finish other than masonry. The siding panels are attached to hat-profile furring channels, which in turn are fastened to intermittent Z supports. The Z anchors span the insulation layer and are attached directly to the wall studs.

FIGURE 10.4B. A grid of metal hat channels is installed over the insulation layer (between the brick piers) to support metal siding panels.

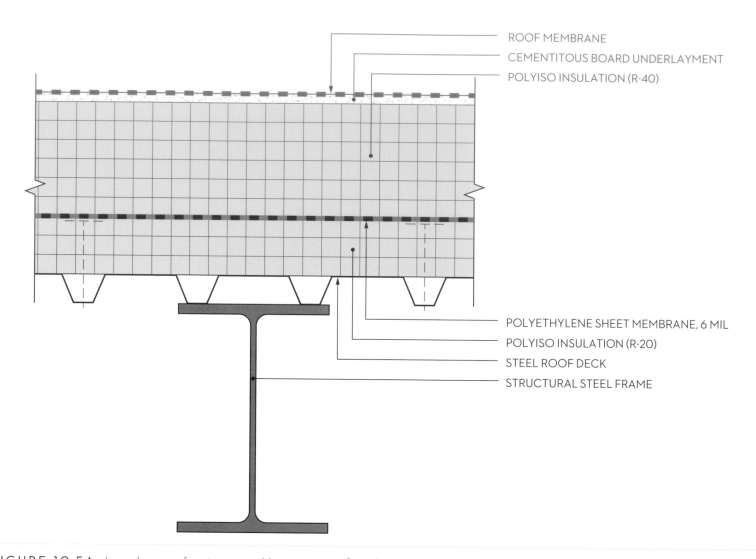

ROOF MEMBRANE

CEMENTITOUS BOARD UNDERLAYMENT

POLYISO INSULATION (R-40)

POLYETHYLENE SHEET MEMBRANE, 6 MIL

POLYISO INSULATION (R-20)

STEEL ROOF DECK

STRUCTURAL STEEL FRAME

FIGURE 10.5A. Low-slope roof, water-control layer on top of insulation: a typical steel-framed, low-slope roof section, with a steel deck supporting the insulation and protection boards and the roof membrane installed on top.

FIGURE 10.5B. A typical low-slope roof under construction, showing the different control layers. The insulation board joints are staggered between layers. (Protection board was not used on top of the insulation in this assembly.)

It should not be located directly on top of the metal decking, because it may be moved by differential air pressure. This can cause taped joints to fail and allow air movement. One risk with this approach is that moist air can get trapped between the air/vapor-control layer and water-control layer with no means of escape. If the air/vapor-control layer is a variable-permeability membrane that changes its permeability with the ambient humidity condition, then air can be stopped and water vapor can escape if it gets to a high level.

If the water-control layer is on top of the insulation, it is exposed to the deleterious effects of the sun and foot traffic on the roof. However, it has the advantage that problems with the membrane are easily detected and repaired.

INVERTED ROOF. With the roof deck, we can make the same perfect building enclosure assembly by taking our wall and turning it 90°, as indicated in figure 10.6a. This allows the water, air, vapor, and thermal layers to be together and under the thermal insulation. A drainage-mat layer is installed directly over the control layers to allow water to travel freely to drains in the roof assembly. While this is inverted from typical roofing installations, it provides the benefit of protecting the roof membrane from sun and people walking on it. This has a significant drawback, however, because leaks in the membrane are difficult to trace and repair. It also means that it is not possible to fasten the insulation, as fastening would put holes in the control layer. Instead, stone ballast is placed on top of the insulation to hold it on the roof. A variation of this system is commonly used, for instance, with green roof system designs.

Common Steel and Concrete Intersections

In this section we address the connections between the wall, roof, floor, and below-grade assemblies. We begin at the base and go up and around the building to cover these conditions.

ABOVE-GRADE-WALL-SLAB-ON-GRADE INTERSECTION. Figure 10.7a shows a typical wall with a combined water-, air-, and vapor-control layer (either a fluid-applied or a peel-and-stick membrane).

Where the water-control layer meets the base of the wall, it is necessary to deflect any water that gets into the wall cavity to the exterior of the wall assembly with through-wall flashings. Metal flashings are the traditional way of doing this, but these expand and contract, making them likely to leak at lapped joints. For this reason, membrane flashing is preferred on top of metal flashings. For masonry veneers, weep holes or corrugated weeps at brick head joints are installed at the bottom of the wall cavity, just above the through-wall flashing, to allow water to drain out through the masonry veneer. Use a mortar mesh at the base of the cavity to prevent mortar droppings during construction from blocking the drainage. While figure 10.7a shows a brick wall, other forms of masonry, panels, or wood siding can be used, requiring the same drainage and protections of the water-, air-, and vapor-control layers. Insect screening should be added at the bottom of the panels or siding to prevent insect intrusion through the gap left for drainage at the bottom of the wall.

Where the above-grade wall assembly meets the slab and frost wall, the continuity of the control layers is crucial. The thermal break at the perimeter of the floor slab aligns with the plane of the exterior wall insulation for continuity of the thermal-control layer. A step in the top of the foundation wall makes this possible. For continuity, the underslab water, air, and vapor membrane must connect with the wall's water, air, and vapor membrane system. This is accomplished by folding the underslab membrane up the edge of the slab and lapping it approximately 6" onto the wall surface. It is lapped behind the wall membrane and through-wall flashing, maintaining positive drainage. Where thinner siding materials are used and the exterior wall is closer to the outside of the foundation, it may be necessary to extend the underslab membrane over the top of the foundation wall. This serves as a capillary break to stop all moisture from wicking up through the footing and foundation wall.

A special intersection condition may exist where concrete piers are required at the exterior foundation, for support of the exterior steel structure. When these piers are engaged with, or integral with, the exterior concrete foundation, and the foundation is insulated on the interior side, these piers interrupt the plane of the insulation and therefore represent a significant thermal bridge to the outside. One way to resolve this is to wrap the interior faces of the piers with the same amount of rigid insulation as the walls. This isolates the top of the pier thermally from the

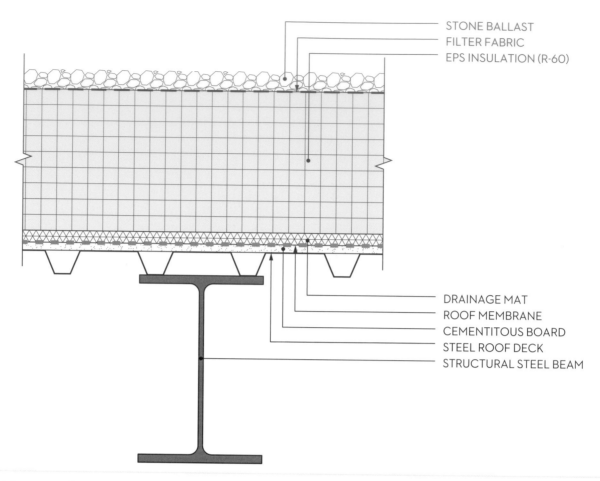

STONE BALLAST
FILTER FABRIC
EPS INSULATION (R-60)

DRAINAGE MAT
ROOF MEMBRANE
CEMENTITOUS BOARD
STEEL ROOF DECK
STRUCTURAL STEEL BEAM

FIGURE 10.6A. Inverted roof: a section through a typical inverted roof assembly, with the combined water-, vapor-, and air-control layer installed below the insulation and ballast.

FIGURE 10.6B. An inverted roof under construction. This is a green roof, with planting medium installed to the right in the photo and a stone drainage channel around the roof perimeter.

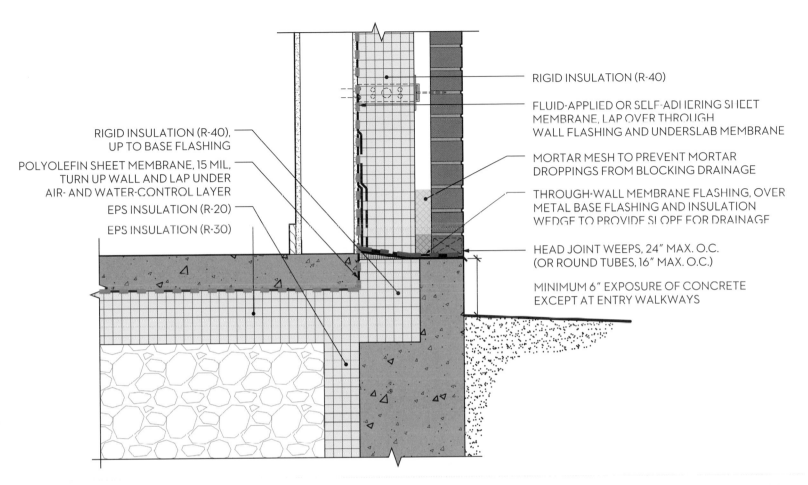

RIGID INSULATION (R-40)

FLUID-APPLIED OR SELF-ADHERING SHEET MEMBRANE, LAP OVER THROUGH WALL FLASHING AND UNDERSLAB MEMBRANE

MORTAR MESH TO PREVENT MORTAR DROPPINGS FROM BLOCKING DRAINAGE

THROUGH-WALL MEMBRANE FLASHING, OVER METAL BASE FLASHING AND INSULATION WEDGE TO PROVIDE SLOPE FOR DRAINAGE

HEAD JOINT WEEPS, 24" MAX. O.C. (OR ROUND TUBES, 16" MAX. O.C.)

MINIMUM 6" EXPOSURE OF CONCRETE EXCEPT AT ENTRY WALKWAYS

RIGID INSULATION (R-40), UP TO BASE FLASHING

POLYOLEFIN SHEET MEMBRANE, 15 MIL, TURN UP WALL AND LAP UNDER AIR- AND WATER-CONTROL LAYER

EPS INSULATION (R-20)

EPS INSULATION (R-30)

FIGURE 10.7A. Above-grade-wall–slab-on-grade intersection: a detail section for a typical masonry veneer wall where it intersects a slab-on-grade, showing through-wall flashing and weeps to direct water out of the bottom of the wall cavity. Note also the insulation used to provide a thermal break between the slab edge and the top of the interior-insulated foundation wall.

FIGURE 10.7B. The edge of concrete slab is aligned with the outside face of sheathing so as to align the insulation that provides the slab edge thermal break with the above-grade wall insulation. Through-wall base flashing has not yet been installed.

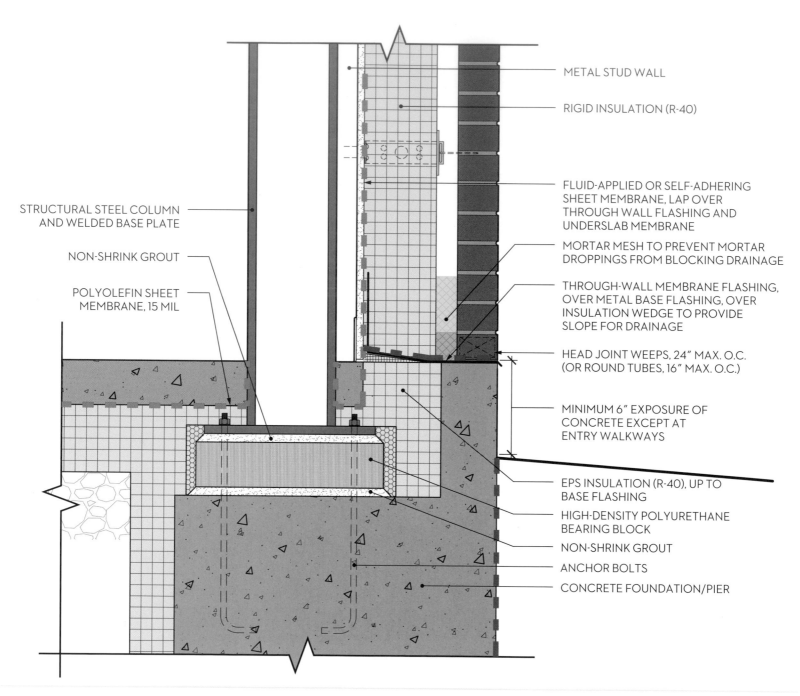

METAL STUD WALL

RIGID INSULATION (R-40)

FLUID-APPLIED OR SELF-ADHERING SHEET MEMBRANE, LAP OVER THROUGH WALL FLASHING AND UNDERSLAB MEMBRANE

MORTAR MESH TO PREVENT MORTAR DROPPINGS FROM BLOCKING DRAINAGE

THROUGH-WALL MEMBRANE FLASHING, OVER METAL BASE FLASHING, OVER INSULATION WEDGE TO PROVIDE SLOPE FOR DRAINAGE

HEAD JOINT WEEPS, 24" MAX. O.C. (OR ROUND TUBES, 16" MAX. O.C.)

MINIMUM 6" EXPOSURE OF CONCRETE EXCEPT AT ENTRY WALKWAYS

EPS INSULATION (R-40), UP TO BASE FLASHING

HIGH-DENSITY POLYURETHANE BEARING BLOCK

NON-SHRINK GROUT

ANCHOR BOLTS

CONCRETE FOUNDATION/PIER

STRUCTURAL STEEL COLUMN AND WELDED BASE PLATE

NON-SHRINK GROUT

POLYOLEFIN SHEET MEMBRANE, 15 MIL

FIGURE 10.8. Steel column and pier intersection, with thermal break below column base: a high-density polyurethane block provides a thermal break between the column base and the concrete pier, which is integral with the interior-insulated foundation wall.

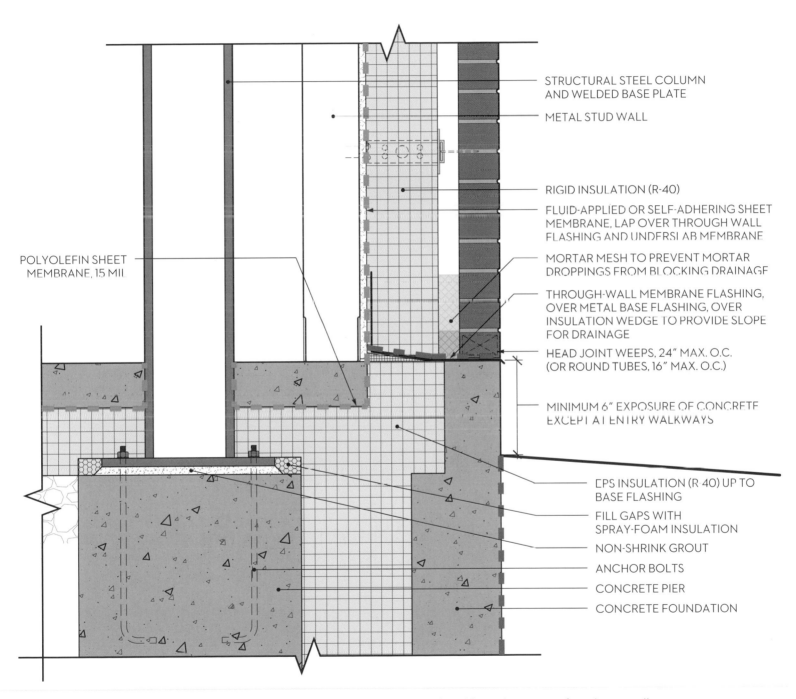

STRUCTURAL STEEL COLUMN
AND WELDED BASE PLATE

METAL STUD WALL

RIGID INSULATION (R-40)

FLUID-APPLIED OR SELF-ADHERING SHEET
MEMBRANE, LAP OVER THROUGH WALL
FLASHING AND UNDERSLAB MEMBRANE

MORTAR MESH TO PREVENT MORTAR
DROPPINGS FROM BLOCKING DRAINAGE

THROUGH-WALL MEMBRANE FLASHING,
OVER METAL BASE FLASHING, OVER
INSULATION WEDGE TO PROVIDE SLOPE
FOR DRAINAGE

HEAD JOINT WEEPS, 24" MAX. O.C.
(OR ROUND TUBES, 16" MAX. O.C.)

MINIMUM 6" EXPOSURE OF CONCRETE
EXCEPT AT ENTRY WALKWAYS

POLYOLEFIN SHEET
MEMBRANE, 15 MIL

EPS INSULATION (R-40) UP TO
BASE FLASHING

FILL GAPS WITH
SPRAY-FOAM INSULATION

NON-SHRINK GROUT

ANCHOR BOLTS

CONCRETE PIER

CONCRETE FOUNDATION

FIGURE 10.9. A pier-wall detail, with the pier structurally and thermally isolated from the exterior foundation wall.

concrete slab and provides a thermally broken base support for the column, reducing thermal conductance from the top of the concrete pier to the steel column. This is illustrated in figure 10.8.

However, the thermal break at the base of the column does not provide the same R-value as the wall, and this detail, while an improvement over no thermal break, represents a compromise to the thermal integrity of the wall. A preferred solution would be to isolate the pier from the exterior foundation wall with the same amount of insulation that the rest of the wall receives, thereby providing a continuous thermal-isolation plane around the foundation (see figure 10.9).

FIRST-FLOOR-BASEMENT-WALL INTERSECTION. In buildings with a basement, the condition at the first floor must respond to likely changing structural conditions as well as differing conditions above and below grade. Figure 10.10 illustrates a wall assembly with metal-panel siding. In this situation the foundation waterproofing is tied directly to the above-grade system, providing continuity of the air- and vapor-control layers. The thermal layer is continuous at this intersection. In buildings with masonry veneer, the weight of masonry must be supported, which requires careful detailing with exterior insulation to avoid thermal bridging at the foundation and floor. Flashing and drainage of the wall cavity is also required.

WALL-UPPER-FLOOR INTERSECTION. The wall at an upper-floor intersection is shown in figure 10.11a. This detail illustrates how the entire structural frame is inside the water-, air-, vapor-, and thermal-control layers to eliminate thermal bridging and to simplify detailing. In addition, figure 10.11a indicates how deflection of steel beams is accommodated in the wall design by allowing the wall studs and exterior insulation to absorb some vertical movement. If not allowed for in the design of control layers, this beam movement can jeopardize the integrity of the control layers over time. A properly designed deflection joint can address this. First, design the beams with a maximum deflection of ½" and preferably ⅜" or less. Use a beam with additional cross-sectional depth and/or additional cross-sectional area, or reduce the span of the beams in exterior walls, where you will not impact the building design. When you minimize deflection, movement at the joint is smaller and more manageable. Limiting deflection also reduces potential issues in other areas

of the building, such as at windows and other wall openings, where the wall might move in relation to the exterior masonry or other finish.

The second step in eliminating air leakage at deflection joints is specifying a truly compressible material for insulating and stopping air movement. We have found two suitable options: an excellent precompressed impregnated foam filler manufactured by Illbruck or a compressible filler fabricated at significantly reduced cost from mattress foam. It is also necessary to install the control membranes at the sheathing with a bend or fold in them, so that the wall materials can contract and separate without stretching the membrane.

ROOF-SIDE-WALL INTERSECTION. A number of factors come into play at this type of intersection. A condition similar to that at the base of the wall (see figure 10.7a) exists above the adjacent roof. Through-wall flashing and weeps are therefore required to divert and drain moisture out of the wall cavity. Continuity with the roof's water-control layer necessitates lapping the roof membrane up the wall and lapping counterflashing over the top of it, then lapping through-wall flashing over the counterflashing to prevent leaking at the joints. The counterflashing is typically metal, and the through-wall flashing is a membrane.

When the roof system employs an air- and vapor-control layer that is separate from and below the roof water-control layer, the air- and vapor-control layer must extend from the roof assembly onto the wall sheathing, where it is overlapped by the wall air-, water-, and vapor-control layers, providing continuity between the two assemblies.

Figure 10.12 illustrates this condition with brick veneer, though the issues are similar with other types of exterior finish materials. Brick and other masonry materials create an additional problem because they need to bear on adequate support below. This is often a structural steel framing member and, as noted before, the steel structure is located on the interior of the thermal and other control layers. An insulation material with the load-carrying capacity to support the veneer above must be used between the interior steel and the masonry on the exterior of the thermal envelope. One such material is Foamglas, a cellular glass product with an R-value of 3.4 per inch. Autoclaved aerated concrete is another material often used for this purpose. Neither of these materials stands

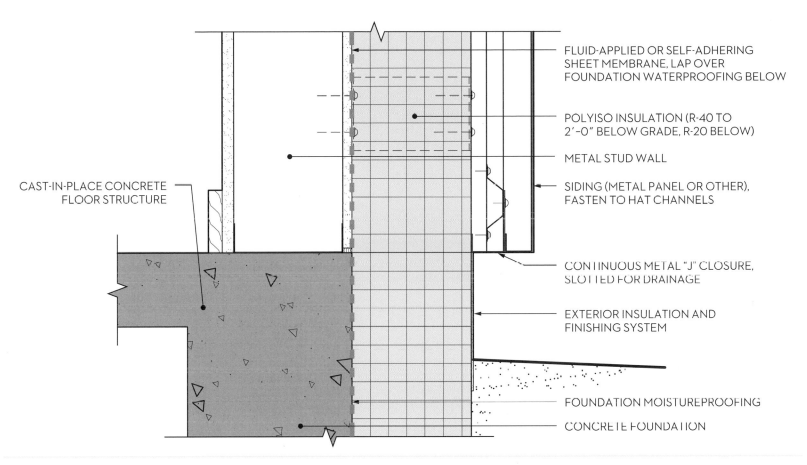

CAST-IN-PLACE CONCRETE
FLOOR STRUCTURE

FLUID-APPLIED OR SELF-ADHERING
SHEET MEMBRANE, LAP OVER
FOUNDATION WATERPROOFING BELOW

POLYISO INSULATION (R-40 TO
2'-0" BELOW GRADE, R-20 BELOW)

METAL STUD WALL

SIDING (METAL PANEL OR OTHER),
FASTEN TO HAT CHANNELS

CONTINUOUS METAL "J" CLOSURE,
SLOTTED FOR DRAINAGE

EXTERIOR INSULATION AND
FINISHING SYSTEM

FOUNDATION MOISTUREPROOFING

CONCRETE FOUNDATION

FIGURE 10.10. Intersection of the first-floor and basement walls: A basement wall that is insulated on the outside and aligned with the above-grade insulation, allowing for continuity of all the control layers from below grade to above.

up well to freeze-thaw cycles, so they must be well protected from moisture intrusion. In addition, whatever material is used, the weight of the masonry veneer above must be calculated to ensure that the compressive strength of the thermal material, which is usually less than that of masonry, is not exceeded.

WALL-ROOF INTERSECTION (PARAPET). The joint of the wall and roof, often a parapet condition in commercial construction, can be an area of significant air leakage in steel buildings. In single-story buildings with large roof spans, this is a greater problem because of structural deflection. As with wall-floor intersections, structural design to limit deflection to ½" or less below steel beams is the first critical step in reducing our infiltration. The total differential movement between the brick and steel

structure must be accommodated at the parapet. To address differential movement, you will need to calculate how much the steel and brick will move as seasonal temperatures change and as the building acclimates during construction. You'll also need to calculate differential movement caused by moisture for brick.

The cap flashing of the parapet sheds water while accommodating movement. Any scuppers at the roof must accommodate movement. Once you have addressed overall and differential movement, you will need to design the connections of the control layers of the roof and wall to be continuous. Figure 10.13a shows a brick wall/parapet assembly intersecting a roof with the water layer on top, separated from the vapor- and air-control layers, which all tie to the wall membrane. Figure 10.14a shows the same wall assembly intersecting a roof

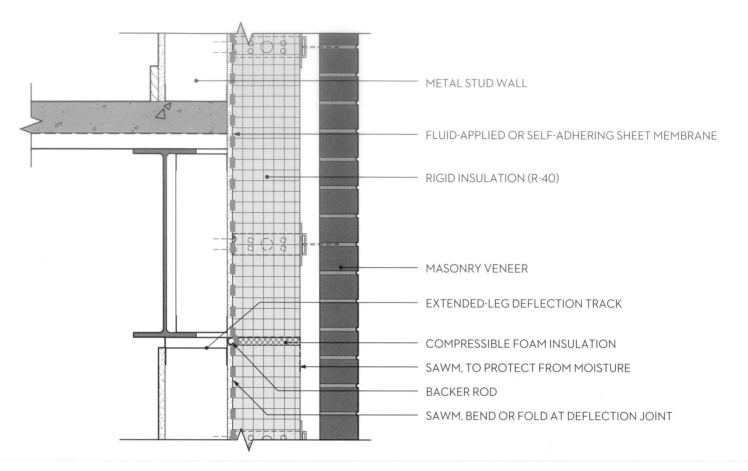

METAL STUD WALL

FLUID-APPLIED OR SELF-ADHERING SHEET MEMBRANE

RIGID INSULATION (R-40)

MASONRY VENEER

EXTENDED-LEG DEFLECTION TRACK

COMPRESSIBLE FOAM INSULATION

SAWM, TO PROTECT FROM MOISTURE

BACKER ROD

SAWM, BEND OR FOLD AT DEFLECTION JOINT

FIGURE 10.11A. Wall at an upper-floor intersection: a detail of a deflection joint located below a floor beam, showing how the stud wall has been designed to absorb beam deflection and the control layers have been designed to flex and absorb movement as well.

FIGURE 10.11B. The horizontal strips of light-colored self-adhering waterproof membrane (SAWM) cover a compressible filler material and provide a durable and flexible joint in the air- and vapor-control layer at the points of structural deflection.

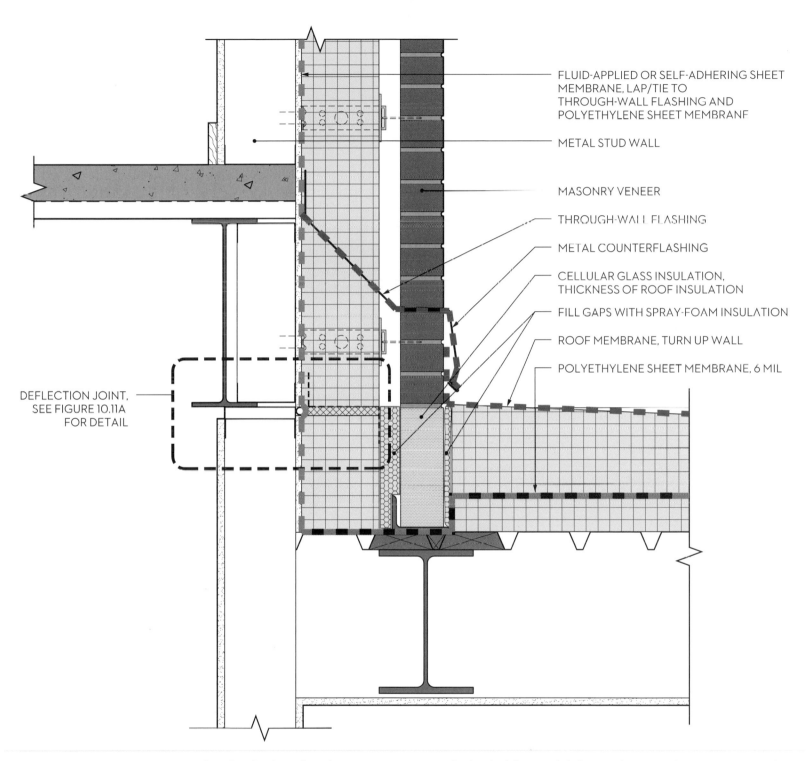

FLUID-APPLIED OR SELF-ADHERING SHEET
MEMBRANE, LAP/TIE TO
THROUGH-WALL FLASHING AND
POLYETHYLENE SHEET MEMBRANF

METAL STUD WALL

MASONRY VENEER

THROUGH-WALL FLASHING

METAL COUNTERFLASHING

CELLULAR GLASS INSULATION,
THICKNESS OF ROOF INSULATION

FILL GAPS WITH SPRAY-FOAM INSULATION

ROOF MEMBRANE, TURN UP WALL

POLYETHYLENE SHEET MEMBRANE, 6 MIL

DEFLECTION JOINT,
SEE FIGURE 10.11A
FOR DETAIL

FIGURE 10.12. Intersection of roof and side wall: in this situation you must deal with differential deflection between the two structures by providing a flexible deflection joint in the control layers. It is also necessary to provide through-wall flashing and weeps to drain water out of the base of the wall cavity above the roof.

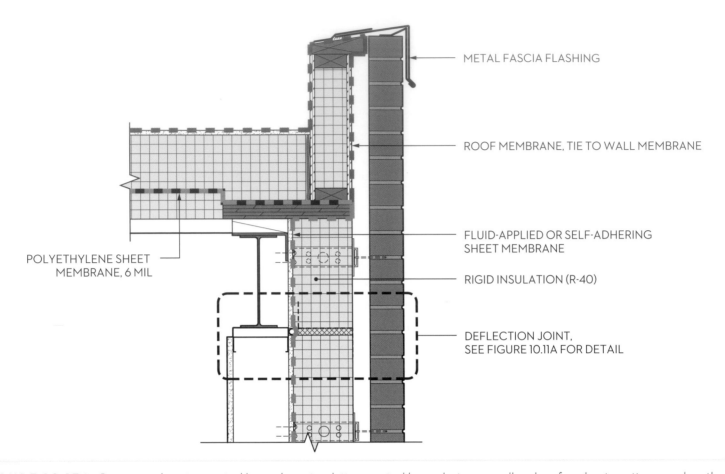

METAL FASCIA FLASHING

ROOF MEMBRANE, TIE TO WALL MEMBRANE

FLUID-APPLIED OR SELF-ADHERING
SHEET MEMBRANE

POLYETHYLENE SHEET
MEMBRANE, 6 MIL

RIGID INSULATION (R-40)

DEFLECTION JOINT,
SEE FIGURE 10.11A FOR DETAIL

FIGURE 10.13A. Parapet with water-control layer above insulation: control layers between wall and roof are kept continuous when the roof water-control layer is above the roof insulation. A flexible deflection joint addresses vertical movement of the roof structure in relation to the wall and its control layers.

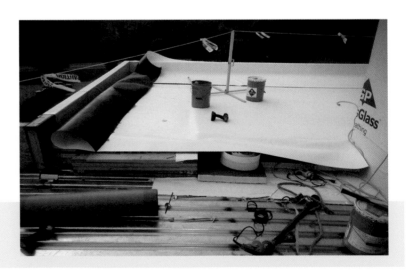

FIGURE 10.13B. The water-, air-, and vapor-control layers in both the wall and the roof are lapped over the top of the parapet wall for continuity.

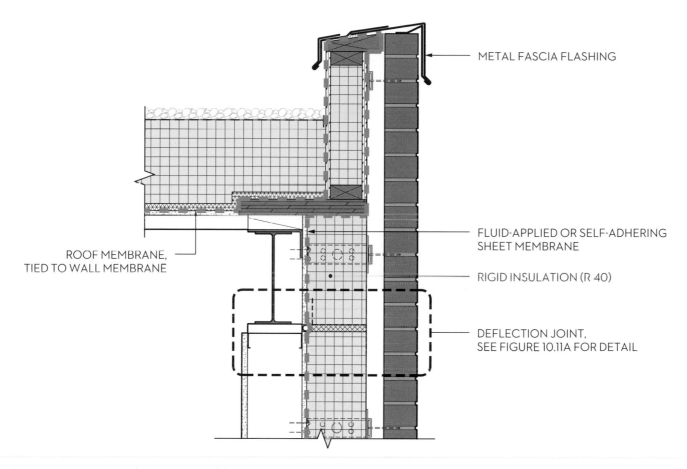

METAL FASCIA FLASHING

ROOF MEMBRANE,
TIED TO WALL MEMBRANE

FLUID-APPLIED OR SELF-ADHERING
SHEET MEMBRANE

RIGID INSULATION (R 40)

DEFLECTION JOINT,
SEE FIGURE 10.11A FOR DETAIL

FIGURE 10.14. Parapet with water-control layer below insulation (inverted roof). A parapet detail at an inverted roof. Continuity of the control layers and a flexible deflection joint must also be addressed with this type of roof as well.

with the combined water-, air-, and vapor-control layer on the bottom of the insulation (an inverted roof). In both cases all of these control layers are continuously lapped and attached.

WALL-ROOF INTERSECTION (NO PARAPET). With a roof assembly that has the water-control layer above the insulation, another common detail omits the parapet and provides a simple fascia flashing at the wall-roof intersection (see figure 10.15a). At this condition the same concerns about structural deflection apply, and additional compressible foam is added at the top of the masonry veneer for deflection at the fascia. Though figure 10.15a shows a brick wall assembly, this detail can be adapted for use with other siding materials with minor modifications.

RELIEVING ANGLE. Due to code requirements, brick veneer walls with steel-stud backing walls cannot be self-supporting if they exceed 30′ in height (38′ at gables) above the foundation. The brick veneer therefore needs to be supported off the structural frame of the building with steel support angles, commonly called relieving angles or shelf angles. It has been a typical practice to install these angles at every floor level, even where not required. As described above, these angles constitute a significant continuous thermal bridge through the insulation layer to the structure and should be used only where required by building codes.

Where relieving angles are used, it is important to minimize these thermal bridges. The continuous relieving angle should

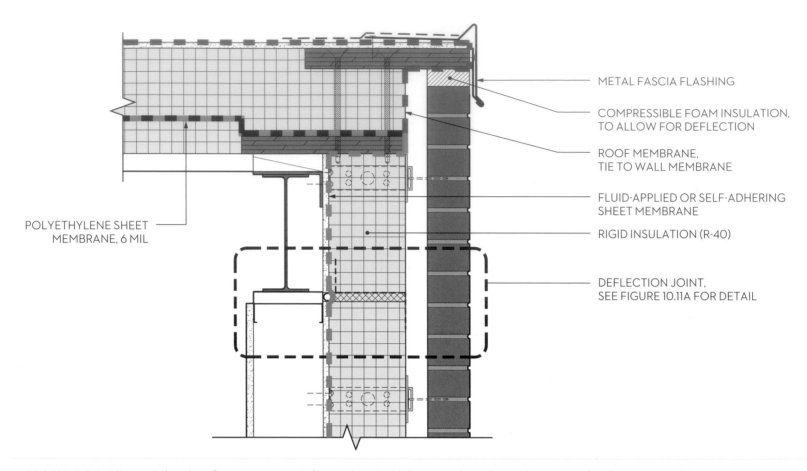

METAL FASCIA FLASHING

COMPRESSIBLE FOAM INSULATION, TO ALLOW FOR DEFLECTION

ROOF MEMBRANE, TIE TO WALL MEMBRANE

FLUID-APPLIED OR SELF-ADHERING SHEET MEMBRANE

RIGID INSULATION (R-40)

DEFLECTION JOINT, SEE FIGURE 10.11A FOR DETAIL

POLYETHYLENE SHEET MEMBRANE, 6 MIL

FIGURE 10.15A. Wall and roof intersection with fascia: this detail illustrates how the roof water- and air/vapor-control layers are wrapped around the perimeter blocking in order to connect with the wall air/water/vapor-control membrane. Note also the accommodation for deflection made both at the roof beam and between the top of the brick veneer and the wood blocking above.

FIGURE 10.15B. The connection is made between the roof vapor- and air-barrier layer to the wall control layer before the installation is installed. The roof water-control layer will then be installed over the insulation and also lapped over the wall to connect with the wall control layer.

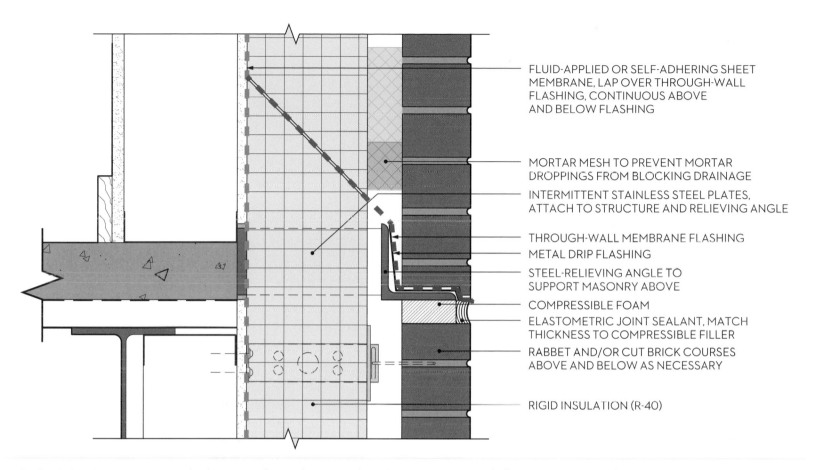

FLUID-APPLIED OR SELF-ADHERING SHEET MEMBRANE, LAP OVER THROUGH-WALL FLASHING, CONTINUOUS ABOVE AND BELOW FLASHING

MORTAR MESH TO PREVENT MORTAR DROPPINGS FROM BLOCKING DRAINAGE

INTERMITTENT STAINLESS STEEL PLATES, ATTACH TO STRUCTURE AND RELIEVING ANGLE

THROUGH-WALL MEMBRANE FLASHING

METAL DRIP FLASHING

STEEL-RELIEVING ANGLE TO SUPPORT MASONRY ABOVE

COMPRESSIBLE FOAM

ELASTOMETRIC JOINT SEALANT, MATCH THICKNESS TO COMPRESSIBLE FILLER

RABBET AND/OR CUT BRICK COURSES ABOVE AND BELOW AS NECESSARY

RIGID INSULATION (R-40)

FIGURE 10.16A. Improved relieving angle: a relieving angle with intermittent standoff supports that significantly reduce thermal bridging compared to a continuous angle connection.

FIGURE 10.16B. These brick relieving angles (near the bottom of the black sections of wall) are supported intermittently from the structure to reduce thermal bridging.

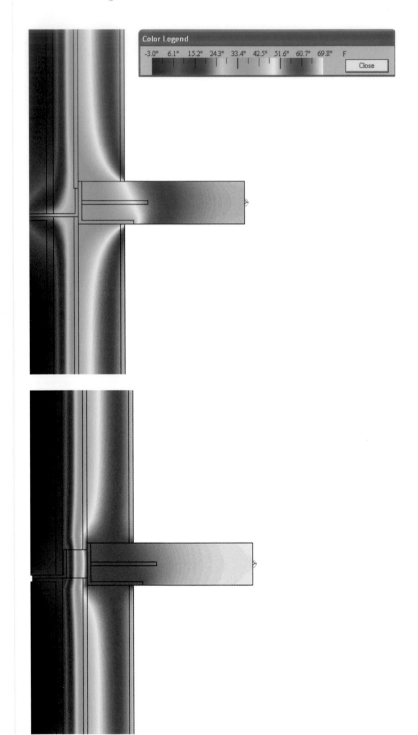

FIGURE 10.17. Poor thermal performance with a continuous steel relieving angle (*top*) versus improved performance with an intermittent angle (*bottom*).

be located outside of the insulation layer, and connections through to the structure should be at intervals of 3′ or more, if possible. Stainless steel, which has roughly one-third the conductivity of normal carbon steel, can be used for these intermittent connections to further reduce the heat loss. Figure 10.16a shows a relieving angle detail with intermittent connections to the structure using vertical stainless-steel plates, an improved condition. There are also premanufactured steel brackets, such as the FAST system by the Fero Corporation, that can be bolted to the structure and have slotted holes to allow for field adjustment to accurately set the height of the angle. The temperature gradient diagrams (figure 10.17) illustrate the relative conductivity and resulting heat loss of both an unmitigated relieving angle detail and an alternate improved detail.

Window, Door, and Skylight Openings

Careful detailing at building openings is critical in maintaining the continuity of the control layers. Breaks, gaps, and holes at these tricky intersections can threaten the integrity of the net zero building envelope through water or vapor intrusion or air infiltration. For successful installation of windows and doors and flashing, be sure you have the involvement of control-layer manufacturers' representatives, make clear construction drawings, train installers, include requirements in the specifications for trial mock-ups in the field, and of course make careful observation during construction. Because this installation method is not typical, it is important to provide clear direction. Figure 10.18 is a drawing we include in our construction documents to show the steps for window installation so that it is easier for the builder.

The quality of the window or door component used in the opening is also an important consideration. Unit selection should take into account thermally broken frames, high-performance glazing, and air- and water-infiltration rates. Using the best-performing windows that the project budget will allow is essential for achieving net zero performance.

WINDOWSILLS. Figure 10.19a shows the sill condition of a window, in this case a triple-glazed window with foam-filled

EXTERIOR SHEATHING

BRICK TIES INSTALLED

2× WINDOW BUCK, LVL AT BOTTOM

LVL PROJECTS 1" PAST JAMB HEAD OF WINDOW BUCK

① STEP 1

FLEX WRAP NF AROUND WINDOW SILL

② STEP 2

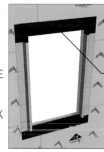

SELF-ADHESIVE WATERPROOF MEMBRANE, LAP OVER FLEX WRAP NF AT SILL

③ STEP 3

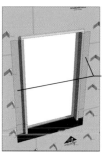

FLEX WRAP NF, LAP OVER SELF-ADHESIVE WATERPROOF MEMBRANE AT JAMBS

④ STEP 4

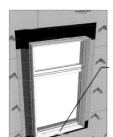

INSTALL WINDOW, USE LOW-EXPANDING FOAM AND SEALANT FROM INSIDE AROUND ENTIRE WINDOW FRAME TO SEAL WINDOW TO MEMBRANES ACCORDING TO WINDOW DETAILS

⑤ STEP 5

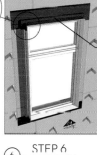

SECOND LAYER OF FLEX WRAP NF, ADHERE TO TOP OF WINDOW BRICKMOLD AND CONTINUE OVER EDGE AND DOWN JAMBS

⑥ STEP 6

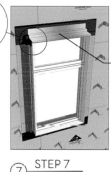

METAL FLASHING, FLASH FROM EXTERIOR SHEATHING OUT OVER TOP OF BRICKMOLD

⑦ STEP 7

MONOLITHIC SPRAY APPLIED AIR AND VAPOR BARRIER OVER SHEATHING, ALL MEMBRANES THAT ARE ADHERED TO SHEATHING, AND METAL FLASHING

⑧ STEP 8

TWO LAYERS OF ⅞" HAT CHANNEL WHERE METAL PANEL WILL BE INSTALLED

INSULATION CLIPS BY BRICK TIE MANUFACTURER

RIGID INSULATION (SHOWN HERE FOR GRAPHIC CLARITY, OWENS CORNING FORMULAR 150 NOT ACCEPTABLE IN EXTERIOR WALLS ABOVE GRADE)

⑨ STEP 9

½" BACKER ROD AND SEALANT (100% EXTENSIBILITY) AROUND SIDE AND SILL OF WINDOW AND UP JAMBS OF METAL PANEL

METAL PANEL RAINSCREEN

BRICK VENEER

⑩ STEP 10

fiberglass frame. Because the thermal-control layer is located on the outside of the wall studs, the window is aligned with the thermal-control layer, outside the plane of the wall studs. This minimizes the thermal bridging found in a typical installation, where the window is installed in the plane of the wall. The insulation layer is not capable of supporting the weight of the window, so alternate means of support must be provided; typically, a wood buck is cantilevered out from the stud wall at the base of the window. With larger windows this buck may need to be made of engineered lumber to support the heavier load. A structural engineer should design the buck for larger windows and the fastening of the buck to the stud wall.

Proper flashing of the window opening with flexible membrane materials is critical to prevent water intrusion. This flashing must cover the sill, lap over the water-control layer on the face of the wall, and turn upward 6″ at the window jambs to provide protection at the corners. We recommend using DuPont FlexWrap NF because of its ability to bend and provide continuous membrane protection at the corners. The interior-most edge of the FlexWrap is turned up behind the window, forming a dam to stop any water that may have gotten through. The gap between the bottom of the window and the sill is not typically sealed at the exterior, to allow any moisture to drain off the sill. Other options include tape products, which need to be cut and caulked at corners, and preformed sill liners, which require gluing or joining different sections to fit the rough opening size. Both of these options can lead to failure at the joints.

The window becomes a component of the envelope's air-control layer and must be sealed to that layer (or combination air/water-control layer). The air-control layer should extend onto the faces of the rough opening adjacent to the window frame. Flexible sealant, with backer rod, that is compatible with the control layer material should be used to seal the control layer to the frame. Blower-door testing must be performed to verify the building meets airtightness requirements before interior finishes are applied that will conceal this sealant joint. This allows any necessary remedial work to be done while the joints are accessible. Low-expanding foam insulation may be used to fill the space between the window and the frame for thermal continuity, but it cannot be considered a substitute for the flexible sealant as part of the air-control layer, because it is not flexible and can lose its bond to the adjacent surfaces when they move with expansion and contraction.

There should be a gap between the window panning and the brick or other exterior finish material to allow for construction tolerances and anticipated differential movement between materials. This gap should be sealed to minimize water intrusion into the airspace/drainage plane behind the finish material.

The sealant must have adequate flexibility and ability to bond to the materials involved, and a backer rod should be used to ensure the proper depth and shape of the sealant bead.

WINDOW JAMBS. Most of the same concerns at the sill apply to the jambs as well, though there are a couple of differences (see figure 10.20a).

The jambs of the rough opening have to support only lateral loads such as wind, not the gravity load of the window. Therefore, it is preferable to omit the wooden buck used at the jamb and replace it with a thinner, rigid material such as a plastic or fiberglass angle. This allows the wall insulation to extend closer to the window frame for better thermal performance.

Also different from the sill detail, the water-control membrane typically laps onto the plastic angle and the window frame, or panning, sealing the gap at the window frame from moisture intrusion. The installation of low-expanding foam insulation in the gap must therefore take place before this step. Installation of the sill flashing must also precede the jamb flashing, so the jamb flashing can lap over and cover the top edge of the upturned sill flashing.

Air sealing occurs on the interior side of the window frame, as with the sill, and before installation of interior finishes. The air-control layer must therefore extend into the window rough opening before the window is installed. Using a combined air/water-control layer results in a double layer—one before window installation to seal the air-control layer and one after, for the water-control layer. Care must be taken to ensure continuity of the sealant around obstructions such as shims and metal anchor clips, which are common with commercial windows.

WINDOW HEADS. The window head is detailed similarly to the jamb (see figure 10.21a). For the water-control layer, however, we recommend using FlexWrap NF, as at the sill, because of its ability to flex around the outer corners of the window frame or panning. The FlexWrap NF must lap over the top of the jamb water flashing, and it must be covered by metal flashing or the air/water-control layer for proper drainage. Where metal head flashing is used, it, too, must be overlapped by the air/water-control layer.

In some cases it may be possible to use a solid masonry or stone lintel to span across a window head. It is more common, however, as in figure 10.21a, to provide a galvanized steel loose

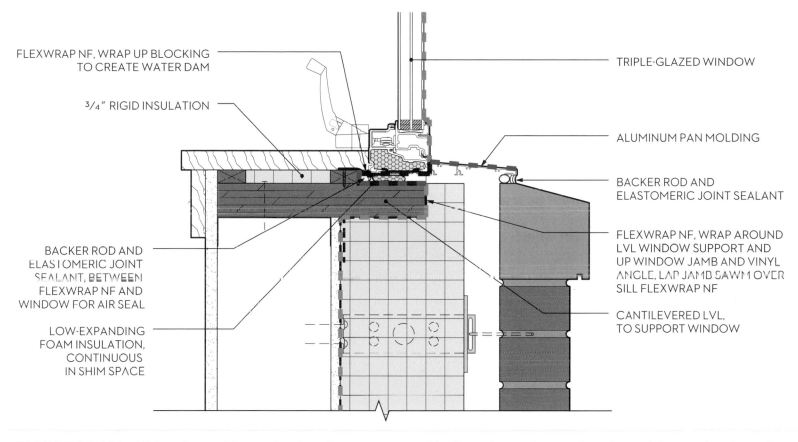

FLEXWRAP NF, WRAP UP BLOCKING TO CREATE WATER DAM

³/₄" RIGID INSULATION

TRIPLE-GLAZED WINDOW

ALUMINUM PAN MOLDING

BACKER ROD AND ELASTOMERIC JOINT SEALANT

BACKER ROD AND ELASTOMERIC JOINT SEALANT, BETWEEN FLEXWRAP NF AND WINDOW FOR AIR SEAL

FLEXWRAP NF, WRAP AROUND LVL WINDOW SUPPORT AND UP WINDOW JAMB AND VINYL ANGLE, LAP JAMB SAWM OVER SILL FLEXWRAP NF

LOW-EXPANDING FOAM INSULATION, CONTINUOUS IN SHIM SPACE

CANTILEVERED LVL, TO SUPPORT WINDOW

FIGURE 10.19A. With wall assemblies insulated on the exterior, a wood buck may be used to cantilever beyond the metal studs, so that the window can be installed in the same plane as the insulation. The control layers wrap around the buck, where they can be sealed under and behind the window frame.

FIGURE 10.19B. The first layer of water control, wrapped around a projecting wood sill buck.

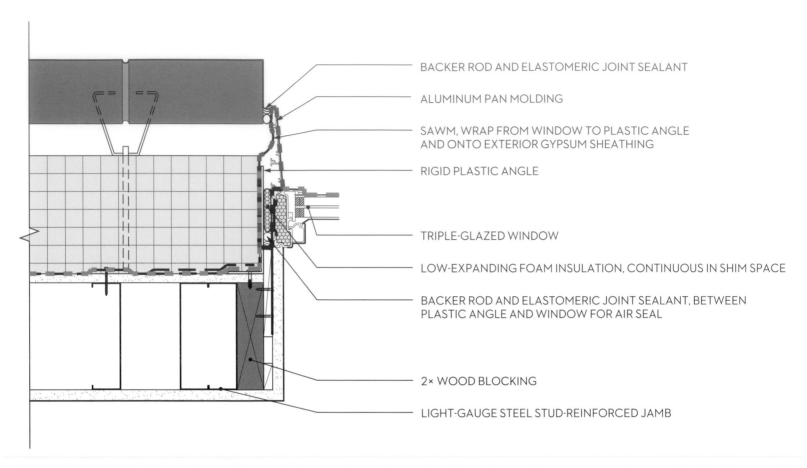

BACKER ROD AND ELASTOMERIC JOINT SEALANT

ALUMINUM PAN MOLDING

SAWM, WRAP FROM WINDOW TO PLASTIC ANGLE
AND ONTO EXTERIOR GYPSUM SHEATHING

RIGID PLASTIC ANGLE

TRIPLE-GLAZED WINDOW

LOW-EXPANDING FOAM INSULATION, CONTINUOUS IN SHIM SPACE

BACKER ROD AND ELASTOMERIC JOINT SEALANT, BETWEEN
PLASTIC ANGLE AND WINDOW FOR AIR SEAL

2× WOOD BLOCKING

LIGHT-GAUGE STEEL STUD-REINFORCED JAMB

FIGURE 10.20A. At a window jamb, a rigid plastic angle may be used to frame the rough opening, providing a surface for the air- and water-control layers to overlap on the outside and to seal the window on the inside, completing the air seal.

FIGURE 10.20B. In this window installation mock-up, the air- and water-control layer is wrapped into the window rough opening, as the first step in flashing the jamb.

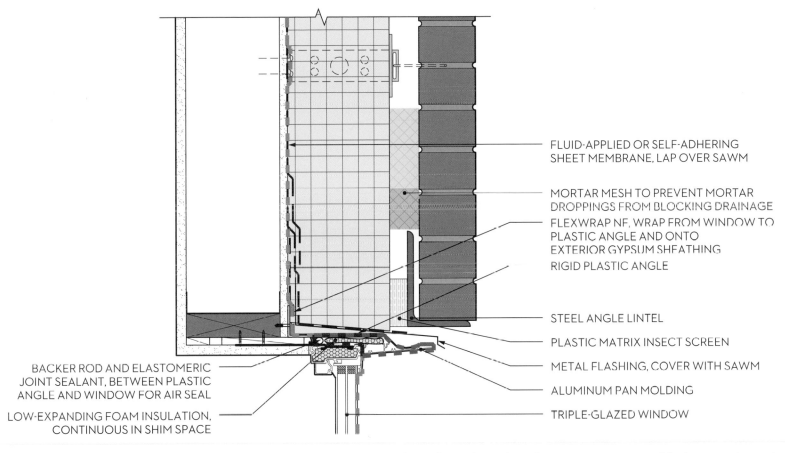

FLUID-APPLIED OR SELF-ADHERING
SHEET MEMBRANE, LAP OVER SAWM

MORTAR MESH TO PREVENT MORTAR
DROPPINGS FROM BLOCKING DRAINAGE

FLEXWRAP NF, WRAP FROM WINDOW TO
PLASTIC ANGLE AND ONTO
EXTERIOR GYPSUM SHEATHING

RIGID PLASTIC ANGLE

STEEL ANGLE LINTEL

PLASTIC MATRIX INSECT SCREEN

METAL FLASHING, COVER WITH SAWM

ALUMINUM PAN MOLDING

TRIPLE-GLAZED WINDOW

BACKER ROD AND ELASTOMERIC
JOINT SEALANT, BETWEEN PLASTIC
ANGLE AND WINDOW FOR AIR SEAL

LOW-EXPANDING FOAM INSULATION,
CONTINUOUS IN SHIM SPACE

FIGURE 10.21A. This detail for a window head uses a rigid plastic angle, similar to the jamb. It also incorporates a metal flashing, overlapped by the water-control layer, to direct any water out beyond the window.

FIGURE 10.21B. Installing the rigid plastic angle at the head of a mock-up window opening.

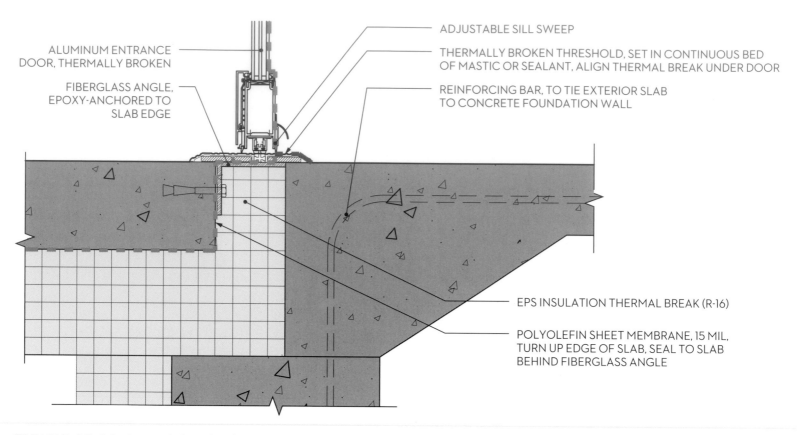

ALUMINUM ENTRANCE
DOOR, THERMALLY BROKEN

FIBERGLASS ANGLE,
EPOXY-ANCHORED TO
SLAB EDGE

ADJUSTABLE SILL SWEEP

THERMALLY BROKEN THRESHOLD, SET IN CONTINUOUS BED
OF MASTIC OR SEALANT, ALIGN THERMAL BREAK UNDER DOOR

REINFORCING BAR, TO TIE EXTERIOR SLAB
TO CONCRETE FOUNDATION WALL

EPS INSULATION THERMAL BREAK (R-16)

POLYOLEFIN SHEET MEMBRANE, 15 MIL,
TURN UP EDGE OF SLAB, SEAL TO SLAB
BEHIND FIBERGLASS ANGLE

FIGURE 10.22. A typical door detail at a slab on grade shows the connection between the underslab water-, vapor-, and air-control layer and the door threshold. A rigid fiberglass angle is used to support the doorsill over the insulated thermal break at the edge of the slab.

lintel that supports the masonry by bearing on the veneer on either side of the opening. With a steel loose lintel, it is customary to install flashing on top of the lintel, with weeps at the masonry head joints to allow water to drain out of the wall. With a rain screen/drainage plane, however, it may not be necessary to tie this flashing back to the water-control layer at the wall plane if there are other means to divert moisture out of the wall above. Metal head flashing, tied to and overlapped by the wall's water-control layer, can be used to provide a positive slope so moisture can drain to the outside face of the window (a small gap should be left above the flashing to allow moisture to drain). The flashing on the loose lintel will divert any moisture that condenses on or penetrates through the brick to the exterior. With other exterior finish materials, it is also usually sufficient to leave a similar gap above the head flashing, unsealed, for drainage of moisture out of the wall

above the window. With all exterior finish materials, the gap or the airspace just above should be provided with screen or a plastic matrix material that will keep insects or other pests out of the cavity.

DOOR SILLS. Door and sidelight components are often parts of an aluminum storefront system. Door/storefront frame members should have an integral thermal break, and doors should have thermally broken stiles and rails with good double- or triple-glazing.

As with windows, doors should be positioned so they are in the plane of the exterior wall insulation to eliminate thermal bridging. Since the floor material in the concrete and steel construction is usually concrete, care must be taken to provide a thermal break at the edge of the slab to isolate the interior slab from the exterior slab and from the foundation wall below (see

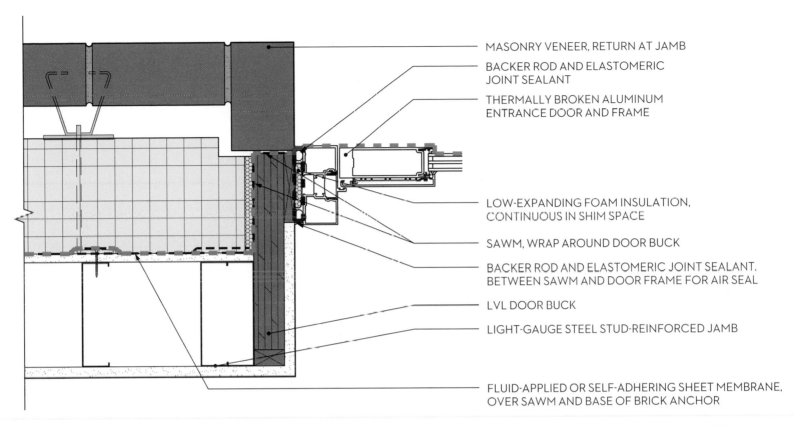

Labels (top to bottom, right side):

MASONRY VENEER, RETURN AT JAMB

BACKER ROD AND ELASTOMERIC JOINT SEALANT

THERMALLY BROKEN ALUMINUM ENTRANCE DOOR AND FRAME

LOW-EXPANDING FOAM INSULATION, CONTINUOUS IN SHIM SPACE

SAWM, WRAP AROUND DOOR BUCK

BACKER ROD AND ELASTOMERIC JOINT SEALANT, BETWEEN SAWM AND DOOR FRAME FOR AIR SEAL

LVL DOOR BUCK

LIGHT-GAUGE STEEL STUD-REINFORCED JAMB

FLUID-APPLIED OR SELF-ADHERING SHEET MEMBRANE, OVER SAWM AND BASE OF BRICK ANCHOR

FIGURE 10.23. A wood buck supports the doorframe beyond the stud wall, in the plane of the insulation layer. The control layer wraps around the wood buck and is water- and air-sealed to the doorframe.

figure 10.22). The top of the foundation wall is dropped several inches at door openings to allow for the slab and the underslab insulation. Sometimes the foundation wall is thickened at the opening to provide a shelf to support an exterior slab and allow for reinforcing bars to connect the exterior slab to the foundation and prevent it from heaving upward under frost pressure. This is especially important in cold climates so that a heaving slab does not prevent egress doors from swinging out.

A vertical thermal break consisting of at least 3″ of rigid insulation (R-15) should be installed between the edges of the interior and exterior slabs. To support the threshold across the top of the insulation, a fiberglass support angle is bolted to the face of the slab. Fiberglass is strong and has low thermal conductivity, making it a good material for this application. The threshold itself, usually aluminum, should have a thermal break to reduce conductive heat loss. The threshold should be installed so the thermal break is positioned directly under the door.

Weather stripping is important at door openings both to prevent water intrusion and to seal the opening from air infiltration/exfiltration. The preferred sill weather stripping is an adjustable silicone sweep strip, which is durable and remains fairly flexible in cold weather.

DOORJAMBS. Door and storefront frames are different from windows, in that they are usually attached to the rough opening directly through the frame, instead of using clips that can offset the attachment point to the interior. Because of this, wood bucks should extend beyond the wall to provide solid attachment for the frame (figure 10.23). Air- and water-control layer flashing wraps around the buck and into the rough opening, where it is sealed to the door or storefront frame on the interior side

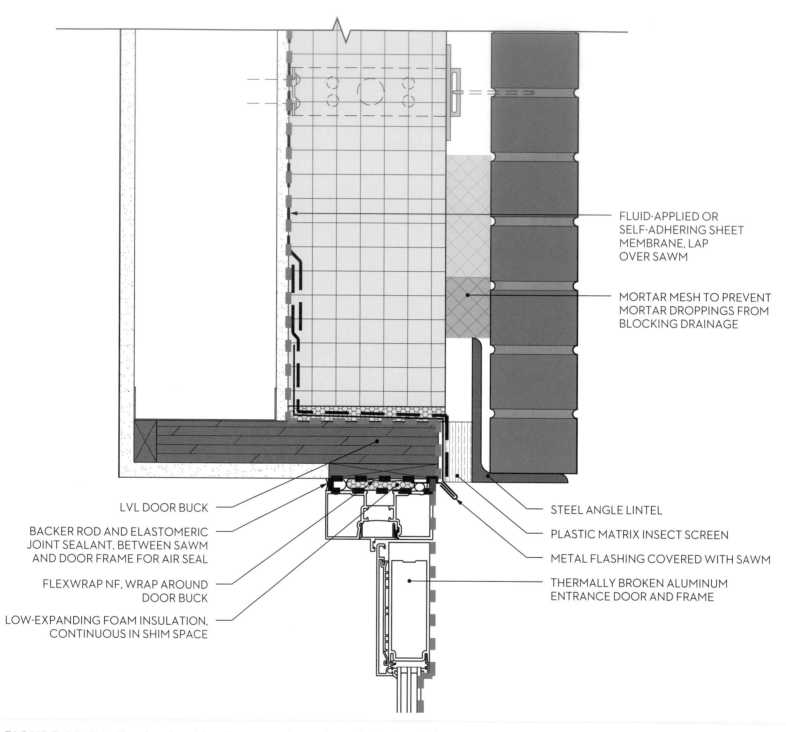

FLUID-APPLIED OR
SELF-ADHERING SHEET
MEMBRANE, LAP
OVER SAWM

MORTAR MESH TO PREVENT
MORTAR DROPPINGS FROM
BLOCKING DRAINAGE

LVL DOOR BUCK

BACKER ROD AND ELASTOMERIC
JOINT SEALANT, BETWEEN SAWM
AND DOOR FRAME FOR AIR SEAL

FLEXWRAP NF, WRAP AROUND
DOOR BUCK

LOW-EXPANDING FOAM INSULATION,
CONTINUOUS IN SHIM SPACE

STEEL ANGLE LINTEL

PLASTIC MATRIX INSECT SCREEN

METAL FLASHING COVERED WITH SAWM

THERMALLY BROKEN ALUMINUM
ENTRANCE DOOR AND FRAME

FIGURE 10.24. This door head detail is very similar to the jamb detail, with the control layer wrapped around a cantilevered wood buck. At the head, additional metal flashing, overlapped by the water-control layer, is added to divert water beyond the doorframe.

of the frame. Since storefront entrances are usually installed after the brick veneer is in place, it is rarely possible to provide water-control-layer flashing over the exterior side of the rough opening. It is therefore important to provide a strong sealant joint where the exterior edge of the frame meets the brick. Where other exterior finishes are used that can be installed after the door or storefront frame, there may be an opportunity to apply a concealed strip of water-control-layer membrane to the edge of the doorframe and onto the door buck.

DOOR HEAD. Detailing of the door or storefront head is similar to the window head, except for a wood buck for frame attachment at the head of the opening. As figure 10.24 shows, the air/water-control layer laps into the rough opening, so the doorframe head can be sealed to the air-control layer from the interior. Loose lintels are typical for masonry veneer, and weeps in the head joints of the masonry above the lintel allow for drainage of any water from the back side of the masonry. Head drip flashing installed above the door head, with the water-control layer lapped over the top, provides drainage. Screening prevents insects from accessing the air cavity.

SKYLIGHTS. Skylights in commercial low-slope roofs require a custom-insulated curb in net zero construction. Elevating skylights for snow and water protection is important in cold climates. To maximize insulation value while providing structural support, we recommend using structural insulated (stressed-skin) panels (SIPs) to frame the curb sides. Check local code requirements. We have been able to use combustible materials to support skylights, even in noncombustible construction types. Figure 10.25a shows a typical detail using SIPs for the skylight curb. The opening in the metal roof deck must be supported by structure. Steel channel members are shown here. The SIPs must be adequately fastened to the perimeter of the opening. The skylight frame sits on top of and is fastened to the curb, after the installation of the air-, water-, and vapor-control layers.

If a separate air-, and vapor-control layer is used, it must turn up the sides of the curb and onto the blocking at the top, where it can be sealed to the skylight frame from the interior.

The water-control layer (roof membrane) must also be turned up and onto the top of the curb and a continuous bead of sealant applied to the top to seal it to the bottom of the skylight frame when it is set in place. Most skylight frames have an integral drip edge on the outside and a gutter on the interior side to catch potential condensate from the inside surface of the glazing.

ROOF CURBS. In commercial/institutional construction with low-slope roofs, roof-mounted ventilation equipment is common. While manufacturers of this equipment can often provide curbs to install their equipment on, these are typically not insulated to a level that is appropriate for a net zero building. Figure 10.26a shows a custom curb detail for net zero construction. This approach is very similar to the skylight curb detail in that it uses SIPs for the sides and the control layers turn up and over the top of the curb, sealed to the bottom of the manufacturer's equipment curb. The equipment curb may provide spring isolation of the equipment where necessary (for acoustic purposes), with a flexible weather and air seal on the outside. A flexible bellows-type joint is also required for the ductwork that comes out of the bottom of the equipment when isolation mounts are used. Since the upper part of the curb is usually uninsulated, it is necessary to insulate the ductwork and the remaining roof surface inside the curb.

Special Conditions in Steel and Concrete Construction

Large buildings frequently need gaps, or joints, in their construction to accommodate thermal expansion and contractions. Additions to existing buildings may also need separation from the adjacent building because the structures may behave differently in seismic events. The covers for these joints are designed to accommodate movement while keeping water out of the assembly. They are installed in or close to the plane of the exterior finish and usually incorporate two flexible water-control layers for redundancy. The air-control layer (or

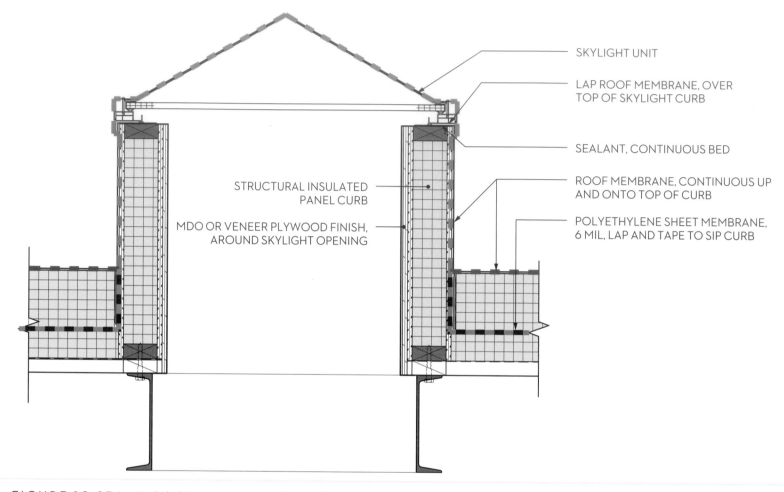

SKYLIGHT UNIT

LAP ROOF MEMBRANE, OVER TOP OF SKYLIGHT CURB

SEALANT, CONTINUOUS BED

ROOF MEMBRANE, CONTINUOUS UP AND ONTO TOP OF CURB

POLYETHYLENE SHEET MEMBRANE, 6 MIL, LAP AND TAPE TO SIP CURB

STRUCTURAL INSULATED PANEL CURB

MDO OR VENEER PLYWOOD FINISH, AROUND SKYLIGHT OPENING

FIGURE 10.25A. At skylights, we recommend using SIPs to support the skylight while providing improved thermal performance compared to typical curbs.

FIGURE 10.25B. Three steps in the installation of the roof control layers at a SIP skylight curb.

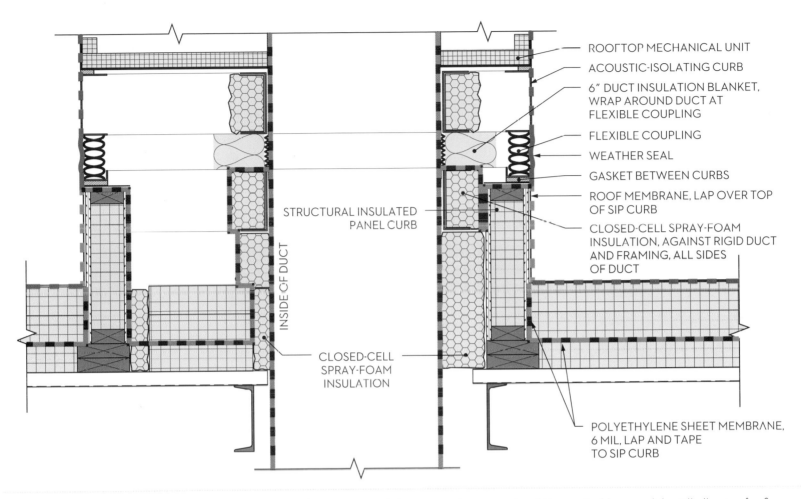

ROOFTOP MECHANICAL UNIT

ACOUSTIC-ISOLATING CURB

6" DUCT INSULATION BLANKET, WRAP AROUND DUCT AT FLEXIBLE COUPLING

FLEXIBLE COUPLING

WEATHER SEAL

GASKET BETWEEN CURBS

ROOF MEMBRANE, LAP OVER TOP OF SIP CURB

CLOSED-CELL SPRAY-FOAM INSULATION, AGAINST RIGID DUCT AND FRAMING, ALL SIDES OF DUCT

STRUCTURAL INSULATED PANEL CURB

INSIDE OF DUCT

CLOSED-CELL SPRAY-FOAM INSULATION

POLYETHYLENE SHEET MEMBRANE, 6 MIL, LAP AND TAPE TO SIP CURB

FIGURE 10.26A. A custom curb detail for a rooftop unit using SIPs to provide continuity of the control layers while still allowing for flexibility and durability at the acoustical isolating mounts.

FIGURE 10.26B. The inside of a rooftop unit curb under construction. The curb is constructed of SIPs and is supporting the isolation mounting frame for the rooftop unit. Because the space inside the curb is uninsulated, the roof deck within the curb is insulated to R-60.

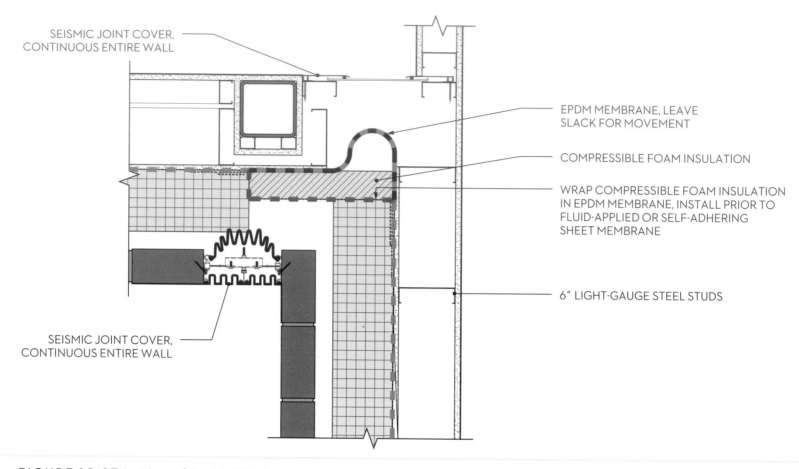

SEISMIC JOINT COVER,
CONTINUOUS ENTIRE WALL

EPDM MEMBRANE, LEAVE
SLACK FOR MOVEMENT

COMPRESSIBLE FOAM INSULATION

WRAP COMPRESSIBLE FOAM INSULATION
IN EPDM MEMBRANE, INSTALL PRIOR TO
FLUID-APPLIED OR SELF-ADHERING
SHEET MEMBRANE

6" LIGHT-GAUGE STEEL STUDS

SEISMIC JOINT COVER,
CONTINUOUS ENTIRE WALL

FIGURE 10.27A. A loop of durable EPDM membrane connects the control layers on either side of a seismic or expansion joint. Compressible foam insulation, protected from moisture, provides continuity of the thermal layer across the joint.

FIGURE 10.27B. EPDM membrane spanning a joint between two wall assemblies to provide continuity of the water/vapor/air-control layer.

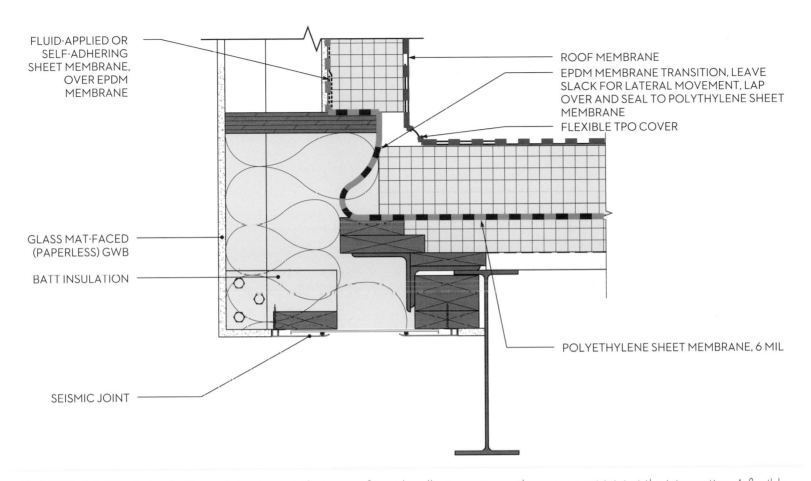

FLUID-APPLIED OR SELF-ADHERING SHEET MEMBRANE, OVER EPDM MEMBRANE

ROOF MEMBRANE

EPDM MEMBRANE TRANSITION, LEAVE SLACK FOR LATERAL MOVEMENT, LAP OVER AND SEAL TO POLYTHYLENE SHEET MEMBRANE

FLEXIBLE TPO COVER

GLASS MAT-FACED (PAPERLESS) GWB

BATT INSULATION

POLYETHYLENE SHEET MEMBRANE, 6 MIL

SEISMIC JOINT

FIGURE 10.28. A step in the roof structure, similar to a roof to sidewall intersection, with a movement joint at the intersection. A flexible EPDM membrane provides the transition between the wall air/moisture/vapor-control layer and the roof air- and water-control layer. A prefabricated flexible cover allows for the necessary movement at the roof membrane intersection.

air/water-control layer) is located behind the exterior finish. Detailing of the air-control layer at this joint is necessary to provide continuity with enough flexibility to accommodate movement between the assemblies on either side of the joint.

SEISMIC OR EXPANSION JOINTS. Figure 10.27a shows a typical wall expansion joint. An exterior expansion joint cover spans the gap where the wall assemblies of two structures meet at right angles, providing protection against moisture and pest intrusion. In line with the insulation layer is compressible foam to provide insulation that spans the gap and can flex with differential movement between the two structures. The foam is covered with a layer of SAWM to prevent it from

absorbing water. Behind the insulation layer, applied to the sheathing, is EPDM roofing membrane, installed with a loop of excess material to allow expansion and contraction of the joint without damaging the control-layer material. The EPDM extends behind the insulation on both sides, where it is tied into the wall air- and vapor-control layer for a continuous seal. On the interior face of the wall, a metal expansion joint cover allows for differential movement without damaging the interior gypsum board finish.

Figure 10.28 shows a roof-to-wall expansion joint condition. A flexible joint cover is installed with the roofing membrane, attached to both roof and wall assemblies. Since the roof assembly in this case has a separate air/vapor-control

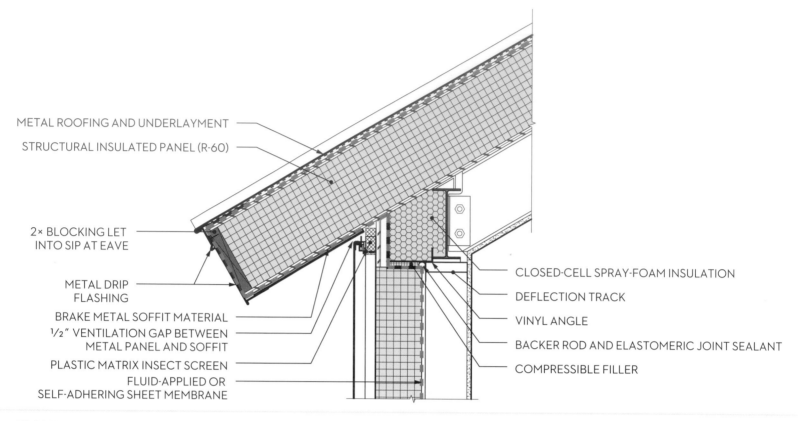

METAL ROOFING AND UNDERLAYMENT

STRUCTURAL INSULATED PANEL (R-60)

2× BLOCKING LET INTO SIP AT EAVE

METAL DRIP FLASHING

BRAKE METAL SOFFIT MATERIAL

½" VENTILATION GAP BETWEEN METAL PANEL AND SOFFIT

PLASTIC MATRIX INSECT SCREEN

FLUID-APPLIED OR SELF-ADHERING SHEET MEMBRANE

CLOSED-CELL SPRAY-FOAM INSULATION

DEFLECTION TRACK

VINYL ANGLE

BACKER ROD AND ELASTOMERIC JOINT SEALANT

COMPRESSIBLE FILLER

FIGURE 10.29A. A SIP provides an insulated extension of the roof over the wall insulation. Roof structural deflection is accommodated with a flexible joint, and the wall and roof control layers are connected for continuity.

FIGURE 10.29B. An insulated wood-framed overhang is being wrapped with peel-and-stick membrane water-, air-, vapor-control membrane to provide continuity of the control layers from wall to roof.

layer, this control layer must be connected to the air-control layer of the wall. As with the wall expansion joint, this connection is made with durable and flexible EPDM roofing membrane, formed with slack to have the ability to accommodate joint movement.

Roof-to-roof expansion joints are also common and, though roofing materials may vary, are generally similar to the roof-to-wall expansion joint approach in that separate exterior water- and interior air-control layers are provided, with the capacity to flex and allow for movement.

ROOF OVERHANGS WITH INSULATED PANELS. Roof overhangs can present challenges to achieving continuity of the control layers. Structural framing of the overhang usually penetrates the top of the wall, presenting many intersecting planes and corners that are very difficult to seal. In addition, the wall air-, water-, and vapor-control layers must be connected to the roof control layers for continuity. One example of how to accomplish this is shown in figure 10.29a, which shows a SIP projecting beyond the wall to form the roof overhang. The bottom and edge of the panel offer a substrate on which the control layers can be installed, thus providing continuity from the wall to the roof control layers. Since this detail is a wall-roof junction, the above-mentioned concerns about accommodating structural deflection also apply, necessitating joints in the control layers that can flex with differential movement of the assemblies.

Note that wood framing is used for the roof overhang in what is otherwise a steel and concrete building, since steel is much more conductive than wood and the many thermal bridges that would result could cause significant energy costs and condensation or mold problems. Code requirements may limit the use of wood in noncombustible building types and, where allowed, it is generally the case that it must be treated with fire retardant. Where steel must be used for the overhang structure, it should be thermally isolated from the interior structure with only isolated fastening points.

BALCONY/CANOPY CANTILEVERS. Balconies and canopies are frequently constructed by cantilevering concrete slabs or steel structures from interior to exterior, penetrating the control layers. This steel and/or concrete wicks significant heat and can cause condensation, mold, and comfort issues.

Figure 10.36 (on page 314) shows concrete balcony bridging and associated heat-loss problems.

Other strategies for thermal isolation exist. One is to build a separate structure outside the building envelope so that loads do not come back to the building structure, calling for only a minimal connection through the envelope. Another strategy, applicable particularly to canopies, is to use cables and/or rods to support canopies in tension. By doing this, a simple connection with relatively small stainless steel bolts (less conductive) and a high-density polyurethane thermal isolation block can be used at the attachment point of the canopy structure and at the attachment for the tension rods or cables. Figure 10.32 shows a detail drawing of this approach. Blocks made from high-density polyurethane or other strong, nonconductive materials can be used both in tension and compression conditions to eliminate thermal bridging through such steel connections. For concrete structures, insulation can be provided to isolate the interior concrete from the exterior concrete, while allowing the reinforcing rods to pass through.

Cantilevered concrete overhangs or balconies are possible using special premanufactured insulation assemblies. One manufacturer, Schöck USA, advertises a 92 percent reduction in heat loss possible with thermally broken connections using their products. Figures 10.30a through 10.30c show a Schöck isolation assembly on a concrete roof overhang. Figures 10.31a through 10.31c show a Schöck isolation assembly for a structural steel balcony overhang.

Enclosure Penetrations

Penetrations through the envelope by pipes, conduit, or ducts must be detailed and executed carefully to ensure that none of the control layers is compromised.

DUCT AND LOUVER WALL PENETRATION. Figure 10.33 shows a penetration of a duct through an exterior wall at a louver. The louver itself is in the plane of the exterior finish and needs to be sealed at the perimeter to repel water. The duct penetrates the backing wall assembly and must be supported at the opening, and all the control layers must be sealed to it. The duct

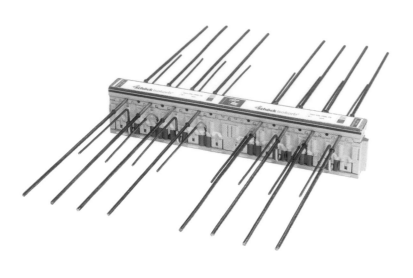

FIGURE 10.30A. A Schöck isolation assembly used for concrete cantilevers.

FIGURE 10.30B. A Schöck isolation assembly installed between the interior concrete and exterior concrete overhang as a thermal break, before the concrete is poured.

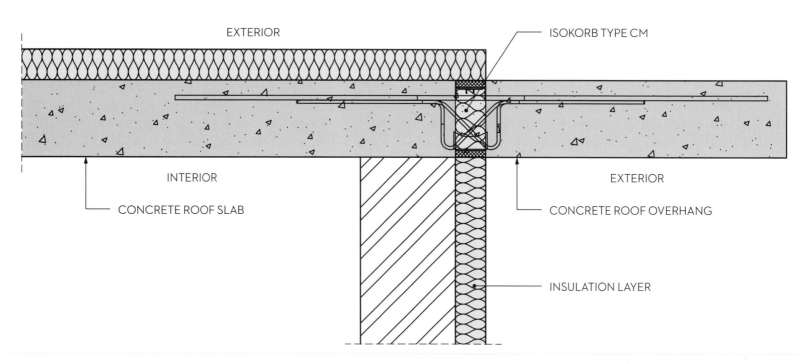

EXTERIOR

ISOKORB TYPE CM

INTERIOR

EXTERIOR

CONCRETE ROOF SLAB

CONCRETE ROOF OVERHANG

INSULATION LAYER

FIGURE 10.30C. This Schöck isolation assembly for concrete cantilevers provides structural continuity of the reinforcing steel rods while still providing a thermal break between interior and exterior concrete.

FIGURE 10.31A. A Schöck isolation assembly for structural steel cantilevers.

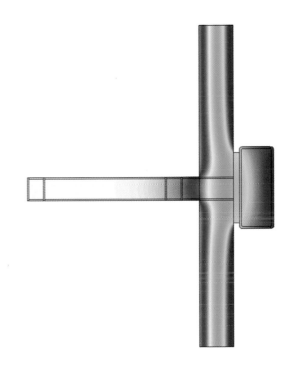

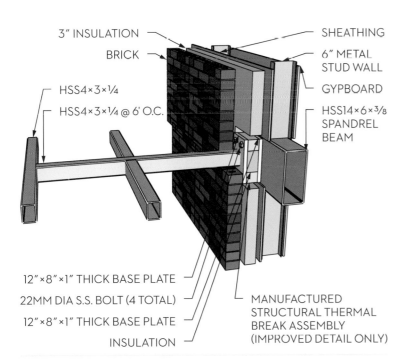

3" INSULATION

BRICK

HSS4×3×¼

HSS4×3×¼ @ 6' O.C.

SHEATHING

6" METAL STUD WALL

GYPBOARD

HSS14×6×³⁄₈ SPANDREL BEAM

12"×8"×1" THICK BASE PLATE

22MM DIA S.S. BOLT (4 TOTAL)

12"×8"×1" THICK BASE PLATE

INSULATION

MANUFACTURED STRUCTURAL THERMAL BREAK ASSEMBLY (IMPROVED DETAIL ONLY)

FIGURE 10.31B. A diagram showing an isolation assembly for structural steel installed at a steel balcony or canopy connection.

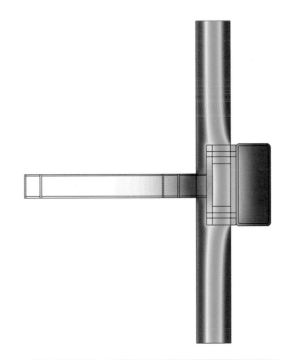

FIGURE 10.31C. These temperature gradient diagrams illustrate the improvement in the thermal performance between a standard steel connection (*top*) and a thermally isolated steel connection (*bottom*).

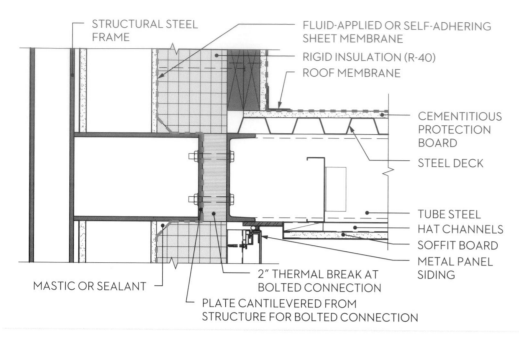

STRUCTURAL STEEL FRAME

FLUID-APPLIED OR SELF-ADHERING SHEET MEMBRANE

RIGID INSULATION (R-40)

ROOF MEMBRANE

CEMENTITIOUS PROTECTION BOARD

STEEL DECK

TUBE STEEL

HAT CHANNELS

SOFFIT BOARD

METAL PANEL SIDING

2" THERMAL BREAK AT BOLTED CONNECTION

PLATE CANTILEVERED FROM STRUCTURE FOR BOLTED CONNECTION

MASTIC OR SEALANT

FIGURE 10.32. This canopy connection was designed with a high-density polyurethane block to provide a thermal break between the canopy and the building structure.

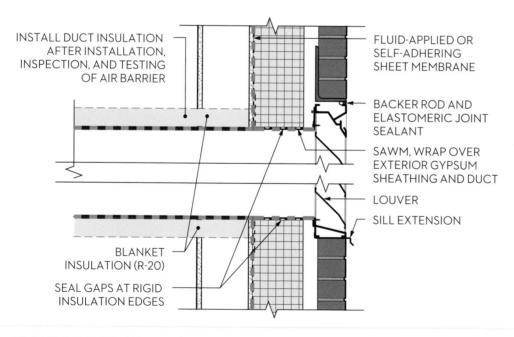

INSTALL DUCT INSULATION AFTER INSTALLATION, INSPECTION, AND TESTING OF AIR BARRIER

FLUID-APPLIED OR SELF-ADHERING SHEET MEMBRANE

BACKER ROD AND ELASTOMERIC JOINT SEALANT

SAWM, WRAP OVER EXTERIOR GYPSUM SHEATHING AND DUCT

LOUVER

SILL EXTENSION

BLANKET INSULATION (R-20)

SEAL GAPS AT RIGID INSULATION EDGES

FIGURE 10.33. Where a duct penetrates an exterior wall, the water/air/vapor-control layer must be wrapped onto the duct, lapped in the proper water-shedding sequence.

must be part of an air-sealed system as well. Make sure the air-control layer is continuous by sealing the supporting angle frame to the air-control layer applied to the exterior sheathing, and sealing the angle frame to the duct. Make sure the water-control layer is continuous by installing FlexWrap NF on the face of the wall and the sides of the duct in the same sequence and with the same overlapping described for window openings. Under the duct the FlexWrap NF will lap over the air- and water/vapor-control layer on the wall, but at the head the air- and water/vapor-control layer must lap over the top of the FlexWrap NF to provide proper drainage. The thermal insulation layer extends to the sides of the duct, using low-expanding foam insulation to fill the gaps around it.

PIPING WALL PENETRATION. See figure 10.34 for a piping penetration through a typical wall assembly with brick veneer. The piping penetration through the brick should be sealed with flexible sealant and backer rod. If the piping connects to a plumbing fixture such as a hose bibb at the exterior wall, the perimeter of the fixture should be sealed with flexible sealant and backer rod. The piping penetration through the wall sheathing is generally somewhat larger than the pipe, and the gap between piping and sheathing should be sealed with a material (often low-expanding foam insulation) that is compatible with the control layer system. In figure 10.34, a 2" wide fillet of mastic or sealant is applied all around the pipe, adhering to both the sheathing and the pipe for an air- and watertight seal. After this has cured, the air/vapor-control layer is applied over the mastic and wall sheathing.

PIPING ROOF PENETRATION. Piping penetrations through low-slope roofs are fairly common, especially for plumbing waste system vents. An example of a single pipe penetration is shown in figure 10.35, with a water-control-layer-on-top roofing system. Where the roof membrane is penetrated, it is lapped up the side of the pipe and attached with a hose clamp. The membrane is fastened to the roof deck around the pipe, and a flexible flashing boot is fitted around the base of the pipe. This is adhered and sealed to the roof membrane, then clamped and sealed to the pipe. The separate air- and vapor-control layers, on top of the first layer of insulation, are also lapped down the side of the pipe and sealed.

ELECTRICAL WALL PENETRATION. In commercial construction electrical wiring is generally routed within metallic conduit. The detailing of the penetration is therefore quite similar to piping wall penetrations, with one difference: the interior of the conduit must be air-sealed because the conduit system is not airtight. This is best accomplished with special putty or sealant specifically made for this purpose. This air seal must be installed after the wiring is pulled through the conduit and—if the conduit is connected to an electrical box on the building exterior—after the majority of the device wiring/handling is complete, so as not to disturb the air seal by tugging on the wires.

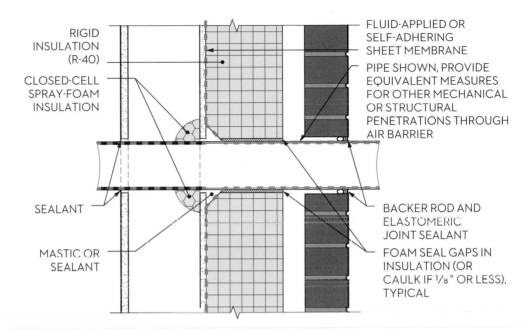

FIGURE 10.34. A vapor-, water-, and airtight seal is made around a piping penetration of an exterior wall using materials compatible with the control layers.

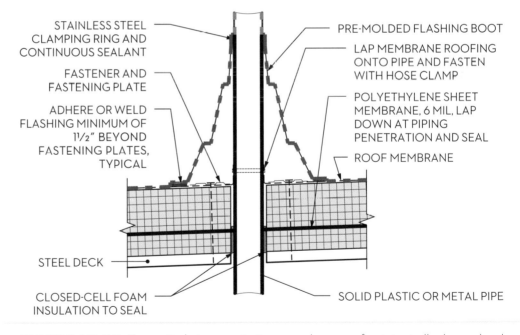

FIGURE 10.35. For vertical pipe penetrations, membrane roofing is typically clamped and sealed to the pipe and a flexible flashing boot is fitted over the pipe, then clamped and sealed to the pipe at the top. Where the vapor-control layer is separate, it must also be sealed to the pipe. Any gaps in the roof insulation around the pipe are filled with closed-cell foam insulation.

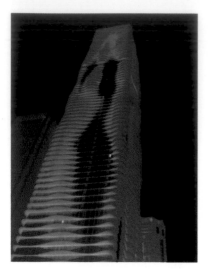

FIGURE 10.36. These cantilevered concrete balconies at the Aqua Tower in Chicago are thermally conductive and represent a significant heat loss from the building. The infrared imagery highlights the heat loss through the thermal bridges at the balcony locations.

11 | Wood-Frame Construction

Many building science professionals recommend putting the framing structure inside the building enclosure so that it is protected from temperature, moisture, pests, or other threats. But wood construction professionals have insulated within the wood structure for more than half a century. This is because wood, unlike steel and concrete, is a reasonably good insulator, with a typical R-value of approximately one per inch. When steel studs are introduced into a wall assembly, the resulting thermal bridging reduces the overall assembly insulation value by 50–75 percent, making the insulation almost useless and a very poor investment. Wood framing, however, reduces the overall insulation value by only 10–15 percent. Insulation in wood-frame construction is thus often used within the wood structure in net zero building construction. However, in net zero wood-frame construction, wood should not extend from the inside to the outside of the insulation layer. Somewhere there should be a thermal break.

Because of the superior thermal performance of wood, the strength of established construction practices, and cost savings in combining wood structure and insulation, we discuss a wide range of wood-framed building enclosure systems, most of which combine the structure and thermal-control layers. For simplicity, we call these structures combined thermal/wood-structure buildings. But before we go into their assembly details, we'll discuss the moisture and other potential problems that need to be addressed when using these combined thermal/wood structures.

Unique Challenges in Wood-Frame Construction

In chapter 6 we discussed the water, air, vapor, and thermal control layers and the critical importance of how these layers are combined in the wall. In thermal/wood structure building assemblies in particular, it is the vapor-control layer that is critical to the design of a resilient and durable wall assembly. Specifically, the key is to avoid conditions that could cause condensation within the structure of the building. In chapter 6 we also discussed how to calculate where the dew point occurs in the building enclosure. Given our focus on cold climates, our rule of thumb is to have a third of the insulation outside the structure in climates up to 6,000 HDD, half on the outside in climates from 6,000 to 9,000 HDD, and all insulation outside the structure in climates above 9,000 HDD. This means for our R-40 wall in a 6,000–9,000 HDD climate a good combination would be 4" of rigid insulation on the outside of the wall, with 5.5" of cellulose inside the wall. All of these variations assume a very effective air-control layer with preferably 0.1 but certainly less than 0.2 cfm50 per square foot of above-grade surface area.

While this rule of thumb is a good guideline, it is also important to take indoor relative humidity into account, as it affects both dew point and temperature. Building Science Corporation has published a chart for determining the ratio of exterior to interior insulation that is required to prevent cold-weather exfiltration condensation for different winter average temperatures and indoor relative humidity (RH) levels (see table 11.1). The winter average temperature is the average of the temperatures for the three coldest months of the year. For a location like Montpelier, Vermont, where the winter average temperature is close to 14°F, at an indoor relative humidity of 35 percent, the ratio of exterior to interior insulation is given as 48 percent—close to the 50 percent figure from our rule of thumb. The indoor relative humidity is affected by climate factors and heating and ventilation systems. However, it is also largely dependent upon the building's use. For instance, a building that generates moisture (such as an athletic facility) or that must be maintained at a higher relative humidity (such as a museum) of 50 percent will require significantly more exterior insulation—a 64 percent exterior-interior ratio. Well-sealed homes, such as net zero homes, may have elevated humidity levels due to bathing and cooking. Offices and schools, however, typically have much lower humidity levels. It's also important to consider that building uses may change over time. It is always best to perform dew-point calculations for each specific combination of wall assembly, local climate, and interior relative humidity.

Given the interconnection of building use, climate, and building enclosure design, calculating the dew point is not easy, even with sophisticated computer programs such as WUFI.

Because of this variability, the building enclosure and assemblies that are detailed in this book are conservative—and when they are not, we will indicate that.

The wall assembly also needs to allow water vapor to escape, so it is optimal for the building enclosure to allow vapor to diffuse to both the outside and inside of the building enclosure. This is accomplished by using materials that diffuse, combined with ventilation cavities. MemBrain acts as a vapor retarder until the humidity rises to levels that could be problematic for wood framing, and then it allows water vapor to pass through. Also, Sheetrock with non-vapor-retardant paint allows for adequate diffusion of water vapor. Once the vapor diffuses to the interior, the vapor is taken up by interior air. On the outside of the building, vapor can move adequately through typical sheathing such as plywood or OSB. However, if there is a control layer and then siding and roofing without an airspace, vapors may not be adequately dispersed and may get absorbed into exterior siding or trapped in the roof assembly, potentially causing moisture problems in the building enclosure. To avoid this, create an airspace between structural sheathing and exterior finishes—at both walls and roofs—to allow the structural and finish materials to stay dry. This space must be combined with a water-control layer such as Tyvek or Typar, which stops water but allows vapor migration. At roofs it is also important to provide ventilation below the roofing, which acts as the water-control layer, as most roofing does not allow for vapor migration.

We recommend that you always have an airspace along with a very tight air-control layer in all roof and wall assemblies. Where there is no airspace, there is a risk of moisture-related problems.

Issues with thermal bridges and/or vapor control also often occur in lighting, electrical, mechanical, and/or plumbing systems located in the building enclosure. The solution is simple: keep all lighting fixtures and equipment out of the building enclosure. Keep lights out of ceilings or use surface-mounted lights. Keep both exhaust fans and HRVs fully inside the building enclosure. Where there are wires, plumbing stacks, HRV inlets, and outlets that have to be located in the building enclosure, take particular care in sealing penetrations for water, air, and vapor, particularly at any control-layer locations. While this is true of all construction types, it is particularly important in combined thermal/wood structure building enclosures.

TABLE 11. 1. EXTERIOR INSULATION REQUIRED TO CONTROL CONDENSATION IN THE BUILDING ENCLOSURE

INDOOR RELATIVE HUMIDITY	20%	25%	30%	35%	40%	50%	60%
INTERIOR DEW POINT (°F)	26.6	32.0	36.6	40.5	44.0	49.9	54.8
Outdoor Temperature (°F)							
50	0%	0%	0%	0%	0%	0%	24%
41	0%	0%	0%	0%	10%	31%	48%
32	0%	0%	12%	23%	32%	47%	60%
23	8%	19%	29%	37%	45%	57%	68%
14	23%	32%	40%	48%	54%	64%	73%
5	33%	42%	49%	55%	60%	69%	77%
-4	41%	49%	55%	60%	65%	73%	80%
-13	48%	54%	60%	65%	69%	76%	82%
-22	53%	59%	64%	68%	72%	78%	84%

Source: Courtesy of Building Science Corporation, from John Straube, "BSD-163: Controlling Cold-Weather Condensation Using Insulation," *Building Science Digest*, November 2011, http://www.buildingscience.com/documents/digests/bsd-controlling-cold-weather-condensation-using-insulation.

Comparing Enclosure-Assembly Options

Once you understand the challenges, you can review your assembly options. We prefer two enclosure assemblies for combined thermal/wood structures for net zero building:

- Conventional framing with insulated cavity and exterior rigid foam insulation
- Double-framing with insulated cavity

However, we will also review the pros and cons of other common enclosure assemblies:

- Conventional framing with insulated cavity
- Conventional framing with sprayed-foam insulation
- Conventional framing with all exterior rigid foam insulation
- Stressed-skin panels, with or without post-and-beam framing

- Truss roofs and walls, insulated concrete form (ICF) and exterior insulation finish systems (EIFS)

While we discuss each of these systems as single unified building enclosures, they can be combined on the same building, with one system used for the walls and another for the roof or the wall or roof assembly, each consisting of more than one system. Where building enclosure systems are combined, extreme care must be used in connecting the water-, air-, vapor-, and thermal-control layers between different systems.

CONVENTIONAL FRAMING WITH INSULATED CAVITY AND RIGID EXTERIOR INSULATION. A common technique for high-performance wood framing is to use conventional framing with cavity insulation and additional rigid insulation on the outside. This assembly is depicted in greater detail in chapter 12.

This assembly is already established within the construction trades and is only a minor evolution from conventional framing. It does not require a major change in common construction practices. However, to comply with our recommendation of how much insulation to place outside the building enclosure, the continuous rigid insulation on the outside of the structure is thicker than current standard practice, which requires some additional care, effort, and expense.

DOUBLE FRAMING WITH INSULATED CAVITY. The concept of double-framed buildings is simple. It is a way to make thicker walls and roofs with fewer materials and less thermal bridging and therefore higher insulation values. These thick, double-framed buildings typically use dense-pack cellulose, so the 12″ overall wall thickness can achieve the R-40 walls for net zero buildings with minimal thermal bridging. Roofs typically are roof trusses with raised heels to gain R-60 or higher of cellulose. This system meets net zero standards and uses cellulose, which as a recycled product is environmentally much better than fossil-fuel-based foams. Thus, the environmental benefits of insulating double-framed buildings with cellulose are clear.

Double framing did not emerge from incremental changes from within the construction industry. Rather, in the mid- to late 1970s, designers in the United States and Canada began modeling, experimenting with, and monitoring highly insulated wood-frame structures. A team at the University of Illinois at Urbana-Champaign coined the term "superinsulation" and created a set of principles for stick-frame buildings, which included double-stud R-30 walls and R-60 roof assemblies. The design was called "lo-cal," and several lo-cal houses, duplexes, and condos were built in the area. The Saskatchewan house in Canada, constructed in 1977, was based on this idea, but an additional space was added in the wall assembly to increase the insulation value to R-40, and superior air sealing (for the time) was used to produce a very-low-energy-consuming home. Later, very simple double-framed ranch houses were built in Canada, with annual heating costs of approximately $100 in cold northern climates, causing a major change in thinking about low-energy buildings and leading to a new trend in double-framed walls and roofs. Double-wall and Larsen truss homes were built with similar ideas. In the 1980s cellulose advocates came up with a 9.5″ cellulose double wall assembly that is the basis for many of today's double-framed buildings.

While this double-framed performance is impressive, this assembly violates the rule of keeping one-third to half of the insulation outside the building enclosure in most cold-climate areas. Some building professionals believe that these assemblies will have the same condensation issues associated with conventional framing. Because cellulose is vapor-permeable and there is typically sheathing on the exterior for structural reasons, it is possible that condensation could occur on the exterior sheathing of the double-wall construction. But double-wall advocates argue that when the envelope is air-sealed to net zero standards, the moisture vapor moving by infiltration or exfiltration is minimized, eliminating the concern. Our view is that although high levels of air sealing will reduce these problems, moisture migration by diffusion is not eliminated by air sealing alone.

To address that, all of our recommended wall details have an airspace with a drainage plane so that drying happens on the outside of the wall, avoiding condensation. We also recommend installing a vapor-control layer on the interior face of the wall to prevent diffusion of moisture from the interior space into the insulated assembly. However, in the winter, when condensation is a concern, the water vapor wants to dry to the warmer side, which is the interior. Thus, a variable-permeability control layer such as MemBrain should be installed on the interior face of the exterior walls. Gypsum wallboard and vapor-permeable paint can also act as a semipermeable vapor-control layer. Both systems allow the cellulose to dry to the interior when needed.

With this assembly, almost all inside air is prevented from moving into the building's exterior enclosure, minimizing the amount of vapor-laden air that could condense. If any air with associated water vapor does get into the assembly, the vapor can escape to the exterior through the vented drainage space or to the interior through the variable-permeability vapor retarder. Lastly, the cellulose can absorb some moisture and will release it slowly, acting as a buffer or moisture sink.

However, this does not address the possibility that different paints or wall treatments could alter the permeability over time. It also is unknown how long "magic" products such as MemBrain will last. Will it be the 100 to 500 or more years that we should expect from our buildings? To increase the safety of this method, our net zero assemblies include a minimum of 2″ of sprayed foam on the inside face of the sheathing, to ensure

FIGURE 11.1. Double-stud cavity awaiting cellulose. These double-framed walls allow for sufficient depth of insulation to meet net zero enclosure standards.

FIGURE 11.2. A double-stud wall after filling with cellulose. The MemBrain film holds the cellulose in place until the gypsum board finish is installed.

FIGURE 11.3. An example of conventional stud framing with fiberglass batt cavity insulation.

FIGURE 11.4. An example of conventional stud framing with spray-foam insulation in the cavities.

protection from condensation. The correct thickness depends on the climate zone and the assembly, whether roof or wall.

CONVENTIONAL FRAMING WITH INSULATED CAVITY. Conventionally framed wood structures—by far the most common frame assembly in traditional building—use nominal 2" wide wood (1½" actual) framing members of various depth dimensions. In new construction fiberglass batt insulation and, more recently, cellulose are typically installed between studs. As noted above, combining the structural and insulation layers has the potential to invite water-vapor migration and condensation—particularly troublesome if there is not an effective, properly installed, continuous air-control layer. Air-permeable insulations, such as fiberglass and to a lesser degree cellulose, allow interior vapor-laden air to move into the wall or roof assembly, which increases the risks of condensation or other moisture-related problems. Therefore, this building enclosure assembly is not recommended for net zero buildings.

CONVENTIONAL FRAMING WITH SPRAYED-FOAM INSULATION. The only insulation that will not allow wood to deteriorate when it is

installed in the framing cavity is high-density closed-cell sprayed foam, which acts as a vapor- and air-control layer and stops the movement of vapor-laden air into the structural assembly. However, the assembly's wood framing acts as a thermal bridge and lessens the insulation value of the wall assembly. While it is possible to get close to achieving the desired R-values for a net zero assembly within a 2×8-framed wall with this assembly, both the high financial and potentially environmental cost of sprayed foam and the wood stud thermal bridges make it a suboptimal choice for a net zero construction. If this assembly is used, the spray foam should be carefully selected to minimize the environmental impact (see chapter 6).

CONVENTIONAL FRAMING WITH ALL EXTERIOR FOAM INSULATION. The wall system closest to the ideal assembly is a conventional wood-framed wall with all of the insulation on the outside of the structural framing and no insulation within the wall cavity. The challenge with this assembly, though, is that 7–10" of rigid insulation is needed outside the wall framing to achieve R-40 walls and 10–15" of insulation is needed on top of the roof. The depth of insulation depends on the specific type of rigid

FIGURE 11.5. Stressed-skin panels used as a structural enclosure assembly.

FIGURE 11.6. Stressed-skin panel installation on the outside of a post-and-beam frame.

insulation used. This creates a very thick building enclosure assembly and also causes challenges in fastening exterior finish materials. This approach, while possible, is usually not very practical or cost effective for net zero buildings. However, it may be worth the trouble and expense if building in very cold climates, above 9,000 HDD.

STRESSED-SKIN PANELS, WITH OR WITHOUT POST-AND-BEAM FRAMING. Stressed-skin panels are not a traditional construction method but are becoming more commonplace. Also known as structural insulated panels, these are manufactured panels that are typically 4' wide by varying lengths up to 24'. They have a rigid foam insulation core, most commonly expanded polystyrene (EPS), sandwiched between two or more structural and/or finish layers. These panels typically have plywood or OSB on the exterior and interior. They can be fabricated with interior and/or exterior finishes, including gypsum board, panel products, tongue-and-groove wood, or almost anything else that can be glued.

When designed as structural panels, stressed-skin panels can provide almost the entire exterior structure for a building, using only a few beams that are either exposed or buried within the panel depth. The depth of panel is determined by structural and insulation requirements. Roof panels can span up to 14' or more, depending on the depth of panel, which generally ranges from 3.5" to 11.25" for the insulation plus the depth of the finishes. In addition to EPS foam, extruded polystyrene (XPS) or closed-cell urethane can be used for improved insulation and/or structural requirements. While they can be structural, stressed-skin panels have most commonly been used nonstructurally, as infill panels with post-and-beam wood frames.

Stressed-skin panels allow for relatively quick and inexpensive construction when they are used for the entire structural system of a building. But when combined with a post-and-beam frame, the cost benefits are lost. Even so, this combination is common, primarily because of aesthetics added by the post-and-beam frame. And with the foam outside the structure, this system complies with the perfect enclosure requirements.

There are drawbacks to stressed-skin panel systems. While all of the proposed wood assemblies use some amount of fossil-fuel-based insulation, stressed-skin panels use this kind of insulation exclusively. This puts them in the same category as all spray-foam assemblies in terms of potential environmental costs. (See chapter 6 for a discussion of environmental consequences of different insulations.)

There are also durability concerns. It is unknown how long the glue between the foam and sheathing in the stressed-skin panel will last, and this issue could potentially affect the entire structure, as the panels hold the building up. The materials are also known to "creep" over time. Additionally, the system has little redundancy, and its lifetime is uncertain—probably less than the 100 or more years that environmentally responsible buildings should last.

Pests are also a concern, as insects and rodents can eat and nest in the foam, lowering insulation values and structural integrity. Although some manufacturers impregnate panels with borates, which can lessen infestations, certain pests such as carpenter ants will make nests even if some of their population dies in the process. Advocates of stressed-skin panels rightfully respond that carpenter ants and other pests also attack wood. While true, it is easier to repair wood framing and restore its structural integrity.

In addition to these concerns, stressed-skin panels, like all other systems we are investigating, require care and effort for proper installation. The weakness with stressed-skin panels is the joint between panels. It is difficult to install them so that there are no gaps in the insulation that allow for air movement. Using foam and splines at the joints helps, but putting large panels together is a challenge, given weather and other conditions encountered at construction sites. Using a fluid-applied membrane or tape at panel joints, as with other air-control systems, can solve those concerns. However, frequent small holes may need to be drilled at panel joints and foam injected, so that

all voids are filled. While this is doable, it is labor intensive. If stressed-skin panels are used, infrared scans with blower door testing should be conducted to detect any insulation gaps that need to be addressed. For all of these reasons, we do not recommend stressed-skin panels as a long-term environmentally appropriate solution for either structural or insulation systems.

TRUSS, ICF, AND EIFS SYSTEMS. The pros and cons of truss roof and wall assemblies are similar to those of double-wall and -roof assemblies. Insulated concrete forms are quite durable; however, standard ICFs do not typically meet the high R-value requirements of net zero buildings. They also do not offer easy protection from insects and rodents, nor do they allow the building to be easily altered in the future, as cutting through concrete is expensive.

Exterior insulation finish systems are typically a synthetic stucco finish installed over rigid board insulation. They can be installed as conventional framing with all exterior insulation or as conventional framing with insulated stud cavity and exterior insulation. While in the past these systems have had major problems due to inadequate moisture drainage and control layers, current EIFS practices have generally addressed these issues. Using the principles and details from this book, you can generate durable and efficient buildings with EIFS, though achieving net zero standards may be more challenging when all insulation is installed on the outside, due to the thickness required to achieve net zero standards.

That said, in our view the two wood construction assemblies most appropriate for net zero buildings are single frame with insulation in the wall cavity and rigid insulation on the exterior and double-frame construction with an insulated cavity.

FIGURE 11.7. Trusses and advanced framing allow for thicker insulation, enhance structural integrity, and reduce thermal bridging, thus increasing energy efficiency.

FIGURE 11.8. Detail of typical stacked ICF wall with expanded polystyrene insulation forms, plastic ties, and rebar installed, waiting for concrete.

FIGURE 11.9. ICF in construction: concrete being added to blocks of cement-bonded wood fiber that are stacked and braced as exterior walls.

12 | Net Zero Wood-Frame Construction

Once you have chosen your frame assembly, there are specific construction steps you'll want to take to ensure you are building to the highest net zero standards. In this chapter we review those steps as they relate to our two preferred construction assemblies.

Advanced Framing

Our two preferred net zero enclosures for wood framing can be optimized through advanced techniques that reduce the amount of wood framing used in order to reduce thermal bridging and increase thermal insulation. These techniques generate energy savings that reduce operating costs, reduce embodied energy, and trim construction costs by reducing the amount of framing lumber required.

Advanced framing is most often applied to single-wood framing, but the same principles provide benefits in double-framed wood walls. Figure 12.1 illustrates many of these techniques. Home or building designers can select which of these features to incorporate into a building design, beginning with the ones that are simplest and deliver the most benefit.

The first and most important step is to design all framing on a 24-inch module instead of the typical 16-inch module of wall framing. This requires aligning the framing (studs, floor joists, and rafters) from top to bottom and sizing and aligning openings to better fit the 24-inch module. Another possibility is to omit the plywood or OSB sheathing and replace it with foam insulation. Be aware, though, that if you remove the plywood or OSB, you will have to take other measures to brace the exterior walls structurally. In addition, you will need to use air and moisture sealing that is significantly different from our typical details, which use the sheathing layer as the air- and sometimes water-control layer.

Another aspect involves eliminating unnecessary framing to reduce thermal bridging. Wall corners are one place where fewer studs can be used: corners are typically framed with three studs to make it easier to attach interior gypsum board, two studs will suffice, and other means can be used to attach the interior gypsum board. Framing can often be reduced at headers by proper sizing, and headers can be omitted in nonbearing walls.

Further reductions include eliminating jack studs that support headers and instead using hangers at the ends of headers as well as using single plates at the tops of walls instead of two. Such steps are made possible by the alignment of the framing members.

Single-Frame Wood Construction

Figure 12.2 shows an overall section of a typical building using single-framed wood-stud wall construction, with insulation on the exterior. This drawing and all our examples to follow show an approach suitable for a cold climate with up to 9,000 HDD with an R-40 wall with 50 percent of the insulation value on the exterior of the building structure. This ratio of exterior to interior insulation should eliminate concerns about moisture vapor condensation within the wood-stud portion of the wall. For the insulation placed within the stud cavity, we recommend dense-pack cellulose for its ability to minimize air movement and absorb some moisture without problems, as well as for its environmental advantages. The exterior insulation is commonly rigid fossil-fuel-based foam because of its high insulation value, and the desired R-20 can be achieved in 4″ thickness or less. This foam is usually installed in two layers, with joints between boards sealed and the joints between layers staggered. Rigid mineral wool boards are an excellent alternative because of their permeability. This allows moisture vapor to escape to the exterior as needed, though the lower R-value of mineral wool requires 5″ thickness to provide R-20. Mineral wool can also absorb moisture, decreasing its R-value, so it should be protected from moisture to maximize the insulation value. The boards must be able to drain at the bottom.

Single-Frame Wall and Roof Assemblies with Exterior Rigid Insulation

On the following pages we provide detailed illustrations for wall and roof assemblies, as well as wall-roof intersections, areas around doors and windows, and other areas of special concern.

The wall assemblies illustrate placement of the air-control layer, either a tape or fluid-applied membrane treatment of the sheathing joints, on the face of the exterior sheathing, which is typically ½″ OSB or plywood for structural rigidity and water vapor permeance. While we generally do not approve of exterior tape products because of concerns about durability, there are a small number of proven, durable products that should provide an airtight seal on sheathing joints for the life of the building.

They also call for a separate water-control layer on the outside of the insulation. This arrangement protects the insulation and air-control layers from moisture and allows less expensive products (Tyvek and Typar) to be used as a water-control layer. An alternative approach is to use a combined air/water-control layer on the face of the sheathing, in the form of a continuous fluid-applied or self-adhering sheet membrane. With this approach, you will want an insulation that is not affected by water and also some means of allowing water to drain between the insulation and the water-control layers. We suggest using insulation that has small drainage channels formed on the back side or installing a water-control layer product that has channels or vertical wrinkles for drainage. Additionally, we recommend the use of a vapor-permeable product to allow moisture to diffuse out of the wall assembly to the exterior when the vapor pressure drive is acting in that direction.

We also recommend the use of a variable vapor-permeable membrane on the inside of the insulation to provide a barrier to moisture migration into the insulation, while allowing it to diffuse to the building interior when necessary. The interior

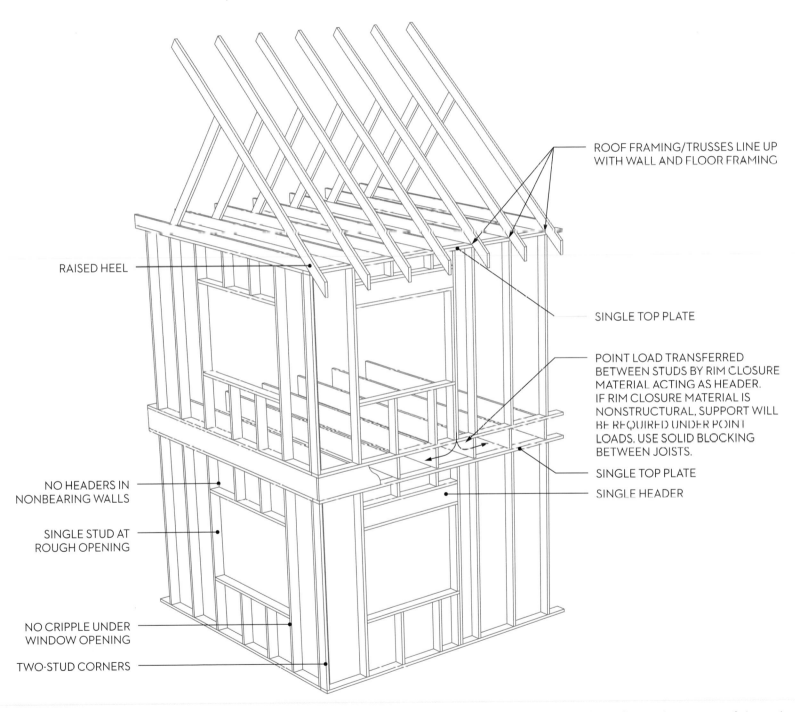

ROOF FRAMING/TRUSSES LINE UP WITH WALL AND FLOOR FRAMING

RAISED HEEL

SINGLE TOP PLATE

POINT LOAD TRANSFERRED BETWEEN STUDS BY RIM CLOSURE MATERIAL ACTING AS HEADER. IF RIM CLOSURE MATERIAL IS NONSTRUCTURAL, SUPPORT WILL BE REQUIRED UNDER POINT LOADS. USE SOLID BLOCKING BETWEEN JOISTS.

SINGLE TOP PLATE

NO HEADERS IN NONBEARING WALLS

SINGLE HEADER

SINGLE STUD AT ROUGH OPENING

NO CRIPPLE UNDER WINDOW OPENING

TWO-STUD CORNERS

FIGURE 12.1. Following these advanced framing instructions will save energy and construction costs by reducing the amount of thermal bridging through the wood framing.

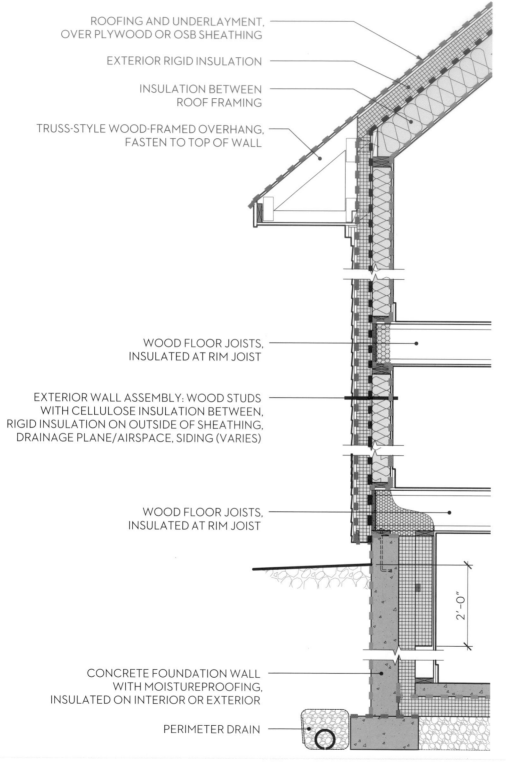

ROOFING AND UNDERLAYMENT,
OVER PLYWOOD OR OSB SHEATHING

EXTERIOR RIGID INSULATION

INSULATION BETWEEN
ROOF FRAMING

TRUSS-STYLE WOOD-FRAMED OVERHANG,
FASTEN TO TOP OF WALL

WOOD FLOOR JOISTS,
INSULATED AT RIM JOIST

EXTERIOR WALL ASSEMBLY: WOOD STUDS
WITH CELLULOSE INSULATION BETWEEN,
RIGID INSULATION ON OUTSIDE OF SHEATHING,
DRAINAGE PLANE/AIRSPACE, SIDING (VARIES)

WOOD FLOOR JOISTS,
INSULATED AT RIM JOIST

CONCRETE FOUNDATION WALL
WITH MOISTUREPROOFING,
INSULATED ON INTERIOR OR EXTERIOR

PERIMETER DRAIN

2'-0"

FIGURE 12.2. A typical wall section for single-frame construction with exterior rigid insulation.

finish is gypsum board, as it includes a reasonable amount of thermal mass, is durable, and can span 2' framing. Glass mat-faced gypsum products are best on the interior face of exterior walls because they do not have paper facing that can provide food for mold growth if moisture problems ever occur.

ABOVE-GRADE WALL WITH STRAPPING. Figure 12.3 shows a single-frame wall assembly with exterior rigid insulation. From the outside of the assembly, the finish material is a horizontal siding, which is attached to vertical wood strapping that is fastened through insulation to the wall framing. Proper fastening of the strapping to the studs is critical. Specialty fasteners have been engineered and tested specifically for this purpose. Manufacturers can provide information on the required horizontal and vertical spacing of their fasteners, using different thicknesses of insulation, to properly support varying dead loads (dependent on insulation and siding type).

The vertical strapping provides an airspace so that the drainage plane will function behind the exterior finish material. With no space, capillary action or atmospheric pressure can counteract the action of gravity, preventing water drainage. For the drainage plane, Tyvek, Typar, or a similar vapor-permeable material is appropriate. Joints between successive sheets of this material must be installed with the upper layers lapped over the lower layers, to prevent water from getting behind the sheets. With these materials, pinholes and small nail holes are tolerable, as there is no water pressure acting on them, and this layer is not acting as an air-control layer. A combined water/air-control layer could be used on the face of the sheathing.

ABOVE-GRADE WALL WITH SHEATHING. If you use shingles, you must install them on continuous sheathing instead of vertical strapping, which means you will need a different means of adding the airspace in front of the drainage plane for ease of fastening. A plastic matrix such as Home Slicker can provide a continuous space about ¼" over the water-control layer and behind the siding. There are also products that combine a matrix with a water-control layer to create an all-in-one air-space, water-control layer, and drainage plane.

Beneath the water-control layer are the secondary sheathing and the insulation layer. These can also be combined in one product, nail base foam insulation, saving on labor costs. However, you should spray foam and/or caulk all panel joints to prevent air movement and loss of insulation value. As in all of our building enclosures, the primary sheathing, attached to the wall framing, is used as the air-control layer. Thus, sheathing joints are sealed with fluid-applied membrane or tape systems.

SLOPED ROOF WITH CATHEDRAL CEILING, EXTERIOR RIGID INSULATION, AND STRAPPING (VENTED). For our typical cathedral roof condition, at least half of the R-value should be rigid insulation outside the structural framing, with half of the R-value inside the cavity. The outside rigid insulation should achieve R-30 to meet the net zero standard of R-60. This can be achieved with multiple layers of rigid board insulation, with overlapping joints, on top of sheathing installed on top of rafters or trusses. The joints of the sheathing on top of the rafters are sealed with a fluid-applied membrane or tape serving as the air-control layer. With this method, an additional layer of sheathing is needed above the insulation so that the roofing can be applied. This sheathing should be fastened onto 2× wood strapping, to provide a vent space to allow moving air to carry moisture under the sheathing and out of the assembly. This airspace is often required to satisfy shingle manufacturers' warranties and is also recommended to ensure a durable and long-lasting roof.

Cellulose should be applied nearly 9" deep to achieve R-30 in the roof cavity, so the rafters should be 2×10s, which are 9¼" actual depth. Even though the full 9¼" of cellulose will slightly exceed R-30, the rafter space must be completely filled with dense pack cellulose for proper thermal performance. As with walls, a variable vapor-permeable membrane should be used on the underside of the rafters to retard moisture migration into the rafter cavity and allow it to escape when needed. Recessed lighting should be avoided with such an assembly, as it will reduce the insulation value of the assembly. Any penetrations of the vapor-control membrane for mechanical, plumbing, or electrical utilities should be minimized as well, since it is challenging to seal such penetrations airtight.

SLOPED ROOF WITH CATHEDRAL CEILING, EXTERIOR NAIL BASE FOAM (VENTED). You can also use vented rigid nailing base panels on top of the cathedral rafter framing and sheathing. First, tape the joints on the structural sheathing or seal them with a fluid-applied air-control product, since this sheathing layer constitutes the air-control layer. Then install a nailing base panel on top of the structural sheathing. (Nail base panels have sheathing on one side of the rigid insulation only, as opposed to a SIP, which has finishes and/or sheathing on two sides.) Long nails or screws then fasten the panels to the framing. Any cracks between panels need to be filled with foam and/or caulk so the insulation layer is continuous. The water-control layer is then installed on top of the nail base panel, followed by the roofing material. Instead of using nail base panels, this same assembly can also be constructed by building it from separate sheathing and insulation materials. As described in the cathedral ceiling assembly above, a variable-permeability vapor-control membrane should be installed on the interior side of the rafters, and recessed lighting should be avoided and penetrations of the membrane minimized.

FLAT ROOF, UNVENTED. Flat roofs are similar to cathedral roofs but lack roof pitch. Because a pitch helps air movement and assists in drying if there is any moisture, a vented flat roof has less drying potential than a sloped roof with a comparable ventilated area. As discussed in chapter 10, the ideal inverted roof approach is the classic ideal wall turned 90°, and it is optimal, as it leaves the rigid insulation outside the water-control layer, so that the rigid insulation is not in an air-sealed space between the air- and water-control layers. Because the insulation is outside the water-control layer, it should be extruded polystyrene, the

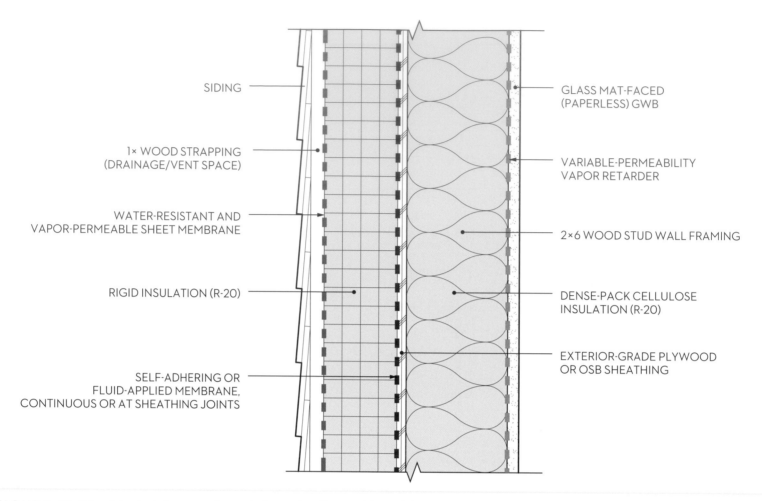

SIDING

1× WOOD STRAPPING
(DRAINAGE/VENT SPACE)

WATER-RESISTANT AND
VAPOR-PERMEABLE SHEET MEMBRANE

RIGID INSULATION (R-20)

SELF-ADHERING OR
FLUID-APPLIED MEMBRANE,
CONTINUOUS OR AT SHEATHING JOINTS

GLASS MAT-FACED
(PAPERLESS) GWB

VARIABLE-PERMEABILITY
VAPOR RETARDER

2×6 WOOD STUD WALL FRAMING

DENSE-PACK CELLULOSE
INSULATION (R-20)

EXTERIOR-GRADE PLYWOOD
OR OSB SHEATHING

FIGURE 12.3A. A typical above-grade single-framed wall assembly, with horizontal siding attached to vertical strapping, which is fastened through the exterior insulation to the wall studs.

FIGURE 12.3B. An above-grade wall using vertical strapping, fastened on the outside of the control layers, to support the siding.

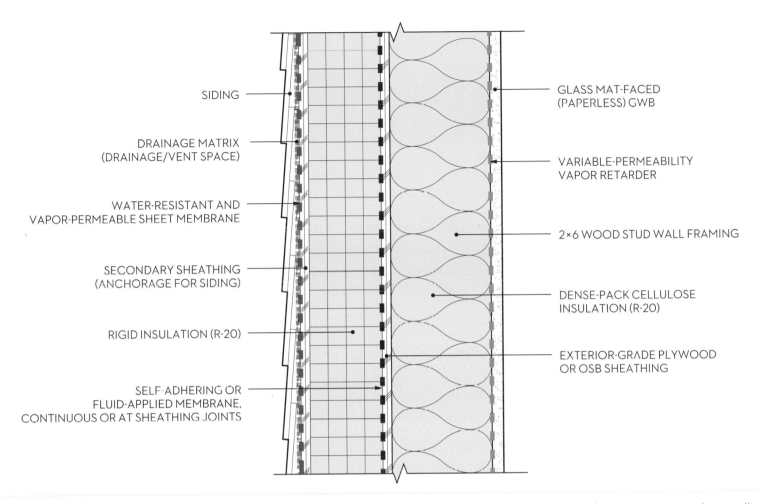

SIDING

DRAINAGE MATRIX
(DRAINAGE/VENT SPACE)

WATER-RESISTANT AND
VAPOR-PERMEABLE SHEET MEMBRANE

SECONDARY SHEATHING
(ANCHORAGE FOR SIDING)

RIGID INSULATION (R-20)

SELF-ADHERING OR
FLUID-APPLIED MEMBRANE,
CONTINUOUS OR AT SHEATHING JOINTS

GLASS MAT-FACED
(PAPERLESS) GWB

VARIABLE-PERMEABILITY
VAPOR RETARDER

2×6 WOOD STUD WALL FRAMING

DENSE-PACK CELLULOSE
INSULATION (R-20)

EXTERIOR-GRADE PLYWOOD
OR OSB SHEATHING

FIGURE 12.4A. A second layer of sheathing is sometimes added for attachment of the siding. In this case a drainage matrix may be installed over the outer sheathing to provide the airspace in front of the drainage plane, instead of strapping.

FIGURE 12.4B. A photo of an above-grade wall with a second layer of sheathing (hidden behind the drainage matrix and water barrier).

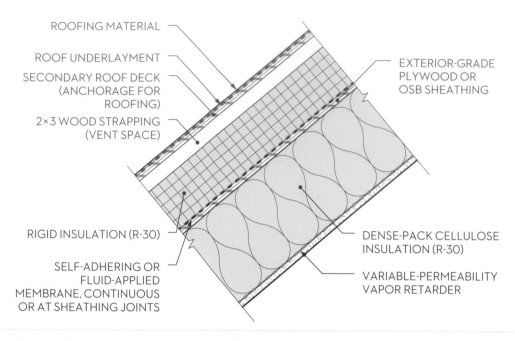

ROOFING MATERIAL

ROOF UNDERLAYMENT

SECONDARY ROOF DECK
(ANCHORAGE FOR
ROOFING)

2×3 WOOD STRAPPING
(VENT SPACE)

RIGID INSULATION (R-30)

SELF-ADHERING OR
FLUID-APPLIED
MEMBRANE, CONTINUOUS
OR AT SHEATHING JOINTS

EXTERIOR-GRADE
PLYWOOD OR
OSB SHEATHING

DENSE-PACK CELLULOSE
INSULATION (R-30)

VARIABLE-PERMEABILITY
VAPOR RETARDER

FIGURE 12.5. Sloped roof with cathedral ceiling, exterior rigid insulation, and strapping: This assembly provides cavity insulation and rigid insulation on the exterior of the structure, with strapping to provide ventilation as well as support for a second layer of sheathing for the roof deck.

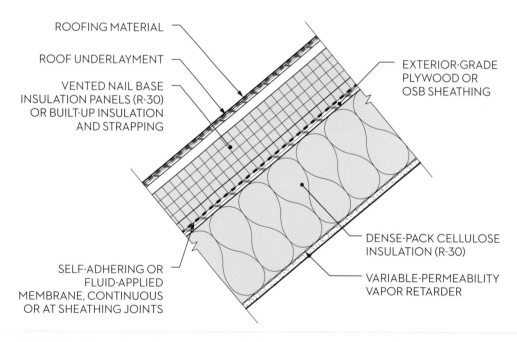

ROOFING MATERIAL

ROOF UNDERLAYMENT

VENTED NAIL BASE
INSULATION PANELS (R-30)
OR BUILT-UP INSULATION
AND STRAPPING

SELF-ADHERING OR
FLUID-APPLIED
MEMBRANE, CONTINUOUS
OR AT SHEATHING JOINTS

EXTERIOR-GRADE
PLYWOOD OR
OSB SHEATHING

DENSE-PACK CELLULOSE
INSULATION (R-30)

VARIABLE-PERMEABILITY
VAPOR RETARDER

FIGURE 12.6. Sloped roof with cathedral ceiling, exterior nail base foam: This assembly uses a nail base insulation panel that provides insulation, internal ventilation, and roof deck in one product, which is screwed on top of the roof structure.

most resistant to moisture of the rigid insulations. On top of the insulation, round ballast stones are needed to hold the insulation down. While this inverted roof is the best from a building science perspective, it is not commonly used, and there may be resistance from installers.

FLAT ROOF, VENTED. The next option is closer to a conventionally framed flat roof, except for added ventilation. This assembly has roof framing with cellulose between and sheathing above, with fluid-applied membrane at joints as the air-control layer. Rigid insulation is installed on top of the structural sheathing, with a 1.5″ airspace above the insulation, before a final layer of sheathing and a roofing membrane are installed on top. In a typical flat roof assembly, the membrane is placed directly on top of the rigid insulation, and water vapor can get trapped in the rigid insulation layer and cause deterioration over time, as it is not easy for water vapor to dry to the inside through the sheathing. Even though the roof is flat and will not move much air, if the air-control layer is carefully installed, the amount of water vapor will be relatively minor and differential air pressures from wind will provide an adequate amount of air for drying.

Common Single-Frame Intersections

At the transition from above-grade to below-grade construction, there are significant moisture conditions to address. Thermal continuity is also important at the junction of the walls and slab. For this reason, we recommend exterior insulation only for slab-on-grade conditions with single-frame walls. With the foundation insulation located on the interior, it is not possible to align the interior foundation insulation with the insulated wall above, thus creating a thermal bridge at this location. This is, however, an acceptable strategy with a thicker wall (see figure 12.30).

WALL/SLAB-ON-GRADE, EXTERIOR INSULATION. If pest-resistant insulation such as mineral wool or rigid fiberglass is used, the insulation layer can continue from the wall down the exterior of the concrete foundation. While mineral wool is not widely used in North America, this approach has the advantage of giving uniform thermal protection. When the foundation wall is insulated on the exterior, the below- and above-grade exterior insulation layers can align, and the slab-on-grade condition is feasible without thermal bridging (see figure 12.9). While we detail a slab-on-grade condition here, for a house with a basement having the thermal mass of the foundation wall inside the insulation is useful in retaining heat and providing a more stable interior temperature. The R-40 insulation levels should be maintained to 2′ below grade, and R-20 levels should be provided below that. Under the slab a minimum of R-20 insulation should be used, with the maximum insulation thickness practical at the edge of the slab.

PEST CONTROL IN WALL/SLAB-ON-GRADE WITH INTERIOR FOUNDATION INSULATION. Mineral wool insulation is not normally subject to infestation by pests, so when

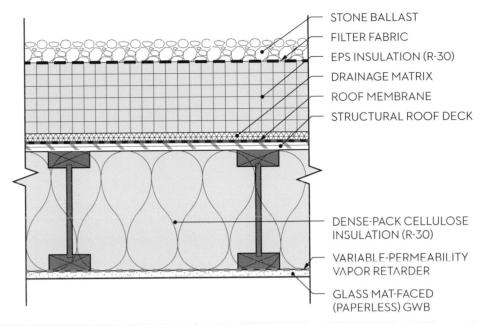

STONE BALLAST
FILTER FABRIC
EPS INSULATION (R-30)
DRAINAGE MATRIX
ROOF MEMBRANE
STRUCTURAL ROOF DECK

DENSE-PACK CELLULOSE INSULATION (R-30)
VARIABLE-PERMEABILITY VAPOR RETARDER
GLASS MAT-FACED (PAPERLESS) GWB

FIGURE 12.7. Flat roof, unvented. In this assembly, an inverted roof, the water-control layer is protected beneath the insulation layer and venting is not necessary.

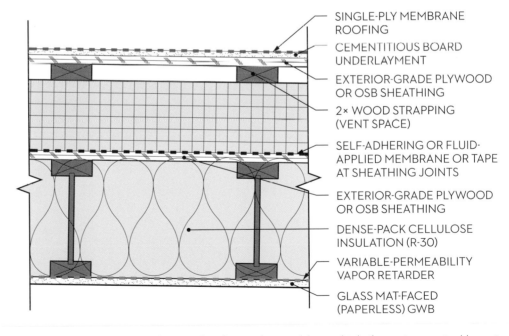

SINGLE-PLY MEMBRANE ROOFING
CEMENTITIOUS BOARD UNDERLAYMENT
EXTERIOR-GRADE PLYWOOD OR OSB SHEATHING
2× WOOD STRAPPING (VENT SPACE)
SELF-ADHERING OR FLUID-APPLIED MEMBRANE OR TAPE AT SHEATHING JOINTS
EXTERIOR-GRADE PLYWOOD OR OSB SHEATHING
DENSE-PACK CELLULOSE INSULATION (R-30)
VARIABLE-PERMEABILITY VAPOR RETARDER
GLASS MAT-FACED (PAPERLESS) GWB

FIGURE 12.8. Flat roof, vented. A flat roof assembly in which the water-control layer is on top, in which case venting below the outer sheathing layer is recommended.

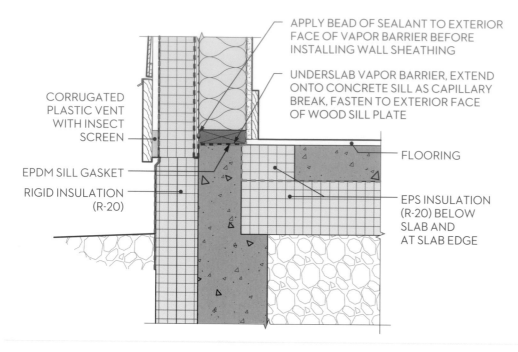

CORRUGATED PLASTIC VENT WITH INSECT SCREEN

APPLY BEAD OF SEALANT TO EXTERIOR FACE OF VAPOR BARRIER BEFORE INSTALLING WALL SHEATHING

UNDERSLAB VAPOR BARRIER, EXTEND ONTO CONCRETE SILL AS CAPILLARY BREAK, FASTEN TO EXTERIOR FACE OF WOOD SILL PLATE

EPDM SILL GASKET

RIGID INSULATION (R-20)

FLOORING

EPS INSULATION (R-20) BELOW SLAB AND AT SLAB EDGE

FIGURE 12.9. Wall/slab-on-grade, exterior insulation: A continuous thermal-control layer is provided on the outside, with additional insulation protecting the concrete slab on grade. (See also figure 12.11 for pest control.)

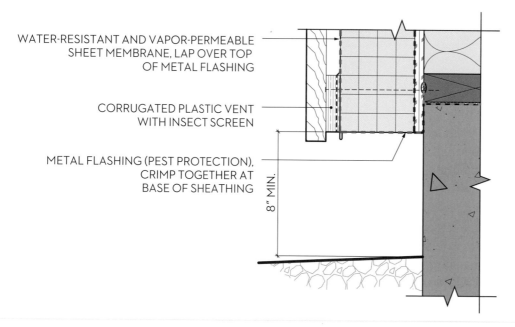

WATER-RESISTANT AND VAPOR-PERMEABLE SHEET MEMBRANE, LAP OVER TOP OF METAL FLASHING

CORRUGATED PLASTIC VENT WITH INSECT SCREEN

METAL FLASHING (PEST PROTECTION), CRIMP TOGETHER AT BASE OF SHEATHING

8" MIN.

FIGURE 12.10. Pest control in wall/slab-on-grade, interior foundation insulation: For pest-susceptible insulation types, metal flashing may be used to prevent pest intrusion.

it is used pest protection is not needed, and through-wall flashing can extend loosely below the insulation to drain water out of the bottom and direct it away from the base of the wall. Foam insulation, in all its various types, however, is susceptible to pests. A vinyl or metal flashing cover such as vinyl-coated metal should therefore be installed at the base of the wall to protect the bottom edge of insulation, as shown in figure 12.10. Because the end joints in the flashing strips are susceptible to pest intrusion, they should be lapped and sealed with a butyl sealant. The flashing detail illustrated here does not allow for any drainage from the bottom of the insulation, but the water-control layer is located on the exterior of the insulation, and most rigid foam insulations (excluding polyisocyanurate) do not absorb water.

PEST CONTROL FOR WALL/SLAB-ON-GRADE WITH EXTERIOR INSULATION. Figure 12.11 shows pest control for the exterior below-grade insulation option. A pest-resistant insulation such as mineral wool should be used for the below-grade exterior insulation, of course. A metal flashing located between the above-grade wall insulation and foundation insulation provides closure and protection of pest-susceptible insulation used on the exterior of the above-grade wall. As noted before, a complete closure is neither necessary nor desirable when mineral wool insulation is used for the exterior of the above-grade wall, since it must be able to drain away any moisture it may have absorbed.

FIRST FLOOR/BASEMENT WALL CONNECTION. The occupied space in the basement also adds concerns regarding moisture.

The connection of the air-control layer between concrete and wood framing is traditionally a weak link, as this is a junction of different structural systems and trades, and this joint needs to accommodate movement between concrete and wood. This can best be accomplished by using a continuous EPDM gasket below the bearing plate, effectively air-sealing the joint with a flexible material. The outside face of the sill plate must also be sealed to the back side of the exterior wall sheathing, for a continuous connection to the air-control layer. The insulation continuity can be maintained on the interior side of the rim joist with layers of rigid foam boards sealed with spray foam around the edges or by installing spray foam at a thickness adequate to provide R-20. (4" of high-density foam or 6" of low-density foam is sufficient).

UPPER-FLOOR RIM JOIST. The rim joist is typically another weak point in the envelope. The thermal-, air-, and water-control layers continue on the outside of the assembly. On the interior the insulation is maintained through the intersecting floor assembly behind the rim joist with layers of edge-sealed rigid foam or spray foam (R-20). Cellulose can also be used at the rim joist, but baffles are required to hold the insulation in place (figure 12.13).

ROOF-WALL, CATHEDRAL CEILING, SMALL OVERHANGS, STRAPPED OR SHEATHED WALLS. At the roof eave detail, the air-control layer needs to connect from the wall to the roof. It is best to make this connection as simple and direct as possible. To optimize the air-control layer,

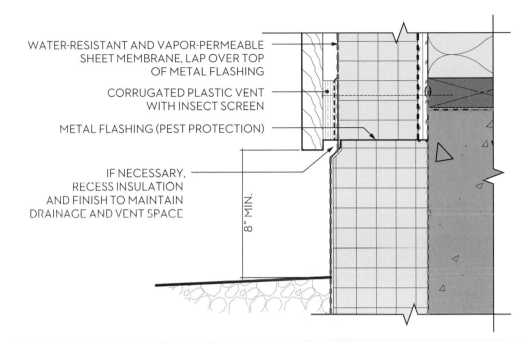

WATER-RESISTANT AND VAPOR-PERMEABLE SHEET MEMBRANE, LAP OVER TOP OF METAL FLASHING

CORRUGATED PLASTIC VENT WITH INSECT SCREEN

METAL FLASHING (PEST PROTECTION)

IF NECESSARY, RECESS INSULATION AND FINISH TO MAINTAIN DRAINAGE AND VENT SPACE

8" MIN.

FIGURE 12.11. Pest control in wall/slab-on-grade, exterior foundation insulation: If the above-grade wall insulation is not pest resistant, there should be pest-control flashing between insulation types.

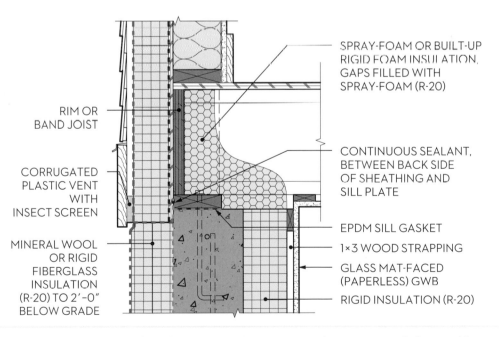

RIM OR BAND JOIST

CORRUGATED PLASTIC VENT WITH INSECT SCREEN

MINERAL WOOL OR RIGID FIBERGLASS INSULATION (R-20) TO 2'-0" BELOW GRADE

SPRAY-FOAM OR BUILT-UP RIGID FOAM INSULATION, GAPS FILLED WITH SPRAY-FOAM (R-20)

CONTINUOUS SEALANT, BETWEEN BACK SIDE OF SHEATHING AND SILL PLATE

EPDM SILL GASKET

1×3 WOOD STRAPPING

GLASS MAT-FACED (PAPERLESS) GWB

RIGID INSULATION (R-20)

FIGURE 12.12. First floor/basement wall connection: The continuity of all control layers must be maintained at this critical connection.

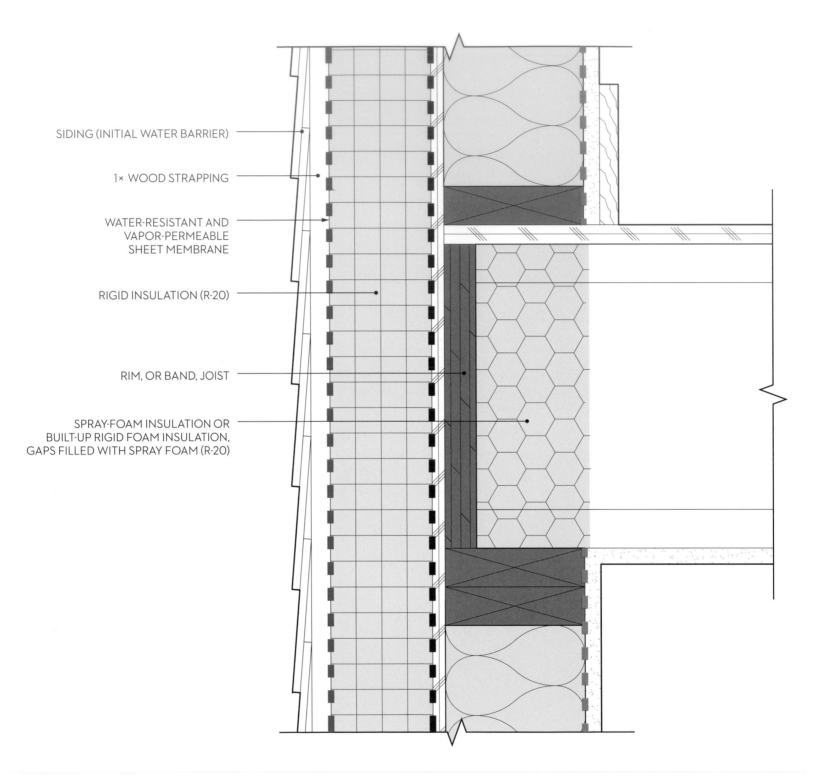

SIDING (INITIAL WATER BARRIER)

1× WOOD STRAPPING

WATER-RESISTANT AND
VAPOR-PERMEABLE
SHEET MEMBRANE

RIGID INSULATION (R-20)

RIM, OR BAND, JOIST

SPRAY-FOAM INSULATION OR
BUILT-UP RIGID FOAM INSULATION,
GAPS FILLED WITH SPRAY FOAM (R-20)

FIGURE 12.13. At the intersection of the floor joists with the wall, the continuity of the water-, air-, and exterior thermal-control layers is easily accomplished. Continuity of the interior thermal layer is provided by adding insulation between the ends of the joists.

the sheathing of the wall and roof should touch, and the air-control layers of the two should overlap. With short overhangs where the eave is supported by extensions of the roof framing, the multitude of framing penetrations through the top of the wall sheathing compromises the control layer. However, as shown in figure 12.14, the air-control layer can wrap out and around the eave blocking instead, with minimal additional framing, to provide continuity between the wall and the roof air-control layers.

ROOF/WALL, CATHEDRAL CEILING, LARGE OVERHANGS. Net zero buildings in cold climates often use large overhangs to protect buildings from the weather. In warmer climates, gutters and downspouts work well in getting water runoff from the roof to the ground without damaging the siding. In cold climates gutters get plugged with ice and snow, so roofs are often designed without gutters, causing backsplash at the ground, which discolors the siding and can shorten its life. Larger roof overhangs of 2 feet or more keep most water off the wall, making this a more durable solution. However, larger overhangs present a challenge in making a continuous air-control layer from the roof to the wall. Continuity can be achieved by wrapping the air-control layer all the way around the soffit sheathing and fascia boards to meet the roof sheathing. While this creates a relatively airtight cavity, any moisture that gets into the cavity may eventually rot the overhang. A preferable approach is to continue the air-control layer directly behind from wall to roof, as shown in figure 12.15. To do this, attach prebuilt, separate trusslike frames to the side of the exterior wall after the air-control layer is installed. These frames can be fabricated on the ground, in a shop, or at a truss-manufacturing facility. This measure also improves construction quality because large rafter overhangs are often difficult to frame, since rafters typically are not straight. The structural roof sheathing is the air-control layer, with joints sealed with fluid-applied membrane. Figure 12.15 shows this condition with sheathed walls, but it is applicable to strapped walls as well. This detail can be used with either a vented or an unvented roof.

ROOF-WALL INTERSECTION WITH FLAT, UNVENTED ROOF. Where an inverted flat roof meets the wall, the wall and roof sheathing can be designed to connect, and the air-control layers can be connected with peel-and-stick membrane or fluid-applied

membrane. Where a parapet occurs, these layers may need to continue up and over the parapet in order to provide the continuity from roof to wall. As with all flat roofs, there need to be scuppers or interior drains to allow water to drain off the roof. The roof side of the parapet should be covered with the roofing membrane so that water can build up against the parapet without damage, in case the scupper or interior drain is blocked and emergency drains or scuppers are blocked as well. The roof should also be designed to carry the additional load of water as high as the parapet wall in the event of such an emergency. As indicated in figure 12.16, additional insulation at the roof-wall intersection on the inside can ensure that insulation levels are maintained.

ROOF-WALL INTERSECTION WITH FLAT, VENTED ROOF. This roof-wall connection detail (shown in figure 12.17) is closer to a typical framed flat roof detail, except that it has an airspace. Wall and roof framing both have sheathing on the outside that connects at the wall-roof intersection, so it is easy to connect the sheathing and membrane air-control layers at this joint. An airspace at the soffit connects with the vent space below the roof deck, allowing air and/or vapor to escape from the wall and/or roof assembly. At the roof-wall intersection there is a small wall and/or blocking that reduces the insulation value at the corner. As in the previous detail, the addition of insulation at the interior framing joint eliminates this thermal bridge.

Single-Frame Window Openings

Window openings are a weak link in the control layers, particularly with the water-control layer. As with all assemblies, windows need to be placed and detailed to keep all control layers continuous. The window needs to be located in the wall so that the insulated glass aligns with the exterior insulation layers. This causes less shading of the glass for better solar gain and daylighting. To do this, window needs to be supported on a projecting sill, or buck, to align it with the insulation plane, and this may need to be made from engineered lumber, especially for larger and heavier windows.

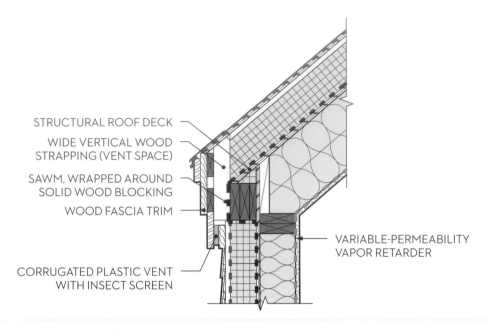

STRUCTURAL ROOF DECK

WIDE VERTICAL WOOD STRAPPING (VENT SPACE)

SAWM, WRAPPED AROUND SOLID WOOD BLOCKING

WOOD FASCIA TRIM

CORRUGATED PLASTIC VENT WITH INSECT SCREEN

VARIABLE-PERMEABILITY VAPOR RETARDER

FIGURE 12.14. The roof-to-wall connection is another place where extra care must be taken to provide continuity of the control layers. Discontinuity of the water-control layer is usually acceptable, however, as long as there is adequate overlap.

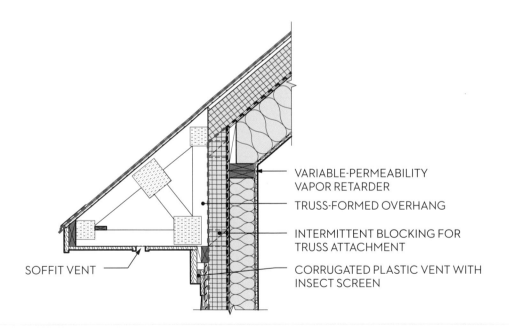

VARIABLE-PERMEABILITY VAPOR RETARDER

TRUSS-FORMED OVERHANG

INTERMITTENT BLOCKING FOR TRUSS ATTACHMENT

CORRUGATED PLASTIC VENT WITH INSECT SCREEN

SOFFIT VENT

FIGURE 12.15. Roof-wall, cathedral ceiling, large overhangs, strapped or sheathed walls: A large overhang, separation of the overhang structure from the main roof structure allows for a simple and direct connection of the layers at the roof-wall intersection. Again, the water-control layers overlap and are not required to be directly connected in this case.

WINDOWSILL. The sill detail for single-frame wood construction is very similar to the concrete and steel sill detail. As figure 12.18 shows, the sill flashing, FlexWrap NF, must lap over and adhere to the water-control layer below the window opening. It must also turn up at the back side of the window frame to form a dam (after installation of low-expanding spray foam to insulate the gap between frame and rough sill). The FlexWrap NF is then sealed to the window frame at this location for the air seal. The ends of the FlexWrap NF must turn up the sides of the rough opening at the jamb. The sill flashing is installed before the window is installed, protecting the corners from water intrusion. This is overlapped by, but not sealed to, a flange on the window (common to residential/light commercial windows) that extends beyond the frame.

WINDOW JAMB. The water- and air-control layer components in the window jamb must also be installed before the window, lapping over the top of the upturned sill flashing, as shown in figure 12.19. The air-control layer is applied to the face of the exterior sheathing—or at least the joints—and the air-control layer is lapped onto a plastic angle at the edge of the rough opening. This angle provides something rigid and impermeable at the edge of the insulation that the window can be sealed to later from the interior, to provide continuity of the air-control layer.

The window nailing flange is often used to attach the window unit to the rough opening. Where possible, this is the preferred way to fasten the window, by means of long screws into the rough opening framing. Clips may also be used at the jambs with many windows, as with the concrete/steel window detail, but they are small thermal bridges and, more important, an obstruction to the installation of the flexible air sealant near the interior edge of the window frame. This detail should be reviewed and approved by the window manufacturer. Given the sill support, fastening through the nailing flange should be more than adequate.

WINDOW HEAD. At the window head (figure 12.20), the air-control layer is lapped onto a rigid plastic angle at the edge of the rough opening, for air-sealing to the window after installation. At the head, strapping is installed across the top of the opening to fully support the wood trim. FlexWrap NF is installed over this blocking. It is lapped over the window flange and top edge of the window frame and turned down at the corners to cover the top of the jamb flashing. Metal head flashing is usually installed over the top of the window to direct water or moisture away. This flashing should be installed over the FlexWrap NF. The water-control layer is installed to lap over the top of the FlexWrap NF and the head flashing for proper drainage. Sometimes drip flashing is installed above the wood head trim, as shown in the detail. It can be installed in front of the water-control layer, as most of the moisture that gets through the siding will drain down the back side of it, diverted by the drip flashing. At the base of the drainage/vent space, installation of a screened vent or plastic matrix is recommended to keep insects out.

As with the jambs and sill, after the window is installed, the gap

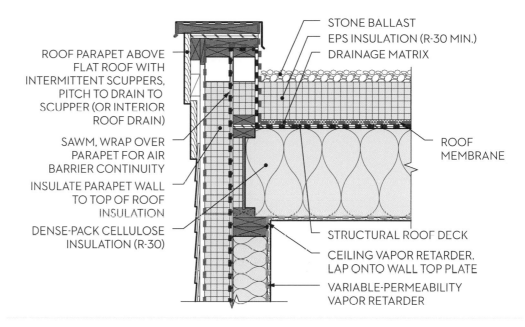

FIGURE 12.16. Roof-wall intersection, flat roof, unvented: The control layers must lap up and over the parapet, so that roof control layers can connect to wall control layers.

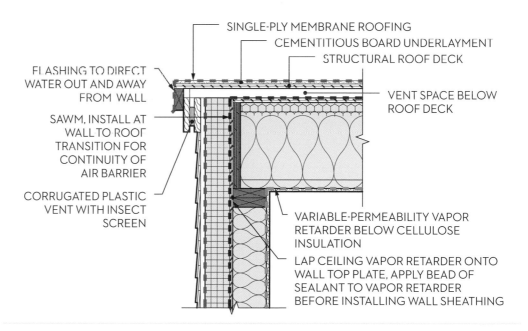

FIGURE 12.17. Roof-wall, flat roof, vented: In this example of a vented roof-wall connection, the roof air- and water-control layers are separate but connected to the wall control layers (with the exception of the overlapping water-control layer).

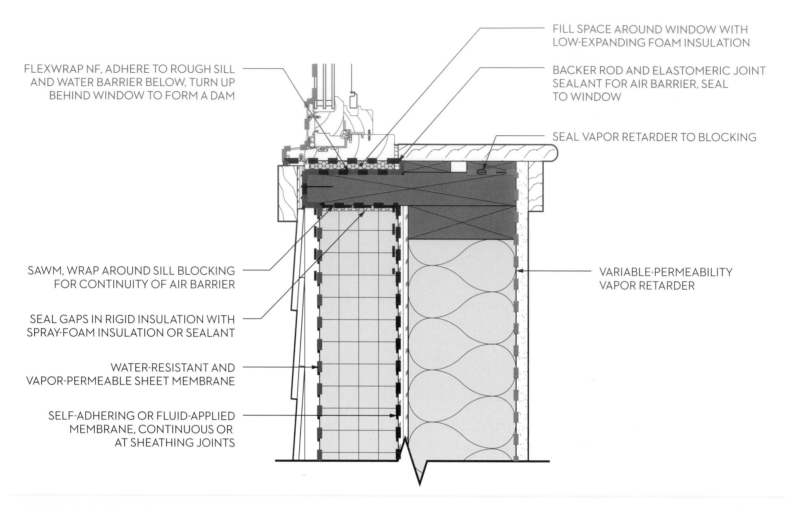

FILL SPACE AROUND WINDOW WITH
LOW-EXPANDING FOAM INSULATION

FLEXWRAP NF, ADHERE TO ROUGH SILL
AND WATER BARRIER BELOW, TURN UP
BEHIND WINDOW TO FORM A DAM

BACKER ROD AND ELASTOMERIC JOINT
SEALANT FOR AIR BARRIER, SEAL
TO WINDOW

SEAL VAPOR RETARDER TO BLOCKING

SAWM, WRAP AROUND SILL BLOCKING
FOR CONTINUITY OF AIR BARRIER

VARIABLE-PERMEABILITY
VAPOR RETARDER

SEAL GAPS IN RIGID INSULATION WITH
SPRAY-FOAM INSULATION OR SEALANT

WATER-RESISTANT AND
VAPOR-PERMEABLE SHEET MEMBRANE

SELF-ADHERING OR FLUID-APPLIED
MEMBRANE, CONTINUOUS OR
AT SHEATHING JOINTS

FIGURE 12.18A. This detail shows a window installed in the plane of the continuous insulation, supported on cantilevered wood blocking, or wood buck. Water- and air-control layers must wrap around this blocking to provide a seal to the bottom of the window frame.

FIGURE 12.18B. This windowsill blocking is wrapped with FlexWrap NF, which can stretch to be turned up at the ends of the sill, a significant improvement over the cut and lapped corners necessary with typical flashing products.

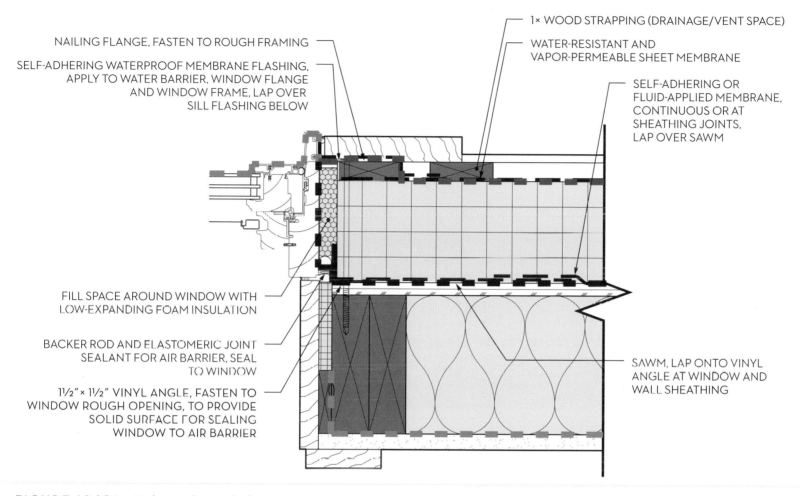

NAILING FLANGE, FASTEN TO ROUGH FRAMING

SELF-ADHERING WATERPROOF MEMBRANE FLASHING, APPLY TO WATER BARRIER, WINDOW FLANGE AND WINDOW FRAME, LAP OVER SILL FLASHING BELOW

1× WOOD STRAPPING (DRAINAGE/VENT SPACE)

WATER-RESISTANT AND VAPOR-PERMEABLE SHEET MEMBRANE

SELF-ADHERING OR FLUID-APPLIED MEMBRANE, CONTINUOUS OR AT SHEATHING JOINTS, LAP OVER SAWM

FILL SPACE AROUND WINDOW WITH LOW-EXPANDING FOAM INSULATION

BACKER ROD AND ELASTOMERIC JOINT SEALANT FOR AIR BARRIER, SEAL TO WINDOW

1½" × 1½" VINYL ANGLE, FASTEN TO WINDOW ROUGH OPENING, TO PROVIDE SOLID SURFACE FOR SEALING WINDOW TO AIR BARRIER

SAWM, LAP ONTO VINYL ANGLE AT WINDOW AND WALL SHEATHING

FIGURE 12.19A. At the window jamb the water-control layer connects to the window at the exterior side of the frame, and the air-control layer is sealed to the interior side of the window frame, making the window an integral part of the control layers.

FIGURE 12.19B. The window has been installed, and self-adhering flashing has been applied to lap onto the window frame and the water-control layer.

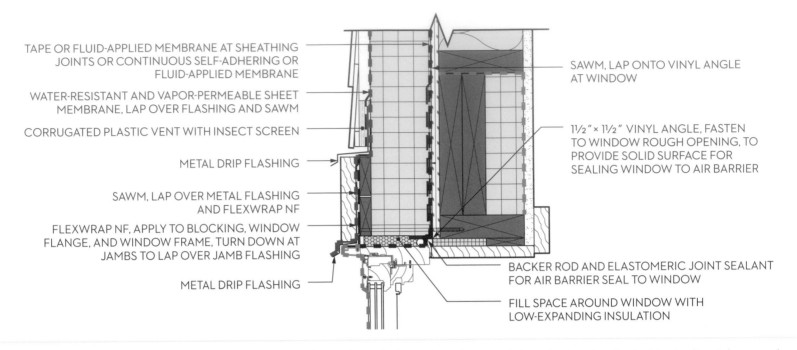

TAPE OR FLUID-APPLIED MEMBRANE AT SHEATHING JOINTS OR CONTINUOUS SELF-ADHERING OR FLUID-APPLIED MEMBRANE

WATER-RESISTANT AND VAPOR-PERMEABLE SHEET MEMBRANE, LAP OVER FLASHING AND SAWM

CORRUGATED PLASTIC VENT WITH INSECT SCREEN

METAL DRIP FLASHING

SAWM, LAP OVER METAL FLASHING AND FLEXWRAP NF

FLEXWRAP NF, APPLY TO BLOCKING, WINDOW FLANGE, AND WINDOW FRAME, TURN DOWN AT JAMBS TO LAP OVER JAMB FLASHING

METAL DRIP FLASHING

SAWM, LAP ONTO VINYL ANGLE AT WINDOW

1½" × 1½" VINYL ANGLE, FASTEN TO WINDOW ROUGH OPENING, TO PROVIDE SOLID SURFACE FOR SEALING WINDOW TO AIR BARRIER

BACKER ROD AND ELASTOMERIC JOINT SEALANT FOR AIR BARRIER SEAL TO WINDOW

FILL SPACE AROUND WINDOW WITH LOW-EXPANDING INSULATION

FIGURE 12.20. This window head detail is very similar to the jamb detail (figure 12.19), with the addition of metal flashing to divert downward-flowing water outward and beyond the window frame.

between window and rough opening needs to be filled with low-expanding spray-foam insulation, then sealed with flexible sealant for the air-control layer.

Single-Frame Door Openings

Door openings also must be detailed and constructed properly so that water does not get into the wall assembly.

DOOR SILL. With concrete slab-on-grade construction, the door sill detail is similar to that for concrete and steel construction. The condition we have illustrated in figure 12.21, however, applies to a sill installed on a wood-floor assembly above a basement, with a wooden deck or porch on the exterior. The door is in-swinging and therefore is not installed as far to the exterior as the windows, though it is still aligned with the insulated stud cavity. The aluminum door threshold is wide enough to extend over the top of the exterior insulation layer and has a thermal break located beneath the door. The outer edge of

the door cannot be supported by the rigid insulation, so the detail incorporates a fiberglass angle, which is less conductive than metal, with 2× blocking on top for attaching the threshold. The angle is fastened securely to the rim joist. In a single-family home without accessibility requirements, a wood threshold is typically used, which is adequate thermally.

Under the sill, FlexWrap NF is installed before the door and threshold are installed. It is lapped over the outside face of the blocking and lapped and adhered to the water-control layer below (installed on the face of the exterior insulation). The FlexWrap NF is turned up 6" or so at the jambs to protect the corners just as it is for windowsills. When the threshold is installed, it is set in a continuous bed of sealant for a watertight seal. In addition, a metal drip flashing may be installed under the outside edge of the threshold to keep water from getting behind the wood apron, or sill trim. The air-control layer is applied to the face of the sheathing and, because it will be penetrated by fasteners for the fiberglass angle, should be a continuous self-sealing product under the sill, such as peel-and-stick membrane or fluid-applied membrane.

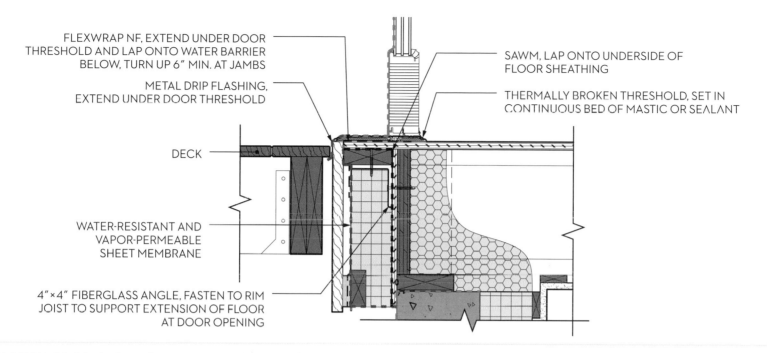

FLEXWRAP NF, EXTEND UNDER DOOR
THRESHOLD AND LAP ONTO WATER BARRIER
BELOW, TURN UP 6" MIN. AT JAMBS

METAL DRIP FLASHING,
EXTEND UNDER DOOR THRESHOLD

DECK

WATER-RESISTANT AND
VAPOR-PERMEABLE
SHEET MEMBRANE

4"×4" FIBERGLASS ANGLE, FASTEN TO RIM
JOIST TO SUPPORT EXTENSION OF FLOOR
AT DOOR OPENING

SAWM, LAP ONTO UNDERSIDE OF
FLOOR SHEATHING

THERMALLY BROKEN THRESHOLD, SET IN
CONTINUOUS BED OF MASTIC OR SEALANT

FIGURE 12.21. At door sills we recommend the use of FlexWrap NF under the door threshold, turned up at the jambs, and folded down over the sill blocking and onto the water-control layer below. The air-control layer must be sealed to the underside of the floor deck for continuity.

DOORJAMB. The door illustrated in figure 12.22 has a clad aluminum frame very similar to the window frame with nailing flange (figure 12.19). For that reason, the treatment of the water-control layer is the same. It is installed after the door is installed and laps onto the nailing flange and edge of the doorframe. At the bottom of the door, it must lap over the top edge of the upturned sill FlexWrap NF.

The air-control layer is treated differently at the door than the window, though, because of the door's location closer to the interior of the wall. Because the door partly aligns with framing for the rough opening, it is not necessary to install a plastic angle. The air-control layer is turned into the rough opening and sealed to the edge of the doorframe with backer rod and flexible sealant.

DOOR HEAD. Again, the door head in figure 12.23 is nearly the same as the window head detail (figure 12.20). The water-control layer and flashings are handled exactly as with the window. As at the doorjamb, the air-control layer should turn into the rough opening, where it can be sealed to the doorframe.

Double-Frame
Wood Construction

As discussed in previous chapters, double-frame wood assemblies reduce thermal bridging and therefore help achieve higher insulation standards. We have also described the potential condensation problems with double-framed and cellulose construction. Because of these concerns, an effective air-control layer to limit moisture transport by air movement is imperative. We also recommend installing a variable-permeability vapor-control product (such as MemBrain) inside the insulation layer to limit moisture migration into the assembly and allow it to escape if it does enter.

Figure 12.24 depicts a full double-framed wood assembly that addresses these concerns. The wall (and some roof) details shown here include a minimum of 2" of spray foam on the inside face of the sheathing. While this reduces the environmental benefit of this system and increases the cost, it is a long-term

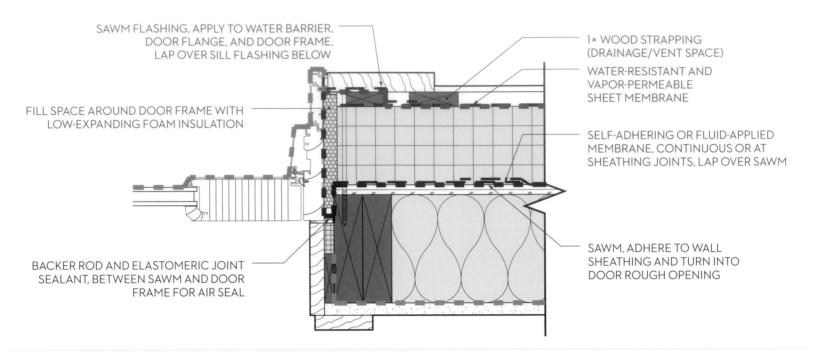

SAWM FLASHING, APPLY TO WATER BARRIER, DOOR FLANGE, AND DOOR FRAME, LAP OVER SILL FLASHING BELOW

1× WOOD STRAPPING (DRAINAGE/VENT SPACE)

WATER-RESISTANT AND VAPOR-PERMEABLE SHEET MEMBRANE

FILL SPACE AROUND DOOR FRAME WITH LOW-EXPANDING FOAM INSULATION

SELF-ADHERING OR FLUID-APPLIED MEMBRANE, CONTINUOUS OR AT SHEATHING JOINTS, LAP OVER SAWM

BACKER ROD AND ELASTOMERIC JOINT SEALANT, BETWEEN SAWM AND DOOR FRAME FOR AIR SEAL

SAWM, ADHERE TO WALL SHEATHING AND TURN INTO DOOR ROUGH OPENING

FIGURE 12.22. At the doorjamb, continuity of the water-control layer is maintained on the outside of the frame, while the air-control layer's sealant connection is made on the interior side of the frame.

durable solution. Most cellulose advocates believe this foam insulation is not necessary, but we suggest you err on the side of caution. In the roof assembly if a typical truss is used with eave and ridge vents, the condensation potential is very low, assuming air-leak control in the ceiling complies with net zero standards. These details thus involve multiple air-sealing measures essential to eliminating possible water-vapor migration and condensation issues. Coordinate this aspect with the designer, builder, trades, and possibly an engineer to avoid problems.

Double-Frame Wall and Roof Assemblies

A special consideration in double-framed wall and roof construction is the weight and pressure of the dense-pack cellulose used on walls and cathedral ceilings. To effectively air-seal and maintain insulation efficiency, dense-pack cellulose must be installed at a pressure of 3.5 lb. per cubic foot. This pressure wants to push apart the double framing in walls and roofs. Although 2×4s spanning up to 9′ in walls and rafters can accommodate these loads, higher walls or larger ceiling framing require either longer framing members or plywood gusset plates tying the two layers of framing together, as shown in figure 12.25. This is critical to avoid bowing of walls and the resulting need for repair during construction. Adequate fastening of the gypsum wallboard is also necessary to withstand pressures.

ABOVE-GRADE WALL WITH DRAINAGE MATRIX OR STRAPPING. Figure 12.25 shows our typical double-wall detail. As with our single-frame wall (figure 12.3), on the exterior we have an airspace, drainage plane, and water-control layer over the sheathing. The sheathing acts as the air-control layer with the same measures we used for the single-frame wall. The wall is shown with drainage matrix, though strapping could be used for horizontal siding. There are provisions for venting the top of the airspace behind the siding, to allow airflow through the space to carry moisture away. These are shown in the roof-wall connection details. A vapor-permeable membrane such as Tyvek or Typar

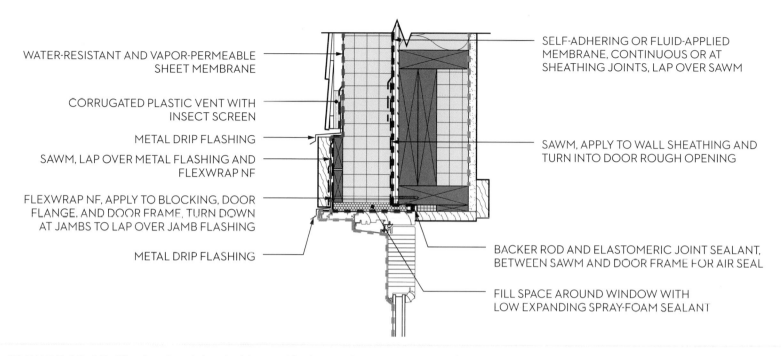

WATER-RESISTANT AND VAPOR-PERMEABLE SHEET MEMBRANE

CORRUGATED PLASTIC VENT WITH INSECT SCREEN

METAL DRIP FLASHING

SAWM, LAP OVER METAL FLASHING AND FLEXWRAP NF

FLEXWRAP NF, APPLY TO BLOCKING, DOOR FLANGE, AND DOOR FRAME, TURN DOWN AT JAMBS TO LAP OVER JAMB FLASHING

METAL DRIP FLASHING

SELF-ADHERING OR FLUID-APPLIED MEMBRANE, CONTINUOUS OR AT SHEATHING JOINTS, LAP OVER SAWM

SAWM, APPLY TO WALL SHEATHING AND TURN INTO DOOR ROUGH OPENING

BACKER ROD AND ELASTOMERIC JOINT SEALANT, BETWEEN SAWM AND DOOR FRAME FOR AIR SEAL

FILL SPACE AROUND WINDOW WITH LOW EXPANDING SPRAY-FOAM SEALANT

FIGURE 12.23. The door head detail adds metal flashing to divert water outward but is otherwise very similar to the jamb detail (figure 12.22).

is used as the water-control layer. On the inside of the sheathing, we have 2″ of spray urethane to protect the sheathing from condensation. On the inside face of the interior wall framing, we have a variable-permeability vapor-control layer such as MemBrain or appropriate interior finish and paint.

Virtually all of the same roof options that apply to single-framed wood walls apply as well to double-framed wood walls, using the outer wall framing for bearing. However, in this section we discuss truss or double-framed roof construction, which has all of the insulation located within the framing layer and none on the exterior. The reason for grouping these together is that these roof assemblies have the same challenges that the double-framed wall assemblies have in terms of moisture vapor and condensation.

Venting of roofs, whether attics or cathedral ceilings, is generally recommended and often dictated by building codes. Some require venting of rafter spaces, while others will allow unvented rafter spaces with air-impermeable insulation applied directly to the underside of the sheathing. In such cases codes may dictate a minimum thickness of such insulation when used in combination with another, air-permeable insulation.

SLOPED TRUSS ROOF WITH FLAT CEILING. The most common and economical wood-frame roof structure is constructed with trusses, which can span relatively large distances with a minimum use of wood resources. Because of the large spans, deflection should be calculated to minimize cracking of gypsum board at the interior ceiling-wall joint with snow loading.

The truss assembly requires ventilation from the eave to the ridge below the roof sheathing and above the insulation layer, to allow any moisture in the insulation layer to dry and prevent condensation on the underside of the sheathing (figure 12.26). Gable end vents cannot adequately vent this assembly. Because of the ventilation space below the roof sheathing, the air-control layer cannot be installed at the surface of the roof sheathing, as shown on the walls and other roof details, but must be installed on the bottom of the truss. MemBrain or other variable-permeability vapor retarder can be fastened to the bottom of the trusses, with the ceiling gypsum board below that.

Proper installation of this air-control layer is both challenging and critical for a durable roof. The control layer must have minimal penetrations, have all penetrations thoroughly

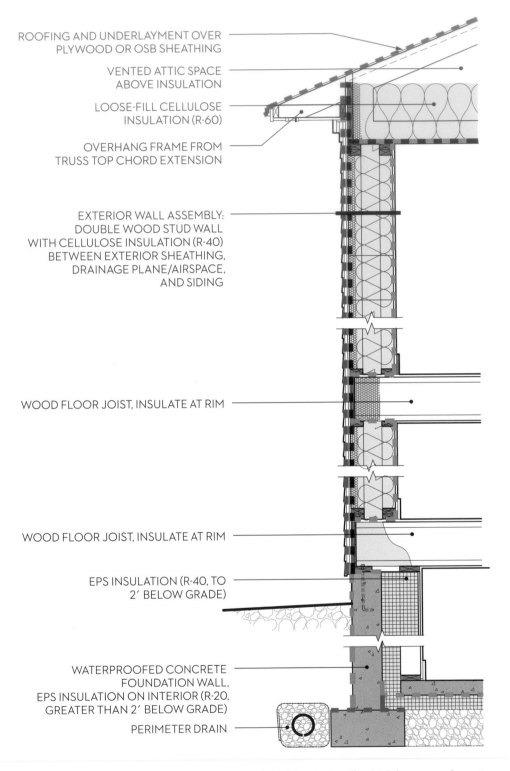

ROOFING AND UNDERLAYMENT OVER
PLYWOOD OR OSB SHEATHING

VENTED ATTIC SPACE
ABOVE INSULATION

LOOSE-FILL CELLULOSE
INSULATION (R-60)

OVERHANG FRAME FROM
TRUSS TOP CHORD EXTENSION

EXTERIOR WALL ASSEMBLY:
DOUBLE WOOD STUD WALL
WITH CELLULOSE INSULATION (R-40)
BETWEEN EXTERIOR SHEATHING,
DRAINAGE PLANE/AIRSPACE,
AND SIDING

WOOD FLOOR JOIST, INSULATE AT RIM

WOOD FLOOR JOIST, INSULATE AT RIM

EPS INSULATION (R-40, TO
2' BELOW GRADE)

WATERPROOFED CONCRETE
FOUNDATION WALL,
EPS INSULATION ON INTERIOR (R-20,
GREATER THAN 2' BELOW GRADE)

PERIMETER DRAIN

FIGURE 12.24. This section shows a typical double-stud wall, which has enough cavity depth to provide an R-40 thermal-control layer.

air-sealed and provide a difficult connection between the wall and ceiling air-control layers. The major challenges to this air-control layer location are the interference of interior wall framing and penetrations for lighting, electrical, and other systems. For this reason, we recommend either a properly installed vapor- and air-control product such as MemBrain or a thin layer of low-density open-cell spray foam on top of the vapor- and air-control membrane for air sealing. The open-cell foam allows for drying potential to the inside as well as the outside. While in theory this is redundant and could be accomplished by air-sealing specific penetrations, the continuous foam layer ensures a well-installed air-control layer. Above the foam, loose-fill cellulose provides the additional insulation to reach the R-60 level for net zero construction.

Even with this design, we still are likely to have some electrical, plumbing, lighting, and mechanical penetrations. At the walls we kept our air-control layer outside of the insulation, which meant that we could have interior wiring and other utilities in the wall cavity without cutting any holes into the air-control layer. When we put the air-control layer on the inside, lights, building, and other utilities may penetrate it. We recommend the use of wall-mounted, table, and floor standing lights, but for lights that must be ceiling-mounted, we recommend only surface-mounted fixtures, which minimize the size of ceiling penetrations. If lights are recessed, then a box with a sealed air-control layer around it must be installed within the insulation large enough so that the light can fit inside it and be totally air-sealed (complying with all code requirements to ensure that the light will not overheat). In addition, the box around the light must not lower the ceiling insulation level, so either insulation must be mounded up over the light or, preferably, the box must be covered with polyisocyanurate insulation, so that the same R-value of insulation fits in less depth.

SLOPED TRUSS OR DOUBLE-FRAME ROOF WITH CATHEDRAL CEILING, VENTED, WITH EXTERIOR AIR-CONTROL LAYER. Previous details showed cathedral ceilings with insulation within framing and exterior insulation outside of framing and sheathing. Cathedral roofs can also be built with separate rafters and dropped ceiling framing, deep I joists, or truss framing and all of the insulation below the roof sheathing. Maintaining the ventilation spaces on the outside of sheathing requires 2× strapping on top of the roof sheathing and a second layer of sheathing for roofing attachment, as indicated in figure 12.27. This system works well for complicated roof forms with dormers, as the 2×2 framing can be installed in multiple directions to connect ventilation spaces from all eaves to ridges. While many building professionals do not ventilate roofs, we think a long-lasting and resilient roof should have ventilation, in case moisture ever gets beneath the roofing. Ventilating a roof seems more important than ventilating walls, as most roofing materials are vapor-impermeable.

With the sloped truss or double-frame roof with cathedral ceiling assembly shown in figure 12.27, the air-control layer

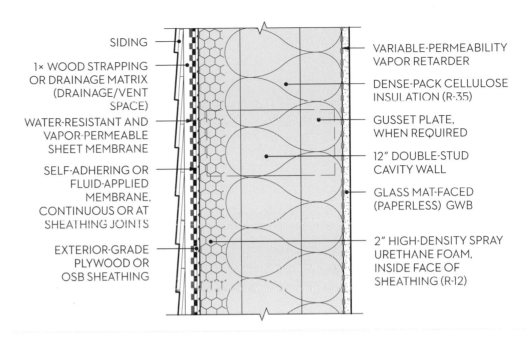

FIGURE 12.25. A double-stud wall assembly with cellulose insulation in the stud cavities, supplemented by 2″ of spray-foam insulation on the inside of the sheathing to control condensation and with the water- and air-control layers on the outside of the sheathing.

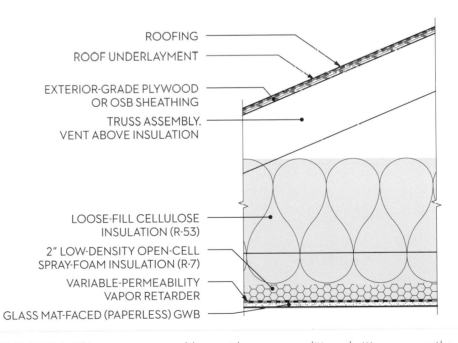

FIGURE 12.26. This common assembly provides an unconditioned attic space, as the thermal-, air-, and vapor-control layers are installed along the flat ceiling. The water-control layer (roofing) is installed on top of the exterior sheathing, which is ventilated below by the attic space.

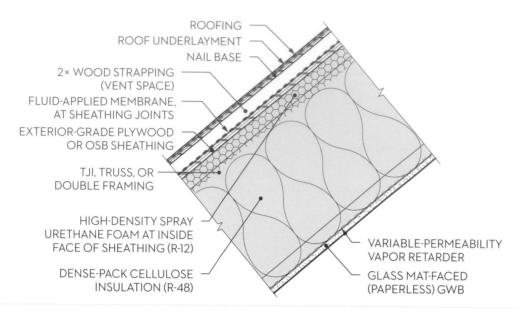

ROOFING
ROOF UNDERLAYMENT
NAIL BASE
2× WOOD STRAPPING (VENT SPACE)
FLUID-APPLIED MEMBRANE, AT SHEATHING JOINTS
EXTERIOR-GRADE PLYWOOD OR OSB SHEATHING
TJI, TRUSS, OR DOUBLE FRAMING
HIGH-DENSITY SPRAY URETHANE FOAM AT INSIDE FACE OF SHEATHING (R-12)
DENSE-PACK CELLULOSE INSULATION (R-48)
VARIABLE-PERMEABILITY VAPOR RETARDER
GLASS MAT-FACED (PAPERLESS) GWB

FIGURE 12.27. This roof assembly has two layers of plywood sheathing on top of the structure, with a ventilation space between. The upper layer, above the vent space, provides the base for the water-control layer. The lower layer of sheathing provides the base for the air-control layer. A variable-permeability vapor-control layer is located at the bottom of the assembly.

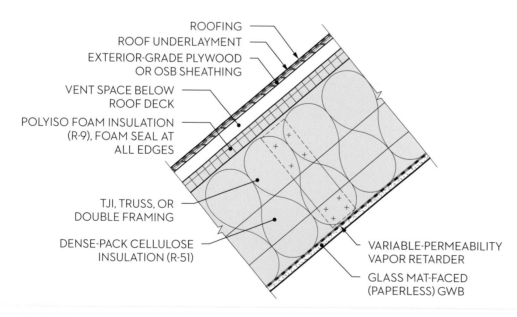

ROOFING
ROOF UNDERLAYMENT
EXTERIOR-GRADE PLYWOOD OR OSB SHEATHING
VENT SPACE BELOW ROOF DECK
POLYISO FOAM INSULATION (R-9), FOAM SEAL AT ALL EDGES
TJI, TRUSS, OR DOUBLE FRAMING
DENSE-PACK CELLULOSE INSULATION (R-51)
VARIABLE-PERMEABILITY VAPOR RETARDER
GLASS MAT-FACED (PAPERLESS) GWB

FIGURE 12.28. This vented roof assembly uses only one layer of plywood sheathing to support the water-control layer. An airspace for ventilation is created below this sheathing, between the framing members. The variable-permeability vapor retarder comprises the air- and vapor-control layers on the underside of the framing.

can be the surface of the lower layer of sheathing, which creates continuity without penetrations. The vapor-control layer must be permeable to allow ventilation. Semi-vapor-permeable paint will encourage the insulation to dry to the interior.

The depth of framing is determined by the level of insulation selected and can approach 18″ for cellulose insulation. Typically, this is deeper than the structural requirements, so a 2×4 or 2×6 dropped ceiling can be installed beneath the roof framing, but trusses and I joists can also be used economically.

SLOPED TRUSS OR DOUBLE-FRAME ROOF WITH CATHEDRAL CEILING, VENTED, WITH INTERIOR AIR-CONTROL LAYER.

Most builders do not want to build double roofs with ventilation above sheathing, as it adds labor and material costs. Another technique is to frame the roof with an airspace below the sheathing. As figure 12.28 indicates, this can be done with 1½″ thick polyisocyanurate insulation installed 1½″ below the sheathing between rafters.

The edges of the rigid foam must be spray-foamed to ensure continuous insulation and stop air movement into the vented space, where it can short-circuit insulation value. Below the rigid insulation, dense-pack cellulose can be installed to fill the cavity to the appropriate thickness if the structural roof framing is not deep enough (which often occurs), then a suspended 2× ceiling is needed to hold insulation. The dropped ceiling below must be designed to bear 3.5 lb. of insulation loading, plus the weight of gypsum board and framing, without sagging. Small plywood gusset plates can also support the dropped ceiling rafters.

This system works well on simple and smaller roofs. However, on more complex roofs ventilating from eaves to ridges requires cutting framing rafters and/or lowering hip or valley rafters and beams, all of which is labor intensive and sometimes nearly impossible. In addition, this system requires the installation of the air-control layer on the interior surface of the lower framing layer. As discussed in the section on roofs with flat ceilings and trusses, this installation is difficult to do well because of interior partitions and mechanical, electrical, and other penetrations.

SLOPED DOUBLE-FRAME ROOF WITH CATHEDRAL CEILING, UNVENTED, WITH HIGH-DENSITY SPRAY FOAM AND CELLULOSE.

Where buildings have complex roofs, ventilated roofs can become very difficult and expensive. While we normally don't recommend this approach, there may be an advantage to using an unvented assembly in such a situation, if allowed by the applicable building codes. With this assembly, the roof sheathing can be the air-control layer, or a combined air- and water-control layer can be applied directly to the sheathing to ensure a continuous, high-performing control layer.

Our recommendation is to use dense-pack cellulose, with a couple of inches of high-density spray foam on the underside of the sheathing. The high-density foam provides the same advantage it does for the cellulose wall assemblies: it is air- and vapor-impermeable, so it eliminates concerns about moisture condensation on the interior face of the sheathing.

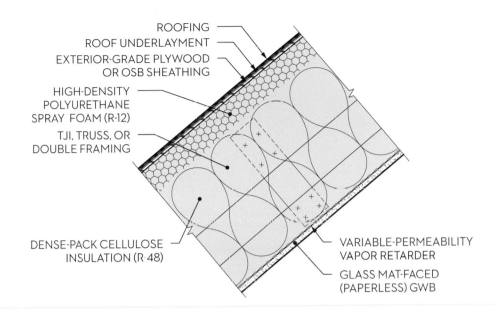

ROOFING
ROOF UNDERLAYMENT
EXTERIOR-GRADE PLYWOOD OR OSB SHEATHING
HIGH-DENSITY POLYURETHANE SPRAY FOAM (R-12)
TJI, TRUSS, OR DOUBLE FRAMING
DENSE-PACK CELLULOSE INSULATION (R-48)
VARIABLE-PERMEABILITY VAPOR RETARDER
GLASS MAT-FACED (PAPERLESS) GWB

FIGURE 12.29. This assembly does not provide venting and relies on a 2″ thick layer of spray-foam insulation to protect the sheathing from condensation. In this assembly, the water- and air-control layers occur on top of the sheathing. It also provides a variable-permeability vapor retarder on the bottom of the framing.

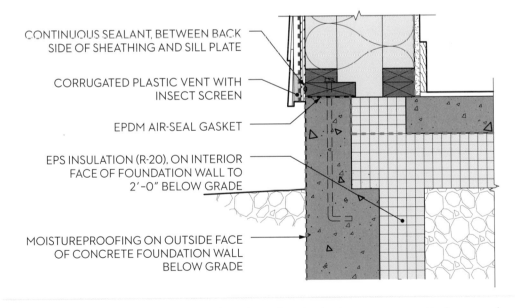

CONTINUOUS SEALANT, BETWEEN BACK SIDE OF SHEATHING AND SILL PLATE
CORRUGATED PLASTIC VENT WITH INSECT SCREEN
EPDM AIR-SEAL GASKET
EPS INSULATION (R-20), ON INTERIOR FACE OF FOUNDATION WALL TO 2′-0″ BELOW GRADE
MOISTUREPROOFING ON OUTSIDE FACE OF CONCRETE FOUNDATION WALL BELOW GRADE

FIGURE 12.30. The slab-on-grade with insulated edge becomes a practical approach when combined with the increased wall thickness of the double-framed wall.

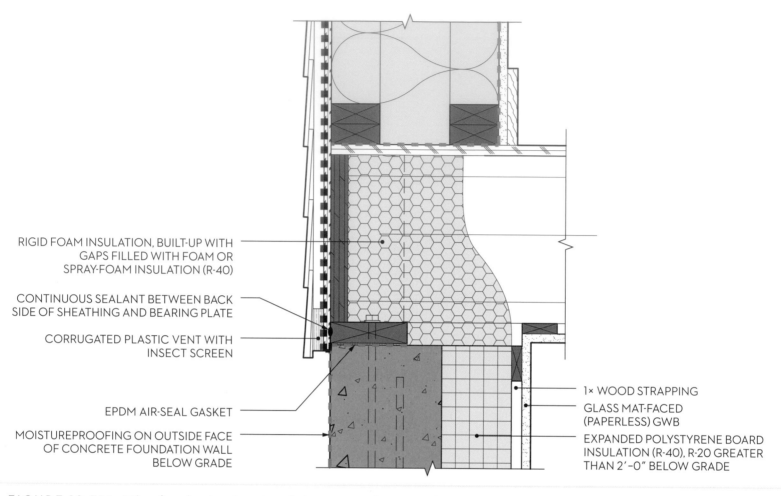

RIGID FOAM INSULATION, BUILT-UP WITH
GAPS FILLED WITH FOAM OR
SPRAY-FOAM INSULATION (R-40)

CONTINUOUS SEALANT BETWEEN BACK
SIDE OF SHEATHING AND BEARING PLATE

CORRUGATED PLASTIC VENT WITH
INSECT SCREEN

EPDM AIR-SEAL GASKET

MOISTUREPROOFING ON OUTSIDE FACE
OF CONCRETE FOUNDATION WALL
BELOW GRADE

1× WOOD STRAPPING

GLASS MAT-FACED
(PAPERLESS) GWB

EXPANDED POLYSTYRENE BOARD
INSULATION (R-40), R-20 GREATER
THAN 2'-0" BELOW GRADE

FIGURE 12.31A. When floor framing sits on top of a basement wall, an air-sealing gasket under the wood sill plate keeps the air barrier continuous. Insulation must be applied to the space behind the rim joist to provide an adequate thermal-control layer between the walls above and below.

FIGURE 12.31B. Spray-foam insulation is installed between the ends of joists above an interior-insulated basement wall.

It is critical to use double framing with this assembly so that there are no framing members extending from the exterior sheathing to the interior finish without a thermal break. With double framing, the depth of the roof structure can be adjusted to provide the depth required to provide an overall R-60 roof insulation value.

Common Double-Frame Intersections

Following is a discussion of common assembly intersections in double-frame wood construction. Some connections have similarities with single-frame intersections, while others require special solutions to maintain the continuity of the control layers.

WALL/SLAB-ON-GRADE WITH INTERIOR FOUNDATION INSULATION. With double framing, the above-grade wall is wide enough that it will conceal the insulated thermal break at the edge of the slab, provided the foundation wall thickness is reduced to 5" (the minimum practical limit) at the top, as in figure 12.30. The underslab insulation becomes the main thermal-control layer, but the rigid insulation on the interior of the foundation wall should continue at least 2' below finish grade.

FIRST-FLOOR-BASEMENT-WALL CONNECTION. Figure 12.31a shows the connection of first-floor framing to a basement wall. Insulating basement walls on the interior is the typical approach with double-framed walls, as they have no insulation on the exterior of the above-grade walls. An airspace and drainage plane is provided behind the siding—either 1×3 wood strapping or drainage matrix. If strapping is used, a screened vent gives pest protection at the base of the airspace. The wall water-control layer extends to the bottom of the exterior sheathing. The wall air-control layer is the exterior face of the sheathing, and continuity with the top of foundation is ensured, ideally with a flexible EPDM gasket. As with this same connection in single framing, the weak link in the thermal-control layer is at the floor framing. One solution for providing insulation behind the rim joist is to install enough layers of rigid foam insulation to reach R-40, cut to fit loosely into the space, then to fill the

gaps around the edges with spray foam. An alternative is to apply enough spray foam to provide insulation value of R-40.

UPPER-FLOOR RIM JOISTS. At the intersection of walls and upper-floor framing, there are no issues with continuity of the air-control layer, as the exterior sheathing serves as the air-control layer, and it is continuous on the outside face of framing. The same options for thermal insulation used for the first-floor framing can be used behind the rim joist here—rigid foam boards to attain R-40, sealed with low-expanding foam at all edges, or all spray foam to provide R-40. Because the air-control layer is continuous on the outside face of the sheathing, the MemBrain on the interior face of the wall can terminate at the top plate of the wall below and the sill plate of the wall above the floor, sealed and stapled through the sealant bead.

SLOPED TRUSS ROOF WITH FLAT CEILING. Roof trusses are typically the most economical way to build a durable, well-insulated roof in cold climates. They work very well for simple roof forms but not with more complex roof forms. As shown in the truss system section (figure 12.33), the attic is ventilated, and it is necessary to locate the air-control layer on the underside of the insulation, at the ceiling. Therefore, our air-control layer is moving from the outside of our wall sheathing to the underside of the roof truss. To connect these air-control layers, we recommend a peel-and-stick membrane applied to the exterior plywood, wrapped over the plate on the top of the stud wall and lapped down the inside of the wall. Then the ceiling-applied MemBrain can be sealed to and attached to the peel-and-stick. The water-control layer should continue up to the top edge of the exterior wall sheathing. It is therefore not continuous with the roof water-control layer, but this is acceptable because of the overhang of the roof deck, and it is a separate layer from the air-control layer.

Since conventional framing does not provide adequate height for insulation and ventilation, maintaining insulation levels at the wall-roof juncture requires some additional effort. Trusses with a raised heel need to be specified to allow the R-60 minimum insulation level to be maintained, along with the 1½" ventilation space. Premanufactured baffles are generally fastened to the underside of the roof sheathing to create the ventilation space. They should continue up above the insulation so the loose-fill insulation cannot be disturbed by air currents. Where the exterior wall sheathing extends up to the vents, there is usually solid blocking between the trusses for structural purposes. This blocking should be covered with 2″ minimum of spray foam to prevent condensation, as with the walls.

CATHEDRAL CEILING. The transition of the air-control layers from the exterior sheathing to the underside of the truss on the interior can be handled the same way as with the flat ceiling truss. As figure 12.34 shows, the major difference in the cathedral-ceiling assembly is the sloped ceiling, which provides a cavity for continuous R-60 insulation between double framing. This space must be ventilated from roof to eave to allow moisture to dissipate to the exterior. This requires continuous baffles from the eave vents to the ridge vents. The baffles must be strong enough to resist compression from the dense-pack cellulose installation, which could close off the vent space. Most premanufactured baffles are inadequate to resist this pressure, but custom baffles can be fabricated from strips of 1½″ thick rigid insulation board, installed with a 1½″ airspace above.

FLAT ROOF, UNVENTED, DOUBLE-FRAMED WITH HIGH-DENSITY SPRAY FOAM AND CELLULOSE. While we normally don't recommend this approach and it may not be allowed by locally applicable codes, there are times that an unvented assembly is used, usually due to cost and complexity. If so, the roof sheathing can be the air-control layer, ensuring a high-performing air-control layer, thereby reducing air and associated vapor movement (figure 12.35).

As with the unvented cathedral ceiling assembly, a 2″ minimum of high-density spray foam should be used on the underside of sheathing, to eliminate concerns about moisture and condensation within the structural framing. Also, double framing should be used with this assembly, to provide a thermal break in the framing.

FLAT ROOF, VENTED, DOUBLE-FRAMED. Figure 12.36 depicts a vented, double-framed flat-roof assembly. Note that like the truss with flat ceiling (figure 12.33) or vented cathedral (figure 12.34) assemblies, this assembly calls for a transition of the air-control layer from exterior sheathing to interior ceiling, and we recommend peel-and-stick membrane for this purpose. This

assembly is also very similar to the double-framed cathedral, except for being flat instead of sloped, which means a constant depth of R-60 insulation is provided between double framing. This space must be ventilated from roof to eave to allow for the dissipation of moisture to the exterior, requiring continuous baffles of 1½″ rigid insulation, leaving 1½″ airspace from the eave on one side of the building to the other.

An alternative approach would be to install 2×2 strapping on top of the roof sheathing and another layer of sheathing on top of that, to create a vented airspace above the roof sheathing. In this case, the sheathing directly on top of the framing can serve as the air-control layer instead of the MemBrain at the ceiling, which, as noted previously, can have challenges with penetrations. This also allows for a simpler transition from the wall air-control layer to the roof air-control layer. As with other similar assemblies, we would recommend installation of at least 2″ of spray foam on the underside of the roof sheathing to prevent condensation damage.

Double-Frame Window and Door Openings

Detailing around openings in double-frame walls presents some unique conditions that must be resolved, as discussed below.

WINDOWSILL. The sill detail (see figure 12.37) for double-framed walls is different from other construction types in this book in one significant respect: there is no exterior insulation and therefore no need for a cantilevered wood buck to support the window. The window sits directly on the rough opening within the framing, simplifying the wrapping of the vapor-control layer. The concept, however, is still the same as with sills at single-framed walls, and the materials and installation steps are identical. The sill flashing, FlexWrap NF, must lap over and adhere to the water-control layer below the window opening. It also must turn up at the back side of the window frame to form a dam (after installation of low-expanding spray foam to insulate the gap between frame and rough sill) and is then sealed to the window frame at this location for the air seal. The ends of the FlexWrap NF must turn up the sides of the rough

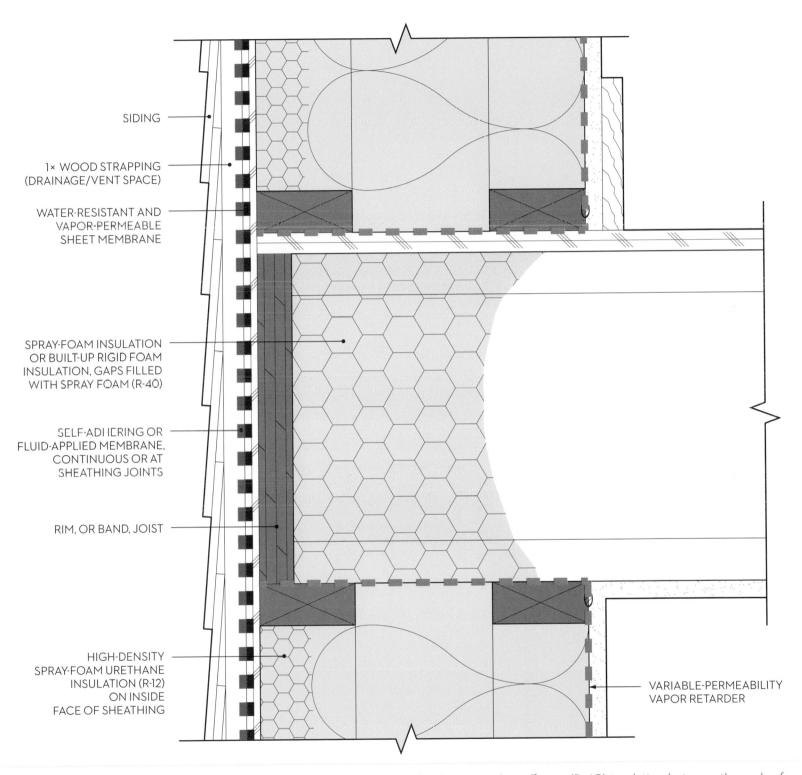

SIDING

1× WOOD STRAPPING
(DRAINAGE/VENT SPACE)

WATER-RESISTANT AND
VAPOR-PERMEABLE
SHEET MEMBRANE

SPRAY-FOAM INSULATION
OR BUILT-UP RIGID FOAM
INSULATION, GAPS FILLED
WITH SPRAY FOAM (R-40)

SELF-ADHERING OR
FLUID-APPLIED MEMBRANE,
CONTINUOUS OR AT
SHEATHING JOINTS

RIM, OR BAND, JOIST

HIGH-DENSITY
SPRAY-FOAM URETHANE
INSULATION (R-12)
ON INSIDE
FACE OF SHEATHING

VARIABLE-PERMEABILITY
VAPOR RETARDER

FIGURE 12.32. Where the joists of elevated floors meet exterior walls, there must be sufficient (R-40) insulation between the ends of the joists.

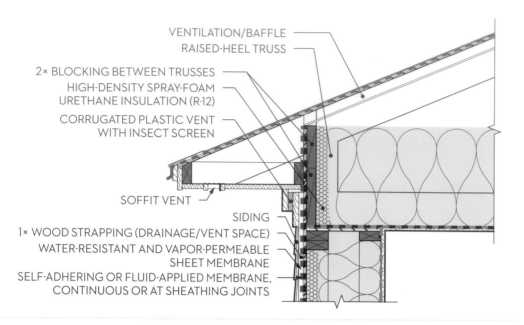

VENTILATION/BAFFLE
RAISED-HEEL TRUSS

2× BLOCKING BETWEEN TRUSSES
HIGH-DENSITY SPRAY-FOAM
URETHANE INSULATION (R-12)
CORRUGATED PLASTIC VENT
WITH INSECT SCREEN

SOFFIT VENT

SIDING

1× WOOD STRAPPING (DRAINAGE/VENT SPACE)
WATER-RESISTANT AND VAPOR-PERMEABLE
SHEET MEMBRANE
SELF-ADHERING OR FLUID-APPLIED MEMBRANE,
CONTINUOUS OR AT SHEATHING JOINTS

FIGURE 12.33. At this connection of a sloped truss roof with flat ceiling and a wall, a plywood bearing plate under the truss provides the transition plane for the air-control layer, from the interior ceiling to the exterior sheathing. The high-density polyurethane foam applied to the inside face of the blocking between trusses protects the blocking from condensation.

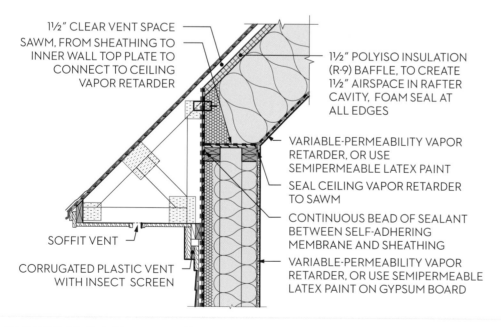

1½" CLEAR VENT SPACE
SAWM, FROM SHEATHING TO
INNER WALL TOP PLATE TO
CONNECT TO CEILING
VAPOR RETARDER

1½" POLYISO INSULATION
(R-9) BAFFLE, TO CREATE
1½" AIRSPACE IN RAFTER
CAVITY, FOAM SEAL AT
ALL EDGES

VARIABLE-PERMEABILITY VAPOR
RETARDER, OR USE
SEMIPERMEABLE LATEX PAINT

SEAL CEILING VAPOR RETARDER
TO SAWM

CONTINUOUS BEAD OF SEALANT
BETWEEN SELF-ADHERING
MEMBRANE AND SHEATHING

SOFFIT VENT

CORRUGATED PLASTIC VENT
WITH INSECT SCREEN

VARIABLE-PERMEABILITY VAPOR
RETARDER, OR USE SEMIPERMEABLE
LATEX PAINT ON GYPSUM BOARD

FIGURE 12.34. The air-control layer must connect from the interior ceiling to the exterior wall sheathing at the top of the wall. The exterior wall's water- and air-control layers continue straight up to the top of the wall, made possible by the separate truss framing for the large overhang.

opening at the jamb as well (where they will be covered after by the jamb flashing), to protect the corners from water intrusion. This flashing and the jamb flashing are put into place before the window is installed and are overlapped by, but not sealed to, a flange on the window (common to residential/light commercial windows) that extends beyond the frame.

In the double-framed wall assembly, we also recommend using a variable-permeability vapor retarder on the interior face of the wall. This sheet membrane must be turned into the framed window opening and sealed and stapled (through the sealant bead) to the window opening framing.

WINDOW JAMB. As figure 12.38 shows, there are differences at the jamb as well, compared to the other assembly window details. Because there is no exterior insulation, and the window is installed in the plane of the outer wall studs, there is no need for the rigid plastic angle for air sealing; the window can be sealed directly to the rough opening. The basic steps and materials are the same as with single-framed walls (figure 12.19), though. The water-control layer components must be installed before the window, lapping over the top of the upturned sill flashing. The air-control layer is, or is applied to, the face of the exterior sheathing and is turned into the rough opening so it can be sealed to the window frame. After the window is installed, the gap between window frame and rough opening is filled with low-expanding spray foam and air-sealed with backer rod and flexible sealant.

Again, the window nailing flange is often used to attach the window unit to the rough opening. This is the preferred way to fasten the window because metal anchor clips are small thermal bridges and obstruct the installation of the flexible air sealant near the interior edge of the window frame.

As with the windowsill, the variable-permeability vapor retarder on the interior face of the wall must be turned into the rough opening, stapled, and sealed.

WINDOW HEAD. At the window head (figure 12.39), the air-control layer is extended into the rough opening for air sealing to the window after installation, just as with the jambs. However, the water-control layer flashing, FlexWrap NF, is installed after the window installation, lapped over the window flange and top edge of the window frame, and turned down at the corners to cover the top of the jamb flashing. Head flashing is usually installed over the top of the window to direct moisture away from the top of the window, and this should be installed over the FlexWrap NF. The water-control layer is installed to lap over the top of the FlexWrap NF and the head flashing for proper drainage. Sometimes drip flashing is installed above the wood head trim, as shown in this detail. Since space must be provided here to allow for drainage, installation of a screened vent is recommended for a strapped wall at the bottom of the airspace to keep insects out.

After the window is installed, the gap between window and rough opening needs to be filled with low-expanding spray-foam insulation, then

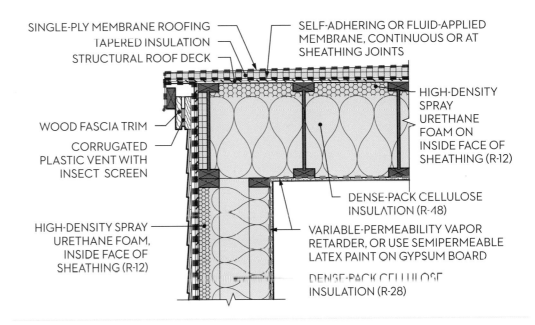

FIGURE 12.35. In this roof-wall connection detail, the roof's air-control layer is on the exterior of the roof sheathing, simplifying the connection to the wall's control layers.

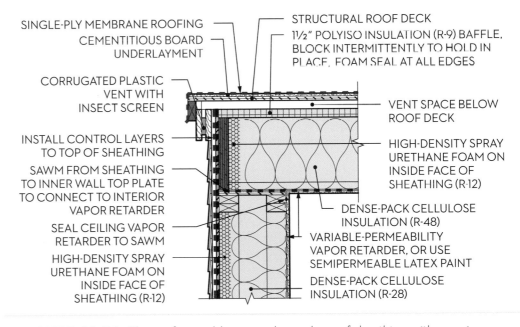

FIGURE 12.36. This roof assembly uses only one layer of sheathing, with a vent space below. Because the sheathing is vented below, the air-control layer is located on the bottom of the framing, and a connection to the outside wall sheathing must be provided.

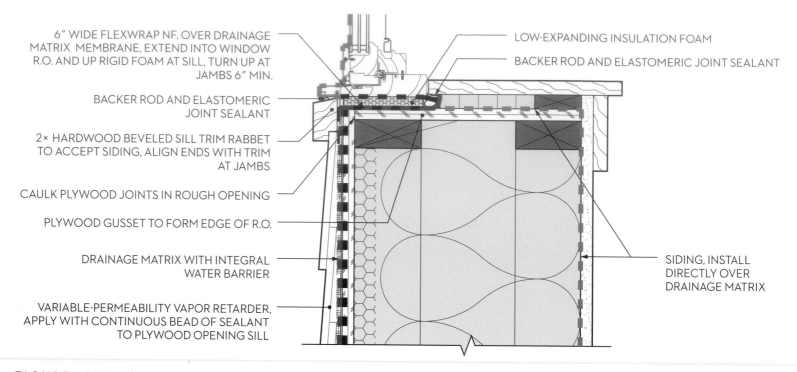

6" WIDE FLEXWRAP NF, OVER DRAINAGE MATRIX MEMBRANE, EXTEND INTO WINDOW R.O. AND UP RIGID FOAM AT SILL, TURN UP AT JAMBS 6" MIN.

BACKER ROD AND ELASTOMERIC JOINT SEALANT

2× HARDWOOD BEVELED SILL TRIM RABBET TO ACCEPT SIDING, ALIGN ENDS WITH TRIM AT JAMBS

CAULK PLYWOOD JOINTS IN ROUGH OPENING

PLYWOOD GUSSET TO FORM EDGE OF R.O.

DRAINAGE MATRIX WITH INTEGRAL WATER BARRIER

VARIABLE-PERMEABILITY VAPOR RETARDER, APPLY WITH CONTINUOUS BEAD OF SEALANT TO PLYWOOD OPENING SILL

LOW-EXPANDING INSULATION FOAM

BACKER ROD AND ELASTOMERIC JOINT SEALANT

SIDING, INSTALL DIRECTLY OVER DRAINAGE MATRIX

FIGURE 12.37. The exterior air- and water-control layers extend under the sill, and the air-control layer is sealed to the back edge of the window frame. The vapor-control layer connects to the windowsill blocking on the interior side.

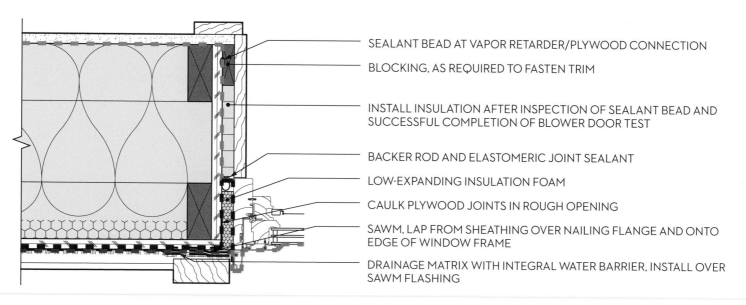

SEALANT BEAD AT VAPOR RETARDER/PLYWOOD CONNECTION

BLOCKING, AS REQUIRED TO FASTEN TRIM

INSTALL INSULATION AFTER INSPECTION OF SEALANT BEAD AND SUCCESSFUL COMPLETION OF BLOWER DOOR TEST

BACKER ROD AND ELASTOMERIC JOINT SEALANT

LOW-EXPANDING INSULATION FOAM

CAULK PLYWOOD JOINTS IN ROUGH OPENING

SAWM, LAP FROM SHEATHING OVER NAILING FLANGE AND ONTO EDGE OF WINDOW FRAME

DRAINAGE MATRIX WITH INTEGRAL WATER BARRIER, INSTALL OVER SAWM FLASHING

FIGURE 12.38. At the jamb the air-control layer extends into the window rough opening and is sealed to the interior edge of the window frame, as with the sill. This window is provided with a nailing flange, and thus the water-control layer is lapped onto the flange and the outside edge of the window frame.

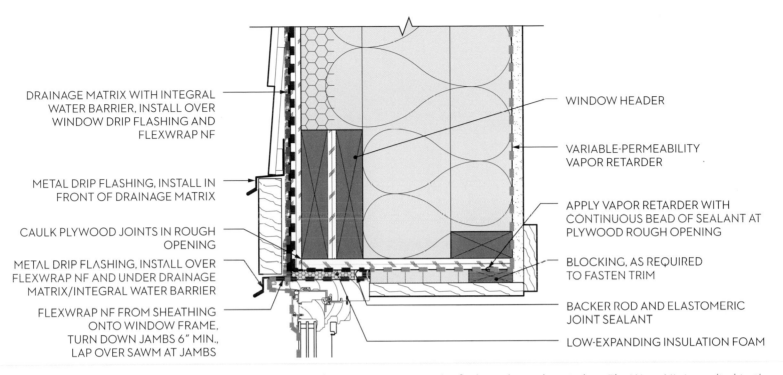

DRAINAGE MATRIX WITH INTEGRAL WATER BARRIER, INSTALL OVER WINDOW DRIP FLASHING AND FLEXWRAP NF

METAL DRIP FLASHING, INSTALL IN FRONT OF DRAINAGE MATRIX

CAULK PLYWOOD JOINTS IN ROUGH OPENING

METAL DRIP FLASHING, INSTALL OVER FLEXWRAP NF AND UNDER DRAINAGE MATRIX/INTEGRAL WATER BARRIER

FLEXWRAP NF FROM SHEATHING ONTO WINDOW FRAME, TURN DOWN JAMBS 6" MIN., LAP OVER SAWM AT JAMBS

WINDOW HEADER

VARIABLE-PERMEABILITY VAPOR RETARDER

APPLY VAPOR RETARDER WITH CONTINUOUS BEAD OF SEALANT AT PLYWOOD ROUGH OPENING

BLOCKING, AS REQUIRED TO FASTEN TRIM

BACKER ROD AND ELASTOMERIC JOINT SEALANT

LOW-EXPANDING INSULATION FOAM

FIGURE 12.39. This detail is similar to the jamb, aside for some revisions to the flashing above the window. FlexWrap NF is applied to the window head and turned down at the jambs (lapped over the jamb flashing), then metal drip flashing is installed to divert water out beyond the window frame. The water-control layer must lap over the top of the metal and FlexWrap NF flashings.

sealed with flexible sealant for the air-control layer. Also, the variable-permeability vapor retarder on the interior face of the wall must be turned into the rough opening, stapled, and sealed.

DOOR SILL. Because there is no exterior insulation, the door sill detail (see figure 12.40) is simpler than the single-framed detail, and the threshold can sit on and be attached to the floor deck instead of a fiberglass angle. The combined air- and water-control layer extends onto the floor deck and will be overlapped by FlexWrap NF, which must turn up at least 6" at the jambs and which will in turn be covered by the jamb flashing. As with sill details in other construction types, the threshold should have a thermal break located underneath the door and should be installed over a continuous bed of sealant or mastic. Insulation behind the rim joist is handled the same as the typical first-floor–basement-wall connection in figure 12.31. The apron trim below the door sill should be installed over strapping or drainage matrix (whichever is used

on the rest of the wall assembly), and drip flashing should be installed at the top of the foundation wall (optional at the top of the apron trim as well).

DOORJAMB. Figure 12.42 shows the installation of a clad wood door in a double-wood-frame wall assembly. Since the frame profile is essentially the same as the clad window jamb detail (figure 12.38), the installation is identical. The air/water-control layer must extend into the door rough opening so it can be air-sealed to the window frame on the interior after window installation. A separate self-adhered membrane flashing is installed over the edge of the window frame and flange and onto the air- and water-control layer on the wall sheathing, lapping over the top of the FlexWrap NF membrane previously installed at the sill below.

As with the window jamb detail for this wall assembly, the variable-permeability vapor retarder on the interior face of the wall must be turned into the rough opening, stapled and sealed.

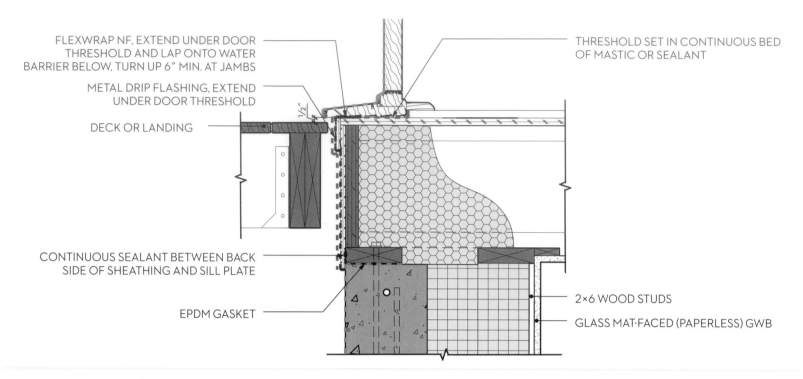

FLEXWRAP NF, EXTEND UNDER DOOR
THRESHOLD AND LAP ONTO WATER
BARRIER BELOW, TURN UP 6" MIN. AT JAMBS

METAL DRIP FLASHING, EXTEND
UNDER DOOR THRESHOLD

DECK OR LANDING

THRESHOLD SET IN CONTINUOUS BED
OF MASTIC OR SEALANT

1/2"

CONTINUOUS SEALANT BETWEEN BACK
SIDE OF SHEATHING AND SILL PLATE

EPDM GASKET

2×6 WOOD STUDS

GLASS MAT-FACED (PAPERLESS) GWB

FIGURE 12.40. FlexWrap NF is used under the threshold and lapped over the wall water barrier. The thermally broken sill is set in a continuous bed of sealant, providing a water- and airtight seal. The space between the end of the joists below is filled with R-40 insulation, extending over the interior basement wall insulation for continuity of the thermal layer.

DOOR HEAD. The installation of a clad wood door in a double-wood-frame wall is illustrated in figure 12.41 and is nearly identical to the window head detail for double-framed construction. The combined air/water-control layer is turned into the window opening, to be sealed to the window frame after window installation. FlexWrap NF is installed over the top of the window and onto the face of the sheathing, turned down at the jambs to lap over the top of the jamb flashing. If head flashing is used, it is installed over the FlexWrap NF, then covered by the air/water-control layer. And as with the window, sometimes drip flashing is used over the top of the wood trim. Drainage matrix is used behind the siding in this detail, but if strapping is used, the bottom of the airspace behind the siding should have a screened vent to keep insects out. The gap between window and rough opening is filled with low-expanding spray foam, and flexible sealant with backer rod is used for the air seal between window and rough framing.

Again, the variable-permeability vapor retarder on the interior face of the wall must be turned into the framed window opening and sealed and stapled (through the sealant bead) to the window opening framing.

Details Common to Both Single- and Double-Frame Construction

The following details and techniques are common to either single-framed or double-framed wood frame construction, as they relate to interior partitions and roof/ceiling openings found in either type.

INTERIOR PARTITION AT INSULATED CEILING WITH CONTINUOUS GYPSUM BOARD (INTERIOR PARTITION AT EXTERIOR WALLS SIMILAR). Figure 12.43 illustrates the condition where the top of an interior

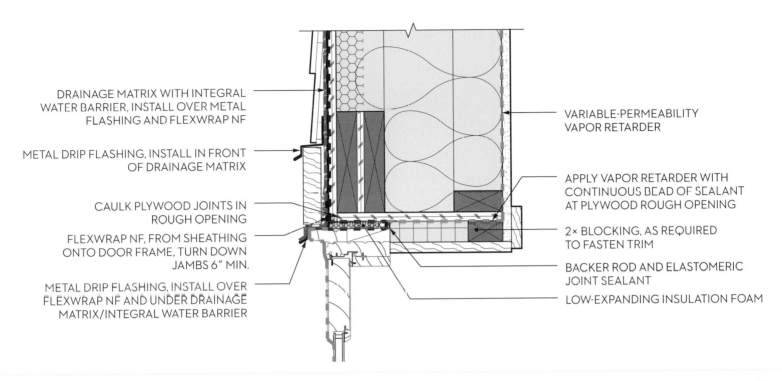

DRAINAGE MATRIX WITH INTEGRAL WATER BARRIER, INSTALL OVER METAL FLASHING AND FLEXWRAP NF

METAL DRIP FLASHING, INSTALL IN FRONT OF DRAINAGE MATRIX

CAULK PLYWOOD JOINTS IN ROUGH OPENING

FLEXWRAP NF, FROM SHEATHING ONTO DOOR FRAME, TURN DOWN JAMBS 6" MIN.

METAL DRIP FLASHING, INSTALL OVER FLEXWRAP NF AND UNDER DRAINAGE MATRIX/INTEGRAL WATER BARRIER

VARIABLE-PERMEABILITY VAPOR RETARDER

APPLY VAPOR RETARDER WITH CONTINUOUS BEAD OF SEALANT AT PLYWOOD ROUGH OPENING

2× BLOCKING, AS REQUIRED TO FASTEN TRIM

BACKER ROD AND ELASTOMERIC JOINT SEALANT

LOW-EXPANDING INSULATION FOAM

FIGURE 12.41. This door head detail is similar to the double-framed window head detail, except that the doorframe does not have a nailing flange. The FlexWrap NF is installed first and laps from the sheathing onto the top of the window frame. The metal flashing covers and protects the FlexWrap NF and is lapped in turn by the water barrier above.

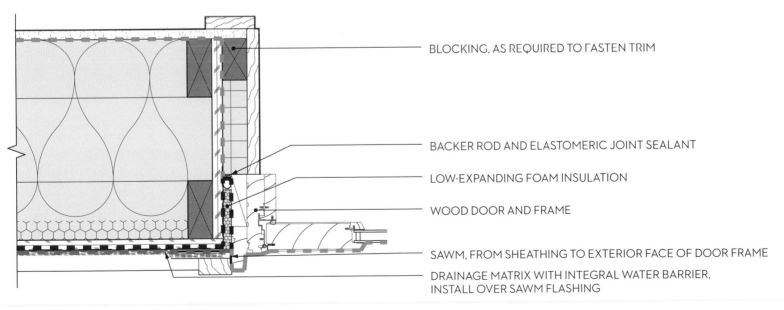

BLOCKING, AS REQUIRED TO FASTEN TRIM

BACKER ROD AND ELASTOMERIC JOINT SEALANT

LOW-EXPANDING FOAM INSULATION

WOOD DOOR AND FRAME

SAWM, FROM SHEATHING TO EXTERIOR FACE OF DOOR FRAME

DRAINAGE MATRIX WITH INTEGRAL WATER BARRIER, INSTALL OVER SAWM FLASHING

FIGURE 12.42. In this jamb detail, the doorframe does not have a flange, but the SAWM laps from the water barrier onto the edge of the doorframe. The air-control layer extends into the rough opening, to be sealed to the doorframe at its interior edge.

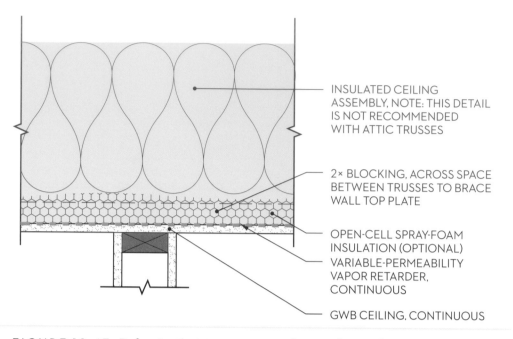

INSULATED CEILING ASSEMBLY, NOTE: THIS DETAIL IS NOT RECOMMENDED WITH ATTIC TRUSSES

2× BLOCKING, ACROSS SPACE BETWEEN TRUSSES TO BRACE WALL TOP PLATE

OPEN-CELL SPRAY-FOAM INSULATION (OPTIONAL)

VARIABLE-PERMEABILITY VAPOR RETARDER, CONTINUOUS

GWB CEILING, CONTINUOUS

FIGURE 12.43. By framing the interior partition after installation of the air/vapor-control layer and gypsum board, you avoid the complicated connections of the air/vapor-control layer that can result from interrupting it with partitions.

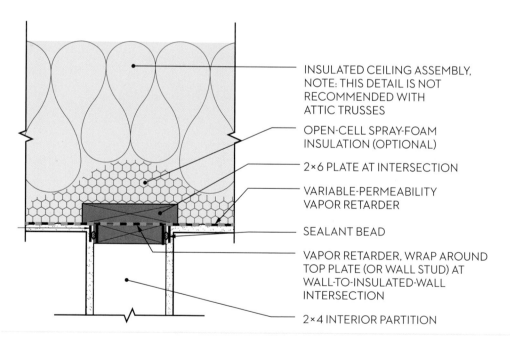

INSULATED CEILING ASSEMBLY, NOTE: THIS DETAIL IS NOT RECOMMENDED WITH ATTIC TRUSSES

OPEN-CELL SPRAY-FOAM INSULATION (OPTIONAL)

2×6 PLATE AT INTERSECTION

VARIABLE-PERMEABILITY VAPOR RETARDER

SEALANT BEAD

VAPOR RETARDER, WRAP AROUND TOP PLATE (OR WALL STUD) AT WALL-TO-INSULATED-WALL INTERSECTION

2×4 INTERIOR PARTITION

FIGURE 12.44. When partitions are put into place before the air/vapor-control layer, it may be necessary to install a strip of the control layer membrane above the partition top plate first, so it can be sealed to the ceiling control layer when that layer is added.

partition meets a typical flat, insulated ceiling, using a variable-permeability vapor retarder on the underside of the ceiling framing. The gypsum board applied to the underside of the ceiling framing members is continuous, and the interior partition is constructed after the installation of the ceiling gypsum board. This simplifies the air sealing, since it is not interrupted by the partition framing. Note that the interior partition is perpendicular to the orientation of the roof framing. When a partition is parallel to the framing and falls between two joists or rafters, it is necessary to install flat 2× blocking between the framing members at intervals to attach the wall top plate to, after installation of the ceiling gypsum board. (For an appropriate detail with truss construction, see figure 12.45. Using the procedures in figure 12.43 for truss construction could cause the wall-ceiling gypsum board joint to crack, since the bottom chords of trusses uplift sometimes during the winter.)

INTERIOR PARTITION AT INSULATED CEILING WITH DISCONTINUOUS GYPSUM BOARD (INTERIOR PARTITION AT EXTERIOR WALLS SIMILAR). Figure 12.44 shows how to handle this connection if the interior partition is framed before the ceiling gypsum board is installed, causing both the gypsum board and the variable-permeability vapor retarder membrane to be discontinuous. This situation requires blocking on top of the wall for the attachment of the ceiling gypsum board. (If 2× blocking is used, as shown, this detail would apply equally well to partitions running perpendicular or parallel to joists.) It also requires careful

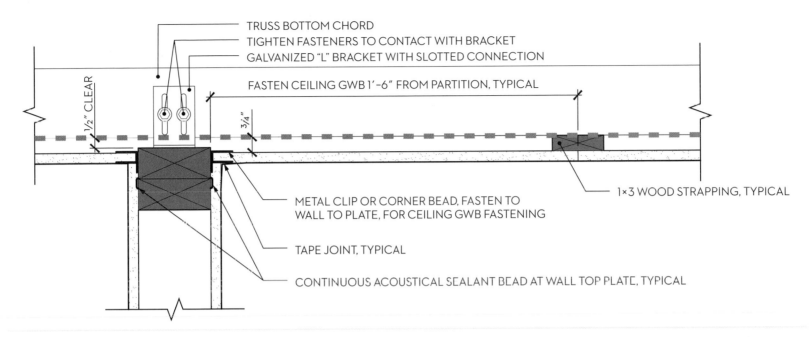

TRUSS BOTTOM CHORD
TIGHTEN FASTENERS TO CONTACT WITH BRACKET
GALVANIZED "L" BRACKET WITH SLOTTED CONNECTION
FASTEN CEILING GWB 1'-6" FROM PARTITION, TYPICAL

1/2" CLEAR

3/4"

1×3 WOOD STRAPPING, TYPICAL

METAL CLIP OR CORNER BEAD, FASTEN TO
WALL TO PLATE, FOR CEILING GWB FASTENING

TAPE JOINT, TYPICAL

CONTINUOUS ACOUSTICAL SEALANT BEAD AT WALL TOP PLATE, TYPICAL

FIGURE 12.45. With attic trusses, the bottom truss chord can move vertically. A slip connection to attach the partition top plate to the truss chord accommodates this movement without cracking the gypsum board.

handling of the vapor retarder membrane, which is serving as the air seal in this assembly. The manufacturer's instructions should always be followed, and this may require installing the membrane on top of the partition top plate and sealing and stapling it to the sides of the plate, then overlapping the ceiling membrane and sealing and stapling it to the wall membrane. Staples at such sheet terminations should always be placed through the bead of sealant. (Again, if working with roof trusses see figure 12.45.)

INTERIOR PARTITION AT CEILING, TRUSS UPLIFT DETAIL. The previous details for interior partition and ceiling junctures were rigid connections. With wood attic trusses, rigid connections do not work well, because the bottom chord of trusses can lift upward in wintertime—a result of the different temperature and therefore relative humidity of the bottom chord, which is covered with insulation, compared to the other truss components, which are exposed to the cold. The upper, exposed truss components are in an environment with higher relative humidity and therefore absorb moisture and elongate, causing the bottom chord to arch upward. The bottom chord may separate from any interior partitions that are connected to it, causing the gypsum board joint to crack unless measures are taken to accommodate this movement.

As shown in figure 12.45, the attachment of the partition top plate to the truss (if perpendicular to truss orientation) or 2× blocking between the trusses (if parallel to truss orientation) should provide a slip connection—a metal angle with a slotted hole for the fastener(s), allowing up-and-down movement of the truss and fastener while keeping the top of the wall from moving side to side. To prevent cracking of the gypsum board joint at the wall-ceiling intersection, the gypsum board must not be fastened to the truss any closer than 18" from the face of the wall. The edge of the ceiling gypsum board must be attached only to the wall top plate and not the truss, either by means of gypsum board clips or by installing wider blocking on top of the wall's top plate as a fastening surface for the ceiling gypsum board edge. This will allow the gypsum board to flex when the truss moves, preventing separation of the joint.

ATTIC HATCH. Figure 12.46 illustrates a custom hatch perimeter detail. While there are some good-quality premanufactured attic hatch products, they generally do not provide the R-60 insulation level that the ceiling of a net zero building requires. A custom hatch can be fabricated from layers of foam insulation board to provide the required R-value (15″ of EPS), adhered to a medium-density overlay (MDO) panel or similar paintable board product, to create a hatch plug that is designed to be pushed up into the attic for access. A plywood box must be built around the hatch opening in order to retain the cellulose insulation all around. A tight air seal is important, so a closed-cell, compressible gasket should be provided at the trim ledge that the bottom of the plug sits on, and a second, flexible gasket should be provided at the top, to seal to the sides of the box. The gap between the plug and the plywood box should be the minimum dimension practical given construction tolerances. It should not exceed ³⁄₈″, or convection currents might result in this gap, which will increase the rate of heat loss.

Where a fire-rated ceiling assembly is necessary, a fire-rated premanufactured attic access panel will be required. It is possible, however, to combine a premanufactured panel that is hinged to open downward with a custom plug that is installed above it in the access opening.

SKYLIGHT, FLAT ROOF. As with skylights in concrete and steel construction, we recommend installation of skylights on a custom curb fabricated from structural insulated (stressed-skin) panels. Figure 12.47 shows a detail of a skylight and curb in a hybrid-insulated flat roof with a water-control layer on top, though the concept is applicable to other flat wood-framed roof types. The SIPs are built on top of the roof deck around the skylight opening, and the air- and moisture-control layers are carried up the sides and onto the top of the curb for continuity. When the skylight is installed, it must be sealed to the control layers for air- and water-tightness. A good triple-glazed skylight is recommended, both for energy savings and reduction of the risk of condensation.

Since the roof surface is not truly flat and must be pitched to interior drains or perimeter scuppers, a cricket must be installed on the upslope side of the skylight curb, to direct water around the curb.

SKYLIGHT, SLOPED ROOF. Figure 12.48 shows a skylight installed in a typical wood single-framed sloped roof. As with the flat roof, we recommend the use of SIPs for custom curbs because of their insulating and structural value. Both the air- and water-control layers must continue up the sides of the curb and be sealed to the skylight when installed, for continuity of the control layers. A flashed cricket must also be provided on the upslope side to divert water around the skylight curb. Again, this detail is applicable to other similar roof assemblies, with minor modifications.

Enclosure Penetrations

Where possible, penetrations in the building enclosure should be avoided, and some that were mandatory in the past can now be eliminated. Vents for clothes dryers, for instance, are now unnecessary if owners choose dryer models that condense moisture rather than channeling it outside via ducts. But, when openings in the enclosure are needed, be sure to apply the following details to make sure they are carefully sealed, and maintain the integration of all control layers.

DUCT AND LOUVER. Louvers associated with mechanical equipment need to penetrate the building envelope for fresh air intake or exhaust air. The louvers are connected to ducts, which are connected to the mechanical equipment, all of which should be part of a sealed system for airtightness. Louvers typically have a hollow frame, so we recommend filling the perimeter frame with rigid insulation before installation.

Figure 12.49 shows installation of a louver frame that has a flange at head and jambs, which must be flashed the same as for window nailing flanges. It sits on a metal subsill, which is installed over FlexWrap NF, similar to windowsills. The louver frame should be fastened from the inside with clip angles to a wood-framed opening and, after installation, the gap between louver and framing and the exterior insulation filled from the inside. The duct should be fastened and sealed to the back side of the louver and the entire perimeter sealed with spray foam, then shaved flush with the interior face of framing. Following successful air-leakage testing, gypsum board can be installed on the wall around the louver and

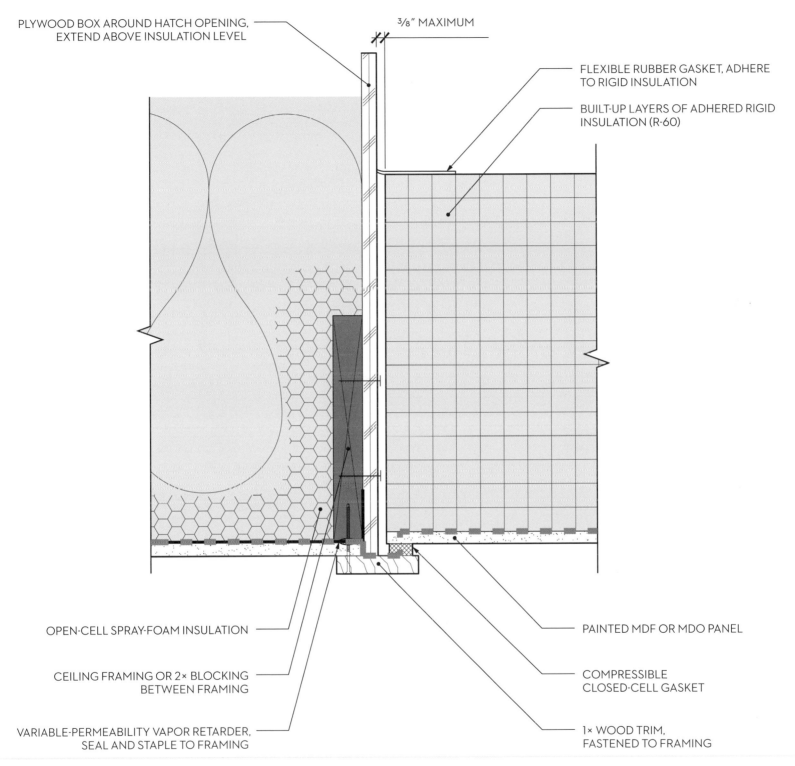

PLYWOOD BOX AROUND HATCH OPENING, EXTEND ABOVE INSULATION LEVEL

3/8" MAXIMUM

FLEXIBLE RUBBER GASKET, ADHERE TO RIGID INSULATION

BUILT-UP LAYERS OF ADHERED RIGID INSULATION (R-60)

OPEN-CELL SPRAY-FOAM INSULATION

CEILING FRAMING OR 2× BLOCKING BETWEEN FRAMING

VARIABLE-PERMEABILITY VAPOR RETARDER, SEAL AND STAPLE TO FRAMING

PAINTED MDF OR MDO PANEL

COMPRESSIBLE CLOSED-CELL GASKET

1× WOOD TRIM, FASTENED TO FRAMING

FIGURE 12.46. A field-fabricated attic hatch provides the required R-60 insulation level and is equipped with double seals around the perimeter.

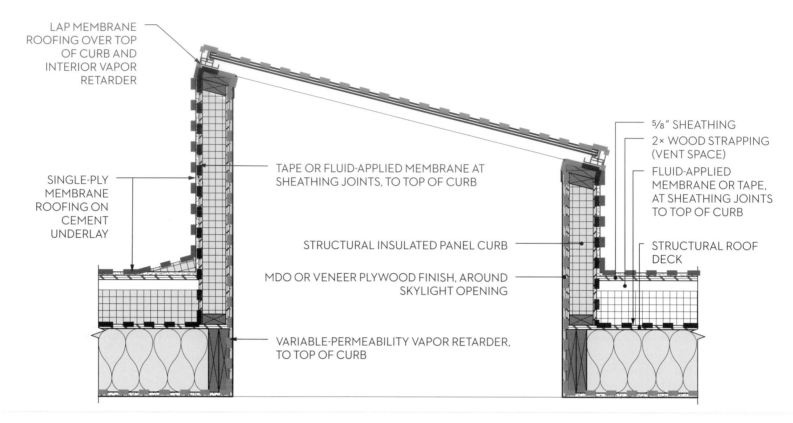

LAP MEMBRANE ROOFING OVER TOP OF CURB AND INTERIOR VAPOR RETARDER

SINGLE-PLY MEMBRANE ROOFING ON CEMENT UNDERLAY

TAPE OR FLUID-APPLIED MEMBRANE AT SHEATHING JOINTS, TO TOP OF CURB

⅝" SHEATHING

2× WOOD STRAPPING (VENT SPACE)

FLUID-APPLIED MEMBRANE OR TAPE, AT SHEATHING JOINTS TO TOP OF CURB

STRUCTURAL INSULATED PANEL CURB

STRUCTURAL ROOF DECK

MDO OR VENEER PLYWOOD FINISH, AROUND SKYLIGHT OPENING

VARIABLE-PERMEABILITY VAPOR RETARDER, TO TOP OF CURB

FIGURE 12.47A. A custom skylight curb fabricated from SIPs provides improved thermal performance compared to premanufactured curbs. The exterior water- and air-control layers extend to the top of the curb, where they are sealed to the skylight frame. The vapor-control layer extends up the interior face. With a flat roof, the curb is constructed to provide a pitch for the skylight, so it will shed water.

FIGURE 12.47B. A custom skylight curb under construction. The roof membrane will be turned up the sides of the curb and lapped over the top, where it will be sealed to the bottom of the skylight frame.

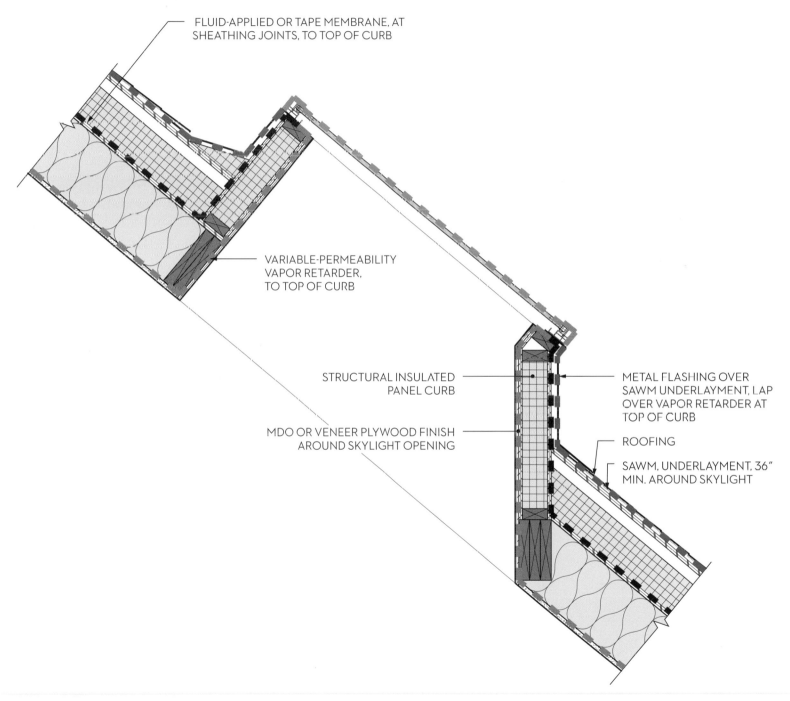

FLUID-APPLIED OR TAPE MEMBRANE, AT
SHEATHING JOINTS, TO TOP OF CURB

VARIABLE-PERMEABILITY
VAPOR RETARDER,
TO TOP OF CURB

STRUCTURAL INSULATED
PANEL CURB

MDO OR VENEER PLYWOOD FINISH
AROUND SKYLIGHT OPENING

METAL FLASHING OVER
SAWM UNDERLAYMENT, LAP
OVER VAPOR RETARDER AT
TOP OF CURB

ROOFING

SAWM, UNDERLAYMENT, 36"
MIN. AROUND SKYLIGHT

FIGURE 12.48. Custom SIP skylight curbs can also be used on sloped roofs. Again, the separate control layers must cover the sides and top of the curb and be sealed to the frame for continuity.

sealed to the sides of the duct. Air-leakage testing should be performed before finishes are installed and, where exterior insulation is used (as in this detail), before insulation is installed over the air-control layer, because it will cover the air-control layer and would make remedial measures much more difficult.

Ducts should be insulated per the mechanical engineer's advice, but we recommend that all ducts be insulated to at least R-38 for a minimum distance of 48″ from the outside wall.

PIPING PENETRATION IN A WALL. Where piping must penetrate the building envelope at a wall, figure 12.50 shows recommended methods for sealing the water-, vapor-, and air-control layers. Blocking fastened between the studs should be drilled for the pipe penetration to provide support for the pipe and to provide fastening for the edge of the sheathing around the penetration. The gap in the sheathing around the pipe should be filled with backer rod and sealant for air-control layer sealing. The gap around the pipe in the insulation layer should likewise be filled, with spray-foam insulation. When the water-control layer is installed, self-adhering waterproof membrane should be lapped onto the sides of the pipe and the water-control layer. As with the duct/louver installation, air-leakage testing should be performed before exterior insulation and finishes are installed.

PIPING PENETRATION IN THE ROOF. Vent pipes for plumbing waste systems create common piping penetration in roofs. Figure 12.51 shows this condition, which is readily adapted to other roof piping penetrations and other wood-framed sloped roof types. The penetrations through the air- and thermal-control layers are similar to the wall piping penetration. Blocking is installed between framing members, which is drilled for the pipe for support and attachment of the sheathing around the opening. The gap between pipe and sheathing is filled with backer rod and sealant in the plane of the air-control layer. Following the successful completion of air-leakage testing, the insulation layer (if used) is installed and sealed with spray-foam insulation around the pipe. The water-control layer at the penetration should be peel-and-stick membrane, tied into the underlayment for the roofing. A flexible rubber boot is installed over the pipe, which has

a flat flange that is fastened to the roof deck and lapped over the shingles below the penetration. The shingles above the penetration are installed to lap over the top of the boot flange for proper drainage.

ELECTRICAL PENETRATION IN A WALL. Through-wall electrical penetrations should be avoided when possible but may be required for exterior waterproof outlets or exterior wall-mounted light fixtures. Both should be detailed in a similar fashion, as shown in figure 12.52. Exterior waterproof boxes typically have a connection for rigid conduit, and we would recommend a conduit stub, at least, through the blocking the box is attached to and the air-control layer into the stud cavity. This will provide a surface for air-sealing the penetration through the sheathing/air-control layer. After wiring is installed, it must be sealed to the conduit with putty or sealant. The water-control layer must be sealed to the sides of the waterproof box, typically with peel-and-stick membrane. With wood siding, a trim block is usually installed around the box, which should be provided with drip flashing at the top.

Interior electrical wall penetrations require attention when a variable-permeability vapor retarder membrane is used on the interior face of studs, as this must be sealed properly to the electrical boxes. It is important to use airtight electrical boxes and to seal the membrane to the box with sheathing tape.

ELECTRICAL PENETRATION IN THE CEILING (WALL PENETRATION SIMILAR). As mentioned earlier, electrical penetrations for ceiling-mounted fixtures or smoke detectors create a challenge when constructing double-framed or truss ceilings that have a variable-permeability vapor retarder for an air-control layer. Airtight boxes or recessed fixtures that are rated for airtightness and for use in insulated ceilings should be used. The vapor retarder membrane must be sealed to the perimeter of the box or fixture with sheathing tape, and wiring must be sealed to the box or fixture (figure 12.53). As an additional precaution, we recommend a layer of open-cell spray foam around the top of the box or rated fixture, or a custom-fabricated box made of board insulation can be constructed around fixtures instead. As noted previously, we would recommend a layer of open-cell spray foam across the top of the whole ceiling where accessible, as in an attic.

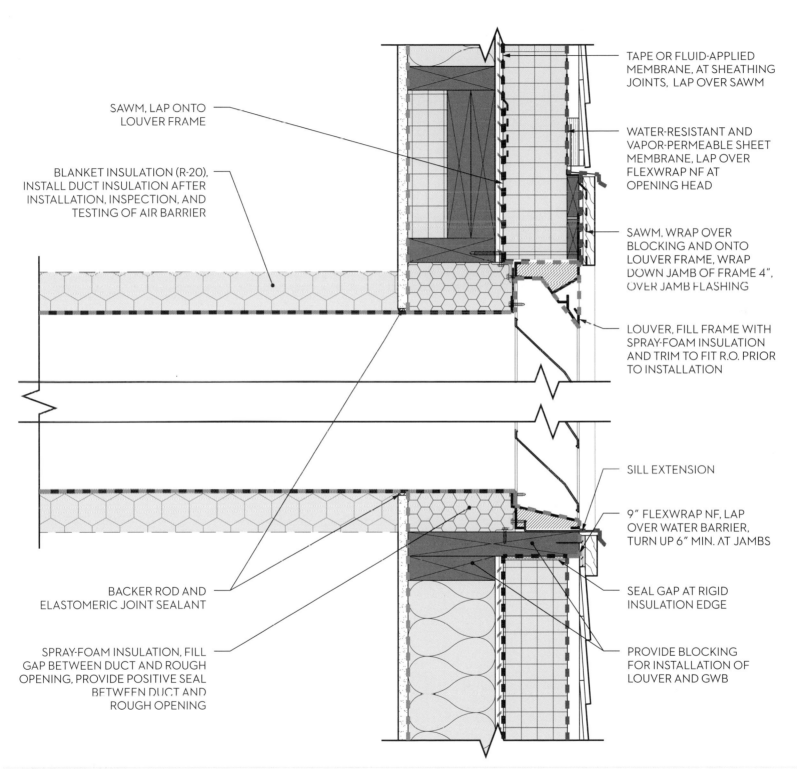

TAPE OR FLUID-APPLIED MEMBRANE, AT SHEATHING JOINTS, LAP OVER SAWM

WATER-RESISTANT AND VAPOR-PERMEABLE SHEET MEMBRANE, LAP OVER FLEXWRAP NF AT OPENING HEAD

SAWM, LAP ONTO LOUVER FRAME

SAWM, WRAP OVER BLOCKING AND ONTO LOUVER FRAME, WRAP DOWN JAMB OF FRAME 4", OVER JAMB FLASHING

BLANKET INSULATION (R-20), INSTALL DUCT INSULATION AFTER INSTALLATION, INSPECTION, AND TESTING OF AIR BARRIER

LOUVER, FILL FRAME WITH SPRAY-FOAM INSULATION AND TRIM TO FIT R.O. PRIOR TO INSTALLATION

SILL EXTENSION

9" FLEXWRAP NF, LAP OVER WATER BARRIER, TURN UP 6" MIN. AT JAMBS

BACKER ROD AND ELASTOMERIC JOINT SEALANT

SEAL GAP AT RIGID INSULATION EDGE

SPRAY-FOAM INSULATION, FILL GAP BETWEEN DUCT AND ROUGH OPENING, PROVIDE POSITIVE SEAL BETWEEN DUCT AND ROUGH OPENING

PROVIDE BLOCKING FOR INSTALLATION OF LOUVER AND GWB

FIGURE 12.49. At louver penetration of the wall assembly, the duct must be sealed tightly to the louver, and the various control layers must be lapped and sealed to the louver or duct.

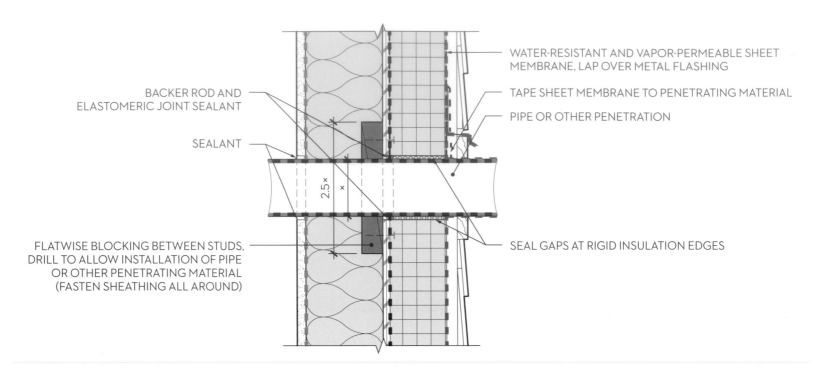

WATER-RESISTANT AND VAPOR-PERMEABLE SHEET MEMBRANE, LAP OVER METAL FLASHING

BACKER ROD AND ELASTOMERIC JOINT SEALANT

TAPE SHEET MEMBRANE TO PENETRATING MATERIAL

PIPE OR OTHER PENETRATION

SEALANT

2.5×

×

FLATWISE BLOCKING BETWEEN STUDS, DRILL TO ALLOW INSTALLATION OF PIPE OR OTHER PENETRATING MATERIAL (FASTEN SHEATHING ALL AROUND)

SEAL GAPS AT RIGID INSULATION EDGES

FIGURE 12.50A. A piping penetration of an exterior wall. All control layers must be lapped and/or sealed to the pipe. A finish trim block is usually provided where the pipe passes through the exterior finish layer.

FIGURE 12.50B. A completed piping penetration is shown here, in this case a round duct. A hooded cap will be installed in the opening for weather protection.

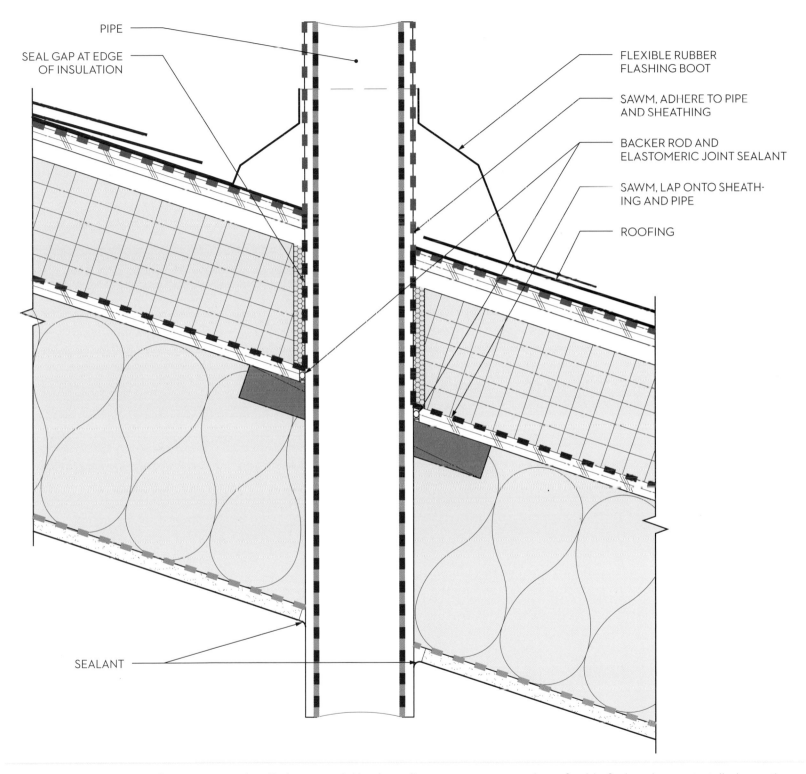

PIPE

SEAL GAP AT EDGE
OF INSULATION

FLEXIBLE RUBBER
FLASHING BOOT

SAWM, ADHERE TO PIPE
AND SHEATHING

BACKER ROD AND
ELASTOMERIC JOINT SEALANT

SAWM, LAP ONTO SHEATH-
ING AND PIPE

ROOFING

SEALANT

FIGURE 12.51. A roof penetration is handled very much like the wall penetration, except that a flexible flashing boot is installed over the pipe for water protection at the same time the finish roofing is installed.

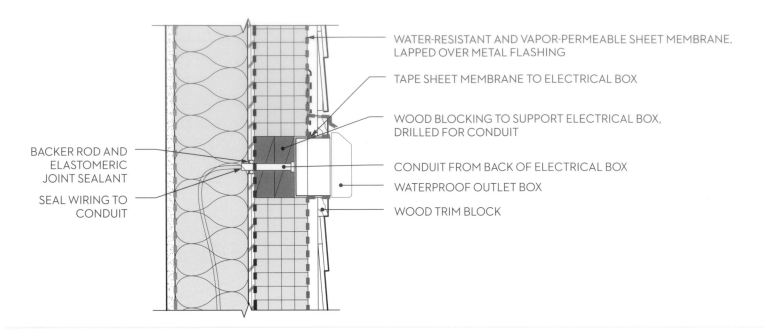

WATER-RESISTANT AND VAPOR-PERMEABLE SHEET MEMBRANE, LAPPED OVER METAL FLASHING

TAPE SHEET MEMBRANE TO ELECTRICAL BOX

WOOD BLOCKING TO SUPPORT ELECTRICAL BOX, DRILLED FOR CONDUIT

CONDUIT FROM BACK OF ELECTRICAL BOX

WATERPROOF OUTLET BOX

WOOD TRIM BLOCK

BACKER ROD AND ELASTOMERIC JOINT SEALANT

SEAL WIRING TO CONDUIT

FIGURE 12.52. With exterior rigid insulation, the electrical device box is often installed on wood blocking for support. In this case conduit should extend through to the stud cavity, so that the conduit can be sealed to the air-control layer. After the wiring is installed, the inside of the conduit must be air-sealed around the wires with putty or sealant.

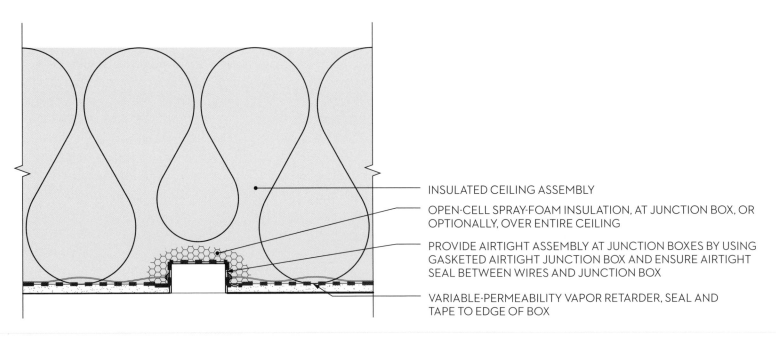

INSULATED CEILING ASSEMBLY

OPEN-CELL SPRAY-FOAM INSULATION, AT JUNCTION BOX, OR OPTIONALLY, OVER ENTIRE CEILING

PROVIDE AIRTIGHT ASSEMBLY AT JUNCTION BOXES BY USING GASKETED AIRTIGHT JUNCTION BOX AND ENSURE AIRTIGHT SEAL BETWEEN WIRES AND JUNCTION BOX

VARIABLE-PERMEABILITY VAPOR RETARDER, SEAL AND TAPE TO EDGE OF BOX

FIGURE 12.53. Recessed electrical boxes can provide a challenge for air and vapor sealing when these control layers occur at a ceiling. The vapor retarder must be sealed and taped to the box. When the wiring has been installed, the top of the box should be sealed as well, before the insulation goes in.

13 | Net Zero Steel and Wood Composite Construction

Steel and wood composite is a niche construction type for midsize buildings. In this type of construction, the insulation is entirely on the exterior of the building enclosure, in alignment with the ideal scenario. The steel components include the structural framework, floor decks, and metal roof decks. The wood-framed walls are nonstructural and provide support for the various control layers. The wood walls may be either single or double framed. Even if wood walls and/or roof assemblies are designed to be nonstructural, it is important that they are designed and installed to avoid moisture-related issues such as those described and illustrated in chapter 12. The roof system can be either a steel-supported metal deck, as described in the concrete and steel construction section in chapter 10, or large-span wood trusses supporting wood sheathing, as described in the double-framed wood section in chapter 12.

The wall section in figure 13.1 depicts a structural steel frame and raised concrete/steel floor combined with wood walls and a wood truss roof. The steel wall structure on the interior of the building enclosure largely eliminates thermal bridging.

Many of the details for the wall and roof are similar to the details shown in the previous chapters. Other areas require special attention, such as the raised floor-wall intersection and the roof-wall intersections. The steel floor and roof beams will deflect under live loads. The connections between these steel components and the wood wall framing that is bearing on the foundation must allow for this movement. It is important to design the structure to limit the steel deflection to a manageable amount (less than ½") so that simple connections can be used to accommodate the differential movement. This improves integrity of the air- and vapor-control layers that are essential for net zero and healthy buildings.

Canopies and balconies must be designed so their supports are not continuous through the control layers, using isolation blocks, as discussed in the steel and

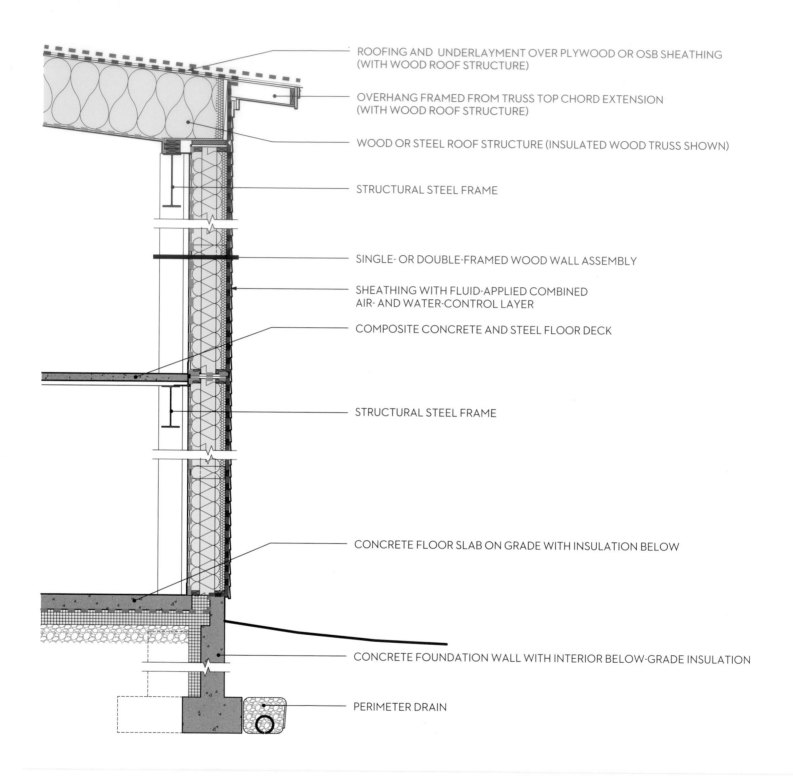

ROOFING AND UNDERLAYMENT OVER PLYWOOD OR OSB SHEATHING (WITH WOOD ROOF STRUCTURE)

OVERHANG FRAMED FROM TRUSS TOP CHORD EXTENSION (WITH WOOD ROOF STRUCTURE)

WOOD OR STEEL ROOF STRUCTURE (INSULATED WOOD TRUSS SHOWN)

STRUCTURAL STEEL FRAME

SINGLE- OR DOUBLE-FRAMED WOOD WALL ASSEMBLY

SHEATHING WITH FLUID-APPLIED COMBINED AIR- AND WATER-CONTROL LAYER

COMPOSITE CONCRETE AND STEEL FLOOR DECK

STRUCTURAL STEEL FRAME

CONCRETE FLOOR SLAB ON GRADE WITH INSULATION BELOW

CONCRETE FOUNDATION WALL WITH INTERIOR BELOW-GRADE INSULATION

PERIMETER DRAIN

FIGURE 13.1. In this example of composite construction, the foundation, slab-on-grade, exterior steel frame, and elevated floor structure are typical of concrete and steel construction. The walls and roof are constructed of wood and are located on the outside of the structure to minimize thermal bridging.

concrete construction section in chapter 10. This is accomplished by providing a separate structure on the outside of the wood-framed walls or supporting the exterior structure on the exterior layer of wood framing. Connections of the perimeter steel structure to the concrete foundation must also be designed to provide thermal breaks because of the high thermal conductivity of steel.

STEEL COLUMN ON PIER. Concrete piers that are contiguous with the foundation wall typically support the perimeter steel columns. If the foundation is insulated on the interior side, the foundation will be exposed to the outside air, and the cold will travel through to the concrete pier and could travel up through the steel column. To prevent the thermal bridging that could lead to condensation and associated moisture issues, a thermal break is necessary between the top of the pier and the base plate of the column. Figure 13.2 shows a typical column installation with a bearing block made from high-density polyurethane, commonly used for this purpose because of its low thermal conductivity and high bearing capacity. The bearing block is embedded in the insulation layer underneath the edge of the slab. Note that the continuity of the air-, vapor-, and water-control layers is maintained between the underslab and the outside wall control layers. Where the column penetrates the underslab membrane, the membrane must be sealed to the sides of the column.

It should be noted that while this is a thermally improved solution, there is still less than the ideal amount of insulation value between the pier and the base plate. A superior solution is actually to isolate the concrete pier from the outside concrete. This can be accomplished by use of a double concrete wall, with R-40 rigid insulation between the inside and outside walls and the pier integral with the interior concrete wall. See chapter 10, figure 10.9 for a description of this solution.

SECOND-FLOOR AND WALL INTERSECTION. The wood wall framing must be attached to the steel floor beam or edge of second-floor slab to brace the wall against lateral loads such as wind and earthquakes. As discussed above, the steel structure will deflect, so this connection must allow for vertical movement of the steel and concrete floor. When deflection is limited by design, a simple slip connection will suffice. Figure 13.3 shows a steel clip angle with a slotted hole. The clip attached to the wood wall remains stationary, while the fastener attached to the concrete floor can slide up and down in the slot when the beam deflects.

The vertical wood wall framing is interrupted at the floor level, and continuous wood blocking at this point can tie the inner and outer wood frames together. This blocking (two layers of ¾" plywood used here) also prevents the spread of fire vertically within the wall cavity. A continuous vertical Larsen truss could also be used to balloon-frame both levels at once as an alternative. Regarding fire blocking, it is becoming much more common to allow the omission of fire blocking when using dense-pack cellulose insulation, which retards the spread of fire, but the regulations should be confirmed with the local building inspector or code official.

ROOF AND WALL INTERSECTION. The connection of the top of the wall to the steel beam and roof truss must accommodate vertical deflection of the roof structure, while providing lateral support. In figure 13.4 this connection is accomplished with a clip angle and slotted hole connection to the interior face of the studs. Since the truss will move vertically with the beam, a deflection joint is also needed between the top of the wall and the truss heel. This gap can be filled with compressible foam, and the air- and water-control layer on the outside of the sheathing should be installed to form a loop at this gap, to allow for movement at this joint without damaging the membrane.

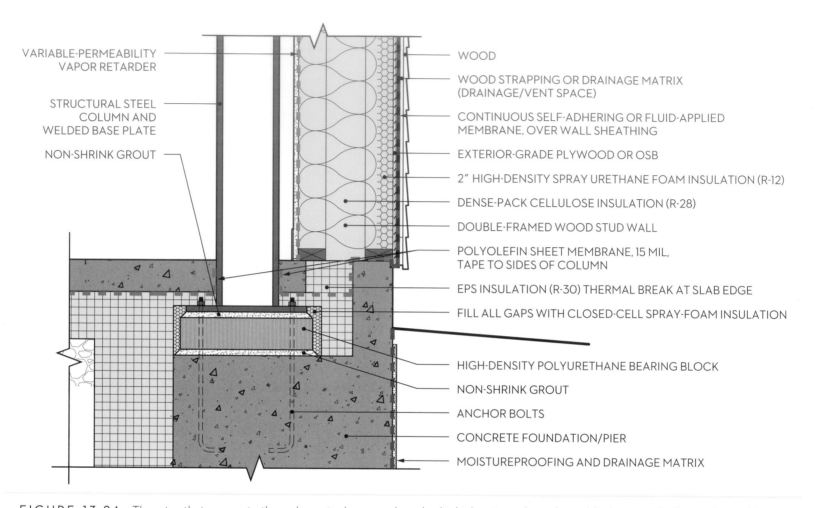

VARIABLE-PERMEABILITY VAPOR RETARDER

STRUCTURAL STEEL COLUMN AND WELDED BASE PLATE

NON-SHRINK GROUT

WOOD

WOOD STRAPPING OR DRAINAGE MATRIX (DRAINAGE/VENT SPACE)

CONTINUOUS SELF-ADHERING OR FLUID-APPLIED MEMBRANE, OVER WALL SHEATHING

EXTERIOR-GRADE PLYWOOD OR OSB

2" HIGH-DENSITY SPRAY URETHANE FOAM INSULATION (R-12)

DENSE-PACK CELLULOSE INSULATION (R-28)

DOUBLE-FRAMED WOOD STUD WALL

POLYOLEFIN SHEET MEMBRANE, 15 MIL, TAPE TO SIDES OF COLUMN

EPS INSULATION (R-30) THERMAL BREAK AT SLAB EDGE

FILL ALL GAPS WITH CLOSED-CELL SPRAY-FOAM INSULATION

HIGH-DENSITY POLYURETHANE BEARING BLOCK

NON-SHRINK GROUT

ANCHOR BOLTS

CONCRETE FOUNDATION/PIER

MOISTUREPROOFING AND DRAINAGE MATRIX

FIGURE 13.2A. The pier that supports the column is depressed, and a high-density polyurethane block is installed as a thermal break between the column base and the pier.

FIGURE 13.2B. A depressed concrete pier and steel column, separated by a bearing block that provides a thermal break.

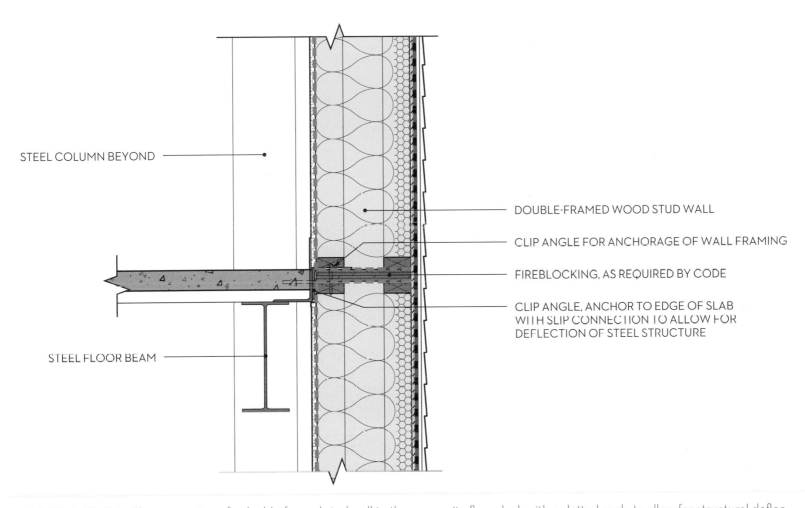

STEEL COLUMN BEYOND

DOUBLE-FRAMED WOOD STUD WALL

CLIP ANGLE FOR ANCHORAGE OF WALL FRAMING

FIREBLOCKING, AS REQUIRED BY CODE

CLIP ANGLE, ANCHOR TO EDGE OF SLAB WITH SLIP CONNECTION TO ALLOW FOR DEFLECTION OF STEEL STRUCTURE

STEEL FLOOR BEAM

FIGURE 13.3A. The connection of a double-framed stud wall to the composite floor deck with a slotted angle to allow for structural deflection. Fire blocking may be required in the exterior wall at the floor level.

FIGURE 13.3B. Before the concrete is poured on the metal deck, the attachment angle for the wall is visible at the edge of the deck.

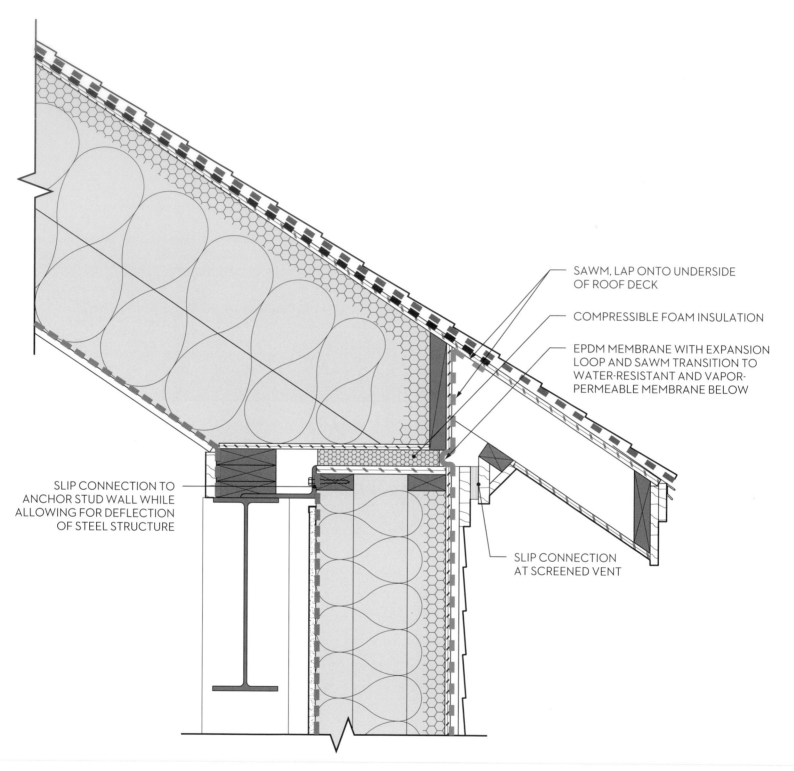

SAWM, LAP ONTO UNDERSIDE
OF ROOF DECK

COMPRESSIBLE FOAM INSULATION

EPDM MEMBRANE WITH EXPANSION
LOOP AND SAWM TRANSITION TO
WATER-RESISTANT AND VAPOR-
PERMEABLE MEMBRANE BELOW

SLIP CONNECTION TO
ANCHOR STUD WALL WHILE
ALLOWING FOR DEFLECTION
OF STEEL STRUCTURE

SLIP CONNECTION
AT SCREENED VENT

FIGURE 13.4. The connection between roof and wall must allow for deflection of the roof, which is supported on steel beams, and the wall. The control layers are connected in such a way as to permit flexibility.

14 | Net Zero for Existing Buildings

The same principles, strategies, technologies, and details that apply to new buildings also apply to net zero improvements and renovations to existing buildings, even historic ones. That said, there are often significant challenges, including expense, when you apply these strategies and details to existing buildings. In chapter 15 we see how to determine whether or not a building is a good candidate for a net zero renovation. In this chapter we cover the details of construction, including common conditions specific to renovating existing buildings to net zero levels and construction types generally found only in older buildings, such as pre-engineered and solid masonry construction.

Each existing building has its own special conditions and challenges, including narrow wall cavities, moisture issues, and thermal bridges. So we'll begin with more general guidelines and strategies, then end with a few above- and below-grade details specific to existing buildings that do not fit our ideal envelope design principles.

Many older building walls have minimal or no wall cavities. Wood framed buildings have some cavities that are too thin to meet net zero standards simply by filling the cavity with insulation, while many brick and stone masonry buildings have no cavities or cavities that are 1" or less. These conditions don't allow for effective insulation levels within the building enclosure itself. Because insulation needs to be protected from the elements, it is typically located beneath finishes in the middle of the assembly. In order to upgrade insulation levels, some finishes must be disturbed. If exterior finishes are in poor repair and need to be replaced during renovation, it makes the most sense to insulate on the exterior of the building structure. If interior surfaces need to be disturbed or removed during the course of renovation, then it makes the most sense to insulate on the interior of the building enclosure. This can cause challenges in the design of the water-, air-, and vapor-control layers. Interior insulation requires a detailed assessment of vapor and air migration in the wall with calculation of the dew point.

When making changes to the building enclosure, you will need to address existing moisture issues and study the insulation properties and the movement of water vapor through the proposed assembly. Similar to new building designs, all renovation designs must address water protection in the roof, wall, and foundation assemblies; all penetrations; and subgrade drainage conditions.

Changes to the building envelope will also reduce air movement through the assembly, commonly referred to as tightening the building envelope. This will alter the moisture characteristics of the building. Water vapor movement and water migration from the ground are particularly important to address, as these can lead to increased humidity levels that can cause mold and moisture problems. These problems in turn can affect building and occupant health. Moisture migration through the slab and subgrade walls from the soil up into the building must be stopped.

Steel and concrete walls are very poor insulators and create thermal bridges. Insulating on the interior of the building envelope in these instances can be quite problematic. In existing buildings, there are often locations where the concrete or steel structure extends through the envelope directly to the outside, causing the direct transfer of heat. These occurrences can be significant in terms of the total heat loss of the building and can cause condensation and moisture problems.

While most of these issues will not prevent renovations, they will limit the options for assemblies and ways to increase insulation. All such conditions in the building must be documented in the existing building assessment to provide the background information needed to develop a sound and durable renovation strategy. Then these issues must be synthesized into an effective strategy, design, and details.

Existing Foundation Assemblies

Existing foundations in net zero retrofits are of particular concern and call for holistic, systems-based solutions. Existing buildings often have moisture issues in basements, grade-level floors, and crawl spaces. These may include water moving through the basement constantly or seasonally and excessive water vapor. If the building is air-sealed for net zero renovation above grade, the moisture levels will increase in the building, as moisture cannot escape as easily as before. Therefore, in existing buildings it is essential to reduce below-grade water and water vapor sources. Methods for doing this are the same as for new buildings, including grading surfaces around the building to move water away from the building and adding permeable backfill with perimeter drains. This is often difficult and expensive, but it is critical for avoiding long-term moisture problems.

It is also necessary to decide whether to insulate on the inside or outside and develop a strategy and details for water and water vapor control, as in most buildings these issues were either ignored or poorly addressed originally. If there is positive drainage away from the building at grade, permeable backfill, adequate moisture protection of the foundation wall, and a functioning perimeter drain, then insulating on either the inside or outside is appropriate. If moisture protection measures are inadequate, then add water protection on the exterior of the building before insulation. If the exterior work is done, add insulation on the outside, the inside, or both. Your course of action will depend in part on whether the foundation walls are uneven, like those made of stone, or flat, like those made of concrete masonry units (CMU) or concrete.

If you are dealing with flat walls, check the structure to make sure it is sound before covering it up, particularly with CMU. If it is sound, rigid insulation and details as for new construction work well, as shown in chapter 9.

Buildings are often surrounded by poorly drained and clay soils that expand and contract as they freeze and thaw, which can cause cracking and structural failure of basement walls. Heat escaping from uninsulated walls keeps the soil from freezing and so prevents structural problems. In insulating basements and crawl spaces, it is critical to address this issue.

Basements and crawl spaces rarely have a proper vapor-control layer. Where there is adequate ceiling height, a new vapor-control layer, rigid insulation, concrete, and new floor finish can be added. Where heights are not adequate, more creative and less perfect solutions may be required.

Insulating from the interior side is generally easiest, since exterior insulation requires excavation around the perimeter of the building. Insulation on the inside of the foundation is also not exposed to potential deterioration from pests or soil contaminants. An interior insulation retrofit for concrete walls should follow the recommendations described in the section on interior basement insulation for new construction in chapter 9, figures 9.1 and 9.2.

Foundations made of stone or brick have special concerns addressed in the following descriptions and details, as do crawl spaces.

STONE MASONRY FOUNDATION WITH INTERIOR INSULATION. Older buildings may have foundations constructed of masonry, typically stone. If the insulation is to be added on the inside of the masonry structure, then the preferred insulation is closed-cell 2.0 lb.-density sprayed urethane foam, as shown in figure 14.1. Urethane foam can tolerate water, does not allow air or water vapor to move through the assembly, and has a high insulation value of R-6 per inch. It must be protected from fire with intumescent paint or a stud wall with gypsum wallboard. The studs, if wood, can go into the foam, as long as the studs are held away from the masonry enough to provide continuous insulation of at least half of the R-value of the total insulation between the masonry and the stud. If studs are metal, they should not be embedded in the insulation at all. Figure 14.2 shows an option for basement walls that are not moistureproofed, where water is allowed to drain down between the stone and the foam and then to an underslab drain. This drain can collect the water and carry it to daylight or to a sump, where it can be removed with a pump. If you follow this detail, make sure soils are permeable so that freeze-thaw cycles will not cause pressure on foundation walls.

CRAWL SPACE AT MASONRY WALLS WITH EXTERIOR DRAINAGE AND INTERIOR INSULATION. As mentioned above, increasing the insulation level of brick

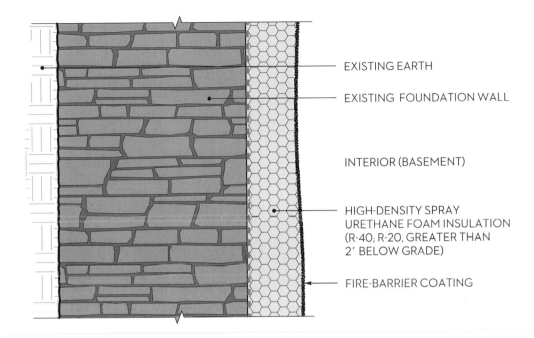

EXISTING EARTH

EXISTING FOUNDATION WALL

INTERIOR (BASEMENT)

HIGH-DENSITY SPRAY URETHANE FOAM INSULATION (R-40; R-20, GREATER THAN 2′ BELOW GRADE)

FIRE-BARRIER COATING

FIGURE 14.1. The easiest approach to insulating an existing foundation wall is often from the interior side. Spray-foam insulation is commonly used because it can be applied over an irregular masonry surface.

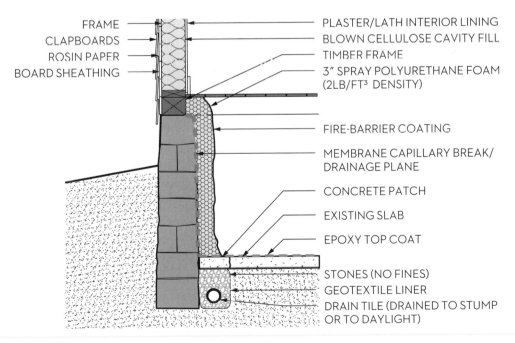

FRAME
CLAPBOARDS
ROSIN PAPER
BOARD SHEATHING

PLASTER/LATH INTERIOR LINING
BLOWN CELLULOSE CAVITY FILL
TIMBER FRAME
3″ SPRAY POLYURETHANE FOAM (2LB/FT³ DENSITY)

FIRE-BARRIER COATING

MEMBRANE CAPILLARY BREAK/ DRAINAGE PLANE

CONCRETE PATCH

EXISTING SLAB

EPOXY TOP COAT

STONES (NO FINES)
GEOTEXTILE LINER
DRAIN TILE (DRAINED TO STUMP OR TO DAYLIGHT)

FIGURE 14.2. Moisture that seeps through a rubble stone wall can be collected in an underslab perforated pipe and drained away.

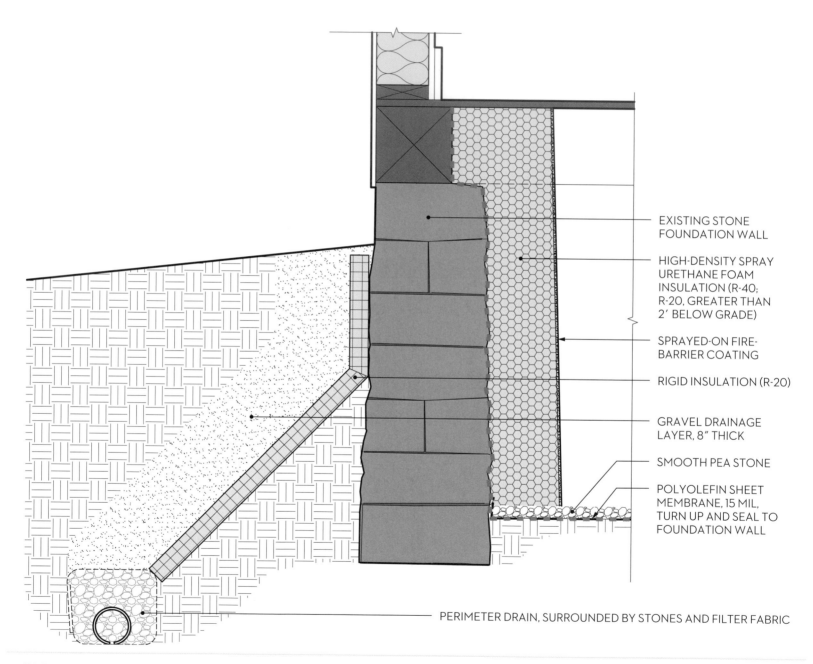

EXISTING STONE
FOUNDATION WALL

HIGH-DENSITY SPRAY
URETHANE FOAM
INSULATION (R-40;
R-20, GREATER THAN
2′ BELOW GRADE)

SPRAYED-ON FIRE-
BARRIER COATING

RIGID INSULATION (R-20)

GRAVEL DRAINAGE
LAYER, 8″ THICK

SMOOTH PEA STONE

POLYOLEFIN SHEET
MEMBRANE, 15 MIL,
TURN UP AND SEAL TO
FOUNDATION WALL

PERIMETER DRAIN, SURROUNDED BY STONES AND FILTER FABRIC

FIGURE 14.3. Exterior insulation and drainage can prevent frost-susceptible soil from freezing and damaging an existing foundation.

or stone foundations can lead to serious consequences where the adjacent exterior soil is susceptible to frost. Frost pressures can result because of the decreased heat loss through the newly insulated foundation walls, leading to bowing of walls or serious structural failure. Testing can help determine the susceptibility of the soils to such problems, though they are especially likely in wet or poorly drained soils. Incorporating drainage measures into the renovation project reduces the likelihood of frost heaving and other moisture problems. The strategy illustrated in figure 14.3, in which below-grade insulation and drainage are installed on the exterior of the foundation, addresses both drainage and frost susceptibility. This technique allows some heat loss to the adjacent insulated soil to protect it from freezing and drains moisture away from the soil adjacent to the building. Figure 14.3 shows a crawl space, but this approach is equally applicable to basements.

Crawl spaces are often problematic because of the likelihood of moisture vapor migration from the soil below. The preferred approach is foam on the inside, drainage on the outside, and a vapor-control membrane over the soil, covered with sand, gravel, or a slab for protection, as indicated in figure 14.3. This detail shows a stone foundation wall. If the existing wall is flat concrete, foil-faced rigid foam board insulation can be used instead of spray-foam insulation. Building codes may also require conditioning of the crawl space to address the potential for moisture problems.

FOUNDATION WALL FOR BRICK VENEER. In steel and concrete construction, it is preferable to insulate on the exterior of buildings, particularly when aesthetics, view, daylighting, and integrated design strategies all combine to justify significant alterations to the exterior design. If insulation is added to the building exterior and masonry is used for the renovated exterior finish, then the masonry moves farther outboard in the wall assembly. However, the masonry still needs support. Preferably, this support is not a lintel with poor thermal performance. Figure 14.4 depicts a detail that provides a new CMU wall outside the existing concrete foundation wall, so that new brick is supported continuously and thermal insulation extends in one plane. Figure 14.5 shows an alternate detail where the foam cannot be run continuously, so insulating masonry is used as a thermal break, maintaining some insulation value, even if reduced.

Existing Wall Assemblies

In existing steel, concrete, and wood-frame wall assemblies, renovating using the strategies described in chapters 10 through 13—by adding insulation to the exterior of the assembly—is the ideal and preferred approach. This is sometimes the cheapest option as well, because many complications arise in the interior insulation approach, which calls for removing existing finishes; removing and replacing baseboard, window, and door trim; and relocating existing baseboard radiators and electrical devices. In some cases adding to or replacing the existing cavity insulation is desirable to achieve net zero levels. With roof construction, the load-carrying capacity of the existing framing should be analyzed to be sure it is not exceeded with the addition of the new materials. In the 1960s and 1970s, buildings were often engineered structurally to rely on melting snow to reduce snow loads. When insulation is added, it is necessary to confirm that both live and dead loads can be supported. In addition to adding insulation, the existing air-, vapor-, and water-control layers will need to be evaluated and possibly altered. While the approaches for steel, concrete, and wood are largely addressed by adapting the ideal details for new construction, brick bearing walls, brick veneer assemblies, and steel buildings are unique. While existing buildings may lend themselves to the approaches outlined in chapters 8 through 12, many existing buildings do not fit into these categories.

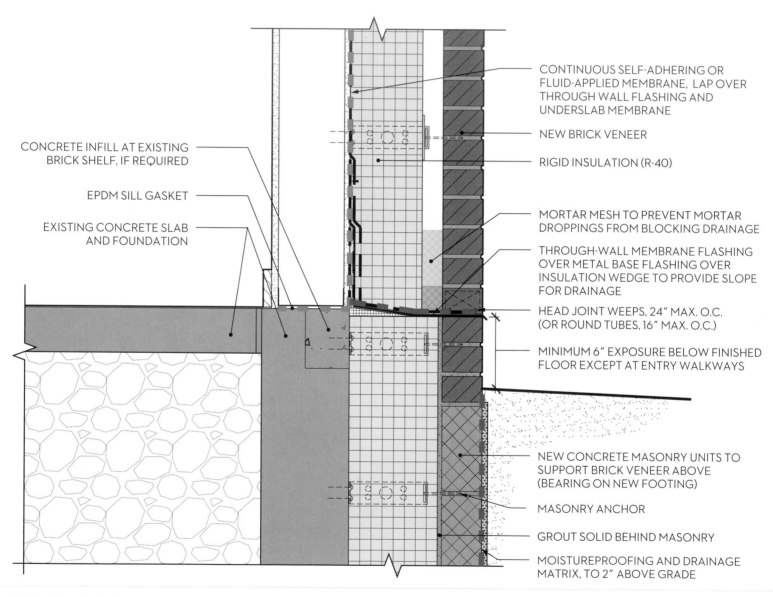

CONTINUOUS SELF-ADHERING OR
FLUID-APPLIED MEMBRANE, LAP OVER
THROUGH WALL FLASHING AND
UNDERSLAB MEMBRANE

NEW BRICK VENEER

RIGID INSULATION (R-40)

MORTAR MESH TO PREVENT MORTAR
DROPPINGS FROM BLOCKING DRAINAGE

THROUGH-WALL MEMBRANE FLASHING
OVER METAL BASE FLASHING OVER
INSULATION WEDGE TO PROVIDE SLOPE
FOR DRAINAGE

HEAD JOINT WEEPS, 24" MAX. O.C.
(OR ROUND TUBES, 16" MAX. O.C.)

MINIMUM 6" EXPOSURE BELOW FINISHED
FLOOR EXCEPT AT ENTRY WALKWAYS

NEW CONCRETE MASONRY UNITS TO
SUPPORT BRICK VENEER ABOVE
(BEARING ON NEW FOOTING)

MASONRY ANCHOR

GROUT SOLID BEHIND MASONRY

MOISTUREPROOFING AND DRAINAGE
MATRIX, TO 2" ABOVE GRADE

CONCRETE INFILL AT EXISTING
BRICK SHELF, IF REQUIRED

EPDM SILL GASKET

EXISTING CONCRETE SLAB
AND FOUNDATION

FIGURE 14.4. Supporting a new brick veneer on masonry beyond the thermal-control layer allows the thermal-control layer to be continuous above and below grade, avoiding offsets in the materials that can cause thermal bridging.

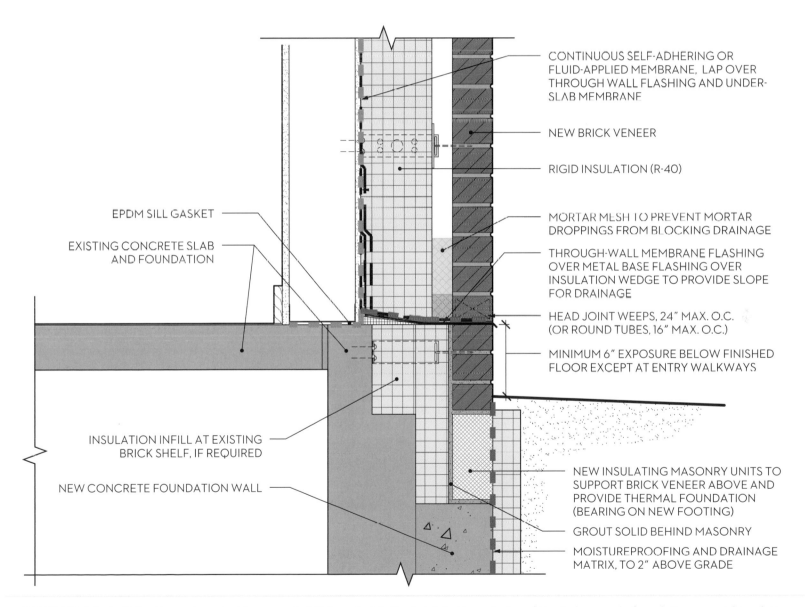

CONTINUOUS SELF-ADHERING OR FLUID-APPLIED MEMBRANE, LAP OVER THROUGH WALL FLASHING AND UNDER-SLAB MEMBRANE

NEW BRICK VENEER

RIGID INSULATION (R-40)

MORTAR MESH TO PREVENT MORTAR DROPPINGS FROM BLOCKING DRAINAGE

THROUGH-WALL MEMBRANE FLASHING OVER METAL BASE FLASHING OVER INSULATION WEDGE TO PROVIDE SLOPE FOR DRAINAGE

HEAD JOINT WEEPS, 24" MAX. O.C. (OR ROUND TUBES, 16" MAX. O.C.)

MINIMUM 6" EXPOSURE BELOW FINISHED FLOOR EXCEPT AT ENTRY WALKWAYS

EPDM SILL GASKET

EXISTING CONCRETE SLAB AND FOUNDATION

INSULATION INFILL AT EXISTING BRICK SHELF, IF REQUIRED

NEW CONCRETE FOUNDATION WALL

NEW INSULATING MASONRY UNITS TO SUPPORT BRICK VENEER ABOVE AND PROVIDE THERMAL FOUNDATION (BEARING ON NEW FOOTING)

GROUT SOLID BEHIND MASONRY

MOISTUREPROOFING AND DRAINAGE MATRIX, TO 2" ABOVE GRADE

FIGURE 14.5. If the thermal-control layer must shift from inside the brick to the exterior of the below-grade foundation, special insulating masonry units may be used to reduce thermal bridging.

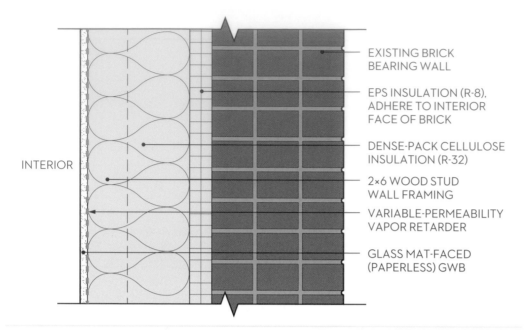

EXISTING BRICK
BEARING WALL

EPS INSULATION (R-8),
ADHERE TO INTERIOR
FACE OF BRICK

DENSE-PACK CELLULOSE
INSULATION (R-32)

2×6 WOOD STUD
WALL FRAMING

VARIABLE-PERMEABILITY
VAPOR RETARDER

GLASS MAT-FACED
(PAPERLESS) GWB

INTERIOR

FIGURE 14.6. A brick bearing wall assembly, with vapor-permeable board insulation installed adjacent to the interior face of brick and a vapor-permeable, insulated finish wall assembly installed to the interior of that.

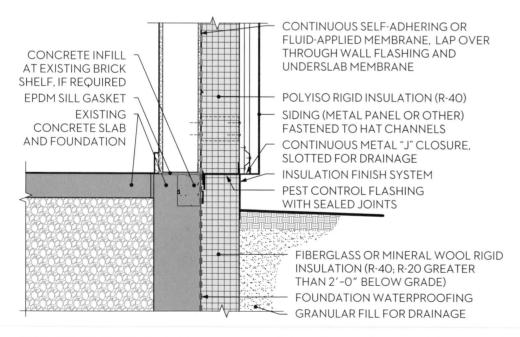

CONCRETE INFILL
AT EXISTING BRICK
SHELF, IF REQUIRED

EPDM SILL GASKET

EXISTING
CONCRETE SLAB
AND FOUNDATION

CONTINUOUS SELF-ADHERING OR
FLUID-APPLIED MEMBRANE, LAP OVER
THROUGH WALL FLASHING AND
UNDERSLAB MEMBRANE

POLYISO RIGID INSULATION (R-40)

SIDING (METAL PANEL OR OTHER)
FASTENED TO HAT CHANNELS

CONTINUOUS METAL "J" CLOSURE,
SLOTTED FOR DRAINAGE

INSULATION FINISH SYSTEM

PEST CONTROL FLASHING
WITH SEALED JOINTS

FIBERGLASS OR MINERAL WOOL RIGID
INSULATION (R-40; R-20 GREATER
THAN 2'-0" BELOW GRADE)

FOUNDATION WATERPROOFING

GRANULAR FILL FOR DRAINAGE

FIGURE 14.7. With the brick veneer removed, the wall assembly can easily be insulated on the exterior, and there are many options for lightweight replacement wall claddings.

Below we discuss potential strategies for a few types of construction.

BRICK BEARING WALL. One common type of exterior wall assembly found in historical buildings is a solid, multiwythe brick or other masonry bearing wall (figure 14.6). From a building science perspective, this wall has some unique characteristics. The brick and mortar absorb moisture to varying degrees, and different kinds of brick absorb different amounts of moisture. Where brick is a veneer and there is a cavity behind the brick, the brick can dry to the cavity or exterior. If brick is a thicker, structural bearing wall, moisture absorbed in the wall dries to the interior. Thus, vapor-control layers and some levels of insulation on the interior can keep the brick from drying, and it can crack and spall in freeze-thaw cycles. It is therefore important to provide vapor-permeable, or at least semi-permeable, insulation and finishes on the interior of such brick walls.

Adding a new brick wall on the exterior may be the best approach in terms of building science approach but not in terms of cost, historic preservation, or aesthetics. If the existing brick exterior is to be preserved, insulating on the interior is the only practical option. To achieve net zero, 2" of vapor-permeable EPS rigid foam or low-density open-cell spray foam can be applied directly to the interior face of masonry. Where board insulation is used, care must be taken to install it tightly to the masonry, with horizontal adhesive beads, to prevent the potential for heat-robbing convective air movement between the insulation and the masonry. On the interior side of the board or spray insulation, new wall studs can be installed with dense-pack cellulose insulation between them. Wood studs are preferable to reduce thermal bridging. On the interior face of studs, a variable-permeability vapor retarder is installed and vapor-permeable paint applied to the gypsum board finish to allow moisture to migrate out of the cavity to the building interior.

VENEER EXTERIOR WALL ASSEMBLY. Concrete and steel is probably the most common construction type used with a masonry veneer wall assembly, with either a light-gauge steel stud or masonry backup wall. In older buildings there is often little or no insulation on the exterior of the backup wall, and the thermal bridging through the metal stud or masonry reduces the wall's overall R-value.

The ideal solution is to add air-, water-, and vapor-control layers and rigid insulation (R-20 or higher, depending on the cavity insulation R-value) on the exterior side of the sheathing to reduce thermal bridging, improve the overall R-value to net zero standards, and install air-, water-, and vapor-control layers equivalent to the standards for new buildings.

This requires removing the existing brick veneer, which is often not economically feasible on larger buildings with a sound veneer and a well-constructed drainage plane and flashing system. If the existing drainage plane was not properly installed and is beginning to show signs of deterioration (which is common in late-twentieth-century buildings), removing brick is frequently justified. It may also prove to be the best strategy on a smaller building or one in which the veneer or the drainage plane and flashing system are compromised. Since the added insulation usually takes up the space the brick once occupied, if the brick veneer is to be replaced in kind, a new concrete shelf wall can be constructed next to the existing foundation to support it (figure 14.4). Other lightweight exterior finishes may be used in place of the brick, supported on furring channels instead of the foundation (figure 14.7).

A less expensive though less than ideal solution for light-gauge stud backup walls that does not require removing the brick veneer is to replace the insulation between the metal studs with a higher R-value insulation and/or add rigid board insulation on the interior face of wall studs. The ideal insulation for retrofitting within the stud cavity from a performance viewpoint (though not

an environmental one) would be high-density spray-foam insulation, because of its high R-value and resistance to air and vapor transmission. For masonry backup walls, rigid board insulation applied to the interior face of masonry and cavity fill insulation, if not already present, will help to increase the wall's R-value. Applying insulation on the interior involves demolishing and replacing the interior wall finishes. Other challenges include floor or roof decks that extend to the outside face of the wall, creating a thermal bridge when the plane of the insulation is within or behind the stud cavity. This strategy should be a last resort. Due to structural framing and metal studs, it is almost impossible for this strategy to achieve our net zero performance standards.

PRE-ENGINEERED STEEL BUILDINGS. Steel buildings, such as warehouses, composed of a steel frame with purlins and exterior metal panels, are typically poorly air-sealed, water protected, and insulated. The steel structure was almost always designed to the minimum code requirements at the time and does not comply with current code. When insulation is added, such structures typically cannot accommodate snow loads and so must be reinforced. Low-pitched roofs with inadequate metal roofing systems almost always leak and need to be replaced with a new membrane roof for proper water protection. For warehouses, however, many users prefer to save money and deal with occasional leaks. In insulating these buildings, the common practice of draping batt pillows over the purlins and fastening the metal panels to the outside of the purlins compresses the batt insulation along the purlins, resulting in heat loss that can cause condensation and corrosion and reduces overall insulating values substantially.

The preferred option for retrofitting this type of building—assuming the structure is adequate—is to replace the wall panels with insulated metal panels and replace the metal roof, usually with new structural metal deck, rigid insulation, and a membrane roof. If the structure is not adequate and needs reinforcement, the real value of the pre-engineered building may only be the foundation—not a very comforting conclusion for the building owner. A less expensive option is to insulate from the interior side, usually by adding interior framing with an insulated space between exterior and interior framing. However, this system is not likely to eliminate thermal bridging and meet net zero energy standards. Figure 14.8 indicates the preferred panel retrofit.

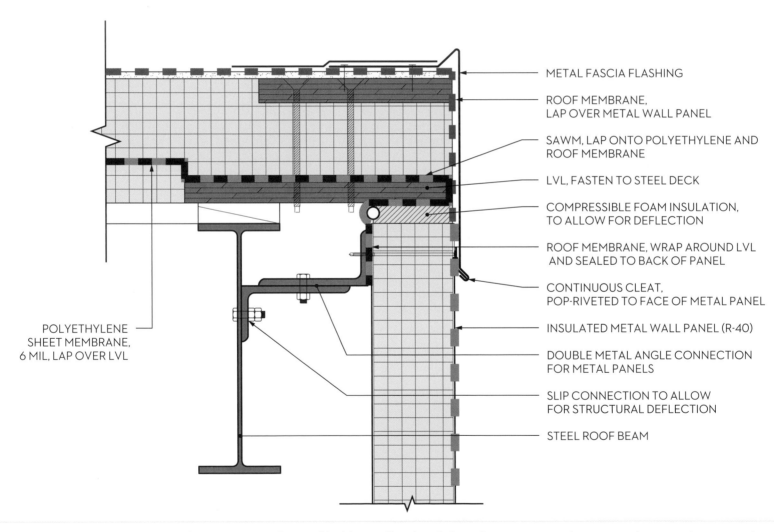

METAL FASCIA FLASHING

ROOF MEMBRANE,
LAP OVER METAL WALL PANEL

SAWM, LAP ONTO POLYETHYLENE AND
ROOF MEMBRANE

LVL, FASTEN TO STEEL DECK

COMPRESSIBLE FOAM INSULATION,
TO ALLOW FOR DEFLECTION

ROOF MEMBRANE, WRAP AROUND LVL
AND SEALED TO BACK OF PANEL

CONTINUOUS CLEAT,
POP-RIVETED TO FACE OF METAL PANEL

INSULATED METAL WALL PANEL (R-40)

DOUBLE METAL ANGLE CONNECTION
FOR METAL PANELS

SLIP CONNECTION TO ALLOW
FOR STRUCTURAL DEFLECTION

STEEL ROOF BEAM

POLYETHYLENE
SHEET MEMBRANE,
6 MIL, LAP OVER LVL

FIGURE 14.8. This detail, at the intersection of a metal building wall and roof, shows how existing inadequate insulation can be removed and replaced with superior insulated wall and roof assemblies. Note that the intersection of these assemblies must be designed to accommodate structural deflection of the roof beams without damaging the control layers.

PART IV

Expanding the Net Zero Horizon

15 | The Case for Renovation

Even as new high-performance and net zero buildings proliferate, there is a common belief that achieving the same performance levels in existing buildings is unrealistic or impossible. These perceptions are wrong. In this chapter we explain why and give you the tools you need to advocate for net zero renovations where practical. While existing buildings typically are challenging and often expensive to improve to net zero levels, thorough assessment and analysis can identify which buildings are viable for net zero renovation and which buildings need more investment, time, or resources than are available.

The results can be surprising. Recently, for instance, the New Buildings Institute investigated deep energy savings in fifty buildings. They found that the average energy savings were greater than 50 percent. And in eleven of the best buildings, the energy intensity (EUI) was less than 39 kBtu/sf-yr.[1]

Why Renovate?

The existing buildings in the United States consume an overwhelming percentage of our nation's overall energy use—48.7 percent, or 47.8 quadrillion Btus annually.[2] To put this into perspective, every year this amount is equal to

- 2.3 billion short tons of coal, enough to fill a train of railroad cars 194,600 miles long (about 72 times across the United States or 7.8 times around the earth's equator);
- 382 billion gallons of gasoline—or 725 million passenger cars each driving 16,550 miles;
- 8.2 billion barrels of crude oil—8,000 days of oil flow in the Alaska pipeline at full capacity;
- 38 days of total world energy use.[3]

When you narrow the scope to just electricity use versus total energy use, the numbers are even more alarming: buildings use 75 percent of all the electricity

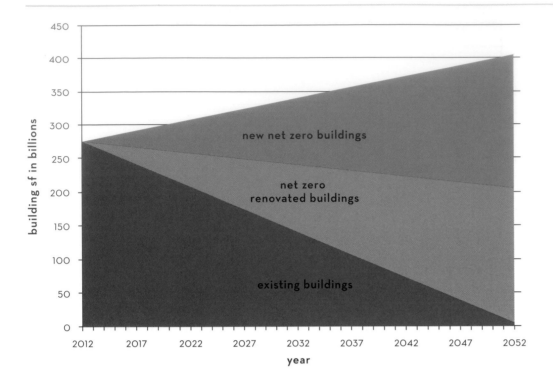

produced in the United States.[4] So not only will net zero renovation go far in reducing the nation's total energy consumption, it is also mandatory if we are going to transition off fossil fuels and keep at least some of our existing buildings.

To develop a viable plan to transition to a net zero future on a schedule that correlates with likely fossil-fuel price escalation, we'll need to examine the trends of building and renovation over time in the United States. The nation's existing building stock comprises approximately 275 billion square feet. Annually, on average, we tear down 1.75 billion square feet, renovate 5 billion square feet, and build 5 billion new square feet.[5] If these rates are maintained, and if all work performed on both new and existing buildings is performed to net zero standards, it would be roughly forty years before all buildings would reach net zero performance as shown in figure 15.1. If we rely only on new construction to reach net zero levels and allow renovation work to continue below these standards, the timeline for achieving our goal stretches to over 150 years. However, with no net zero requirement in place the time frame for every building in the United States to reach net zero extends much longer.

With diminishing fossil-fuel reserves and increasing energy prices, the timetables described in these scenarios indicate the need to begin in earnest the process of improving our existing building stock to net zero or net zero ready performance levels.

FACTORING IN EMBODIED ENERGY

Existing buildings also account for a significant amount of embodied energy—or energy beyond what they consume for operation. In the process of constructing buildings, energy is required to extract or produce building materials, as well as transport them to and place them on the site. Every product in our buildings contains a varying amount of embodied energy, an important factor when considering whether to renovate an existing structure or which products to choose. Wood, for example, has little embodied energy, while cement, which requires the mining of nonrenewable raw materials, has 43 percent more embodied energy by volume.[6]

Research shows that operational energy accounts for 83 to 94 percent of total energy during a fifty-year life cycle.[7] That doesn't mean, though, that embodied energy

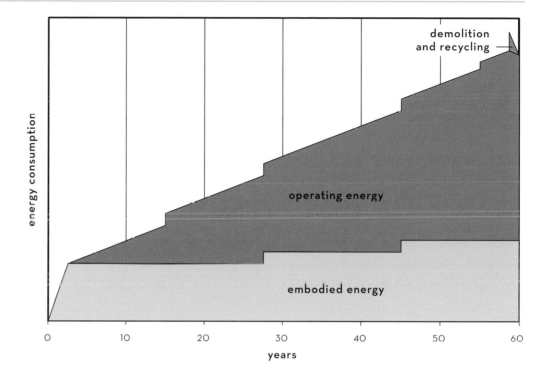

FIGURE 15.2. Construction of a building involves embodied energy—energy consumed in producing the building materials, transporting them to the site, and constructing the building. However, in a typical building the majority of energy is consumed operating the building, with a small amount for demolition at the end of the building's life. In net zero buildings the operating costs are much smaller than what is shown here for a typical building.

is insignificant—rather, it shows that building energy use is exceptionally high. And in net zero buildings, the embodied energy is proportionally much greater, as there is increased energy in materials compared to significant energy reductions in operations. Thus, we recommend calculating the embodied energy when assessing existing buildings for renovation or replacement. Table 15.1 shows the widely varied embodied energy between building materials, although materials that are more heavily processed or less locally sourced typically have higher embodied energy contents.[8]

UNDERSTANDING LIFE CYCLES FOR MATERIALS AND BUILDINGS

We should also analyze the life cycles of building materials and assemblies. For instance, if a product has high embodied energy and a short life cycle, this clearly is not an efficient use of resources. From a sustainability perspective, durability and life cycles are even more important than embodied energy. For instance, stone, which was traditionally used structurally in institutional projects, lasts for hundreds or even thousands of

years. Important buildings in Europe and ancient civilizations last much longer then new buildings of steel and concrete with thin veneer finishes. Some buildings erected in the last century may last twenty years or less due to building science issues.

THE IMPACT OF TRANSPORTATION

Looking at how much energy a building consumes for its daily operation, though, tells just half the story. The other half of a building's total energy consumption and carbon footprint comes from the transportation of people, goods, and utilities to the building. Much of our older building stock is located in urban areas, where mass transportation reduces the energy consumed to move people and goods. If we compare renovating an existing building in an urban location to building a new one in a suburban or rural location, the annual energy consumption will almost always be significantly lower for the existing building in the centralized location when transportation energy is included.

Clearly, location and proximity to mass transportation and goods and services have a dramatic impact on the total energy

TABLE 15.1. EMBODIED ENERGY OF BUILDING MATERIALS BY WEIGHT

	EMBODIED ENERGY (MJ/Kg)	EMBODIED CARBON (KgCO$_2$/Kg)
Concrete Block (medium density)	0.67	0.074
Concrete (1:1.5:3 cement:sand:aggregate)	1.11	0.159
Cellulose	0.94–3.3	. . .
Brick	3	0.22
Timber (general)	8.5	0.46
Steel	24.4	1.77
Fiberglass (glass wool)	28	1.35
PVC Pipe	67.5	2.5
Aluminum	155	8.24
Monocrystalline PV Modules	4,750	242

Source: Geoff Hammond and Craig Jones, "Inventory of Carbon and Energy (ICE)" University of Bath, Version 1.6a, http://web.mit.edu/2.813/www/readings/ICE.pdf.

consumption of a building. If we compare the total energy consumption for a family in a rural net zero home with a car (or multiple cars) to an urban family in an uninsulated apartment using public transportation, it is likely that the total energy consumption of the family in the apartment is significantly less than the family living in the rural, net zero home. Rejuvenating our existing downtowns and our existing infrastructure and not just continuing to build structures farther from our downtowns is an essential consideration in creating our net zero future.

How to Assess Existing Buildings

The first step of a net zero renovation is a critical assessment of the existing building. And the first decision to be made is whether to renovate a building at all. Some existing buildings are not a prudent investment and should be removed, reusing and recycling as much material as possible, rather than renovated. Others have net zero renovation potential but also inherent challenges arising from the fact that they weren't created using integrated design principles and so are unlikely to meet all of the design guidelines we would recommend for net

zero buildings. That said, in many building renovations, changes in the design process can result in metrics as low as those for new net zero buildings.

The process of achieving a net zero renovation is in some ways similar to the process of building a new net zero building. You must still consider location, siting, massing/orientation, and daylighting. But there are also some key differences. You must assess existing structural integrity, existing insulation, moisture concerns, indoor air quality, building science, environmental controls/mechanical systems, embodied energy, life cycle, and historic considerations.

Let's walk through all these assessment points in the context of renovation.

LOCATION

First we must consider the location of the building in relation to its total energy consumption, asking the following questions:

- Is the building located near public transportation?
- Is the building located near amenities?
- Are there opportunities for mixed use that can reduce the overall energy consumption and carbon emissions of the occupants or users?

There also may be some considerations that offset location concerns. An historic building may be a significant cultural asset. Or it may have important community value that makes it worth relocating to a better site—a more common practice in the past. Think of other reasons an existing building may be an asset and worth keeping before it is too late.

BUILDING SITE/MASSING AND ORIENTATION TO SUN AND VIEWS

Whether renovating an existing building or building a new building, a preliminary assessment includes the constraints of the site, including planning and building codes, existing permit requirements, wetland restrictions, past pollution issues, market constraints, stormwater permits, traffic requirements, and any other municipality-enforced requirements. Achieving net zero goals means evaluating additional site constraints as well, including shading from adjacent buildings and vegetation, view opportunities, and surrounding land uses that affect future mixed-use potential. At this stage you should ask such questions as:

- What is the solar potential of the site, including passive, active, and PV options?
- Are existing outside spaces pleasant to use?
- Are there changes to the site that can enhance the user experience?
- Are there site constraints that limit net zero goals?
- If this is a brownfield site, are the costs manageable for site restoration?
- Are there funding or market opportunities to offset constraints?

At this stage it is important to assess how the existing building compares to typical integrated design strategies and practices overall, and in particular those strategies related to mass and orientation. As we discussed in greater detail in chapter 3, ideally buildings are elongated along the east–west axis, so that there's an opportunity to maximize south-facing glass for passive solar heating. This massing and orientation also mean that there is an opportunity for more north-facing glass, which doesn't have the overheating problems that east–west glass does but is still very useful for daylighting. One of the largest challenges when considering existing buildings is

that they have been sited in every possible orientation. While picking up and reorienting the building on the property is not typically a viable solution, it is possible for some small buildings.

BUILDING FUNCTION AND FIT

The existing building must be assessed in terms of how the overall building size and shape will suit the needs of the future users. Whether the use will remain the same or a new use will be accommodated in the existing building envelope, keep in mind the following questions:

- Does the size of the building suit the future needs of the client and users?
- Does the building footprint need to be expanded? If so, can it be expanded, and how difficult and expensive is that to do?
- Can the building be opened up or changed to improve performance?

Adaptive reuse of buildings is both a significant challenge and often a great opportunity for creativity and innovation.

DAYLIGHTING

The daylighting potential of a building is directly interconnected with the building massing and orientation. If the building is well oriented along the east–west axis, there is an opportunity to maximize daylighting and/or passive solar heating while minimizing glare and overheating issues. This is valid regardless of whether daylighting or solar is being used effectively in the existing building. Some questions to consider at this point include the following:

- Is the building so wide that daylight is not able to penetrate well? Generally, buildings wider than 50 feet in any one direction do not allow for the effective use of daylight in the center of the building.
- What are the floor-to-floor heights? The higher the floor, the deeper the light can penetrate into the building. Lower floor-to-floor heights reduce the potential for daylight penetration.
- How tall are existing windows? And how far off the floor are existing windows? This affects view, daylight, and glare.

Many buildings that are over 100 years old were designed to use daylight effectively because artificial lighting was dim and expensive. Often older buildings that have been previously renovated have been retrofitted with modern lighting and mechanical systems. They may have windows or skylights that have been closed off when dropped ceilings were installed. In many old buildings, these existing openings can be reopened to provide daylighting and can make the existing building consistent with net zero daylighting strategies. In contrast, many of the buildings constructed in the twentieth century were designed to rely on artificial illumination, which can cause major challenges for renovation when considering daylighting strategies.

Windows can be enlarged or heightened, but such modifications to the exterior envelope may mean a major impact and expense, especially when somewhat immovable materials, such as brick, were used for the exterior finish. If the building is wider than ideal, skylights can increase the daylighting opportunity for a single-story building; light wells and multistory atriums can provide better opportunities for daylighting in multistory buildings. Although alterations to improve daylighting do result in additional cost, if these updates are connected to creating better spaces for circulation or gathering, the multiple benefits can make the change an easier investment. Daylighting strategies are covered in greater detail in chapter 4.

STRUCTURAL SYSTEMS

In a new building the structural system can be designed specifically to fit net zero requirements, but in a renovation the existing building has a structure that needs to be evaluated for reuse. While that structure can be modified to meet net zero goals, there can be significant expense.

Here are some of the many questions that can guide the evaluation of the existing structure:

- What is the overall condition of the structure? Is there evidence of rust, rot, or termites? Are the walls, floors, or roofs bowed or sagging?
- Has deterioration occurred since the building was built? Has the building been well maintained? Are there deferred maintenance issues?

- Is there failure within the structure? Do basement walls, beams, or other structural members have cracks or breaks? Are structural members such as columns and beams separating at joints?

These, though, cover just a few of the possible problems with existing buildings. To thoroughly evaluate the structure, you will likely need a structural engineer to conduct a careful review of the existing conditions, determine whether the structure has deteriorated, and evaluate its appropriateness for reuse. Use a structural engineer with renovation experience and preferably net zero experience.

Second, the structure must be evaluated for its ability to support any proposed new use for the building. For instance, if the building was designed as a mill and will be renovated for use as an office, the loads will likely be less for the new use and the structure will likely be adequate. Conversely, if the proposed design includes large gathering spaces or storage spaces, these spaces may call for structural amendments. As building uses change, so do codes, and the structure might need to be changed to meet current guidelines. This is particularly relevant for roof loads in climates with snow but can also apply to floor loading. While an initial visual inspection is often helpful for renovation projects because of the complications of these requirements, it is essential that an engineer perform a detailed structural evaluation, including both overall existing condition and new load requirements.

Sometimes work associated with the renovation of a building will also impact the structure. To meet net zero building goals, the roof must be insulated, increasing the snow loading on the building structure and therefore requiring structural reinforcement. And while the installation of a green roof is not required for a net zero renovation, they have become more and more popular in green building designs. However, in existing buildings they will typically increase roof loads beyond their designed structural capacity and thus may require further reinforcement of the roof structure.

It is also important in reviewing the building structure to consider how flexible it is for renovation. For instance, renovation and updates to interior partitioning in buildings with a bearing wall type of construction will often be more challenging than in structures using open columns and beams, which greatly

Vermont Energy Investment Corporation's mission is to reduce financial and environmental costs of energy in Vermont and beyond. It manages energy-efficiency programs to save millions of energy dollars per year and reduce significant amounts of carbon.

For its office expansion, the company selected an historic cotton mill with a floor plate the size of a football field. The project demonstrated that an old industrial building can be successfully repurposed for high-performance office use, despite a footprint that at first seemed antithetical to high-performing workspace.

The mill was built in the mid-nineteenth century, before electric light, and therefore was designed for maximizing daylight. Even though the floor plate was 100 feet wide, the typical floor-to-floor height was 15 feet 9 inches, allowing light to penetrate deeply from two sides. Renovation during the twentieth century dropped ceilings, closed off high windows, and put executive offices on the perimeter, leaving an unattractive, artificially lit open office area for support staff. With the windows opened up and dropped ceilings eliminated, the space could again use daylight as the primary source of light.

The question was whether the large space could be converted into a satisfying and productive workspace. The redesign used a "neighborhoods" concept, with a connected block of meeting, storage, and support spaces at the center of the building to break up the space. A "street" for circulation connects the center with "neighborhoods," giving a village or small-town feeling. At the center is the heart of the organization's physical space, a two-story café that serves as town center, a place for whole-company gatherings, eating, and informal meetings.

To conserve energy, a strategy was developed for incremental insulation and daylighting improvements.

FIGURE 15.3. The interior of the Vermont Energy Investment Corporation's headquarters: *top left*, previous office space, with low ceilings and a cube format; *bottom left*, new offices with "neighborhoods"; *right*, "town center" for eating and company or small meetings.

Brick buildings have specific concerns related to moisture issues. When bricks get wet, they absorb varying levels of moisture. Generally, harder brick absorbs less moisture, making it more durable, and softer brick needs to have softer, more absorbent mortar so that the wall is less affected by freeze-thaw cycles. In a building assembly, brick walls typically dry to the inside in the wintertime. Thus, as the exterior brick wall gets wet, the moisture gets drawn into the brick, then dries to the interior of the building. If during renovation you install a vapor barrier on the wall, then in the future moisture from the brick can no longer dry to the inside of the building. This can cause the bricks to freeze, creating freeze-thaw cycles where the bricks perform differently from the mortar, which can cause the bricks to deteriorate as a result. When working with existing brick buildings, assess the bricks and mortar to determine if they are compatible with proposed wall assembly changes.[9]

enhance the flexibility of a renovation. While any of these structural issues can be addressed in a renovation, there may be additional costs associated with meeting net zero standards.

BUILDING INSULATION

In renovating an existing building to net zero standards, often the largest change is boosting insulation levels. Interestingly, the worse the situation seems in terms of insulation levels in an existing building, the easier it is to justify upgrading insulation to net zero standards. Conversely, the more insulation that is already in the existing building enclosure, the harder it is to justify the expense of energy upgrades to net zero improvements.

Given the goal of meeting net zero standards, assessing the existing insulation is central to our purpose. Determine the type, thickness, and insulating value of insulation around the entire building enclosure. Assess the insulation conduction. Has its effectiveness been reduced by water, insects, building user alterations, or other concerns? Has the appropriate insulation been used in the appropriate location? Is there a vapor barrier, and is it properly installed? Is there leaking into the insulation and/or structure due to poor roof, wall, window, and/or door details? Review chapters 8 through 13 for new construction to see whether insulation has been properly installed. Determine whether to remove and/or reuse existing insulation.

Once we evaluate the current levels of insulation in the building and decide how much insulation needs to be added to reach our net zero metrics, then we need to determine where this added insulation will occur. To upgrade insulation we typically have choices: adding insulation on the interior of the existing building enclosure, the exterior of the building enclosure, or a combination. In chapter 14 we explored how to approach this in greater detail based on the conditions encountered, including a consideration of the interior and exterior finishes, as well as the water, air, and vapor barriers and the dew point in the new net zero assembly.

WATER AND VAPOR

Building science, particularly as it relates to water and vapor migration, has generally been inadequately understood and addressed in the building profession. Only recently have building science concerns factored into standard construction techniques. When we consider existing buildings, the issue of moisture can be significant in relation to occupant health and building durability. Assessing moisture issues in existing buildings requires a firm foundation in building science and the principles discussed in chapter 4.[10]

Older building assemblies are simple constructions of wood and stone. As we renovate these structures, we alter this simplicity and must be careful not to create a building enclosure that causes moisture issues and increases the potential for mold growth or other indoor air-quality problems.

All too often it is determined that renovation to net zero standards cannot be performed in existing buildings due to vapor and moisture issues. Then these buildings undergo a standard renovation to deal with outstanding deferred maintenance issues. In these standard renovations, what is often overlooked is that any tightening of a building envelope with existing moisture issues may result in significant negative consequences to building durability and occupant health. In old buildings water vapor from the ground frequently travels to upper floors, migrating through vapor-permeable walls and escaping to the outside. However, when the building is tightened up, this migration is slowed significantly. If there are places where mold and mildew already exist, these problems could be exacerbated. If any vapor barrier currently does exist in the building, it needs to be assessed in terms of condition and effectiveness. Sometimes a damaged moisture barrier can cause more damage as rain and direct water is trapped within the building envelope. How to address these conditions in a net zero renovation is covered in the building assemblies in chapter 14.

ENVIRONMENTAL CONTROL

An overall building assessment should consider the existing mechanical systems, including heating, cooling, and ventilation. While net zero structures should be designed to last at least 100 years, mechanical systems typically will be replaced in twenty to twenty-five years. If the mechanical systems are already in need of replacement, it can make a net zero renovation more cost effective, because more of the building improvements can be accounted for under deferred maintenance needs. In assessing the reuse of environmental control systems, we must consider existing and/or potential indoor air-quality issues along with the possible reuse of part or all of the existing systems. Some questions we might ask under this assessment include:

- Is the current ventilation adequate? Will it be adequate to meet the changes resulting from renovation work?
- Are there duct linings that currently do or could harbor biological growth and cause health issues?
- Are return air plenums used that can distribute contaminants?
- Is the boiler or furnace exhaust system located in such a way that contamination of the air intake could occur?
- Are air intakes located near truck loading, trash, or other possible pollution sources?

Again, these questions address just a few of the areas that should be investigated in relation to the environmental control systems. These systems are complex, and evaluation by a knowledgeable and experienced MEP engineer is critical.

Special Concerns with Historic Buildings

The renovation of historic buildings to net zero standards presents unique challenges and opportunities over and above the renovation of typical existing buildings. Sensitivity to the character and integrity of the historic building provides the foundation for all changes. As with the reuse of any historic building, we should begin by assessing the significant historic aspects of a building and asking question such as:

- Are the exterior and interior well preserved?
- Are there elements or parts of the building where historic character has been compromised?
- Are there historic elements that are deteriorating? Does this relate to the design of the building structure and environmental control systems?
- Will historic details that are poorly designed from a building science and durability perspective be more difficult to fix because it is a historic building?

Prior to proposing any energy improvements, conduct an overall historic assessment to address all historic elements and determine whether each element is worth preserving. While most of this discussion will focus on the challenges

There has long been a conception in the design world that renovation projects cannot achieve the same levels of energy performance as new construction. The Wayne Aspinall Federal Building and US Courthouse, a prominent building in downtown Grand Junction, Colorado, refutes this notion. Built in 1918, this 41,562 sf building is designed to be net zero.

The federal government has set a target for all agencies to achieve energy independence by the year 2030. When the Wayne Aspinall Federal Building project was granted $15 million in American Recovery and Reinvestment Act funds to modernize the building, the owner set a target for this to be the first site net zero building listed on the National Register of Historic Places. Performance targets also included achieving LEED Platinum and total energy performance 50 percent better than code.

The design concept for the Wayne Aspinall Federal Building and US Courthouse combines the needs of both the historic building and energy-performance upgrades. It was found that many of the original building features had been heavily altered, so the redesign took into account both historic and energy concerns to restore the building to its original grandeur. The main lobby was converted from a small vestibule to an open, airy entry; the historic grand curved stairwell that connects three floors was reopened; original arched windows were exposed after being hidden behind dropped ceilings; and the original skylight was restored, providing increased daylighting throughout the building.

New, high-performance mechanical systems were integrated into the building, but in such a way as to differentiate between the new and historic elements. A geo-exchange system rejects or provides heat to the building using the constant temperature of the earth, which is tied to the high-efficiency HVAC system that filters and conditions air for comfortable cooling and heating for building occupants. Additional features incorporated into the renovated building are advanced metering and building controls, high-efficiency lighting systems, and a thermally enhanced building envelope. A 123 kW PV array located on an elevated canopy above the building's north edge is expected to cover the building's annual energy needs.

of balancing historic building standards and net zero building standards, it is critical to begin with recognizing the opportunity that historic buildings offer. Historic buildings are typically high-quality buildings that usually are durable and well designed. They represent our history and culture and add value to our lives. They also represent a chance to integrate our diverse and rich heritage into the future that we create.

Unfortunately, there has been some conflict between historic preservationists and energy advocates, and some of the most widely discussed disagreements surround embodied energy, building deterioration, and energy consumption.

Some energy advocates argue that the cost of renovating historic buildings is too expensive and thus only the most historic buildings should be preserved. However, when we factor embodied energy into the discussion and couple it with a building's cultural importance, the additional cost to renovate historic buildings can be justified—so the design process should begin with an historic assessment that specifically addresses embodied energy.

FIGURE 15.4. *Top left*, the Wayne Apsinall Federal Building, a community icon, is on the National Register of Historic Places and is net zero. *Right*, the original arched windows were exposed throughout the building, and an additional storm window and solar-control system was installed to increase thermal performance. *Bottom left*, the roof contains a 123 kW PV system sized to provide enough energy to cover the building's use on an annual basis.

Addressing building deterioration issues also poses specific challenges in historic structures. Historic preservation advocates often oppose changes to the building enclosure, such as insulating walls, roofs, and foundations, which impact energy and moisture migration due to visible impacts on historic elements. Taken to the extreme, some have proposed that no changes should be allowed to historic building enclosures to ensure that the historic structure is not harmed. However, as mentioned above, older buildings typically allowed for abundant moisture vapor and air migration through the building enclosure, allowing buildings to dry themselves and therefore limiting deterioration. This generally works. And obviously the underlying concern for the durability of the structure is valid and relevant. If we save energy in the short term and rot the structure in the long term, we have not created a truly sustainable and net zero solution. That said, there are often changes that can be made to improve building performance without causing harm.

First of all, not all historic structures were well designed: there may be leaking due to poor initial design details; the site

Kimberley Quirk bought an historic building in Enfield, New Hampshire, with the goal of creating a net zero demonstration project with commercial and retail space and a home for herself. Living in a village, she would save travel to work and enjoy other amenities. She worked with her local historic commission to achieve both her energy and preservation goals.

The envelope was first sealed and insulated to net zero standards. A whole-house heat-recovery ventilation system was used to efficiently provide fresh air to the tight building. The building is heated with a solar evacuated-tube hot water system with seasonal storage and an on-demand electric hot water backup that will also boost the temperature from the tank as needed. Electric backup was needed in the coldest winter months, when the solar thermal tank could not provide enough heat. Continued monitoring to optimize the systems and size an appropriate PV system to offset all of the electric use is currently in the works.[11] Quirk put together a financial analysis and determined a simple seven-year payback and a fifteen-year internal rate of return (IRR) of 14 percent.[12]

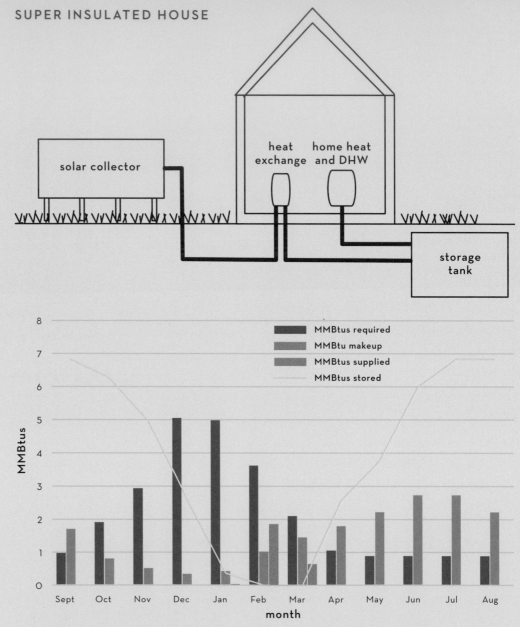

SUPER INSULATED HOUSE

FIGURE 15.5. The renovation used an innovative solar hot water and PV system for heating and electricity that allowed for energy to be stored for months when supply exceeded demand.

FIGURE 15.6. The restoration retained the historic character and improved the envelope to net zero standards. The renovated exterior (*top*), the historic exterior (*bottom left*), and a detail of the interior during construction (*bottom right*).

THE EMPIRE STATE BUILDING

The Empire State Building, opened in 1931, is the icon of American skyscrapers. It is 2.7 million sf, and yet its existing energy intensity is 88 kBtu/sf-yr, which is much better than that of many newer skyscrapers. Building owner Malkin Holdings worked with a core team that included the Clinton Climate Initiative as the project advisor, Jones Lang LaSalle as the project manager, Johnson Controls as the energy service company, and Rocky Mountain Institute as the design partner. The goal was to improve energy performance and reduce carbon emissions through a $550 million renovation project, of which $106 million was energy related. Due to window, mechanical, and enclosure improvements that reduced mechanical and cooling loads and hence capital costs, the incremental cost for energy improvements was only $13.2 million, with annual savings of $4.4 million; the simple payback is less than three years.[13]

The owner and project team engaged many stakeholders and created an iterative and collaborative process that enabled the team to achieve the project goals. Then they identified all possible technically achievable energy-efficiency measures and packaged these to compare cumulative energy

FIGURE 15.7. The integrated approach to energy savings: comparing the capital costs for efficiency measures (*yellow*) to the initial project savings due to reduced mechanical system requirements (*blue*) and yearly energy savings (*green*) shows overall project benefits, even within the first year.[14]

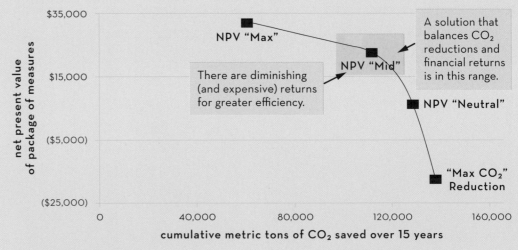

FIGURE 15.8. The range of energy-efficiency measure packages and the resulting net present value of savings generated compared to CO_2 emissions reduction. The "mid" value was chosen for the project in order to optimize those two variables.

savings that could arise. Additionally, carbon-offset strategies were packaged together in a range of offset outcomes in order to compare the financial savings and the carbon offsets. Figure 15.8 shows the three levels of cost saving and carbon offset based on the fifteen-year net present value. As more efficiency measures are added to the package, additional CO_2 savings are realized, but there are diminishing returns on the net present value of these energy savings because the upfront cost is greater.

A particularly unique innovation was the on-site remanufacturing of 6,500 existing glass units into super windows, which reduce heat loss in the winter and solar gain in the summer. Other measures included radiant barriers, dimmable lights and photosensors on the lighting, tenant load reduction, and chiller and mechanical system improvements.

While these measures did not get the Empire State Building to a net zero ready status, the technical potential of using all of the energy efficiency measures was a 48 percent reduction in existing energy use, or 46 kBtu/sf-yr. The final design EUI is 55 kBtu/sf-yr, which is still a substantial accomplishment for a historic, commercial, 102-story office building.[15]

The process used in this project is fully applicable to net zero projects.

THE BYRON G. ROGERS FEDERAL OFFICE BUILDING

The Byron Rogers Federal Office Building, built in 1964 for the US General Services Administration, is another example of what can be accomplished with a historic high-rise. The renovation of this nearly 500,000 sf building had to take into account the preservation of the midcentury modern architecture. Without changing the look of the building, the renovation cut energy consumption 70 percent, from 90 kBtu/sf-yr to an estimated 27 kBtu/sf-yr EUI plus 25.7 kBtu/sf-yr with renewables, which is within the net zero ready range.[16]

FIGURE 15.9. Byron Rogers Federal Building, Denver, Colorado.

may be wetter than anticipated or prone to flooding; or the building may experience "rising damp," moisture in foundation walls migrating from the ground. While fixing these deficiencies may have some impact on the historic character, leaving the exact historic details in place may threaten the long-term health of the building. Second and often more common, the use of the building has changed, and this new use and the systems supporting it can lead to building deterioration. For example, an historic building may have been minimally heated or cooled by early users, but modern standards of comfort have caused a major increase in the heating and/or cooling of the building. This can cause ice damming on roofs or moisture issues in walls or ceilings, as moisture condenses in the building enclosure. An even more common problem is that insulation or vapor and air barriers have been added incrementally over time and are already causing major durability issues.

All of these factors, and their tendency to compound and cause greater problems, underscore the need to conduct a thorough investigation of the building based on building science. This investigation should include an evaluation of the original design and an evaluation of the building at the time of inspection. It should also include options for the long-term health and preservation of the building, at different levels—including a return to the original envelope design, maintenance as is, net zero ready, and high-performing options. Typically, when building science is used as the foundation of assessment, it is possible to achieve net zero goals *and* improve the long-term durability of the historic building.

The real question when balancing historic and energy concerns is how much alteration to the historic structure is acceptable. Most people would not want noticeable changes to landmark buildings but would allow alterations to sections of historic buildings that have already lost their historic quality. The vast majority of historic buildings fall somewhere in between these states, and an in-depth energy analysis combined with historic assessment should be conducted to find an appropriate balance between historic preservation and energy. Finding that balance is quite important, because many historic buildings include no or very minimal insulation, which means that rising energy costs might soon make these properties unviable to use. For unique or landmark historic properties, these rising costs often can be accommodated. However, when the building is being evaluated for adaptive reuse to housing, retail, commercial, or anything else where it will be competing with new and non-historic properties, the rising energy costs may edge the historic building out of the marketplace. Without incorporating energy conservation at higher levels, many historic buildings may be abandoned.

If energy conservation measures are addressed in places that are not visible, the concerns are minimal. Adding attic or basement insulation, for example, is typically not a controversial energy conservation measure. Similarly, if wall cavities can be filled to net zero ready standards without altering finishes and wall thickness, almost no one objects to doing so. But especially when insulating to net zero ready standards, wall insulation can rarely be added in such a manner. To meet net zero ready standards in most historic buildings, the exterior walls need to be thickened, a reasonable and appropriate alteration on all but the most significant historic buildings. Some preservationists, however, oppose this almost across the board. Although some superinsulating technologies achieve very high insulation levels in minimal depths, these currently are ultra-high-tech methods that are extraordinarily expensive. This then raises the discussion of whether to insulate on the inside or the outside of the building or a combination. Altering the wall thickness can impact window trim and trim at the wall-ceiling juncture on the interior or overhang depth and other proportional relationships on the exterior. These alterations also add expense beyond the insulation upgrades. This work must be completed with sensitivity to the recommendations in the historic assessment, following a design approach that preserves historically significant surfaces. Typically, you should not alter these surfaces unless both the inside and outside are historically significant, leaving no other tactic for improving performance.

Windows are another major issue in historic buildings. Historic windows are usually a single layer of glazing in frames that are drafty and often include counterweights that create uninsulated, drafty cavities in the wall next to the windows. The mullions, which allow small panes of glass to be used, have thick and articulated profiles that are difficult to replicate. The glass often transmits a different color of light and reflects light differently from modern, energy-efficient glass. There are a variety of solutions possible, ranging from new windows to rebuilt windows to interior and exterior storm windows. If windows are original and in reparable condition, it is generally best to repair them and add storm windows. It is very important to investigate multiple options and balance historic, energy, and cost concerns.

Where to Find the Energy Savings in Renovations

In sum, while renovation to net zero standards is achievable, it typically takes greater care and cost than for new buildings to attain net zero standards. But it is doable, cost effective in most cases, and necessary if our goal is a net zero future. Aside from attention to building science, possible occupancy changes, and historic features, keep these rules of thumb in mind when planning a net zero renovation:

DAYLIGHTING/LIGHTING. Maximize daylighting and integrate with high-efficiency lighting and controls.

HVAC. Assess applicability of heat pumps, controls, and heat-recovery ventilation. Particularly in cooling-dominated buildings, investigate building systems with enclosure improvements for combined savings.

BUILDING ENCLOSURE. Assess multiple levels of upgrades of building enclosure, including windows.

CONTROLS/MONITORING. Install control and monitoring systems with multiple-level metering and tracking.

			Maclay Architects' Office	Dartt House
Building Profile	Building Name:		**Maclay Architects' Office**	**Dartt House**
	Location:	Waitsfield, Vermont		
	Square Footage:		2,568	2,207
Energy Profile	Total Energy Consumption:		97,948 kBtu	42,240 kBtu
	Total Energy Production:	63,712 kBtu (produced on-site)	41,726 kBtu	42,240 kBtu (produced off-site)
	Energy Intensity:	Actual:	38 kBtu/sf	19 kBtu/sf
		Actual with Renewables:	-3 kBtu/sf	0 kBtu/sf
Building Envelope	Construction Type:	Renovation of historic structures of wood construction		
	Insulation Values:	Walls:	R-40, fiberglass-filled walls were filled with dense-pack cellulose; rigid foam was added to the interior walls in lower studio space	R-40, existing cellulose and fiberglass insulation in 2×4 cavity, 5–6″ polyurethane spray foam in a new interior stud wall held 2″ off exterior wall for thermal break
		Roof:	R-60, loose-fill cellulose added to the attic	R-60, 10″ spray urethane foam in rafter bay
		Foundation:	2″ XPS insulation added to perimeter of foundation walls; 2″ XPS insulation added under new radiant slab in slab on grade portion of building; R-40 insulation added below floor above crawl space	Walls: R-20 below grade, R-40 above grade, combination of rigid foam insulation on the exterior and spray foam on the existing stone foundation
	Air Infiltration:	Final Blower Door:	N/A	1100 cfm50
	Windows:	Windows:	R-5, fiberglass tri-pane windows	R-5, triple-glazed
Mechanical/ Electrical Systems	Heating System:		Air-source heat pumps with water distribution	Air-source heat pumps
	Cooling System:		Minisplit	None
	Ventilation System:		Heat-recovery ventilation system	Heat-recovery ventilation system
	Lighting System/ Controls:		Added south-facing windows for natural daylighting; light-guiding blinds; occupancy sensors; efficient task-lighting fixtures	CFL fixtures
	Hot Water:		Electric instantaneous hot water	two 60-gal electric hot water tanks
	Renewable System:	Combined system:	17.55 kW solar carport	
			2 kW tracker	
			20 kW equivalent of trackers at Maclay residence in Warren	

DARTT HOUSE AND MACLAY ARCHITECTS' OFFICE
Mixed-Use Renovation in an Historic Village Center

Built by Joshua Dartt in the 1850s, the Dartt House is located on the Mad River in the historic village center of Waitsfield, Vermont. In 1998 William and Alexandra Maclay purchased the property, with an historic house and carriage barn, and planned to use the carriage barn as the office for Maclay Architects and retain the house for residential use. Since the purchase, the goal has been to make the property into a model sustainable and historic retrofit, today called a deep energy project. The project illustrates the value of integrating upgrades to the net zero level over time and demonstrates that net zero is achievable in mixed-use and historic projects and is financially sound.

Project Overview

Both buildings on the property underwent deep energy retrofits. The carriage barn, which was partially renovated by previous owners, was incrementally improved as office space to net zero ready standards over thirteen years. The approximately 2,000 sf house was larger and more expensive to heat than tenants wanted. In 2009 it was renovated and converted into two apartments to improve marketability and reduce operating and maintenance expenses. Creating two apartments increased overall rent, making it a prudent investment for the owners. The tenants enjoyed increased comfort, and having control over energy costs has made the two apartments more affordable and desirable.

One challenge of this project was to perform the energy upgrades while preserving the historic exterior. Above-grade insulation upgrades are primarily on the interior of the building. While this approach decreased the interior square footage slightly, it left the historic façades untouched. Additional care was taken to reuse materials and to replace materials only to increase energy efficiency.

Throughout both projects Maclay Architects has experimented with sustainable materials, technologies, and strategies, gaining direct experience that we use on client projects to ensure their performance.

Energy and Site

This site, located on the Mad River in a historic village, presented multiple challenges in providing renewable power with PV. The historic buildings have no south-facing rooflines, making roof-mounted PV a poor investment. While there is open land on the property adjacent to the road, there is public objection to solar collectors along scenic roads in general and with historic properties specifically. Existing trees along the river shade other optimum solar sites for PV, and the town has restrictions on cutting down trees along rivers.

After site and energy-load analysis, our strategy was to maximize on-site production with a tracking collector and solar carport to supply office needs and off-site collection at the

Maclays' home for the apartment. In 2008 we installed a 2 kW tracking collector on site to cover a portion of the electric needs of the office. When adding the solar carport at the site in 2011, we developed a river restoration plan that removed larger trees, retained medium and smaller trees, and planted new native trees and bushes. We selected trees and shrubs that restore river ecosystems and wildlife but stay relatively small. The PV installation on the carport raised collectors higher off the ground and lessened shading by trees. The collectors are installed at 17°, which maximizes summer solar gain and reduces annual gain by less than 10 percent, decreasing the impact of summer tree shading. This flatter angle also mimics the shape of traditional shed structures that are more typical of and compatible with the historic village. A hemlock hedge in front of the cars completes the form of the shed with softer-feeling vegetation. This design also maximizes site utilization, with parking below the carport, while adding weather protection for cars. Site planning included an easement for the Mad River Path, allowing public access along the river and linking the village and valley. The carport is owned by the office

and funded with a grant from US Rural Development, the local utility, and a loan.

To supply power for the apartments, an off-site location 9 miles away at the Maclay home was selected. These equivalent 20kW trackers are sized to provide all apartment needs and over 50 percent of the Maclay home's power as well. Thus, through group net metering, this project helped another project get closer to net zero. This remote PV used a power purchase agreement that eliminated any additional capital expense.

The first renovations to the house included adding rigid insulation on the roof, improving foundation drainage, pouring concrete on the outside of the stone wall for stabilization, and adding insulation, plastic, and new gravel for drainage on the outside. Other early-stage work included adding dense-pack cellulose on ceilings and walls and upgrading glazing and jamb liners on windows.

In 2010 net zero ready improvements further reduced energy loads. Secondary walls were built inside the building perimeter, providing space between the two walls for insulation, and 5–6″ of polyurethane spray foam was applied on

PV carport   Dartt House   office beyond

all walls. The gap between wall framing allows depth for the desired level of insulation and a thermal break so that heat is not lost through the wood studs. Rigid insulation was added to the underside of the roof. Triple-glazed R-5 replacement windows were installed within the existing window openings and frames, providing maximum energy performance while retaining the historic character. In the basement spray foam was added to the R-40 standard above grade and R-20 below grade.

The carriage barn was also improved in multiple phases to net zero ready standards. First, in the upstairs new triple-glazed R-5 fiberglass windows were installed, fiberglass-filled walls were filled with dense-pack cellulose, and loose-fill cellulose was added to the attic. Three later phases of work included further window upgrades to R-5 units, renovation of walls with composite rigid and cellulose assemblies, improvements to floor insulation levels, and installation of foundation insulation. Eventually, we brought the entire building up to our desired R 20/40/60/5 standards.

On the south side of the building, windows were added to increase passive solar gain and improve daylighting.

Light-guiding blinds improve daylighting in the offices on both levels. The daylighting combined with high-efficiency lights throughout reduce lighting loads. On the second floor, shades that reduce glare in the workspaces also allow occupants to see outside to the river.

The house is heated with air-source heat pumps. The office is heated with air-source heat pumps with water distribution. This system allowed for a connection to the existing hydronic heating system with reduced costs. Both buildings have heat-recovery ventilation systems.

Healthy Materials

Healthy materials selected for both buildings include no-VOC paints, formaldehyde-free wheat board, and medite particle board. Cherry harvested from the Maclays' home property and locally harvested maple are used throughout the building. Many reused and recycled content materials were also used throughout both projects.

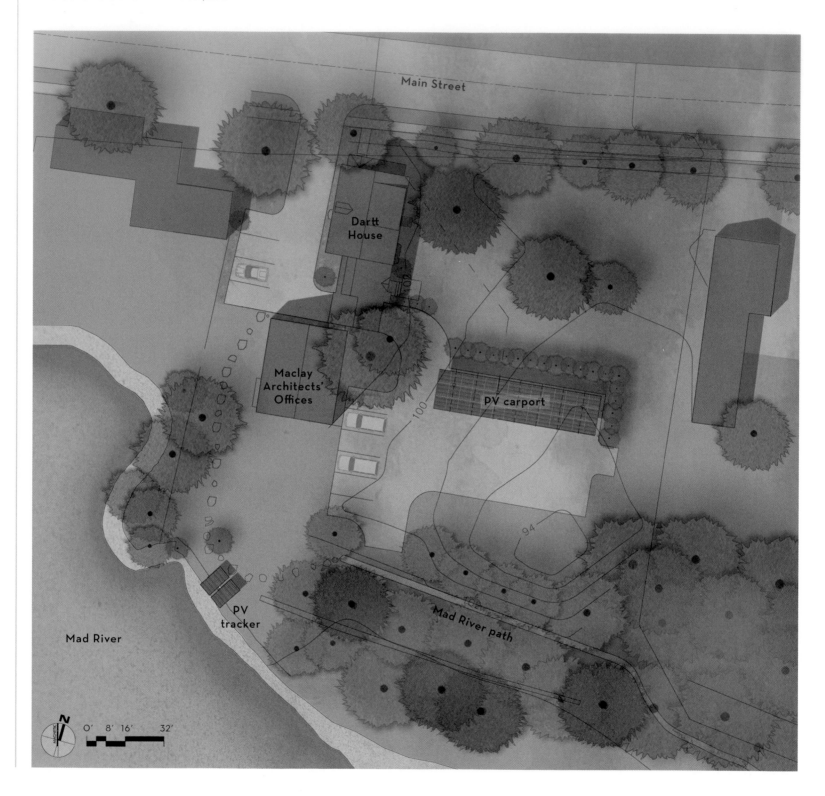

Main Street

Dartt House

Maclay Architects' Offices

PV carport

PV tracker

Mad River

Mad River path

N

MAGNETIC

0' 8' 16' 32'

FIGURE CS6.4. Equivalent 20 kW solar trackers at the Maclay home provide power for the apartments.

FIGURE CS6.5. The 17.6 kW carport that provides power to Maclay Architects' office.

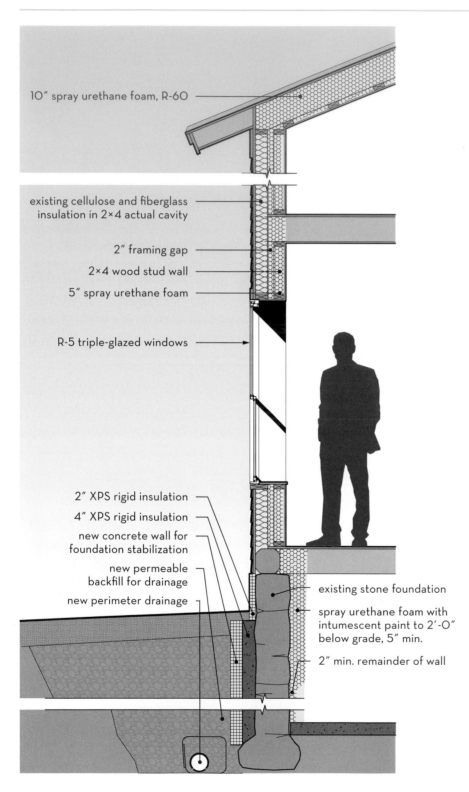

10" spray urethane foam, R-60

existing cellulose and fiberglass insulation in 2×4 actual cavity

2" framing gap

2×4 wood stud wall

5" spray urethane foam

R-5 triple-glazed windows

2" XPS rigid insulation

4" XPS rigid insulation

new concrete wall for foundation stabilization

new permeable backfill for drainage

new perimeter drainage

existing stone foundation

spray urethane foam with intumescent paint to 2'-0" below grade, 5" min.

2" min. remainder of wall

16 | The Case for Net Zero Homes

Across the United States and beyond, people are growing more aware of the environmental impact of personal behaviors and lifestyles. More and more individuals are taking small steps to minimize and mitigate their environmental and carbon footprints, such as washing clothes in cold water, air-drying clothes, composting, and performing energy-efficient upgrades on homes. We have less control in our offices and our public spaces, but we do have control over where and how we live. Building net zero homes or renovating homes to net zero standards is one way for people to model stewardship and care for the earth, take responsibility for their impact on the earth, and take concrete action to create a better world for the future.

While the material throughout this book applies to homes as well as larger buildings, there are a few considerations for homes worth exploring further.

Beauty in the Net Zero Home

Homes are special places. They are the center of the world for their inhabitants, embodying their rhythms, spirit, and dreams. A home should be simply but elegantly designed to fit the site and enrich the lives of the users. It should provide comfort while minimizing energy consumption. And it should be practical and durable in design to reduce ongoing maintenance and operational costs.

The art in home design emerges from enhancing people's daily living, learning, work, and play. The beauty emanates from the flow, health, and meaning that the space provides. Beauty is more than just visual image or sculpture; it includes design for all senses. Daily living in the home, not just the home itself, should be like a work of art—allowing people to move through their most personal space in harmony with the patterns of nature (see figure 16.1).

Net zero homes offer inspiring places for people to live, reduce global warming, and protect their owners from likely fuel escalation shocks in the future. They are also healthy, connecting people to nature and providing optimum indoor air quality. And they minimize our negative impacts on the environment. Our homes are places where we can take a personal stand with concrete action to begin to make a net zero world.

Settlement Patterns and Quality of Life

Our society's use of oil has resulted in dispersed settlement patterns and sprawl, and the suburban and rural areas indicative of these patterns are home to many of our single-family homes. Most of the additional consumption related to homes is directly tied to transportation, specifically cars. While building and living in a net zero home is a big and extraordinary step, without widespread smart-growth development, our reliance on fossil fuels will remain an issue.

Additionally important to consider is quality of life and how the home fits into the surrounding community. If you are in a pedestrian-friendly community, you can walk or bike to school, work, the market, and other destinations. As you walk by your neighbor's house, you see your neighbor and decide to have dinner together. This keeps you physically healthy and socially connected. When we build with or create a community, the quality of life can shift and support net zero living beyond the walls of the home.

So when selecting your home's location, think about the neighborhood. Consider cohousing or a deep energy retrofit to an existing home.

The Size of the House

Size is a key consideration when building any home and even more critical in a net zero home. First, the size of the house directly corresponds to the amount of resources and materials that go into building it. Second, the amount of energy consumed and the associated renewables required to provide energy are greater in a larger home. Manufacturing these renewable energy sources consumes energy, materials, and natural resources. For example, PVs contain rare earth minerals. So

while the home may be net zero in terms of operation, the overall energy footprint of the home grows with the size of the home. The average American home has grown from 983 sf in 1950 to 2,349 sf in 2004.[1] This is why the best metric for homes is energy consumed per capita, as it includes the size of the buildings as well as energy intensity.

Long-Term Investment

Building a net zero home is an investment in the future, both financially and ecologically. The first roadblock people express is usually, "I can't really afford a net zero home; it costs too much money." But the real consideration should be how much it costs per month to pay a home's mortgage and operation, including monthly energy bills. Thus, the real question is, "How can I minimize finance and operation costs of my home?"

Size dominates this conversation as well. If you build your home a third smaller than what you originally planned, the money saved by reducing the square footage can be put into making the home more heavily insulated and installing renewable energy to power the home. This upfront investment to make a net zero home will eliminate utility costs in the future while minimizing environmental impact. When you look at the big picture, is there really anyone who cannot afford to build a net zero home? If you can afford to build a new home, the question is whether you invest in long-term value or savings or in a larger home. The net zero ready home adds only around 5 percent to the cost of the home. While PV may cost $25,000 to $50,000 for a home, it can be phased, leased, or attained through a power purchase agreement.

All of these things remain true when purchasing an existing home. If you buy a larger home, it may not have the best envelope, and you will have little money for efficiency upgrades. In the same general location, you can find a smaller, less expensive home that will leave you with more money for renovating the home to net zero. Thus, while many people say they want a net zero home but cannot afford one, the reality is that for middle-income families and above, it really is a choice. If they want a net zero home, they have the financial capability to make it happen. And with a little education, they can.

FIGURE 16.1. Daylight and natural finishes enhance the connection to the outdoors in this entry hall.

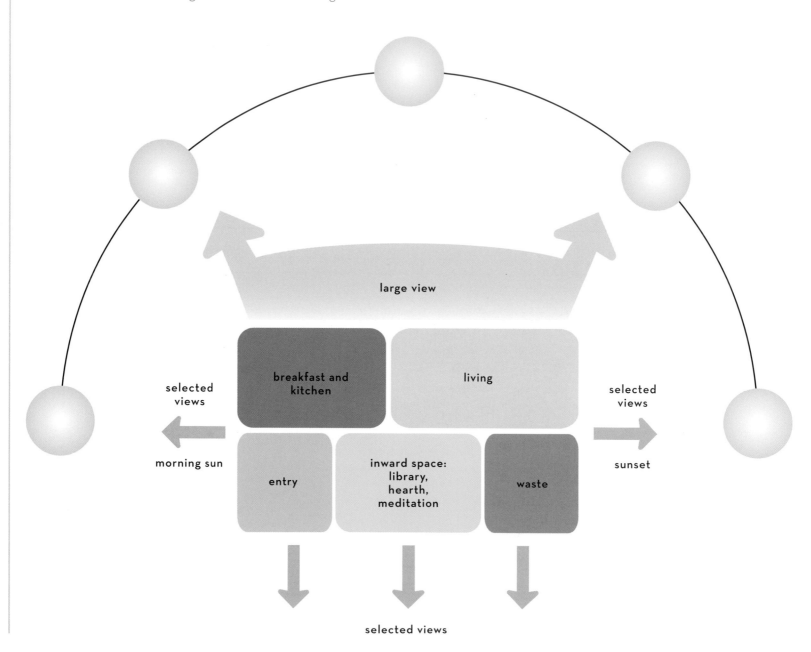

FIGURE 16.2. The daily flow of interior lives and space can interconnect with outside living and nature in a well-designed home.

large view

breakfast and kitchen

living

selected views

selected views

morning sun

sunset

entry

inward space: library, hearth, meditation

waste

selected views

Integrated Design

The principles of integrated design for net zero buildings are in some instances much easier to accomplish at the scale of a home. While we follow the core principles of elongating along the east–west axis, limiting east and west glazing, and maximizing southern glazing, we balance this by designing beauty and comfort into the home for example, by including a breakfast room with east-facing glass for sunlight and solar energy first thing in the morning, generating warmth and comfort. Likewise, it may include a den or living space on the west side, with a view to the sunset. Each individual may have different ways to relate the spaces in the home to the times of the day based on routines and patterns of living, and each site is unique in terms of connection to special outdoor spaces or views (see figure 16.2).

The connection to outdoors and use of outdoor space is not unique to rural sites. In urban Japanese settings, meditation gardens create a whole world in very small spaces. New York and Philadelphia have a tradition of row houses with front steps where people sit to talk with neighbors or watch passersby as well as incredibly small backyards that residents can use to grow food, socialize, or relax.

EXAMPLES FROM THE FIELD

The best case for net zero homes, though, can be made by those who are building them and living in them. So here we introduce you to some net zero innovators.

CARTER SCOTT'S TRANSFORMATIONS: AFFORDABLE NET ZERO

Carter Scott has been a leading proponent, innovator, and practitioner in transforming single-family homes from fossil-fuel addicts to fossil-fuel-free, affordable dwellings. His Massachusetts-based company, Transformations, Inc., specializes in delivering net zero homes cost-effectively. All of their homes meet or exceed net zero standards, typically using high-efficiency air-source heat pumps and solar PV. Some homes add PV to garages to accommodate electric vehicles. And with current technology, the car battery can be used to provide power during power outages.

Homeowners can select from saltbox, Greek revival, and other more traditional designs that satisfy the broad spectrum of the real estate market (see figure 16.3). Typical costs for a custom net zero ready home run about $140 to $250 /sf.[2] Transformations estimates that installed costs for PV run about $5/watt, and they usually install an 8.25 kW system for a cost of around $41,000 before tax credits, SRECs, or other incentives or grants.[3] And if that capital cost is too much, there are options to lease systems.

MARC ROSENBAUM'S "SHALLOW ENERGY" RETROFIT TO NET ZERO

In 2010, Marc Rosenbaum, a nationally recognized engineer, purchased a 1,589 sf house built in 1999–2000 on Martha's Vineyard, Massachusetts, with the goal of living a comfortable, low-carbon life in a net zero home that could meet both the Thousand Home Challenge and Passive House standards without investing a lot of money.[4] Because the house was relatively new with good interior and exterior finishes and his family had no reasons to make changes or renovations, he realized the traditional deep energy retrofit strategies of adding insulation on the inside or outside would not be cost effective.

Rosenbaum wanted to reduce energy costs from around $3,300 per year with an estimated EUI of 58 kBtu/sf/yr to around $700 per year and an EUI of 11–12 kBtu/sf/yr before renewables. After making improvements in the first year, he and his family achieved that goal. And with their 4.76 kW PV system, they had a net export of over 3,000 kWh—enough to drive an electric car over 10,000 miles. They managed all of this with an investment of

FIGURE 16.3. Roof-mounted PV on traditional and modern home designs.

FIGURE 16.4. The energy efficiency renovations to the Rosenbaums' home cost just $26,000 but will save $2,600 annually, eliminating energy bills.

FIGURE 16.5. The breakdown of energy use in the Rosenbaums' house with efficient appliances, use of a clothesline, and high-efficiency lighting.

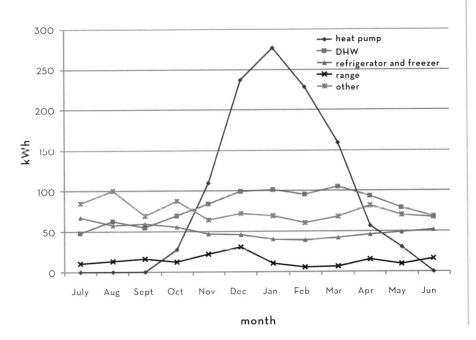

$26,000, saving around $2,600 annually with a simple payback of less than ten years. In addition, they live in a more comfortable house with no energy bills at all (see figures 16.4 and 16.5).

So how did they accomplish this feat? They used an approach that Rosenbaum calls a "shallow energy" retrofit. They made improvements in four areas: envelope, mechanical, appliances, and renewables. Having been built in the late 1990s, the envelope was decent: 2×6 walls and a combination of 2×10 rafters and 14" attic insulation. These were left unchanged, but basement insulation was added, increasing insulation from 1" to 3". Air infiltration was cut in half. Large double-pane windows got EcoSmart double honeycomb cellular shades with tightly sealing tracks.

The heating system was changed from an oil burner to a 16,000 Btu/hr single-zone minisplit air-source heat pump with a single wall heater. The single heat source in the winter keeps open living space at the desired temperature, with second-floor bedrooms 2 degrees cooler (and as much as 4 degrees cooler when the outside temperature drops to 10°). A third bedroom

was closed off when not used to reduce energy consumption. Hot water is provided for the most part by a heat-pump water heater.

Rosenbaum replaced the old refrigerator with a new, more energy-efficient model, switched to an induction cooktop, and replaced a gas clothes dryer with drying racks and a clothesline. He only minimally improved lighting, as the house already had mostly compact fluorescent lights.

The "shallow energy" retrofit approach, then, is a combination of simple, inexpensive envelope improvements based on careful investigation of energy options to reduce consumption to very low EUI numbers, making the renewables affordable. The moderate size and creativity in optimizing energy conservation measures make this an innovative model for a cost-effective, single-family renovation.

THE PILL-MAHARAM HOUSE

In a rural area with a moderate wind resource, David Pill's and Hillary Maharam's home in Charlotte, Vermont, depicted in figures 16.6 and 16.7, demonstrates that net zero homes can

FIGURE 16.6. The Pill-Maharam House, with wind generator.

FIGURE 16.7. Sun and passive solar in the open living area.

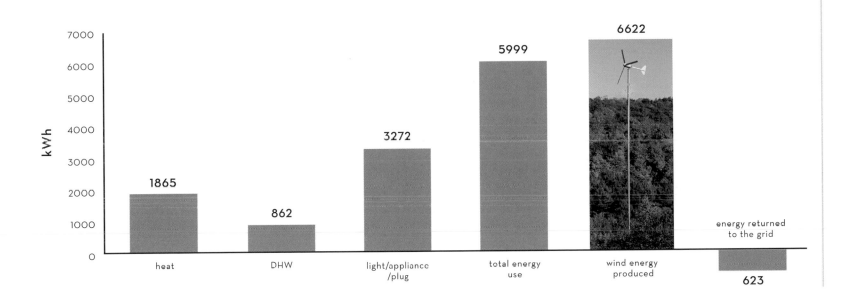

FIGURE 16.8. Annual energy use by load: Because of the ground-source heat pump for heating and domestic hot water, these loads are less than all other loads and more than offset by wind energy.

6622

5999

3272

1865

862

energy returned
to the grid

623

kWh

7000

6000

5000

4000

3000

2000

1000

0

heat   DHW   light/appliance/plug   total energy use   wind energy produced

FIGURE 16.9. Month-to-month comparison of energy used in the home and energy produced by the family's 10 kw wind turbine.

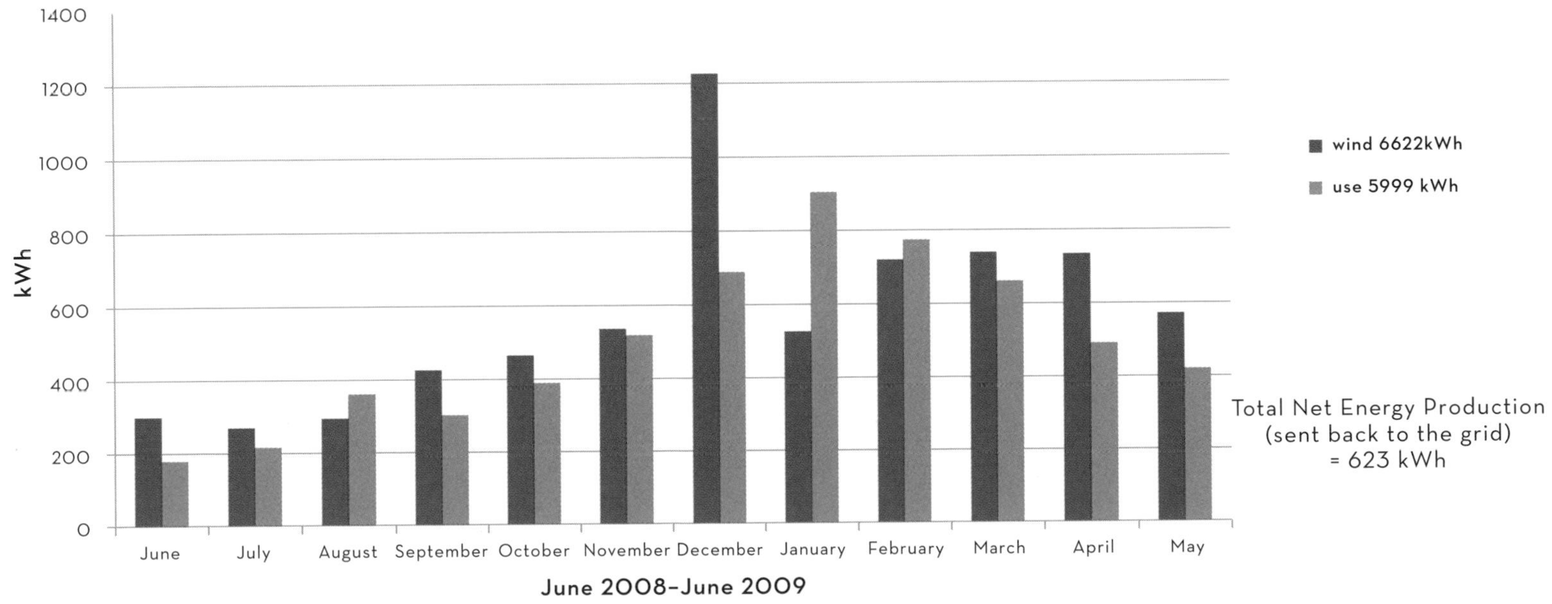

kWh

1400

1200

1000

800

600

400

200

0

June July August September October November December January February March April May

June 2008–June 2009

■ wind 6622kWh
■ use 5999 kWh

Total Net Energy Production
(sent back to the grid)
= 623 kWh

FIGURE 16.10. A Vermont Healthy Home with PV in Moretown, Vermont.

FIGURE 16.11. A positive-energy Vermont Healthy Home plan with added PV to generate excess energy annually.

FIGURE 16.12. Passive House in the Woods, Hudson, Wisconsin uses a 4.52 kW PV system and solar domestic hot water to power a positive-energy home.

combine low energy consumption, high-quality contemporary design that fits a rural site, and Vermont's architectural traditions. Light-filled interior spaces connect to nature, making a pleasant and inspiring place for the family. To accomplish their net zero goal, the family optimized passive solar collection, built a tight and very well insulated envelope, used a ground-source heat pump for heating and hot water, reduced loads with high-efficiency lighting and appliances, and powered their home with a 10kw wind turbine (see figures 16.8 and 16.9).

Net Zero Homes Transforming the Future

Net zero homes are beginning to enter the single-family-home marketplace, but in a limited way. How can net zero homes become the rule rather than the exception? Green entrepreneurs are eager to find ways for net zero and ultra-low-energy-consuming homes to dominate the housing market, through home plans, panelization, prefabrication, and manufacturing.

Our own office has developed home plans for the Vermont Healthy Home and the Energy Plus Healthy Home, (see figures 16.10 and 16.11) two programs that focus on homes that are healthy for people and the environment. We offer net zero house plans that any builder can purchase and follow.

PASSIVE HOUSE

Different from but related to the net zero movement, Passive House, or Passivhaus, is a comprehensive, very-low-energy-consuming building and construction concept that originated with Wolfgang Feist and Bo Adamson, who launched a pilot project in Germany in 1990. Passive House designation does not mean that a home relies solely on passive solar, although passive solar heat is used in Passive House buildings. Rather, it means that the home consumes minimal energy and has no active heating other than a heating coil in the ventilation system.

The Passive House design, certification, and construction process has introduced innovation and higher levels of energy conservation in design and construction details. This includes the elimination of thermal bridging, ultra-high-performing windows,

FIGURE 16.13. The Green Mountain Habitat for Humanity Passive House in Charlotte, Vermont, is an example of very-low-energy-consuming manufactured housing with traditional New England design.

and durable and efficient ventilation equipment. Other benefits include comfort, durability, and resilience. Passive House standards can encourage investments in energy conservation, which are more costly than investments in renewables to offset the energy conservation investment. Overall the Passive House movement has helped chart a course for a fossil-fuel-free and renewable future, since all certified Passive Houses exceed net zero ready standards and can become net zero easily by adding renewables. Currently, over 20,000 living units have been Passive House–certified in central Europe, and many more residential, commercial, and institutional projects—including a high-rise—have been certified around the world, in all climate zones. Passive House is making a difference.

A 1,940 sf home in Hudson, Wisconsin, called Passive House in the Woods, (see figure 16.12) uses modern design strategies on the interior and exterior to provide comfort and connection to nature in a cold climate. ICF and EIFS building systems were used, and the resulting assemblies meet Passive House standards. R-70 walls, R-95 roof, high-performance windows, low air infiltration, heat-recovery ventilation, a 600-foot earth loop for preheating and precooling fresh air, and wastewater heat recovery all contribute to minimizing loads, as required for Passive House certification. Solar domestic hot water and a 4.52 kW tracker and roof-mounted PV system supply more energy than consumed to make the home net energy positive.

In Vermont Green Mountain Habitat for Humanity worked with Albert, Righter and Tittmann Architects; Peter Schneider; Preferred Building Systems; and others to bring passive-house thinking and technologies to the larger marketplace with long-term, affordable housing.. The ultra-low-energy-consuming (or net zero ready, in our terms) modular house in figure 16.13 is heated with one air-source heat pump and has been extensively monitored to demonstrate superior comfort with minimal energy use, and it is Passive House certified.

In Switzerland a low-cost certified net zero Passive House incorporates an innovative vertical south solar wall made of paraffin phase-change material that stores and releases energy as it goes from solid to liquid and back. The heating load of 1,000 kWh/yr is supplied by PV, which can provide up to 2,500 kWh/yr. The passive windows and phase-change

FIGURE 16.14. Dark gray areas with phase-change material on the south façade.

FIGURE 16.15. An open space plan, with south-facing glass for views, and passive solar as well as a thermal storage wall.

FIGURE 16.16. The original Unity House.

material incorporated on the south exterior façade fit with the open-plan interior layout in the simple, modern design (see figures 16.14 and 16.15).

UNITY HOMES

Unity House, built for the president of Unity College in Maine (figure 16.16), is part of Bensonwood's mission to create a new model for the design, fabrication, and assembly of housing in the United States. Following on Unity House, Tedd Benson began Unity Homes™ to offer affordable, very energy-efficient, net zero ready, net zero, and/or Passive House homes to the larger public.[5] With four models, from traditional to modern, ranging in size from 1,113 to 2,896 sf, Unity Homes achieves construction costs from $160 to $170 per square foot, with home prices beginning under $200,000. Their goal is to bring the cost down to $130 per square foot, which is lower than the $140 per square foot for homes on the resale market. The homes are built with a goal of a 250- to 500-year life, clearly achieving life-cycle material and energy savings many times the initial cost of the building.

In addition to Unity Homes, many other prefabricated and manufactured housing companies are entering into the net zero and Passive House single-family homes market to create affordable net zero homes for the future. In chapter 19 we explore additional opportunities available in building net zero multifamily housing and communities to achieve greater energy savings by integrating buildings and transportation.

DESIGN PROFILE			
Building Profile	Building Name:	**Newton House**	
	Location:	Newton, Massachusetts	
	Square Footage:	5,329	
	Certification:	LEED Platinum anticipated	
Energy Profile	Energy Reference Year:	November, 2011–October, 2012	
	Total Energy Consumption:	11,620 kWh (39,659 kBtu)	
	Total Energy Production:	13,276 kWh (45,310 kBtu)	
	Energy Intensity:	Actual:	7 kBtu/sf-yr
		Actual with Renewables:	-1 kBtu/sf-yr
Building Envelope	Insulation Values:	Walls:	R-40, 2″ polyiso rigid insulation, dense-pack cellulose in 2×8 wall cavity
		Roof:	R-67, 18″ loose fill cellulose
		Foundation (slab perimeter):	R-20, 4″ XPS rigid insulation
		Foundation (sub-slab):	R-20, 4″ XPS rigid insulation
	Air Infiltration:	Final Blower Door:	1,111 cfm50
			0.13 cfm50/sf exterior surface area
	Windows/Skylights:	Windows:	Low-e, tri-pane, argon-filled
			U-value: 0.20, SHGC: 0.24, VT: 0.39
Mechanical/ Electrical Systems	Heating System:	Mitsubishi air-source heat pump	
	Cooling System:	Air-source heat pump, as needed	
	Ventilation System:	ERV	
	Lighting System/Controls:	High-efficiency fluorescent and LED fixtures	
	Hot Water:	Solar thermal: three 4×8 collectors with 120-gallon tank, 3,200 kWh-yr	
	Renewable System:	42 SunPower, 225W modules	
		Installed System Size:	9.45 kW

THREE HIGH-PERFORMANCE HOMES

Newton House
Net Zero in a Traditional Neighborhood

Inspired by a career dedicated to energy and conservation issues, the owners built this net zero home in harmony with their values and beliefs. At the same time, the owners wanted a beautiful and traditional family home that fit in with other houses in their neighborhood in the Boston suburb of Newton. Balancing both these needs, their home is exceeding the owners' net zero energy goal after two years of occupancy, with a surplus of site-generated renewable energy.

One of their main criteria for choosing their site was close proximity to a high-frequency train stop, allowing them to use public transportation regularly. An adjacent park provides recreation out the front door, and the town center within walking

FIGURE CS7.1. South façade of the house, with roof oriented for PV panels. Entry oriented to the street in keeping with street presence of the neighboring houses.

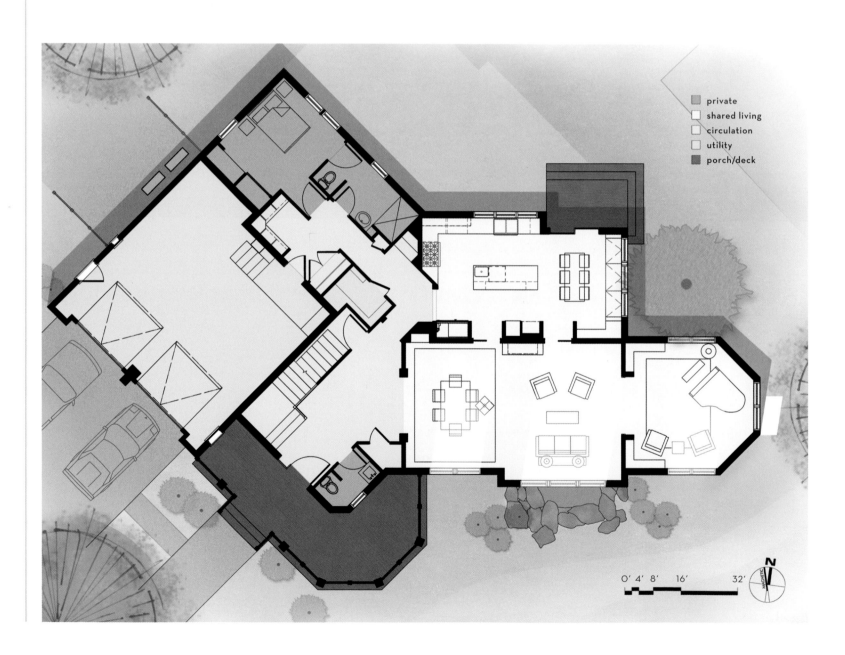

FIGURE CS7.2. The living, dining, and music rooms are oriented
to the south to maximize daylight and passive solar.

private

shared living

circulation

utility

porch/deck

FIGURE CS7.3. High-performance building assembly.

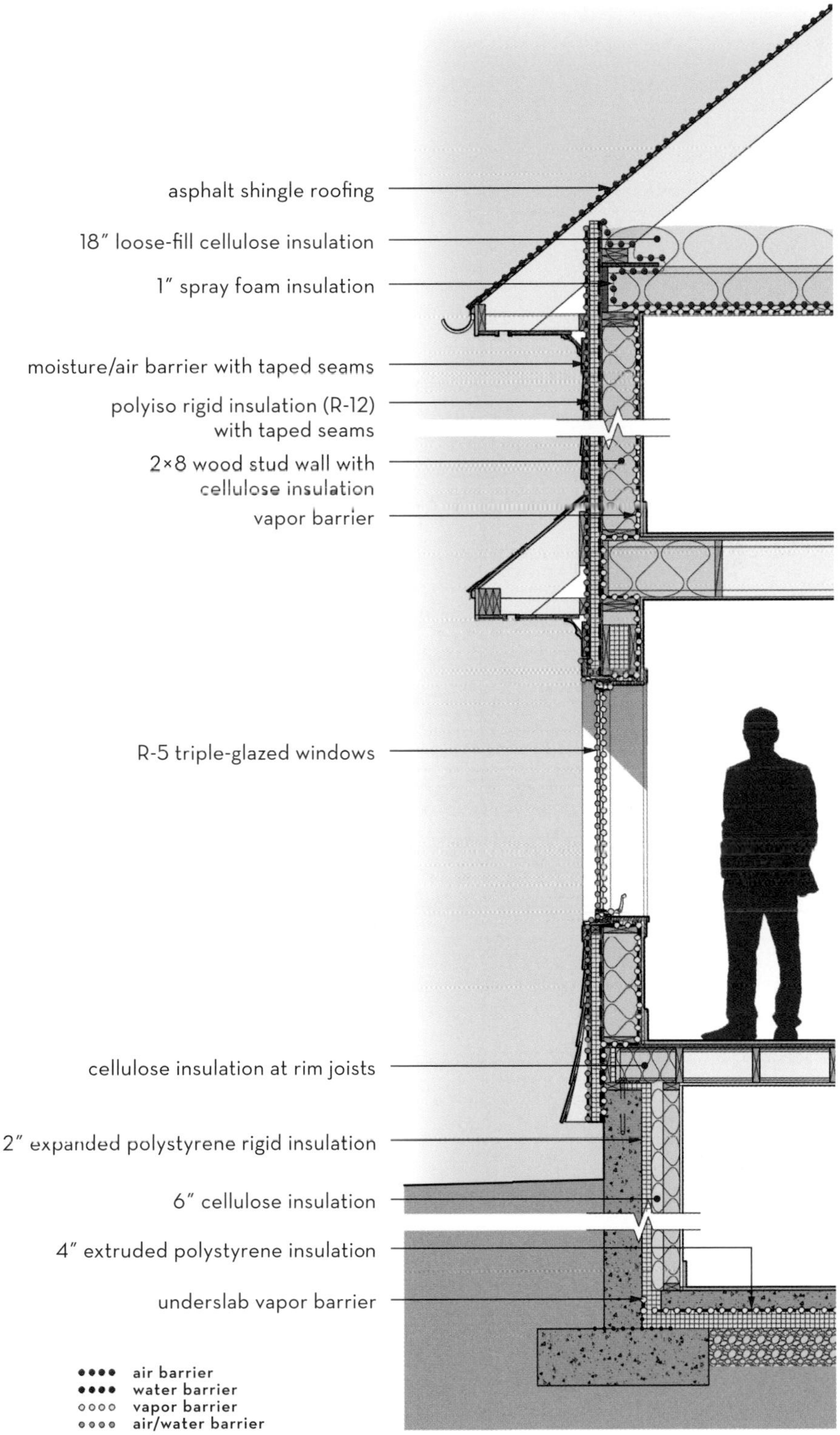

asphalt shingle roofing

18" loose-fill cellulose insulation

1" spray foam insulation

moisture/air barrier with taped seams

polyiso rigid insulation (R-12) with taped seams

2×8 wood stud wall with cellulose insulation

vapor barrier

R-5 triple-glazed windows

cellulose insulation at rim joists

2" expanded polystyrene rigid insulation

6" cellulose insulation

4" extruded polystyrene insulation

underslab vapor barrier

●●●● air barrier
●●●● water barrier
○○○○ vapor barrier
●○●○ air/water barrier

distance has restaurants and shops to minimize transportation energy consumption and maximize community life. A small, deteriorating home on the property was deconstructed and building materials salvaged for reuse to the greatest extent possible. The size of the new home is only in the twenty-ninth percentile for homes built during the last ten years in the neighborhood but provides comparable amenities and fits market conditions.

The constrained site in an existing neighborhood called for creative design solutions. The site property boundaries were 45° off south, and adjacent trees made siting and solar access a challenge. To fit in with the neighboring shingle-style and Victorian houses, the home has an angled plan. A street-facing entry 45° off south preserves a formal and street presence, while the main building form is angled away from the street, with southern orientation for passive and active solar gain. South-facing windows optimize passive solar gain, connect the family to the nature of the native landscape in the yard, and create a light-filled main living space.

The south-facing roof is covered in PV panels that generate all of the home's energy needs, and then some, on an annual basis. Two solar domestic hot water panels are situated on the southeast-facing slope of the front gable roof. The house is superinsulated, with an R-20 basement, R-40 walls, R-5 windows, and an R-60 roof. Heating and cooling, when needed, are provided by an air-source heat pump, powered by the electricity from the home's PV panels. The home is on track for LEED Platinum status.

The home uses 88 percent less energy than the family's previous townhouse, which was built in 2005 with an actual EUI of 7 kBTU/sf-yr and an EUI of -1 kBtu/sf-yr with renewables. Additionally, the production of energy on site will save the couple approximately $6,000 annually. Combining energy rebates with reduced energy costs, the renewable energy system is on track to pay for itself after only four years.

While these energy savings are significant, the owners also actively play a role in the home's reduced energy consumption and have adopted lifestyle choices that support their commitment to addressing climate change. The home includes two home offices, one for each parent. While the offices result in increased size and energy demands, working from home results in a smaller overall carbon footprint for the family. In addition, clothes are air-dried, timed thermostats are aligned with occupancy of individual rooms, and a comprehensive monitoring system generates performance data. Careful tracking of this data provides the owners with the information necessary to make adjustments to improve performance and maintain the net zero goal over time. Most important, this family was able to build a new home that creates a satisfying and inspiring place while meeting their commitment to minimize energy and live lightly on the planet.

Building Profile	Building Name:	**Stone House**	
	Location:	Moretown, Vermont	
	Square Footage:	4,500	
Energy Profile	Total Energy Consumption:	13,000 kWh (44,356 kBtu)	
	Total Energy Production:	13,650 kWh (46,574 kBtu)	
	Energy Intensity:	Actual:	9.86 kBtu/sf-yr
		Actual with Renewables:	-0.5 kBtu/sf-yr
Building Envelope	Insulation Values:	Walls:	R-60, 10″ spray polyurethane insulation in 12″ thick double-wall cavity
		Roof:	R-60, 10″ rigid polyisocyanurate above structural sheathing
		Foundation (slab perimeter):	R-20, 4″ XPS rigid insulation
		Foundation (sub-slab):	R-20, 4″ XPS rigid insulation
	Windows/Skylights:	Windows:	Low-e, tri-pane, argon-filled U-value: 0.20, SHGC: 0.24, VT: 0.39
Mechanical/ Electrical Systems	Heating System:	Ground-source heat pump with 600′ deep wells	
	Cooling System:	AC in sleeping spaces only	
	Ventilation System:	HRV	
	Lighting System/Controls:	High-efficiency fluorescent or LED fixtures on Lutron controls	
	Hot Water:	Solar thermal and GSHP, 600-gallon tank, seven 4×8 SDHW panels	
	Renewable System:	Installed System Size:	14 kW

Stone House
Passive Solar Living Connected to a River

The owners wanted to create a home that was intimately connected to a unique site on the Mad River in Vermont where a major dam blew out in the famous 1927 flood. They also loved the character and manner of Frank Lloyd Wright's work and had high environmental hopes for the home, including carbon-neutral and net zero goals. The site is a large outcropping of ledge rock along the river and next to a stone abutment, which is all that is left of the wooden crib dam. The original dam was approximately 40 ft high, with stone on both sides of the river.

The stone portion of the dam with the old penstock hole still remains immediately adjacent to the house site.

The linear form of the dam was used to organize the building layout. Beautiful views looking upriver toward the south allowed for easy orientation toward both the sunlight and the spectacular view of a turn in the Mad River. The result is a classic passive solar house, long and skinny, with south-facing glass into all living spaces and bedrooms and largely bermed into the earth on the north. A sedum-covered green roof with

FIGURE CS7.4. The private and shared wings of the house are separated by the entry, which connects through to the riverside stone terrace.

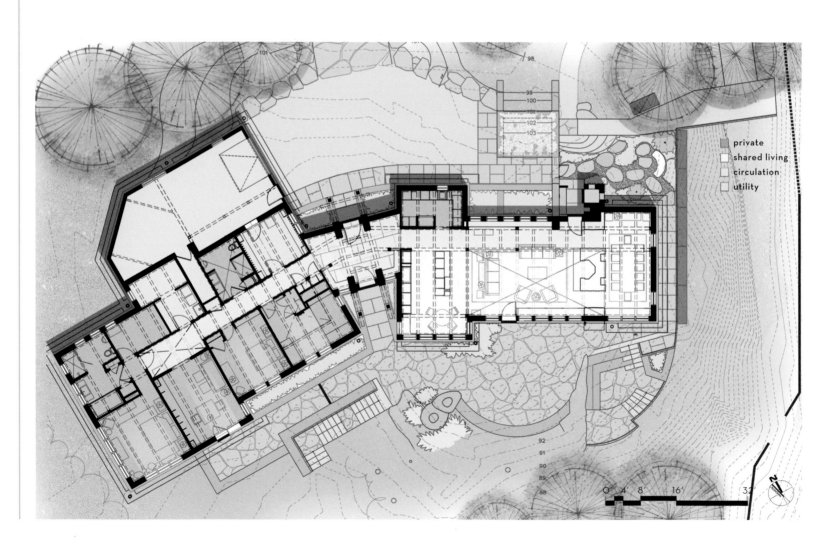

private
shared living
circulation
utility

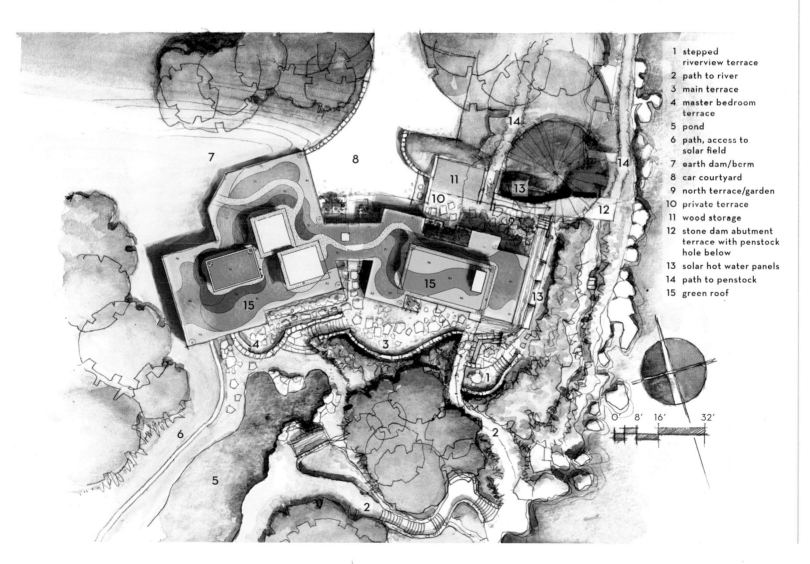

FIGURE CS7.5. This early conceptual site plan depicts the strong connection to the surrounding landscape, river, and dam.

1 stepped riverview terrace
2 path to river
3 main terrace
4 master bedroom terrace
5 pond
6 path, access to solar field
7 earth dam/berm
8 car courtyard
9 north terrace/garden
10 private terrace
11 wood storage
12 stone dam abutment terrace with penstock hole below
13 solar hot water panels
14 path to penstock
15 green roof

0'   8'   16'   32'

FIGURE CS7.7. View from across the pond.

berming causes the house to nearly disappear from the north and an adjacent small dirt road, addressing the owner's desire for privacy and security.

To the south, terraces cascade down toward the river and a swimming pond that reflects the house. To the east, the flat top of the former stone dam abutment creates a dramatic viewing platform 40 feet above the river, with picturesque ledge rock descending into the rapidly flowing current. A forged metal railing with elements derived from dam remains provides safety while allowing viewers to experience the full drama of the site. From inside the house low windows in the dining and living rooms allow constantly changing views of the river below.

The layout and interior materials of the home reinforce the connection to nature and sustainable design. The entry acts as a narrow, transparent threshold from the roadside through the center of the home, providing access to the southern river views and the series of terraces, stairways, and pathways to the river and pond. The entry also serves as a connector between the two wings of the house, the living wing and the sleeping wing. The two wings bend slightly to enclose the site and to orient the larger southern windows toward the sun and maximize river views. The large stone fireplace and chimney anchor the building to the stone of the site and the dam remnant. The green roof reduces stormwater impact on the site, with runoff water fed to native plantings around the home.

The energy performance of the home is supported by the robust thermal envelope with 12″ double stud walls filled with spray foam (R-60), an R-50 roof assembly, and R-20 below-grade insulation. The home's systems include a ground-source heat pump with a 600′ well, a 600-gallon solar hot water soft tank for heat storage for the radiant heating and for domestic hot water, and a 14 kW PV array with a 10 kW battery backup and a wood-burning boiler.

DESIGN PROFILE

Building Profile	Building Name:	**Tepfer House**	
	Location:	Putney, Vermont	
	Square Footage:	2,733	
Energy Profile	Total Energy Consumption:	9,180 kWh (31,325 kBtu)	
		0.75 cords of wood (15,000 kBtu)	
	Total Energy Production:	9,215 kWh (31,442 kBtu)	
	Energy Intensity:	Actual:	16.95 kBtu/sf-yr
		Actual with Renewables:	5.49 kBtu/sf-yr
Building Envelope	Insulation Values:	Walls:	R-44.4, dense-pack cellulose in 12″ thick double-wall cavity
		Roof:	R-69.2, 16″ dense-pack cellulose, min 1.5″ rigid tapered insulation on roof
		Foundation (slab perimeter):	R-20, 4″ XPS rigid insulation
		Foundation (sub-slab):	R-20, 4″ XPS rigid insulation
	Air Infiltration:	Final Blower Door:	566 cfm50
			0.12 cfm50/sf exterior surface area
	Windows/Skylights:	Windows:	Low-e, tri-pane, argon-filled
			U-value: 0.20, SHGC: 0.24, VT: 0.39
Mechanical/ Electrical Systems	Heating System:	Daikin air-source heat pump	
	Cooling System:	Air-source heat pump, as needed	
	Ventilation System:	ERV	
	Lighting System/Controls:	High-efficiency fluorescent or LED fixtures	
	Hot Water:	Solar thermal: two 4×8 collectors	
	Renewable System:	36 Suntech 210s	
	Installed System Size:	7.5 kW	

Tepfer Residence
Carbon Neutral in Putney, Vermont

Harriet and Burt Tepfer nurtured and improved a beautiful farm property for decades as their children grew and then left. They had always cherished a special spot in a secluded meadow on rolling terrain behind their old farmhouse. It had a serene and pastoral view of hayfields, with Mt. Monadnock in the distance. With their children gone, it no longer made sense for them to maintain an old farmhouse. They knew the location, and they knew they wanted a new home that would steward and live lightly on the land they loved. They wanted a healthy, energy-efficient, and easy-to-maintain home for retirement. As

FIGURE CS7.8. The home nestled in the field, with solar hot water on panels on the roof.

residents of the Putney community, the owners were familiar with and inspired by the nearby net zero Putney School field house. The idea of net zero resonated with their environmental goals as well as their desire to control costs and avoid energy cost escalation and/or volatility.

The house is insulated to net zero energy ready standards and meets the definition of net zero in terms of amount of energy consumed. They decided to install an air-source heat pump with PVs, solar domestic hot water panels, and a wood-stove. They have a wood lot that can easily and sustainably supply all they need for heating, they enjoy harvesting wood off their land, and they love wood fires. Under the definitions outlined in chapter 2, the on-site PV combined with on-site harvesting of wood for heating categorizes the home as carbon neutral, while under many other definitions the home would be classified as net zero.

The house was designed so that now they can burn wood for about 30 percent of their heating needs. The 7.5 kw PV array was sized to supply all of their electricity needs, including all normal uses, plus the balance of their heating need. Because of this the house is classified as carbon neutral based on the wood energy used. However, the air-source heat pump could heat their house, and they have selected a site where they can add PV in the future, so the home can easily be net zero. And with the wood backup they are already prepared to keep their home warm if the electricity goes out.

Having lived many years on the land, they were in love with the views east to the mountain. The site presented a challenge in terms of designing a house that would take advantage of the views while controlling the eastern solar gain, which could lead to overheating and excess heat loss. The resulting design is an elongated house on the east–west axis, allowing for the majority of glass to be south facing. This allows passive solar gain into all of the major occupied spaces, including the bedroom, study, and living spaces. In addition, the living room and dining room enjoy direct eastern views of the meadow and mountain. The open plan also allows for views from the kitchen through the dining room and living room.

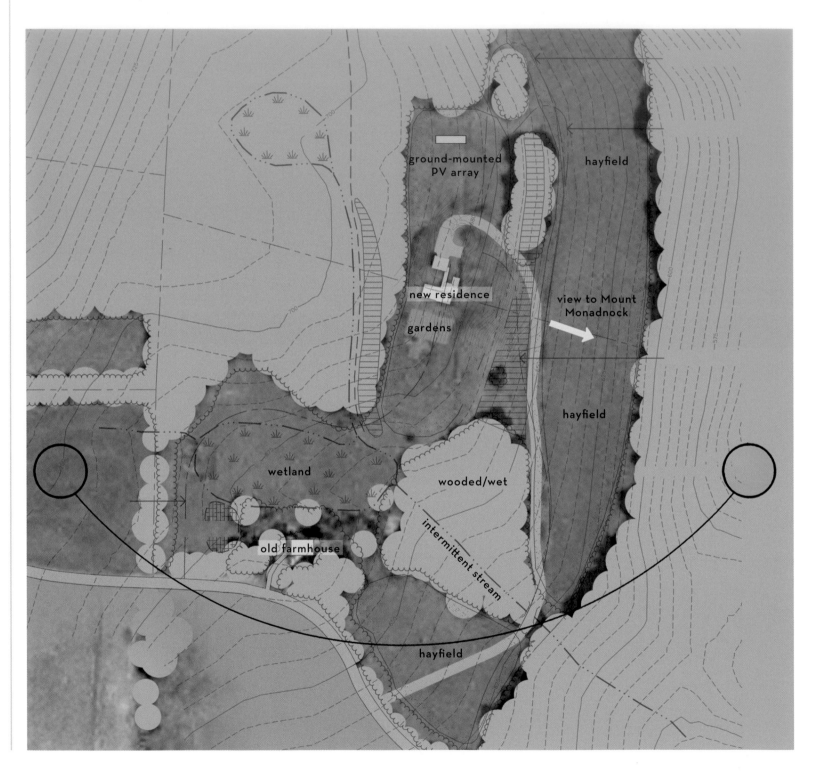

ground-mounted
PV array

hayfield

new residence

view to Mount
Monadnock

gardens

hayfield

wetland

wooded/wet

intermittent stream

old farmhouse

hayfield

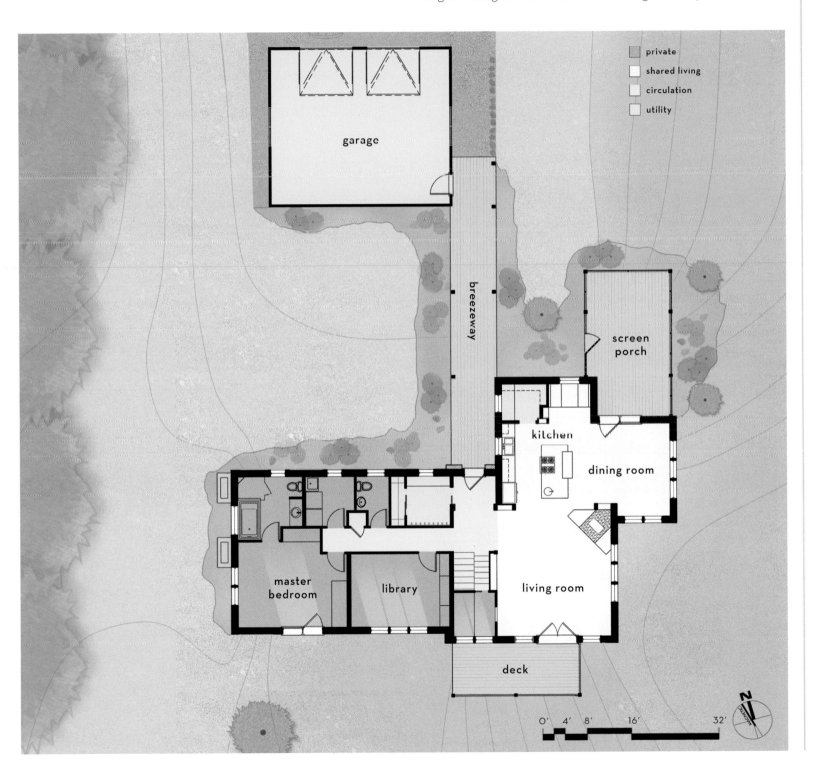

FIGURE CS7.10. First floor with master suite for single-story living and living room connected to south gardens by deck.

private
shared living
circulation
utility

garage

breezeway

screen porch

kitchen

dining room

master bedroom

library

living room

deck

0' 4' 8'   16'   32'

N

From a building massing and overall energy perspective, this design approach both optimizes solar gain by its overall orientation on the east–west axis and incorporates important views and connection to nature to the east. And this design allows the current owners to live in their carbon-neutral home now, enjoying the warmth of their woodstove, while providing them or future owners an easy path to full net zero performance with the simple addition of PV.

We worked with the owners to blend their desire for a home that offers an inspiring and satisfying way of life with minimal environmental and energy impacts. In the design of their home, they sought a welcoming experience and lifestyle, filled with sunshine and connected to the outdoors. Living spaces have direct access to the south, where a large vegetable garden and orchard border the home. The owners grow and preserve much of their own food, so a root cellar with passive temperature control is in the basement. The north side of the kitchen and dining area opens to a screened porch with eastern views. To the west an existing forested area leads to a meandering stream and hill, with trails to enjoy the surrounding beauty. The trees and hill also provide some protection from winter winds. To the north the solar array sits beyond the drive on the north edge of the hayfield. In the interior at the end of the hall to their bedroom and library, a skylight brings natural light to enliven and accent the connection to their private space. During the day the house is flooded with natural light.

The character of the house sprung from the owners' past travel and attraction to the textures and colors of the Tuscan landscape and sympathetic building design. Exterior stucco, stone, and interior plaster walls in the central living area were incorporated in the design to support this desire. Oak and cherry trees were harvested from their land and used as interior finishes. Quarter-sawn oak was used for flooring in the main living spaces, beams, trim, stair treads, and built-in bookcases. The site-harvested cherry was used for hand-carved doors and the built-in dining nook. All were finished with low- or no-VOC finishes. All of these details were used to further deepen the connection of the owners to their unique property and to nature in general.

17 | Why the Cost Is Right

M ention net zero buildings and most people ask about the added cost and payback. They also might believe that net zero is a good idea but assume that it is impossible to include in the budget for most projects. In reality, though, there is no feasible choice *except* net zero: it is the only prudent investment. Not only do net zero buildings now pay for themselves, but they also increase real estate values and protect their owners from increasing fossil-fuel energy costs and other trends.

The Big Trends
Affecting Net Zero Cost Benefits

We already know that reason number one for going carbon neutral is to reduce climate change. We also know that if the cost of cleaning up environmental, health, and carbon impacts were included in economic assessments, fossil-fuel use would be totally unviable. Amory Lovins estimates that these costs triple actual fuel costs.[1] But a less obvious economic argument can be found in an analysis of fossil-fuel price volatility, its link to declining oil supplies, and its correlation to improving energy standards.

THE IMPACT OF ESCALATING FUEL COST

During the twentieth century, oil prices remained relatively steady, with only one large spike in the 1970s during the Arab oil embargo and another at the end of the century, after 1999. In fact, when rates are adjusted for inflation, a barrel of oil cost the equivalent of $21.83 in 1913 and $31.40 in 2000, with an average annual fuel escalation rate of 0.5 percent, as figure 17.1 illustrates. In comparison, the annual average fuel escalation rate between 2000 and 2013 was 15 percent. Since this recent price volatility is likely due to oil depletion, not a political crisis, as in the 1970s, the rising escalation rates are probably indications of long-term trends. When oil prices spiked in the 1970s, energy

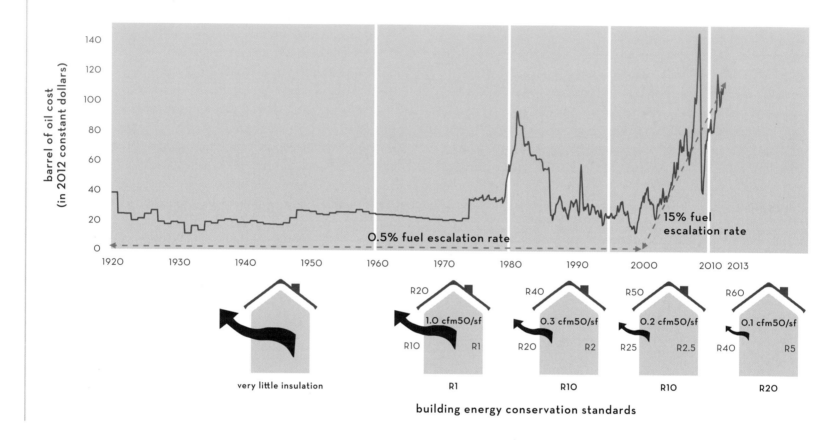

FIGURE 17.1. From 1920 to 2000, average annual oil cost escalation was 0.5 percent; from 2000 to 2013 it was 15 percent. With the rise in energy prices has come a rise in energy conservation standards, such as increased insulation values, which doubled in the 1970s and will likely double again in the 2010s.[2]

conservation standards in buildings doubled (see figure 17.1 and "Historical Trends in Energy Cost and Insulation Practices" sidebar); the steady climb has caused those standards to get tighter—despite initial concerns about cost—and now, with over-all price escalation upon us, we are likely to see the widespread adoption of net zero standards in the relatively near future.

So how do we know what's heading our way? When calculating the financial performance of a building for a client, we estimate approximate fuel escalation rates. Since we can only speculate on future energy prices based on past prices, we use a range. Figure 17.2 shows an actual range of oil prices

from 2000 to 2013, suggesting an escalation rate of fuel cost, drawn from the highs and lows in that span that varies between 2 percent and 42 percent. We extrapolate from this depending on the specific project's circumstances, using a low range of 3–5 percent and a high range of 6–15 percent. All of our calculations adjust for the effects of inflation, so that costs are in "constant" dollars (not adjusting for inflation has led to skewed views of fuel cost increases in the past). The US Energy Information Administration provides estimates for fossil-fuel prices based on a longer stretch of the past, making their numbers very conservative for estimating future fuel escalation

Before the 1940s insulation was rarely used, and directly after World War II standard insulation levels were quite low: generally R-11 walls, R-19 roofs, single-pane glass, and no foundation insulation. Additionally, little thought was given to reducing air infiltration through the building envelope. As a result, buildings did not provide comfortable living and working spaces for their occupants. Since energy used for heating was relatively inexpensive at this time, the practice of insulating began as much to provide increased comfort as it did to save money. For most individuals, environmental stewardship rarely figured into the evaluation of energy sources.

With the first energy crisis in the United States in the 1970s, insulation standards effectively doubled to R-19 walls, R-30 roofs, and double-pane glass. Builders, bankers, and real estate professionals believed that these energy-saving measures would stop construction and hurt the economy.

Today, however, these insulation standards are considered the minimum in colder climates and are typically exceeded in all new construction and significant renovation. While concerns about energy security and global climate issues have risen to the forefront and have contributed to the increase in insulation levels, energy cost is and likely will continue to be the major impetus for increased energy conservation.

As we transition away from fossil fuels to more expensive options, we are poised for another jump in insulation levels. Energy costs will rise, and the financial justification for further increasing insulation standards to save energy seems a foregone conclusion.

Will again doubling these standards be cost-effective and get us to the appropriate level? Should we increase standards by more or less? If the goal is to design and construct buildings that can produce as much energy as they consume, what is the right level of conservation?

rates in times of energy source transition, such as today, and given the increasing energy prices we expect. We think that fuel escalation rates should consider twenty-first-century trends.

THE RENEWABLE COST PLATEAU: ENERGY PARITY

From 2008 to 2013 the cost of solar PV dropped significantly, from over $6/peak watt installed to $4/peak watt installed for small installations and roughly $2/peak watt for large utility installations. It is likely renewable energy will continue to

decrease so that the cost of energy produced from renewables will at some point equal the cost of energy produced from fossil fuels. Then, as fossil-fuel prices continue to rise, the cost of energy from renewables will become the least expensive energy source, and energy investments will be based on renewable energy costs, not fossil-fuel costs.

So when we use the term "new net zero," we are saying that future buildings will be based on a renewable energy economy, not a fossil-fuel economy. We will eventually reach what we call the renewable solar cost plateau, where fossil-fuel and PV costs equalize and PV then becomes more cost effective (see

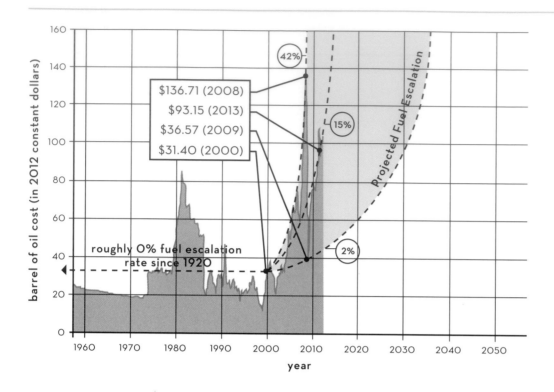

FIGURE 17.2. The average oil price from 1920 to 2000 was $25.14 a barrel. The current fuel cost volatility is evident when we look at the high and low prices between 2000 and 2013. The cost of oil in 2000 was $31.40. The highest oil price, recorded in July 2008, was $136.71, with an annual fuel escalation rate of 42 percent. The lowest oil price since 2000 was recorded in February 2009, at $36.57, with a resulting annual fuel escalation rate of only 2 percent. The price of oil was $93.15 in January 2013, which gives an annual fuel escalation rate of 15 percent.[3]

figure 17.3). We have projected this renewable energy plateau by estimating future market rates for different energy sources and estimating when renewable and fossil-fuel energy prices equalize, the point of grid parity. This may sound simple, but in reality it is a complex projection.

Energy produced by renewables has already reached grid parity in some nations, but the real tipping point will not occur until a certain "pain factor" is reached with their existing fuel prices, causing the majority of people to shift to renewable energy. The delay in reaching grid parity is caused by numerous factors connected to changing from fossil fuels to renewables. For existing buildings, these factors include owners' prior investments in fossil-fuel heating and cooling equipment, as well as time needed for shifts in perception and buying habits. For new buildings, this transition will happen sooner, as their owners do not face the cost and complexity of replacing an existing system. However, the fact that consumers resist change and uncertainty will slow advances even in new buildings.

Yet the plateau brought on by price parity may not be enough, right away, to force a swift transition. To understand why, we can first look at our current options and practices when purchasing energy to meet our electricity needs. In Vermont, due to power purchase agreements, all homeowners and most businesses can purchase their electricity for the same price or less from solar developers and companies typically with a guaranteed rate for 5 years. This would seem to indicate that the solar plateau has arrived for solar PV in Vermont. And yet most people have not switched. Why? First, this is not as easy as just asking your power company to change their billing procedure. You need to call the solar developer company to determine if your site is feasible. You have to switch providers and engage in a seemingly complicated agreement, new and different in the marketplace. You need to put the solar on your home or your land, or on other land in the territory of your utility. All of this takes effort and causes resistance by the consumer. Thus, the effective solar plateau happens after the theoretical solar plateau.

If you do not have easy solar access to make this change, you have to wait until your utility switches from fossil fuels to renewables, and this is likely to be much later. Utilities will probably wait until there is a greater price difference between renewables and fossil fuels, because utility companies already have major investments in fossil-fuel generating plants. So, while a homeowner may arrive at the solar plateau when fossil fuels are slightly more expensive than renewables, say 1.25 times PV prices, a utility likely won't change until energy from fossil fuels is closer to twice the cost of energy from renewables. The utilities will also change more slowly as net-metering laws mandate that utilities pay net-metered users the retail price for renewable power, which is not the typical purchase price for utilities.

While the theoretical solar plateau is when grid parity occurs, our estimate is that people will switch at varying times from when renewable energy and fossil-fuel energy cost the same to when fossil fuel energy is twice as expensive as renewable energy. This variance is based on multiple factors, including viability of PV on-site or off-site, existing systems, utility company decisions, and each individual's or organization's environmental mission.

So let's look in greater detail to figure out the plateau for building owners, managers, and users, as well as the best time to convert to renewables. Our interest lies in determining when PV will reach the tipping point in the United States, by determining for our clients the financial analysis of an installed PV system in relation to traditional fossil-fuel options. We use PV in our analysis because it is the most common renewable technology for electrical needs, and so, the most likely candidate for net zero energy construction.

All of our estimates of the renewable solar plateau are based on 2013 PV costs and use $4/watt for installation costs of small- and medium-size installations of a durable, high-efficiency module. We chose a thirty-year lifetime of the PV panels (although they will likely last longer), a panel degradation of 0.5 percent per year, one inverter replacement in the thirty years (which is not discounted), a fixed-tilt array, and 1.1 kWh/yr-Wp peak rating (typical of New England). Drawing on these assumptions, we would expect the PVs to produce energy for a price of $0.14/kWh for typical electric uses without any incentives in New England.

If we made the same assessment for Colorado Springs, Colorado, with a 1.5 kWh/yr-Wp peak rating, the PV system would produce energy for a price of $0.10/kWh (without incentives) because of the increased solar radiation of Colorado. Depending on your location and incentives available, the costs for energy from PV are better than, or are approaching, the 2013 national residential electric rate of $0.12/kWh. When PV systems are paid for up front by the owner, it seems as if the cost is much higher than using grid electricity, but over the lifetime of the system the cost is in fact lower.

So far we have discussed the solar plateau in relation to an existing user's electricity bill. What if we want to use renewable energy for heating or cooling? Does this change? Likely it does, because of the efficiency of all-electric heating using heat pumps. Ground-source and air-source heat pumps are 2.3 to 3 times more efficient than electricity used for direct resistant heating. With heat pumps the relative efficiency of electricity increases, making it more cost effective as a heating source. In other words, it lowers the solar plateau by roughly 60 percent compared to electricity for other typical uses. However, if you are switching from an existing fossil-fuel heating system to a heat pump you will be less eager to change because you have a functioning system, and you may wait until fossil-fuel energy moves well beyond the cost of renewable energy.

In table 17.1 and figure 17.3, we converted each energy source to cost per MMBtu in order to compare the cost of fossil fuels and electricity from PV. Table 17.1 indicates that PV electricity for our general use or for direct-resistance electric heat is equal to propane at $3.76/gal, oil at $5.58/gal, or natural gas at $4.10/therm. However, we do not use fossil fuels directly for typical electrical uses so we need to incorporate heating efficiencies into the analysis.

The range of heat pump efficiencies is typically between 2.3 and 3 in cold climates. Our analysis assumes a heating COP of 2.3 for air-source heat pumps, meaning they are 230 percent efficient (based on a high-efficiency, variable-refrigerant-flow heat pump operating in a cold climate). Using electricity from PV at a cost of $0.14/kWh, the heat delivered is $0.06/kWh ($17.58/MMBtu), which is equivalent to fossil fuels if you are paying $1.61/gal for propane, $2.39/gal for oil, or $1.76/therm for natural gas (see table 17.1). These costs are well below 2013 oil and propane rates in Vermont as shown in table 17.2. If you have an existing building, the renewable solar cost plateau would occur at double these rates, as shown in table 17.1, at $35.17 /MMBtu.

Table 17.2 shows heating comparisons from various fuel sources with their adjusted efficiencies in Vermont from December 2013. The cost per MMBtu and heating efficiencies reported by the Vermont Public Service Department for each

TABLE 17.1. HEATING COSTS COMPARING SOLAR PV TO FOSSIL FUELS

	ELECTRIC (kWh)	PROPANE (GAL)	OIL (GAL)	NATURAL GAS (THERM)	$/MMBtu
2013 cost of heat comparing direct electric resistance and PV	$0.14	$3.76	$5.58	$4.10	$41.03
Plateau for heating sources, when retrofitting with heat pumps	$0.12	$3.22	$4.78	$3.52	$35.17
2013 cost of heat comparing heat pumps and PV	$0.06	$1.61	$2.39	$1.76	$17.58
2013 cost of heat pumps and PV with 30 percent federal tax credit for PV	$0.04	$1.07	$1.59	$1.17	$11.72

Source: Analysis completed with the assistance of Andy Shapiro, Energy Balance.

TABLE 17.2. COST COMPARISON OF HEATING FUELS IN VERMONT

TYPE OF ENERGY	Btu/UNIT	ADJUSTED EFFICIENCY	PRICE PER UNIT	COST PER MMBTU
Fuel oil, gallon	138,200	80%	$3.77	$34.09
Kerosene, gallon	136,600	80%	$4.19	$38.36
Propane, gallon	91,600	80%	$2.91	$39.75
Natural gas, therm	100,000	80%	$1.46	$18.28
Electricity, kWh (resistive heat)	3,412	100%	$0.15	$43.46
Electricity, kWh (cold climate heat pump)	3,412	300%	$0.15	$14.49
Wood, cord (green)	22,000,000	60%	$193.33	$14.65
Pellets, ton	16,400,000	80%	$247.00	$18.83

Source: Vermont Department of Public Service, Vermont Fuel Price (December 2013), 3, http://publicservice.vermont.gov/publications/fuel_report

fuel source confirms our assumptions and are the starting point for the fuel prices in figure 17.3.

We prepare a customized financial analysis for projects, and assume fuel escalation rates for energy that are discussed and agreed upon with our clients. In figure 17.3, we offer an example of this analysis. We begin with the costs for different energy sources without tax credits. In this case we used residential energy costs in Vermont in December 2013 as the starting point, but these costs should be adjusted to each individual project. In this example we use $3.77/gal for oil, $2.91/gal for propane, and $1.46/therm for natural gas. We used an annual fuel escalation rate of 4 percent. Once the renewable cost plateau is reached, we assume fuel escalation rates are zero and the only cost increases are due to inflation, which

we have disregarded in this analysis. For PV electric rates we show three alternative solar plateaus: electricity from PV and direct resistance heat, retrofitting heat pumps for fossil fuels, and heat pumps in new installations. In order to account for delivered energy per fuel type, efficiencies of heating systems are taken into account. Heat pumps have a COP of 2.3, while other fuel sources have an efficiency of 0.8. Heat pumps in new installations are already at the solar plateau for all fossil fuel sources (with natural gas reaching it by 2014). If you are retrofitting your existing heating system the plateau is at $35.17/MMBtu or $0.12/kWh. Propane is already above this plateau, oil will likely reach this solar plateau in 2015, and natural gas will reach it in 2027. If local PV incentives of federal tax credits are included, the solar plateau decreases by 30 percent, making

FIGURE 17.3. This example of the renewable solar cost plateau when heating efficiencies are used shows three plateaus: new construction with PV electric and heat pumps, retrofitting using PV and heat pumps, and electricity from PV. This graph confirms that heat pumps in new construction are already cost effective for all fuel sources, and even retrofits will become cost effective by 2027, depending on fuel prices and options.

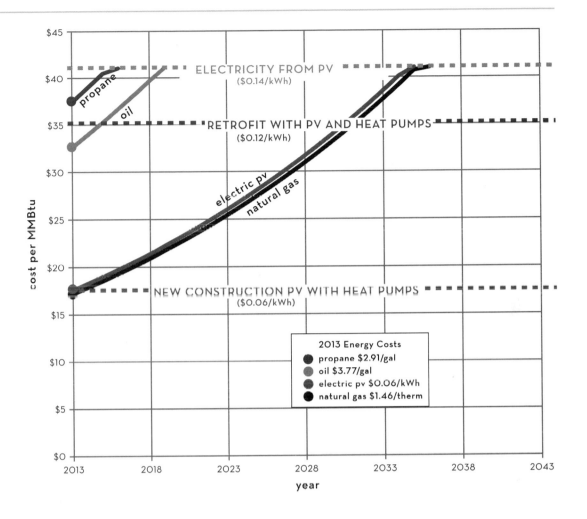

Assessing Intangibles: Productivity, Health, Resilience, Market, and Other Benefits

People value buildings they love. Net zero buildings, beyond their energy performance, incorporate healthy, integrated, sustainable design strategies and provide higher levels of occupant comfort, health, productivity, satisfaction, and even inspiration than typical buildings. These strategies are all oriented toward creating wonderful places to be, work, and play. The financial rewards related to these additional benefits are difficult to quantify but appear to be much greater than the value of energy savings.

The transition sooner. And if a business is undertaking these improvements, depreciation and other benefits may further expedite the solar plateau.

The value of a building comes from its ability to create a beautiful, healthy, and productive place for occupants, owners, guests, and the larger public. It is this value that will ultimately generate more interest in net zero buildings and communities. If building users love their buildings, they will care for them, and the buildings will last through the centuries. In this way these healthy net zero buildings can add long-term value to the built environment. Evaluated on their life cycles, net zero buildings can be the least expensive buildings.

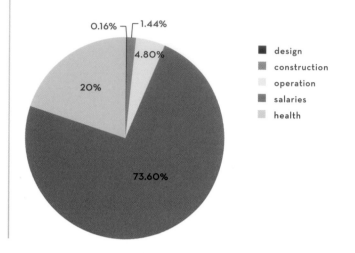

FIGURE 17.4. The estimated life-cycle cost of buildings over 30 years includes less than 5 percent total for design and construction, which indicates that relatively small additional costs for high-performing buildings are profitable over a building's lifetime.

	TWENTY-YEAR NPV
Energy value	$5.79
Emissions value	$1.18
Water value	$0.51
Waste value (construction only; 1 yr)	$0.03
Commissioning operations and maintenance value	$8.47
Productivity and health value	$55.33
Less green cost premium	($4.00)
Total twenty-year NPV	$67.31

TABLE 17.3. FINANCIAL BENEFIT OF GREEN BUILDING (PER SQUARE FOOT)

Source: Greg Katz, *The Costs and Financial Benefits of Green Buildings: A Report to California's Sustainable Building Task Force*, Capital E (October 2003), 55.

While the building stock of net zero and green buildings is small and concrete research is limited, multiple studies have documented the broader financial benefits of green building design, including increased worker productivity, decreased absenteeism, and increased product sales. Calculating the actual value of these benefits is not as straightforward as calculating energy savings, but research has found that these benefits have a larger impact on the bottom line of businesses than the energy savings associated with net zero buildings. Employee-related costs account for 89 percent of the life cycle costs of buildings, while energy is 5 percent of the total costs. Increased productivity due to reduced absenteeism and increased efficiency, then, is substantial.[4] A widely recognized study indicates employee-related productivity savings in LEED Gold and Platinum buildings to be ten times greater than energy savings alone, as shown in table 17.3.[5]

INCREASED PRODUCTIVITY

Occupant productivity can be attributed to a range of design features, including daylighting, outside air ventilation, green indoor finishes, and other healthy interior conditions.

Many findings have shown the potential value of increased productivity:

- Improved lighting has led to median productivity gains of 3.2 percent and saved $1,600 per employee based on twenty-five studies analyzed by Carnegie-Mellon University.[6]
- Absenteeism is reduced by one day per year for employees in green buildings.[7]
- Indirect savings of reduced employee turnover (due to employee efficiency and reduction of training) in green buildings is $294,000 per year or $1.72 per square foot.[8]

DAYLIGHTING

A study of major retail stores in California showed 40 percent higher sales in well-daylit stores, plus higher employee satisfaction. In addition, the value of higher sales was worth nineteen times more than the energy savings, the initial impetus for the daylighting.[9] The findings also challenge conventional retail dogma that lighting must be refined and controlled.

Results like these, though, are little surprise, given that daylighting enhances the quality and aesthetics of buildings,

In 1986 the Reno, Nevada, post office underwent a phased renovation to the ceiling and lighting above their two sorting machines. The design features included enhancing the indirect lighting by changing the ceiling slope and minimizing the direct downlighting with more efficient and pleasant lights. After a test section of these design changes was completed, the post office calculated how the design improvements affected mail-sorting errors. They found an 8 percent increase in productivity of the workers in the new section compared to no change for workers in the old section. After the complete renovation, the facility's increased productivity stabilized around 6 percent, and the rate of sorting errors by machine operators dropped to 0.1 percent, the lowest in the western region.[10] Altogether the energy and maintenance savings of the new ceiling and lighting came to $50,000. In comparison, the productivity gains of the increased working efficiency and reduced error rates were worth between $400,000 and $500,000 per year. The renovation cost the post office only $300,000, so this productivity increase was clearly a beneficial investment.[11]

Another example of the financial benefits of energy efficiency through boosted worker productivity is the International Netherlands Group (ING) Bank headquarters completed in 1987 in Amsterdam. The 538,000 sf building is broken into ten towers that house 2,400 employees on narrow floor plates where all desks are located within 23 feet of a window. ING's previous headquarters building consumed primary energy at a level of 422 kBtu/sf-yr, whereas the 1987 building consumes only 35 kBtu/sf-yr. Costs associated with the increased energy performance were estimated at $700,000.[12] Annual savings were estimated to be $2.6 million.[13] At such prices the energy savings will pay for themselves in three months. Additionally, absenteeism in the new building is 15 percent lower than in the bank's old headquarters.[14]

FIGURE 17.5. The ING Bank headquarters in Amsterdam is a community icon and a leading example of energy-efficient office design with productivity gains.

means less strain for our eyes, and decreases overall stress levels, and the windows that bring the natural light in also allow views to the outside. Good daylighting design can also result in decreased energy consumption for lighting, which can in turn reduce air-conditioning loads (though these energy reductions are usually relatively small).

INDOOR AIR QUALITY

The improved indoor air quality in net zero and green buildings also brings significant benefits—particularly since an estimated $15 to $40 billion in US health care costs are directly related to "sick" buildings.[15] Twenty-six peer-reviewed papers showed an average of 43 percent reduction in symptoms of indoor-air-quality health impacts in buildings with green attributes.[16]

Net zero buildings provide healthy indoor air by using low-toxicity materials, eliminating combustion systems, including moisture-control strategies, and carefully controlling ventilation. All of us have felt sleepy in conference rooms, for instance, but likely didn't know that increased CO_2 found in many buildings may have caused it. But elevated CO_2 levels are just one health concern. Hal Levin and the Environmental Protection Agency have thoroughly documented sick building syndrome, caused by inadequate ventilation, chemical contaminants from interior or exterior materials, and biological contaminants such as mold from interior stagnant moisture.[17]

PHYSICAL COMFORT

A well-insulated building has warmer mean radiant temperatures on its exterior wall surfaces than a building with lower insulation levels. Because of this, occupants in well-insulated buildings feel warmer than those in less-insulated buildings, even when the air temperature is the same. Similarly, employees are more comfortable sitting close to higher-performing windows that provide views and daylight, which can enhance overall satisfaction and productivity. Net zero buildings also incorporate ergonomic design to minimize such health issues as carpal tunnel syndrome and the negative impacts of a sedentary lifestyle.

In general, studies show a 36 percent reduction in symptoms of poor health when occupants have access to natural views, natural ventilation, indoor plants, and daylight.[18] But the benefits of building comfort have been particularly discernable in hospitals. Behavioral scientist Roger Ulrich has shown that green, comfortable hospitals, with access to views, had better outcomes for patients—helping them feel better, recover sooner, and have fewer hospital stays.[19]

BUILDING LIFE CYCLE

A building's efficiency level dramatically impacts its life cycle. Some insurance companies already recognize this: they reduce casualty insurance by 5 percent on LEED-certified buildings because they consider them to be a lower risk.[20]

However, for the last half century in the fossil-fuel era, owners have generally accounted for energy improvements separately from structural improvements. This makes little sense today. Insulation is located within the building enclosure. It cannot be easily added after initial construction or renovations. Under either new construction or renovation scenarios, the insulation is only a small part of the building enclosure cost. Interior and exterior finishes and mechanical, electrical, and structural systems make up the major costs of the building enclosure. Opportunities to increase the level of insulation in a building occur when other improvements are financed. It is appropriate, then, to consider financing energy improvements as a long-term investment over the life of those upgrades rather than justifying the improvements with simple payback. This approach significantly improves the return on investment and/or cash flow.

This means that unless you add insulation to the interior of the building, usually a costly decision, the insulation levels that you choose to employ in your building today should be adequate for the life of the envelope. If later you consider insulation upgrades in the building enclosure that are not a part of interior or exterior building renovations, they will likely not be a good investment. Because it is appropriate to consider energy enclosure upgrades over a longer time frame, the fiscally prudent insulation levels should not be based on the current cost of energy. These decisions should instead be based on a projection of what energy costs will be over the lifetime of the building enclosure. Therefore, fuel escalation is important to include in your assessment.

Studies by the Heschong Mahone Group (HMG) have indicated a statistical correlation between daylighting in elementary school classrooms and the performance of students on standardized tests. HMG's 1999 study of daylighting in California schools focused on skylights, which separate the factor of natural daylighting from other factors related to windows (such as views out) that could also affect student performance. With a test group of more than 21,000 second-through fifth-grade students, the results showed that "students with the most daylighting in their classrooms progressed 20% faster on math tests and 26% on reading tests in one year than those with the least."[21]

Additional tests in Seattle and Fort Collins, Colorado, which used a slightly different testing metric, showed that "students in classrooms with the most daylighting were found to have 7% to 18% higher scores than those with the least."[22] Because these three school districts have significantly different curricula, school building designs, and climates, the consistency in the results makes a strong case for a positive correlation between daylighting and student performance. Additional reanalysis was performed in 2001 and 2003 to minimize external variables and study new student populations. The 2001 reanalysis study accounted for teacher bias and found that the classrooms with the most daylighting had a 21 percent student learning rate improvement over classrooms with the least amount of daylight.[23]

Wal-Mart initiated an experimental store in 1993 to examine environmental implications as well as design for high energy efficiency. Because the company opted to locate skylights over only half of the roof, it could see as well the effects of daylighting on retail sales. With real-time tracking of the activity at each cash register, Wal-Mart soon recognized that the daylit side of the store generated significantly higher sales per square foot than the departments on the non-daylit half of the store. Overall sales for the daylit departments were higher compared to the same departments in Walmarts without daylighting. Employee satisfaction was also noticeable: workers in the half of the store without skylights wanted to move to the daylit side of the store.[24]

FIGURE 17.6. A high-performance classroom at the DaVinci Middle School in Portland, Oregon, designed by SRG Partnership, Inc. The large skylight provides daylighting through a fabric diffuser that evens out the light in the classroom and was designed in partnership with the Energy Studies in Buildings Laboratory.

The Vermont Studio Center had several buildings that were causing occupant discomfort and had high energy bills and durability issues. Maclay Architects teamed with Andy Shapiro of Energy Balance and Steve Pitkin, a construction estimator, to perform an assessment of two structures for energy performance, maintenance, and durability. This project also served as a template for a larger-scale campus capital investment plan. The assessment of the two buildings offered recommended improvements and associated costs that the Studio Center could implement to achieve three different levels of energy improvements. Specifically, we compared an option of taking energy conservation measures (ECMs) to net zero ready standards today to an option where net zero ready levels are achieved with partial ECMs today and additional measures later. The two-step process is a much poorer investment, as finishes and systems are disturbed two times rather than once. Our findings (see figure 17.7) demonstrated the significant financial benefits of implementing the highest level of energy improvements at the beginning of a thirty-year period rather than making incremental upgrades.

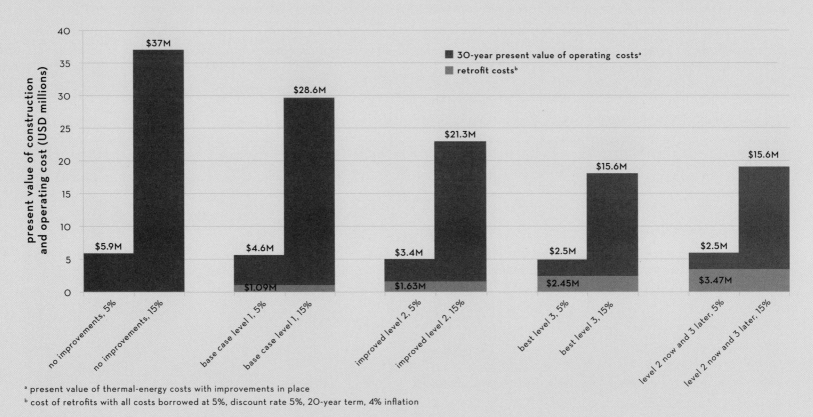

ᵃ present value of thermal-energy costs with improvements in place
ᵇ cost of retrofits with all costs borrowed at 5%, discount rate 5%, 20-year term, 4% inflation

FIGURE 17.7. A strategic energy plan for the Vermont Studio Center. Above is an analysis of a representative building, the Barbara White Studio, using both a 5 percent and 15 percent fuel escalation rate with no solar plateau. It shows a thirty-year operating and capital costs comparison of three levels of energy performance and a phased implementation of level-two and level-three improvements.

RESILIENCE

Resilience is the ability to adapt and withstand changes to the environment, and net zero buildings are well poised to be resilient. In this time of increased weather-related disasters and fuel-price volatility, more and more people are interested in buildings that perform on a long time frame and across a wide range of conditions. In fact, the US Department of Homeland Security and the US military are embracing and mandating net zero building design to make themselves more resilient.[25]

With higher-performing, better-insulated buildings, owners can be more comfortable during power outages in the winter. They will be protected from an immediate descent to freezing temperatures, and there will be no frozen pipes or associated damage to worry about. Additionally, if occupants of net zero homes lose heat on a cold evening, a very small electric space heater can maintain comfortable temperatures.

This overall resilience comes at a relatively small price: green and net zero construction added between 0 percent and 4 percent to the price of three-quarters of the buildings in one study, with most between 0 percent and 1 percent. The typical cost increase for the green features was $3.04/sf.[26]

LEASE AND MARKET CONSIDERATIONS

Operating a building throughout its lifetime typically costs 80 percent or more of a building's total costs.[27] As energy costs continue to rise and become more volatile, building owners, renters, property management companies, and the general public are becoming increasingly aware of the growing energy-related building operation costs. Prior to the 1970s, energy costs did not factor heavily into the discussion when buildings were evaluated for lease. Since then, though they have played a larger role, they are still not a primary determinant in real estate decisions—particularly since renters have traditionally paid the energy costs for their spaces. Today, potential building owners, real estate professionals, and appraisers are beginning to recognize the value of high-performance and net zero buildings, particularly as these buildings combine energy performance with healthy workplace and lifestyle design. The National Association of Realtors has even developed a tool kit to help members address, list, and promote green features in buildings.[28]

Companies often want to rent or own green buildings to align with their mission as a sustainable business, which simultaneously improves their image. As building owners are able to charge higher rental rates for higher-performance buildings, we will continue to see an increase in the market value of these buildings. Trends already point in this direction:

- US buildings labeled under the LEED or Energy Star system charge 3 percent higher rent, have greater occupancy rates, and sell for 13 percent more than comparable properties.[29]
- A McGraw-Hill survey of design and construction professionals expected a 10.9 percent increase in green building value and a 9.9 percent increase in return on investment in 2008.[30]
- The Solaire, a LEED Gold residential building in Manhattan, had a 10 percent to 15 percent higher sale price than non-green buildings in the same location.[31]
- 78 percent of respondents to a consumer survey said they would give preference to a buying a green home, and a majority would pay a premium for energy-efficient design and systems.[32]
- 50 percent of survey respondents said they would pay an additional $100 a month in mortgage payments for a green home.[33]
- Energy Star–labeled buildings have a 3.6 percent higher occupancy rate than nonlabeled buildings, while LEED-rated buildings have a 4.1 percent higher occupancy rate than nonrated buildings.[34]
- Reducing energy costs on an annual basis below $1/sf will add $10/sf in property asset value.[35]

COMMUNITY AND SOCIETAL BENEFITS

Society and communities benefit from green building through reduced carbon emissions, healthier outdoor environments, and reduced operating costs of public buildings, but many of these externalities are often omitted from financial analysis. But if we are to fully examine the benefits of net zero and green buildings, the larger context of benefits to society must be acknowledged. Certain cities are becoming known for their progressive green building codes and green building incentives, which have become a catalyst for additional growth and redevelopment. Chicago, a leader in reducing greenhouse gas emissions from buildings, has implemented policy that encourages greening existing buildings and new construction and considers it key to creating a stronger environmental and economic future.[36]

Again, the data point to positive trends:

- One study showed that simple building and site features such as light-colored roofs and shade trees could reduce the number of days of noncompliant ozone quality in Los Angeles by 12 percent. This would lead to a reduction of $360 million in health care costs related to community air quality.[37]
- Each 1,000 sf of light-colored roof surface is equivalent to reducing CO_2 emissions by 10 tons.[38]
- The increased benefit to society for green schools is $5/sf for reduced carbon emissions, indirect energy savings, and employment.[39]
- Many nonprofit organizations attract funds for capital projects by including green features and reduced operating costs.[40]
- Americans living in areas served by public transportation save 865 million hours in travel time and 450 million gallons of fuel on an annual basis due to reduced congestion.[41]
- For every dollar communities invest in public transportation, $4 in economic returns is generated through job creation and other societal benefits.[42]

Net Zero Building Costs

Net zero buildings are new to the design and construction industry, and estimates for costs associated with them can vary significantly. Advocates may aim for minimal additional costs to bring a project to net zero; others may estimate astronomical additional costs. Actual data are limited due to the small number of net zero buildings. However, when considering net zero building costs, it is helpful to break them down into energy conservation, renewable energy, and green and healthy building costs.

In the previous chapters we documented our process for determining metrics for net zero buildings' EUI numbers. The cost difference between our net zero building renewable-ready EUI numbers and a code-compliant building can be determined relatively easily. Much of the energy savings can be attained with no additional cost to the project through integrated design features such as optimizing building massing and glazing (without overglazing), minimizing heat loss, and downsizing mechanical and control systems. Overall we have been able to provide energy efficiency to net zero standards at an increased construction cost of $5 to $10 per square foot—a relatively minor premium.

In addition to these energy conservation costs, net zero buildings have renewable energy costs that are typically significant, despite rapidly declining production costs for the systems. Tax incentives and grants can make renewables an attractive investment now. Also, when renewable energy installation costs are financed, they typically have monthly payments similar to current utility bills. So by shifting renewable costs from a capital to an operating expense, the renewable energy becomes a prudent investment in today's economy. As we've seen in case studies throughout this book, integrated design practices can add some capital expense but allow savings in other areas. This reduces the overall capital costs so that net zero buildings do not need to cost much more than code-compliant buildings.

The third potential area of expense is in green and healthy building design costs. Many of these costs come as an unquantified benefit of net zero buildings. Features such as improved indoor air quality and benefits from daylighting, views, and operable windows are included in the expense of net zero buildings. Some other green components—composting toilets and green roofs, for example—are likely not included in the energy conservation and renewable energy expenses but do add to the overall building costs. But these additional costs not only add other environmental benefits but may also boost productivity and occupant satisfaction—enough to outweigh initial costs.

As we will see later, if both energy conservation and renewables are evaluated based on cash flow rather than cost alone, they have the potential to be cash-flow-positive investments.

Funding Mechanisms for Net Zero Buildings

How do you fund the increased energy conservation, renewable energy, and other possible green and healthy building design measures? There are two potential ways to pay for these additional costs: capital sources and financing sources.

Additional capital costs can be paid for up front, by the owner, donations, grants, tax credits, or other incentive programs. If owners pay, effectively it means they are prepaying their future energy cost. Most owners either do not have access to the money to do this or do not want to tie up their money in capital improvements for efficient, renewable, and healthy buildings. Capital contribution can be reduced by state and federal tax credits. Donations are also possible, particularly for tax-exempt nonprofits. A database for finding local, state, and federal incentives can be found at the Database of State Incentives for Renewables and Efficiency (DSIRE).[43]

Even if capital sources are used, often they do not cover all the efficiency and renewable costs and are usually applicable only to specific parts of the project. To meet this need, the owner can finance the additional costs directly, or a third party can finance the costs. Some lending institutions offer lower interest rates for efficiency and renewables. Third-party financing includes power purchase agreements, leases, and performance contracting, such as an energy savings company or energy service company (ESCO). The specifics of the mechanisms vary significantly.

Leases are the simplest mechanism for third-party financing of energy conservation measures or renewable energy. Most often the lease is from the seller of the equipment, who maintains ownership of the system, gets any rebate or tax credits, and pays for maintenance or replacement of system components. The customer pays "rent" to the lease company, which ultimately is similar to or lower than their current energy costs. The lease terms vary from no down payment to some portion of the system cost. If a building owner has limited access to resources for a large down payment and plans to be in the home for a long time, leasing a PV system is an attractive option.

ESCOs most often finance only energy conservation measures, typically sharing the energy savings with owners for an agreed-upon period, after which the benefits typically accrue to the owner alone. Before investment, the ESCO conducts an energy audit to decide which conservation measures are appropriate for the project and will provide the greatest return. The ESCO borrows the necessary money, engineers and installs the energy conservation plan, measures and verifies the results, and, finally, guarantees savings to the owner. Thus, owners limit their own risks.

ESCOs are very attractive because the building owners or tenants make no capital investment. But because the companies are looking for the highest returns, they tend to pick the low hanging fruit and fund only those energy retrofits that have the quickest return. Currently, ESCOs are usually not interested in funding the longer-term and lower-return investments needed for net zero buildings. However, with either increased tax incentives for energy conservation measures or increased energy costs, these businesses may become more receptive to net zero buildings.

While ESCOs are generally only for energy conservation, the same or a similar agreement can be used for renewable energy. Power purchase agreements are for renewable energy systems and are usually provided by the installer. With a PPA, the provider guarantees a monthly energy cost to the owner or tenant for a specific time period, usually five years. The rate is typically the same as or slightly less than the owner is paying at the beginning of the PPA. Thus, if the energy cost increases, the owner saves money. At the end of the period, the owner can buy the equipment at market value at the time, most often assumed around 30 percent of the initial cost, or the owner can renew the PPA on a rate close to the market rate at the time. The PPA provider finances the improvements and uses any available tax credits to make the investment profitable. Thus, if the owner purchases the system later, tax credits are not available.

The specifics of PPAs vary with different companies, but they generally follow the outline above. The benefit is that the owner n Vermont there are over 2,000 mobile home lots in non-profit and cooperatively owned trailer parks. These homes consume around twice as much energy per square foot as stick-built homes and are less comfortable. The Housing and Conservation Board and Efficiency Vermont initiated a Mobile Home Innovation Pilot project to bring high-performance building technologies to mobile homes.

Figure 17.9 shows the proposed energy conservation measures—such as increased airtightening, HRV, a more efficient envelope, and more insulated windows—for a mobile home in Vermont. These measures can reduce monthly maintenance and operating costs while achieving longer-term savings for mobile home owners. The additional capital costs are offset by the less expensive heating/cooling system required if these efficiency measures are taken.

Due to the additional conservation measures and a PV system, monthly mortgage payments rise from $193/month to $451/month (based on a thirty-year term and 5 percent interest rate), while the energy costs per month decrease from $318/month to $16/month on average. The average overall monthly cost is reduced by $44. Figure 17.10 shows the cumulative monthly payments over ten years of a HUD-compliant home compared to a high-performance home. By year eight the overall monthly payments for the HUD-compliant home (*red line*) surpass the high-performance home (*green line*), and from then on the high-performance home will continue to save homeowners money.

FIGURE 17.8. High-performance mobile home design increases initial capital costs but will result in a home with little to no monthly energy costs.

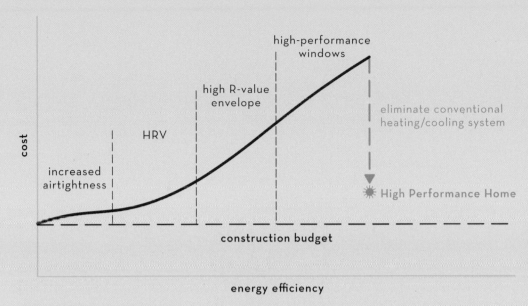

FIGURE 17.9. Additional energy conservation measures in the high-performance home add to the capital costs, but the elimination of the conventional heating/cooling system brings down most of these costs.

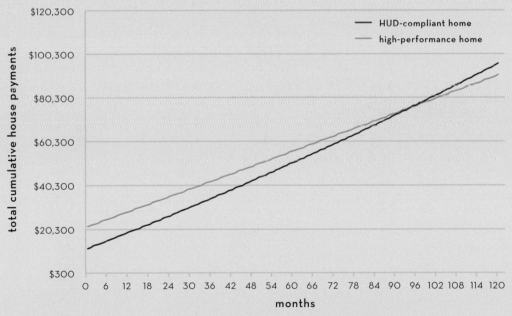

FIGURE 17.10. With net zero building strategies, monthly mortgage and energy payments are less for a high-performance mobile home, but the down payment was $21,000 versus $9,000, so the position at year one varies. By year eight the cumulative costs for the high-performance home are less than a typical HUD-compliant home.

of a net zero ready building can get renewable energy with no investment and minimal effort. The down side is that the net zero building owner is still paying energy costs, and the owner does not get the tax benefits or any available state rebates.

Financial Assessment

How do you determine which energy improvements are worth investment? This is particularly relevant since energy savings happen over time, while the investment is at the beginning. Generally, building owners want their money back at the end of the period of investment with interest that is competitive with other possible investments and that covers inflation.

To analyze the investments in energy improvements that our clients are making, we assess energy conservation and renewable and other green features separately as well as together. In our financial assessment, we use six investment strategies: simple payback, return on investment (ROI), net present value (NPV), internal rate of return (IRR), twenty-year capital and operating cost, and cash flow with and without financing. .

Each of these analysis methods has advantages and disadvantages for different building owners and users. All of these methods use the current cost of money (present value) in their evaluation, and other than the simple payback and the return on investment, all account for fuel escalation—which is not a standard practice, though it is entirely appropriate in a time of energy transition. Let's take a look at each analysis tool.

SIMPLE PAYBACK

Often clients want to know how long it will take to recoup their initial investment through savings. The easiest way to calculate this is with a simple payback that takes the initial cost of the investment and divides it by the cost savings per year. When fuel costs are constant and you will spend the same amount of money to heat your building in five years as you do today, a simple payback analysis makes sense. Unfortunately, this method does not account for the time value of money, including interest, inflation, and fuel escalation rates, which can greatly impact the savings per year. When fuel costs are rising, prudent financial analysis includes the rate of fuel escalation. In

this situation a simple payback analysis will often suggest that increased energy improvements are not cost effective, yet they are if fuel cost escalation is included.

To calculate the simple payback (SP) on an investment, divide the cost of the energy investment (I) by the cost of savings during one year (S):

$$SP = \frac{I}{S}$$

RETURN ON INVESTMENT (ROI)

The return on investment is the rate of annual gain or loss indicated as a percentage of the initial investment. Interest, inflation, and fuel escalation are not included in the calculation, but ROI can be compared to an interest rate for borrowing money. A high ROI, compared to the real or perceived cost of money, means the gains are favorable compared to the initial investment. This assumes the annual savings are constant, but it is a simple way to compare profits from the initial investment to other investment sources. This method also changes the perceived value of energy performance. Thus, while a ten-year simple payback is often seen negatively, a 10 percent ROI is generally perceived positively.

$$ROI = \frac{S}{I} \times 100\%$$

NET PRESENT VALUE (NPV)

The analysis of NPV is a central tool in finance to appraise the viability of long-term projects, such as energy improvements, taking into account the value of money over time. NPV determines how much investment in energy conservation measures is prudent today based on certain assumptions. It considers a sum of cash flows due to energy improvement savings to determine a present value of energy improvements above a chosen discount rate. In this calculation the interest rate, called the discount rate, is assumed based on the investor's minimum interest criteria for making investments of similar risk.

We calculate the present value of future savings over a given period, typically twenty years, and subtract the initial investment to get the net value. The present value is based off the following formula, where R_t is the cash flow, t is the time period of the cash flow, N is the total number of periods, and d is the discount rate, or rate of return that could be earned on an investment in a market with similar risk:

$$PV = \sum_{t=0}^{N} \frac{R_t}{(1+d)^t}$$

To determine the NPV, subtract the total savings from the initial investment (I):

$$NPV = PV - I$$

If the NPV is greater than 0, then the investment would add value based on the investor's criteria, and the project should be accepted. The higher the NPV, the better the investment. If, however, the NPV is less than 0, then the investment would subtract value, and the project should be declined based on the investor's criteria.

INTERNAL RATE OF RETURN (IRR)

The internal rate of return (IRR) assesses a specific investment as compared to other investments that could be made with the same money. Many businesses have a minimum internal rate of return that is a threshold for making any investment. The IRR identifies whether the investor's threshold criteria are met or not, and if so by how much.

To determine the internal rate of return, we need to know the capital cost of the energy improvements, the first-year annual energy savings, the assumed fuel escalation rate, the cost of borrowing money, and the rate of return derived from the level of anticipated risk.

The IRR determines the discount rate where the net present value of the costs of the initial energy investment equals the net present value of the savings from the energy investment. This calculation is best done through a spreadsheet program.

The following equation derives the IRR using a given positive time period (n), cash flow of that period (C_n), total number of time period (N), and the net present value (NPV):

$$NPV = \sum_{n=0}^{N} \frac{C_n}{(1+IRR)^n} = 0$$

TWENTY-YEAR CAPITAL AND OPERATING COST

Perhaps the simplest means of evaluating the costs of a net zero building is to consider the twenty-year capital and operating cost. To perform this analysis, we need to determine the capital cost and twenty-year operating cost for each of the building performance levels being considered. Because it allows increasing energy costs to be included in the analysis, we often determine the twenty-year operating cost for both a low and high fuel escalation rate, usually 3 percent and 15 percent, based on the owners' preference. This range can provide owners with useful information as to which building performance level is right for their needs.

The calculation to determine the total costs (C) combines the initial investment (I), the present value of energy costs to operate the building (Epv), and the present value of other costs, such as operation, maintenance, finance, end-of-life salvage, and replacement costs (Opv). Our typical analysis disregards maintenance, finance, salvage, or replacement costs, but depending on the desired analysis these other optional costs can be accounted for by adding them to the equation.

$$C = I + Epv + Opv$$

When all of these costs are included and are based on the lifetime for improvements, the evaluation is called a life-cycle cost analysis. The federal government uses this analysis with specific protocol for all of their building projects.[44] The benefit of assessing the twenty-year capital and operating cost is that it is simple and easy to comprehend. It provides a very useful analysis for government, educational institutions, and health care providers who will own and operate their buildings with similar use patterns for decades. It is also a helpful tool for individuals who are nearing retirement age and need to be able to budget for longer-term operating expenses. These specific organizations or individuals are in a position to benefit from long-term investments that avoid long-term cost escalation and the associated risk, which could burden them with unsustainable operating expenses. Unfortunately, institutions are typically under short-term pressure to meet a budget and spread capital expenditures over both new and deferred maintenance projects. Educational institutions have particular challenges with some of the energy-efficiency projects because donors are often interested in funding new projects but have little enthusiasm for funding deferred maintenance projects.

CASH-FLOW ANALYSIS

Calculating the capital and operating costs can estimate the relative costs and savings between approaches for a specific period, but it does not inform homeowners or businesses who are budgeting monthly payments for their buildings. Typically, mortgage costs are considered without including monthly energy costs. As energy costs increase, leaving them out of the calculation makes it increasingly inaccurate for determining the ability to meet monthly expenses. Cash-flow analysis determines if energy improvements generate savings in monthly or yearly operating costs. Good investments are considered cash-flow positive, in that the cost of the energy improvement reduces the combined energy and mortgage costs enough to generate a positive monthly cash flow.

Cash-flow analysis compares the monthly payments, including both mortgage and energy costs, for the base case, or the scenario without any energy improvements, against the energy improvement option. Cash-flow analysis can be financed or not financed. If financed, cash flow will be either positive or negative by the same amount for the life of the loan and then will have savings only when the loan is paid off. However, if the energy improvement cost is included in the first year's cost, the cash flow for the first number of years will be negative and will become positive later. While this approach eliminates all interest costs, it requires up-front investment.

When energy investments are included in major renovations or new construction, it is easier to finance.

If most energy improvements are cash-flow positive, annually and/or over the life of an improvement, why aren't more energy investments undertaken? In many cases decisions are driven by first costs, because owners do not have capital available and can borrow only a limited amount of money, as most banks will not expand loan limits to include higher levels of energy performance. Additionally, property appraisals typically do not increase based on energy improvements, or some owners see better investment opportunities in different venues, where they could raise enough money to pay for higher fuel costs in the future. However, the marketplace is beginning to transition: more banks are offering better interest rates for energy performance upgrades, and some properties are beginning to see higher prices for their better energy performance.

Optimizing Your Energy Investment

To assess what level of energy performance is appropriate for a specific building, we need to assess what is possible as well as what is perceived as financially viable and desirable for building owners and users. Figure 17.11 depicts a pyramid of energy conservation and renewable levels for buildings, beginning with what is possible at the bottom going to what is readily accepted in the marketplace at the top. The base includes energy conservation measures, technologies, and strategies at the boundary of the possible, without regard to cost. This base level is unlikely to have much impact on buildings in the near future. In the next higher level of technological potential are energy conservation and renewable measures that are technologically feasible but still not likely to be included in building projects. Above this the measures are considered economically feasible but not commonly realized in most new or existing buildings following today's practices. The final level, the market viability level, includes measures realized in most buildings today (with minimal regard to what energy conservation measures are economically viable and able to be implemented on any given project).

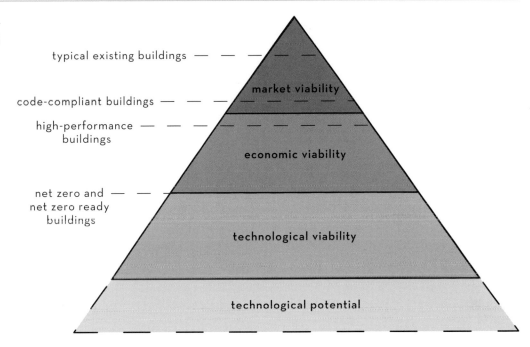

FIGURE 17.11. The levels of building performance relative to market, economic, and technologies available.

typical existing buildings — — — — —

market viability

code-compliant buildings — — — — —

high-performance — — — — — —
buildings

economic viability

net zero and — — —
net zero ready
buildings

technological viability

technological potential

Thus, given the time lapse for the real estate market to adjust to the changing energy reality, existing buildings are well within the realm of what is viable in the current market and likely are not fully valued due to the higher energy costs associated with typical existing buildings. Code-compliant buildings, as representing the norm for new buildings, are typically located around the average by owners and users, while high-performing buildings are perceived as being at the lower end of the market viability portion of the pyramid. Net zero and net zero ready are at the boundary of what is economically and technologically viable. They make sense financially and technologically, but they are new, and the market has not yet realized they are what will become the standard in the future.

To find what levels of energy conservation are appropriate, we use two strategies that are helpful in analyzing, estimating, assessing, and implementing energy conservation, renewable energy, and net zero energy decision making: energy optimization and strategic energy master planning.

ENERGY OPTIMIZATION

We use the following process to optimize energy performance:

1. Identify energy performance levels.
2. Assess the financial energy performance of the relative levels.
3. Assess financial opportunities and benefits beyond operational performance.
4. Select the desired energy level.

We identify four and sometimes five levels of energy performance. The standard levels for new and existing buildings are code-compliant, high-performing, net zero ready, and net zero (including renewables). The fifth level is existing building performance. For an existing building, we use its documented energy performance before improvements. For new buildings, we may compare our new options to a typical existing building of the same type.[45] Sometimes, when biomass is considered as a fuel source, we also use the carbon-neutral building distinction. At the beginning of each project, we determine what level is the best fit.

The purpose in providing multiple levels in our analysis is to provide comparative financial estimates based on clear, well-estimated, and documented choices for the client, so that choices are based on the best information available.

The Bennington Superior Courthouse and State Office Building provides a useful financial story. The project consisted of a major renovation and addition to an existing courthouse and state office building. During the initial schematic design, we identified a significant opportunity to adapt the renovation concept: rather than renovating both the existing one-story and three-story sections, we could demolish the one-story portion and build a three-story addition to provide needed square footage. This change reduced the surface area of the building by 31 percent on the above ground five sides and by 45 percent when including the slab. This reduction in surface area will significantly reduce the heating demand. Cost analysis during phase one of the project determined that this building massing change would add no capital cost to the project while providing energy savings, which results in an infinite ROI.

In addition, we considered three other options that involve removal of the existing brick and insulating the envelope to different levels, including code-compliant and net zero ready. We also considered other energy improvements, including more detailed enclosure commissioning and the installation of a high-performance ground-source heat pump system. Increased enclosure performance added $240,000 to the project costs, and the high-efficiency ground-source heat pump and the addition of a solar hot water system added $130,000. These features save $49,000 annually in operating costs. In total these net zero ready improvements added just under $6/sf to the project cost, an increase of only 3 percent to the project budget. This analysis includes the investment to make the project net zero ready.

SIMPLE PAYBACK. The additional financial investment to get to net zero ready standards over just completing a code-compliant project was calculated at $370,000. In comparison, the annual energy savings are estimated at $49,000. Therefore, the simple payback for the project is $370,000/$49,000, or 7.6 years.

RETURN ON INVESTMENT. To calculate the ROI, we divide the savings from the initial investment and multiply it by 100 percent: $49,000/$370,000 × 100 percent, or 13 percent return on investment.

NET PRESENT VALUE. To calculate the net present value of energy costs to operate the code-compliant building versus the net zero building, we multiply the building energy savings per year for each case by the fuel price each year. We calculated two charts, one with a low fuel escalation rate (3 percent) and one with a high fuel escalation rate (6 percent) using the solar plateau. We used a 3 percent discount rate and determined the net present value of energy savings over the twenty-year operating period.

The net zero building energy savings above the code-compliant building for the low fuel escalation scenario is $2,432,583 and the high fuel escalation is $2,891,060.

INTERNAL RATE OF RETURN. The internal rate of return for the net zero building, using the code-compliant building as the example to extrapolate energy savings, is 6.2 percent based on a 3 percent fuel escalation rate, and 8 percent based on a 6 percent fuel escalation rate using the solar plateau, as described earlier.

CAPITAL AND OPERATING COSTS. We considered the twenty-year capital and operating cost of the two building options in comparison to the do-nothing approach; one analysis took the solar

TABLE 17.4. DIFFERENCE IN COST BETWEEN ENERGY-CODE-COMPLIANT AND NET ZERO READY PROJECT AT THE BENNINGTON SUPERIOR COURTHOUSE AND STATE OFFICE BUILDING

BUILDING COMPONENT	CODE COMPLIANT	NET ZERO READY (AS BUILT)	ADDED COST
Windows	Double-glazed windows	Triple-glazed windows	$30,557[a]
Insulation	Install 2" of rigid insulation under slabs	Install 4" of rigid insulation under slabs	$32,500
	Install 3" of rigid insulation on exterior face of wall framing	Install 4" of rigid insulation on exterior face of wall framing	$22,500
	Insulate seismic joint between new and existing wings to R-9	Insulate seismic joint between new and existing wings to maximum R-value	$22,500
	Standard detailing of steel support for exterior sunshades	Custom detailing of steel support for exterior sunshades to minimize thermal bridging	$8,000
	Standard detailing of steel relieving angles for brick veneer	Custom detailing of steel relieving angles for brick veneer to minimize thermal bridging	$14,000
	6" isocyanurate on the roof	9" minimum polyisocyanurate on the roof	$40,040[b]
Air/Vapor Barrier	Vapor barrier only[c]	Combined air barrier and drainage plane	$39,000
Commissioning	NA	Full envelope commissioning and blower-door testing	$27,000
Solar Hot Water	Not a required system	Solar hot water system installed	$31,000
HVAC	Standard HVAC replacement[d]	High-efficiency ground-source heat pump HVAC replacement	$105,000
	Total added cost		$372,097[e]
	Total added cost per square foot		$5.72
	Total added cost as a percentage of total construction cost		3.04%

[a] 9 percent more for triple-glazed windows than double-glazed (per Accurate Dorwin)

[b] Polyiso cost from RSMeans: $1.82/sf per 3" thickness. From RSMeans: *Building Construction Cost Data*, 65th Annual Edition, 2007, 184

[c] 50 percent cost of combined air and vapor barrier

[d] Standard HVAC replacement: high-efficiency boiler and chiller for cooling

[e] Original cost without owner-elected change orders: $12,246,000, or $188.40/sf

plateau into account, and the other did not. Figure 17.12 considers the cost of three options without considering the solar plateau. It is easy to see here that the net zero ready building is a better investment than the code-compliant building when considered at either a 3 percent or 6 percent fuel escalation rate and using the solar plateau. The do-nothing approach is much more expensive to operate, and at the 6 percent fuel escalation rate the cost of doing nothing over twenty years is more than three times more expensive than renovating to net zero ready standards. In figure 17.13 we consider the same investments while taking into account the solar plateau. The difference between the 3 percent and 6 percent fuel escalation rates is minimal when we consider the energy cost under the solar plateau.

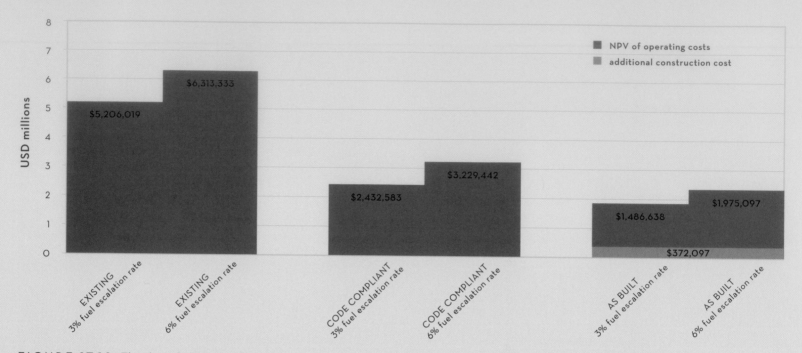

FIGURE 17.12. The three building scenarios, comparing the total twenty-year operating costs to the additional capital costs.

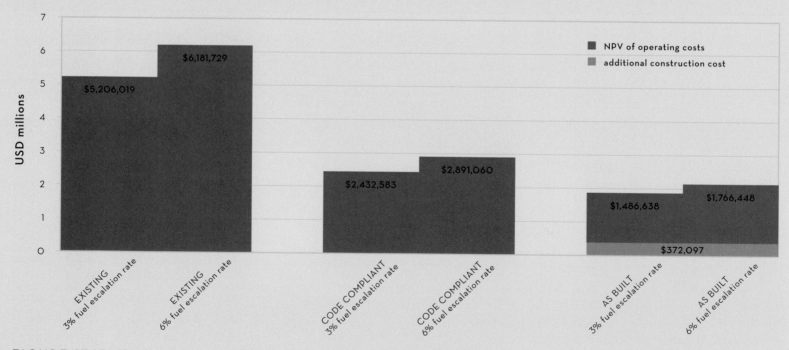

FIGURE 17.13. The three building scenarios, comparing the total twenty-year operating costs to the additional capital costs and including the solar plateau.

CASH-FLOW ANALYSIS. For the cash-flow analysis for this project, we considered the energy savings of the net zero ready building above the code-compliant. There are two options to pay for the additional costs to make the building net zero: additional capital costs and financing. In this project the additional energy conservation measures were included in the capital costs and financed. The option showing cash flow based on a first-year single payment for energy conservation measures is included for illustrative purposes and demonstrates how this method initially generates negative cash flow then positive cash flow, since there is no interest cost for borrowing. For the financing option, assume the PV system is paid for through bond payments over twenty years with an interest rate of 3 percent. This method spreads out the capital cost to make the project net zero ready, without the necessary capital costs. In certain cases it makes sense to consider the funds for the energy improvement in one lump sum at the beginning of the project.

When examined from a cash-flow perspective with the solar plateau and financing for the net zero ready building, figure 17.14 shows that cash flow is positive from the first year because the energy savings above the code building are more than the annual bond payment. Paying the additional capital cost in year one option shows a negative cash flow for the first seven years, then positive after that from energy savings.

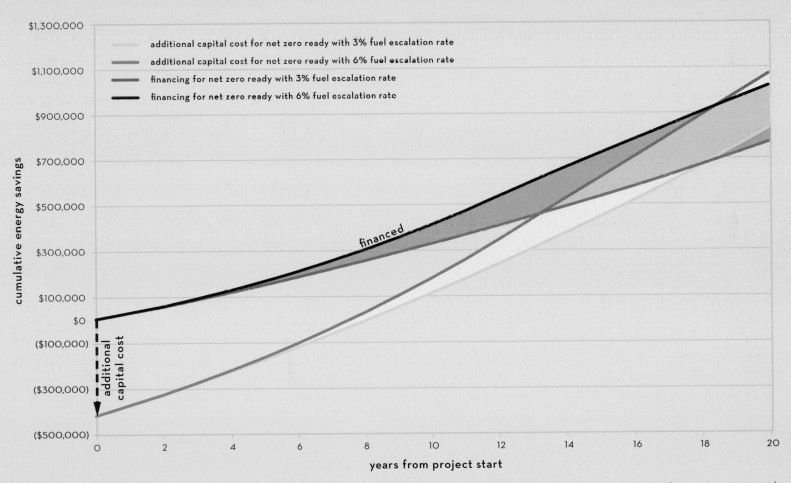

FIGURE 17.14. Savings of the net zero ready building compared to the code-compliant building over twenty years. It shows a positive cash flow beginning after year seven for both the low and high fuel escalation rates.

Typically, initial integrated design measures can lower building costs, while energy conservation and renewable energy costs increase initial capital costs as the overall building EUI is lowered. Before renewables, a net zero ready building need only be slightly more expensive than a code-compliant building. If renewables are financed, then net zero buildings do not need to cost much more than typical buildings. This analysis does not quantify the benefits of green and healthy building design on occupant productivity or reduced absenteeism, though many of these green design benefits are a part of net zero buildings with no additional cost.

While predicting the future is impossible, we have found that offering a clear and coherent process for assessment and evaluation of different energy alternatives or scenarios is invaluable in building support for net zero projects. Clients use the resulting information to explain their decisions to donors, users, investors, stockholders, stakeholders, and the press, all of whom ask about the fiscal prudence of net zero buildings. In general, the questions come from advocates as well as thoughtful skeptics and sometimes opponents.

The primary focus of our analysis is on energy investments, but putting these assumptions on the table opens discussion on other features, such as composting toilets or living machines for sewage treatments, green roofs for stormwater treatment, and other healthy, green, and sustainable design features. In all cases we estimate additional construction costs for features as well as savings, then calculate the return on investment based on life-cycle costing. Where features include productivity and health benefits, it is more difficult to estimate financial savings, despite the fact that these benefits typically outperform energy savings. Generally, we look only at energy savings, since those are easiest to quantify, the most directly related to net zero buildings, and the element our clients are most focused on.

STRATEGIC ENERGY MASTER PLANNING

Hopefully, by now we have demonstrated the fiscal prudence in building net zero buildings, and the choice is clear and simple. However, finding money and even financing net zero improvements is not easy. If you need to borrow most of the capital for your project, the lending institution may not be willing to loan the money necessary for net zero energy conservation and renewable energy. You may, then, have to figure out ways to make improvements incrementally to get to net zero. For both new building and renovation projects, it is easy to design the buildings so that the renewable energy systems are added later. Simple conduit for wiring and/or plumbing can be installed inexpensively for roof- or ground-mounted PV or other renewable resources to make renewable installation easier and less expensive in the future. Since the renewable system expense is the major additional construction cost for a net zero building, this strategy can be very effective in achieving net zero goals little by little.

However, when it comes to saving through energy conservation and integrated design strategies in the building, it is not so easy. If you have to make choices, windows will not last as long as the envelope, so spending less on windows is possible but could be problematic if they increase heating and cooling loads. Although we do not recommend this strategy, it is better than compromising the envelope insulation.

When working on existing buildings, you may find more potential issues and opportunities to make incremental improvements toward a net zero building. With additions and renovations our strategy is to design and build all incremental improvements to net zero standards. This way, as you and future owners make building improvements over time, you eventually will meet the net zero standards. So if you are renovating a kitchen, bathroom, or other room in your home, you want to build the outside walls and ceilings to the eventual net zero standards. The same strategy applies if you are working with commercial or institutional buildings.

To make this process successful, you need to look at your whole building before doing your renovation or addition. You will want to figure out how to upgrade your building envelope, provide mechanical systems, and power your buildings. You will address questions discussed in the renovation chapter, such as whether to insulate on the inside or outside of the building. You also will want to figure out how you will address air, vapor, and water barriers to prevent building deterioration. Once you have the overall strategy and design and building detail concepts, then you can apply that strategy to each improvement you make so that eventually the net zero building performs effectively.

Typically, when we develop this plan, we indicate performance levels, building enclosure details, system improvements, and renewable energy systems for the eventual net zero building. We will figure out construction costs and ROI and other financial assessments to implement these improvements if done at the time of our strategic energy master plan. This then allows for building owners to implement these phases as it fits their building use, budget, and other needs. We usually develop a phasing plan and approach as well, so that improvements can occur as coherently and cost effectively as possible.

In the past the conventional wisdom was to do energy conservation first and renewable energy afterward. When we do the strategic energy plan, we identify and size the eventual renewable system—usually PV. Once the owners know this size, they can install the PV before doing some or any of the energy conservation or systems upgrades, allowing them to take advantage of grant and tax incentives, donor interest, or other opportunities to move toward a net zero project.

Additions are the same as new buildings in terms of designing and building to net zero standards. In the past construction professionals have suggested that it is not worth insulating additions and renovations to new building standards because the existing building is poorly insulated. But if you build to net zero standards on additions, you may not need to add any new heating/cooling load to your building. For instance, if you added to one entire side of your building with net zero standards, you would be reducing your existing load significantly through the upgraded envelope. And if you added on to the south side, you might include passive solar heating to cut overall heating loads. While additions usually do not cover an entire wall and often do not add passive solar heating, the increased load due to the net zero addition is minimal and often reveals that the existing heating/cooling system is adequate for the extra space. To provide even more energy reduction, strategic energy planning can be used for building complexes and campuses and/or portfolios of properties owned by commercial or institutional owners and investors.

Net Zero Is Free Now

If you have read this book and are not yet convinced that net zero is free today, there are other ways that net zero is free. Let's assume you are truly committed to a net zero goal for your project, but you don't think you can afford a net zero building. Also, for the purpose of this example, let's say that there's an additional 15 percent cost to construct your net zero building. If net zero performance is critical, you first can see if you can accomplish your net zero goals through financing net zero improvements based on strategies outlined in this chapter. If that does not work or you have a fixed budget and are not financing the project, you can investigate ways to cut costs that are not net zero related; for instance, reducing the level of some finishes or amenities. Another option is to reduce the square footage of your building by 10 to 15 percent. This can offset the added net zero cost and will result in no additional cost to making the house net zero. One way to do this is to use a more open floor plan, which still feels large but allows for mixed use and flexibility. For instance, when considering an office building, instead of thinking about traditional, private offices or even open offices, you can start to think about the office as a whole ecosystem and how people work together. Some people are in the office very little and really do not need a full-time desk. From this thinking you can start to save on cost by reducing the size of the building.

If these measures still are not enough, you can see if your project can be phased through strategic energy master planning. Finally, owners who make their buildings net zero now will never have energy bills in the future; they have prepaid. This is particularly valuable to nonprofits, educational and public institutions, the elderly, and others on a fixed income.

BENNINGTON SUPERIOR COURTHOUSE
AND STATE OFFICE BUILDING

		DESIGN PROFILE	
Building Profile	Building Name:	**Bennington Superior Courthouse and State Office Building**	
	Location:	Bennington, Vermont	
	Occupancy Date:	April, 2012	
	Square Footage:	65,032	
	Certification	LEED Gold anticipated	
Energy Profile		Modeled:	24 kBtu/sf-yr
Building Envelope	Construction Type:	Steel structure, DensGlass, air/moisture/vapor barrier, 4″ polyiso, masonry and panels	
	Insulation Values:	Walls:	R-27, 4″ continuous polyisocyanurate
		Roof:	R-60, 9″ continuous polyisocyanurate
		Foundation (slab perimeter):	R-20, 4″ XPS panel to 36″ depth
		Foundation (slab edge joint):	R-20, 4″ XPS
		Foundation (sub-slab):	R-20, 4″ XPS under whole slab
	Air Infiltration:	Final Blower Door:	6,298 cfm50
			0.114 cfm50/sf exterior surface area
	Windows/Skylights:	Windows:	U-value: 0.19, SHGC: 0.34, VT: 0.41
		Skylights (offices):	U-value: 0.1 (C.O.G.) 0.3 (unit, estimated), SHGC: 0.54, VT: 0.5
Mechanical/ Electrical Systems	Heating System:	Open-loop ground-source shallow aquifer with plate and frame heat exchangers and console heat pumps	
		Annual COP (estimated):	3.6
	Cooling System:	Open-loop ground-source shallow aquifer with plate and frame heat exchangers and console heat pumps	
	Ventilation System:	Dedicated ventilation, constant volume in private offices and lobbies, variable volume in all other spaces, controlled by occupancy sensors in small meeting rooms and CO_2 sensor in large meeting areas (occupancy over four)	
	Energy Recovery System:	Thermotech enthalpy wheel	
		Average Effectiveness:	70 percent
	Lighting System/Controls:	High-efficiency fluorescent and LED lamps throughout, open-loop daylight harvesting in all third-floor conference and courtrooms and north-facing offices, dual switching in all other rooms, Lutron GRAFIK Eye with EcoSystem	
	Hot Water:	60 percent SDHW, 40 percent propane	

BENNINGTON SUPERIOR COURTHOUSE AND STATE OFFICE BUILDING

Breathing New Life into a Renovated State Building

The renovated Bennington Superior Courthouse and State Office Building is now one of the healthiest and most energy-efficient buildings in the state of Vermont. The vision for the project focused on the development of a healthy indoor work environment for state employees and a high-performing, energy-efficient building. The building addition was sited to improve the building orientation for energy and site connections, to create a more welcoming entry experience, to simplify courtroom circulation and operations, and to minimize internal building volume. Lobby spaces and large public circulation corridors are located to the south to take advantage of the views to the nearby Bennington monument and minimize east and west glazing. With an anticipated project cost of just over $200 per square foot and energy-intensity numbers modeled at only 24 kBtu/sf-yr, this building meets net zero ready energy standards on a competitive budget.

FIGURE CS8.1. Entrance façade of the newly renovated Bennington Superior Courthouse and State Office Building.

Project Overview

The existing Bennington Superior Courthouse and State Office Building was composed of the original one-story building with a three-story section tied to a one-story addition. Initially, the state planned to renovate both portions of the building. However, during programming it became evident that the existing single-story building did not function well for courtroom or energy purposes, and it created an unattractive and unwelcoming entrance. More specifically, this massing created conflicts with courtroom circulation and security. It also was oriented to maximize east and west windows, causing potential daylighting and overheating conflicts as well as maximizing the exterior surface area of the building, causing energy and budget issues.

The design team offered multiple design alternatives with costing to resolve these issues. Through this process the state decided to tear down the one-story section of the building and locate a three-story addition oriented directly south. This solution lowered the surface-area-to-volume ratio and improved the efficiency of court operations, daylighting opportunities,

employee and public connections to the site, and the public entry experience. In addition, this option was less expensive than the preliminary design options. For these reasons, the state decided to pursue this path.

Vision and Goals

A leading project goal was to create a model, productive, and inspiring workplace by producing optimized indoor air quality through ventilation, building science, materials selection, and elimination of nearly all fossil-fuel combustion; increasing the views to the natural world; and enhancing daylighting. High environmental goals are anticipated to win this project a LEED Gold rating.

Another goal was to establish the state of Vermont as a leader in net zero ready energy performance and to demonstrate that deep energy retrofits can transform poor-performing

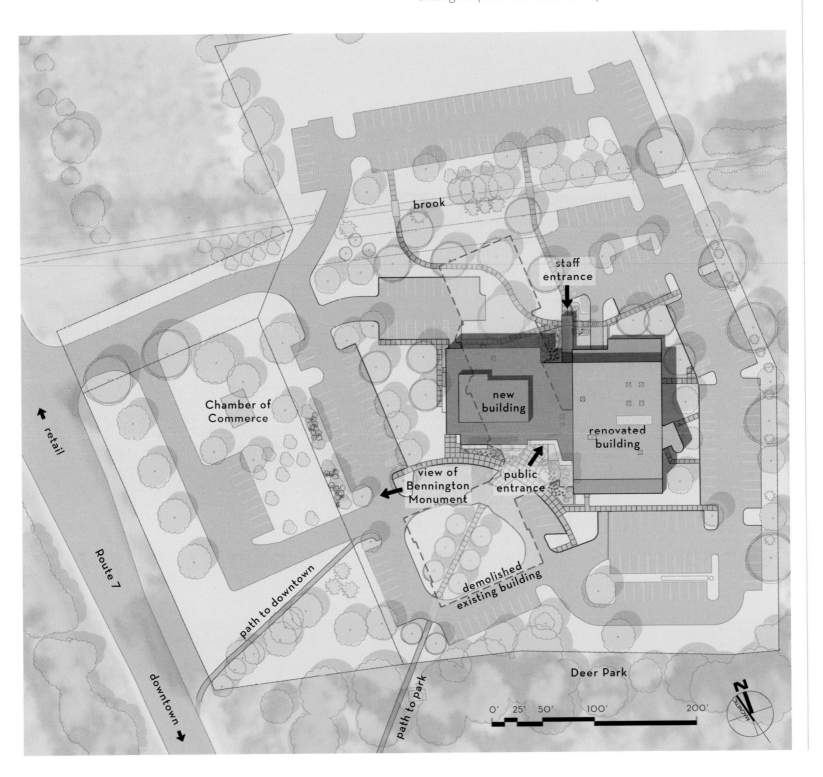

brook

staff entrance

new building

Chamber of Commerce

renovated building

retail

view of Bennington Monument

public entrance

Route 7

path to downtown

demolished existing building

downtown

path to park

Deer Park

N

MAGNETIC

0' 25' 50' 100' 200'

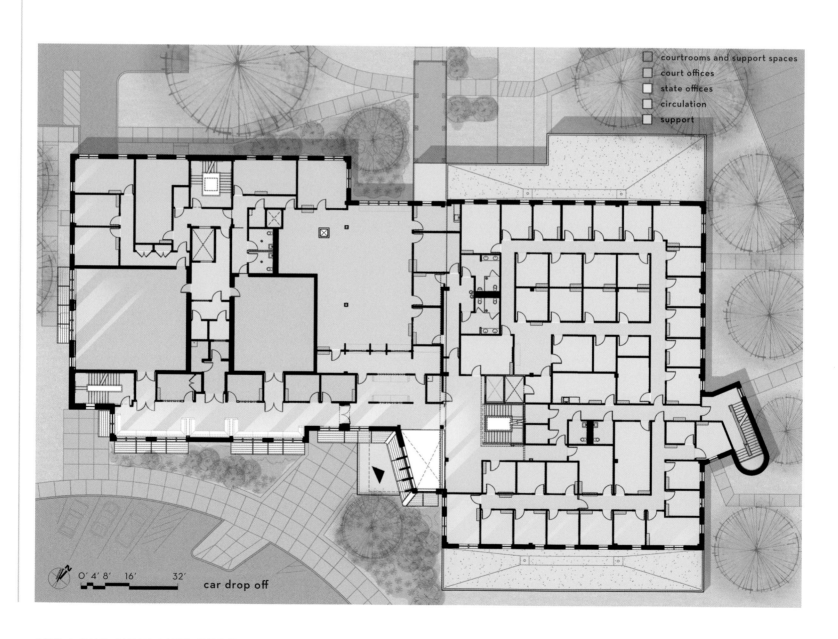

FIGURE CS8.4. The floor plan depicts the daylit gallery and courtrooms in the new portion of the building and the private offices in the existing portion of the building.

courtrooms and support spaces
court offices
state offices
circulation
support

0' 4' 8'   16'   32'   car drop off

buildings into net zero ready standards within budgets set for code-compliant construction.

And of course the renovation needed to provide functional, safe, and pleasant state-of-the-art court space for the public and staff—and to exemplify prudent, long-term investment in capital, energy, and maintenance costs.

Energy

The Bennington Superior Courthouse and State Office Building achieves a net zero ready design, with a minimum 13 percent rate of return on energy investments. Energy modeling predicts a 78 percent reduction in energy consumption over the existing facility and a 40 percent reduction in energy over a similar code-compliant building. The energy intensity has been reduced from 110 kBtu/sf-yr in the existing building to 24 kBtu/sf-yr, saving the state $180,000 in annual energy costs the first year. Based on energy modeling, the building is anticipated to be the best-performing Vermont state office building. Heating and cooling are provided with a ground-source heat pump. The building uses only a very small amount of fossil fuel for domestic hot water. The state plans to convert the hot water system to an electric system in the near future. This change in conjunction with the addition of PV panels acquired through a PPA will result in a net zero building.

Envelope

During the schematic design phase, the team investigated several levels of thermal performance. Wall and roof system options were evaluated based on expected energy performance, initial construction cost, and long-term operating costs. Three alternatives for wall construction were analyzed for performance and capital and operating costs:

- Leaving the existing exterior brick in place and insulating from the inside by using spray foam behind the existing veneer.
- Demolishing the existing exterior brick and insulating from the outside using rigid foam, plus installing a new metal-panel rain screen.
- Demolishing the existing exterior brick and insulating from the outside using rigid foam, plus installing a new ventilated brick veneer rain screen.

The design team investigated each of these wall options with multiple levels of insulation. Comparing the potential return on investment for each of the options, the team determined that the optimum value was achieved by demolishing the existing brick and installing 4″ of polyisocyanurate board insulation under a combined brick-veneer and metal-panel rain screen wall assembly.

AIR SEALING

In addition to the high thermal performance achieved by the wall assembly, a combined air/water/vapor barrier was applied continuously over the entire building envelope. This spray-applied barrier combined with membrane layers, used at corners and nonadhesive surfaces, was specifically detailed to ensure that the resulting building would be one of the tightest commercial buildings in Vermont. In final blower-door testing the building reached a result of 0.11 cfm50/sf exterior surface area, which put this building in the top 10 percent of buildings tested in Vermont.

LIGHTING AND DAYLIGHTING

Daylighting and artificial lighting systems were carefully integrated into the design for maximum user satisfaction and energy savings. To create inviting and pleasing spaces for the public, lobbies and corridors were located on the south side of

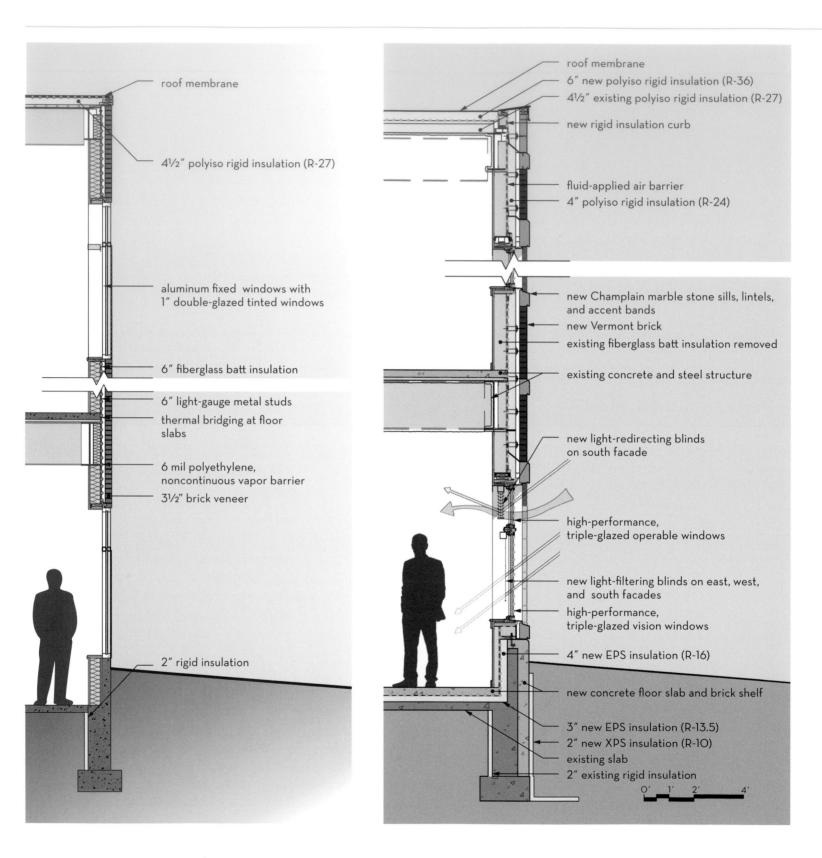

roof membrane

4½" polyiso rigid insulation (R-27)

aluminum fixed windows with 1" double-glazed tinted windows

6" fiberglass batt insulation

6" light-gauge metal studs

thermal bridging at floor slabs

6 mil polyethylene, noncontinuous vapor barrier

3½" brick veneer

2" rigid insulation

roof membrane

6" new polyiso rigid insulation (R-36)

4½" existing polyiso rigid insulation (R-27)

new rigid insulation curb

fluid-applied air barrier

4" polyiso rigid insulation (R-24)

new Champlain marble stone sills, lintels, and accent bands

new Vermont brick

existing fiberglass batt insulation removed

existing concrete and steel structure

new light-redirecting blinds on south facade

high-performance, triple-glazed operable windows

new light-filtering blinds on east, west, and south facades

high-performance, triple-glazed vision windows

4" new EPS insulation (R-16)

new concrete floor slab and brick shelf

3" new EPS insulation (R-13.5)

2" new XPS insulation (R-10)

existing slab

2" existing rigid insulation

0'   1'   2'   4'

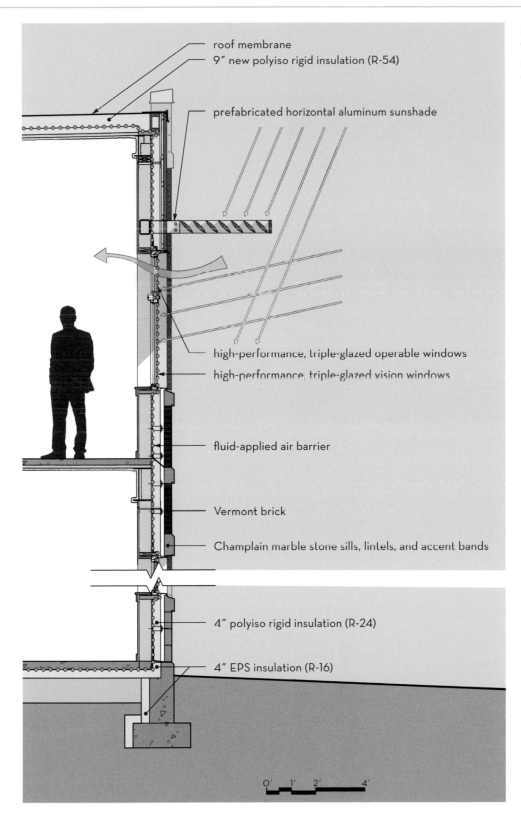

roof membrane
9" new polyiso rigid insulation (R-54)

prefabricated horizontal aluminum sunshade

high-performance, triple-glazed operable windows
high-performance, triple-glazed vision windows

fluid-applied air barrier

Vermont brick

Champlain marble stone sills, lintels, and accent bands

4" polyiso rigid insulation (R-24)

4" EPS insulation (R-16)

0' 1' 2' 4'

FIGURE CS8.5. *Left*, existing wall section with minimal insulation and thermal bridging. *Middle*, improved retrofit wall section. *Right*, new wall section.

the building, decreasing the need for artificial lighting in these spaces. All east-, south-, and west-facing windows in occupied spaces include glare-controlling, light-filtering blinds to ensure comfort for building occupants. South-facing transom windows are designed into many occupied spaces, using light-guiding blinds to reflect daylight deep into the building's interior. Exterior sunshades are located on the south and west façades of the building to reduce unwanted summer solar heat gain. This building uses an open-loop, daylight-harvesting system, which automatically adjusts the artificial lighting levels in many of the offices, conference rooms, and courtrooms depending on the availability of daylight.

HEATING AND COOLING

Space heating and cooling is supplied by an open-loop, ground-source heat pump system. This system uses a high-volume, shallow, flowing aquifer on the site, in combination with

a water-source heat pump, to provide high-efficiency heating and cooling at all times of the year. The heating and cooling is delivered through console heat pumps, with an individual console unit located in each occupied space, to allow for individual thermal comfort control.

Healthy and Sustainable Strategies

All mechanical systems and controls were designed to optimize indoor air quality, an important keystone to this project. Environmental standards for indoor air quality were determined at the beginning and maintained throughout design and construction. Polished concrete flooring in office areas minimizes the collection of dust and allergens, while low- or no-VOC-emitting stains, paints, and adhesives reduce

off-gassing. Rigorous air-quality testing following EPA protocol demonstrated that containment concentrations were well below allowable levels. Additionally, when construction was complete, a prolonged ventilation flush out was conducted in conformance with LEED standards, further ensuring optimum indoor air quality levels.

In the selection of materials, life-cycle costs and proximity of production and/or extraction sites were carefully considered. As much as reasonable, Vermont materials were incorporated, including Vermont-manufactured brick; locally quarried marble sills, lintels, and accent bands; and locally quarried slate flooring for public corridors and lobbies. Additionally, more than half of the wood-based materials used for the project are FSC certified.

Low-flow sinks, toilets, and urinals contribute to a projected 40 percent reduction in potable water consumption compared to an average building. A solar hot water system is projected to supply over half of all the hot water needs for the building. And outside the building, irrigation-free landscaping further reduces the building's water consumption.

Collaborative Process

Our firm led a team of eight consultants, nine state departments, and various other stakeholders through the design and planning of this project. At the start of the project, a collaborative effort between the architect, the commissioning agent, the mechanical engineer, and the owner identified the owner's project requirements. Subsequently, meetings with stakeholders and state department leaders established the program and required adjacencies for the building. Once the building program, functional adjacencies, and OPR were understood and agreed upon, the design team was able to use these tools to help guide the decision-making process. This clarity helped the large team execute a complicated design in a relatively short time frame.

PART V

The Net Zero Journey

18 | The Twelve Steps to a Net Zero Building

Creating a net zero building is a twelve-step process. Bear in mind that the steps are not intended to be necessarily sequential. Design is an iterative process—more like a loop or spiral progressing toward the desired vision and outcome. Along the way you will experience bursts of insight; at other times you may hit confusing plateaus. But if you take each of these steps, applying the principles and techniques in the earlier chapters, you can ensure that you cover the ground necessary to complete a successful net zero project. You'll note that some of these steps are foundational, some deal with design methodology, some with mechanics and implementation, and some with enjoying what you've created.

All of them, however, require a shift away from traditional design construction practice. Most buildings are one-of-a-kind projects, and often clients and other stakeholders expect perfection. Designing a unique building is similar in complexity to designing a new computer or car—products with extensive design processes that include modeling, testing, and debugging to minimize problems. Unfortunately, the relative design budget for a building is much smaller than that for mass-produced goods. And designing a net zero building—which requires an even more in-depth process of design, fabrication, and testing—demands rethinking the entire conventional design system.

It follows, then, that the twelve steps by definition are practices and procedures that are innovative and require change—change that will help us deal with the other changes our society will encounter as we transition off fossil fuels. If enough leaders take on the net zero design challenge, we can make sure that what lies at the other end of that transition is a more secure and sustainable future.

Step 1: Build and Empower Your Team

Net zero buildings are innovative; they are not business as usual. For success, you need a unique team that is equally innovative. The net zero team needs to work together so that all disciplines understand buildings as interconnected systems where all systems and design are one, integrally connected to everything else.

All team members need to be able to work collaboratively and demonstrate leadership, expertise, experience, and competence in their respective fields. Track records are important. Specifically, all team members need sustainable design and net zero or near-net-zero knowledge and experience, including involvement in the design of buildings with EUI numbers below 30 kBTU/sf-yr (or preferably better).

Clarity in roles, vision, goals, objectives, and metrics generates team alignment, and alignment is critical through the many hurdles and bumps that are inevitable on the path to net zero success. The team's role is first to help the owner clarify the vision and purpose and second to implement the vision, which includes establishing objectives, metrics, and strategies to create the client's desired outcome. As the team leader, the architect carries the commitment, responsibility, and accountability for meeting the net zero and other design goals. Ultimately, though, clarity in direction can come only from the client. Without client commitment and vision, net zero projects will not happen. The client needs to keep the challenge of the project in front of the team.

The traditional design process for projects and buildings has been linear. In a fixed, mechanistic universe, this may work adequately. In the volatile, changing, and frequently unpredictable world that is now transitioning to a non-fossil-fuel-based economy, a more dynamic, interactive, and responsive process and practices are more effective. This integrated design practice is based on the following components:

FRONT-END LOADING. Rapid discovery and viability assessment are included before the concept/schematic design phase. This saves time later and lowers risk.

OPTIMIZED COLLABORATION. Even with a stellar team, the path to net zero is not always straight and obvious. Ultimate success results from long hours exploring and conversing as a team to develop great ideas and visions and test them. All of this requires an ongoing dialogue between the client and the design and construction team. So to ensure that whole is optimized and designed within an innovative framework, an integrated team will need many more small interactions than in the traditional design and construction process.

A PULSING DESIGN FLOW. Rather than thinking of the design process as linear, as many of us were trained to do, think of it more as a pulsing, spiral process that moves forward but also expands and contracts at times. The project is entwined in an interactive dance with its surrounding world like an organism in an ecosystem.

Step 2: Engage with a Collaborative Process

Without an effective collaborative and integrated design methodology—a way of working together that unifies process, practices, and procedures—even an extensive knowledge of net zero, ecological, and sustainable strategies and technologies will not generate success.

Step 3: Explore, Understand, and Discover

Exploring and understanding the context from which a project emerges is the foundation for design and requires listening and eliciting ideas, concerns, potential problems, and issues connected to the project—the worlds of the project.

In every project there are four larger, interconnected worlds or overall areas of concern to observe and understand: the environment, including local ecosystems and biological concerns; the human, social, and cultural context; the economic and operational systems; and our spiritual connection to all living systems and the universe. We need to look through all these lenses if we hope to generate projects that exist in an evolutionary context—in other words, that are designed for both the present and a future that is emerging and not yet clear.

At a more practical level, this includes discovering issues and goals relating to programming, functioning, aesthetics, neighbors, permitting, regulations, and energy and construction cost volatility, all of which can significantly impact a project for better or worse. This requires including more diverse stakeholders in the process from the very start and tweaking the project purpose and essence so that it stays in touch with the reality of the outside world.

Step 4: Embrace a Bold Vision

The ultimate vision for any project is to create spaces and buildings, places and communities that are productive, satisfying, healthy, and inspiring places for people to inhabit—regardless of whether the building itself is designed for living, playing, working, or socializing.

The visioning process begins with an open mood of curiosity, possibility, exploration, and even wonder and awe at the opportunity to create and contribute to a better world. To move the process into action, collect any ideas you encounter—from images, diagrams, and model projects to inspiring quotes, random thoughts, and even dreams and fantasies. Engage in lively conversation and brainstorming with others on your team. Broaden these conversations to include people who have done similar projects, community members, users, people affected by your project, and even

people who may not want your project. There is some magic in an inquiring dialogue with others; we can uncover and explore ideas much more quickly and deeply this way than we could by working alone or just with like-minded people. Sketch ideas and generate diagrams to document your thinking and discoveries. Explore and diagram how the project will branch out into the worlds of the environment, society, economy, and spirit. Have fun, summarize what you find out, and share your learning. Repeat this process multiple times with different groups and you will begin to disclose a vision more beautiful and amazing than you could have imagined at the beginning.

We have also found that imagining scenarios is extremely helpful. Think about the daily and seasonal life patterns that people and systems will experience in and around the building. Ask questions about the environmental, energy, social, and spiritual impacts of different scenarios. In the process of doing this, we find stakeholders in projects can become clearer about what their real choices are, to select a path with the greatest consensus and buy-in.

As these scenarios are refined, move toward finding a scenario that fits, as an organism fits in an ecosystem. Relax and remind yourself that this vision will grow in clarity and strength as you keep pursuing your project. It might even have some big changes. Remember that an underlying goal is creating an inspiring, beautiful, and healthy future for you, your community, all living systems, and the planet.

As alternative scenarios are suggested, stakeholders can envision themselves living in these scenarios and assess what works well and what does not. Based on this imagining, the scenarios can be revised, adjusted, and enhanced so that the fit between scenarios, lifestyle, and goals creates a vibrant vision and new reality. This iterative design process is at the heart of an exciting and fun process that begins with envisioning a project and extends to the final details of construction. As the process continues with engagement, the level of detail increases.

Step 5: Commit to Metrics

Great visions often fail. The nitty-gritty detail—and steps in between—are often missing. What are the critical elements needed to implement the vision successfully? It is the interconnection of vision and implementation that determines success or failure of net zero (and other innovative) projects. Remember these basics as you begin to implement your design:

PURPOSE. Without purpose there is no project. Connect to your concerns and what you care about in taking on your project. For a net zero project, this includes the use of no fossil fuels, as well as creating a quality and way of life that is interconnected to others, including people, nature, and the planet. With clear purpose it is easier to articulate goals.

GOALS. Goals are broad, and there are often far-reaching intentions for a project. Once you have engaged others in generating your goals, break them into subareas, such as environmental, economic, social, and spiritual goals.

OBJECTIVES/METRICS. Establish objectives and metrics. They are quantifiable ways to see if goals are being met, and they identify precise outcomes and numbers that can be measured to determine success or failure. Net zero and energy-intensity numbers are two of the essential metrics for net zero projects.

OWNER'S PROJECT REQUIREMENTS. Before beginning the design process, create an OPR document that states the agreed-upon project understanding, vision, goals, metrics, and strategies. This document summarizes the larger vision and implementation measures and establishes a clear foundation and a benchmark for project success.

PROGRAMMING. In the typical design process, programming lists rooms, sizes, adjacencies, qualities, and specific requirements. For a net zero building, the program is also a necessary foundational document. In addition to traditional programming requirements, a net zero building program needs to assess all building energy loads accurately, including all equipment, hours of occupancy, and occupant use.

Step 6: Design Living Buildings and Places

Modern architecture has been driven by the motto "form follows function." But in the new world order, form follows life and living systems. Both of these ways of thinking can influence and generate the order, form, and shape of our buildings, neighborhood centers, landscapes, and even regions and nations.

Life-centered design creates places that support and nurture human life and all living systems in a symbiotic interconnection and dance. When we create places that connect to nature and other people through view, daylight, layout, and the connection of activities, aesthetics, and materials, we begin to generate buildings and communities where people feel alive and engaged.

In this analogy, we can interpret our buildings and communities as integrated systems that behave with similarities to living organisms, inescapably connected to ecosystems. As humans and other organisms breathe, building systems must provide fresh air and exhaust stale air. Just as our skeleton supports us, columns, beams, walls, and roofs hold up our buildings to allow human activities inside them. Our buildings have circulating systems of hallways, stairs, and elevators, and our cities have streets allowing for the movement of goods, services, and people. Our buildings and communities have wires that enable communication much like our nervous system.

The key organs of our buildings are less analogous, but still at the core of a building's activity and life. We can think of the heart and soul of buildings bringing life to spaces and places. We can think of living rooms, religious spaces, parks, and urban plazas as places that act as the heart of an organization, building, community, or city. The brain might be the offices or meeting spaces, with communication networks providing connections within and beyond the building. As these systems support the operation and activity of the living organism, similarly, in buildings and communities, these systems support human activity, purpose, and functioning.

When we design a building, we strive to create a pattern of spaces that bring people together for a larger purpose, such as work, play, sociability, community, or spirit. And in doing this, the organization of activities creates a larger organism such as a business, school, church, neighborhood, village, or city. The design creates a linked organizational pattern or form of a building that fits the energy, activity, and purpose of those inside. The form can generate and nurture a feeling of aliveness, beauty, and inspiration in the proportions and details from the whole to each of the parts.

Step 7: Minimize Energy Loads

To build cost-effective net zero buildings, we must minimize loads. As we discussed in chapter 7, by adding all of the energy a building consumes annually and dividing by the building's size, we get the energy-use intensity number—similar to fuel mileage for a car. For net zero buildings, this number should be in the range of 10–20 kBtu/sf-yr , excluding process loads such as commercial kitchens and manufacturing plants. In buildings with process loads, these loads should also be substantially reduced with use of waste heat.

To reduce energy, first investigate building energy requirements for all anticipated uses. Typical building loads include envelope heating and cooling, ventilation, lighting, plug, and process loads. Use room-by-room analysis to estimate all energy consumption and disaggregate consumption into subcategories. After estimating different loads, compare lighting, heating, cooling, ventilation, and plug loads to disaggregated targets for components of the overall EUI number.

Use integrated passive solar, massing, building orientation, energy conservation, and daylighting strategies to significantly reduce energy consumption. See the discussion in chapter 6 and use table 6.1 for envelope insulation and air infiltration guidelines to meet the heating and cooling load metrics for net zero buildings cost effectively. Use iterative energy modeling, and adjust envelope design to achieve the EUI metric.

Step 8: Optimize Systems for Comfort and Efficiency

Net zero buildings perform very differently from typical buildings. Because of the ultra-energy-conserving envelope, internal temperatures go up and down very slowly. Exterior surfaces, including glass, do not feel cold to occupants, as radiation losses from the body are reduced. Heating and cooling distribution can be reduced while still providing occupant comfort. Integrated design strategies that reduce energy consumption in one area can help in other areas. The following are four key elements to consider in building environmental control systems:

RIGHTSIZE SYSTEMS. Building systems are typically oversized, as designers are afraid the building will not perform as designed. This can waste energy, increase capital expense, and lower performance and comfort. Accurately calculate loads, and properly size systems for comfort, efficiency, and cost.

SIMPLIFY SYSTEMS. Given the reduced loads and high insulation levels, mechanical systems can be less complex, with simpler controls.

MINIMIZE DISTRIBUTION. Reduce ductwork and/or piping. Because exterior enclosure surfaces are warmer (or cooler in summer) than in typical buildings, it is not necessary to provide HVAC to exterior walls and also windows. Rooms such as bathrooms, interior rooms, and utility rooms may not need heating and cooling and can use heat-recovery ventilation circulation to provide comfort and fresh air.

SEPARATE VENTILATION AIR FROM HEATING AIR. Separation saves energy and simplifies performance. When ductwork serves both functions, duct sizing and controls may cause unnecessary energy consumption and expense.

These combined measures can lower mechanical costs, leaving money to be invested in a higher-performing building enclosure.

Step 9: Power with Renewables

Use EUI metrics with reduced building energy loads to appropriately and cost effectively size renewable energy systems. Renewable technology is well established, so supplying renewable energy is one of the easiest steps to achieve. Renewable costs have dropped dramatically, and when combined with grants, credits, leasing, and power purchase options, renewables are more affordable than ever.

There are four central aspects to powering net zero buildings with renewables:

RIGHTSIZE RENEWABLES. Calculate the annual energy load for all energy uses. Balance energy conservation measures and renewable energy expense to optimize renewable energy capacity and production. Add about 10 percent as a safety factor to account for occupant use, climatic, and renewable production variations. Educate the building owner that user behavior and operation is significant and can vary loads by 25 percent or more.

EVALUATE RENEWABLE OPTIONS. Evaluate different solar, wind, and biomass options as well as manufacturer and installer options. While wind, hydro, methane, biomass, and other sources are all possible, almost all net zero buildings are solar powered. They are either 100 percent powered by PV energy or PV with solar hot water for heating domestic hot water and/or possibly space heating. For small buildings and/or hot water loads, buildings are typically all electric and use PVs alone with electric backup. PVs are simple to use and require minimal maintenance in comparison to solar hot water systems. In rural areas carbon-neutral buildings may be powered with high-efficiency wood heating. Powering net zero buildings with wind, methane, or hydro requires more complicated research, assessment, design, and construction procedures. With all of these systems, find experienced renewable energy companies for equipment, installation, service, and maintenance.

CONSIDER COST, OPERATION, MAINTENANCE, AND FUNDING. In evaluating options, compare installation, operation, and maintenance costs. Ask the installer for detailed capital and operating cost estimates as well as for grant, tax, and other funding opportunities. The financial consequences of renewables are constantly changing and vary state by state, but up-to-date knowledge can make a huge difference in the financial feasibility of your system.

EXPLORE ON-SITE RENEWABLES AND OFF-SITE POWER PURCHASE OPTIONS. While typical net zero projects install all renewables on site, if your state allows net metering, you may be able to install renewables off-site and credit the energy to your property. Or you may be able to lease or purchase renewable power from a company that installs PV or other renewables on your property and sells you renewable power at comparable rates to your electric utility.

Step 10: Detail and Build

As outlined below, a net zero project involves thorough preparation by the design team before construction, care and attention during construction, as well as follow-up thereafter:

DOCUMENTATION FOR SUCCESS. Because many parts of net zero buildings differ from conventional ones, you should provide clear and detailed construction drawings and specifications of all building elements, particularly the unique and critical net zero requirements. Documentation must also include testing and commissioning procedures.

BUILDING WITH CARE, COMMITMENT, AND TEAMWORK. Construction requires mutual commitment, alignment of net zero goals, teamwork, and clear communication and project management procedures. This includes all construction subs and design team consultants. Ensure detailed ongoing communication and project management procedures that encourage a strong, unified team of the owner, design team, and the construction team. At initial meetings the design team should clarify the ways this project is different from typical projects and help the construction team anticipate construction and scheduling challenges. Construction mock up procedures must be followed throughout construction for success.

CONFIRMING PERFORMANCE THROUGH INSPECTION, TESTING, COMMISSIONING, AND INITIAL MONITORING. At critical milestones during construction, test so that you can take any necessary corrective action immediately, minimizing delays and expense. The process of commissioning begins with reviewed design and proceeds throughout construction until final testing and commissioning are completed at the end of construction. While construction is often considered complete when the building is occupied, typical projects have a one-year warranty period. On net zero projects the building performance should be carefully monitored for a full year minimum after occupancy. This includes review of energy consumption, including disaggregated loads, monthly and at seasonal changes. Through this process the building should be operating on track for the first year. Remember, though, that the goal is net zero operation throughout the lifetime of the building—100 years and longer.

MONITORING. To help guide operations, monitoring systems should allow building occupants to observe and correct performance if operation is inconsistent with design metrics. With an all-electric building with submetering, this monitoring can be accomplished easily by reading electric meters for the building subpanels. More complex and extensive systems with public display and interaction can also be used but are not necessary.

Step 11: Learn and Operate

Continued net zero performance requires building operation consistent with the procedures and practices identified during design and documented in an operations manual. Annual building and systems maintenance as outlined in the warranties and operations manual is also necessary to ensure proper performance. While the project team should monitor a building in its first year of performance, occupants and/or owners will need to monitor the building thereafter. Building users need education so that their behavior supports net zero goals: net zero buildings work only with net zero occupants. Education about net zero projects should be broader as well, extending to building visitors and the public, so that more net zero buildings are built in the future.

Step 12: Celebrate

Construction is a huge effort by a diverse and complex team, so the end of any building project should be an occasion for celebration. Given the additional challenge, care, and effort needed to complete a net zero project, celebration is even more important.

Celebrating the fact that you have met your goals is an important step in keeping building occupants inspired to maintain net zero operation into the future. A building opening in particular allows an opportunity to thank individuals and organizations who have supported a net zero project through funding, grants, volunteering, labor, and other ways. Celebrations can also build public support for other net zero projects and a renewable future for the planet.

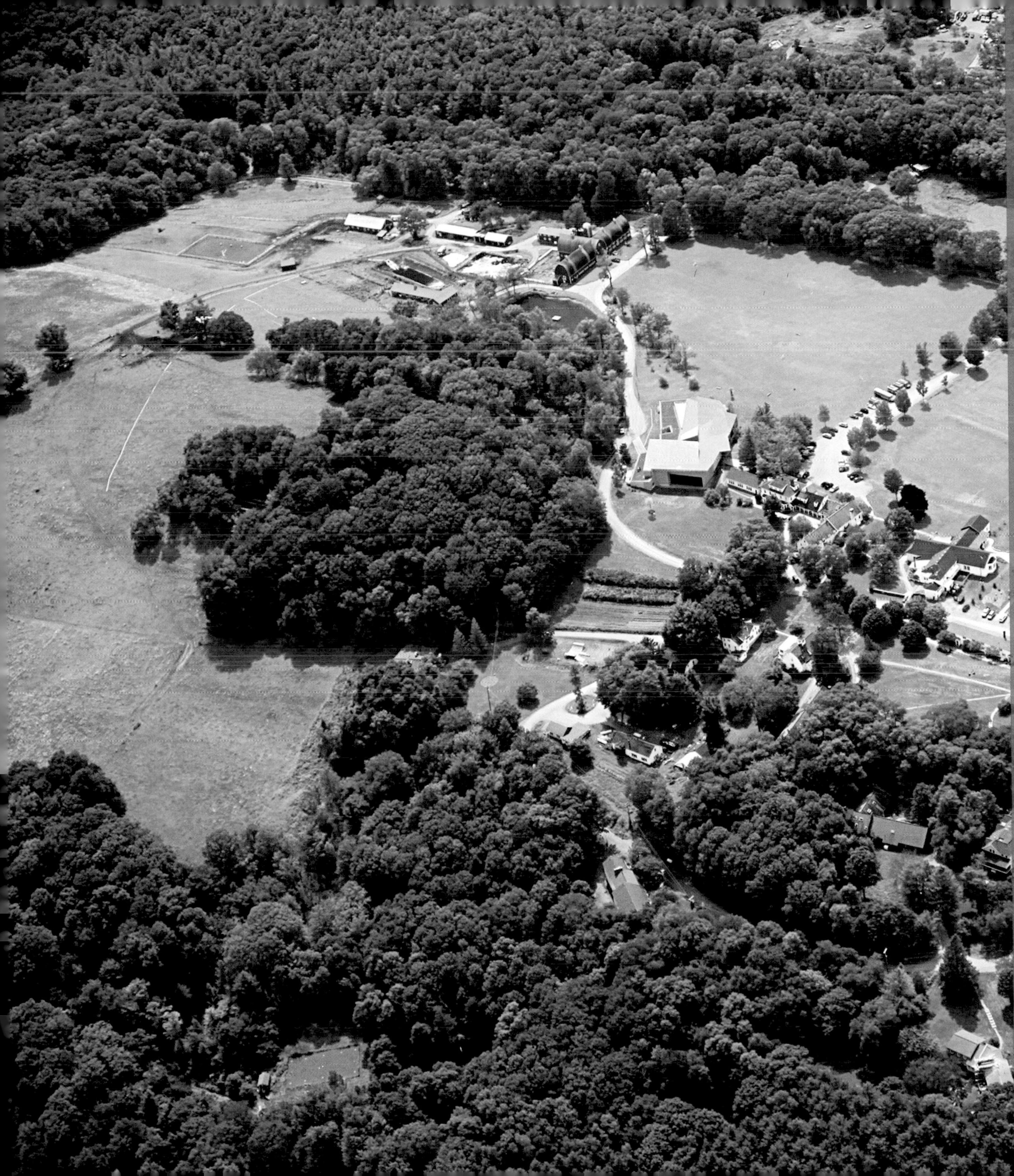

THE PUTNEY SCHOOL MASTER PLAN

THE PUTNEY SCHOOL MASTER PLAN
A Focused Plan for a Net Zero/Carbon-Neutral Future

With fuel-oil prices tripling in recent years and the success of their net zero field house (see The Putney School Field House case study in chapter 5), The Putney School saw both the necessity and feasibility of major energy reduction. While the field house construction was under way, the school realized that their real challenge lay in their forty existing buildings. If the school were going to protect itself against fuel price increases, then it would have to deal with the fuel use of all of its buildings, not just new buildings on campus. So with the completion of the field house project, the school embarked upon a new mission: a master plan for the campus, including a net zero energy goal for the school.

The final master plan presents a means for financial planning with focused environmental stewardship. The future reduction of energy use on campus, as articulated in the master plan, will further establish the school as a leader in environmental stewardship and protect against rising energy costs and price volatility. The evolution of the master plan was driven by the school's desire to walk their environmental talk. As part of the plan, energy conservation standards were developed for all future renovations and new construction on campus, and renewable energy sources were recommended to meet reduced building energy loads. The plan also outlines the concrete actions required to achieve the goal of a net zero/carbon-neutral school.

Project Overview

The Putney School campus is located above the town of Putney, Vermont, in a saddle between two hilltops that flank the campus to the north and south. Broad expanses and corresponding long views open to the west and east. The school's programs function in an eclectic mix of buildings. Before the school's founding in 1935, a few of today's buildings were part of two neighboring farming operations. The current Putney School's core building infrastructure includes just over 190,000 square feet of heated space, including nine buildings with classrooms or dedicated to academic uses, ten dormitories or buildings including dormitory functions, twenty attached faculty apartments, and twelve faculty houses that exist at the periphery of the campus.

The long-term strategy for the campus, as indicated in the master plan, includes a few new buildings and significant renovation of existing buildings to address program, deferred maintenance, and energy needs. The master plan maintains and preserves the school's unique character and history while recognizing the need for improved facilities, new infrastructure, parking, utilities, and defined open space.

Vision and Goals

The vision and goals were developed with broad-based community support. While some of the goals identified here do not relate specifically to energy use or the net zero/carbon-neutral goal of the energy master plan, they provide context for the entire master plan.

MORE EFFICIENTLY SUPPORT THE SCHOOL'S ACADEMIC MISSION.
Most importantly, the master plan is focused on connecting the physical place with the academic mission of the school.

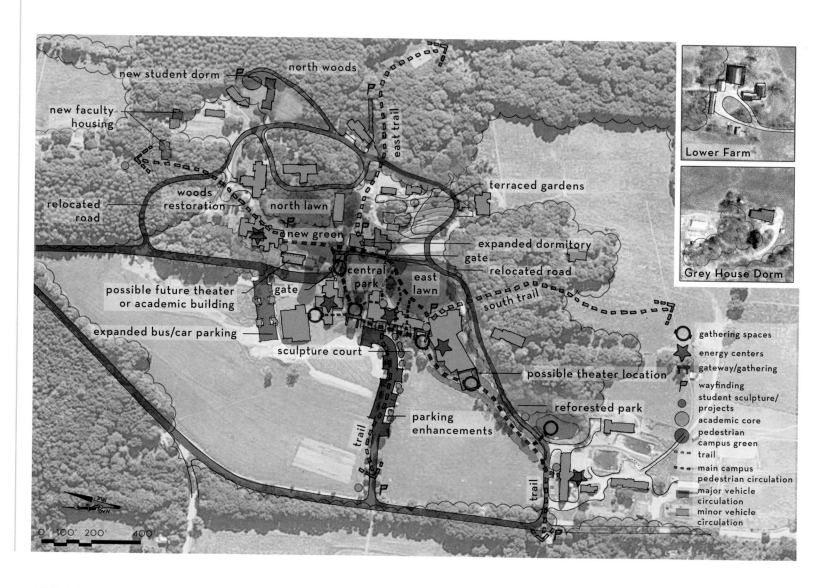

FIGURE CS9.1. The overall master plan for the campus shows gateways, linkages, buildings, gathering spaces, and spots for student sculptures.

DEVELOP A CAMPUS CORE THAT EMBODIES COMMUNITY SPACE. The plan provides strategies to enhance the campus core, to enliven the buildings' outside spaces, and to create a space that supports student and staff interaction and learning, allowing for open communication between all levels and ownership of place.

DEVELOP HOUSING THAT NURTURES AND FOSTERS COMMUNICATION. Because the school is a residential community, housing and living spaces play an important role in shaping the context of place. The plan envisions future growth and development of the housing stock that reinforces the sense of community by developing small neighborhood enclaves that connect to the larger academic community.

ENHANCE NATURAL CONNECTION TO THE ENVIRONMENT. The school is fortunate to be located in an extraordinary setting. The master plan encourages future development that takes advantage of the magnificent Vermont mountaintop setting and natural areas, while preserving, enhancing, and sustaining those environments for the future. The plan also promotes a clear sense of place, respecting the history and diversity of the school and land, and commits to the preservation of key historic buildings and open spaces that make The Putney School a stimulating learning environment.

DEVELOP A NET ZERO, HEALTHY, AND DURABLE CAMPUS. A sustainable campus integrates ecological conservation, economic viability, and social equity through design, planning, and operation. Sustainability goals inform campus decisions on energy, the built environment, and relationships with the adjoining community. The master plan explicitly calls for creating a net zero/carbon-neutral campus and for implementing concrete steps to get there. The school strives to become a local, regional, and national leader in the ongoing practice of sustainability embedded through teaching, research, and outreach. The master plan aligns with these goals.

ENCOMPASS STUDENT WORK IN THE CAMPUS EXPERIENCE. The Putney School students are known for their creativity, including art installations throughout the campus. The plan identifies spaces for student work to be exhibited.

DEVELOP ROADS AND UTILITIES. The plan addresses the infrastructure that is needed to make this campus operate smoothly.

INTEGRATE THE THEATER INTO THE CAMPUS EXPERIENCE. The Putney School is recognized for the artistic expression of its students. A theater at the center of the campus is planned to replace the seasonal theater on the campus perimeter.

Energy

The development of the energy components of the master plan for The Putney School started with an evaluation of the current energy usage of the campus. In 2010 the campus used the following energy, for buildings only, not transportation, at a cost of about $440,000.

- 800,000 kWh electricity
- 75,000 gallons of oil
- 14,000 gallons of propane
- 20 cords of wood

As depicted in CS9.2, a picture was derived as to where energy consumption was the highest and where energy savings offered the greatest opportunity. The total campus energy use was broken down by building. The kitchen/dining unit has the highest EUI of any building on campus. The next three buildings with the highest energy-intensity ratings burn cordwood at a low efficiency.

With its stated goal of developing a net zero/carbon-neutral future, energy and financial analysis in the master plan, and the positive experience with the net zero field house project, the school decided that all future construction would be completed to net zero ready standards. This financial model used in the master plan assumes future buildings and renovations will employ renewables, not fossil fuel. So if an energy conservation measure costs less than renewables to provide the amount of energy that the improvement will save, then the energy conservation is justified. If not, then renewables are justified.

For example, if it costs $500 to insulate a roof to R-60 and that saves enough energy to avoid installing $800 of PV, it would make sense to invest in the insulation. However, if adding

FIGURE CS9.2. This graph indicates the EUI (kBtu/sf-yr) of each building in order to understand how efficient the building is for its size. The range of energy intensity that is required to meet the net zero goal is noted as two dashed red lines, at 19 and 32 kBtu/sf-yr. The energy data presented here are an average of the 2008–09 and 2009–10 academic years.

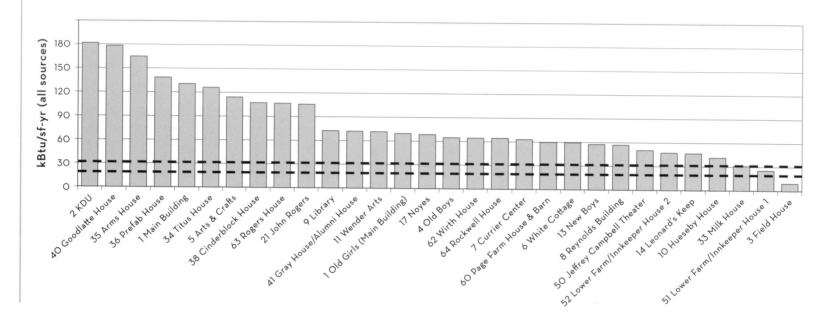

additional insulation, to go from R-60 to R-80, will cost $300 more and only avoids installing $200 worth of PV, it would justify the installation of the PV. It is important to note that this net zero financial metric approach is unlike that for typical energy conservation projects, which look at payback. The master plan metric instead focuses on the installed cost of the energy source versus the installed cost of the conservation measure.

Drawing on this financial analysis, The Putney School has adapted the following building efficiency standards for all new and renovation projects:

- R-5 windows
- R-20 below-grade walls and slabs
- R-40 above-grade walls
- R-60 roofs
- Air leakage rates of less than 0.1 cfm50/sf aboveground surface area

In general, meeting these net zero levels in building enclosure improvements will result in building energy consumption between 15 and 30 kBtu/sf-yr for total energy utilization. Some of the older and more articulated buildings, especially those with historic constraints, will cost more per unit area for energy improvements, so the higher end of the energy use range will be appropriate for those projects. Simpler and less significant historical façades can be upgraded at a lower cost, so energy retrofits would target the lower end of the range.

Once the future energy load for the campus was estimated, the second part of the energy master planning process was to calculate the renewable energy needed to cover the expected loads. Because The Putney School owns hundreds of acres that are managed as forestland, the biomass resource on the property is sufficient to supply heating needs. However, in the long term it is more sensible to use most of the forested land for a higher use than for fuel.

Renewable Energy Type[a]	Strategy Name	Number of Boiler Rooms	Source for Electrical Loads	CENTRAL BUILDINGS		PERIPHERAL BUILDINGS	
				Source for heat	Source for hot water	Source for heat	Source for hot water
Net Zero (Class 1 and Class 2 Net Zero)	PV/ASHP[b]	0	PV[c]	Air-source heat pump w/PV	Solar hot water w/electric backup w/PV	Air-source heat pump w/PV	Solar hot water w/electric backup w/PV
Carbon Neutral (Class 3 Net Zero)	Biomass Central	1	PV[c]	Boilers, fired by wood chips	Solar hot water w/boiler backup	Woodstove or pellet stove w/ ASHP or only ASHP w/PV	Solar hot water w/electric backup w/PV
Carbon Neutral (Class 3 Net Zero)	Biomass Distributed	3 to 5	PV[c]	Boilers, fired by wood pellets	Solar hot water w/boiler backup	Woodstove or pellet stove w/ ASHP or only ASHP w/PV	Solar hot water w/electric backup w/PV

[a] Net zero classification system from Shanti Pless and Paul Torcellini, *Net-Zero Energy Buildings: A Classification System Based on Renewable Energy Supply Options*, National Renewable Energy Laboratory Technical Report , NREL/TP-550-44586, June 2010; http://www.nrel.gov/docs/fy10osti/44586.pdf.

[b] ASHP = air-source heat pump.

[c] PV is most likely all ground mounted, in large arrays, possibly at several locations, net metered to all buildings on campus.

In terms of the traditional renewable energy sources, there are no hydro resources available on the campus, and the wind resources on the site are less cost effective than solar PV. Three options were investigated in the master plan: solar PV providing all needs, a central biomass system with PV for electricity, and a mini-district pellet system for heating central campus buildings with PV for electricity and peripheral campus heating. Ultimately, the school decided that a mix of PV for general electric use, solar thermal for domestic hot water, and biomass and PVs for heating would best provide its future energy needs. The school did not look into cogeneration with the biomass options, as there are few uses for cogenerated electricity in the summer.

Buildings at the center of the campus are close together, while small, peripheral buildings are dispersed, making the campus as a whole inappropriate for district heating. Even the core buildings are far enough apart that a single district heating system was not cost effective. However, several small district heating systems serving three to four buildings each made sense. So the school opted for a hybrid system, with PV to provide all electricity, a wood pellet mini-district heating system for thermal energy to the central campus, and either pellet boilers or air-source heat pumps to provide thermal energy to the peripheral buildings.

Implementation Strategy

The path to a carbon-neutral/net zero campus consists of two separate but related pieces: conservation and renewable energy implementation. While conservation has typically been pursued before renewables, the master plan recommends that conservation and renewables be pursued in tandem. There are three reasons:

INCREMENTAL ENERGY CONSERVATION. This strategy takes advantage of energy conservation opportunities as they arise. If a building is being worked on for programmatic, deferred maintenance, or other reasons, then improvements will meet the net zero ready energy standards by incrementally moving toward net zero.

INCREMENTAL RENEWABLE ENERGY AND BIOMASS IMPLEMENTATION. Since renewable strategies have been identified, the school can use outside funding as opportunities arise. Given frequent changes to government programs and differing funding interests of donors, this strategy allows the school to take advantage of these opportunities with minimal effort. This approach was effective for the field house in securing a grant from a state clean energy development fund, which was available only for a short period.

IMPLEMENTATION OF NET ZERO/CARBON-NEUTRAL GOALS. To meet the school's mission and to proactively address climate change, the best course for moving quickly toward a net zero future is to address conservation and renewables simultaneously.

The Putney School, like most academic institutions, faces the challenge of many older buildings with deferred maintenance and programmatic needs that require repurposing or remodeling. Meeting the multiple needs of The Putney School requires integrating energy improvements with all programmatic and deferred maintenance upgrades. To accomplish this, the master plan indicates that all building improvements, however small, should be completed to net zero ready standards. Including net zero standards improvements with programmatic or deferred maintenance upgrades makes projects more fundable, as donors can see multiple benefits. This approach also allows the school and its contractors to become more proficient at accomplishing these deep energy retrofits, which require great attention to detail.

Cost Analysis

The cost analysis performed for the master plan included the cost of the building energy-efficiency upgrades and the installation of the renewable technologies. Each of the three renewable energy scenarios was vetted for cost implications and determined to be the following.

- Net zero, all-PV: $18.7 million
- Carbon-neutral, mini-district, wood pellets: $15.5 million
- Carbon-neutral, single-district, wood chips: $16.4 million

TABLE CS9.2. COSTS OF PREDICTED ENERGY SCENARIOS

	NET ZERO, PV	CARBON NEUTRAL, WOOD PELLETS	CARBON NEUTRAL, WOOD CHIPS
Description	More load reduction + all PV/NPs	Pellet nodes + major load reduction + PV	Central wood chip plant + major load reduction
Costs for Efficiency Upgrades	$8,757,000	$8,757,000	$8,757,000
Costs for Biomass Systems[a]	$0	$1,991,000	$2,872,000
Costs for PV2[b]	$6,571,429	$4,011,429	$4,011,429
Costs for Solar Hot Water	$295,000	$295,000	$295,000
Costs for Air-Source Heat Pumps[c]	$3,032,000	$472,000	$472,000
Total Cost	$18,700,000	$15,500,000	$16,400,000

[a] Pellet system and piping costs based on recent cost experience with the pellet system for the Main Building.

[b] Based on 1.05 kWh/year per peak watt installed; cost of $6 total per peak watt installed (before tax credits, if available).

[c] Costs for air-source heat pumps include electrical service upgrades where appropriate.

All options assume improvements done at one time with 2011 dollars. (Although the improvements will be done incrementally, calculating the costs as a onetime expense makes comparison easier.) Table CS9.2 outlines the full, detailed, up-front costs of each of the three renewable energy implementation scenarios based on DEW Construction company's cost estimate and the work of Andy Shapiro.

The net zero, all-PV scenario has the highest initial capital cost; the carbon-neutral, mini-district, wood-pellet scenario the lowest. However, the net zero, all-PV option has no ongoing fuel cost, whereas both of the biomass options do. Figuring in capital and operating costs as well as ongoing cash flow thus changes the relative cost of these systems. For the purpose of the master plan, the costs were evaluated based on the net present value of the investments over the next thirty years, taking both the energy costs and the installation costs into account. The base case, or campus as-is scenario, included oil, propane, electricity, and cordwood being consumed consistently at the same rate that the campus uses these sources today. The three future scenarios all assume the significant reductions in energy use that had been outlined throughout the master plan.

Table CS9.3 illustrates two versions of net present values, one at 5 percent real escalation and one at 10 percent real escalation. Since future fuel escalation rates are unknown, we use two rates to show a range of costs, assuming that the future will fall somewhere in between and the school can make its own judgment as to the most likely rate. In these calculations inflation is assumed to be 2 percent, and we used a discount rate of 3 percent. These results demonstrate very significant financial benefit to The Putney School in securing a stable renewable-energy future and minimizing long-term financial stability.

Negative values in table CS9.3 represent costs to school, while positive values indicate deferred costs. If tax credits are able to be taken under the net zero, all-PV scenario, then it is the only scenario that over this thirty-year period has a positive net present value of $1.78 million. In comparison, doing nothing to improve the school's energy future will result in a cost of $13 to almost $15 million over three decades.

Recommended Net Zero Strategy

The final recommendations made to The Putney School to implement their net zero goal include the following:

TABLE CS9.3 THIRTY-YEAR NET PRESENT VALUE OF INVESTMENT

	LOW FUEL ESCALATION (5%)	HIGH FUEL ESCALATION (10%)
Campus As Is	($13,000,000)	($14,910,000)
Net Zero, PV	($2,690,000)	($780,000)
Net Zero, PV with Tax Credits[a]	($142,523)	$1,780,000
Net Zero, Wood Pellets	($5,020,000)	($7,690,000)
Net Zero, Wood Pellets with Tax Credits[a]	($3,420,000)	($6,090,000)
Net Zero, Wood Chips	($4,450,000)	($4,680,000)
Net Zero, Wood Chips with Tax Credits[a]	($2,850,000)	($3,080,000)

Note: Includes cost of full implementation plus cost of electricity, oil, propane, cordwood, pellets, wood chips, fuel, and cost for added or savings from decreased maintenance. All fuels escalate at the same rate (5 or 10 percent), up to cost of energy from PV, except cordwood, which goes up with general inflation only. Includes $0.06 credit per kWh exported.

[a] 40 percent combined federal and state credits. No accelerated depreciation credit is taken. Applied only to PV cost.

- Perform microload retrofits whenever a building (or portion of a building) is worked on in any capacity.
- Install a biomass mini-district heating system for the largest users in the core of the campus. As building energy usage is decreased with energy upgrades, connect wood-pellet heat to adjacent buildings.
- Retrofit one or two (preferably one larger and one smaller) peripheral buildings with microload building enclosure retrofits, air-source heat pumps, and solar hot water to gain experience with this approach.
- Raise funds for PV arrays, and install incrementally as funds from donors and/or grants and/or investments become available.
- Continue to raise funds for and implement microload retrofits, air-source heat pumps, solar hot water, and PVs, concentrating first on peripheral buildings and any central core buildings not served (or not servable) by biomass systems. The final step would include the addition of air-source heat pumps and solar hot water to the central buildings first served by biomass systems, after they receive microload retrofits.

- Develop an annual monitoring protocol for all buildings and the campus overall to track the effectiveness of each of the measures pursued and update total energy and individual building energy consumption annually.
- Annually review the net zero plan with the net zero team to assess progress in the previous year and prioritize projects for the upcoming year. Reprioritize implementation measures for the energy plan annually.
- Update the full net zero plan every five years to address changes in technology, finance, and school needs.

The strategy laid out in the master plan lowers fuel costs in the short term, moves toward a net zero or carbon-neutral future, and preserves flexibility to accommodate future unknown conditions. Changes at the school and energy cost will affect the choices available and the factors favoring different choices. The net zero energy master plan will help The Putney School to achieve its educational vision and mission as a leader in proactive response to global climate change and environmental innovation.

19 | Net Zero Communities and Beyond

magine living in a world where earth and air are healthy and unpolluted; where your food is grown nearby and is nutritious and delicious; where your home is in a neighborhood with close friends and in a village, town, or city where community life flourishes; where people care for others and nature; where nature is closely connected to your daily life; where the energy you use is endless and renewable; where people live with meaning, joy, and love for others as well as wonder for life; and finally, where we are stewards contributing to the future evolution and continuation of life on the planet.

It doesn't have to be a fantasy. We can choose to create a healthy and vibrant future for humans and nature. An important step along the way is transforming our buildings to net zero standards. But this will solve just 40 percent of our energy problems. Tackling the other 60 percent requires changes in transportation and infrastructure—and these changes can be made only at the community level.

In fact, communities are the key to creating a net zero future, and projects around the world are experimenting with sustainable community design. That's because we can really only scale up renewable energy in a community framework. A renewably powered future is not going to emerge from the independently powered buildings that were the focus of sustainable design in the 1970s. To truly build a net zero world, we not only have to account for the energy required to get to and from a building or home but also the way the building or home meshes with the surrounding social, transportation, ecological, and energy frameworks. And we need to create a new web of renewable power sources that interconnect with community-scale human settlements that have realigned their energy infrastructure to benefit from renewables.

If we look carefully, we can see that this new world is already emerging; there are patterns and trends heading in the right direction. There is increasing intention, commitment, and concrete action demonstrating this is a viable path to the future. Our quality of life and settlement patterns are changing. People are moving out of suburbs and back to more urban communities, where community life is more vibrant and offers more choice and opportunity. This is particularly true for smart-growth communities, like Hammarby Sjöstad in Sweden, and Hamburg, Germany, with their nature-friendly planning, mass transit options, strong local economies, and local food networks.

Transitioning to Energy Systems That Strengthen Communities

As nonrenewable energy sources decline and renewable energy production becomes relatively less expensive, there will be a rapid move to renewables. Renewable energy production will be dispersed around the globe at the locations where it is most abundant and distributed to where it is used. This new distribution system will adapt to accommodate the seasonal, daily, and hourly variations in both production and consumption of energy. New energy control and storage systems, such as smart grid technology with networked distributed storage of batteries, hydrogen, or other innovations, or larger, utility-based storage systems will play a bigger role. These technologically advanced networked systems will even out differences in energy sources and usage in an integrated energy supply distribution storage system that is as different from today's power grid as the Internet is from fax machines. Larger renewable systems will become more common, including large-scale utility projects and community partnerships to gain economics of scale and reduce cost and complexity.

The first steps to creating this system include improving and transforming the electric grid by adding to our existing major hydro resources in the Northwest with major solar production in the Southwest and major wind generation in the Midwest and on the two coasts. Combined with local and smaller renewable resources throughout the United States, these steps can create a decentralized network scaled to renewable energy supply and demand.[1] Figure 19.1 illustrates this concept with national, regional, local, and building energy scale.

Already there has been major progress. In Europe, where renewable energy development is encouraged, villages, cities, and nations are achieving high levels of renewable production, and this production is rapidly expanding. Europe also has developed a grid that allows for higher renewable energy utilization without disruption of the grid from the fluctuation of renewable energy generation. Denmark has increased wind production from 1.9 percent in 1990 to 28.1 percent in 2011.[2] The majority of wind power in Denmark is funded and owned by cooperatives with over 100,000 members.[3] In Germany renewably powered electricity has increased from 3.8 percent in 2000 to 22.9 percent in 2012.[4] About 46 percent of this gain is from wind, 41 percent from biomass, 28 percent from PV, and 21 percent from hydropower.[5] Spain in 2010 generated 23 percent of all its electricity from wind and solar.[6] Even in the United States, renewable energy accounted for 14.3 percent of domestically produced electricity in the first six months of 2011, which surpasses nuclear power production. Over 60 percent of this was produced by hydro, and 23 percent came from wind.[7]

Because renewable energy functions at more of a community scale than fossil-fuel-based energy does, communities are becoming more resilient in the process. The island of Samsø in Denmark is a remarkable example of a carbon-neutral, near-net-zero renewable community. This 44-square-mile island with over 4,000 residents produces 100 percent of its electricity from wind power. Islanders funded, own, and run this system, which produces significant investment returns to many islanders.[8] Eleven land-based wind turbines supply all of the island's electricity needs; another ten offshore turbines sell surplus energy to the mainland.[9] The offshore wind turbines supply 20 percent of Denmark's total electricity needs. In addition, 70 percent of the island's total heating needs are produced from solar and biomass, including four district heating systems using local straw and wood chips.[10] Local biofuels such as canola oil even provide a portion of the fuel for vehicles.[11]

The islanders' goal is to be entirely fossil fuel–free toward 2030.[12] Perhaps most important, Samsø has gained near energy independence through local initiative and cooperation. From a project that was initially supported only by a mayor, this initiative has become a community resource and source of pride.

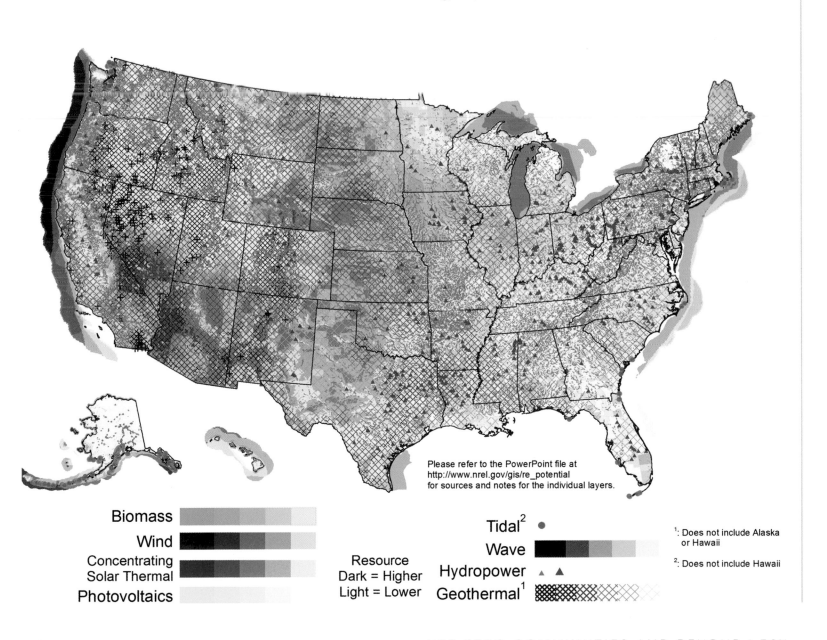

FIGURE 19.1. Renewable energy sources across the United States combined with a decentralized grid can power future energy requirements.

Please refer to the PowerPoint file at http://www.nrel.gov/gis/re_potential for sources and notes for the individual layers.

Biomass

Wind

Concentrating Solar Thermal

Photovoltaics

Resource
Dark = Higher
Light = Lower

Tidal[2]

Wave

Hydropower

Geothermal[1]

[1]: Does not include Alaska or Hawaii

[2]: Does not include Hawaii

REFOCUSING TRANSPORTATION

As rising fuel prices increase the cost of transportation, more and more people are turning to mass transit—not to mention pedal power and foot power—and more and more businesses are finding ways to reduce transportation distances, create new distribution systems, and increase efficiencies of existing systems. In the future our automobiles are likely to be hyper-cars, and our primary mode of transportation will likely be mass transit.[13] Algae, or other bio-based fuels that do not compete with food production, will supply reduced liquid fuel needs.[14] High-speed rail will increase convenience for short- and medium-distance travelers. Air transportation will decline dramatically, as its high consumption of concentrated fossil fuels makes it extremely expensive. Water-based transportation, including the use of large sailing cargo ships, will experience a rebirth, especially for the movement of goods around the planet. In the longer term, other transportation options may emerge. In the process our communities will change to accommodate the kind of pedestrian-oriented development that allows for the practical use of mass transportation. These denser, walkable communities will improve the quality of life and reduce environmental impacts.

Of course much innovation in transportation has begun. High-speed rail is already replacing interurban air transportation in some areas of the world. Cars in Europe already achieve fuel mileage over 40 mpg on average. We've already seen that when energy prices go up, automobile use declines, fuel mileage improves, and mass transit use increases. Government action could accelerate the transportation transition by improving mass transit and encouraging better automobile mileage through regulation and incentives. But again, how communities are conceived or reshaped has enormous impact on how rapidly our transportation systems can evolve.

CREATING COMMUNITY-ORIENTED SETTLEMENTS

As we rely more on mass transit and pedestrian or bicycle paths, new settlement patterns will evolve. A world built around the automobile will give way to clustered, mixed-use development that allows people to work, play, shop, and carry out other aspects of their lives closer to home. It will cost less to move people and goods. And as the automobile-dominated culture that has separated people physically and lessened their human connections fades, community life will strengthen.

Since the existing oil-based infrastructure will not serve us well as we shift back to a renewable foundation, we will need to find creative ways to revise our existing infrastructure. Adapting our older village, town, and city centers that evolved prior to oil-based, sprawl-based settlement patterns will be relatively easy, though it will require significant energy conservation retrofits to buildings and a reinvestment in mass transit. Repurposing and reusing our suburban infrastructure will require much greater effort and creativity. Houses and buildings will need to be reorganized into more dense settlement patterns—not just to improve quality of life and encourage mass transit but also to recapture agricultural and conservation lands. Moving buildings, deconstruction, reconstruction, and reuse of existing building materials will become more common.

RESTORING REGIONAL AGRICULTURE AND ECOSYSTEMS

Moving away from fossil fuel also allows us to reenvision our foodsheds and restore healthy ecosystems—both critical aspects of creating viable sustainable communities in a net zero world.

As people have grown concerned over the quality of food produced by industrial agriculture, the amount of energy it takes to produce and transport that food, and the vulnerability of depending on food grown far away, there has been intense focus on encouraging local agriculture and improving local food-processing and distribution options. We can only expect this focus to increase as the energy-related costs of producing and transporting food grow higher. Currently, food production uses ten times more energy from fossil fuel than energy from the sun during the process of planting, growing, transporting, and selling food products to the marketplace. In the short term food production will evolve to eventually eliminate the use of fossil fuels, requiring more human and animal power to be used for agriculture. We can also expect to see agriculture return to systems-based cultivation, where waste equals food, as it does in successful biological systems.

As our settlement patterns get denser, nature will be allowed to move back closer to our homes. Wood and trees will be required to replace metals and oil-based plastics, putting pressure on forest resources while encouraging appropriate management to improve forests and forest habitat. Wildlife will have more opportunity to reclaim former habitat. In the process, ecosystems will have the chance to revive, and the connection between their health and ours—that of humans, our communities, and our planet—will become even more apparent.

Initial Steps toward Net Zero Communities

Hopefully by now the importance of larger-scale net zero energy projects is becoming clear. The next question is how to get more of them under way. The following are a few examples of projects, by our firm and others, that take steps beyond building construction to create a net zero world.

BRINGING BACK BUFFALO

Buffalo was once a vibrant, industrial city, an epicenter for grain production and transport and home to steel, iron, and other manufacturing. In 1900 it was the eighth largest city in the United States.[15] By the 1970s, manufacturing trends had shifted, causing industry to decline and Buffalo's middle class to shrink dramatically as jobs vanished. Today it is the third poorest among US cities with over 250,000 residents, and it has the third largest number of vacant properties.[16] Its story is a classic example of the decline of American industrial cities, and its struggle to transition itself to a more resilient future embodies the challenge facing many other urban areas in the nation. Many efforts to boost the local economy, green the city, and revive community life are under way.

A local, membership-based community organization, People United for Sustainable Housing (PUSH), is working to revitalize neighborhoods and address affordable housing through community participation and empowerment. PUSH is leading efforts to renovate housing stock and weatherize existing residential and commercial properties to increase energy efficiency and reduce operating costs to the future owners. It has established a Green Development Zone, where it focuses on establishing affordable green housing renovation and reconstruction and community-based renewable energy projects, in keeping with its mission to "mobilize residents to create strong neighborhoods with quality, affordable housing, expand local hiring opportunities and to advance economic justice in Buffalo."[17] Revitalization has also been aided by the city's Urban Homestead Program, which allows abandoned buildings or vacant lots to be purchased for $1.[18]

ADDRESSING COMMUNITY-SCALE ISSUES IN VERMONT

Our office is located in Waitsfield, Vermont, at the upper end of a watershed in a distinct valley between two mountain ranges. The Mad River Valley, as it is called, includes parts or all of five towns. As residents here, we wondered if we could apply our twelve steps to net zero at the scale of our valley. To accomplish this we first estimated the entire energy load of our valley—all the loads from every building, business, institutional, manufacturing, transportation, and other endeavors of local residents and businesses based on the total number of residents. We did not include the energy load of the local ski resort, or transportation energy loads of tourists, which would be associated with their own towns. To estimate energy numbers for residents, we used statewide averages from the Vermont Department of Public Service Utility Facts from 2013, which include residents' automobile transportation both in our valley and beyond.

Once we estimated the existing energy consumption, we made assumptions about energy conservation sector by sector. This gave us a net zero ready number for the entire valley. Then we investigated the renewable resources in our valley, including sun, wind, and biomass (see figure 19.2). While there is some amount of hydro today and the possibility of a small increase, we did not include more hydro. We then estimated the amount of renewable energy required by source if only one energy source were used to supply all valley energy needs. While this does not specifically address how transportation fuels would be supplied, it does include the energy. In reality, transportation fuel could be biomass or electrically based or a more likely mix

FIGURE 19.2. The Mad River Valley is an example of how the twelve steps to net zero can be used in developing proactive energy strategies for towns and regions. This map projects possible sites for a mix of renewable-based technologies such as solar, wind, biomass, hydro, and methane, as well as community-oriented settlement and transit.

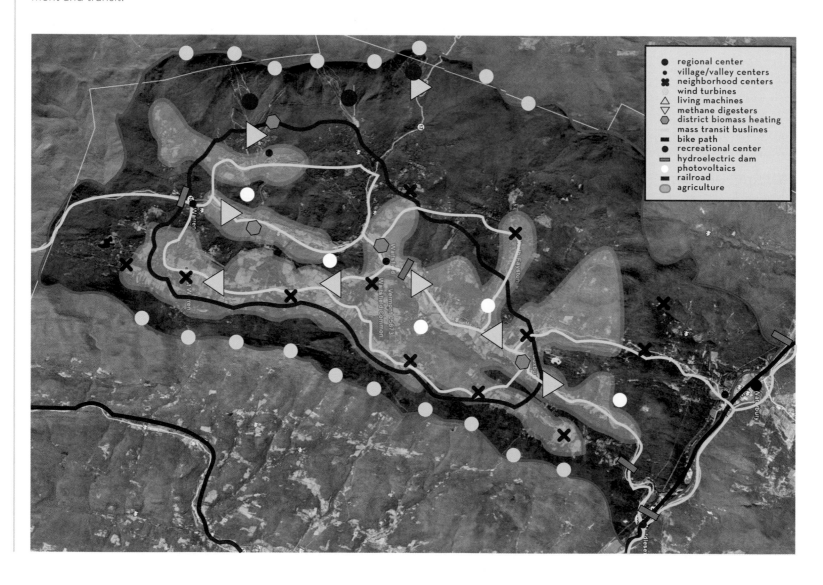

of the two. With no energy conservation, the Mad River Valley would need 108,000 cords of wood from 216,000 acres of sustainably managed woodlot, over two times all of the land in the valley; 377,000 kW on 3.5 square miles of installed PV; or 52–2.3 MW wind turbines with 100-meter blades to produce its own energy. With energy conservation we can realistically expect to reduce total energy needs by at least 50 percent, cutting these numbers to 108,000 acres of sustainably managed woodlot, 1.75 square miles of installed PV, or 26–2.3 MW wind turbines to provide the valley's energy needs.

In Vermont there is much vibrant dialogue and argument about the pros and cons of each energy source. While most residents favor a renewably powered state and valley, there are strong opponents to each of these sources, with little discussion based on what alternative should be used to achieve a commonly shared goal. Our assessment is that a mix of sources is the best alternative. This will help to balance loads from different intermittent energy sources and soften the aesthetic impacts.

MODEL ECO-COMMUNITIES

New residential projects are forming a foundation for larger-scaled net zero projects, creating more livable communities and an improved quality of life. New neighborhood-oriented projects are being built that bridge the gap between single-family homes and cities.

The Beddington Zero Energy Development, more commonly known as BedZED, shown in figure 19.3, is an environmentally focused eighty-two-unit housing project with over 10,000 sf of workspace. Built in 2000–2003 in a borough of London, this community was England's largest and first carbon-neutral eco-community. BedZED receives its power from a small combined heat and power (CHP) plant that produces hot water and distributes it around the site via a district heating system. This CHP plant is powered by offcuts from tree surgery that would otherwise become trash. At the time it was built, it was a pioneer in larger-scale renewably powered design.

In Freiburg, Germany, the solar community Schlierberg is composed of fifty-nine residential homes and a 65,000 sf mixed-use commercial, retail, and office building. The entire community in figure 19.4 is designed to be net zero. Actual energy data analyzed for twenty homes show an average residential use of 31 kBtu/sf-yr before renewables, compared to 59 kBtu/sf-yr for the average house built to German building code.[19] Heat pumps provide heat for the community, and a 455 kW PV system on the roofs provides the electrical power.

INNOVATION IN THE WORKPLACE

While a net zero world needs net zero homes, it also needs net zero workplaces, and more and more businesses, government agencies, and institutions are stepping up to reduce their carbon footprints through changes in their buildings.

One of the main drivers of business is computing power. Server farms alone represent around 2 percent of US total electric energy use and are one of the fastest expanding sources of CO_2 emissions. Google's data centers, which use considerable energy despite efficiencies, are the company's largest source of CO_2 emissions.[20] In 2012, 34 percent of Google's electricity came from renewable sources. The remaining 66 percent came from nonrenewable energy, for which the company invested in carbon offsets.[21] Using offsets, Google has been carbon neutral since 2007 and has supported the expansion of renewable energy by purchasing electricity directly from utility and wind farms close to their data centers. Purchasing 630 MW of wind energy—equivalent to the yearly amount of energy used by more than 210,000 US households—is a step toward their long-term goal of achieving 100 percent renewable energy use without including offsets. They have also used PPAs to spur on clean energy developers and projects and have committed to investing over $1 billion to large-scale wind and rooftop solar projects.[22] To address companywide carbon impacts, they offer employees bus and car sharing transportation options.

Other large corporations are also adopting measures that could have far-reaching impacts in the transition from fossil fuels to renewables. Wal-Mart is using a combination of on-site photovoltaics, off-site wind turbines, and long-term PPAs to achieve their ultimate goal of being powered by 100 percent renewable energy.[23] Their goal for 2020 is to create 7 billion kWh of annual global renewable energy and to reduce the kWh/sf energy intensity of their buildings worldwide by 20 percent from 2010 levels, thus generating annual savings of $1 billion after 2020.[24] In 2012, Wal-Mart had reduced their greenhouse emissions by 20 percent, and as of October, 2013, they had installed 89 MW of

FIGURE 19.3. BedZED is England's largest and first carbon-neutral eco-community.

FIGURE 19.4. This aerial view of the solar mixed-use community of Schlierberg shows the commercial and retail building in the foreground, with residential units beyond.

solar systems at 215 locations, with plans to install solar systems at 6,000 stores before 2020. Costco, Kohl's, Apple, Ikea, and Macy's also have significant plans to install solar capacity.[25]

In general, the building stock and infrastructure of businesses are moving toward net zero and ultra high-energy performance. In 2009 Manitoba Hydro built a new headquarters in Winnipeg, Canada, (see figures 19.5 and 19.6) one of the coldest cities in North America. The building features innovative passive and active strategies developed by the energy consultants Transsolar, reducing the building's energy requirement by 65 percent compared to a typical office building.[26] Passive building design takes advantage of the climate and solar opportunities, including a 377 sf tower to act as an outflow for stack ventilation and a double façade that provides a buffer to the interior spaces and includes plants and shading devices. The heart of the building is oriented around a new public space and covered walkway through the city block that encourages the public to pass through and interact with the building. Radiant heating and cooling with ground-source heat pumps provide space conditioning. Preconditioned fresh outside air is supplied at all times, and occupants have access to operable windows and shades.[27] While not net zero, with an EUI of 28 kBtu/sf-yr it is net zero ready and an excellent model for urban high-rise office design.[28] Because the building is located near many public transportation lines, 50 percent of the employees (1,600 people) use public transportation, boosting the economy of the adjacent areas. Thus, it is a workplace that contributes to the quality of life and community in Winnipeg.

In Austria, where the Passive House certification process is well established, Passive House design principles, practices, and certification are even being used for the design of high-rise office buildings (see figure 19.7).

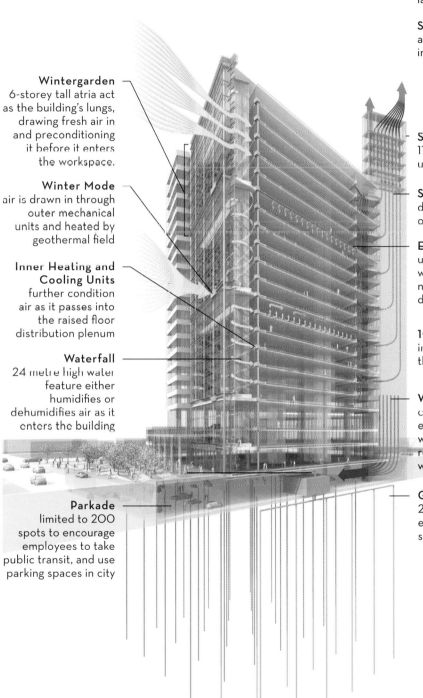

FIGURE 19.5. The Manitoba Hydro Place building systems, showing the design features that are at work in the building.

Wintergarden
6-storey tall atria act as the building's lungs, drawing fresh air in and preconditioning it before it enters the workspace.

Winter Mode
air is drawn in through outer mechanical units and heated by geothermal field

Inner Heating and Cooling Units
further condition air as it passes into the raised floor distribution plenum

Waterfall
24 metre high water feature either humidifies or dehumidifies air as it enters the building

Parkade
limited to 200 spots to encourage employees to take public transit, and use parking spaces in city

Shoulder Seasons/Summer Mode:
air is drawn naturally in through large operable windows

South Gusting Winds
abundant in Winnipeg, direct air into south wintergardens

Solar Chimney
115 metre high solar chimney uses stack effect

Shoulder Seasons/Summer Mode
draws used air up and exhausts it out of the building

Exposed Ceiling Mass
uses radiant heating and cooling; warm air rises and is drawn into north atria via natural pressure differences

100% Fresh Air, 24/7
in all office spaces is drawn through the raised access floor

Winter Mode
chimney closes, fans drawn warm exhaust air down, and recirculate it to warm the parkade. Heat exchangers re-capture heat and return it to south wintergardens to preheat incoming air

Geothermal System
280 boreholes, 125 metres deep draw excess heat or cold stored within the soil to condition the building.

fresh air
exhaust air
heating and cooling systems

FIGURE 19.6. View of Manitoba Hydro Place from the street, showing ventilation tower.

FIGURE 19.7. With a highly efficient façade, mechanical system, and PV on the roof, the RHW.2 is a twenty-story Passive House–certified office building in Vienna. It is a leading example of optimized performance on high-rise buildings.

So what should net zero buildings look like? Should they evolve their own design aesthetic? Should their aesthetic be based on context or historical traditions? Steinhude Sea Recreation Facility, shown in figure 19.8, located on an 11-acre island in Steinhude, Germany, explores a new design paradigm. Describing his approach to its design, architect Randall Stout said, "The energy needs tell me what the building looks like. The end result is new to the world. It doesn't look like any other building. We let concepts of harvesting energy inform and inspire design."[29] Designed by Randall Stout Architects and Archimedes GmbH, this carbon-neutral building uses passive and active solar heating and hot water systems as

well as ground-source heat pumps and a seed-oil-fueled co-generation microturbine. Excess solar electric energy powers a fleet of eight boats. A glazed observation tower with café is the focal point of activity, connecting water activities and views with the ecosystems, wildlife, and birds in a nature preserve.

EXAMPLES FROM THE MIDDLE EAST

In Abu Dhabi in the United Arab Emirates, the proposed Masdar City Centre will have over 1 million square feet of hotel, commercial, residential, entertainment, and retail space. Inspired by the

FIGURE 19.8. Iconic view of the Steinhude Sea Recreational Facility observation tower and café.

FIGURE 19.9. Zira Island features biophilic architecture: the buildings look like seven mountain peaks in Azerbaijan.

FIGURE 19.10. A PV solar roof filters light into Masdar City's center.

dry climate and a vision for a life beyond oil, it has been referred to as the "oasis of the future" (see figure 19.10). Key goals include carbon neutrality, 100 percent renewable energy utilization, 50 percent water and waste reduction, and a dynamic and modern, pedestrian-oriented social center for a new community.

In the Caspian Sea, off Azerbaijan, the architecture firm BIG has developed a master plan for Zira Island, nearly 11 million square feet of mixed-use spaces, including recreation, culture, and residential. The buildings are being designed to be reminiscent of the seven famous peaks of Azerbaijan, as seen in figure 19.9, creating diverse ecological zones connected by a central valley between buildings. Zira Island will be self-sufficient in water and energy. Heat pumps connected to the Caspian Sea will provide heating and cooling; power will be provided by offshore wind combined with solar thermal and PV. Wastewater and rainwater will be cleaned and reused.[30]

MODEL SUSTAINABLE CITIES

Today several models for sustainable cities are emerging. In the warmer climate of Brazil, Curitiba, with 1.7 million people, is considered among the greenest cities in the world. With almost no budget, former mayor Jaime Lerner and his successors left a sustainable legacy by creating a renewable urban environment

FIGURE 19.11. Aerial view of Hammarby Sjöstad's mixed-use development integrated with waterfront and nature.

over the last forty years. Work began in 1972 with the creation of a pedestrian street. At a cost of 1 percent of a subway system, a mass transit system with articulated three-section buses was then added so that no point in the city is more than 1,200 feet from a bus stop. Green space—with sheep for grass mowing—was increased tenfold since the planning began in the 1960s, and innovative strategies improved the quality of housing. GDP per person is 60 percent higher than average for Brazil.

Stockholm, too, has been called one of the most sustainable cities. It has one of the largest district heating and energy systems in the world and a strong focus on waste and energy systems. It is also converting an old industrial area and harbor into a modern neighborhood, Hammarby Sjöstad (see figure 19.11), with an eventual population of over 25,000 people, plus workplace and supporting community amenities. Goals for Hammarby Sjöstad, expected to be fully built by 2015, include decontaminating polluted soils, conserving nature, adding new green public spaces, and encouraging healthy lifestyles. Rail, ferries, and carpooling will minimize transportation-related energy consumption. Buildings will be built to high-performance

standards and will use solar energy. There will be solid waste and wastewater energy recovery, as well as district heating, cooling, and power. Energy consumption is projected to be cut in half over similar recent developments in Stockholm. This is a leading example of large-scale integrated urban design and long-range planning.

Fukuoka, a Japanese city of over 1.4 million inhabitants, needed a new office and civic building with exhibition hall, museum, conference facilities, retail, and parking. To meet the project requirements for a building larger than 1 million square feet, it was proposed that about half of the 5-acre Tenjin park in the heart of the city be eliminated. The architect, Emilio Ambasz and Associates, proposed a fifteen-story building with lush, green step garden roofs cascading down (see figure 19.12). Not only is this reminiscent of a mountain connecting to a park but it helps mitigate the loss of park space. In addition to providing space for relaxation, meditation, and views of the bay of Fukuoka and surrounding mountains, it includes over 35,000 plants representing seventy-six species and provides habitat for birds and natural systems. Since construction, birds have brought over

FIGURE 19.12. The step gardens cascade to the central park at the heart of Fukuoka, Japan.

forty new varieties of plants and over 10,000 new plants to the garden.[31] The large plantings keep the roof temperature about 27 °F lower than surrounding roofs and reduce CO_2 impacts.[32] New gardens and atrium spaces open to the public (and nature) offer a compelling vision of how we can build places that bring an enhanced quality of life to people and ecosystems.

Leaders and citizens in the city of Hamburg are taking action to improve their quality of life and reduce their carbon footprint on a 13.5 square mile district with 55,000 people through reduced energy consumption and increased local renewable energy production. To do this they plan to produce enough renewable power to provide all electric needs by 2025 and all heating demand by 2050. They are experimenting with new technologies, including building to Passive House standards.

A core part of Hamburg's plan involves establishing five decentralized district heating networks. One district is proposing to use renewable energy, including solar thermal, waste industrial heat, a wood chip boiler, and a biomethane cogeneration (CHP) plant. This district will provide heat to around 3,000 homes and electricity to over 1,000. Another heating district is investigating

geothermal energy using 10,000-foot-deep geothermal wells. Yet another district heating network has put forward a community energy association with a grid approach allowing for power to be fed in or out by users or supplied by a central plant. In the city's Elbe Island district, the Energy Hill project (see figure 19.13) is turning a former landfill into an energy park that will power 4,000 households—20 percent of homes in the district—by capturing and using landfill gases, erecting two 3.4 MW wind turbines, and installing a PV array that covers 2.47 acres.[33]

When we hear of China's energy-related issues, the news is often bleak. It is one of the largest producers of greenhouse gases, its residents endure extremely poor urban air quality, and pollution in general is a tremendous problem. The nation is rapidly developing coal plants and acquiring oil and gas fields globally. Simultaneously, though, China has taken steps toward a renewable, ecological future. It is a leader in large-scale wind and solar energy development, and it is beginning to take pollution seriously and address it.

China is building and rebuilding cities at a scale that is unprecedented in human evolution. Entire cities are currently

being designed and built to accommodate populations well over 1 million. It has been estimated that 70 percent of China's population will be living in an urban environment by 2050. To anticipate this influx of people, China is adopting a more integrative and ecological approach to city design and planning as a way to rethink how people engage in complex and richly populated environments. For many years, China has accepted sustainability as a sound strategy for future planning, and they are looking to push the boundaries to develop new models of sustainable urbanism, creating cities that function as true, healthy ecological systems.

Tianjin Eco-city is one example of sustainable urbanism in China that looks to be practicable, replicable, and scalable. When fully completed around 2020, it will be home to 350,000 residents. Its vision is to be "a thriving city which is socially harmonious, environmentally friendly and resource efficient."[34] At the core of the master plan is an eco-city concept with a network of rivers, canals, and a lake for recreation and wildlife. Vegetative corridors will act like a green lung for the city. The urban fabric will be composed of eco-cell modules to form a city center network with smaller neighborhoods and larger districts. Key performance indicators provide quantitative and qualitative ecological, social, and economic metrics.

As diverse as these examples are, they represent just some of the trends emerging to create societies that live within natural flows and cycles and to restore vibrant and healthy human and ecological communities. Net zero buildings are just part of the way forward. Future generations demand that we all think of the larger community, including cities, regions, and countries, every time any of us plan or build a new home, workplace, or community space. The net zero path is a journey we all need to follow for the sake of our children and their children.

NOTES

CHAPTER 1: ENERGY IN TRANSITION

1. *American Anthropologist* 45, 3, part 1 (July–September 1943), 335.

2. International World History Project, "The Neolithic Transition," accessed September 26, 2013, http://history-world.org/neolithic1.htm.

3. Amory Lovins, *Reinventing Fire: Bold Business Solutions for the New Energy Era* (White River Junction, VT: Chelsea Green Publishing, 2011), 119.

4. "Building Energy Data Book," US Department of Energy, updated 2010, accessed September 24, 2013, http://buildingsdatabook.eere.energy.gov/ChapterIntro1.aspx.

5. Lovins, *Reinventing Fire*, 4.

6. Millennium Ecosystem Assessment, *Ecosystems and Human Well-Being: Our Human Planet—Summary for Decision Makers* (Washington, DC: Island Press, 2005).

7. Robert Costanza, Ralph d'Arge, Rudolf de Groot, Stephen Farber, Monica Grasso, Bruce Hannon, Karin Limburg, Shahid Naeem, Robert V. O'Neill, Jose Paruelo, Robert G. Raskin, Paul Sutton, and Marjan van den Belt. "The Value of the World's Ecosystem Services and Natural Capital," *Nature* 387 (15 May 1997), 253.

8. Paul Hawkins, Amory Lovins, and L. Hunter Lovins, *Natural Capitalism: Creating Industrial Revolution* (New York: Little, Brown and Company, 1999).

9. Gerhard Knies, "Global Energy and Climate Security through Solar Power from Deserts," Trans-Mediterranean Renewable Energy Cooperation (TREC), July 2006, 1.

10. "About the Solar Office," US Department of Energy: Sunshot Initiative, accessed September 25, 2013, http://www1.eere.energy.gov/solar/sunshot/about.html.

11. International Energy Agency, *PVPS Report: A Snapshot of Global PV 1992-2012* (Paris: IEA, 2013), 5.

12. Todd Woody, "Wind Power Now Competitive with Coal in Some Regions," Grist.org, accessed September 26, 2013, http://grist.org/article/2011-02-07-report-wind-power-now-competitive-with-coal-in-some-regions/.

13. Global Wind Energy Council, *Global Wind Statistics: 2012* (Brussels: GWEC, 2013), 2.

14. Stacy C. Davis, Susan W. Diegel, and Robert G. Boundy, *Transportation Energy Data Book*, edition 32, produced by Oak Ridge National Laboratory for the US Department of Energy's Office of Energy Efficiency and Renewable Energy (2013), 2–3.

15. Timothy Searchinger, Ralph Heimlich, R. A. Houghton, Fengxia Dong, Amani Elobeid, Jacinto Fabiosa, Simla Tokgoz, Dermot Hayes, and Tun-Hsiang Yu, "Use of US Croplands for Biofuels Increases Greenhouse Gases through Emissions from Land-Use Change," *Science* 319 (29 February 2008), 1238.

16. David J. Murphy, Charles A. S. Hall, and Bobby Powers, "New Perspectives on the Energy Return on (Energy) Investment (EROI) of Corn Ethanol," *Environment, Development and Sustainability* 13 (2011), 179–202.

17. Eviana Hartman, "A Promising Oil Alternative: Algae Energy," *Washington Post*, January 6, 2008, http://www.washingtonpost.com/wp-dyn/content/article/2008/01/03/AR2008010303907.html.

18. Peter H. Diamandis and Steven Kotler, *Abundance: The Future Is Better Than You Think* (New York: Free Press, 2012), 163.

19. Joint Center for Artificial Photosynthesis, "Overview," accessed September 27, 2013, http://solarfuelshub.org/about/.

20. Joseph Tainter, *The Collapse of Complex Societies (New Studies in Archaeology)* (Cambridge, United Kingdom: Cambridge University Press, 1988), 91.

21. Albert Einstein Site Online, accessed January 8, 2012, http://www.alberteinsteinsite.com/quotes/.

CHAPTER 2: DEFINING THE NEW NET ZERO

1. American Society of Heating, Refrigerating and Air-Conditioning Engineers, *ASHRAE Vision 2020*, ASHRAE Vision 2020 Ad Hoc Committee, 2007, https://www.ashrae.org/about-ashrae/strategic-planning-documents.

2. "Steering Through the Maze #2, Nearly Zero Energy Buildings: Achieving the EU 2020 Target," European Council for an Energy Efficient Economy, February 2011, 6.

3. National Renewable Energy Laboratory, *Net-Zero Energy Buildings: A Classification System Based on Renewable Energy Supply Options*, Technical Report, NREL/TP-550-44586, June 2010.

4. "Living Building Challenge Net-Zero Energy Building Certification," accessed August 7, 2013, http://living-future.org/node/188/#net.

5. "Living Building Challenge Net-Zero Energy Footnotes," accessed August 7, 2013, http://living-future.org/node/212.

6. See the US Environmental Protection Agency, Green Power Partnership, for more information on PPAs, http://www.epa.gov/greenpower/buygp/solarpower.htm, or the US Department of Energy, Energy Efficiency and Renewable Energy, On-Site Renewable Power Purchase Agreements, https://www1.eere.energy.gov/femp/financing/power_purchase_agreements.html.

7. See the US Environmental Protection Agency, Green Power Partnership, for more information on RECs, http://www.epa.gov/greenpower/gpmarket/rec.htm.

8. See the US Energy Information Administration, *Commercial Buildings Energy Consumption Survey*, 2003, http://www.eia.gov/consumption/commercial/, and the US Department of Energy, *Building Energy Data Book* 2012, http://buildingsdatabook.eere.energy.gov/ChapterIntro1.aspx, for more information.

9. Paul Torcellini, Shanti Pless, and M. Deru, *Zero Energy Buildings: A Critical Look at the Definition*, Conference Paper NREL/TP-550-39833, June 2006.

10. National Renewable Energy Laboratory, *The Design-Build Process for the Research Support Facility*, presented at the 2011 Sustainable Operations Summit, http://www.nrel.gov/docs/fy12osti/51387.pdf.

11. National Renewable Energy Laboratory, *NREL's Research Support Facility: An Energy Performance Update*, Commercial Buildings Research Group, December 2011, http://www.nrel.gov/sustainable_nrel/pdfs/rsf_operations.pdf.

12. M. Deru and P. Torcellini, *Source Energy and Emission Factors for Energy Use in Buildings*, Technical Report NREL/TP-550-38617, revised June 2007.

13. Environmental Protection Agency, *Unit Conversions, Emissions Factors, and Other Reference Data*, November 2004, http://www.epa.gov/appdstar/pdf/brochure.pdf; Energy Information Administration, *Updated State- and Regional-level Greenhouse Gas Emission Factors for Electricity* (March 2002), accessed from http://www.eia.gov/oiaf/1605/ee-factors.html.

14. EIA, *Updated State-and Regional-level Greenhouse Gas Emission Factors for Electricity*.

15. American Institute of Architects, "AIA/COTE Top Ten Green Projects, 2007," accessed August 6, 2013, http://www2.aiatopten.org/hpb/energy.cfm?ProjectID=946.

CHAPTER 3: THE ROOTS OF NET ZERO DESIGN

1. Le Corbusier, *Towards a New Architecture* (New York: Dover, 1986).

2. N. J. Habraken, *The Structure of the Ordinary: Form and Control in the Built Environment* (Cambridge, MA: MIT Press, 2000), 7.

3. For more information, see Stephen Kellert, Judith Heerwagon, and Martin Mador, *Biophilic Design: The Theory, Science, and Practice of Bringing Buildings to Life* (New Jersey: John Wiley & Sons, 2008); E. O. Wilson, *Biophilia* (Cambridge, MA: Harvard University Press, 1984); Stephen Kellert, *Biophilic Design: The Architecture of Life*, produced by Bill Finnegan (Burlington, VT: Tamarack Media, 2011), DVD; Stephen Kellert, *Building for Life: Designing and Understanding the Human-Nature Connection* (Washington, DC: Island Press, 2005).

4. Roger S. Ulrich, "Health Benefits of Gardens in Hospitals," paper presented at the Plants for People conference, International Exhibition Floriade, The Netherlands, 2002.

5. Janine M. Benyus, *Biomimicry: Innovation Inspired by Nature* (New York: HarperCollins, 1997).

6. Lynne Peeples, "The Secret Right under Our (Bottle)noses: What Dolphins Can Teach Us about Hydrodynamics," *Scientific American*, June 29, 2009, http://www.scientificamerican.com/blog/post.cfm?id=the-secret-right-under-our-bottleno-2009-06-29; Paul W. Weber, Laurens E. Howle, Mark M. Murray, and Frank E. Fish, "Lift and Drag Performance of Odontocete Cetacean Flippers," *Journal of Experimental Biology* 212 (2009): 2149–2158.

7. "Learning from Lotus Plants How to Clean without Cleaners," *Biomimicry* 3.8, accessed August 21, 2013, http://biomimicry.net/about/biomimicry/case-examples/natural-cleaning/.

8. "Building Insulation," *Ecovative*, accessed August 21, 2013, http://www.ecovativedesign.com/products-and-applications/insulation/.

9. "Eastgate Development Harare," Mick Pearce Official Website, accessed August 21, 2013, http://www.mickpearce.com/works/office-public-buildings/eastgate-development-harare/.

10. William McDonough, *Cradle to Cradle: Remaking the Way We Make Things* (New York: North Point Press, 2002).

11. "About Eco-Machines," John Todd Ecological Design, accessed August 22, 2013, http://www.toddecological.com/eco-machines/.

12. "Regenerative Design," Regenesis Group, accessed August 22, 2013, http://www.regenesisgroup.com/RegenerativeDevelopment.

13. For more information, see the US Green Building Council website: http://www.usgbc.org/leed.

14. International Living Futures Institute, *Living Building Challenge 2.1: A Visionary Path to a Restorative Future* (Seattle, WA: ILFI, 2012), 5.

15. Oberlin Environmental Studies Program, "Design Philosophy: Home," accessed August 22, 2013, http://buildingdashboard.net/oberlin/ajlc/#/oberlin/ajlc/.

16. "Bullitt Center," Miller Hull Partnership, accessed August 2013, http://www.millerhull.com/html/nonresidential/Bullitt.htm.

17. Franklin Becker and Fritz Steele, *Workplace by Design: Mapping the High-Performance Workspace* (San Francisco: Jossey-Bass, 1995), 6.

18. Jane Jacobs, *Death and Life of Great American Cities* (New York: Random House, 1992), 50.

19. Humberto Maturana and Francisco Varela, *Autopoiesis and Cognition: The Realization of the Living* (Dordrecht, The Netherlands: D. Reidel, 1980), 78.

20. N. John Habraken's website, accessed August 22, 2013, http://www.habraken.org; Francis Duffy, "Measuring Building Performance," *Facilities* 8, 5 (1990): 17–20.

21. Stewart Brand, *How Buildings Learn: What Happens After They're Built* (New York: Viking, 1994).

22. Ibid., 13.

23. Brand, *How Buildings Learn: What Happens After They're Built*, 13.

24. Ibid.

25. For more information on these projects, visit: http://architecture.mit.edu/house_n/ and http://www.openprototype.com/.

CHAPTER 4: INTEGRATED DESIGN FUNDAMENTALS

1. Walter T. Grondzik , Alison G. Kwok, Benjamin Stein, and John S. Reynolds, *Mechanical and Electrical Equipment for Buildings* (Hoboken, NJ: John Wiley and Sons, 2011), 153.

2. Heating degree days can use different base numbers and calculation methods. Depending on the detail of data available for a site, half-hour increments can be used to determine the HDD for the site. For our calculations, we assume 65°F as the standard temperature measurement and use the daily average temperature compared to 65°F to determine the HDD for one day. These are then summed for an annual number of HDD65 for a specific site.

3. Smartphone software that predicts the solar access of a site will continue to improve. For more information on smartphone applications, see George Musser's blog post, "20 Solar Apps for Your iPhone," *Scientific American*, August 1, 2011, http://blogs.scientificamerican.com/solar-at-home/2011/08/01/20-solar-apps-for-your-iphone/.

4. Gaëtan Masson, Marie Latour, and Daniele Biancardi, *Global Market Outlook for Photovoltaics until 2016* (Brussels: European Photovoltaic Industry Association, 2013), 42.

5. "The Center of Chacoan Culture," National Park Service, accessed August 16, 2013, www.nps.gov/chcu/historyculture/index.htm.

6. "Circadian Rhythms Fact Sheet," National Institute of General Medical Sciences, last reviewed June 12, 2013, http://www.nigms.nih.gov/Education/Factsheet_CircadianRhythms.htm.

7. Anjali Joseph, "The Impact of Light on Outcomes in Healthcare Setting," (Concord, MA: Center for Health Design, 2006).

8. Ben Stein, "Do White LEDs Disrupt Our Biological Clocks?" *Inside Science*, October 14, 2011, http://www.insidescience.org/content/do-white-leds-disrupt-our-biological-clocks/679.

9. Andrew Pressman, ed., *Architectural Graphic Standards*, 11th ed. (Hoboken, NJ: John Wiley and Sons, 2007), 476.

10. See the most recent *Lighting Handbook* by the Illuminating Engineering Society publication for current light level standards, available from http://www.ies.org/.

11. Edward Allen and Joseph Iano, *The Architect's Studio Companion: Rules of Thumb for Preliminary Design*, 5th ed. (Hoboken, NJ: John Wiley and Sons, 2012), 155.

12. There are many computer-modeling software programs being developed for daylighting analysis that work with different building information modeling software, as listed in Grondzik et al., *Mechanical and Electrical Equipment for Buildings*, 1735. Additionally, Autodesk has described some of the current options at http://sustainabilityworkshop.autodesk.com/buildings/daylight-analysis-bim. For a comparison of performance from different programs, see a paper by H. Bryan and S. M. Autif, "Lighting/Daylighting Analysis: A Comparison," School of Architecture, Arizona State University, 2002. Additional information is available from Grondzik et al., *Mechanical and Electrical Equipment for Buildings*, 610. Physical model testing can be very informative for designers and clients, see Grondzik et al., *Mechanical and Electrical Equipment for Buildings*, 621. For a sample of information for physical model construction, see Pacific Energy Center, "Daylight Model Construction and Analysis," accessed September 16, 2013, http://www.pge.com/includes/docs/pdfs/about/edusafety/training/pec/inforesource/daylighting_photometry.pdf.

13. Grondzik et al., *Mechanical and Electrical Equipment for Buildings*, 105.

14. Victor Olgyay, in his classic book *Design with Climate: Bioclimatic Approach to Architectural Realism* (Princeton, NJ: Princeton University Press, 1973), offers numerous design strategies to optimize cross-ventilation and stack ventilation.

15. P. Torcellini, R. Judkoff, and S. Hayter, "Zion National Park Visitor Center: Significant Energy Savings Achieved through a Whole-Building Design Process," National Renewable Energy Laboratory, conference paper for American Council for an Energy-Efficient Economy Summer Study on Energy Efficiency in Buildings, 2002. Accessed September 16, 2013, www.nrel.gov/docs/fy02osti/32157.pdf.

16. Ibid.

17. Alex Wilson, "The Folly of Building-Integrated Wind," BuildingGreen, accessed August 16, 2013, http://www.buildinggreen.com/auth/article.cfm/2009/4/29/The-Folly-of-Building-Integrated-Wind/.

18. Agriculture-based pellets are not viable in many situations as they require special burners and a very detailed maintenance procedure. Though agricultural-based pellets should be discussed in the context of biomass options, the viability of their use requires a much more complicated investigation than we will undertake in the context of this book.

CHAPTER 5: INTEGRATED DESIGN PROCESS

1. An excellent source for more in-depth information about the integrated design process is 7group and Bill Reed, *The Integrative Design Guide to Green Building* (Hoboken, NJ: John Wiley and Sons, 2009).

2. Tony Buzan has written many books on mind mapping; for more information see his series, beginning with *The Mind Map Book: How to Use Radiant Thinking to Maximize Your Brain's Untapped Potential* (London: BBC Books, 1993).

3. National Institute of Building Sciences, "NIBS Guideline 3-2012: Building Enclosure Commissioning Process BECx," April 2012, www.wbdg.org/ccb/NIBS/nibs_gl3.pdf; American Society of Heating, Refrigerating and Air-Conditioning Engineers, "ASHRAE Guideline 0-2005, The Commissioning Process," 2005, https://www.ashrae.org/File%20Library/docLib/Certification/Guidebooks/Commissioning-Process-Management-Professional-Long.pdf.

4. Marc Rosenbaum, "Zero-net Possible? Yes! Energy Performance of Eight Homes at Eliakim's Way," South Mountain Company, created June 16, 2011, http://www.energysmiths.com/resources/documents/EliakimsEnergyMediaReportFullwCopyrightv2.pdf.

PUTNEY FIELD HOUSE CASE STUDY

1. American Society of Heating, Refrigerating and Air-Conditioning Engineers, "ANSI/ASHRAE/IESNA Addendum r to ANSI/ASHRAE/IESNA Standard 90.1-2007 (Appendix G)," *Energy Standard for Buildings Except Low-Rise Residential Buildings* (Atlanta, GA: ASHRAE, 2009).

CHAPTER 6: THE PRINCIPLES FOR NET ZERO BUILDING ENCLOSURES

1. For greater investigation of building science, refer to the research and work by Building Science Corporation at http://www.buildingscience.com/.

2. "How R-Value Is Calculated," BuildingGreen, August 1, 2011, http://www.buildinggreen.com/auth/article.cfm/2011/7/1/How-R-Value-Is

3. John Straube, "BSD-011: Thermal Control in Buildings," Building Science Corporation, available at http://www.buildingscience.com/documents/digests/bsd-011-thermal-control-in-buildings.

4. For additional information, see "Info-502: Temperature Dependence of R-values in Polyisocyanurate Roof Insulation," April 11, 2014, Building Science Corporation, available at http://www.buildingscience.com/documents/information-sheets/info-502-temperature-dependent-r-value. Also, see "Info-502: Temperature Dependence of R-values in Polyisocyanurate Roof Insulation," April 11, 2014, Building Science Corporation, available at http://www.buildingscience.com/documents/information-sheets/info-502-temperature-dependent-r-value.

5. John Straube, "RR-901: Thermal Metrics for High-Performance Enclosure Walls: The Limitations of R-Value," Building Science Press, 2009, available at http://www.buildingscience.com/documents/reports/rr-0901-thermal-metrics-high-performance-walls-limitations-r-value.

6. For more information on air barriers, see Joseph Lstiburek, "BSD-104: Understanding Air Barriers," Building Science Corporation, available at http://www.buildingscience.com/documents/digests/bsd-104-understanding-air-barriers.

7. Joseph Lstiburek, "BSD-106: Understanding Vapor Barriers," Building Science Corporation, available at http://www.buildingscience.com/documents/digests/bsd-106-understanding-vapor-barriers .

8. John Straube and Eric Burnett, *Building Science for Building Enclosures* (Westford, MA: Building Science Press, 2005), 450–458.

9. Joseph Lstiburek, "RR-0412: Insulations, Sheathings and Vapor Retarders," 4, Building Science Corporation, available at http://www.buildingscience.com/documents/reports/rr-0412-insulations-sheathings-and-vapor-retarders.

10. For more information on windows, see Alex Wilson of Building Green's article "The Revolution of Window Performance—Part One," March 20, 2012, http://www2.buildinggreen.com/blogs/revolution-window-performance-part-one.

11. For more information on NAFS and to access the 2011 standard, see http://www.aamanet.org/upload/file/CMB-5-11.pdf.

12. Passive House windows require additional performance numbers to accurately account for thermal performance, which are not listed in the NAFS or the NFRC. A list is currently being developed by Passive House US For more information, see http://www.passivehouse.us/passiveHouse/CertifiedWindowData.html.

13. For additional information, see John Straube, "BSD-163: Controlling Cold-Weather Condensation Using Insulation," Building Science Corporation, available at http://www.buildingscience.com/documents/digests/bsd-controlling-cold-weather-condensation-using-insulation.

14. Lstiburek, "Insulations, Sheathings and Vapor Retarders."

CHAPTER 7: THE ESSENTIAL ELEMENTS OF NET ZERO BUILDINGS

1. US Department of Energy, *Buildings Energy Data Book* (October 2010), table 1.3.1; http://buildingsdatabook.eren.doe.gov/TableView.aspx?table=1.3.1.

2. Typical existing building EUI numbers are sourced from the 2009 *Buildings Energy Data Book* (tables 2.1.11 and 3.1.13), published by the US Department of Energy and updated periodically.

3. "Office Workers Spend Too Much Time at Their Desks, Experts Say," *Science Daily*, January 15, 2012, http://www.sciencedaily.com/releases/2012/01/120113210203.htm.

4. Christopher K. Wilkinds and Mohammad H. Hosni, "Plug Load Design Factors," *ASHRAE Technical Journal*, May 2011.

5. For more information, see Edward Mazria, *The Passive Solar Energy Book* (Emmaus, PA: Rodale Press, 1979). In addition, the National Renewable Energy Lab has an online program called PV Watts, which will determine PV production for your location, array orientation, tilt angle, and panel efficiency. Visit: http://www.nrel.gov/rredc/pvwatts/.

6. Andy Walker, "Solar Water Heating," Whole Building Design Guide, August 24, 2012, http://www.wbdg.org/resources/swheating.php.

CHAPTER 15: THE CASE FOR RENOVATION

1. New Building Institute, *A Case Study for Deep Savings: 11 Case Studies of Deep Energy Retrofits in support of NEEA's Existing Building Renewal Initiative and NBI's Getting to 50 Work* (September 2011), 3.

2. "Architecture 2030 Will Change the Way You Look at Buildings," Architecture 2030, accessed August 22, 2013, http://architecture2030.org/the_problem/buildings_problem_why.

3. US Department of Energy, *2009 Building Energy Data Book* (Silver Springs, MD: D&R International, Ltd, 2009), pg 1–29.

4. "Architecture 2030 Will Change the Way You Look at Buildings," Architecture 2030.

5. "By 2035 Approximately 75% of the Built Environment Will Either Be New or Renovated," Architecture 2030, accessed August 22, 2013, http://architecture2030.org/the_solution/buildings_solution_how.

6. Edward Allen and Joseph Iano, *Fundamentals of Building Construction: Materials and Methods* (Hoboken, NJ: John Wiley and Sons, Inc., 2009).

7. P. Reppe and S. Blanchard, "Life Cycle Analysis of a Residential Home, Report 1998-5," Center for Sustainable Systems, University of Michigan, 1998; R. Cole and P. Kernan, "Life-cycle Energy Use in Buildings," *Building & Environment*, Vol. 31, No. 4 (1996), 307–317.

8. Data from University of Bath, Inventory of Carbon and Energy (ICE), Version 16.a, Prof. Geoff Hammond and Craig Jones, www.bath.ac.uk/mech-eng/sert/embodied.

9. For more information, see Joseph Lstiburek, "BSI-047: Thick as a Brick," Building Science Corporation, created March 15, 2011, http://www.buildingscience.com/documents/insights/bsi-047-thick-as-brick?topic=doctypes/insights.

10. For additional resources, Building Science Corporation has substantial research available on their website. http://www.buildingscience.com/index_html.

11. For more information, visit Kimberley Quirk, Energy Emporium, "78 Main St-Renovation," http://energyemp.com/78-main-st-renovation/.

12. Kimberley Quirk, "ZEB in a Historic Shell: 78 Main Street, Enfield, NH" (presentation at the Northeast Sustainable Energy Association Building Energy 12, Boston, MA, March 6–8, 2012).

13. Eric Harrington and Cara Carmichael, "Project Case Study: Empire State Building," Rocky Mountain Institute: RetroFit and RMI Initiative, 2009, http://www.rmi.org/Content/Files/ESBCaseStudy.pdf, 1.

14. Ibid.

15. The kBtu/sf-yr calculations are based on energy reduction percentages as shown in the "True Stories: Empire State Building, New York," Rocky Mountain Institute, Presentation Case Study, accessed August 27, 2013, http://www.rmi.org/PDF_retrofit_true_stories_empire_state_building_overview_deck.

16. Molly Miller, "Project Case Study: Byron Rogers," Rocky Mountain Institute: RetroFit, an RMI Initiative, 2009, http://www.rmi.org/Content/Files/ByronRogersCaseStudy.pdf, 1.

CHAPTER 16: THE CASE FOR NET ZERO HOMES

1. National Association of Home Builders, *Housing Facts, Figures and Trends* (Washington, DC: NAHB Public Affairs and NAHB Economics, 2006), 14.

2. "Affordable Zero Energy Home Construction, an interview with Carter Scott," Zero Net Energy Homes, posted August 2, 2012, http://www.zerohomes.org/2012/08/02/affordable-zero-energy-home-construction-an-interview-with-carter-scott/#sthash.NhgsWf4s.dpuf.

3. Martin Holliday, "Just Two Minisplits Heat and Cool Whole House," Green Building Advisor, created on August 17, 2012, http://www.greenbuildingadvisor.com/blogs/dept/musings/just-two-minisplits-heat-and-cool-whole-house.

4. For more information, visit http://thousandhomechallenge.com/.

5. For more information, visit http://unityhomes.com/ and http://bensonwood.com/.

CHAPTER 17: WHY THE COST IS RIGHT

1. For detailed assessment of these costs, see Amory Lovins, *Reinventing Fire*.

2. Data updated from "US Crude Oil First Purchase Price (Dollars per Barrel)," Energy Information Administration, accessed August 27, 2013, http://www.eia.gov/dnav/pet/hist/LeafHandler.ashx?n=PET&s=F000000_3&f=A.

3. All fuel rates are adjusted to 2012 dollars and use 2000 as the price comparison. Fuel price data from Energy Information Administration, "US Crude Oil First Purchase Price (Dollars per Barrel)," Accessed August 23, 2013, http://www.eia.gov/dnav/pet/hist/LeafHandler.ashx?n=PET&s=F000000_3&f=A.

4. Greg Kats, et al., *The Costs and Financial Benefits of Green Buildings: A Report to California's Sustainable Building Task Force*, Capital E (October 2003), 55.

5. Ibid., ix.

6. Carnegie Mellon University Advanced Building Systems Integration Consortium, "High Performance Lighting," accessed August 30, 2013, http://cbpd.arc.cmu.edu/ebids/pages/strategy.aspx?group=3&strategy=1.

7. Martin Melaver and Phyllis Mueller, ed. *The Green Building Bottom Line: The Real Cost of Sustainable Building* (New York: McGraw Hill, 2009), 205.

8. Ibid., 207.

9. Heschong Mahone Group, "Daylight and Retail Sales." (Fair Oaks, CA: California Board for Energy Efficiency, 2003).

10. Joseph J. Romm and William D. Browning, *Greening the Building and the Bottom Line: Increasing Productivity Through Energy-Efficient Design* (Snowmass, CO: Rocky Mountain Institute, 1998), 4.

11. Ibid.

12. Olivier, David, *Energy Efficiency and Renewables: Recent Experience on Mainland Europe* (Herefordshire, England: Energy Advisory Associates, 1992), 27–28.

13. Brenda Vale and Robert Vale, *Green Architecture: Design for an Energy Conscious Future* (Boston: Little Brown, 1991), 156-168.

14. Romm and Browning, *Greening the Building and the Bottom Line*, 12.

15. Melaver and Mueller, ed. *The Green Building Bottom Line*, 206.

16. Greg Kats, *Greening Our Built World: Costs, Benefits, and Strategies* (Washington, DC: Island Press, 2010), 10.

17. Hal Levin is the editor of BuildingEcology.com, a resource for articles and research on indoor air quality for sustainable buildings; "Indoor Air Facts No. 4: Sick Building Syndrome," United States Environmental Protection Agency, Research and Development (February 1991), accessed August, 2013, http://www.epa.gov/iaq/pubs/sbs.html.

18. Kats, *Greening Our Built World*, 50.

19. Roger S. Ulrich, "Recovery from Surgery," *Science* 224 (1984): 420.

20. Kats, *Greening Our Built World*, 75.

21. Heschong Mahone Group, *Daylighting in Schools: An Investigation into the Relationship Between Daylighting and Human Performance* (San Francisco: Pacific Gas and Electric Company, 1999), 3.

22. Ibid., 4.

23. Heschong Mahone Group, *Re-Analysis Report, Daylighting in Schools*, California Energy Commission (New Buildings Institute, 2001).

24. Romm and Browning, *Greening the Building and the Bottom Line*, 11.

25. Alex Wilson, "Resilient Design—Smarter Building for a Turbulent Future," *Environmental Building News*, 21:3, March 1, 2012, http://www.buildinggreen.com/auth/article.cfm/2012/2/28/Resilient-Design-Smarter-Building-for-a-Turbulent-Future/.

26. Kats, *Greening Our Built World*, 48.

27. Jerry Yudelson, *Green Building Through Integrated Design* (New York: McGraw-Hill, 2009), 139.

28. National Association of Realtors, "Green MLS Tool Kit," accessed August 30, 2013, http://www.greenthemls.org/.

29. Nadav Malin, "Non-Green Office Buildings Sacrifice 8% in Rent Revenues," Buildinggreen.com, November 9, 2010, http://www.buildinggreen.com/auth/article.cfm/2010/11/9/Non-Green-Office-Buildings-Sacrifice-8-in-Rent-Revenues/.

30. McGraw Hill Construction, "Green Outlook 2009" (New York: McGraw-Hill Construction, 2008).

31. Jeff Martin, Brian Swett, and Doug Wein, "Residential Green Building: Identifying Latent Demand and Key Drivers for Sector Growth" (Master's thesis, University of Michigan, Ross School of Business, 2007).

32. Martin, Swett, and Wein, 2007.

33. Martin, Swett, and Wein, 2007.

34. Yudelson, *Green Building Through Integrated Design*, 96.

35. Tom Hootman, *Net Zero Energy Design: A Guide for Commercial Architecture* (Hoboken, NJ: John Wiley and Sons, 2013), 343.

36. "Green Buildings and Homes," City of Chicago, accessed August 29, 2013, http://www.cityofchicago.org/city/en/progs/env/green_buildings_andhomes.html.

37. Arthur H. Rosenfeld, Joseph J. Room, Hashem Akbari, and Alan C. Lloyd, "Painting the Town White—and Green." *MIT Technology Review*, February/March 1997, 5.

38. Hashem Akbari and Arthur Rosenfeld, "White Roofs Cool the World, Directly Offset CO2 and Delay Global Warming," Lawrence Berkeley National Laboratory, Heat Island Group, November 2008, 10.

39. Kats, *Greening Our Built World*, 85.

40. Yudelson, *Green Building Through Integrated Design*, 115.

41. "Public Transportation Benefits," American Public Transportation Association, accessed September 9, 2013, http://www.apta.com/mediacenter/ptbenefits/Pages/default.aspx

42. "Public Transportation Benefits," APTA.

43. For more information and state-specific incentives visit DSIRE's website: http://www.dsireusa.org/.

44. For the specific requirements of this procedure see: Sieglinde K. Fuller and Stephen R. Petersen, *Life-Cycle Costing Manual: for the Federal Energy Management Program*, National Institute of Standards and Technology Handbook 135, (Gaithersburg, MD: Building and Fire Research Laboratory, Office of Applied Economics, 1995) or Thomas Hootman, *Net Zero Energy Design: A Guide for Commercial Architecture* (Hoboken, NJ: John Wiley and Sons, Inc. 2013), 335.

45. We usually use the Department of Energy Building Energy Databook for typical existing building EUIs.

CHAPTER 19: NET-ZERO COMMUNITIES AND BEYOND

1. For additional information on the US Energy sector see the US Energy Information Administration, *Electric Power Monthly: With Data for June 2013* (Washington, DC: US EIA, 2013), accessed August 23, 2013, http://www.eia.gov/electricity/monthly/pdf/epm.pdf.

2. Danish Energy Agency, "Energy Statistics, 2011: Data, Tables, Statistics and Map," (Danish Energy Agency, December 2012), 9.

3. Jens H. Larsen, *The World's Largest Off-Shore Windfarm, Middelgrunden 40 MW* (Copenhagen, Denmark: Copenhagen Environment and Energy Office, 2004), 33.

4. "Renewable Energy Sources 2010," Federal Ministry for the Environment, Nature Conservation and Nuclear Safety (March 23, 2011), 5.

5. "Development of renewable energy sources in Germany 2012," Federal Ministry for the Environment, Nature Conservation and Nuclear Safety, Version: February 2013), 3–4.

6. Brad Molnar, "Renewable Theology vs. Economic Reality, Part 2," created November 24, 2012, http://www.billingsnews.com/index.php/commentary/3991-renewable-theology-trumps-economic-reality.

7. Ron Pernick and Clint Wilder, *Clean Tech Nation: How the U.S. Can Lead in the New Global Economy* (New York: HarperCollins Publishers, 2012), 5.

8. David Biello, "100 Percent Renewable? One Danish Island Experiments with Clean Power [Slide Show]," Scientific American, last modified January 19, 2010, http://www.scientificamerican.com/article.cfm?id=samso-attempts-100-percent-renewable-power.

9. "Renewable Energy Island," Samsø Commerce and Visitor Center, accessed September 29, 2013, http://www.visitsamsoe.dk/en/oplevelser/vedvarende-energi-o/.

10. David Biello, "100 Percent Renewable?"; "Renewable Energy Island," Samsø Commerce and Visitor Center.

11. David Biello, "100 Percent Renewable?"

12. "Fossil Free Island: Objective 1," The Energy Academy on Samsø, accessed September 29, 2013, http://energiakademiet.dk/en/fossilfri-o/mal-1/.

13. Amory Lovins and Rocky Mountain Institute, *Reinventing Fire: Bold Business Solutions for the New Energy Era* (White River Junction, VT: Chelsea Green Publishing, 2011), 60.

14. Peter H. Diamandis and Steven Kotler, *Abundance: The Future Is Better Than You Think* (New York: Free Press, 2012), 163.

15. "Table 1. Rank by Population of the 100 Largest Urban Places, Listed Alphabetically by State: 1790–1990," US Census Bureau, retrieved August 23, 2013.

16. Green Renaissance of Western New York, "Urban Revitalization: What is going on today?" accessed August 28, 2013, http://growwny.org/issues/urban-revitalization.

17. PUSH Buffalo, "About Us: Mission Statement," accessed August 28, 2013, http://pushbuffalo.org/about-us.

18. For more information visit: City of Buffalo: Urban Homestead Program, http://www.ci.buffalo.ny.us/Home/City_Departments/RealEstate/UrbanHomesteadProgram.

19. Mira Heinze and Karsten Voss, "Goal: Zero Energy Building: Exemplary Experience Based on the Solar Estate, Solarsiedlung Freiburg am Schlierberg, Germany," *Journal of Green Building*, 4:4 (2009) 93-100, accessed August 28, 2013. doi: http://dx.doi.org/10.3992/jgb.4.4.93

20. "Google's Zero-Carbon Quest," CNNMoney, accessed December 5, 2013, http://tech.fortune.cnn.com/2012/07/12/google-zero-carbon/.

21. "Google Green: The Big Picture," Google, accessed December 10, 2013, http://www.google.com/green/bigpicture/.

22. "Google Green: Purchasing Clean Energy," Google, accessed January 22, 2014, http://www.google.com/green/energy/use/#purchasing.

23. "Renewable Energy," Walmart, accessed December 17, 2013, http://corporate.walmart.com/global-responsibility/environment-sustainability/renewable-energy.

24. "Walmart Targets Ambitious Renewable Energy, Energy Efficiency Standards By 2020," CleanTechnica.com, accessed December 17, 2013, http://cleantechnica.com/2013/04/23/walmart-targets-ambitious-renewable-energy-energy-efficiency-standards-by-2020/.

25. Joao Peixe, "Walmart: the next clean energy giant?" The Christian Science Monitor, created October 30, 2013, http://www.csmonitor.com/Environment/Energy-Voices/2013/1030/Walmart-the-next-clean-energy-giant.

26. Manitoba Hydro Place, "Energy Performance and Sustainable Design," accessed August 28, 2013, http://www.manitobahydroplace.com/Post-Occupancy-Performance/Performance/Detail/?rid=42.

27. KPMB Architects, "Manitoba Hydro Place," accessed August 28, 2013, http://www.kpmb.com/index.asp?navid=30&fid1=50&fid2=37&minyearx=&maxyearx=#desc.

28. Manitoba Hydro Place. "Energy Performance and Sustainable Design."

29. Mary Guzowski, *Towards Zero Energy Architecture: New Solar Design* (London: Lawrence King Publishing, 2010), 167.

30. Sergi Costa Duran and Julio Fajardo Herrero, *The Sourcebook of Contemporary Green Architecture* (New York: Collins Design, 2010), 577.

31. "About ACROS Fukuoka: Step Garden," accessed October 4, 2013, http://www.acros.or.jp/english/about/03.html#02.

32. Meili Gault, "ACROS Fukuoka's Step Garden," last modified October 15, 2009, http://www.greendesignetc.net/Nature_09/Nature_Gault_Meili_paper.pdf.

33. Uli Hellweg, Neil Veilleux, and Galen Nelson, "A German City Confronts Climate Change: IBA Hamburg's holistic plan for generating heat and electricity locally," *Northeast Sun* 31, no. 3 (Spring 2012): 9–13.

34. "Tianjin Eco-city: Background," Singapore Government, accessed October 4, 2013, http://www.tianjinecocity.gov.sg/bg_intro.htm.

RESOURCES

PART I

BOOKS AND ARTICLES

Alexander, C. *A Pattern Language*. Oxford: Oxford University Press, 1977.

Baer, Steve. *Sunspots: An Exploration of Solar Energy Through Fact and Fiction*. Seattle, WA: Cloudburst Press, 1975.

Becker, Franklin, and Fritz Steele. *Workplace by Design: Mapping the High-Performance Workspace*. San Francisco: Jossey-Bass Publishers, 1995.

Benyus, Janine M. *Biomimicry: Innovation Inspired by Nature*. New York: HarperCollins, 1997.

Bower, John. *Healthy House Building: A Design and Construction Guide*. Unionville, IN: The Healthy House Institute, 1993.

Brand, Stewart. *How Buildings Learn: What Happens After They're Built*. New York: Viking, 1994.

Butti, Ken, and John Perlin. *A Golden Thread: 2500 Years of Solar Architecture and Technology*. New York: Van Nostrand Reinhold Company, 1980.

Capra, Fritjof. *The Hidden Connections: Integrating the Biological, Cognitive, and Social Dimensions of Life into a Science of Sustainability*. New York: Doubleday, 2002.

Capra, Fritjof. *The Web of Life: A New Scientific Understanding of Living Systems*. New York: Doubleday, 1996.

Costanza, Robert, Ralph d'Arge, Rudolf de Groot, Stephen Farber, Monica Grasso, Bruce Hannon, Karin Limburg, Shahid Naeem, Robert V. O'Neill, Jose Paruelo, Robert G. Raskin, Paul Sutton, and Marjan van den Belt. "The Value of the World's Ecosystem Services and Natural Capital." *Nature* 387 (1997).

Denning, Peter J., and Robert Dunham. *The Innovator's Way: Essential Practices for Successful Innovation*. Cambridge, MA: The MIT Press, 2010.

Diamandis, Peter H., and Steven Kotler. *Abundance: The Future Is Better Than You Think*. New York: Free Press, 2012.

Diamond, Jared. *Collapse: How Societies Choose to Fail or Succeed*. New York: Penguin Group, 2005.

Egan, M. David. *Concepts in Thermal Comfort*. Englewood Cliffs, NJ: Prentice-Hall, Inc., 1975.

Gottfried, David. *Explosion Green: One Man's Journey to Green the World's Largest Industry*. New York: Morgan James Publishing, 2014.

Gould, James, and Carol Grant Gould. *Animal Architects: Building and the Evolution of Intelligence*. New York: Basic Books, 2007.

Habraken, N.J. *The Structure of the Ordinary: Form and Control in the Built Environment*. Cambridge, MA: MIT Press, 2000.

Hawken, Paul, Amory Lovins, and L. Hunter Lovins. *Natural Capitalism: Creating Industrial Revolution*. New York: Little, Brown and Company, 1999.

Heinberg, Richard. *Powerdown: Options and Actions for a Post-carbon World*. Gabriola Island, BC, Canada: New Society Publishers, 2004.

Heschong, Lisa. *Thermal Delight in Architecture*. Cambridge, MA: MIT Press, 1979.

International Living Future Institute. *Living Building Challenge 2.1: A Visionary Path to a Restorative Future*. Seattle, WA: ILFI, 2012.

Jacobs, Jane. *Death and Life of Great American Cities*. New York: Random House, 1992.

Johnson, Steven. *Emergence: The Connected Lives of Ants, Brains, Cities, and Software*. New York: Scribner, 2001.

Kellert, Stephen. *Building for Life: Designing and Understanding the Human-Nature Connection*. Washington, DC: Island Press, 2005.

Kellert, Stephen, Judith Heerwagen, and Martin Mador. *Biophilic Design: The Theory, Science, and Practice of Bringing Buildings to Life*. Hoboken, NJ: John Wiley & Sons, 2008.

Le Corbusier. *Towards a New Architecture*. New York: Dover, 1986.

Leopold, A. The Land Ethic. Pp. 201–226. In *A Sand County Almanac and Sketches from Here and There*. New York: Oxford University Press, 1987 [1949].

Lovins, Amory. *Reinventing Fire: Bold Business Solutions for the New Energy Era*. White River Jct, VT: Chelsea Green Publishing, 2011.

Maturana, Humberto, and Francisco Varela. *Autopoiesis and Cognition: The Realization of the Living*. Dordrecht, The Netherlands: D. Reidel, 1980.

Maturana, Humberto R., and Francisco J. Varela. *The Tree of Knowledge: The Biological Roots of Human Understanding*. Boston: Shambhala Publications, 1987.

McDonough, William. *Cradle to Cradle: Remaking the Way We Make Things*. New York: North Point Press, 2002.

McHarg, Ian L. *Design with Nature*. New York: Wiley, 1995 [1969].

McLennan, Jason F. *The Philosophy of Sustainable Design*. Kansas City, MO: Ecotone Publishing Company, 2004.

Millennium Ecosystem Assessment. *Ecosystems and Human Well-Being: Our Human Planet—Summary for Decision Makers*. Washington, DC: Island Press, 2005.

Millennium Ecosystem Assessment Board. *Living Beyond Our Means: Natural Assets and Human Well Being*. United Nations: MEA, 2005.

Odum, Howard T. *Environment, Power, and Society for the Twenty-first Century: The Hierarchy of Energy*. New York: Columbia University Press, 2007.

Olgyay, Victor. *Design with Climate: Bioclimatic Approach to Architectural Realism.* Princeton, NJ: Princeton University Press, 1973.

Orr, David W. *Ecological Literacy: Education and the Transition to a Postmodern World.* Albany, NY: State University of New York Press, 1992.

Rudofsky, B. *Architecture Without Architects.* Albuquerque, NM: University of NM Press, 1987 [1965].

Steadman, Philip. *Energy, Environment and Building.* New York: Cambridge University Press, 1975.

Tainter, Joseph. *The Collapse of Complex Societies: New Studies in Archaeology.* Cambridge: Cambridge University Press, 1988.

Vitruvius Pollio, M., translated by M. H. Morgan. *The Ten Books of Architecture.* New York: Dover, 1960 [1st Century BC].

White, Leslie A. *The Evolution of Culture: The Development of Civilization to the Fall of Rome.* Walnut Creek, CA: Left Coast Press, Inc., 2007.

Wilson, E.O. *Biophilia.* Cambridge, MA: Harvard University Press, 1984.

WEBSITES

American Society of Heating, Refrigeration, and Air-Conditioning Engineers, www.ASHRAE.org

Kellert, Stephen. *Biophilic Design: The Architecture of Life*, produced by Bill Finnegan. Burlington, VT: Tamarack Media, 2011. DVD, www.biophilicdesign.net

National Climatic Data Center, www.ncdc.noaa.gov

National Renewable Energy Lab, www.nrel.gov

RMI, www.rmi.org

US Green Building Council, www.usgbc.org

PART II

BOOKS AND ARTICLES

7group and Bill Reed. *The Integrative Design Guide to Green Building.* Hoboken, NJ: John Wiley & Sons, 2009.

Allen, Edward, and Joseph Iano. *The Architect's Studio Companion: Rules of Thumb for Preliminary Design.* 5th edition. Hoboken, NJ: John Wiley & Sons, 2012.

American Society of Heating, Refrigerating and Air-Conditioning Engineers. *Handbook of Fundamentals.* Many editions.

Ander, G. D. *Daylighting Performance and Design.* New York: John Wiley & Sons, 2003.

Anderson, Bruce, and Michael Riordan. *The Solar Home Book: Heating, Cooling and Designing with the Sun.* Andover, MA: Brick House Publishing Co., 1976.

ASTM. *International Standards for Sustainability in Building.* 3rd edition. CD-ROM.

Bainbridge, David A., and Ken Haggard. *Passive Solar Architecture: Heating, Cooling, Ventilation, Daylighting, and More Using Natural Flows.* White River Jct, VT: Chelsea Green Publishing, 2011.

Brown, G. Z., and Mark DeKay. *Sun, Wind, and Light: Architectural Design Strategies,* 2nd edition. New York: John Wiley & Sons, Inc., 2001.

Buzan, Tony, and Barry Buzan. *The Mind Map Book: How to Use Radiant Thinking to Maximize Your Brain's Untapped Potential.* London: BBC Books, 1993.

Daniels, Farrington. *Direct Use of the Sun's Energy.* New Haven, CT: Yale University Press, 1964.

Givoni, B. *Man, Climate and Architecture.* New York: Elsevier Publishing Company Ltd., 1969.

Grondzik, Walter T., Alison G. Kwok, Benjamin Stein, and John S. Reynolds. *Mechanical and Electrical Equipment for Buildings.* Hoboken, NJ: John Wiley & Sons, 2011.

Illuminating Engineering Society of North America (IESNA). *Lighting Handbook Reference,* 10th edition. www.iesna.org.

Lam, William M. C. *Sunlighting: As Formgiver for Architecture.* New York: Van Nostrand Reinhold Company, 1986.

Masson, Gaëtan, Marie Latour, and Daniele Biancardi. *Global Market Outlook for Photovoltaics until 2016.* Brussels: European Photovoltaic Industry Association, 2013.

Mazria, Edward. *The Passive Solar Energy Book.* Emmaus, PA: Rodale Press, 1979.

Mendler, Sandra, and William Odell. *The HOK Guidebook to Sustainable Design.* New York: John Wiley & Sons, 2000.

National Oceanic and Atmospheric Administration (NOAA). *Climatography of the United States.* Asheville, NC: National Climatic Data Center, 2008.

Olgyay, Aladar, and Victor Olgyay. *Solar Control and Shading Devices.* Princeton, NJ: Princeton University Press, 1957.

Pacala, S., and R. Socolow. "Stabilization Wedges for Solving the Climate Problem for the Next 50 Years with Current Technologies." *Science* 305 (2004): 968-972.

Pressman, Andrew, ed. *Architectural Graphic Standards.* 11th edition. Hoboken, NJ: John Wiley & Sons, 2007.

Racusin, Jacob Deva, and Ace McArleton. *The Natural Building Companion: A Comprehensive Guide to Integrative Design and Construction.* White River Jct, VT: Chelsea Green Publishing, 2012.

The Underground Space Center, University of Minnesota. *Earth Sheltered Housing Design: Guidelines, Examples, and References.* New York: Van Nostrand Reinhold Company, 1979.

U.S. Department of Energy. *2009 Building Energy Data Book.* Silver Springs, MD: D&R International, 2009.

Van der Ryn, Sim, and Stuart Cowan. *Ecological Design.* Washington, DC: Island Press, 1996.

Yudelson, Jerry, and Ulf Meyer. *The World's Greenest Buildings: Promise Versus Performance in Sustainable Design.* New York: Routledge, 2013.

WEBSITES

Architecture 2030, www.architecture2030.org

Building Science Corporation, www.buildingscience.com

Center for Maximum Potential Building Systems, www.cmpbs.org

Illuminating Engineering Society, www.ies.org

New Buildings Institute, newbuildings.org

PART III

BOOKS AND ARTICLES

Allen, Edward, and Joseph Iano. *Fundamentals of Building Construction: Materials and Methods.* Hoboken, NJ: John Wiley & Sons, 2009.

Balcomb, J.D., ed. *Passive Solar Buildings.* Boston: MIT Press, 1992.

Lstiburek, Joseph. "BSI-062: Thermal Bridges Redux," Building Science Corporation, July 2012. http://www.buildingscience.com/documents/insights/bsi062-thermal-bridges-redux.

Lstiburek, Joseph. *Energy and Environmental Building Association Builder's Guide: Cold Climates.* Westford, MA: Building Science Corporation, 2001.

Lstiburek, Joseph, and John Carmody. *Moisture Control Handbook: Principles and Practices for Residential and Small Commercial Buildings.* New York: Van Nostrand Reinhold, 1993.

Marshall, B., and R. Argue. *The Super-Insulated Retrofit Book.* Toronto, Canada: Renewable Energy in Canada, 1981.

Nisson, J. D., and G. Dutt. *The Superinsulated Home Book.* New York: John Wiley & Sons, 1985.

WEBSITES

Green Building Advisor, www.greenbuildingadvisor.com
GreenSpec and *Building News*, www.buildinggreen.com

PART IV
BOOKS AND ARTICLES

Barnett, D. L., and W. D. Browning. *A Primer on Sustainable Building*. Snowmass, CO: Rocky Mountain Institute, 1995.

Bower, John. *The Healthy House*. New York: Carol Communications, 1989.

Chiras, Daniel D. *The Natural House: A Complete Guide to Healthy, Energy-Efficient, Environmental Homes*. White River Jct, VT: Chelsea Green Publishing, 2000.

Chiras, Daniel D. *The Solar House: Passive Heating and Cooling*. White River Jct, VT: Chelsea Green Publishing, 2002.

Edminster, Ann V. *Energy Free: Homes for a Small Planet*. San Rafael, CA: Green Building Press, 2009.

Edwards, B., ed. *Green Buildings Pay*. New York: Spon Press, 2003 [1998].

Fuller, Sieglinde K., and Stephen R. Petersen. *Life-Cycle Costing Manual for the Federal Energy Management Program*. National Institute of Standards and Technology Handbook 135. Gaithersburg, MD: Building and Fire Research Laboratory, Office of Applied Economics, 1995.

Johnston, David, and Scott Gibson. *Toward a Zero Energy Home: A Complete Guide to Energy Self-sufficiency at Home*. Newton, CT: Taunton Press, Inc., 2010.

Kats, Greg. *Greening Our Built World: Costs, Benefits, and Strategies*. Washington, DC: Island Press, 2010.

Kats, Greg, Leon Alevantis, Adam Berman, Evan Mills, and Jeff Perlman. *The Costs and Financial Benefits of Green Buildings: A Report to California's Sustainable Building Task Force*. Report to California's Sustainable Building Task Force, 2003.

Melaver, Martin, and Phyllis Mueller, eds. *The Green Building Bottom Line: The Real Cost of Sustainable Building*. New York: McGraw-Hill, 2009.

Olivier, David. *Energy Efficiency and Renewables: Recent Experience on Mainland Europe*. Herefordshire, England: Energy Advisory Associates, 1992.

Romm, Joseph J., and William D. Browning. *Greening the Building and the Bottom Line: Increasing Productivity Through Energy-Efficient Design*. Snowmass, CO: Rocky Mountain Institute, 1998.

Rousseau, David, W. J. Rea, and Jean Enwright. *Your Home, Your Wealth, and Well-being*. Berkeley, CA: Ten Speed Press, 1988.

Vale, Brenda, and Robert Vale. *Green Architecture: Design for an Energy Conscious Future*. Boston: Little Brown, 1991.

Wilson, Alex. *Your Green Home*. BC, Canada: New Society Publishers, 2006.

Yudelson, Jerry. *Green Building Through Integrated Design*. New York: McGraw-Hill, 2009.

WEBSITES

BuildingEcology.com, buildingecology.com
Department of Energy Buildings Energy Databook, buildingsdatabook.eren.doe.gov
DSIRE, www.dsireusa.org
Energy Information Administration, www.eia.gov
Heschong Mahone Group, www.h-m-g.com
Passivhaus Institut, www.passiv.de and www.passivhaus-info.de
Resilient Design Institute, www.resilientdesign.org

PART V
BOOKS AND ARTICLES

Buchanan, Peter. *Ten Shades of Green: Architecture and the Natural World*. New York: The Architectural League of New York, 2005.

Corbett, Judy, and Michael Corbett. *Designing Sustainable Communities: Learning from Village Homes*. Washington, DC: Island Press, 2000.

Corbett, Michael N. *A Better Place to Live: New Designs for Tomorrow's Communities*. Emmaus, PA: Rodale Press, 1981.

Duran, Sergi Costa, and Julio Fajardo Herrero. *The Sourcebook of Contemporary Green Architecture*. New York: Collins Design, 2010.

Gissen, David, ed. *Big and Green: Toward Sustainable Architecture in the 21st Century*. New York: Princeton Architectural Press, 2002.

Goodman, Paul, and Percival Goodman. *Communitas: Means of Livelihood and the Ways of Life*. New York: Vintage Books, 1947.

Guzowski, Mary. *Towards Zero Energy Architecture: New Solar Design*. London: Laurence King Publishing Ltd, 2010.

Hall, Kenneth B., and Gerald A. Porterfield. *Community by Design*. New York: McGraw-Hill, 2001.

Hart, Sara. *EcoArchitecture: The Work of Ken Yeang*. West Sussex, UK: John Wiley & Sons, Ltd., 2011.

Hootman, Tom. *Net Zero Energy Design: A Guide for Commercial Architecture*. Hoboken, NJ: John Wiley & Sons, 2013.

Hopkins, Rob. *The Transition Handbook: From Oil Dependency to Local Resilience*. Cambridge, UK: Green Books Ltd, 2008.

Knowles, Ralph L. *Energy and Form*. Cambridge, MA: MIT Press, 1974.

Kostof, Spiro. *The City Shaped: Urban Patterns and Meanings Through History*. London: Thames and Hudson Ltd., 1991.

Lerch, Daniel. *Post Carbon Cities: Planning for Energy and Climate Uncertainty*. Sebastopol, CA: Post Carbon Press, 2007.

Macaulay, David R. *Integrated Design*. Bainbridge Island, WA: Ecotone Publishing, 2008.

Pahl, Greg. *The Citizen-Powered Energy Handbook: Community Solutions to a Global Crisis*. White River Jct, VT: Chelsea Green Publishing, 2007.

Pernick, Ron, and Clint Wilder. *Clean Tech Nation: How the U.S. Can Lead in the New Global Economy*. New York: HarperCollins, 2012.

Van der Ryn, Sim, and Peter Calthorpe. *Sustainable Communities: A New Design Synthesis for Cities, Suburbs and Towns*. San Francisco: Sierra Club Books, 1986.

Weisman, A. *Gaviotas: A Village to Reinvent the World*. White River Jct, VT: Chelsea Green Publishing, 1998.

Wilson, Alex, Jenifer L. Uncapher, Lisa McManigal, L. Hunter Lovins, Maureen Cureton, and William D. Browning. *Green Development: Integrating Ecology and Real Estate*. New York: John Wiley & Sons, Inc., 1998.

Wines, James. *Green Architecture*. Cologne, Germany: Benedikt Taschen Verlag Gmbh, 2000.

Yeang, Ken. *The Green Skyscraper: The Basis for Designing Sustainable Intensive Buildings*. Munich, Germany: Prestel Verlag, 1999.

Yeang, Ken, and Arthur Spector, eds. *Green Design: From Theory to Practice*. London: Black Dog Publishing Ltd., 2011.

WEBSITES

Terrapin Bright Green, www.terrapinbrightgreen.com

CASE STUDY TEAMS

BOSARGE FAMILY EDUCATION CENTER AT THE COASTAL MAINE BOTANICAL GARDENS

PROJECT TEAM	
Owner's Team	
Owner	The Coastal Maine Botanical Gardens
Commissioning Engineer	Investment Engineering
Design Team	
Architect	Maclay Architects & Scott Simons Architects
Energy Consultant	Energy Balance Inc.
Sustainability Consultant	Thornton Tomasetti
Structural Engineer	Becker Structural Engineers
Mechanical and Electrical Engineer	Allied Engineering Inc.
Civil Engineer	Knickerbocker Group
Landscape Architect	AECOM Inc.
Specification Writer	Lowell Specifications Inc.
Lighting Designer	J&M Lighting Design Inc.
Acoustical Consultant	ACENTECH
Construction Team	
Construction Manager	HP Cummings Construction
Building Systems Fabricator	Bensonwood

GEORGE D. AIKEN CENTER

PROJECT TEAM	
Owner's Team	
Owner	The University of Vermont
Design Team	
Architect	Maclay Architects
Energy Consultant	Energy Balance Inc.
Building Codes, Life Safety, and Access Consultant	Rolf Jensen & Associates
Structural and Civil Engineer	Engineering Ventures
Mechanical and Plumbing Engineer	Kohler & Lewis
Electrical Engineer	Pearson & Associates
Fire Protection Engineer	Chase Engineering
Landscape Architect	University of Vermont
LEED Consultant	Linda Samter
Lighting Designer	Naomi Miller Lighting Design and Pearson and Associates
Construction Team	
General Contractor	PC Construction

THE PUTNEY SCHOOL FIELD HOUSE

PROJECT TEAM	
Owner's Team	
Owner	The Putney School
Design Team	
Architect	Maclay Architects
Energy Consultant	Energy Balance Inc.
Cost Consultant	DEW Construction Inc.
Civil Engineer	Heindel & Noyes
Structural Engineer	Engineering Ventures
Mechanical Engineer	Kohler & Lewis
Electrical/FP Engineer	William Bissell
Landscape Architect	Cynthia Knauf Landscape Design
Lighting Designer	Naomi Miller Lighting Design
Construction Team	
Construction Manager	DEW Construction Inc.

MIDDLEBURY SOUTH VILLAGE PROFESSIONAL OFFICE BUILDING

PROJECT TEAM	
Owner's Team	
Owner	MSV Partners LLC
Energy Consultant	Efficiency Vermont
Design Team	
Architect	Maclay Architects
Structural Engineer	Ina Hladky
Mechanical and Plumbing Engineer	Thomas Engineering Associates
Civil Engineer	Otter Creek Engineering
Electrical Engineer	Lane Associates
Fire Protection Engineer	Chase Engineering
Construction Team	
Construction Manager	Naylor & Breen Builders Inc.

NRG SYSTEMS

BUILDING ONE PROJECT TEAM	
Owner's Team	
Owner	Wind NRG Partners LLC
Design Team	
Architect	Maclay Architects
Energy Consultant	Energy Balance Inc.
Civil Engineer	Krebs & Lansing Consulting Engineers
Energy Efficiency Consultant	Efficiency Vermont
Cost Consultant	Erickson Consulting
Structural Engineer	Engineering Ventures
Mechanical, Electrical, and Plumbing Engineer	Salem Engineering
Lighting Designer	Naomi Miller Lighting Design
Integrated Art Designer	Sarah-Lee Terrat
Construction Team	
General Contractor	Bread Loaf Corporation

BUILDING TWO PROJECT TEAM	
Owner's Team	
Owner	Wind NRG Partners LLC
Design Team	
Architect	Maclay Architects
Energy Consultant	Energy Balance Inc.
Civil and Structural Engineer	Engineering Ventures
Energy Efficiency Consultant	Efficiency Vermont
Construction Manager	Erickson Consulting
Mechanical, Electrical, and Plumbing Engineer	LN Consulting
Landscape Architect	T. J. Boyle and Associates
Fire Protection	Chase Engineering
Lighting Designer	Naomi Miller Lighting Design
Integrated Art Designers	Sarah-Lee Terrat and Carolyn Shapiro
Construction Team	
Construction Manager	HP Cummings Construction

DARTT HOUSE AND MACLAY ARCHITECTS' OFFICE

PROJECT TEAM	
Owner's Team	
Owner	Bill and Alex Maclay
Design Team	
Architect	Maclay Architects
Energy Consultant	Energy Balance Inc.
Construction Team	
General Contractor	Brothers Building
General Contractor	Cedar Tree Builders
HVAC	Vermont Heating and Ventilating
HVAC	Chuck's Heating and A/C
Electrical	Middlesex Electric
PV	Alteris Renewables

STONE HOUSE PROJECT TEAM	
Design Team	
Architect	Maclay Architects
Mechanical Engineer	LN Consulting
Energy Consultant	Energy Balance, Inc.
Lighting Designer	Naomi Miller Lighting Design
Interior Designer	Cooper, Robertson & Weatherly
Landscape Architect	Cynthia Knauf Landscape Design
Construction Team	
General Contractor	Michael Ellis Builder
Stone Mason	Mike Eramo Masonry

THREE HIGH-PERFORMANCE HOMES

NEWTON HOUSE PROJECT TEAM	
Design Team	
Architect	Maclay Architects
Landscape Architect	Matthew Cunningham
Interior Designer	LDa Architects
Lighting Consultant	Lam Partners
Mechanical Engineer	Kohler & Lewis
Civil Engineer	Everett Brooks
Energy Consultant	Energy Balance Inc.
Construction Team	
Contractor	Affinity Builders
Site and Foundation	Stevens-Burke LLC

TEPFER RESIDENCE PROJECT TEAM	
Design Team	
Architect	Maclay Architects
Energy Consultant	Energy Balance Inc.
Construction Team	
General Contractor	Jonathan Klein Builders

BENNINGTON SUPERIOR COURTHOUSE AND STATE OFFICE BUILDING

PROJECT TEAM	
Owner's Team	
Owner	Buildings and General Services, State of Vermont
Design Team	
Architect	Maclay Architects
Court Architect	RicciGreene Associates
Energy Consultant	Energy Balance Inc.
Cost Consultant	DEW Construction Inc.
Structural Engineer	Engineering Ventures
Mechanical Engineer	Kohler & Lewis
Civil Engineer	Engineering Ventures
Electrical/Lighting Engineer	EDM-AE Services
Landscape Architect	Cynthia Knauf Landscape Design
Geothermal Consultant	Haley and Aldrich Inc.
Commissioning Agent	Cx Associates
FP Engineer	Chase Engineering
Construction Team	
	DEW Construction Inc.

THE PUTNEY SCHOOL MASTER PLAN

PROJECT TEAM	
Owner's Team	
Owner	The Putney School
Design Team	
Architect	Maclay Architects
Energy Consultant	Energy Balance Inc.
Cost Consultant	DEW Construction Inc.
Historic Consultant	Lyssa Papazian
Civil Engineer	Stevens & Associates PC
Landscape Architect	Stevens & Associates PC
Landscape Architect	Cynthia Knauf Landscape Design
Theater Consultant	Don Hirsch Design Studios LLC
Forestry Consultant	Future Generations Forestry

FIGURE CREDITS

Macchu Pichu photograph by Martin St-Amant, Wikimedia Commons, http://upload.wikimedia.org/wikipedia/commons/0/01/80 _-_Machu_Picchu_-_Juin_2009_-_edit.2.jpg (CC-BY-SA 3.0)

Fig. P.1 Photograph courtesy of Boyd Norton, http://www.flickr.com /photos/usnationalarchives/7065981017

Fig P.2 Photo courtesy of Jim Sanford

Fig. P.3 Adapted from figure N1101.10 (R301.1) Climate Zones and reproduced with permission from International Code Council, *2012 International Residential Code* (Washington, DC: International Code Council, 2011), p. 40

Fig. P.4 *Top left*, photograph by Cynthia Knauf; *top right*, photograph by Carolyn Bates, www.carolynbates.com; *bottom left*, photograph by Robert Benson; *bottom right*, photograph by Jim Westphalen

Fig. 1.1 Adapted from World Nuclear Association/Unesco Courier

Fig. 1.2 Adapted from Innovative Clean Energy, Inc.

Fig. 1.3 *River Landscape* by Jan Brueghel the Elder, photograph courtesy of the National Gallery of Art, Washington, DC

Fig. 1.4 Photograph by Michigan Department of Transportation, Wikimedia Commons, http://upload.wikimedia.org /wikipedia/commons/7/77/US_131%2C_M-6%2C_68th _St_interchange.jpg

Fig. 1.7 *Data Source*: David J. Murphy and Charles A. S. Hall, "Year in Review—EROI or Energy Return on (Energy) Invested," *Annals of the New York Academy of Sciences* 1185 (2010): 102–118

Fig. 1.8 *Data Sources: BP Statistical Review of World Energy, June 2012* (London, BP, 2012); IPCC Special Report on Renewable Energy Sources and Climate Change Mitigation; 2010 Survey of Energy Resources, World Energy Council

Fig. 1.9 Photograph by Alan Radecki, Wikimedia Commons, http://upload.wikimedia.org/wikipedia/commons/4/44 /Solarplant-050406-04.jpg, (CC BY-SA 3.0)

Fig. 1.10 Photograph by Harald Pettersen, courtesy of NHD-INFO, http://www.flickr.com/photos/nhd-info/8033151828/ (CC BY 2.0)

Fig. 1.11 Photograph from Tswgb, Wikimedia Commons, http:// upload.wikimedia.org/wikipedia/commons/e/eb /Barrage_de_la_Rance.jpg

Fig. 1.12 Photograph by Gretar Ívarsson, Wikimedia Commons, http://upload.wikimedia.org/wikipedia/commons/9/9f /NesjavellirPowerPlant_edit2.jpg

Fig. 1.13 Photograph by Le Grand Portage, Wikimedia Commons, http://upload.wikimedia.org/wikipedia/commons/a/ab /ThreeGorgesDam-China2009.jpg (CC BY 2.0)

Fig. 1.14 Photograph by Andrew Carlin, Tracy Operators, NREL 06665

Fig. 1.15 Photograph by John Fowler, Wikimedia Commons, http:// upload.wikimedia.org/wikipedia/commons/3/31/Cliff _Palace_%284016037924%29.jpg, (CC BY 2.0)

Fig. 1.16 Photograph by La Citta Vita, http://www.flickr.com/photos /la-citta-vita/4758188317/ (CC BY-SA 2.0)

Fig. 2.4 Photograph by Dennis Schroeder, NREL 19350

Fig. 2.5 Rendering by RNL Design, NREL 18471

Fig. 2.6 Photograph by Dennis Schroeder, NREL 17830

Fig. 2.7 Photograph by Dennis Schroeder, NREL 19913

Fig. 2.9 © The Kubala Washatko Architects, Inc. / Mark F. Heffron

Fig. 2.10 © The Kubala Washatko Architects, Inc.

Fig. 2.11 © The Kubala Washatko Architects, Inc. / Mark F. Heffron

Fig. 3.1 Reprinted from David Lloyd Jones, *Architecture and the Environment* (Woodstock, NY: The Overlook Press, 1998). 34

Fig. 3.2 and 3.3 Photographs by David Brazier

Fig. 3.4 *Left*, adapted from diagram of the Eastgate Center designed by the Pearce Partnership and The Urgency of Change by Eugene Tsui; *right*, photograph by David Brazier

Fig. 3.5 Photograph by David Brazier

Fig. 3.6 Photograph courtesy of Nedlaw Living Walls

Fig. 3.7 *Left and right*, photograph courtesy of Ocean Arks International

Fig. 3.8 *Left*, photograph by Robb Williamson, NREL 10856; *right*, photograph by Ed Hancock, NREL 11666

Fig. 3.9 Copyright © 2013 by T. R. Hamzah & Yeang Sdn. Bhd.

Fig. 3.10 Copyright © by Alan Karchmer

Fig. 3.11 Image courtesy of Miller Hull Partnership

Fig. 3.12 Photograph by Paul g. Wiegman

Fig. 3.13 Copyright © by The Design Alliance Architects

Fig. 3.16 Photographs courtesy of Bensonwood

Fig. 4.5 Reprinted from *Passive Solar Architecture*, copyright © 2011 by David A. Bainbridge and Ken Haggard, with permission from Chelsea Green Publishing (www.chelseagreen.com)

Fig. 4.7 Adapted from NOAA Heating and Cooling Degree Day Maps, http://www.ncdc.noaa.gov/oa/documentlibrary /clim81supp3/clim81.html

Fig. 4.9 This map was created by the National Renewable Energy Laboratory for the Department of Energy

Fig. 4.12 Image from Clark Wissler, Wikimedia Commons, http:// upload.wikimedia.org/wikipedia/commons/4/4d/The _American_Indian_Fig_54.jpg

Fig. 4.13 Photograph by Massimo Catarinella, Wikimedia Commons, http://upload.wikimedia.org/wikipedia/commons/3/35 /MesaVerdeNationalParkCliffPalace.jpg, (CC BY-SA 3.0)

Fig. 4.15 *Top*, photograph courtesy of Museo24, Wikimedia Commons, http://upload.wikimedia.org/wikipedia /commons/4/44/Hovilanhaara_paper_mill_interior_1915 .jpg; *bottom*, photograph by Pascal Reuch, Wikimedia Commons, http://upload.wikimedia.org/wikipedia/commons /6/61/Cologne_Cathedral_interior.JPG, (CC BY-SA 3.0)

Fig. 4.16 Photograph by Danny Choo, Wikimedia Commons, http:// upload.wikimedia.org/wikipedia/commons/a/a7 /Kadokawa_office_%282%29.jpg, (CC BY-SA 2.0)

Fig. 4.17 Adapted from *Passive Solar Architecture*, copyright © 2011 by David A. Bainbridge and Ken Haggard, with permission from Chelsea Green Publishing (www.chelseagreen.com)

Fig. 4.22 Photograph courtesy of TRC Energy Services, copyright © 2009 by TRC Companies, Inc.

Fig. 4.26 Photograph by Rob Williamson, NREL, 10026

Fig. 4.27 *Left*, photograph by Peellden, Wikimedia Commons, http://upload.wikimedia.org/wikipedia/commons/b/b1 /WorkdGame2009_Stadium.jpg (CC BY-SA 3.0); *right*, photograph by Akendall, Wikimedia Commons, http:// upload.wikimedia.org/wikipedia/commons/8/87 /UO_Lillis_Front.jpg (CC BY-SA 3.0)

Fig. 4.29 *Left*, photograph by Southwest Windpower, NREL 14936; *top right*, photograph by Magnus Hæroldus Laudeus, http:// www.flickr.com/photos/haerold/2423094158, (CC BY-ND 2.0); *middle right*, photograph by Joe Smith, NREL 18461; *bottom* right, photograph courtesy of Dave Stackpole

Fig. 4.30 Photograph courtesy of Mac Rood

Fig. 4.31 Photograph courtesy of www.froeling.com

Fig. 5.1 Courtesy of 7group and Bill Reed, graphics by Corey Johnston

Fig. 5.8–5.10 Courtesy of Marc Rosenbaum

Fig. 5.11 *Right*, photograph by Tim Greenway

Fig. 5.12 *Left*, photograph by Jim Westphalen; *middle,* photograph by Tim Greenway; *right*, photograph by Robert Benson

Fig. 5.13 Photograph by Tim Greenway

Fig. 6.1 *Top*, photograph by Jibi44, Wikimedia Commons, http:// upload.wikimedia.org/wikipedia/commons/e/ef/084Skellig _Michael.JPG (CC BY-SA 3.0); *bottom*, photograph courtesy of Department of the Interior, Bureau of Indian Affairs

Fig. 6.5 Photograph courtesy of John Straube

Fig. 6.6 Photograph by Achim Hering, Wikimedia Commons, http://upload.wikimedia.org/wikipedia/commons/5/5d /Rockwool_4lbs_per_ft3_fibrex3.jpg, (CC BY-SA 3.0)

Fig. 6.10 Photograph by FSEC/IBACOS, NREL 13607

Fig. 6.11 Courtesy of Andy Shapiro, Energy Balance

Fig. 6.13 Photograph by Bauthermografie & Luftdichtheitsprüfung Lutz Weidner / Thüringen, Wikimedia Commons, http://upload.wikimedia.org/wikipedia/commons/d/d5 /BlowerDoor.jpg (CC BY-SA 3.0)

Fig. 6.14 Courtesy of Building Science Corporation

Fig. 6.16 Courtesy of John Straube

Fig. 6.24 Courtesy of Building Science Corporation

Fig. 7.1 EUI numbers for a typical educational building are sourced from the 2009 *Buildings Energy Data Book* (table 3.9.1), published by the US Department of Energy.

Fig 7.7 *Right*, photograph by Steve Lakatos

Fig. 8.1 Courtesy of John Straube

Fig. 8.2 Courtesy of John Straube

Fig. 10.17 Courtesy of Russ Miller—Johnson/Modern Steel

Fig. 10.30a and 10.30b Courtesy of Schöck USA, Inc.

Fig. 10.30c Adapted from drawing courtesy of Schöck USA, Inc.

Fig. 10.31a Courtesy of Schöck USA, Inc.

Fig. 10.31b Courtesy of Raquel Ranieri, from Modern Steel Construction, March 2012

Fig. 10.31c Courtesy of Dave DeLong, from Modern Steel Construction, March 2012

Fig. 10.36 *Inset*, photograph courtesy of Fluke Corp.; *main*, photograph by George Showman, http://www.flickr.com /photos/gshowman/3668250139, (CC-BY 2.0)

Fig 11.5 Photograph courtesy of Foam Laminates of Vermont

Fig. 11.7 Photograph by Sara Farrar, NREL 07139

Fig. 11.8 Photograph by Kent Baxter, Wikimedia Commons, http:// upload.wikimedia.org/wikipedia/commons/7/71/FEMA _-_5754_-_Photograph_by_Kent_Baxter_taken_on_11-23 -2001_in_Oklahoma.jpg

Fig. 11.9 Building Science Corporation, NREL 13546

Fig. 12.1 Courtesy of Building Science Corporation

Fig. 14.2 Adapted from Building Science Corporation

Fig. 15.1 *Data Source:* Architecture 2030, "By 2035 Approximately 75% of the Built Environment Will be Either New or Renovated," accessed January 7, 2014, http://architecture 2030.org/the_solution/buildings_solution_how

Fig. 15.2 *Data Source:* David Lloyd Jones, *Architecture and the Environment* (Woodstock, NY: Overlook Press, 1998), 36.

Fig. 15.4 Photographs by Kevin G. Reeves, courtesy of GSA/The Beck Group/Westlake Reed Leskosky

Fig. 15.5 and 15.6 Courtesy of Kimberley Quirk, Energy Emporium

Fig. 15.7 and 15.8 Courtesy of Rocky Mountain Institute

Fig. 15.9 Courtesy of GSA

Fig 16.1 Photograph by Carolyn Bates, www.carolynbates.com, www.carolynbates.com

Fig. 16.3 Photograph by Transformations, Inc.

Fig. 16.4 and 16.5 Courtesy of Marc Rosenbaum

Fig. 16.6 and 16.7 Photographs by Jim Westphalen

Fig. 16.8 and 16.9 Courtesy of Pill - Maharam Architects

Fig. 16.12 Photograph courtesy of TE Studio, Ltd.

Fig. 16.13 Photograph courtesy of www.jensencarter.com

Fig. 16.14 and 16.15 Photographs by Frédéric Comtesse, Dietrich Schwarz Architects, Zurich

Fig. 16.16 Image Courtesy of Bensonwood

Fig. 17.3 Analysis completed with the assistance of Andy Shapiro, Energy Balance

Fig. 17.4 Adapted from *Passive Solar Architecture*, copyright © 2011 by David A. Bainbridge and Ken Haggard, with permission from Chelsea Green Publishing (www.chelseagreen.com), 36.

Fig. 17.5 Photograph courtesy of Sybolt Voeten, Wikimedia Commons, http://upload.wikimedia.org/wikipedia/commons/4/43/ING _Headoffice_Amsterdam_%282%29.jpg (CC BY-SA 3.0)

Fig. 17.6 Photograph courtesy of Charles Ingram

Fig. 17.8 Courtesy of Pill - Maharam Architects

Fig. 17.9 and 17.10 Courtesy of Peter Schneider

Fig. 17.11 Adapted from Rocky Mountain Institute

Fig. 19.1 Map created by the National Renewable Energy Laboratory

Fig. 19.3 Photograph by Tom Chance, http://www.flickr.com/photos /tomchance/1008213420/in/photostream/ (CC BY-SA 2.0)

Fig. 19.4 © Rolf Disch Solar Architecture

Fig. 19.5 Image courtesy of KPMB Architects, diagram by Bryan Christie Design

Fig. 19.6 Photograph by Maris Mezulis

Fig. 19.7 Photograph by Manfred Burger

Fig. 19.8 Photograph by Peter Hubbe, Design by Randall Stout Architects, Inc.

Fig. 19.9 Photograph courtesy of BIG

Fig. 19.10 Copyright © by LAVA

Fig. 19.11 Photograph courtesy of Jan Aınalı, Wikimedia Commons, http://upload.wikimedia.org/wikipedia/commons/d/d5 /S%C3%B6dra_Hammarbyhamnen.JPG (CC BY-SA 3.0)

Fig. 19.12 Photograph by Kenta Mabuchi, Wikimedia Commons, http://upload.wikimedia.org/wikipedia/commons/b/b3 /ACROS_Fukuoka_2011.jpg (CC BY-SA 2.0)

Fig. 19.13 Image © IBA Hamburg GmbH / bloomimages

Bosarge Family Education Center Case Study opening image by Robert Benson

Fig. CS1.2 Courtesy of Scott Simons Architects

CS1.3 Photograph by Robert Benson

Fig. CS1.5 Photograph by Robert Benson

Fig. CS1.7 Courtesy of Scott Simons Architects

Fig. CS1.8 and CS1.9 Photographs by Robert Benson

George D. Aiken Center Case Study opening image by Jim Westphalen

Fig. CS2.1, CS2.4, CS2.5, CS2.8, and CS2.11 Photographs by Jim Westphalen

Fig. CS2.10 Courtesy of Matt Beam, Designer of Eco-Machine™

The Putney School Field House Case Study opening image by Jim Westphalen

Fig. CS3.1, CS3.5, CS3.6, CS3.9, and CS3.11 Photographs by Jim Westphalen

Middlebury South Village Case Study opening image by Jeffry Glassberg

Fig. CS4.4 Photograph by Jeffry Glassberg

NRG Systems Case Study opening image by Carol Bates

Fig CS5.1 Photograph courtesy of Renewable NRG Systems

Fig CS5.5 *Top*, photograph by Jeff Clarke; *bottom*, photograph by Carolyn Bates

Fig CS5.8, CS5.9, and CS5.10 Photographs by Carolyn Bates

Fig. CS7.6 Photograph by Carol Stenberg

Bennington Superior Courthouse and State Office Building Case Study opening image by Jim Westphalen

Fig. CS8.1, CS8.6, CS8.7, and CS8.8 Photographs by Jim Westphalen

The Putney School Master Plan opening image courtesy of The Putney School

INDEX

Note: Page numbers in *italics* refer to photographs and figures; page numbers followed by *t* refer to tables.

John Earle

William Maclay, founder and principal of Maclay Architects, pursued architecture to create a healthy, vibrant world for people and all living systems. Maclay is committed to creating a non-fossil-fuel-based future and began using renewable energy in 1970. He developed, designed, and built one of the first renewable communities in the United States and continues to design leading-edge projects today. He has lectured and taught extensively at colleges, universities, and conferences focused on environmental design. He is past president of the Vermont Chapter of the American Institute of Architects (AIA) and has served on the board of directors of the Vermont Businesses for Social Responsibility and the Yestermorrow Design/Build School. He is a recipient of the Terry Ehrich Award for Excellence in Socially Responsible Business. Maclay has a BA from Williams College and a Master of Architecture from the University of Pennsylvania.

Maclay Architects is an award-winning architecture and planning firm specializing in ecologically oriented and net zero planning and design for more than forty years. Projects include institutional, commercial, multifamily and single-family residential buildings, interiors, and communities. Maclay Architects has experience and expertise with net zero, LEED, Living Building Challenge, Passive House, and other high-performance rating systems, metrics, and standards. Maclay Architects is involved in education and in research on all aspects of environmental design—including sustainable design, indoor air quality, building science, and material selection. Maclay Architects' innovative renewable and energy-conserving projects have been exhibited and published internationally.

Maclay Architects is located in Waitsfield, Vermont. For additional information on Maclay Architects and net zero buildings, see www.maclayarchitects.com and www.maclayarchitects.com/net-zero.

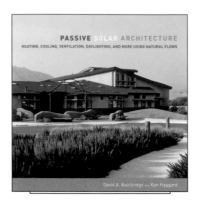

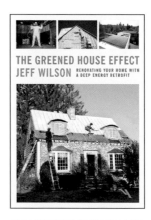